◆ ◆ ◆ ◆

Social Stratification

The Interplay of Class, Race, and Gender

◆ ◆ ◆ ◆

Second Edition

Daniel W. Rossides

Bowdoin College

Prentice Hall
Upper Saddle River, New Jersey 07458

Library of Congress Cataloging-in-Publication Data

Rossides, Daniel W.
[American class system]
Social stratification : the interplay of class, race, and gender / Daniel W. Rossides. — 2nd ed.
p. cm.
Originally published: The American class system: Boston : Houghton Mifflin. © 1976
Includes bibliographical references and index.
ISBN 0–13–192535–0
1. Social classes—United States. 2. Social classes—Cross-cultural studies. I. Title.
HN90.S6R68 1997
305.5.0973—dc20 96-470
CIP

Editor in chief: Nancy Roberts
Acquisitions editor: Fred Whittingham
Associate editor: Sharon Chambliss
Editorial/production supervision: Patty Sawyer (Pine Tree Composition)
Editorial assistant: Pat Naturale
Buyer: Mary Ann Gloriande

This book was set in 10/12 Palatino by Pine Tree Composition, Inc., and was printed and bound by Courier Companies, Inc. The cover was printed by Phoenix Color Corp.

Printed in the United States of America
10 9 8 7 6 5 4 3 2 1

ISBN 0-13-192535-0

Prentice-Hall International (UK) Limited, *London*
Prentice-Hall of Australia Pty. Limited, *Sydney*
Prentice-Hall Canada, Inc., *Toronto*
Prentice-Hall Hispanoamericana, S.A., *Mexico*
Prentice-Hall of India Private Limited, *New Delhi*
Prentice-Hall of Japan, Inc., *Tokyo*
Simon & Schuster Asia Pte. Ltd., *Singapore*
Editora Prentice-Hall do Brasil, Ltda., *Rio de Janeiro*

For Marilyn, as always

Contents

Preface

Social stratification has been studied scientifically and with considerable success on a relatively sustained basis since the 1920s, but it cannot be said that a consensus has emerged about the main issues in the field. However, it is no longer as necessary as it was during the early 1970s, when the first edition of this text was written, to argue the case that social classes are real. Today, almost all sociologists accept the reality of social classes and reject the classless ideology that still controls most popular and most elite opinion. This development is to the good, since the achievements of stratification analysts are considerable and make up one of the best (if not the best) ways to understand the nature of individual societies as well as their relations to each other.

As a text, this study is designed for students with some background in social science and is especially directed at the introductory social stratification course. It focuses on the American class system, the current state of the field of social stratification, and on other forms of inequality, especially race, ethnicity, and gender.

In tackling the broad and complex materials of social stratification, every effort has been made to introduce ideas in an orderly sequence and to allow students to extend their grasp of these materials in a cumulative manner. I have also assumed that a pedagogically effective text must provide background on specialized topics; thus, I discuss marriage and the family as a context for understanding the relation of class to family life, the sociology of law and deviance as a context for understanding the relation between class and law, and so on. Above all, I have tried to locate the levers of power so that knowledge can be wedded to policy.

Given the lack of consensus about social stratification, I have tried to represent rival positions as accurately and as fairly as possible, hoping in this way to let readers form their own judgments about the complex issues of stratification analysis while at the same time making it as easy as possible for instructors to follow their own bent in designing their courses. This new edition simplifies the contrast between evolutionary liberalism and evolutionary Marxism. It has also added a few words about the interpretive philosophy that has appeared in creative liberalism (represented by Anthony Giddens), as well as a word about postmodern currents (too diffused to be represented by a single figure).

No study can avoid organizing assumptions even when presented in the name of science (as this one is). Accordingly, I have tried to state where I stand as early and as clearly as possible. The book's basic theoretical framework is derived from two aspects of Max Weber's work (as well as the work of others): one, Weber's insistence on clear analytical models, which in the case of stratification analysis means that the dimensions of class (the economic hierarchy), prestige or status (subjective forms, consumption, and interaction in social groups), and power (political-legal hierarchies) must be kept analytically separate; and two, Weber's unique comparative-historical perspective, which not only provided an empirical foundation to his work, but led him to stress the diversity, relativity, and instability of social phenomena. In contemporary stratification language, Weber had both a conflict and a functional approach to industrial (capitalist) society, seeing it, on the whole, as inherently unstable because of its rich, complex, and contradictory institutions, but at the same time as subject to deep stabilizing pressures from bureaucratization and state centralization.

In adopting the Weberian orientation, I have not interpreted his multidimensional approach to mean that modern society is a hodgepodge of hierarchies with no coherent or structured system of inequality, or that it can be understood as a system of inequality making progress toward becoming an open, equal-opportunity society. And in adopting his anti-Marxian perspective, I have tried to avoid the temptation (which is so strong in American society and sociology) to overemphasize subjective (prestige) factors or to give them priority over economic (class) variables. Weber himself was more than aware of the preeminent role of economic forces and would no doubt have disavowed some of the uses that have been made of his multicausal approach in stratification analysis.

In analyzing the American class system, I have tried to present a balanced and relatively full treatment of the nature and interrelations of all three major stratification dimensions. Not only do neglected areas, such as law, politics, government, and legislation, receive extensive treatment, but there is also a relatively full treatment of class variables, such as wealth, income, occupation, and education, as well as prestige variables, such as self-perception and attitudes, consumption, and differences in associational life. My analysis also contains a major emphasis on minorities. There is an extended discussion of African Americans and Mexican Americans (with case studies of Puerto Rican and Cuban Americans) and a summary of the social class position and prospects of racial and ethnic minorities in general. There is a major focus on gender inequality as well as discussions of age groups, the disabled, and gays and lesbians. The materials on race, ethnicity, and gender have now been grouped into separate chapters for easier access. In addition, the chapters on minorities feature the views of leading African-American and feminist theorists.

This edition has three new substantive additions: extensive descriptions and analyses of America's professions, its mass media, and its legitimation process. The role of elite occupations in the creation and maintenance of the American class system, oddly enough, has been neglected in stratification analyses (actually, the professions have been neglected in most areas of sociology, including the introductory text). Also neglected has been the growing power of the mass media, not only journalism, but popular culture (entertainment and sports). The ideology of the professions and the content of the mass media also figure in the new chapter on how the power structure of American society legitimates itself.

This edition also contains a stronger emphasis on a theme that appeared in the 1990 edition. That edition suggested that important and unique changes had occurred in the American class system. By the late 1980s, it was apparent that wealth and income inequality were widening and that the United States was no longer raising living standards. These changes were explained by reference to changes in the American economy and to the economic, political, and ideological militancy of the upper classes. Characterized in brief, what appeared to be happening when I wrote the 1990 edition was a strengthening of the upper classes, a corresponding weakening of the lower classes, and a squeeze on middle-income groups. Since then, the American economy has continued to concentrate and the political power and militancy of the upper classes has intensified. Aided by higher education and government, broad occupational changes have occurred to facilitate these trends. Thanks largely to the computer, corporations are now able to move to any area of the country or part of the globe, including the major communist countries of China and Vietnam, to take advantage of cheap labor, low taxes, low environmental protection, and compliant governments. The computer, incidentally, was having other novel impacts: for the first time in the history of technology it was displacing labor without creating an equivalent number of good jobs (in the United States); it was making possible economic concentration on an unprecedented scale; it was making possible command structures that could tightly monitor labor, including professionals, on a scale unimaginable in the past; and it was leading to concentration in the realm of symbol making and dissemination.

These trends were aided by a willingness by American business to cut American wages, pensions, and health insurance; to use surplus labor to render the strike ineffective; and to use their political power to undermine legal protections for workers, labor unions, the poor, and minorities. In addition, American business mounted an onslaught against the welfare state and a wide variety of public services, forcing many into the labor market, thus further weakening labor. By the late 1980s, surplus labor had appeared in many areas (including among the professions and managers) and a widespread use of temporary and part-time labor appeared.

The above trends have intensified since the last edition of this text. By the mid-1990s, the bipolar income structure was well developed, wealth had become even more concentrated than the previous high levels, the stagnation of real wages since 1970 continued, and the squeeze on middle-income groups had intensified. The collapse of Soviet, East German, and Central European communism in 1990 has opened vast new areas for American (and Western) capital to move into. The movement of the People's Republic of China and Vietnam toward market economies has, in effect, made the entire globe a capitalist world. None of this is good news for ordinary Americans (or ordinary Europeans or Japanese); what has happened is that the power of scarce capital has been magnified enormously by its access to the globe's superabundant labor (aided, of course, by the NAFTA and GATT treaties).

Internally, the political mobilization of business and allied groups has continued, and an open repudiation of the welfare state, affirmative action, and environmental and consumer protection occurred with the 1994 congressional election victory of the Republican party. An insecure, atomized electorate had been mobilized against government and minorities in the name of an anarchistic liberalism (laissez-faire individualism). America's tradition of equal opportunity has been transformed into the very different concept of an "opportunity society"—that is, all are invited to compete for shrinking rewards, which of course means that upper-level individuals and organized groups are enormously advantaged.

The 1990 edition amply demonstrated the well-known fact that America had not made good on its ideals of equal opportunity, equality before the law, and equal political power. It suggested that realizing these ideals was much more difficult than most Americans were aware of. Today, the class (plutocratic) nature of American society is so far advanced that the dominant classes are even arguing that this is a good thing as they exploit their opportunities for gain in the new world-market capitalism.

The present edition interprets the conservative backlash of the past few decades, not as an aberration but as consistent with the core power structure of the United States since its inception two centuries ago. The right-wing success of the past few decades represents not the failure but the success of America's essential liberal philosophy—abstract ideals such as equality, liberty, happiness, and individualism are essentially ideological covers for the property-based upper classes, including the human-capital-rich professions. The excesses (ignorance and greed) of the present conservative onslaught could well generate a reaction toward left liberalism. There are deep divisions among the upper classes that could appear once their common interest in subduing labor and bending federal and state governments to their wishes is accomplished. What this edition now suggests is that a return to the liberal Democratic party and its reform programs will not only be difficult, but may not be worth the effort. What this suggests is that neither right nor left liberalism holds much promise for the effective management and democratization of an advanced, world-market capitalist society.

The role of social science is not to prescribe, but to present evidence indicating what given courses of action have led to in the past or will lead to in the future. The present text widens the choices for readers by suggesting that America's conventional choices are too narrow. It also indicates that the major creative currents in sociology (and elsewhere) have now moved away from the old-fashioned, modern perspective of nonpolitical, value-free, objective science (because it is impossible) and toward an open, honest, interpretive science that sees knowledge as a primer for private and public action and negotiation.

Instructors may or may not find students who can easily conceptualize the United States as a macrosystem. They may or may not find students ready to politicize knowledge or see their individual fortunes bound up with the fortunes of others in this macrosystem ("the sociological imagination"). But they will find that college students are aware of competitive pressures and tight employment opportunities. This text contains themes that build on that awareness. It has a pronounced theme on the professions and how they too are being adversely affected by the new economy. It shows readers how the latent, or subtext, themes in education, popular culture, and journalism are ideological covers for the new economy. Its overall conclusion about the wealth-income-occupational-legal-political system is that oscillations between the Republican and Democratic parties, and oscillations between more and less inequality and misery, may hide a deeper reality, namely, that the United States is a directionless, largely illegitimate class society mired in ascriptive property relations and liberal ideology. Above all, the text asks readers to examine American institutions and the shades of liberalism that endorse them and decide if they are suitable for the kind of world they'd like to live in.

Though books usually have one author, they are never written alone. Authors owe a heavy debt to scholars, teachers, students, colleagues, spouses (especially heavy in my case), and reviewers. I was particularly fortunate in having conscientious reviewers and I should like to extend my thanks to Cliff Brown (Emory University), Joan Morris (University of Central Florida), and Michael J. Sherman (Flagler College) for their valuable criticisms and suggestions, even for those that I lacked the wit to accept.

Daniel W. Rossides

1

An Introduction to Stratification Analysis

◆ ◆ ◆ ◆

◆ ◆ ◆ ◆

Inequality is a pervasive feature of human society and a subject that has fascinated both social theorists and laypeople from time immemorial. Social inequality is the stuff of which the drama of history is made: the power and pageantry of kingship, the struggle for supremacy among feudal barons, the executioner's block, the stench and brutality of a slave galley, the vast chasm between Brahman and untouchable, the mind-deadening routine of an assembly line, the factory owner, and the welfare mother all evoke vivid images of the ways in which stratification has been manifested at different times and places.

American history also evokes dramatic images of inequality, such as the bonded servant, the plantation owner and slave, the robber baron, the immigrant, the Depression, and the Dust Bowl. Americans have also witnessed some unique efforts to institute relations of equality, such as the Bill of Rights, the Homestead Act, the Fourteenth and Fifteenth Amendments, the sit-down strike, collective bargaining, the war on poverty, and the civil rights movement. In trying to understand these and other manifestations of the ceaseless drama of inequality and equality, sociologists must ask many questions: Who or what process determines who shall work in the fields and who in a factory, office, or laboratory? Who or what process decides who shall stand in an unemployment line or suffer the humiliation of welfare allotments? How is it possible in a democracy that millions have second homes while many live in rat-infested tenements or are homeless? Why do people tolerate hardship in the face of plenty when they have the franchise? Has rising prosperity made Americans more nearly equal? Have reforms made any headway against the forces of ascription, exploitation, and unequal opportunity? Is the United States a meritocracy, and if not, is it making progress in that direction?

As a distinct discipline within modern social science, sociology has long studied such questions. Despite decades of creative research and theorizing, however, there is still no integrated body of research and theory to account for the way in which social inequality is produced, maintained, and transmitted from one generation to the next. Given the complexity of this subject, it is understandable that there are many rival theories about the nature and destiny of social inequality, ranging from those that describe industrial society as spearheading a long-term drive toward equality, personal achievement, and consensus to those that interpret it as characterized by privilege, conflict, and repression.

We begin, therefore, by considering a theme basic to Western social thought—the attempt to understand the relationship between human nature and inequality. Because the literature that addresses this theme is exceedingly rich, we can do no more than discuss representative examples of the two major positions: the view that seeks to explain social inequality in terms of factors in human nature (the biopsychological position) and the view that seeks to explain it in terms of social variables (the sociocultural position).

THE ARGUMENT THAT INEQUALITY COMES FROM HUMAN NATURE

The Biopsychological Explanation of Inequality

The type of stratification theory that is most pervasive and influential in Western society attributes inequality to differences among individuals *qua* individuals. This explanation can be called *biopsychological* (or *naturalistic* or *ahistorical* or *nonsocial*) in that it argues that deep innate differences exist among human beings and that society derives (or should derive) its structure from the hierarchy of "talent" identifiable among human beings. This position assumes, in other words, that behavior is a function of human nature, and differences in the behavior of individuals result from differences in their natures.

One of the most famous and influential expressions of the biopsychological view is Plato's *Republic.* Plato was not the first to articulate the idea that there is a congruence between human nature and society, but he gave it a revolutionary cast by combining it with the novel assumption that the nature of that congruence could be identified by means of rational analysis. Society, argued Plato, has always been nonrational, or even irrational, based more on blind than on conscious cooperation. Instead of being founded on and governed by reason, society is governed by myth and custom. And because human beings have not understood themselves, they have not understood the nature of society. As a result, they have argued over the worth of their respective roles in the social division of labor, causing widespread inefficiency, instability, and civil war.

To bring about the good society, Plato insisted, one must derive social and ethical conclusions from rational analysis. The division of labor that is the essence of society can be likened to the division of labor in the human personality. According to Plato, the structure of the personality is hierarchical: reason is at the top, followed by the "spirited" or executive capacity, and then the appetites. This specialization within the human being is matched by specialization *among* human beings. In the aggregate, human beings have different aptitudes. Some men and women have the capacity to reason, some are specially equipped to manage, and others are suited for work and work alone. In his famous metallic analogy, Plato described the hierarchy of human talent as composed of three groups of individuals who correspond respectively to gold, silver, and iron-brass.

The structure of society, therefore, corresponds to the division of labor in the human personality. In order to function, it must have a reasoning element (philosopher-king or -kings), administrators, and workers. To establish a rational society, one must see to it that the human beings suited by nature to each of these functions are identified and appropriately educated. Doing this would not be easy since Plato complicated his prescription by introducing another revolutionary idea. Gold parents, he argued, can have iron-brass children, and iron-brass parents can have gold or silver children; in other words, the distribution of talent is not determined by family birth, nor is it insured by property or a function of sex. For Plato, society could not be constituted on any of the traditional grounds. Only when the innate hierarchy of individual ability (enhanced by education) matches the intrinsic hierarchy of social functions can one speak of the good—and thus stable, just, and happy—individual and society.

Plato's interpretation of society as a functional system, staffed by those innately equipped to perform certain social functions, has had a long and varied career in Western social theory. But it is one thing to posit an ideal society free from the imperfections of history and another thing to talk about how people and societies actually behave. As we shall see when we examine some contemporary thinking about inequality, whenever the biopsychological, ahistorical, functional definition of society predominates, the concept of social class—especially its emphasis on illegitimate and exploitative-ascriptive factors—is relegated to a secondary position.[1] And we will also find that the rulers of society invariably depict their dominions as a harmonious, equitable, and natural division of functions based on human nature and avoid forms of thought that stress ascription, exploitation, and conflict. In brief, this social philosophy takes the form of what Ossowski has called *nonegalitarian classlessness,* or the belief that social inequality is based on natural factors and not on arbitrary definition or the use of force.[2] In the United States, nonegalitarian classlessness is expressed as the belief that inequality is determined by the innate differences in individuals as revealed by equal opportunity and competition.

Biopsychological Inequality: The Liberal World View

The emergence of capitalism gave rise to the novel proposition that society and social position should directly reflect the personal natures of individuals as individuals, a social philosophy known as liberalism.[3] Expressed in its fullest earliest form in the social contract theories of Thomas Hobbes (1588–1679) and John Locke (1632–1704), this revolutionary redefinition of human nature (and thus of society) gradually broadened and deepened, and eventually triumphed over the feudal view of human nature and society. Expressed in terms of stratification theory, liberal thought attacked the hereditary principle and fixed hereditary estates of feudal society, and in their place sought to establish the achievement ethic. Henceforth, it declared, inequality was to be a function of personal ability, especially in economic pursuits.

The new focus on achievement in the West acquired a deep biopsychological cast in the period between 1650 and 1850. During this unusually creative period in social thought, theorists in their efforts to explain behavior and inequality catalogued an enormous variety of biological and psychological forces: pugnacity, reason, hunger, sex, the will to power, self-interest, moral traits, genius, mental power, and so on. In French thought, the fathers of sociology, Saint-Simon (1760–1825) and Auguste Comte (1798–1857), found the explanation for behavior and inequality directly in human nature. Both theorists divided human beings into brain men, sensory men, and motor men, each category having special functions to perform for society.[4] According to Saint-Simon and Comte, these three biopsychic capacities, while shared by all individuals, are distributed unevenly. Education can develop the dominant capacity in individuals but it cannot change the category in which nature has placed them.

In English social thought, the biopsychological approach is a prominent feature of the work of Herbert Spencer (1820–1903). Spencer never developed a rigid classification of biopsychological types, but his thought—the first to be based on the scientific theory of evolution—was heavily influenced by biological analogies. The basic capacity in nature, according to Spencer, is the ability to adjust to conditions, a capacity that is not solely a function of thinking. For Spencer, the individual is a real but unknown quantity in the operation of society. Because it is not possible to identify the capacities of individuals precisely, it is necessary for society to provide competitive situations; thus Spencer's emphasis on the free market, private property, limited government, and open competition.

The idea that inequality stems from differences among individuals is the dominant theme of American political and social theory. James Madison, for example, argued in the *Federalist* paper number 10 that government is necessary because of conflicts over property, and that differences in amounts and types of property individuals own are due to "diversity in the faculties of men." Because social conflict has this natural basis, it cannot be eliminated without doing violence to nature. "The protection of these faculties is the first object of government," argued Madison, and its proper role is to contain or control the effects of conflict, not to eliminate conflict as such. The main virtue of representative government, Madison concluded, is that it transfers natural economic conflicts and inequalities to a different arena and mitigates their impact on the body politic.

In American sociology, the thought of William Graham Sumner (1840–1910) best exemplifies the biopsychological approach. Like Madison, Sumner emphasized the importance of economic conflict in human behavior. History, he argued, is a struggle between economic interests. Modern society has evolved to a point at which this struggle can be made explicit and thus more "rational." All societies, according to Sumner, are divided into the masses and the classes; the former embody the society's *mores* and resist change, while the latter introduce variation and change. Society cannot change individuals, but it can select and develop those who best serve its interests. There is a natural distribution of human talent, ranging from the few individuals of genius and talent to the defective and delinquent. Modern society, which has evolved from a system based on customary status to one based on rational contract, provides individuals with an opportunity to prove themselves. Merit is inherent in the individual; society merely brings it out by means of education and competition. Thus, concluded Sumner, all schemes to help the weak and less talented are wrongheaded interferences with nature.

The biopsychological approach constituted the core of the liberal world view from the seventeenth through the nineteenth centuries, and reflected the needs of emerging capitalism. The liberal emphasis on equality of opportunity and inequality of native endowment was both a metaphysical attack on feudalism and a legitimation of the emerging liberal society. With the consolidation of liberal society, the same position was used to attack theories of reform and assorted forms of socialist thought. Eventually, however, the biopsychological explanation of social inequality had to be drastically modified, not only on scientific grounds, but because it no longer suited the needs of a maturing industrial society. A complex industrial society requires a great deal of coordination, and many of its members require long years of preparation for adult roles. It is not surprising, therefore, that the idea that society should simply reflect the natures of individuals was gradually questioned and modified. The shift to a more sociocultural explanation of behavior has been the major trend in liberal intellectual-scientific circles during the past century.

This is not to say, however, that American society as such is characterized by beliefs or values that have been updated to suit the needs of an advanced urban-industrial system. Quite the contrary, as our analysis will show, most Americans still live in the nineteenth century. Actually, recent decades have seen a resurgence of demands, especially by the Republican party and conservative Democrats, that the United States return to the laissez-faire competitive individualism of the past. Few realize that that world never existed except as ideology.

THE ARGUMENT THAT INEQUALITY IS A SOCIAL PHENOMENON

Rousseau and the Sociocultural Explanation of Inequality

The other influential theme in Western social theory treats inequality as the outcome of social variables. Rousseau's remarkable essay the *Discourse on the Origin of Inequality* (1754) argued that those who attribute inequality to human nature are mistaken; they are confusing the effects of society on human beings with their original constitution. Humans in their original state, Rousseau suggests, can only be hypothesized about. At best, they are merely compassionate bundles of emotions motivated by their own welfare and self-preservation, and repelled by others' pain and death. By and large, they are equal to their fellows in their weakness and nakedness. Only in the society of others do they develop language, property, law, and inequality; in this process their original nature is distorted and corrupted by reason and civilization. Above all, the division of labor and the attendant convention of property create mutual dependence and enslave not merely the subordinate groups in society but everyone.

Rousseau's thesis is an outstanding example of the sociocultural view of behavior and inequality. Of special importance is the fact that his analysis contains a conception of the division of labor totally different from Plato's (and from those of most "functional" theorists). While Rousseau defined society as a network of functional specialization, unlike Plato he saw the division of labor as resulting not in mutual profit or peace but only in corruption, injustice, and violence. He was an adherent of the "conflict school of inequality," which regards social factors, and often the basic structure of society, as detrimental to human beings and incompatible with social harmony and justice.

Sociocultural Inequality: Karl Marx and Max Weber

The sociocultural explanation of inequality has many sources, but its most influential contributors have been Karl Marx (1818–1883) and Max Weber (1864–1920). Indeed, the basic conceptual elements both of the contemporary sociocultural explanation of social stratification and of conflict theory are found in their original forms in the theories of these two men. Both Marx and Weber explicitly rejected the Anglo-American liberal view that capitalist society and the inequality that characterizes it stem from the individual. Despite serious disagreements, both theorists maintained that the biopsychological approach was a thorough mistake. The reasons for their rejection of it transcend the undoubted genius of these two men. Gradual economic growth and small-scale enterprise had misled English and American theorists into believing that individualism had caused capitalism. As Germans, Marx and Weber had not grown up in a social environment permeated by the logic of individualistic explanations. The growth of capitalism in Germany was an abrupt, disruptive process spawned largely by military and political considerations. Lacking the long phase of small-scale enterprise characteristic of capitalist growth in other countries, German capitalism took the form of a relatively large-scale factory system from the outset. This abrupt growth, due to corporate formation and state action, made it as impossible for Germans to develop a theory of individualism and laissez-faire as it was for them to explain capitalism and its resulting system of social stratification in biopsychological terms.[5]

Karl Marx: Social Classes as Property Relations

Though Marx and Weber agreed that behavior is the outcome of sociocultural forces, they disagreed markedly about the nature of these forces. Marx, who was greatly influenced by such classical liberal economists as Adam Smith and David Ricardo, by and large accepted their definition of society as a functional division of economic and social labor.[6] But Marx rejected the notions that an individual's place in the functioning of society rested on his or her innate talents and that the division of labor (as found in any known society) was compatible with social harmony and justice. For Marx the key determinant of human behavior and human consciousness is the relationship of humans to nature. Marx referred to this relationship as *the forces of production* or *the material conditions of life* (resources, technology, and technical skills). A given level of production, he argued, leads to a distinctive set of social relations or *mode of production.* The core of these social relations is the legal order, especially property forms; forms of the state; and the ideological order, including religion, philosophy, and art. In brief, as Marx put it, "the hand mill will give you a society with the feudal lord, the steam mill a society with the industrial capitalist."

History is essentially the story of the changing relation of humans to nature. As the forces of production change, they come into conflict with the mode of production (or superstructure), leading to a conflict between classes and eventually to revolution. As the forces of production crystallize into a new modal technology, they give rise to a new set of social relations that corresponds to the new needs it creates, including a new type of human being. For Marx, therefore, society derives its essential structure from the prevailing level of technology, and it is the individual's relation to the means of production, rather than innate abilities or drives, that determines one's class level, personality, and consciousness. Rather than seeing economic and social structures as the result of human talents, drives, or needs, Marx always focused on social variables, particularly technology and the economic system in which it was embedded.

Strictly speaking, the crucial factor in the creation of classes is not technology as such but the ownership of technology, or the means of production. The simple dichotomy between owner and nonowner is the ultimate basis of Marx's conception of social stratification. All other factors, such as income, occupation, education, and political power, are derivative and secondary.[7] Fundamental to Marx's conception of class is the fact that all material value is the result of labor. But because of the power inherent in property, the owners of the means of production receive more than they produce by their own labor. Therefore their interests and those of the nonpropertied (labor) are inherently antagonistic (see Box 1–1).

Economic classes (determined on the basis of the ownership and nonownership of land, tools, factories, and the like) are synonymous with social classes, according to Marx, because beliefs and values (consciousness) and overt behavior outside of work correspond to economic behavior, beliefs, and values. Also crucial to Marx's explanation of class formation, as well as his theory of the dynamics of class struggle and social change, is his assumption that one can distinguish between progressive and reactionary technological forces. The basic criterion that Marx used to make this distinction is the concept of *human fulfillment.* Some technological forces (and the social systems that embody them) retard and some promote the progress of human beings toward emancipation from historical necessity. A class is progressive when it represents the emergence of new forms and levels of liberating technology; an example is the middle class between the sixteenth and

BOX 1–1 *Professional Sports and the Labor Theory of Value*

The deep conflict between owners and athletes in professional sports is a contemporary example of a question that we encountered earlier in both Plato and Rousseau: How does one establish a division of labor complete with agreed-upon duties and rewards?

Arguments over the respective contributions of capital and labor have permeated capitalism from its start. The emergence of specialized groups such as hospitals, law firms, and research institutes has complicated matters. The issue has been further complicated by the demands of feminists that similar pay be given to occupations that appear dissimilar and that we cease thinking of housework and parenting as nonwork.

Professional sports is an area where this issue can be seen more clearly than, say, in manufacturing or banking. The owners of professional sports teams make monopoly profits (30 percent) despite the fact that the values in a baseball, football, or basketball game are created by athletes (labor). Understandably, athletes have demanded an unlimited right to get the most income from their scarce talents. The already extremely high pay of athletes raises the issue of excessive income for all American upper-level occupations. It also raises the issue of artificial scarcity—are good athletes—or doctors, lawyers, and so on—really scarce naturally or are they scarce because of how society produces them? Is the high income of both owners and players a way to justify excessive profits and salaries elsewhere? Sports provide many insights into the American class system and are discussed more fully in Chapters 10, 17, and 19. For now, sports help us understand Marx's labor theory of value by raising a question: Exactly what is the contribution of capital to a sports match?

nineteenth centuries. Inevitably, however, such a class becomes conservative and reactionary—a "ruling class"—because it can make larger and larger profits without distributing the fruits of the machine to the general populace; examples from American history are the monopoly-based robber barons of the nineteenth century.

For Marx, therefore, economic growth under private property will not end either exploitation or the distortion of the human personality. Only when economic growth is conducted under democratic auspices will the promise of science and industry result in the elimination of both material and moral scarcity. The spectacular economic growth of the century since Marx's death has borne out his suspicion that abstract economic growth is not the same as the growth of democracy. Only when material abundance is democratically produced and distributed will historical systems of inequality (caste, estate, and class), and the corresponding structures of moral scarcity (original sin, noble versus ignoble birth, master-slave, lord-serf, owner-worker, government-citizen, policeman-criminal) disappear and a "classless" society of human fulfillment emerge.

Max Weber: Social Classes as Multicausal and Nondirectional

Marx's identification and analysis of economic causation was perhaps the most important contribution to social science in the nineteenth century. However, the monocausal or deterministic version of economic causation that he proposed had to be considerably modified before it was accepted into stratification theory and sociology. The theorist largely responsible for its modification was Max Weber. While acknowledging the importance of economic causes in the formation of social strata, Weber insisted that noneconomic sociocultural variables are not only influential but regardless of their origin often take on a life of their own and become more influential than economic factors in controlling the distribution of material and symbolic benefits. Religious beliefs and values, for example, significantly influence the relationship of humans to nature, the definition of work, and the worth of material values. And such factors as family beliefs and values, canons of taste or consumption, considerations of race or ethnicity, and philosophical, political, legal, or military beliefs and values can often exert powerful controls over economic forces.

Weber developed his multicausal theory of behavior in a lifelong analysis of the rise and nature of capitalism.[8] While acknowledging the importance of the economic factor, Weber came to the conclusion that the economic breakthrough to capitalism would have been impossible had medieval Europe not possessed a congenial religious and social tradition. With regard to social stratification, Weber concluded that a simple economic determinism was not consonant with the historical record.[9] He insisted, therefore, that the analysis of social inequality required the analytical separation of three major causal variables: class (market factors, property, technology, income, wealth), status (cultural evaluations expressed in group life, involving such matters as family, religion, race, morality, ethics, consumption, breeding, and general style of life), and party (access to the state, ability to create and enforce law).

In developing this analytical model, Weber raised all the problems that confront contemporary stratification theory, especially those associated with his stress on multiple causation. The many causes influencing the formation and composition of social classes and the reciprocal relations between causes, he argued, make it necessary to think of causation as mutual action and reaction. Economic wealth, for example, can be used to obtain prestige and political-legal power, and, conversely, one can use prestige (in the form, say, of noble birth or skin color) to secure economic wealth or political-legal benefits. So too, one can use political-legal power (such as military skill or the ability to organize voters) to secure economic benefits or prestige.

Max Weber also rejected both the liberal and the Marxian belief that modern society represented humanity's march toward an ever better future. On the contrary, he felt that the impersonal, cost-benefit, instrumental rationality of capitalism (efficiency as determined mostly by property owners) would eventually undermine and erode the moral capital of the West. And he would not have been surprised at what contemporary research has discovered about the class system of the capitalist countries: a nondirectional oscillation between high inequality and higher inequality with no progress toward eliminating capitalism's departures from its ideals of merit, competence, and equality (see Chapter 5).

The other prophetic contribution by Max Weber was his interpretive sociology: science, he argued, cannot be objective, nonpartisan, and value-neutral because the scientist is always embedded in a particular social class at a particular time and place. The multicausal, nondirectional nature of society means that there is no objective world to uncover. To avoid seeing only in terms of the narrow assumptions of time and place, scientists must become aware that they must use unverifiable assumptions and try to balance them with opposing viewpoints. Since science can lead only to knowledge, not truth, its purpose is to assist individuals and groups to make personal and public value decisions (a fuller picture of the growing role of Weber's interpretive sociology in current stratification analysis is given in Chapters 4, 5, and 6).

But there is no need to stress any further the differences between Marx and Weber. It is their similarities that are relevant to our present task of distinguishing the theories that focus on human nature from those that focus on society as the cause of inequality. Marx and Weber agreed that no such phenomenon as human nature can be identified as a cause of behavior; what we call human nature is the result of sociocultural forces, and the deep observable differences among human beings are the *result* of social stratification, not its cause.

A WORKING DEFINITION OF SOCIAL STRATIFICATION

Social Differentiation versus Social Stratification

All human societies are differentiated by various forms of specialization, only one of which should be called *social stratification.* The advantages of specialization are obvious and every society is characterized by a division of labor, no matter how rudimentary. Simple societies, for example, use sex, age, and kinship to ascribe rights and duties to their members. That these three biological attributes are universally used to assign people to social functions, however, does not mean that sex, age, and kinship actually cause behavior. We have become too aware of the wide variations in behavior within each of the sexes and age groups, and among parents and children, to accept a simple biopsychological explanation of behavior. The way in which power groups *define* these human attributes is the crucial determinant of how people are assigned to social functions. Despite historical variations, the differentiation of social tasks on the basis of age, sex, and kinship leads to certain forms of inequality. Specifically, the old are usually given authority over the young, parents over children, and males over females.

But simple society cannot generate social stratification even if it has outstanding individuals. Imagine, for example, a hunting and gathering tribe in which all males are fairly equal in hunting ability, and therefore equal socially. Then imagine the appearance of an individual who is exceptionally fleet of foot and keen of vision. Social stratification begins when he becomes the leader of the hunting party and is given authority, prestige, and a larger share of the catch. It is crucial to note that both he and his family will rank above those who are average in ability and who in turn will rank above those who are lame or nearsighted. But such a stratification hierarchy is only a partial system because the superior hunter cannot ensure his son's future position as a leader. His wife and children will enjoy more food and prestige during his lifetime, but unless the son inherits his father's physical traits he will sink in the hierarchy upon reaching adulthood. Indeed, if no biologically superior or inferior individuals emerge in our hypothetical society, the stratification hierarchy itself will disappear. A full system of social stratification emerges only when parents can see to it that their children inherit or acquire a social level equal or superior to their own regardless of innate ability.

The key to intergenerational transfer of social level is the development of high occupational positions that can be filled only by those who possess or acquire a given range of *social* assets, such as property, leisure, motivation, education, personality traits, noble birth, military or other skills, and so on (or those who have socially defined, valued, and cultivated biopsychological abilities associated with such occupations as basketball player, opera singer, or mathematician). Thus, *stratification inequality* is the condition in which social positions are ranked in terms of importance, rewarded differentially, acquired by individuals (and thus their families), and transmitted over generations quite independently of biological or psychological attributes. Furthermore, the definition of what is functionally important and the ways specified to achieve given social functions are quite arbitrary and based as much on force as on rationality, moral insight, or social necessity. The fact that modern society allows some individuals to rise above their parents' station (or to drop below it) does not alter the fact of social stratification. There is far less mobility than is popularly believed, and it neither diminishes the distance between tops and bottoms nor interferes much (despite considerable rhetoric to the contrary) with the hereditary transmission of stratification level.

Caste, Estate, and Class Forms of Stratification

Once a society achieves a degree of economic surplus, social stratification inequality emerges prominently.[10] Economic surplus is easily translated into prestige and power and readily transmitted from one generation to the next. In short, economic surplus provides the wherewithal for social stratification: If property is esteemed, parents can guarantee that their children will be esteemed by giving them property; if abstinence from economic work is valued, those who can live off property or the work of others will be elevated above those who must work; if education is necessary to attain high occupations, those whose parents can motivate and support them through long years of schooling will have a decided edge over those who cannot.

Though economic variables are crucial to social stratification, they do not function in any mechanical or unitary fashion. As Weber pointed out, moral relationships (status or, in our terms, prestige) emerge to legitimate property relations and often become strong enough to disguise and even counteract economic forces. The diversity of causation and the variety of structures that social stratification assumes make it difficult to impose conceptual order on this form of inequality. However, for our immediate purpose of developing a brief working definition of social class, we need only note that it is generally accepted that social stratification, considered in the abstract, takes three general forms:

1. Caste stratification, in which an agrarian society defines social level and function in terms of a hierarchy of religous worth (or a hierarchy of racial worth in some approximations)
2. Estate stratification, in which an agrarian society defines social level and function in terms of a hierarchy of family worth
3. Class stratification, in which an industrial society defines social level and function in terms of a hierarchy of differential achievement by individuals, especially in economic pursuits

Class Stratification

Class stratification appears in societies with expanding economies and is a phenomenon peculiar to industrial society. Essentially, an expanding economy requires functional expertise in many sectors of its specialized occupational system, and needs flexibility in its labor, commodity, and credit markets (to use Weber's breakdown of class variables). Because of these needs, expanding economies undermine feudal norms and practices based on static lineage, prestige, and legal criteria. Thus the emergence of class over estate stratification occurred in modern Western Europe.

Much of the widespread confusion over the meaning of class inequality results from a failure to note two things: (1) class stratification emerged primarily in societies with well-developed systems of estate stratification; and (2) class stratification in such countries has undergone two distinct stages: an initial period during which classes crystallized into relatively self-conscious antagonistic strata,[11] followed by a stage in which an expanding standard of living, political-legal equality, and state welfare programs have succeeded in muting class hostility and eroding class consciousness.

Though the United States was spared the early stage of class crystallization experienced by most European nations, it would be a mistake to assume that social classes do not exist in the United States. The essence of class stratification is that economic status prevails openly, steadily, and strongly over all other statuses. What Americans are worth on the labor, commodity, and credit markets is the primary determinant not only of their standard of living but also of their worth in the realms of prestige and power. As we shall see, American social classes do not form a strict and clearly defined set of strata. There are multiple dimensions of inequality, which, while under the general sway of economic status, remain distinct and somewhat independent. Thus our overall analytical model, based on the general orientation provided by Max Weber, assumes, first, that the causes of behavior are sociocultural rather than biopsychological, and it accepts the primacy of economic factors even as it stresses multiple causation. Because of the number of factors affecting social stratification, analysis is made easier if these factors are grouped under three broad headings—class, prestige, and power, each of which has subdimensions. (See Table 1–1.)

Values within the dimension of class range from affluence and economic power and security at the top to destitution and economic powerlessness at the bottom. Some of the variables or subdimensions of class are listed in Table 1–1: income, wealth, occupation, education, family stability and values, and the education of children. In general, class refers to those who have similar life chances (goods, living conditions, personal experiences) because of a similar ability or power to turn goods or skills into income in a given economic system.

The variables that compose the dimension of prestige are occupational prestige, certain aspects of personality, associational life, and consumption or style of life. At one end of this scale are individuals who have integrated personalities and enjoy personal fulfillment through valued associations and consumption. At the other end are those who have distorted, underdeveloped personalities and live lives of isolation and despair.

The dimension of power is made up of rights to political participation and access to public office, political attitudes, legislative benefits, and governmental treatment, including the distribution of justice. In all areas, and

TABLE 1–1 Basic Dimensions of Social Stratification (with examples of values in the top and bottom classes within each dimension and examples of subdimensions)[a]

	(ECONOMIC) CLASS VARIABLES INCOME WEALTH OCCUPATION EDUCATION FAMILY STABILITY EDUCATION OF CHILDREN	PRESTIGE VARIABLES OCCUPATIONAL PRESTIGE SUBJECTIVE DEVELOPMENT CONSUMPTION PARTICIPATION IN GROUP LIFE EVALUATIONS OF RACE, RELIGION, ETHNICITY	(POLITICAL-LEGAL) POWER VARIABLES POLITICAL PARTICIPATION POLITICAL ATTITUDES LEGISLATION AND GOVERNMENTAL BENEFITS DISTRIBUTION OF JUSTICE
HOUSEHOLDS IN THE UPPER SOCIAL CLASS	Affluence: economic security and power, control over material and human investment Income from work but mostly from property	More integrated personalities, more consistent attitudes, and greater psychic fulfillment due to deference, valued associations, and consumption	Power to determine public policy and its implementation by the state, thus giving control over the nature and distribution of social values
HOUSEHOLDS IN THE LOWER SOCIAL CLASS	Destitution: worthlessness on economic markets	Unintegrated personalities, inconsistent attitudes, sense of isolation and despair; sleazy social interaction	Political powerlessness, lack of legal recourse or rights, socially induced apathy

[a]For expository purposes, religious-ethnic and racial rankings are omitted.

perhaps especially in this one, it is necessary to see beyond the rhetoric of formal institutional analysis to the operational reality. As we will see in abundant detail later, the people at the upper end of this scale have far more power to influence the state, and thus the distribution of values in all dimensions, than do those at the bottom, protestations of democracy and equal rights notwithstanding.

Weber's cross-cultural comparisons and his acute eye for historical variations enabled him to see things that most stratification theorists overlooked. For Weber, class was no simple dichotomy between the propertied and nonpropertied (though he, like Marx, considered this phenomenon central to social stratification), but rather a series of hierarchies that interact to produce the inequality of social stratification. Thus the importance of Weber's insistence that the various dimensions and subdimensions of social stratification be kept analytically separate so that their relationships could be disclosed on an empirical rather than verbal basis.

The basic objectives of stratification analysis, therefore, are to locate a population along the axes of class, prestige, and power and to understand the causal processes that produce social classes, that is, households characterized by common benefits and behavior across the dimensions of class, prestige, and power.

To understand social stratification comprehensively, however, one must also account for related forms of inequality based on race, ethnicity, gender, age, disability, and sexual orientation. Let us explore these briefly starting with the complexities of age and gender inequality.

AGE AND GENDER INEQUALITY

Age and gender relations both differ from social stratification because the latter is a hierarchy of households, said households having at all class levels members of different ages and both sexes.

Age has a bearing on what one is worth on economic, prestige, and political markets, and is not irrelevant to class analysis. How much is spent on the education of the young or the support of the elderly has a significant impact on income distribution and here again one can see the significance of age for class stratification. The strong push by the Republican majority in Congress (1994–96) to curtail the medical cost of our aging population has a direct bearing on class inequality. The various groups up and down the class hierarchy feel the cost pressure of free medical care under Medicare (for retirees under Social Security) and under Medicaid (for the poor, with two-thirds of the funds going to care for the elderly poor in nursing homes). Taxes must be paid by the nonelderly to cover these costs and that means less capital for the rich, less income for working Americans, less money for the young (student grants, loans, and education), and so on.

Gender inequality is also different from class inequality because households at all levels have women in them. Thus even if men at all class levels do not consider women their equals, wives and daughters in the upper classes are generally better off than their counterparts in the lower classes. The power of class continues even when women move into the labor force: their chances of upward or downward mobility in their initial occupation is similar to that of men (see Chapter 19). In other words, the ability of both females and males to obtain good or poor jobs is very much affected by the class they are born and raised in with more or less equal results for both.

Gender inequality appears strongly inside the household and in the occupational careers of women. Focusing on the latter, women are an exploited portion of the labor force even after education, type of work, and lifetime experience are taken into account. That women are concentrated in low-paying occupations is not the main issue here; so are many men. Central to gender stratification is the fact that women are not treated as men's equals once they enter the labor force. They receive less pay for the same work, are not subject to the same standards of evaluation and promotion as men, and are prevented from entering certain occupations. Furthermore, when their husbands die or disappear they must assume the extraordinary burden of heading the household (which means that many widows and abandoned mothers and their children sink to and remain at the bottom of the social hierarchy). When we analyze the relation between gender and class inequality, we must distinguish between inequalities, just and unjust, to which men and women are both subject and those that pertain only to women (or, for that matter, only to men).[12]

Gender relations, therefore, must be analyzed as both class phenomena and as power relations in their own right.

RACIAL-ETHNIC INEQUALITY

The inequality of ethnic and racial groups can be related to social stratification much more easily than can age or sex, for a simple reason. In a society with an ethnic-religious or racially diverse population, a hierarchy based on ethnic-religious or racial status is easily established using the traditional ranking unit, the family. The upper classes must contain all ages and both sexes, but they need not include all ethnic, religious, and racial groups. Thus, a relatively sharp hierarchy based on ethnicity, religion, or race can easily be established and maintained over generations. Indeed, the clustering of economic and political power around distinctive ethnic, religious, or racial statuses is a commonplace of social stratification, not only in the United States but in all societies that are or have been heterogeneous in these regards.

INEQUALITY AND THE HANDICAPPED

The handicapped (who prefer to be called the differently abled) of the United States number over 40 million (approximately 15 percent of the total population). They are extremely diverse, ranging from those with learning disabilities, the severely and mildly retarded, the physically disabled, including the blind and deaf, the physically different, and the mentally ill. We will assume that the handicapped are largely, indeed mostly, the products of society (of poverty, especially inadequate prenatal care, of dangerous work, of dangerous leisure, of unsafe consumer products, of biased professional judgments, of faulty socialization, and contradictory norms and values). To be handicapped is to stay at the bottom of the class system or, if well off, to sink to the bottom or to lose out on many of the benefits of social life. Class analysis helps us identify how society generates handicapped people and thus how the social production of disease and disability can be prevented. It also helps us in understanding the many ways in which the handicapped can lead more productive lives.

INEQUALITY AND SEXUAL ORIENTATION

Societies have also treated unequally those individuals who look to members of their own gender for companionship and sex. Homosexuals (or gays and lesbians as they prefer to be called) form anywhere from 1 to 5 percent of the population, or somewhere between 2½ to 13 million individuals. The economic position and problems of gays and lesbians deserves study though they cannot be compared to the class system directly because in theory, gays and lesbians do not reproduce and there are no offspring to transmit class positions to. Theory aside, it should be noted that many gays and lesbians are in heterosexual marriages and a small number outside marriage are adopting children. In any case, gays and lesbians are denied important social benefits despite the fact that sexual preference appears to be irrelevant for the performance of occupation roles, and now that reproduction is not as vital for social survival as it was in the past, irrelevant for citizenship too. Or said differently, the denial of full rights to gays and lesbians is another way in which the American achievement ethic and its class system fails Americans.

SUMMARY

The purpose of this chapter was to provide a broad overview of the general field of social stratification. To do so we examined and discussed the relative merits of the biopsychological and sociocultural explanations of inequality, finding the latter more persuasive. In developing a working definition of social stratification, we relied heavily on Max Weber, and especially on his insistence that the various areas of inequality—the economic (class), the social (prestige), and the political (power)—be kept analytically separate. We explained that the purpose of stratification analysis is to locate social units on each of these three dimensions (and their subdimensions) over time, and to relate the various hierarchies to each other, also over time. Again following Max Weber, we assumed that though these dimensions vary in importance over the course of history, they tend with time to coalesce and form either castes, estates, or classes—that is, aggregates of households whose members share given social benefits across all three dimensions, largely on the basis of economic power.

All this means that the popular explanation for American inequality is unacceptable: Americans are not made unequal by their biopsychological natures but by social variables, which are for the most part ascriptive in nature. In other words, social class at birth explains success or failure for Americans in the aggregate better than does the idea of talent or innate individual ability (nonegalitarian classlessness). Social stratification, as the institutionalized ranking of family units containing both sexes and all ages, was carefully distinguished from gender- and age-related inequality. It was also pointed out that since religious-ethnic and racial aggregates are composed of family units, they can be stratified as aggregates by more powerful religious-ethnic or racial groups. We pointed out too that the handicapped are a numerous and varied group who also suffer from a socially induced and maintained inequality. Finally, we added a brief word about inequality on the basis of sexual orientation, indicating that being gay or lesbian appears to be irrelevant to the performance of both occupational and citizenship roles.

NOTES

1. For an historical survey of functional stratification thought that notes this similarity between apologists for very different social systems, see Stanislaw Ossowski, *Class Structure in the Social Consciousness,* trans. Sheila Patterson (New York: Free Press, 1963), pp. 172–180.
2. Ossowski, *Class Structure in the Social Consciousness,* chap. 7.
3. The meaning of the term *liberalism* will unfold gradually, especially over the next few pages. Essentially, it refers to the acceptance of private property, private economic motives and actions, and political and legal equality as central social institutions. Thus, both Democrats and Republicans in the United States are liberals; that is, both accept the validity and superiority of capitalist (liberal) society while disagreeing on how to run it. For a fuller discussion of liberal social theory, see *The International Encyclopedia of the Social Sciences* (New York: Macmillan and Free Press, 1968) or *Encyclopedia of Sociology* (New York: Macmillan, 1992).
4. Comte used the terms *men of intellect, men of feeling,* and *men of action.*
5. In this connection, see Norman Birnbaum, "Conflicting Interpretations of the Rise of Capitalism: Marx and Weber," *British Journal of Sociology* 4 (June 1953): 125–141.
6. The substance of Marx's theory of social stratification may be found in *The Communist Manifesto* and, on a more sophisticated level, in *The German Ideology.*
7. The importance of wealth, or the income and power derived from the ownership of the means of production, was neglected by American stratification theorists until quite recently. For its importance and for attempts to incorporate it into stratification theory, see Chapter 7.
8. For Weber's summary of the rise of capitalism, see his *General Economic History,* trans. Frank H. Knight (New York: Greenberg, 1927), Collier paperback, 1961, pt. 4.

9. Weber's theory of stratification is outlined in his influential essay "Class, Status, Party," in H. H. Gerth and C. Wright Mills, trans. and ed., *From Max Weber: Essays in Sociology* (New York: Oxford University Press, 1946), chap. 7. The introduction to this volume by Gerth and Mills is invaluable.
10. For an ethnographic study of fourteen aboriginal Polynesian cultures that finds a direct relationship between productivity and degree of social stratification, see Marshall D. Sahlins, *Social Stratification in Polynesia* (Seattle: University of Washington Press, 1958). This general point has been usefully elaborated by Gerhard Lenski; for a fuller discussion of his work, see Chapter 4.
11. The terms *social class* and *social stratum* will be used interchangeably throughout this text, though this is not always the case in the literature of stratification.
12. For example, men are uniquely subject to military service, and inequitably burdened by muscular and dangerous wage labor and the anxieties and hurts of economic insecurity and failure.

2
Stratification Through History

◆ ◆ ◆ ◆

◆ ◆ ◆ ◆

SOCIAL INEQUALITY AND TYPE OF SOCIETY

The best way to break the stranglehold of our familiar social world is to compare it with other worlds. In stratification analysis, this means analyzing how forms of inequality vary by type of society and by stage of social development.

HUNTING AND GATHERING SOCIETY

Imagine a hunting and gathering society based on age and sex differentiation. Men and women both perform important economic duties. All work hard and there is little economic surplus. By and large, families are equal—equally poor, equally rich, equal in a shared scarcity. Those who have outstanding abilities that are directly beneficial to society will stand out. An outstanding male hunter may well get a larger share of the catch and some prestige because of his hunting ability. People will listen to him when organizing hunts. A female hunter who is more dextrous (in hunting small animals) will also gain some extra benefits and be listened to with extra attention. The families of these individuals will share their fortune, and one can thus see the beginnings of economic, political, and social stratification. But a full system of social stratification cannot appear because these successful individuals have no way to guarantee the superiority of their offspring after they die. It is possible, of course, that they can pass on their attributes to their children through biological inheritance. But there is no guarantee.

COMPLEX HORTICULTURAL SOCIETY

The transition from hunting-gathering to horticultural society resulted from an economic revolution, the cultivation of plants. Simple horticultural societies produce food in family plots using simple tools and methods (and sometimes by herding animals). The emergence of more advanced methods of plant cultivation between 9,000 and 6,000 years ago soon led to complex or advanced horticultural societies. A key technological element in crossing the threshold to complex society was the development of metallurgy.[1]

The advanced horticultural societies of Mesopotamia, Egypt, India, China, Mesoamerica, and Peru were marked by permanent settlements, population increase, a marked growth in specialized occupations, technological and normative creativity, and the emergence of separate political institutions. One striking feature of the more advanced horticultural societies is the large increase in nonproductive activities: warfare, religious ritual and ceremonies, prestige practices and consumption, and administration. Also striking is the growth of specialized occupations: political heads, priests, warriors, tax collectors, merchants, artisans, servants, tenant-workers, serfs, slaves, entertainers, prostitutes, and bandits.

Perhaps the most striking feature of advanced horticultural society is the growth and formalization of special economic and political statuses. These statuses, which revolve around property rights, the organization of the labor force, and political authority, represent a significant change in power relations. Of special significance is the fact that these statuses become the attributes and transferable possessions of private individuals. Society is not only reconstituted but also its operation and maintenance over time are achieved through hereditary rights and processes. Another striking feature of advanced horticultural (and advanced herding societies) is the development of *monotheism* (doctrine or belief that there is one God). In some advanced horticultural societies there is also the momentous development of writing and mathematics, both outcomes of the need to record and direct complex economic and social transactions.

Complex horticultural societies are marked by considerable internal rivalry among elites, by population pressures both internal and external, and by economic problems (water shortages, pests, plant disease). The basic flow of resources is toward the top, although there are some downward redistribution processes, most of them token and symbolic. The essential power structure derives from ownership of or control over land, which in turn leads to occupations dependent on land ownership or control either directly or indirectly: king, nobility, priests, artisans, servants, serfs, slaves. The essential problem of power in this type of society (not necessarily seen clearly or fully) is how to maintain the overhead of nonproductive activities in the face of population growth, disease, crop failure, water shortages, and so on.

The power groups of advanced horticultural societies establish granaries to provide for lean years, institute welfare programs, undertake public works, some with direct economic significance such as irrigation and road building projects, and expand their economic base by conquest and plunder. The association of advanced horticultural society (out of which grew some of the great agrarian civilizations) with irrigation and flood control is striking. Also striking is the independent emergence of an autonomous state in societies that geared their economies to water control.[2]

COMPLEX AGRARIAN SOCIETY

Five Thousand Years of Hereditary Landlords and Servile Labor

The first agrarian societies emerged out of advanced horticultural societies in the Middle East approximately 5,000 years ago. An agrarian society is unique because it can produce food, tools, and other things, including belief and value systems, on a scale far exceeding even an advanced horticultural society. New technology, especially iron metallurgy and the plow, along with other productive techniques such as irrigation and the harnessing of animal energy—combined with such economically central sociocultural inventions as slave and serf labor, family-tenant labor, administrative structures, standing armies, forms of taxation (including forced labor), money, writing, mathematics, religion, and legal codes—result in a unique type and level of social existence.

The revolution implicit in the domestication of plants and animals soon expressed itself in the "domestication" of human beings. A sedentary farm or village life became the characteristic form of human behavior in a number of places. Within a few thousand years there emerged that momentous transformation in the quality and quantity of social interaction, namely the city. The unique advantages of an urban division of labor augmented technological advances.[3] Once established, the new agrarian economy became the basis for a continuous growth of the productive arts (despite setbacks) until a series of technological-economic plateaus were reached in the high civilizations of India, China, and medieval Europe.

The complex agrarian society develops a considerable economic surplus, thanks to an advanced technology and division of labor. Literacy, restricted to the elite in power, leads to the accumulation of technical knowledge and of a corpus of sacred writings, all easily transmissible under the custody of a privileged profession of priests or scholars. Agrarian society is characterized by mighty public works such as aqueducts, temples, roads, and fortresses, but little accumulation of productive capital; most production is for consumption. Any surplus over subsistence is expended on luxury, on "public" buildings glorifying the upper estates and the beliefs and values that benefit them, and on warfare. The surplus produced by the masses, in other words, is used to reinforce and perpetuate the system that dominates and exploits them.

Advanced agrarian societies (as found, for example, in the river-valley civilizations of the Middle East, India, and China) are typically large both in population and territory and exhibit a marked degree of institutional specialization. Above all, they everywhere exhibit a sharp cleavage between a small governing elite and a large unarmed peasant mass. Feudal-absolutism (or state feudalism) was given considerable impetus by the development of centralized irrigation and water-control systems. The so-called hydraulic societies[4] everywhere set up a leader and a state machine that legitimated itself in terms of an alleged derivation from both the supernatural and the people, and an alleged devotion to their service.

In addition to advances in technology, agrarian society develops a variety of labor forms. The tenant family is the most productive unit where crops require intensive labor; a militarized slave force is productive in some forms of agriculture and transportation (slave galley), in mining, road building, and other public works. Productivity is also enhanced by the emergence of specialized crafts. The outstanding characteristic of advanced agrarian society is a concentration of land worked in a variety of ways by human and animal muscle. The essential economic power relation is between the owners/controllers of land and the landless. As a result, the goods and services produced by the economy are not distributed equally nor are they distributed widely enough to raise per capita living standards. The essential flow of goods and services is upward into the coffers and service of the landlord (in the form of rent, interest, labor, or goods).

Advanced agrarian societies are marked by pronounced expansionist tendencies.[5] Once productive levels reach their limits, the only way to increase an elite's holdings—to make up for reverses caused by drought or disease, to replenish a labor force, or to gain psychic benefits—is physical expansion, invariably through conquest. A key perspective on complex agrarian societies is that they have the technological and organizational capacity to utilize their own as well as captured labor forces.[6]

The high agrarian civilizations are also marked by fully developed universalist, monotheistic religions. Monotheism and monarchy support and reinforce each other, and religious and political institutions are formally intertwined; indeed, religious values and norms permeate all institutional areas. In addition, complex agrarian society develops practices and symbols in the realms of law, education, and art that reinforce and maintain elite domination. A marked feature of these developments is the explicit division of a population into two static categories, a tiny elite and a huge mass, and the explicit parallel between inequality in law, education, and art with the sharp inequality in economic and political power. Ultimately, the basic symbolic system portrays the interests of the monarch and elite as synonymous with the interests of the masses.[7]

The central problem in building an agrarian state is the decentralizing thrust of the local, self-sufficient economy. The central authority must subdue not the masses but the local landlords, who in turn are intent on subduing the masses on their self-sufficient estates. Because the power that accrues to those who control land is enormous, the agrarian state never succeeds in fully freeing itself from its social base—its essential characteristic is a tension-filled collaboration between hereditary landlords and a central power (the monarch who is also a hereditary landlord).

Nonetheless, a developed agrarian society is characterized by a nobility that has been harnessed to serve a centralized state. In addition to civil servants and the military, there is further specialization and professionalization—for example, priesthood, astronomers and astrologers, theologians, physicians, mathematicians, scholars, philosophers, and artists. Though king and nobility are at odds in some ways, their interests are reconciled somewhat by the fact that the upper reaches of the various professions are recruited either by law or de facto from the hereditary stratum of landlords. *The essential definition of complex agrarian society is domination by a landed, propertied group that has specialized to control all functional areas—or, expressed differently, the propertied elite monopolizes the means of production, administration, warfare, belief, and meaning.*[8]

Agrarian societies are stable, and yet comparative standards of stability are difficult to establish either in contrast to simpler societies or to industrial systems (whose time span has so far been very small). Advanced agrarian systems, however, experience unique types of instability. In addition to the palace rivalries that occur in horticultural systems, advanced agrarian societies face a new problem—challenges from below. A marked feature of advanced agrarian feudalism is peasant and slave revolt (and crime). Stated more broadly, class polarization and struggle are widespread in advanced agrarian society.

Advanced agrarian society is also more politicized than earlier societies. Government takes an active role in managing the economy, providing public works, and storing food and other provisions for time of need. Despite notable achievements, however, agrarian society has instability built directly into its power relations—the masses work hard, do not receive much in return, and can identify their oppressors.[9] Many reforms are "revolutions from above"—segments of the dominant oligarchy seeking to oust other segments, to institute "reforms." A characteristic feature of Greece and Rome, for example, is *caesarism*—a reform movement initiated at the top in populist language but which leaves class relations substantively intact and distracts the masses by providing bread, circuses, and moral exhortation as substitutes for equality and justice.[10]

These societies never solved the economic problem that was the cause of their malfunctioning. The best-documented pictures of the instability caused by economic troubles and inequality are for ancient Greece and Rome. Strictly speaking, these are both hybrid societies (that is, they have complex economies consisting not only of subsistence horticulture and agriculture, but extraction, construction, moneylending, manufacturing, and export agriculture and manufacturing) and complex political-legal institutions (that stemmed largely from the need to manage their complex economies). Nonetheless, their essential system of inequality was based on land and unfree labor (slaves and a variety of semifree serfs, tenants, and laborers). Without the consensus that marked this relation in the more straightforward agrarian systems, such as Egypt or China, this system was regarded as illegitimate (exploitative) by many and resulted in a chronic condition of class struggle.

The cleavage between rich and poor not only led to internal dissension but also spilled out to cause instability among the Greek city-states and between Rome and its neighbors.[11] Under pressure to pay higher taxes, the wealthier elements were always ready to lead and unite with the poor to seek booty in war. This relation between inner and outer power relations is a characteristic feature of all complex societies down to the present day.

Agrarian society has two similar yet different forms of social stratification—the caste system and the estate system. Each deserves a special word.

The Caste System: India

A caste system forms when an ascriptive condition, usually religious birth or condition of servitude, becomes an unalterable and inviolate basis for the unequal distribution of all social benefits. While a number of societies (for example, Ceylon, and parts of Africa, Japan, and the United States) have developed approximations of caste stratification, probably the only true example is India.[12]

Disregarding origins and historical irregularities, what appears to have happened on the Indian subcontinent is that the Hindu religion crystallized in such a way as to transcend class and power, and came not only to express economic and political forces but also to dominate them. This is not to minimize the importance of economic and political factors. It should be kept in mind that India was an agrarian society, the vast bulk of whose population worked in a labor-intensive, low-technology agricultural economy dominated by large landlords. Given a static village economy, it is not surprising that a complex, sophisticated religion such as Hinduism could provide the simple productive system with a religious sanction and eventually envelop it altogether.

The same is true of family, governmental, and military relations. Together with economic functions, these realms too were eventually absorbed into a hierarchic mosaic of religiously defined castes and subcastes. With behavior in all areas of life subject to a religiously determined division of social labor, the individual castes were self-sufficient in terms of marriage and reproduction, the socialization of the young, eating patterns, kin obligations and mutual help, the settlement of disputes, and the practice of religion per se, while at the same time they were committed to occupations and caste relations that incorporated them into villagewide, regional, and all-India divisions of social labor. On a very abstract and relatively unrealistic level, Indian society was a hierarchy composed of four *varnas* (broad all-India castes) and the *untouchables* (the outcaste). This scheme was derived from a religious literary tradition about 3,000 years old; while it is not accurate empirically—the reality of Indian stratification is its thousands of subcastes—it provides a first approximation of the essential spirit of caste.[13]

Formally speaking, therefore, the classic caste system of India was based on the all-pervasive importance of religious status at birth (Hinduism). Both the Hindu religion and the social system it eventually brought under its sway were vastly different from the religions and societies that Westerners are accustomed to. They lacked the theology, explicit organizational structures, functional staff (clergy, civil servants), and degree of legalization and formal political authority that Westerners associate with religion and society. Despite the apparent formlessness of the Indian caste system, however, it effectively controlled Indian society for well over 2,000 years. This is all the more remarkable in light of the fact that the caste and subcastes could never be precisely identified, described, ranked, or even numbered. Each of the four main castes—the Brahmans (priests and scholars), the Kshatriyas or Rajputs (princes and warriors), the Vaishyas (merchants), and the Sudras (peasants, artisans, laborers)—contained many subcastes, and the total numbered in the thousands. Below these, the outcastes (untouchables) made up approximately 20 percent of the population.

It is impossible to understand the absolute inequality that prevails under the Indian caste system without understanding the main tenets of Hinduism:

1. *Samsara,* or reincarnation, is life after death—in this world, not another.
2. *Dharma,* or correct ritual behavior, specifies the behavior appropriate to one's caste.
3. *Karma,* or causality, is dependent on how well one adheres to correct ritual behavior (dharma) independently of social conditions.

In Hinduism, there is no supreme creator: Life, or the soul, has always existed and manifests itself in caste. One can improve one's caste in the next (social) life, and failure to adhere to the dharma of one's caste can cause one to be downgraded either in this social life or the next one, but no one can climb the social hierarchy during any given lifetime.

There is little that is obligatory for all Hindus. All must respect the Brahmans, believe in the sacredness of the cow, and accept the castes into which they are born. The main thrust of Hinduism (and thus of Indian culture) is toward prescribing different modes of behavior and different benefits for each caste. There is no universal standard of right and wrong, no improvement is possible in this life, all deprivations and hardships are ordained and explained by religion, and the only recourse against worldly suffering and the only avenue to social mobility is the possibility of a better life in some future reincarnation. Unlike Christianity, which has universal moral rules (the Ten Commandments), universal ethical ideals (love and brotherhood), and declares all individual souls equal before God, Hinduism sets a radically different course for each caste and subcaste, saying in effect that different castes are worth different amounts in the divine scheme of things.

The enormous power and stability of the Indian caste system resulted from the extension of religion into every aspect of behavior, occupation, marriage, eating and drinking, friendship, and so on. The radical particularism of religion thus resulted in a social and cultural particularism so deep that it precluded even a minimal degree of equality. The Indian subcaste was a prestige group without parallel in the history of stratification. It constituted the consciousness of its members and controlled their economic and political relationships down to the smallest particular. A Westerner's deeply implanted sense of the public, ingrained universalism, and easy use of abstractions in dealing with oneself, others, and nature make the cultural diversity (particularism) represented by India's thousands of subcastes almost incomprehensible. Nevertheless, the caste system was not random or unpatterned. Relations between the subcastes were strictly prescribed according to a logic provided by the Hindu concept of ritual purity—a concept blurred obviously by such phenomena as conquest, migration, British imperial control, urbanization, and industrialization.

Given this strict and narrow definition of identity, there is no formal consistency between the hierarchies of class, prestige, and power. Formally, each of the top three castes monopolized the top of one hierarchy and each was formally positioned hierarchically in relation to the others: Brahmans (prestige), Kshatriyas or Rajputs (power), and Vaishyas (class). But beneath the forms of the Indian caste system there is a general consistency of status in the major dimensions of stratification: All three of the top castes, for example, enjoyed high or substantial economic status and were roughly equivalent in their other statuses. Only a minority of Brahmans, for example, followed a priestly calling; while Brahmans could not pursue certain occupations, such as medicine and moneylending, without jeopardizing their caste positions, they were landlords and practiced all the learned professions. Hinduism, and its rigid, religious system of inequality, like racism in the plantation American South, was in the final analysis an ideology of economic domination.

Stratification by Estates: Feudal and Feudal-Authoritarian Societies

Inequality by estates is the most common system of stratification among precommercial horticultural and agricultural societies. Two subtypes can be distinguished:

1. *Feudalism,* or the highly localized and personalized lord-vassal relation based on hereditary linkages to land, in which the lord has explicit governmental, religious, military, and economic power over his dependents.
2. The *feudal-authoritarian* form, in which a relatively strong central government emerges and is superimposed on the feudal system. Ordinarily, a hereditary absolute monarchy rules bureaucratically through officials recruited from the nobility.[14]

A feudal or *simple* agrarian society is not much different from a horticultural society—in some ways it is less differentiated and less developed culturally. A simple feudal system is centered on the economically self-sufficient *latifundia, manor,* or *hacienda.* It has a natural economy—little is produced for exchange. Simple feudal society is also marked by political self-sufficiency: the local lord (or patron, or gentry) enforces laws and settles disputes. Decentralized feudalism generates simple market relations, mostly of a local character. Its outstanding characteristic is that land and labor are not commercialized. Work and nature are given fixed definitions and the economy is embedded in political, religious, and family institutions.[15]

Like the caste system, the estate system is focused formally on prestige rather than economic status. However, institutionalized inequality in estate society relies much more explicitly and heavily than does caste society on power (monarch, magistrate, state religion, tax collector, the military). Although economic variables are important in the origin of such societies, they eventually succumb to such power and prestige variables as military force, law and administration, a mighty religion, styles of consumption, traditions of family honor, and intellectual-educational forces.

The estate system of stratification is similar to the caste system in other ways. Both caste and estate societies lack a coherent and viable state or system of public authority relative to modern society. When estate stratification is compared only with the Indian caste system, however, one finds that it has a much higher degree of formal definition, especially in the area of law. While the estate system is also governed by ascription, it is family, not religious status at birth, that is the crucial determinant of social position in an established estate system.

Medieval society in the West is our best known example of estate stratification. Because of the prime importance of force during the settlement of barbarian Europe after the fall of Rome, skill at warfare became the most important form of social power. The retreat into the countryside and the primitive technology of the time made land the most important economic value. The warrior soon turned his skill at violence into an economic asset through plunder and control of land under a system in which protection was exchanged for food and labor, and eventually succeeded in legalizing and legitimizing his ascendant position through chivalry, *noblesse oblige,* and privilege or superior legal rights.

While the full-fledged estate system has a relatively higher degree of explicit social specialization than does the caste system, it is much less specialized and differently specialized than modern society. The modern social system specializes the behavior of individuals according to an intricate occupational system, but also demands considerable versatility from individuals. Thus, individuals (especially males) are Jacks-of-all-functions in that they must obtain education, work, attend to the formation and functioning of their families, be responsible for the legality and morality of their actions, seek out salvation, participate in public affairs, and fight in their nation's wars. The feudal system specializes a population by families. In the feudal system the upper stratum of noble families (its males) did the fighting, administered the manors, dispensed justice, engaged in "politics," and did the thinking and praying.[16] The serfs were a dependent group who followed the decrees of custom and lord. They raised families, of course, and went to church, and were even pressed into military service on occasion, but by and large the religious and secular normative tradition and social practice confined them to manual work, a dishonorable activity regarded as punishment for sin.

The estate legal system in the West stipulated that legal status was a function of family birth and provided for different rights and duties (privilege) depending on social position. The noble was not subject to arrest or trial in the same manner as were commoners; his fiefs were not inherited in the same way as were other properties; his rank gave the nobleman exclusive access to high religious position; his person was specially protected against his inferiors; he had the right of private vengeance; he enjoyed special rights with regard to consumption and personal adornment; and he was able to substitute military service for the usual burdens of taxation.

The feudal idea of privilege must be seen in the context of a pronounced system of cultural particularism. Feudalism was characterized by few abstractly defined functional institutions, and there was little that was shared by all. Its emphasis, rather, was on the different rights and duties of the different strata. The relation between lord and serf was a highly personal, rigid, and pervasive structure of supersubordination that encompassed all spheres of existence. Of great significance to this system was the privatization of political power; what today is defined as public authority or public office was defined under feudalism as the attribute or possession of private persons.

Despite the static nature of feudal stratification, a certain measure of social mobility was both possible and legitimate. In the Western estate system, for example, marriage between social unequals (strictly forbidden in a caste system) was possible though not common, non-nobles could be knighted in exceptional circumstances (usually military), noble status and high office could be purchased, and the nature of the Christian Church blurred the strict distinction between noblemen and serfs by permitting the latter to become priests. Furthermore, Christianity tended to give all people a common religious and moral status, thus lending the moral force of religion to a minimal acknowledgment of equality.

Western feudalism was modified, of course, by the emergence of absolutism or feudal-authoritarian society. Attempts to impose absolute monarchy on feudalism account for a great deal of the histories of England, France, Prussia, Russia, and other countries. The essential new contribution by the authoritarian estate system was bureaucratic administration in government, a hierarchy of governmental occupations requiring training and other ways to attach individuals to a centralized means of administration. While this subtype emerged throughout the world, it developed most fully in the West, where it was eventually transformed into the class system when the "state" passed out of the hands of the monarch and nobility into the hands of the middle class. As Gideon Sjoberg[17] points out, however, the emergence of liberal democracy represented less of a break with the past than we imagine. Agrarian societies are exceedingly durable. Despite large-scale problem-solving failures, they successfully resist revolt from below and changes from above. In only one place—the West—did agrarian society succumb to a new form of society and even there it imparted many of its characteristics to its successor. With their monopolistic control of symbol formation, technical intelligence, and administrative-military-legal-political skills, along with their highly developed forms of etiquette and taste, it is not surprising that agrarian feudal elites were highly influential in shaping the modern West. In England the feudal aristocracy had a profound impact on liberal society and one must think in terms of the blending of interests and values between the feudal elite and the developing middle class rather than an abrupt break and reversal.[18] The feudal nobility was a powerful force in France well after the French Revolution, while feudal elites remained dominant in industrial Germany[19] and Japan. Thus, while the class system of stratification will be treated as a distinct type, important continuities and similarities with the estate system will be noted.

INEQUALITY IN THE MODERN WORLD: CAPITALIST SOCIETY

The Rise of Capitalism

The transformation of feudal to industrial society is the most momentous event ever directly experienced and reflected upon by human beings (if we are right in assuming that the advent of agriculture was too gradual and too absorbed in mythology to stimulate much reflection). Many social scientists in the eighteenth and nineteenth centuries interpreted the rise of modern (capitalist or liberal) society as the outcome of "individualism." They assumed that human nature, suppressed for millennia by the forces of ignorance and superstition, had at last freed itself. Human beings they felt were now manifesting their natural biopsychological structures (or drives, instincts, needs, rights). Today, a sociological perspective would insist that the order of causality be reversed, that capitalism emerged first and then developed individualism (including the full range of vices and virtues termed the *modern Protestant-bourgeois personality*) as its necessary personality type. If there's no human nature, then, where did capitalism come from?

Our best answer comes from Max Weber. According to Weber, capitalism was the outcome of the following conditions that came together by chance during the late Middle Ages:

1. Greek philosophy with its emphasis on abstraction, its assumptions about the lawfulness of human nature and nature, and its well-developed structures of logic (teleology and mathematics)
2. Greek and Roman political and legal theories with their distinctions between law and other types of norms, between the responsible and irresponsible exercise of power, and between public and private offices and norms
3. The Judaic-Christian religious-moral orientation with its abstract theology (rational monotheism), its this-worldly counterbalance to excessive otherworldliness, and its sharp separation among the realms of God, human nature, and nature
4. An advanced material culture (plows, carts, the harness, hearths, bellows, wind and watermills, ships)
5. A favorable natural environment (good soil, adequate rainfall, a temperate climate; good energy and other resources such as timber and ores; cheap water transportation)
6. Military factors
7. Luxury trade

8. But "in the last resort the factor which produced capitalism is the rational permanent enterprise, rational accounting, rational technology and rational law, but again not these alone. Necessary complementary factors were the rational spirit, the rationalization of the conduct of life in general, and a rationalistic economic ethic."[20]

Indispensable to the capitalist spirit, argued Weber, was Protestantism. Protestant Christians, especially Calvinists, were called on, one and all, to do God's work in this world and to accept the world's problems as a challenge to their character. As Protestants they could neither withdraw from the world into mysticism nor accommodate themselves to it under the guidance of others (the medieval Catholic Church). Given the need to avoid creatural temptations, Calvinism soon came to see work as a calling in which one administers what God has given. Eventually, argued Weber, there emerged a methodical, impersonal, individualist type of conduct, especially in economic affairs, which, combined with a religious brake on personal consumption, stimulated both capital formation and the spirit of capitalism. Out of the Reformation came a merger of religious and economic behavior in which economic success signified religious worth and religious status provided economic motives and credentials.

Weber did not think of religion as the only or even as the major cause of capitalism. If anything, his major emphasis was on economic factors, followed by political and then religious factors. But while his approach was multicausal, he put no emphasis on establishing priorities or on finding the unifying thread of human history as Marx had done. If anything, argued Weber, capitalism occurred because a large number of causes came together by chance. Thus, he emphasized such economic factors as the emergence of technology, especially in the textile industry; the preeminent importance of coal and iron, which freed industry from inorganic and organic limitations; and the rise of new forms of economic organization such as the joint-stock company. But he also cited political factors such as law, administration, warfare, and types of urban existence as important causes. All these, along with Protestantism, said Weber, caused capitalism.

Weber (as did Marx) emphasized *internal* factors in his explanation of the rise of capitalism. In recent years theorists have argued that capitalism could not have risen without the help of factors *outside* society. No understanding of the rise of capitalism is complete, therefore, until international trade and imperial expansion are included.[21] And the rise of science was also dependent on an international network of stimulation and support.[22]

The Nature of Capitalism

The essence of capitalism is the private ownership of aspects of nature (land, water, mineral or grazing rights, air space, and so on), technology, including knowledge, and labor power (including professional skills), and their employment for gain (profit, rent, salaries, wages) through exchange relationships. Understood differently, capitalism means the transformation of nature and human nature into productive forces. Under a capitalist (market or exchange) economy, the bulk of productive property (land, animals, factories, offices, and so on) is in private hands and its owners strive to profit from the use of their property. Under capitalism, work is performed by legally free individuals who sell their labor time. In classic capitalist theory, it is assumed that economic units are small and competitive, and that the free exchange of goods, services, and labor is the most rational way to allocate resources. The reality of capitalism is otherwise: The vast bulk of economic activity is conducted by giant, oligarchic corporations and there are numerous distortions and barriers to the free exchange of goods, services, and labor; distortions and barriers that are both legal and illegal and which often represent other respectable social values.

Another distinctive feature of capitalism is its many-sided process of capital formation. Unlike even the highly productive agrarian society, capitalism channels significant portions of economic surplus into productive uses. While part of its surplus goes toward a rising standard of living and part for social overhead, part also goes for capital investment. Paying labor less than it produces, thrift, safeguarding property rights, tax policies that favor investments, norms of efficiency, the substitution of technology for labor, the subsidization of necessary but unprofitable capital investments (such as canals, railroads, highways, airports, water supply, sanitation, fire and military protection) by public revenues are all part of the process of capital formation.

Historic capitalism based itself on a number of key beliefs: that its institutions expressed fundamental forces in human nature, that science and knowledge embedded in capitalist institutions are an unmixed good, and that the encouragement of self-interest is compatible, indeed, a requisite for social health. These beliefs were based on the master assumption that a hidden logic synthesizes the selfish, short-term initiatives of profit-oriented egos. The magical belief in the hidden logic of social institutions, especially economic markets (laissez-faire market economy), political markets (representative government), and intellectual markets (competitive education, professionalism, research, free press), has no basis in fact. Nonetheless, it dominates, nay monopolizes, American culture and serves as a mind-numbing legitimation of power and the status quo.

Both history and social science make clear that capitalism is simply another type of society constructed haphazardly over time using half-understood natural and cultural resources and opportunities. It is no more rooted in human nature or the cosmos than hunting-gathering, horticultural, or agrarian societies. Beneath its ideology of progress through abstract individualism and competition lies a very different world. The essential dynamic of the American economy is supplied by huge corporations aided by government, higher education, the professions, and a variety of voluntary groups. The record of American elites in managing American capitalism is spotty: while economic growth occurred from 1850 on, it was marred by numerous busts and panics. Of the utmost importance is the fact that the improved standard of living after 1850 ceased after the 1960s even though economic growth continued. Related to this development is the fact that not only has economic growth failed to produce more equality for Americans, but inequality has increased since 1970!

Inequality in American society allegedly derives from the natural hierarchy of ability in human beings. America's biopsychological explanation of inequality often takes the form of racism and sexism. While there is much talk of equality of opportunity in all spheres and a strong normative tradition stressing equality of competition, in reality most competition takes place within classes. While a powerful ideology stresses individual achievement, in reality the majority of wealthy individuals inherited their property. In addition, occupational placement is also hereditary, either directly or through class-based socialization processes, including the private and public educational systems. Underlying the overall process is deep economic concentration linked to political and social power.

SUMMARY

Equality and inequality vary with type of society. The only known relatively equal society is the hunting-gathering type. Complex societies such as horticultural, agrarian, and industrial are very unequal.

The economic system is the main source of inequality. Using different means and different ideologies, horticulture, agrarian, and industrial societies channel surplus resources upward into concentrated economic and political control by small numbers of elite households.

American capitalism, despite its ideology of individualism, competition, and equality, is a very unequal class society. Despite on-average economic growth for upwards of 150 years, the United States has neither reduced its hierarchy of classes nor increased overall levels of equal opportunity. More ominously, economic and class differences have grown in the past two or three decades and all indications are that they will continue to grow into the future.

NOTES

1. I am indebted to Gerhard Lenski, Patrick Nolan, and Jean Lenski, *Human Societies: An Introduction to Macrosociology*, 7th ed. (New York: McGraw-Hill, 1995), ch. 6–7, for their informative analysis of horticultural and agrarian societies.

2. Morton H. Fried, "On the Evolution of Social Stratification and the State," in Robert A. Manners and David Kaplan, eds., *Theory in Anthropology* (Chicago: Aldine, 1968), pp. 251–260. For more general discussions, see Morton H. Fried, *The Evolution of Political Society* (New York: Random House, 1967), and Elman R. Service, *Origins of the State and Civilization: The Process of Cultural Evolution* (New York: W.W. Norton, 1975).
3. Two essays, by Robert J. Braidwood, "The Agricultural Revolution," and Robert M. Adams, "The Origins of Cities," both in *Scientific American*, September 1960 (reprints 605 and 606), give quick introductions to this period. For fuller treatments, see the highly readable accounts by V. Gordon Childe, *Man Makes Himself*, rev. ed. (New York: Mentor, 1951), and *What Happened in History*, rev. ed. (Baltimore: Penguin, 1954); William Howells, *Back of History* (New York: Doubleday, 1954); and Leslie A. White, *The Evolution of Culture* (New York: McGraw-Hill, 1959).
4. Karl Wittfogel, *Oriental Despotism: A Comparative Study of Total Power* (New Haven, CT: Yale University Press, 1957).
5. Complex societies in general tend to be expansionist—see Chapter 3 for a discussion of the imperialism of empire (found among advanced horticultural, agrarian, and early capitalist societies) and the imperialism of the world-market economy (found among contemporary industrial systems).
6. Industrial societies also know how to utilize foreign labor at home (immigrants, brain drain, guest labor, illegal aliens). In addition, industrial capitalists use foreign labor abroad by exporting capital to compliant countries with large pools of cheap labor; for example, American capital goes abroad to manufacture television sets in Taiwan, textiles in the Republic of Korea, and automobile engines in Mexico.
7. The historic middle class of the modern West did much the same—it proclaimed a universal humanity and gave itself as the definition of the human.
8. Important continuities and similarities between state feudalism and liberal democracy will be pointed out in due course.
9. These are also the conditions that lead to economic and technological stagnation and that propel elites toward war as a way to maintain revenues.
10. The similarity with reform in contemporary liberal societies will be noted in due course. And revolution from above is a distinctive feature of contemporary developing societies.
11. Alvin W. Gouldner, *Enter Plato: Classical Greece and the Origins of Social Theory* (New York: Basic Books, 1965), pt. 1; Robert Antonio, "The Contradiction of Domination and Production in Bureaucracy: The Contribution of Organizational Efficiency to the Decline of the Roman Empire," *American Sociological Review* 44 (December 1979):895–912; Andrew Lintott, *Violence, Civil Strife and Revolution in the Classical City* (Baltimore: Johns Hopkins University Press, 1981); G.E.M. de Ste. Croix, *The Class Struggle in the Ancient Greek World: From the Archaic Age to the Arab Conquests* (Ithaca, NY: Cornell University Press, 1981); and Alexander Fuks, *Social Conflict in Ancient Greece* (Jerusalem: Hebrew University Press, 1984).
12. For a wide-ranging historical and comparative analysis of various stratification systems, which sees class forces behind caste divisions including racial slavery in the American South, see Oliver Cromwell Cox, *Caste, Class and Race* (Garden City, NY: Doubleday, 1958).

13. For an excellent formal description of the Indian caste system, see Egon E. Bergel, *Social Stratification* (New York: McGraw-Hill 1962), pp. 35–67. For a theoretical discussion of caste, see Anthony de Reuck and Julie Knight, eds., *Caste and Race: Comparative Approaches* (London: J. and A. Churchill, 1967), especially ch. 1, 5, and 7. Probably the best introduction for the beginning reader is Taya Zinkin, *Caste Today* (London: Oxford University Press, 1962).
14. For a broad sociological analysis of an example of the feudal-authoritarian form of estate stratification, see Hsiao-Tung Fei, "Peasantry and Gentry: An Interpretation of Chinese Social Structure and Its Changes," *American Journal of Sociology* 52 (July 1946):1–17.
15. For a useful distinction between types of economies and their societies, see C. B. Macpherson, "Status, Simple Market, and Possessive Market Societies," in his *The Political Theory of Possessive Individualism: Hobbes to Locke* (London: Oxford University Press, 1962), pp. 46–68. As we see in Chapter 3, societies with a horticultural or simple feudal background (black Africa and Latin America) have had a more difficult time "modernizing" than have societies with a feudal-authoritarian background (Western Europe and Sino-based societies).
16. The upper clergy were eventually drawn only from noble families. Thus, the disputes between Church and State, however real, were disputes between two estates that shared fundamental stratum (class, prestige, and power) attributes and interests.
17. Gideon Sjoberg, "Folk and 'Feudal' Societies," *American Journal of Sociology* 58, no. 3 (November 1952):231–239.
18. Walter L. Arnstein, "The Survival of the Victorian Aristocracy" in F. C. Jaher, ed., *The Rich, the Well Born, and the Powerful* (Urbana: University of Illinois Press, 1973), pp. 203–57.
19. For an interesting analysis of how feudal and bourgeois values of inequality blended in Germany, which has implications for all modern societies, see Walter Struve, *Elites Against Democracy: Leadership Ideals in Bourgeois Political Thought in Germany, 1890–1933* (Princeton, NJ: Princeton University Press, 1973).
20. Weber's only summary of his position is in his *General Economic History*, trans. F. H. Knight, 1927 (New York: Collier, 1961), pt. 4. The quotation is on p. 260.
21. This perspective will be developed more fully in Chapter 3.
22. Robert Wuthnow, "The Emergence of Modern Science and World System Theory," *Theory and Society* 8 (September 1979):215–243.

3

Stratification Among Societies

◆ ◆ ◆ ◆

◆ ◆ ◆ ◆

Societies are characterized by "political" relations; they discuss, argue, and moralize among themselves, negotiate trade and military agreements, and agree or disagree on matters as varied as air rights, mail, customs, the rights of citizens, cultural and scientific exchange, and so on. Societies spy on each other and finance political movements in other countries that favor their interests. Political relations among societies can lead to mutual respect, a concern for the rights of the weak and of minorities, including political opponents, and a willingness to compromise. But intersocietal relations are also characterized by domination, conquest, exploitation, and dependence, in short, by stratification and imperialism.

INTERSOCIETAL STRATIFICATION: EMPIRE AND WORLD-MARKET SYSTEMS

The fact that societies interpenetrate as part of larger systems, culminating in imperialism, has received various explanations. Karl Deutsch has identified them as:

1. Folk theories (biologic-instinctive, demographic-Malthusian, geographic-strategic, cultural organicism, or the people as a psychological entity), theories that today command little respect
2. Conservative theories (Julie Ferry, Disraeli, Rhodes, Kipling), which advocated imperial expansion to provide economic stability at home
3. Liberal theories (John Hobson and Norman Angell), which argued that imperialism was unnecessary and stood in the way of competition
4. A sociological/psychological theory (associated with Joseph Schumpeter), which argued that imperialism was learned behavior and thus not inevitable
5. Marxian theories of imperialism (especially those of Vladimir Lenin, Jon Galtung, and Samir Amin), which argued that capitalist economies necessarily reach outward to acquire colonies to support themselves (with Leninists arguing that imperialist nations weaken themselves by investing abroad and other Marxists arguing that they strengthen themselves by creating dependent, complementary colonial economies and societies)[1]

Perhaps the first systematic analysis of imperialism to influence mainsteam sociology is Immanuel Wallerstein's *The Modern World System: Capitalist Agriculture and the Origins of the European World Economy in the Sixteenth Century.*[2] Wallerstein argues that a society's internal development is greatly affected by its relations with other societies. The uniqueness of capitalism is its commitment to economic growth through economic activity. The empires acquired by the capitalist societies were not ordinary empires. They were part of a new international division of labor roughly divided into technically advanced countries and countries that specialized in food, staples, ores, fuel, and labor. Gradually modern imperialism shifted to a new kind of imperialism, one in which advanced societies could dominate others through new imperialist mechanisms such as free markets, trade agreements, loans, and investments (as well as in conquest and colonies). Historically, the imperialism of the new world-market economy emerged as a mercantile-financial operation (*portfolio investment*, or loans to the governments of colonies and dependent countries, characteristic of British imperialism) and then shifted to *direct investment* in productive, especially industrial enterprises (characteristic of American imperialism).

In analyzing international stratification, therefore, one must distinguish between the imperialism of an empire, in which a society expands by absorbing other societies (often becoming a larger society composed of different ethnic, religious, or linguistic groups), and the imperialism of the capitalist era in which a society expands by developing an economic superiority to other societies (as well as by territorial expansion) within an international division of labor.

AGRARIAN EXPANSIONISM: THE IMPERIALISM OF EMPIRE

Empires in some form or another have existed for 5,000 years and were made possible by the advent of agriculture. Their beginnings are the great river-valley civilizations in the Middle East and their endings are in the dissolution of the Hapsburg Empire in 1918, the collapse of Imperial China between 1900 and 1945, the containment and contraction of the Ottoman Empire between 1450 and the 1920s, the dissolution of the British Empire and the overthrow of the French Empire after World War II, and the end of Portugal's empire in 1975. The essence of an empire is expansion through military or political conquest, and an attempt to control and profit from the economy of a conquered territory through military and political means. Empires are not able to integrate themselves through homogenization (because of feudal particularism and because they invariably contain a variety of racial and ethnic groups) though they are often accompanied by religious, missionary zeal (world religion).

Empires often last for considerable periods, but they exhibit chronic internal turmoil and all have decayed and disintegrated. Empires are marked by considerable economic surplus since they are based on a well-developed agriculture and a relatively advanced technology (irrigation, aqueducts, metallurgy, power from animals, water, wind, and sail, and from human muscle, especially serfdom and slavery). Characteristically, economic surplus is consumed in nonproductive activities: war, luxurious life-styles, inefficient administration, public spectacles, art, and the construction of monuments, arenas, palaces, temples, churches, and tombs. Indeed, the costs of these activities, especially the military and administrative costs of maintaining empires, invariably become so great that they stagnate the economy. A stagnant or declining economy creates political and social unrest that requires more coercion, more unproductive activities, and more conquest.

Empires may expand in terms of geographical size, population, and production but they are not dynamic systems. Unlike modern industrial systems they do not result in increased per capita living standards and do not provide incentives for productivity, technological advance, or capital investment. Actually, they institutionalize *disincentives* for production and efficiency. Their servile serf and slave labor, nonbureaucratic (nonrational) administration, punitive systems of tribute and taxation, otherworldly values, and institutionalized "waste" (prestige and military-political expenditures militate against productivity, efficiency, and capital formation). The elites of feudal systems see the acquisition of territory as the main way to enlarge the economic pie (which means that enemies are created because someone else's pie shrinks).

The mounting and conflicting claims that converge on the central state of empires lead to more inefficient centralization, political intrigue and conflict, ethnic and class rivalries, labor repression, and the suppression of political dissent through force. Ultimately, the military and political costs of running such a system outstrip the economy's ability to sustain them.

THE NEW IMPERIALISM: THE CAPITALIST WORLD-MARKET SYSTEM

New insight into the rise and nature of capitalism, modern class formation, the nation-state, imperialism, and international stratification is provided by Wallerstein's concept of a capitalist world economy, or as we will refer to it, the world-market system. Using neo-Marxian ideas concerning imperialism, Wallerstein argues that solitary societies (except for simple subsistence societies) are not ultimate entities. On the contrary, all contemporary societies must be conceived as part of a uniquely modern international division of labor. Unlike the inner structure of a single (precapitalist) society in which economic and political institutions are explicitly related, capitalist society separates its economy and politics both in its domestic life and in the relations among societies. The essence of the international system is that an expansive world economy comes into being in which all benefit, but because unequal units are transacting business, the more powerful benefit disproportionately. And because there is no government common to the unequal and often exploitive economic relations of the world-market economy, there is no way to focus conflicts, bring about compromises, assign blame and responsibility, and the dominant societies do not (at least at first) have to pay the full costs of maintaining order or institutionalizing exploitation.

Core, Semiperiphery, and Periphery

According to Wallerstein, three different types of units interact in the capitalist world-market system that emerged in the sixteenth century: *core states, peripheral areas,* and *semiperipheral areas.* The core state develops an expanding economy based on capitalist agriculture (gentry, yeoman farmers), trade (for example, the East India and Hudson's Bay companies), manufacture (textiles, china, and ironware), and services (banking and insurance). A large component of this expanding economy is made up of foreign trade. Essentially, a core state specializes its economy (and its internal system of social stratification) to complement the specialization of its international trading partners. Over time it acquires many trading partners, whereas peripheral and semiperipheral areas acquire few. Gradually, its labor force is upgraded in skills and responsibilities, and a strong state emerges to supply the conditions of internal economic expansion (roads, law, currency) and external economic expansion (army, navy, foreign ministry).

Peripheral areas are marked by a distinctive form of development known as *underdevelopment.*[3] Development for them means the creation of unskilled, coerced, slave, or serf labor organized in extraction (for example, silver, gold, tin, oil, bauxite, copper) or in the production and export of labor and agricultural staples (slaves, cheap "immigrant," "migrant" or "guest" labor, sugar, cotton, coffee, rubber, tea, bananas, or cash crop specialty fruits and vegetables). Such areas are also politically underdeveloped. At first they are colonies but even after independence they are governed by a native upper and middle class that benefits from and thus has a stake in the new international division of labor.

The term *semiperipheral* denotes societies that for one reason or another were able to avoid being subordinated by the capitalist core long enough to develop as core states themselves (Russia and Japan), or societies that are large enough, developed enough, or have enough special assets to have some of the features of core societies (India, the People's Republic of China, Brazil, Spain, Greece, Turkey, South Korea, and others). Here one is dealing with *dependent development* as opposed to underdevelopment. The society in question has a growing economy, perhaps with considerable industry, and an active national state. Nonetheless, it is still subject to both its own past and to the imperatives of the world market.

The concept of semi-periphery also serves as a caution against a mechanical one-way conception of the imperialist causal process. Every state, no matter how weak, has unique traditions and sources of strength and resilience. Thus, dependent societies all have some power vis-à-vis dominant countries even if it only means the ability to participate in setting the terms of their dependence.

The Disruption of Preindustrial Economies

The impact of the advanced nations of the West on preindustrial societies has been varied. British imperialism stressed elite control through British administration in cooperation either with a native elite or a white-settler elite. British colonial government tended to be relatively efficient and honest. In addition, roads and ports were built and hygienic measures were instituted. The French thought of their colonies as extensions of French civilization and tended to avoid the overt racism and ethnocentrism of Britain. Variations of the British and French models can be found in the imperial policies of Portugal, Spain, Germany, the Netherlands, Belgium, and Italy. Russian and then later Soviet imperialism is somewhat different in that

Czarist and Soviet Russia simply incorporated conquered lands into Russian society. English imperialism also consisted of incorporating contiguous areas, succeeding with Scotland and Wales, failing with Ireland. The United States has also expanded by incorporating new territory unto itself, some through conquest, some through purchase.

Despite variations, Western imperialism has had one outstanding feature: everywhere traditional subsistence economies were transformed into export-oriented economies. From relative self-sufficiency, traditional societies became dependent on world markets (and internally, rural and urban areas became dependent on each other). Colonial powers everywhere introduced and promoted cash-crop agriculture and (where resources permitted) the extraction and export of raw materials. The colonial powers developed an infrastructure of roads, water and power supply, sanitation and medicine, currency, ports, railroads, land-use patterns, law, tax and other money incentives, and education, all of which furthered economic development in keeping with their needs. Even the white-settler colonies of British North America (the American colonies, Canada), Australia, and New Zealand were shaped to suit the needs of England.

The dissolution of the European empires after World War II changed little in the economic relations between developed and developing nations. The former colonies were now independent nations, but their economies were still geared to the world economy. Most former colonial powers adopted foreign aid programs, especially for their former colonies, and development loans were now made through international (Western-dominated) bodies such as the World Bank. The developing countries were still subject to private groups: multinational corporations, churches, universities, and foundations, professional groups, and so on. The basic thrust of development aid—whether in the form of loans, grants, education, technical aid, or capital investment—has been the same: to develop the human and natural resources of the developing world in keeping with the needs of the developed world.

SOCIETIES IN THE CONTEMPORARY WORLD: DEVELOPED, DEVELOPING, UNDERDEVELOPED

The developed world refers to the industrialized capitalist nations led by the United States (see Table 3–1). All are liberal (capitalist) democracies. With the exception of Japan, all are white and derive from the European Judaic-Christian, Greco-Roman tradition. The basic economic interests of the developed capitalist countries are threefold: economic growth through private capital and an exchange economy, trade and investment abroad, and the importation of raw materials. The small group of developed capitalist countries outproduce by far the rest of the world, conduct most of the

TABLE 3–1 The Developed World (Industrial Capitalist Countries) Ranked By GDP[a] (With Per Capita Income based on Purchasing Power Parity, 1993)

	GDP (IN BILLIONS, U.S.)	PER CAPITA INCOME
1. United States	$6,260	$24,302
2. Japan	2,559	20,523
3. Federal Republic of Germany	1,503	18,510
4. France	1,079	18,709
5. Italy	1,018	17,830
6. United Kingdom	985	17,036
7. Canada	554	19,278
8. Australia	302	17,103
9. The Netherlands	269	17,593
10. Belgium	195	19,517
11. Switzerland	161	23,195
12. Sweden	147	16,831
13. Austria	103	19,128
14. Denmark	100	19,335
15. Norway	84	19,476
16. New Zealand	54	15,493
17. Luxembourg	11	28,368

[a]Gross Domestic Product (GDP) differs from Gross National Product (GNP) in that it excludes property income from other countries.

Source: U.S. Bureau of the Census, *Statistical Abstract of the United States, 1995* (Washington, D.C.: U.S. Government Printing Office, 1995), Table 1374; derived from Organization for Economic Cooperation and Development, *National Accounts* (Paris, annual), Vol. 1.

world's trade among themselves, and consume far more of the earth's resources than the rest of the world combined. The United States alone, for example, with only 6 percent of the world's population, consumes 33 percent of its energy.

The outstanding characteristics of most developing countries are their low technological levels, low energy consumption, an unskilled and surplus labor force, specialized economies geared toward exporting food and raw materials, and their inability to create capital fast enough to yield self-sufficiency and self-direction. Many of these characteristics have their origin in foreign economic (and political-military-educational-religious) penetration, and all are reinforced by continued outside influences.

The developing countries are highly diversified by size, natural environment, previous forms of social development, including experience with imperialism, and by the nature of their economy. Some, like the People's Republic of China, India, Brazil, and Nigeria, are very large and exert considerable influence on world and regional affairs. Others are oil-rich, whereas some are extremely poor with bleak prospects. Some nations are semideveloped with good prospects, while still others are floundering and in revolutionary ferment.

The impact of imperialism on the non-West is extremely complex, and its interpretation has understandably become a source of considerable controversy. Probably the best strategy in assessing the impact of imperialism is to keep the issues in close contact with concrete cases. Two studies are presented in the following sections illustrating the two forms of dependency (underdevelopment and dependent development) and their respective systems of internal stratification.

UNDERDEVELOPMENT: EL SALVADOR

An inflow of technology, money, and know-how into a simple feudal society results in economic concentration, especially in land. A road, a new supply of water, tractors, or a dependable customer for a product—each in its own way makes land more valuable. Before the arrival of imperial powers, the landlord had to develop labor-intensive methods of utilizing the land. Landlords and serf-tenants needed each other. The introduction of Western technology and supporting institutions made the land more valuable and labor cheaper. Everywhere in such societies landlords began to abrogate traditional relations with tenants, serfs, and other forms of labor. Unneeded labor was dispossessed and a gradual concentration of land took place in keeping with economic power and the economies of scale. Today, most such societies are in a peculiar position: food production, even where it has risen dramatically, can no longer keep up with population growth (which has also risen spectacularly because of Western sanitation and medicine). Neither the Green Revolution nor food from abroad (whether bought or given free) seems to help.

Like much of Central and South America, El Salvador has outgrown its social form, namely the simple feudal society. *Simple feudalism* is a customary society centered on subsistence farming. The society is decentralized and revolves around a series of haciendas or large self-sufficient estates. The *patron* (invariably male) is head of the hacienda, similar to the lord of the manor of yesteryear. He supervises an estate that is labor-intensive and provides for its own needs—furniture, clothing, leather goods, repairs, sickness, old age, and so on. A rudimentary polity, created and operated by large landowners, provides a few services. There is no government in the sense of national educational, health, transportation, postal, or energy services (some of these are provided especially in the few urban centers).

From the nineteenth century on, but especially in the past fifty years or so, El Salvador gradually developed a more specialized division of labor, and its simple feudal system eventually broke at the seams. In clear view of the United States government (actually with its help), American and other foreign companies brought new technology to El Salvador and introduced new products and services. The El Salvador government grew to provide more services to handle the increased economic activity, but ominously there was no extension of political participation. Essentially, political power remained in the hands of a few landowners and the tiny urban business and professional elite. Economic development resulted in a changeover from subsistence, labor-intensive farming to cash-crop, export-oriented, technologically intensive farming. As in the rest of the Third World, the *patron* asserted absolute legal ownership of the estate and renounced all customary rights based on the previous feudal, patron-tenant relations. This was a preliminary, of course, to dispossessing the peasants and turning the estate into a business.

Gradually a new economy emerged under the euphemism of the *Green Revolution.* The Green Revolution refers to the many-sided effort by the United States (and other industrial countries) to increase the agricultural output of Third World countries through technology (new seeds, fertilizer, irrigation systems, tractors, harvesters). The same technology has made the United States incredibly productive in food and staples. When Third World countries needed more food, the United States simply assumed that what worked here would work there. But even in the United States the Green Revolution has not been an unmixed blessing. Millions of Americans, for example (of all skin colors and ethnic backgrounds), were dispossessed by the surge of agricultural technology and forced to enter cities that were only partially ready for them.

The Green Revolution in El Salvador (and in the Third World) did not have an industrial revolution to soak up the labor it dispossessed from the countryside. Although it raised agricultural production, the Green Revolution seems to have had the ironic outcome of increasing food dependency, making people poorer than they were and hungrier as well. The Green Revolution has promoted cash-crop agriculture, which means production to stock the pantries and dining tables of America, Europe, and Japan: coffee, sugar, cotton, bananas, cocoa, nuts, artichokes, and so on. The Green Revolution means economic concentration in land and the dispossession of former tenants. The Third World landlords import seed, fertilizer, and farm machinery and pay for them by exporting food and staples. The World Bank, other international agencies, the United States government, and a landlord-dominated home government provide ports, energy, and roads. The police become a National Guard to protect the economy. The value of the exports can never match the value of what is being imported (farm technology, Coca-Cola, television sets, arms for the National Guard), and a classic example of a dependent right-wing society has been helped into being by the Green Revolution.

When food aid is sent either by the United States government or private charities to feed the dispossessed masses, the basic power structure is reinforced. The free or subsidized food is used to keep the National Guard, the civil service, and urban workers fed and quiet. Some of the food is used to put rural labor to work—building roads, for example. But roads benefit landlords who can now get their crops out to be sold abroad. Food aid simply postpones the day of reckoning—the day the masses question a society in which economic growth produces poverty for most of the people.

Despite some growth of industry and urban services, El Salvador's new economy could not absorb the dispossessed labor. People crowded into the cities, most of them as squatters without jobs. Government employees and other workers are insecure and dependent because their jobs are precarious—a slight change in the price of coffee or energy and many are out of work. The government is under the influence of landlords, banks, import companies, and manufacturing firms, many of them branches of multinational (mostly American) corporations. But all efforts by civil servants, workers, and peasants to obtain a voice in setting government policy are rebuffed. Gradually, a revolutionary situation develops in plain sight of all, including the United States Embassy, and American executives and professionals.

The major trend is clear: the fruits of economic growth were being hogged by a small set of oligarchic elites. The masses, who were always poor, are now poor in a new way: their poverty lacks meaning—they are idle while things around them are humming. Workers and civil servants are insecure, surrounded by consumer goods they cannot afford. Both the poor and the insecure employed can see the flow of profits to both native and foreign elites. Eventually, after repeated demands for reform are rebuffed, increasingly by violent means, the situation becomes polarized. Armed insurrection breaks out (using weapons supplied from abroad, especially the Soviet Union and Cuba, but also purchased from private dealers in the United States or stolen from the inept El Salvador military). There is also support from social democratic governments and forces in Europe as well as from the one-party conservative government of Mexico. The El Salvador government quickly schedules elections, which nobody takes seriously. It also beefs up its antiquated National Guard (with emergency aid from the United States) in an effort to suppress the rebellion.

Official United States policy is that El Salvador is trying to develop representative government and that Soviet and Cuban forces are causing all the trouble. But the American government is not believed by even its own people, let alone the rest of the world. Everyone knows that the main problem lies in the outmoded, unworkable institutions of El Salvador itself,[4] an institutional disarray that the United States has helped to produce. With U.S. help the El Salvadorean oligarchy prevails. Today, El Salvador continues to supply the United States with cheap food and now has a thriving export trade in textiles (see Box 3–1) and other items, all based on exploited labor, yielding high profits to American multinational corporations, helping to depress American labor, and helping to keep U.S. inflation low.

BOX 3–1 *The Progresso Free Trade Zone, or the World Market as Free Labor Peonage*

New York Times reporter Bob Herbert secretly interviewed a mother working in El Salvador's Progresso Free Trade Zone, a huge compound of sweatshops walled by concrete and barbed wire and patrolled by armed guards (*New York Times,* October 9, 1995, p. A17). The woman earned $.56 an hour, not enough to feed herself and her daughter (it is not uncommon for workers to faint from malnutrition). Her plant makes jackets for Liz Claiborne that sell for $178 each in well-known American retail stores; the labor cost for each jacket is $.77.

The president of one of the factories agreed that wages were not fair, but he added that he and the workers had to compete in the world market; or rather, the brand-name American clothing companies were always ready to move to cheaper labor areas, and he had no choice about how he conducted his business.

As we see in future chapters, the impact of accessible cheap labor in the world market has had and is having a sizable negative impact on American labor.

DEVELOPING SOCIETY: THE REPUBLIC OF SOUTH KOREA

Land and People

Korea[5] occupies a peninsula on the northeast coast of Asia. Korea has a distinctive language and culture although it has been massively influenced by its giant neighbors, China and Japan.

The population of South Korea in 1994 was 43.9 million. The religion of South Korea is primarily Buddhist but Confucianists and Christians represent sizable minorities. South Korea is not well endowed with natural resources. It lacks minerals and fuels, its topography is mountainous, its soil poor, and overcutting has denuded it of trees. Aside from its hardworking, disciplined people, perhaps its most valuable resource is its fishing waters.

Korea has a continuous history of settlement that stretches back into Paleolithic times. The various groups on the Korean peninsula were united in the seventh century, and Korea remained a unified kingdom until 1905 when it was occupied by Japan (Korea was formally annexed by Japan in 1910). Feudal Korea was similar to Imperial China and in general conformed to authoritarian or state feudalism rather than manorial, decentralized, stateless feudalism. Land is the basis of power under all forms of feudalism. In advanced agrarian systems large landowners supplement their local power by participating in a central power structure. Under the Chinese system the landowning gentry prepared their sons to take rigorous examinations in the classics, the gateway to highly prized positions in the emperor's civil service. Confucianism supplied the legitimating ideology for China's power structure. As is common in feudal symbolic systems, Confucianism gave central position to the family, or rather the patriarchical family. The authority of the father, and thus the superiority of males, is the linchpin of the entire system. Filial piety is the most important obligation, and the hierarchical family is the model for thinking about society. The ultimate image in Confucian as well as feudal thought in general is of a harmonious, finished hierarchy that extends from one end of human nature to nature at large. The essential value for all to seek, in keeping with their station in life, is the world's harmony.

Economy

For various reasons, including influence and pressure from the outside, Korea's economy[6] and polity tended to promote concentrated landholding. For much of its history feudal Korea was subsistence-oriented. Under Japanese rule Korea developed as a typical colonial economy. Japan treated Korea as booty—it took over all land, businesses, and government, and colonized it with a thick strata of Japanese who occupied all important positions. The Korean agricultural sector became export-centered to supply Japan with food and staples while Japan supplied Korea with manufactured products.

World War II and the Korean War of 1950 to 1953 brought new forms of economic devastation to Korea. After the stalemate and negotiated peace of 1953, massive American aid and investment in the 1970s wrought a significant transformation in the Korean economy. During the 1960s Korea had one of the highest economic growth rates in the world. Essentially its economy was oriented toward exporting from a labor-intensive manufacturing sector. Using imported capital, Korea also imported most of its raw materials and exported them in the form of finished goods.

Korea's agricultural sector was bypassed by its industrial boom. Land reform after World War II had ended its long history of large feudal landholding. Korea took back its economy after the defeat of Japan and redistributed the large Japanese-held lands to its own people. The effect, however, was not to produce a balanced economy or a greater equality of political power. Korean autocracy and elitism switched from agriculture to industry and services. The impact of China during Korea's early history had helped to produce a hierarchical, concentrated bureaucratic agrarian economy and society. The Japanese reinforced this structure by deliberately using it to dominate and exploit Korea between 1910 and 1945 (the United States also relied on the feudal-authoritarian tradition during its occupation between 1945 and 1948, thereby giving it added legitimacy. Korea's modernization after 1948, based on its own efforts, massive American aid and military protection, and American and Japanese investment, took place within this feudal-authoritarian system.

Korea's economic development deviates considerably from other Third World countries. Significant steps toward industrialization have been taken; its standard of living has shown a steady increase; and its inequality, while considerable, is more in line with developed rather than developing countries. Its gross national product (GNP) of $91.7 billion (1986 estimate) yielded a per capita income of $2,032 (1985). Korea's economic success is due to a number of factors. Japan's occupation, which lasted to 1945, and land reform brought about by the American occupation following World War II, left Korea without a landed oligarchy to oppose modernization and industrialization. In addition, an uprooted population fell back on a cultural tradition that stressed discipline, hierarchy, state service, and respect for education. And Korea's government has provided a wide variety of support facilities and services, including reliable statistics and planning services.

It should be noted that Korea's economic success since the 1960s is no miracle of free enterprise and did not result from Korean efforts alone. Korea's economic success should also not be attributed to abstract forces like Confucian values or education.

Chinese hierarchical feudal forms certainly played a part. But Korea is also a result of Japan's imperial expansion from the late nineteenth century through World War II. The Japanese conquest and colonization provided Korea with much of what it needed to become part of the capitalist world. Korea is also a result of American policy since World War II. The United States' major foreign-policy goal in Asia has been to contain and roll back communism. To that end it fought the Korean war and it supported Korea with massive economic aid of various sorts, including making its own giant market available to Korean exports.[7] It has also provided a home for significant numbers of Koreans displaced by Korea's industrialization.

There can be little doubt about one thing, however: Korea's economic success is real and puts it in a select group of Third World countries that have managed to achieve significant growth, *including relative gains against the developed world.* As is true of the various capitalist countries, Korea's industrial sector is not organically linked to the Korean people. In Korea, as in other parts of the developing capitalist world, American and First World aid and investment have promoted a highly concentrated dual economy and an authoritarian political regime.

Polity

Korea's political institutions, like its economy, have been massively influenced by outsiders.[8] Korea did not develop as a decentralized, self-sufficient feudal society. The landed elite of a self-sufficient manorial economy fears the state and retards its growth as it develops enough state power to maintain the status quo. In the modern world, oligarchies whose power is based on self-sufficient estates or derived from horticulture have had great difficulty in developing successful nation-states. It is quite different with societies with a feudal-authoritarian background. Political institutions in China, Korea, Japan, Prussia, and Russia were based on the absolute authority of the ruler, an authority, it must be noted, that extended over the nobility and not just the masses.

Korea has also modernized successfully, owing in large part to its feudal-authoritarian experience. Korea's social order and political system came largely from its giant neighbor, China. That system was reinforced by Japan and the United States. Korea's status as a Japanese colony strengthened the authoritarian system. The American occupation after World War II did not alter the feudal-authoritarian system. Independence led to a liberal political constitution and land reform (similar to the pattern that occurred in the American military occupation of Japan). But land reform had no real significance (except perhaps to facilitate the neglect of the agricultural sector), and the liberal political constitution became a dead letter thanks to the Korean War and to the fact that electoral politics threatened the power of Korea's tiny elite.

Violent political protests in 1987 finally forced the government to agree to free elections. Under the new constitution both the president and the national legislature are elected by secret ballot and share power. Korea now has a typical system of representative government, one that reflects but does not change its class system.

Family, Religion, and Education

As is common in countries with a well-established agrarian tradition, the family has first claim on the energies, time, and resources of Koreans. The Korean family is male-oriented and is explicitly conceived as the permanent foundation of society over time. In the ideal agrarian Korea, the household is a three-generation extended family. In practice, the eldest son and his family (as the eventual inheritors of the family property and authority) continue to live with his parents while other sons establish separate households (primogeniture). Further reflecting Confucian values and beliefs, age and sex were carefully defined as a hierarchy. Grandparents received considerable respect, while elder brothers had authority over younger brothers, brothers over sisters, and husbands over wives.

Given the large concentration in landholding in feudal Korea, the hierarchical, ascriptive family form was generalized into a model for all social relations. Confucian religion and philosophy stressed filial piety and argued that all social relations must be modeled on authority relations derived from a father-headed family. Social harmony would ensue if all obeyed the obligations of their ascriptive stations in life.

In today's Korea the family has changed in keeping with urbanization and industrialization. As in other countries experiencing economic growth, Korea's urban families have become neolocal (married couples establish their own residence), nuclear (the family consists of parents and children), smaller, and the status of Korea's urban women has been changing, though slowly.

Korea's religious institutions are relatively diverse, ranging from shamanism and nativist eclectic forms to Buddhism, Confucianism, and Christianity. While the largest group of religious adherents are Buddhist, the most influential has been Confucianism. Ever since the end of the nineteenth century a significant Christian sector has established itself largely because Christianity brought with it Western values that Koreans wanted.

Education is highly valued by both Korea's elite and its people. However, the Chinese practice of gearing education to the development of officials has been a burden. Confucian educational precepts emphasized the memorization of classics and the acquisition of basic ethical norms. The goal of education was wisdom, and it was assumed that wise officials could solve problems through the application of what they had learned from the classics.

Nonetheless, after 1945, Korea witnessed an extraordinary development of education leading to mass literacy. The educational system is no doubt part of the explanation for Korea's economic success. Education is highly graded and extremely competitive, with a pronounced emphasis on credentials, although it is still deficient in scientific and vocational programs. The emphasis on academic learning has two consequences. First, it cuts back on the supply of qualified (that is, credentialed) job applicants, for it is easier to inflate academic as opposed to technical requirements; and, second, it created a reservoir of politically active students who brought down one government and has challenged others from the 1970s on.

Despite Korea's traditional preference for the classics (which has been carried into the present), it has not lacked trained technical personnel. Whether derived from training programs in Korea, or through its own efforts, Korea's economic success is in no small measure due to its supply of trained economists, civil servants (including military, intelligence, and police), engineers, and technically oriented business leaders. It is also important to note that Korea appears far more successful than other countries in getting its citizens to extract meaning and benefits from utilitarian, lower-level schooling.[9]

Class and Dependency

Korea is an unequal country with a considerable disparity among the upper and lower reaches of its system of social stratification. Perhaps the most remarkable thing about Korean inequality is the ease with which authoritarian-feudal forms have transferred themselves to urban-industrial conditions.[10] In any case, the fruits of economic growth have not been distributed evenly to the Korean people nor has economic growth equalized income and wealth. This pattern is not uncommon, especially in capitalist countries, both developed and underdeveloped—economic expansion raises general living standards without producing more equality.

Korea is one of the few developing countries whose class system has been studied in some depth. In making this study, Hagen Koo has argued that we cannot simply use Marx's central criterion of property owner vs. nonproperty owner and purchaser vs. seller of labor power to understand social stratification. One must also analyze the occupational system, especially nonmanual vs. manual status. Combining these criteria, Koo argues, yields these basic social classes: capitalist and state elite, new middle class, petty bourgeoisie, working class, marginal class, plus farmers who are relatively equal. Between 1965 and 1975 the new middle class (white collar), petty bourgeoisie, and the marginal class all grew while the working class expanded rapidly and farmers declined significantly.

Household income inequality declined during the 1960s (largely because manufacturing reduced the number of unemployed and underemployed) but increased during the 1970s. The top 20 percent of households increased their share of the total from 41 to 45 percent while the bottom 40 percent declined from 19 to 16 percent. Beyond income inequality, Korea's class structure went from one that was relatively fluid and amorphous to one with more clearly defined boundaries and overall hierarchy. First, there is an extremely wealthy and politically powerful capitalist class anchored in highly concentrated economic groupings called *Jaebols* (the largest twenty Jaebols, for example, controlled 33 percent of total manufacturing). By and large, the capitalist class refers to large industrialists as well as the political elite who are joined at the hip. Hagen Koo notes that there is considerable resentment of this class by the Korean people, more than any resentment of foreign capital. The people resent this class because they know it has received its wealth through political favoritism. Second, there is now a distinct working class. By and large, Korean workers receive higher wages than their counterparts in other developing countries, but there is still considerable resentment over the injustice of its relative share in Korea. The white-collar class has enjoyed a good share of economic growth along with the owners of small businesses. Farmers, marginals, and especially industrial workers have lost out.

Koo argues that while Korea is a case of dependent development, it is different from such dependency in other countries, most notably in Latin America.[11] Korea's development is a result primarily of state action with foreign capital and multinationals playing only a small role. The other difference with dependency elsewhere is that development has not led to a dual economy and the marginalization of significant portions of the population. The benefits of economic growth have been distributed widely though not fairly or equally.[12]

Korea's dependency takes a number of forms. One, it is dependent on world markets and has accumulated considerable debt (which its economy can service as long as its exports remain strong). And it is dependent in the sense that it is still subject to what outsiders do. Dependence on outside powers is such a marked feature of Korean history that it is remarkable that Korea could emerge as a distinct ethnic-linguistic group. American policy since 1945 has openly supported South Korea's survival and development as part of larger American interests in the Far East.[13] Although President Carter was on the verge of removing American troops in 1977, the step was never taken and the United States is still directly tied to Korea's military security.

South Korean governments have worked hard to promote national pride and have even begun to purge the Korean language of Chinese characters and of words borrowed from China, Japan, and the United States. But dependency is structured deep into the fabric of Korean life. Despite its highly centralized political tradition and its explicit intertwining of state and economy, Korea's radical dependence on world markets makes it extremely vulnerable to the vagaries of the world economy. The political turbulence of the late 1970s, climaxed by the assassination of President Park Chung Hee in 1979, is directly linked to the painful economic recession that accompanied the dramatic rise in oil prices after 1973 and the surge in world prices for raw materials. Efforts to intensify exports to pay for the higher cost of imports left Koreans with fewer consumer goods and high inflation. A government-promoted recession further violated domestic expectations. Korea's internal political instability is directly linked to its economic dependency.[14]

South Korea's internal political instability is unlikely to end as long as an authoritarian government is geared to the defense of an economy that does not benefit the Korean people directly and equitably. Authority is undermined when followers can no longer connect the actions of powerholders with their interests. The flow of benefits from economic expansion and the manner in which economic troubles and political protests have been handled have made it clear whose interests Korean society serves. The move toward representative government in 1987 was followed by considerable labor-union activity, including strikes, demanding better wages and working conditions. By the late 1990s, representative government seems to have taken root and South Korea appears to be on its way toward becoming a developed class society, the trappings of democracy helping to disguise and stabilize a property-based society.

SUMMARY

Relations among societies are characterized by domination, conquest, exploitation, and dependence—in short, by stratification and imperialism.

Leaving aside the discredited folk theories based on biology, theorists tend to agree that imperialism occurs for economic reasons. Liberal (capitalist) theorists argue that imperialism is unnecessary and should be curbed as a barrier to competition and efficiency. Marxists, following Lenin, argue that imperialism is a necessary stage of mature capitalism and will lead eventually to vigorous competition from colonies and the downfall of capitalism. Dependency theorists, similarly influenced by Marx, also argue that imperialism is necessary for capitalism to continue but say that it creates dependency among colonies and former colonies.

Empire imperialism is characteristic of agrarian society and consists of conquering other lands and peoples. *World market* imperialism is when *core* societies exploit their economic superiority toward *peripheral* societies. *Semi-peripheral* societies, while economically backward, manage to avoid being turned into underdeveloped, dependent countries.

Nationalism in the West emerged as part of the surge to power by the middle class. Nationalism destroyed feudal particularism and resulted in central government (common currency, taxation, laws, transportation) and large domestic markets. Nationalism outside the West is often part of a liberation movement directed against imperialist powers.

The international system from 1450 to 1950 was marked by acute rivalry among the capitalist countries of the West and the dominance of these countries over most of the world. From 1950 to 1990, the *First World* (the developed capitalist societies) was united under American leadership because of challenges from the *Second World* (the developed socialist societies led by the Soviet Union) and the *Third World* (the developing nations).

The developed capitalist countries, with their advanced technologies, high energy consumption, and intricate division of labor, produce the bulk of the world's output and conduct most of its trade among themselves.

As opposed to the developed capitalist societies, the developing world of approximately 150 of the world's 180 nation-states is economically weak and dependent.

Imperialist core societies tend to turn colonies and dependencies into exporters of food, labor, and raw materials while they diversify and upgrade their own economies. When developed societies collide with simple feudal or horticultural societies, the result is *underdevelopment* (a society's labor force and economy are geared to remain suppliers of food and raw materials). When advanced societies act on smaller feudal-authoritarian systems, the result is *dependent development* (a society develops a labor-intensive export-oriented manufacturing sector but is dependent on the outside world for markets, raw materials, and capital).

NOTES

1. For a valuable analysis of these theories, including the fine shades of meaning that my summary has obscured, see Karl W. Deutsch, "Theories of Imperialism and Neocolonialism," in Steven J. Rosen and James R. Kurth, eds., *Testing Theories of Economic Imperialism* (Lexington, Mass.: D.C. Heath, 1974), chap. 2.

2. New York: Academic Press, 1974; two more of the projected 4 volumes have appeared: Vol. II, *The Modern World System: Mercantilism and the Consolidation of the European World Economy, 1600–1750* (New York: Academic Press, 1980) and Vol III, *The Modern World System: The Second Era of Great Expansion of the Capitalist World Economy, 1730–1840s* (New York: Academic Press, 1988).
3. In this respect Wallerstein's work builds on the revisionist wing of Marxist imperialist theory; for two pioneering essays, see Paul A. Baran, "On the Political Economy of Backwardness," *Manchester School of Economics and Social Studies* (January 1952), reprinted in Robert I. Rhodes, ed., *Imperialism and Underdevelopment: A Reader* (New York: Monthly Review Press, 1970), pp. 285–301; and Andre Gunder Frank, "The Development of Underdevelopment," *Monthly Review* (September 1966), reprinted in Andre Gunder Frank, ed., *Latin America: Underdevelopment or Revolution: Essays on the Development of Underdevelopment and the Immediate Enemy* (New York: Monthly Review Press, 1969), pp. 3–17.
4. For a brief but meaty background on El Salvador, see Roland H. Ebel, "Political Instability in Central America," *Current History* 81 (February 1982):56ff. For more extensive data on the extreme and growing inequality in El Salvador, the brutality with which the tiny elite rules, and the complicity of the United States in perpetuating an unworkable system, see Enrique A. Baloyra, *El Salvador in Transition* (Chapel Hill: University of North Carolina Press, 1982); Tommie Sue Montgomery, *Revolution in El Salvador: Origins and Evolution* (Boulder, CO: Westview Press, 1982); Robert Armstrong and Janet Shenk, *El Salvador: The Face of Revolution* (Boston: South End Press, 1982); and Raymond Bonner, *Weakness and Deceit: U.S. Policy and El Salvador* (New York: Times Books, 1984). For an eyewitness account by a priest of the role of local Christian communities in supporting insurrection in El Salvador, Guatemala, and Nicaragua (influential in the latter's success), see Philip Berryman, *The Religious Roots of Rebellion: Christians in Central American Revolutions* (Maryknoll, NY: Orbis Books, 1984).
5. *South Korea: A Country Study*, 3rd ed. (Washington, D.C.: U.S. Government Printing Office, 1982), compiled by Foreign Area Studies of American University, provides invaluable background on all aspects of Korean history, culture, and society, including the division of North and South Korea after World War II. An indispensable companion to this volume is *North Korea: A Country Study*, 3rd ed. (Washington, D.C.: U.S. Government Printing Office, 1981). Other sources will be cited below, but towering over all accounts is the sophisticated and comprehensive analysis by Norman Jacobs, *The Korean Road to Modernization and Development* (Urbana: University of Illinois Press, 1985).
6. For indispensable background and analysis of all of Korea's institutions, see Norman Jacobs, *The Korean Road to Modernization and Development* (Urbana: University of Illinois Press, 1985).
7. For a valuable analysis placing the economic success of Korea (as well as Taiwan and Japan) into its historical context, including the role played by Japanese and American imperialism, see Bruce Cumings, "The Origin and Development of the Northeast Asian Political Economy: Industrial Sectors, Product Cycles, and Political Consequences," *International Organization* 38 (Winter 1984):1–40.
8. For an analysis of Korean political institutions that provides valuable historical contrasts and continuities, see Gregory Henderson, *Korea: The Politics of the Vortex* (Cambridge, MA: Harvard University Press, 1968); Edward Reynolds Wright, ed., *Korean Politics in Transition* (Seattle: University of Washington Press, 1976); and especially Norman Jacobs, *The Korean Road to Modernization and Development* (Urbana: University of Illinois Press, 1985).

9. R. P. Dore, "South Korean Development in Wider Perspective," *Pacific Affairs* 50 (Summer 1977):196–198.
10. This has parallels in the West as we saw in Chapter 2.
11. For an original contribution to the theory of dependent development, see Peter Evans, *Dependent Development: The Alliance of Multinational, State, and Local Capital in Brazil* (Princeton, NJ: Princeton University Press, 1979).
12. Hagen Koo, "Transformation of the Korean Class Structure: The Impact of Dependent Development," in Robert V. Robinson, ed., *Research in Stratification and Mobility*, vol. 4 (Greenwich, CT: JAI Press, 1985), pp. 129–148. Koo focuses on 1960 to 1980 and cannot be completely faulted for failing to put Korea's development in deeper historical context, including the role of Japanese and American imperialist expansion and policies.
13. For background on American foreign policy toward Asia and Korea, see Frank Baldwin, ed., *Without Parallel: The American-Korean Relationship Since 1945* (New York: Pantheon, 1973).
14. Chong-Sik Lee, "South Korea 1979: Confrontation, Assassination, and Transition," *Asian Survey* 20, no. 1 (January 1980):63–76.

4
Theories of Social Stratification

◆ ◆ ◆ ◆

◆ ◆ ◆ ◆

The goal of every field of science is to develop a unified depiction of its subject matter and a comprehensive causal theory that explains how that subject matter behaves. The heart of such a unified or general theory in social stratification would consist of generalizations applicable to all systems of stratification. Our task in this chapter, therefore, is to review the progress that has been made toward a general theory of stratification and to identify some of the barriers standing in the way of its realization.

The bulk of stratification theories claim that the phenomena of stratification exhibit an objective pattern of evolution representing social progress. These theories take two forms, Marxian and liberal. A different perspective denies that a unitary pattern of stratification exists and argues that stratification is an irreducible diversity.

Irreducible diversity means that human inequality is historical in nature, at once the result of time, place, and power. This perspective runs counter to all transhistorical (metaphysical) theories, both Marxian and liberal. Developed by Max Weber, this position has no exact contemporary representative (most theorists shy clear of Weber's relativism). However, Anthony Giddens, a leading sociological theorist working in the liberal tradition, is a contemporary exponent of Weber's interpretive sociology. Giddens is useful because he is a capitalist thinker who has recognized that there is no cosmic context for capitalism; his work is analyzed later in this chapter.

EVOLUTIONARY MARXISM

Marx's Vision of a Unitary Line of Historical Development

Marx's great drama of secular salvation through the inexorable march of economic development and class struggle culminating in a classless society (see Chapter 1) has not been borne out in the more than one hundred years since his death. Even before Marx's death in 1883, historians and anthropologists were outlining a world of sociohistorical diversity that Marx's theory could not encompass. The time scales characteristic of hunting-gathering, horticultural, agrarian, and capitalist societies and their radical diversity do not lend themselves to useful generalizations.

A dynamic economy is the exception, not the rule, in world history. All non-Western societies, including the great civilizations of China and India, reached a certain point of economic development and then stagnated. Even in the West, Marx's prediction of the future of capitalism has failed to materialize. Industrial society has not been split apart by polarized classes, and the working class has not risen to proclaim the end of private property and thus of social exploitation. What appears to have happened instead is that modern society has been diversified internally into a number of social classes, and has evolved a number of practices for adjusting (and disguising) the relations between them. To refute Marx's metaphysics, however, is not to accept evolutionary liberalism or "nonegalitarian classlessness." Modern society is a class structure that is not easily related to any of the explanations offered on its behalf.

It is true that Marx foresaw future developments quite accurately in many respects. Modern society is characterized by a high concentration of economic power and a deep interpenetration of economic and political power. It is exploitative and wasteful, and its legitimating symbols contain much ideology (the symbolic justification of an outmoded status quo) and even hypocrisy. And there is also a considerable amount of "false consciousness," or acceptance by the lower classes of upper-class symbols that are not in their true interests. But modern society has not fulfilled Marx's prediction of class polarization and struggle. In all industrial countries, including those where class hostility was once pronounced, the forces of economic expansion and political reform have diversified and diffused the structure of social classes. As a result, class society is far more stable and adaptable than Marxists (and others) are wont to believe. Instead of a dynamic system containing the seeds of its own destruction, one must think of capitalism as a society that successfully reproduces itself generation after generation despite and often because of exploitation and misery. We will explore the various agencies by which this is accomplished in due course, but central to any study of social stability are the ascriptive processes inherent in the idea of social class itself.

The image of a classless society (about which Marx said very little) is surprisingly similar to the liberal idea of nonegalitarian classlessness. By positing a society based on the fulfillment of all individuals, it sets a high standard for human hopes and aspirations. But, as Marx himself understood only too well, moral values reflect the realities of economic life. As we examine the realities of class in the United States, we will find ample proof of the power of economic life over society and of the way in which it reflects and disguises itself in appealing moral terms, not the least of which is the belief that a classless society has already been achieved.

Creative Marxian Currents

Marxist theorists have long since understood all of the above. As early as Edward Bernstein (a Marxist revisionist in the German Social Democratic Party at the end of the nineteenth century) and Vladimir Lenin (the leader of the Communist party that seized power during the military defeat of Czarist Russia), Marxist scholars have grappled with the ambiguous legacy left by Marx.

The main thrust of creative Marxian thought has been twofold: one, to find a place for noneconomic forces, especially political action, in the promotion of socialism, and two, to extend Marxian analysis beyond the single nation-state and to make the relation among societies one of the variables explaining domestic inequality (and vice versa).

In the developed capitalist societies of Europe, Marxists from Bernstein to Louis Althusser,[1] Perry Anderson,[2] Nicos Poulantzas,[3] and Erik Olin Wright[4] have all found value in the capitalist political system, in effect, advocating the use of liberal political institutions, including alliances between workers and other classes, to bring about socialism. Orthodox Marxists have resisted this approach as a dilution and distraction from class struggle.

Marxists outside the developed West have also placed their faith in political action, but here politics has taken an aristocratic, elitist turn. The two main figures are Lenin in Russia, who saw the need for a vanguard to lead the proletariat, and Mao Tse-Tung in China.

The other current in creative Marxism is its theory of imperialism. Capitalism, argue Marxists in this tradition, has been able to forestall class polarization and the pauperization of its working class because of its profits from colonies and investments abroad.[5] Lenin, who was one of the founders of imperialist theory, argued that the development of colonies would soon lead to the demise of the mother countries. Contemporary dependency theorists argue that imperialism will postpone the demise of capitalism for the foreseeable future.

Creative Applications of Marxism to Understanding the United States

Marxist scholars have produced new images of American history and social development. Gabriel Kolko has interpreted the rise of the regulatory state from the late nineteenth century on as a capitalist device to stabilize markets under corporate capitalism.[6] William Appleman Williams has interpreted American foreign policy in the nineteenth century as imperialist because of pressure from domestic groups, especially farmers, eager for foreign markets.[7] And Michael Harrington has produced a Marxian picture of American politics since the New Deal of the 1930s that ranks as high as any image produced by liberal thinkers.[8]

In an important test of Marx's idea that workers would be "proletarianized" under advanced capitalism, Wright and Martin subjected the overall American occupational system between 1960 and 1980 to close empirical scrutiny. Contrary to Marx's belief that the labor force faced deskilling and declining income, Wright and Martin found evidence that white-collar, supervisory (managerial) occupations have grown. Relying on Marxian economic causation theory (imperialism and technology), Wright and Martin argue that, (1) American class relations were internationalized during this period, and, (2) economic concentration (made possible by technology and bureaucracy) made more managerial jobs necessary.[9]

Wright argues that Marx's concept of labor exploitation is still central to class analysis but must be elaborated to distinguish the different ways in which surplus value is extracted from the working class. The owners of the means of production along with managers get more income than is warranted even when education, occupational status, age, and job tenure are held constant.[10] There is also a second form of exploitation that results in undeserved income and the use of organizational assets. The larger the organization the more unwarranted income (big business and upper-level managers getting significantly more than small business and single-person enterprises). The third form of exploitation is through control of skills and credentials. Here better-educated and skilled people get more income than is warranted by their education (Wright says this form is not as clearly established or as important as the first two forms of exploitation).

These three forms of exploitation are obviously found in mixed and combined form in large corporations. But Wright's argument and empirical findings should also be seen as pertaining to hospitals, schools, voluntary groups, professions, and state officials. Wright's findings can also be seen in the large number of supervisory occupations in the United States (much larger than in capitalist Sweden), which act both as a buffer between the upper classes and the masses and which serve to produce America's large number of "working class" individuals and households with "contradictory class positions" (that is, they are both exploiter and exploited).

Despite many similarities in technology and standard of living, capitalist Sweden is different from the United States. It has a strong trade union and socialist movement and the capitalist segments of the society have not been able to depoliticize the polity the way they have in the United States. It has far fewer supervisory occupations and college graduates, and 40 percent of its labor force works for the state as opposed to 20 percent in the United States. Despite these differences, class consciousness is similar in both countries—the further up the three dimensions of exploitation one goes the more pro-capitalist the attitudes. Swedish workers are more likely to be polarized on issues, largely because they have a supportive union and political environment.

Wright's fascinating empirical contrast between the United States and Sweden also allows him to develop a picture of historical development somewhat different from Marx's (and orthodox Marxists) but one that he feels is still fully consistent with Marx. Wright argues that the case of Sweden (and other evidence) shows that capitalism can have "multiple futures"—either statism or communism. Those who are interested in the democratization of capitalist society should try to use the state (as Sweden has done) to reduce the unwarranted income of those who own or control the three forms of exploitation. Not only can this be done through class alliances, taxation, and public services, but the policy-making positions of organizations can and should be democratized.[11]

The search within Marxism for a unified picture of social development continues, and we will come across further creative applications of Marx's ideas in later chapters.

EVOLUTIONARY LIBERALISM

The main metaphysical legitimation of capitalist society has also taken an evolutionary form—that of evolutionary liberalism.[12] Though the evolutionary theory of social development was rejected by social science in the early decades of this century as teleologically biased and contrary to the facts, the idea was too firmly planted to be erased, even in social science. It lives on in various guises: "nonegalitarian classlessness"; functionalism in sociology; the theory of convergence; faith in markets, faith in progress, especially through economic growth; and the denial that classes exist. In its simplest form, it is a belief that industrial capitalism is the end of history and is uniquely capable of carrying humanity toward a better future for all. Let us examine some of the variations of this position, beginning with the ideology of liberal functionalism.

The Ideology of Liberal Functionalism: Davis and Moore

In 1945 Kingsley Davis and Wilbert E. Moore published an essay on social stratification at the level of general theory; that is, they articulated what they claimed were the universal principles of stratification. Written in the spirit of functionalism and with only an implied evolutionary framework, Davis and Moore argued that phenomena that occur universally must stem from the inherent needs of society itself.

Working in this tradition, and leaving aside "variable" or historical issues, Davis and Moore argue that the "main functional necessity explaining the universal presence of stratification is precisely the requirement faced by any society of placing and motivating individuals in the social structure."[13] Assuming that different positions in society require different incentives and rewards, they conclude that "social inequality is an unconsciously evolved device by which societies ensure that the most important positions are conscientiously filled by the most qualified persons." The thrust of their argument is that despite historical variations in the way inequality manifests itself and the failure of given societies to live up to their own values and norms, inequality as such is generic to society, intrinsic to its nature. All societies, say Davis and Moore, simply must define some positions—in general, the leadership of major institutional areas—as more important than others and must structure the distribution of social, cultural, and personality benefits so as to ensure an adequate supply of personnel for these positions, which require various talents, arduous training, and heavy responsibility.

The first criticism of Davis and Moore's functional position is that it is really a discussion of differentiation, not stratification. Secondly, the critics of the Davis-Moore position, Tumin especially, have sensed the basic emptiness of their generalization.[14] By and large, conflict theorists—those who see society and inequality as a means by which the strong can induce the weak to do more for less—tend to bypass the Davis-Moore analysis. It is one thing to argue that differentiation must take place—that individuals must be motivated and trained to occupy different statuses in the hierarchies of work, or leisure, or warfare, or whatever—and quite another to decide how all this is to be done. Invariably, the placement of individuals has been a result of social stratification, not individual achievement or natural social processes, which is to say that at some point in history families are ranked with regard to general economic, social, and political power and worth, and that this hierarchy of families then becomes the basis for the next generation's hierarchy of families. Equally important, the hierarchy of strata that emerges eventually controls the definition of functional positions and recruitment into them. It is this radical inequality of economic birth that lies at the heart of stratification analysis, regardless of the type of society, argue conflict sociologists. The fact that liberal democracies (or communist dictatorships, for that matter) generate high levels of achievement does not alter the fact that birth into the class hierarchy determines, by and large, who will be socialized to succeed and who to fail.

The Davis-Moore view of stratification was not consistent with stratification research nor with history or anthropology. After Davis and Moore, liberal theorists sought to make the functional view consistent with the historical record by adopting an evolutionary perspective.

The Evolutionary Liberalism of Gerhard Lenski

Gerhard Lenski has made a notable contribution to stratification analysis at the level of classification and description.[15] To appreciate Lenski's theory and obtain its many potential benefits, one must focus mainly on his fascinating description and classification of the ways in which inequality has manifested itself throughout history. Basically, says Lenski, the variety of inequality a society exhibits depends upon how the "power" system distributes material surplus, especially food. Focusing his analysis on the basic techniques of subsistence, Lenski identifies a main line of development from hunting and gathering societies to horticultural, advanced horticultural, agrarian, and industrial with offshoots such as herding, fishing, maritime, and hybrid societies. Each type has a distinguishable degree of inequality. As production grows, says Lenski, so does inequality, reaching its greatest height in agrarian society.

The emergence of an industrial technology represents a profound change in the "means of subsistence" available to society. As a consequence, sharp increases take place in production and in specialized economic activity. Lenski claims that the resulting material surplus does not lead, as in the past, to increases in inequality but to a reversal of this historic trend. While economic, prestige, and political inequality is still considerable, it is less marked than in agrarian societies. The top 2 percent of income units, for example, receive at most 15 to 20 percent of the total income, as opposed to 50 percent in agrarian societies, and the emergence of universal suffrage represents a diffusion and popularization of political power. The main reason for this reversal of the trend toward increased inequality is that industrial society is too complex to be run personally or arbitrarily. The upper groups tend to find it in their interests to involve the lower and intermediate groups in economic and political processes.

The foregoing is only a rough sketch of Lenski's rich portrayal of human inequality through the ages. Indeed, the materials he presents are so rich that they could easily be interpreted as irreducibly diverse and nondirectional. Lenski's description of human inequality and his classification of a wide variety of societies would have been perfectly acceptable scientific procedure had he limited himself to searching for their similarities. But locating his types in a scheme of evolutionary development begs all the important questions in social science. Above all, Lenski never addresses himself to the basic question of why one agrarian society—Western feudalism—transformed itself into industrial society while the rest "stagnated." What was to Max Weber and most of the classical theorists of sociology a great novelty in need of explanation presents no problem for Lenski, since he assumes that the basic ideas and values of capitalism are normal to human nature. Instead of trying to explain the unique historical phenomenon of liberal society, he unabashedly attributes liberal values and behavior to human nature. To assume that liberal society is natural to humans is also to assume that all other societies are distortions or pale reflections of that norm.

Lenski's description of the reduction of certain forms of inequality by industrial society is useful and important. Who cannot be impressed with the fact that all individuals (of both sexes) have for the first time in human history been defined as moral entities with the legal right to engage in economic pursuits of their own choice, participate equally in political decision making, and be treated as legal equals by the state? And it is significant, as Lenski emphasizes, that the top economic elite in industrial society claims a smaller portion of the economic pie than the economic elite of agrarian society. However, these are not important enough to warrant Lenski's central theme emphasizing the reduction of inequality as the salient feature of modern capitalism. The same transformation can also be interpreted as the displacement of one unique historical set of social inequalities by another. The unique inequalities of industrial society are steep, stable, and illegitimate enough to warrant caution in making overall judgments. Lenski, however, minimizes the problem of inequality in industrial society by framing his analysis primarily as a broad comparison with the past, and, reflecting the optimism of the 1960s, by stating that the full flowering of industrial society is yet to come, claiming that modern society will continue to reduce inequality.[16]

Lenski's argument that capitalism represents a reversal of the historical trend in which economic surplus is turned into increased economic concentration has continued into the seventh edition of his textbook *Human Societies: An Introduction to MacroSciology*.[17] Lenski's comparison is empirically true, but if highlighted, takes on a meaning that is misleading. Such a comparison represents the main thrust of American stratificiation theory down through the 1960s and 1970s. It lingers on in Lenski's work and is prominent in various stratification texts.

Comparisons among types of society are fraught with difficulties that distort reality. Feudal society is unequal in ways that are different from industrial society. To see how slippery such concepts in this area are, consider this: the vast majority of the inhabitants of ancient Egypt, Rome, Imperial China, and the Ottoman Empire were far more equal in their occupations, their material existence, and their life expectancy than the majority of present-day Europeans or Americans. True, the elite of feudal society received a larger percentage of the total income than today's industrial elites, and wealth was more concentrated. But that is only a small part of the total inequality picture. Puting elite comparisons aside, the remaining population in contemporary industrial countries is more steeply graded than the mass of people in the agrarian societies of either the past or present. In addition, it is not clear that there is much difference in the nature of economic power (control over the use of material and human resources) between the elites of complex societies in the past and those of the present. When judged by economic concentration, all complex societies are heavily concentrated. Lenski says nothing about the fact that wealth concentration in contemporary society is so large that private property owners, both in the economy and policy, make all the important decisions affecting the economic lives of the rest of the population. In their capacity as owners of newspapers, the mass media, higher education, and voluntary groups, they also determine how modern populations think and feel about the world.

Lenski claims that political democracy has played an important part in the dramatic reversal of the historic process in which economic growth is associated with a growth in inequality. Most studies have found that once economic growth is accounted for, political democracy plays little or no role in reducing economic inequality. As part of this argument, Lenski also claimed that strong trade union and democratic socialist movements reduce economic inequality. This aspect of Lenski's argument has received some support.[18]

Lenski has rightly focused on economic variables as the movers of society. But by taking capitalism at face value he has missed its main stratificational outcome: the emergence of deep and persistent inequality on a new and unique set of economic dimensions. The result of his overemphasis on a comparison of fedual authoritarianism and industrial society is to hide contemporary class society from view. Since it refutes his major perspective, it is understandable that Lenski does not say much about the stagnation and decline in American living standards since 1970, and the significant growth of income and wealth inequality in the past decade or so.

Anthony Giddens and the Revision of Evolutionary Liberalism: Liberal Society as a Self-Directing, Undefinable Juggernaut

The easy optimism and certainties about modern society in the immediate post–World War II period no longer characterize creative liberals. In an effort to update liberal social theory, the British sociologist Anthony Giddens tackled both the theory of class and social theory. His class theory, written during the 1960s, is now rather dated.[19] His full-length treatment of class theory consists of endless qualifications about what Marx and Weber said, ending in a fairly conventional late liberal theory:

1. Classes in capitalist society cannot become structured because there is social mobility.
2. The state is a positive force in managing the economy from which classes emerge.

3. The economy and state are separate and each reflects different interests and mediating power.
4. Developed capitalist societies are different because central economic planning and collective bargaining have muted and lubricated class tensions.
5. There is a distinction among "governing class," "ruling class," "power elite," and "leadership groups," and one does not imply any of the others (we are never told which or what combination of these is characteristic of advanced capitalism, though his bias in favor of liberal pluralism is clear).

Giddens's theory was dated even in the 1960s. There is no reference to empirical studies showing the pronounced and illegitimate class character of communities throughout the United States. Separating economy and state into functional parts is a mistake unless the strong bond between the upper classes and state activity in American history, to the detriment of others, is also noted. Giddens could not have predicted the collapse of collective bargaining in the United States but he should have been aware that "central planning" in the United States has always taken place in keeping with the interests of the upper classes.

In this and later works, Giddens has developed a view of modern society that abandons the evolutionary premise behind so much of American class theory. For this reason, and because Giddens has exerted considerable influence on sociology, his social theory deserves a word.[20] Giddens's creativity stems from his wide familiarity with the history of sociological theory,[21] with history itself, and with a variety of knowledge fields outside of sociology. The break with traditional liberalism can be seen from the following conclusions he has drawn from his studies:

1. The state, and its administrative reach, is an integral part of the emergence of modern society (this is clearly stated and is a mark of Giddens's late liberalism, but his own theory as we see is curiously apolitical).
2. Modern society is unique and should not be thought of as evolving out of the past (it is "discontinuous" with it). There is no linear development of history from simple to agrarian to modern society, though each of these can be typified and some continuities identified. On the other hand, modern society, which is now omnipresent on the globe and busily becoming itself fully, could be superseded.
3. Generalizations about all human societies are not possible. Generalizations about modern society, however, are possible. The purpose of sociological theory, however, is not to make generalizations.
4. The grounding of theory is not possible, but relativism and postmodernism are wrong—valid truth statements can be made, at least about modern society. On the other hand, his own perspective is perhaps one of many. The best path to take against positivist or naturalistic empiricism is a moderate phenomenology (reflexive, interpretive epistemology). In any case, all laws in social science are provisional and change because society changes. History is powerful, but historicity means we can learn from history to manage our affairs. All knowledge is contextual, but that does not lead to relativism.

Giddens's own theory about society and how to reconstruct sociology is called *structuration.* Society, he argues, is not an external entity imposing itself on individual actors, as an assortment of structuralists have claimed, but an interplay between the actor as a socialized being and other actors. In this interplay, "knowledgeable actors" engage in a give and take. By give and take, Giddens means interpreting each other's behavior and learning from each other (Giddens's terms for this foundational process are "double hermeneutics" and "reflexive monitoring"). Here it is obvious that Giddens is using the interpretive tradition to say that subjectivity is a knowable phenomenon both to the observer and the actor. It is also clear that his emphasis on the "knowledgeable actor" puts him in the liberal camp of phenomenology.

For Giddens, the concept of *structure* is not an objective thing but consists of "rule [norms] and resources [economic]"—more or less similar to Parsons' concept of "abstract disposable facilities." *Social system* refers to concrete interaction regularities (institutions). Together, structure and social system both *constrain* and *enable* individual actors. The concept of power, he argues, should be incorporated into this scheme by thinking of rules and resources as a *transformative capacity,* that is, as abstract forces that allow change to take place. One must be careful, Giddens warns, to avoid the dichotomy or dualism of individual versus society or subjective versus objective. Instead, he argues, and this is the linchpin of his theory, there is a "duality of structure," actors and rules and resources are one and the same thing, opposite sides of the same coin. All of the above is what Giddens calls the theory of structuration.

Fundamental to Giddens's thought is the concept of the knowledgeable agent, the individual actor as rational cause. Individuals have a *practical consciousness* exhibited in a huge inventory of both simple and complex social skills. These skills, acquired from society, harden into *routines,* which simultaneously ward off the unconscious and its anxieties (yielding "ontological security") and produce the overall social system. Individuals are capable, when pressed, of explaining why they behave as they do ("discursive consciousness"). The double hermeneutic also applies to knowledge elites—much of the knowledge generated by the professions and disciplines is about what lay people already know. Any new knowledge is absorbed by lay people as they come into contact with knowledge elites. All in all, the knowledgeable activities of actors, both lay and professional, reproduce society as well as change it in the light of new knowledge. Human actors are learners and society is thus a learning machine.

Though generalizations about society, like the ones he has just made, are possible, society itself cannot be defined, says Giddens, and he warns against using the allegedly autonomous nation state as a bounded and definable entity. Modern society is now global and societies interpenetrate. Society is not definable because it is also becoming something else as actors learn and because it is also filled with unanticipated consequences. Social behavior, remember, is highly structured and reproduced at the micro level by the enormously skillful interaction displayed by ordinary individuals, and by a process of creativity represented by the interaction of knowledge elites, especially those in social science. The latter, remember, is itself in a double hermeneutic relation with its subject matter. It gets to know what actors already know and adds knowledge that eventually becomes part of society. Social science is not lagging behind natural science because it is not standing detached from its field of study in search of laws. It *is* its field of study and has had considerable success in generating what it is that actors are behaving according to.

Giddens advocates adopting this approach as the way to think of policy as well as sociological method and theory. One does not develop knowledge first and then intervene. Just as actors monitor their own interactions and negotiate their meanings, thereby improving themselves, just so reformers should immerse themselves in the world they are studying, thereby gaining a better position to bring insights from other areas into whatever context they are in.

The methods of natural science and social science are now understood, says Giddens, to be postempirical, by which he means postpositivist. The subject matter of each is different (the natural world is not subjective and cannot act back to initiatives by natural scientists), but both natural and social scientists use, whether they know it or not, an interpretive method. Sociological theory in the nineteenth and early twentieth century mistakenly coalesced, argues Giddens, around the core concept of industrial, modern, scientific society in contrast to agrarian or sacred, feudal society. By imitating the false empirical method of the natural sciences, says Giddens, sociological theory hardened into the "orthodox consensus" of "functionalism and naturalism" in the 1960s led by Talcott Parsons. Giddens feels that he has escaped the dead end of functionalism and naturalism by blending its good parts with phenomenology or interpretive sociology, and by redefining the nature of modernity.

Though Giddens carefully mentions everything important about society and theory in his commentaries, his own theory is curiously selective. He argues that power is a pervasive part of society, but it does not figure much in his own theory. Actually, there is a conspicuous absence of hierarchical power and social class in his theory, and little emphasis on groups as actors, though on occasion he mentions that the state and social movements are important (he has almost no reference to corporations and other complex organizations and certainly overlooks them as the central actors in current capitalism). Giddens also states that social life is a process of negotiating, but there is little emphasis on this idea in his own theory—the idea remains a liberal one, meaning negotiation among equals leading to contracts, with no acknowledgment that the differentials of power in modern society make negotiation decidedly one-sided (workers–owners, men–women, and so on).

Giddens's most explicit statement about modern society, not buried in his commentaries on other theories, in his small essay *The Consequences of Modernity*.[22] In it, he develops a theory that he claims is different from those of Marx, Durkheim, and Weber, who were too deeply embedded in false comparisons of modern and premodern, as well as different from the post-modern outlook of Jean-François Lyotard (the latter sees "a shift away from attempts to ground epistemology and from faith in humanly engineered progress"). Rather, Giddens claims, we are witnessing a period in which "the consequences of modernity are becoming more radicalized and universalized than before."

The modern period, or society in the West from the seventeenth century on, is marked by discontinuities, by rapid and comprehensive change, and by distinctive institutions. The dimensions of modern society and its achievements, dangers, and discontinuities must be seen as a series of processes:

1. The separation of time and space from any locality or type of experience and the use of these abstractions to order life
2. The disembedding of social systems, or the lifting of social relations out of particular contexts, and restructuring them in terms of abstract time and space
3. The reflexive ordering and reordering of social relations by the continuous generation of knowledge

Knowledge elites are engaged in a "double hermeneutics," the observer interpreting the observed, the latter interpreting the former, and both incorporating each other's observations. Thus, "sociological knowledge spirals in and out of the universe of social life, reconstructing both itself and that universe as an integral part of that process."

Modernity, concludes Giddens, is not Weber's "iron cage" of instrumental reason or Marx's oppressive property system, but rather a "juggernaut—a runaway engine" whose speed and direction cannot be known or controlled. The juggernaut of modernity (modern society) has many good features and many bad features, all in complex interaction with each other.

But underneath Giddens's argument is an unabashed liberal focus on the adaptability of existing society through knowledge (though he hedges continuously) and a faith in the hidden logic of unintended outcomes (the liberal market mentality). By saying everything, by giving all sides of every issue, Giddens creates the impression of Olympian objectivity. What he has done, though, is to endorse capitalism by openly identifying its warts, but saying it also has the most good features possible: integration, self-identity, growth, openness, and so on. Nowhere in his discussion of modern institutions does he refer to the concentrated economy, the primacy of the corporation as a social actor, the plutocratic polity, the poor, chronic unemployment and underemployment, minorities (including pronounced gender inequality and inequity), the state as a supporter of a capitalist way of life, or imperialism. Giddens argues that a focus on the nation-state as society is a mistake, but the net result is not to show the outward thrust of the main engine in the modern world, the political economy of the Western nations and its five centuries of imperialism. The result is to hide that engine in abstract talk of global processes.

Giddens emphasizes regionalism to remind us that nation-states are not integrated, but this is not to emphasize the need to overcome disparities within society (Giddens says nothing about the profound cleavages of race and ethnicity in the United States); his comments are really a way to say society cannot be integrated and therefore existing ways of managing are all we can do.

Perhaps the most important thing about contemporary capitalist societies is that its leaders in practical life, public life, and in the world of knowledge seem incapable of running their domains with any degree of certainty or equity. There seems no awareness in Giddens that contemporary societies, while continuing to produce economic growth, have been unable to turn that growth into growing standards of living, or to curb what appear to be mounting pathologies, including deeply alienated electorates. One reason could be that much of liberal social science is a grappling with ideas, not the structure of social power.

Despite many references to how the abstract processes he is identifying reach out to bring individuals to life (the enabling process), what his selective abstracting has done is to remove the impact of society on the aggregate of individuals, thus giving their fate over to existing power groups. In other words, Giddens is guilty of committing modernism, the use of selective ideas to create a fictitious, depoliticized, nondemocratic world based on noninterpretive, objective analysis. In short, there is more than a hint of functionalism and evolutionism in Giddens's thought. Deep down he has provided a late liberal appreciation of the social nature of behavior and of the uses of the state in the emergence and maintenance of capitalism, something much needed in mainstream American theory. But he has also cut that world off from scrutiny by:

1. Emphasizing that there is no continuity with the past
2. Stressing that there is no better future
3. Saying nothing about creating a better future through political action

Instead we are a "juggernaut" beyond control lurching into the future. Giddens seems unaware that his depiction of society as a juggernaut contradicts the heart of his earlier theory—society as a duality of structure in which human interaction constrained and enabled by an abstract culture continually reproduces itself and adapts through new knowledge. In the final outcome, Giddens's theory is a defense of corporate world-market capitalism against early liberalism, socialism, and postmodernism alike.

Though he rejects the idea of such a goal for social theory, Giddens is a grand theorist producing a grand narrative no more or less than Marx, Spencer, Durkheim, or Parsons. Giddens's extensive forays into the history of social theory have resulted in a convergence theory (à la Talcott Parsons), though he explicitly rejects the possibility of convergence. He could have concluded from his history of theory that the best way to enable actors in today's enormously diverse and novel world, including at the political level, is to keep the theories of the past in clear contrast in order to facilitate political choices about alternative structures of power. Enabling actors in politics, however, requires more than a choice among theoretical outlooks. History clearly shows that creative politics occurs only when there is genuine pluralism, that is, when economic and political power are relatively equal, and this Giddens nowhere mentions.

SUMMARY

The goal of every field of science is to develop a unified picture of its subject matter and to derive a comprehensive causal theory that explains how that subject matter behaves.

The historical diversity of social inequality, suggesting that human inequality is a function of time, place, and power, presents a challenge to both liberal and Marxist theorists as well as to governing classes.

In social stratification, a unified or general theory would consist of generalizations that are applicable to all systems of inequality.

The two major attempts to produce a general theory of social stratification are *evolutionary Marxism* and *evolutionary liberalism.*

Marx's identification of economic causation was the single greatest contribution to nineteenth-century social science. His theory of linear development of society through class struggle (resulting in a classless society) has not stood the test of time and research. Liberal theorists, and even some socialists, argue that capitalist society in the West has managed to raise living standards and to mitigate class struggle through reform.

Marxist theorists have struggled to find a place in Marx's general theory for noneconomic variables, especially political action. And they have argued that capitalism has managed to raise living standards, and to avoid class struggle only through imperialism, that is, by its ability to exploit colonies and the Third World.

Evolutionary liberalism also argues that history is a linear development toward a classless society, that is, a society based on achievement and knowledge, which will eliminate ascriptive and other nonrational forces. In the case of liberals, however, capitalist society (usually referred to as industrial society) is already based on achievement criteria, functional differentiation, and either has or is trying to eliminate nonrational vestiges from the past.

Variations among liberal thinkers are:

1. Some argue that the logic of industrialization is leading to or has led to a classless society.
2. Some argue that inequality based on functional need is inherent in society.
3. Some argue that industrial society is marked by institutions promoting equal opportunity, especially mass education, and by referee institutions, especially government, law, the professions, and voluntary groups. These institutions have greatly modified—some even say eliminated—the power of property.

Research has failed to confirm liberal theory. To the extent that such a comparison can be made, industrial society is more equal than agrarian societies, but this is a misleading comparison. Contemporary society is steeply graded and highly unequal on a stable basis in every arena of life. Birth into economic classes as well as such birth factors as race, ethnicity, and sex are still enormously important in modern society. And few today are able to say that mass education, government, law, the professions, and voluntary groups counteract ascriptive (illegitimate) inequality or offset the power of property.

Liberal theory appears to be an ideology (the biased defense of a particular society). By claiming that capitalist society has either overcome the forces of ascription or can overcome them through the application of science, technology, and modest reforms, liberal theorists have asked us to take the capitalist economy and other institutions at face value, in short, to overlook the many ways in which modern society deviates from its stated ideals.

The success of the conservative (right liberal) backlash against efforts to remove the ascriptive factors of class, race, ethnicity, and gender from 1980 into the late 1990s means that nineteenth-century liberalism is still dominant in American life.

Sensing difficulties in traditional evolutionary liberalism, Anthony Giddens has revised it, arguing that generalizations about all societies are not possible. However, generalizations about capitalism are possible. Capitalism, says Giddens, reveals no pattern of progress and has no fixed, objective structure. It generates personalities that can respond and adapt to social conditions but never fully understand or control them. In the final analysis, modern society is an undefinable, uncontrollable juggernaut carrying humans with it as it lurches along toward no particular destination.

Given all of the above, it appears that general theory is still a distant goal. Theorists have been unable to escape the assumptions of their own time and place, and they have been unable to account for the radical diversity of social stratification through time and place. For the time being, theorists of stratification must confine themselves to understanding particular systems of inequality while keeping an eye on what these systems all have in common.

NOTES

1. *Reading Capital,* with Etienne Balibar (London: New Left Books, 1970), and *For Marx* (London: New Left Books, 1977).
2. *Lineages of the Absolutist State* (London: New Left Books, 1974).
3. *Political Power and Social Classes* (London: New Left Books, 1973).
4. *Classes* (London: Verso, 1985).
5. For an earlier discussion, see Chapter 3.
6. Gabriel Kolko, *The Triumph of Conservatism: A Reinterpretation of American History* (New York: Free Press, 1963).
7. William A. Williams, *The Tragedy of American Diplomacy,* 2nd rev. and enlarged ed. (New York: Dell, 1972).
8. Michael Harrington, *The Twilight of Capitalism* (New York: Touchstone, 1976), pt. 2.
9. Erik Olin Wright and Bill Martin, "The Transformation of the American Class Structure, 1960–1980," *American Journal of Sociology* 93 (July 1987):1–29.
10. For details, see the section "Power Over Income," in Chapter 7.
11. Wright, *Classes.*
12. For this term, see the valuable critique of American stratification theory by John Pease, William H. Form, and Joan Huber Rytina, "Ideological Currents in American Stratification Literature," *American Sociologist* 5 (May 1970):127–137.
13. Kingsley Davis and Wilbert E. Moore, "Some Principles of Social Stratification." *American Sociological Review* 10 (April 1945):242–249.
14. Melvin M. Tumin, "Some Principles of Stratification: A Critical Analysis," *American Sociological Review* 18 (August 1953):387–397.
15. Gerhard Lenski, *Power and Privilege: A Theory of Social Stratification* (New York: McGraw-Hill, 1966).
16. Harold Lydall, *The Structure of Earnings* (London: Oxford University Press, 1968), pp. 344, 397, 400–402, stresses the difficulties, if not the impossibility, of comparing economic inequality in agrarian and industrial societies.
17. Written with Patrick Nolan and Jean Lenski (New York: McGraw-Hill, 1995).
18. For a further discussion of these studies, see Chapter 7.
19. Anthony Giddens, *The Class Structure of the Advanced Societies* (New York: Harper and Row, 1973), especially ch. 6, 7, and 15.
20. Giddens's discussion of methodology can be gleaned from his wide-ranging commentary on a variety of epistemologies in his *New Rules of Sociological Method: A Positive Critique of Interpretive Philosophies* (New York: Basic Books, 1976). Giddens's substantive theory emerged gradually in *Central Problems in Social Theory; Action, Structure and Contradiction in Social Analysis* (London: MacMillan, 1979), *Profiles and Critiques in Social Theory* (Berkeley: University of

California Press, 1992), and *The Constitution of Society: Outline of the Theory of Structuration* (Berekely: University of California Press, 1984).

21. Anthony Giddens, *Capitalism and Modern Social Theory: An Analysis of the Writings of Marx, Durkheim, and Max Weber* (Cambridge, England: Cambridge University Press, 1971), and *Social Theory and Modern Sociology* (Stanford, CA: Stanford University Press, 1987).
22. Stanford, CA: Stanford University Press, 1990.

5
Creative Advances in Stratification Analysis: Functional and Conflict Perspectives

◆ ◆ ◆ ◆

◆ ◆ ◆ ◆

HISTORICAL BACKGROUND

American social scientists have discussed stratification from the earliest days of American social science. William Graham Sumner railed against plutocrats and masses in defense of the individualistic middle class. Thorstein Veblen denounced the unproductive and parasitic rich and celebrated productive professionals and workers. And Charles Horton Cooley's penetrating analysis focused on the social power of wealth and the "vicious circle" that minimized the life chances of the poor. Cooley is of special interest because he also enunciated America's characteristic faith that the United States was on its way to an evermore functional and just system of inequality. Along with most Americans, Cooley assumed that the United States was a free society and inequality reflects the natural distribution of talent among human beings. And, being natural, inequality and the conflicts that resulted from it posed no threat to American society, although it did create problems of adjustment. If these adjustments could not be made by free economic markets, they could be undertaken by the nation's free political markets. And the purpose of reforms, even when they involve extensive changes in the social environment, was not to change society but to make it more consistent with its basic principle—the emancipation of unequal individual talent through equality of opportunity—and thus produce a natural and just society (or system of "nonegalitarian classlessness"). To accomplish this, however, it was necessary to know how society promotes or retards personal achievement. Along with the other social sciences, sociology responded to this challenge, and the development of stratification research and theory was an important part of its response.

The formative period of empirically oriented sociology (1920s–1960s) was a golden, if innocent, age in American sociology. It developed new methods for investigating the factual world and employed a variety of perspectives. To help us through sociology's long struggle to understand the various forms of inequality, these perspectives can be put into two categories. The dominant one, liberal-functionalism, had both a micro-orientation (W. I. Thomas, the Chicago School, the social-problems approach, the small-town focus) and a macro-orientation (Charles Horton Cooley, Davis-Moore, Talcott Parsons, Blau-Duncan). The second perspective was a many-sided conflict approach (the economist Thorstein Veblen, Robert and Helen Lynd, the Frankfurt School, C. Wright Mills).

The Small-Town Focus

The American tradition of stratification research and theory emerged as a focus on the small town. From the 1920s on, American social scientists developed a complex set of skills for analyzing social class (and "caste") in small-town America. While an important aspect of this tradition was a search for the typical community, almost every kind of community and region was studied. From this effort emerged a rich and colorful picture of regional and other variations in inequality: from the well-established and differentiated class structure of the Northeast and South to the frontier communities of the middle and far West, from complex industrial communities to homogeneous farm and mining communities, from ethnically and racially homogeneous communities to those richly diversified by ethnicity and race, and from small towns to metropolitan centers and suburbs.[1]

Regardless of orientation, the sociologists (and other social scientists) who studied small-town America revealed a world at variance (in conflict) with American beliefs and values. The Middletown (Muncie, Indiana) studies (1927 and 1936) were especially revealing in this regard largely because the Lynds placed American society in a historical frame and tried to understand Muncie as it went from a farming to an industrial world.

The pioneer small-town studies had common characteristics. Virtually all researchers chose communities of manageable size—small enough for the observer (often a team) to get to know it fairly well, and, even more importantly, for the inhabitants to identify and evaluate each other in terms of stratification categories. Thus, community members subjectively evaluated families on a number of different bases (income, amount and type of wealth, occupation, club memberships, breeding, power, and so on), and the observers presumably allowed the reality of social class to emerge.

The main outlines of this tradition stemmed from the work of the social anthropologist W. Lloyd Warner, who with many collaborators investigated a number of communities, starting in 1930 with Yankee City (Newburyport, Massachusetts). In 1949 Warner and his associates published a manual[2] in which they formalized their method, presenting two different procedures for determining social classes: Evaluated Participation, or the subjective determination of social classes by community members, and the Index of Status Characteristics, or an average of weighted scores for occupation, source of income, and house type and location. The results from these two procedures were found to correlate quite well in the case of a small town; and presumably the Index of Status Characteristics could be substituted for the more cumbersome interview procedure to allow for the study of larger population complexes whose members do not know each other well enough to judge others' class positions.

Small-town stratification theory is characterized by many difficulties, notably its basic assumption that studying the small town is tantamount to investigating the nature of the United States.[3] This assumption was probably not justified even at the time such studies were being conducted, and their current relevance to the dynamics and structure of the American system of stratification is even more problematic. Aside from their diverse orientations and conclusions, these studies all focused on something that has since virtually disappeared, small-town America. The great creative period of small-town stratification research lasted from the mid-1920s to the early 1940s; it occurred, in other words, at the same time that the United States was rapidly becoming an urban society dominated by a national economy and governed by a national state. And as we stressed earlier, even the concept of an autonomous nation-state is inadequate; one must think in terms of an international political economy that has important consequences for class structure. Wal-Mart—a chain of retail stores commanded by computer and based on cheap labor, state highways, and cheap gas, straddling the United States, Mexico, and Canada, selling products from around the world, and upsetting local businesses and class hierarchies—symbolizes the new America.

The Shift from Subjective to Objective Data

The limitations of a narrow concentration on small communities was sensed by Warner, who eventually developed a more efficient procedure for analyzing stratification phenomena than the reputational approach he had used. However, credit for the transition, both theoretical and practical, from the study of the small town to the study of the metropolitan center, belongs to August B. Hollingshead. Early in his career, Hollingshead had used the reputational approach to study the impact of social class on education in Morris, Illinois, a small Midwestern town of 6,000 inhabitants.[4] But later, when he wanted to tackle the relation between social class and mental illness in New Haven, Connecticut, a metropolitan center of 240,000, Hollingshead could not rely on subjective awareness of social class. Instead, he developed an "objective" substitute, the Index of Social Position.[5] After intensive interviews with a cross-sectional random sample of 552 households, Hollingshead and his associate Jerome K. Myers ranked the families. Working independently, they agreed, by and large, on the ranking of the families in a scheme of five classes. They then extracted the basic three criteria they had used to rank the families: (1) location of residence, (2) occupation, and (3) education (which was taken to indicate associational and cultural life). Each of these factors was scaled and weighted, and the resulting range of scores produced five distinct classes, the upper classes containing 2.7 percent, 9.8 percent, and 18.9 percent of the total number of families and the two lower classes containing 49.4 percent and 20.2 percent.

Stratification theory and research has flourished since the 1950s. Its story can best be told in terms of the effort to understand the American occupational system and social mobility. Its initial development in tackling the problem of social mobility was continuous with the main tradition in American liberalism and functionalism: the interpretation of behavior in individualistic terms under the unstated assumption that the United States is a meritocracy or is on its way toward becoming one. It developed as part of the major thrust of American sociology, its preoccupation with developing a scientific methodology and becoming a science. In the immediate post–World War II period, this meant functionalism and quantitative analysis. Unfortunately, it also meant the continuance of powerful American mores (the liberal consensus, or nonegalitarian classlessness, that had been expressed by Cooley in 1920 and had reappeared in Davis and Moore in 1949).

THE LIBERAL-FUNCTIONAL FOCUS ON OCCUPATIONS

Talcott Parsons: The Professions as the Spearhead of an Evolving Liberal Society

Talcott Parsons (1902–1973) was America's leading sociological theorist from the end of World War II until his death in 1973. Primarily a specialist in general theory, and the United States' leading exponent of the evolutionary-functional perspective, Parsons devoted considerable attention to social stratification.[6] Like Lenski, his depiction of the American system of stratification was also derived largely from an abstract contrast with feudal society. He emphasized the decline of ascriptive forces and the rise of equality, choice, pluralism, and functional inequality based on achievement processes over the past few centuries. His depiction of stratification was also based on a refutation of Marx (he asserted that property is declining in importance); he saw social class, in the traditional sense, as a transitional phenomenon.

In his contribution to stratification analysis, Parsons stressed the importance of egalitarian forces, especially equality of opportunity, mass education, and civic rights in government and private associations. These forces, Parsons claimed, tend to have real effectiveness in controlling and moderating inequality. The "competence gap" produced by achievement and competition is also modified by fiduciary mechanisms located most prominently in law, government, and the professions. Some ascriptive advantage accrues in the families of the upper classes, but Parsons did not see this as a great problem. Actually, he argued that the concept of social class should be divorced from kinship and property and that we should instead think in terms of hierarchical differentiation. A social class should now be thought of as an aggregate of people who "in their own estimation and those of others" occupy achievement positions of approximately equal status. Basically, social classes "represent a more or less successful resultant of mechanisms dealing with integrative problems of the society, notably those having to do with the balance between factors of equality and of inequality."[7]

Parsons saw the professions as the spearhead of the developing democratization of modern society. Just as the early capitalists superseded feudal aristocrats, argued Parsons, the professions lead the way past property and toward meritocracy. The emerging professions represent a marriage of objective knowledge and its applications.[8]

The early functional perspective on the professions bore a deep kinship with the innocent optimism of early sociology. Pioneer sociologists such as Condorcet and Saint Simon down through Lester Ward and Charles Horton Cooley equated modern society with the growth of knowledge through science. Parsons's functional view of the professions saw them as an integral part of the modernization process in which sacred-agrarian-ascriptive society gives way to a secular-industrial-achievement society based on the institutionalization of knowledge.

On all of the above counts, Parsons is wrong, a record that cannot be excused given the knowledge available to him. By Parsons's time, and in his lifetime, a burgeoning empirical tradition had unearthed an America that was widely divergent from its beliefs about itself (beliefs that Parsons never questioned). The Lynds, for example, had uncovered in *Middletown* (1927 and again in 1936) an America that should have inhibited Parsons from assuming a correspondence between American ideals and behavior. A vital tradition of social stratification research, starting with the seminal works of W. Lloyd Warner, John Dollard, James West, St. Clair Drake and Horace Cayton, August B. Hollingshead, and Floyd Hunter, had splashed itself all over mainstream sociology in the 1940s and early 1950s to question the alleged meritocratic basis of America's class system. In 1951, C. W. Mills's *White Collar* raised serious questions about the bureaucratization and concentration of the American economy. Michael Harrington's *The Other America* (1962) raised still further questions about American society (especially the question of why there is a large and chronic amount of poverty in a society with well over a century of industrialization). All of the above books were current and well known during Parsons's creative years. In addition, Parsons, who ignored Marx when he canvassed ideas for his social theory, did not pick up on the Marxian-influenced theory of imperialism, known as dependency theory, that emerged in the 1950s starting with Paul A. Baran and then blossomed in the 1960s and 1970s with such figures as André Gunder Frank and Immanuel Wallerstein.

Over and beyond all of the above were the personal experiences that Parsons had: the Great Depression was no imbalance to be dismissed by asserting that society had mechanisms to deal with such things (it was war that reequilibrated American society, not social cybernetics). The civil rights battles and the War on Poverty of the 1960s could certainly have been causes for optimism, though it was clear well before Parsons's death that the United States was not really succeeding in extending the achievement ethic to excluded groups. The Vietnam War was perhaps an aberration, but many during Parsons's lifetime were arguing that it was a necessary outcome of the American power structure.

Parsons's reluctance to cite the overall polity as an integrative mechanism is significant. American elites have consistently denied a positive role for the state, even though they use it extensively. Essentially, the negative view of the polity from Madison and Jefferson through Sumner and then to indifference to it by Cooley, Thomas, and Parsons is part of a pervasive pattern in American liberalism that allows American elites to use the state for their interests while denying its use to the masses. Parsons does emphasize the integrative function of law, but this is part of his misplaced faith in the nonpolitical professions and the nonpartisan state.

The trouble with Parsons's stratification theory, of course, is that he simply stated as fact what society itself claims to be. As we see later in more detail, much of what modern society (actually, its power-holders) says about itself is not true, is highly dubious, or is as yet incapable of being tested. Many favorable judgments about modern society are based on highly abstract and dubious comparisons with the feudal-monarchical past. But the contemporary United States still has many powerful ascriptive forces, including class ascription, and it is not even possible to say that their efficacy has been reduced during the course of American history.[9]

Blau and Duncan: Occupations and Social Mobility

In 1967, Peter Blau and Otis Dudley Duncan published their landmark study, *The American Occupational Structure*.[10] Its landmark status derives from its creative (quantitative) methodology, which is employed to analyze the occupational mobility of a representative sample of males, aged 25–64, in the labor force in 1962.

Social mobility refers to movement (or lack of movement) by individuals and households up and down the hierarchy of social class.[11] Caste and estate systems have little movement and are known as *closed systems of mobility*. Industrial systems have considerable movement up and down and are known as *open systems*.

The analysis of social mobility can focus on:

1. Intergenerational mobility, or the relation between parents' class position and that of their children
2. Intragenerational mobility, or the career of individuals over their life course
3. The class origins of particular occupations and other statuses (Where do teachers, government officials, corporate executives, the wealthy, and so on come from?)
4. Ascriptive barriers to mobility such as race, ethnicity, and gender (in some usage, class birth is also referred to as ascription)

Blau and Duncan used education and income to create a Socioeconomic Index for All Occupations (SEI). Their index correlated well with the astonishingly high consensus among Americans on how they subjectively rated the prestige of occupations. Their analysis revealed high immobility at the top and bottom with wide movement up and down in the middle layers of occupations (more up than down). Their causal analysis, focused on the father's occupation and education and the son's education, first job, and current job, did not find a conclusive pattern of causation: father influenced what happened to son but son seemed to influence himself, especially by doing well or poorly in school.

The Blau-Duncan study largely coincided with earlier studies on mobility, providing valuable insight into American society—the United States has had considerable upward mobility in the middle reaches, plus downward mobility (less than upward, but still considerable), and rigidity at the top and bottom throughout its history. In a study that connects the Blau-Duncan study and a similar one in 1973 with more recent data from the General Social Survey, Robert Hauser has found that while the overall pattern persists, upward mobility decreased somewhat in 1972–1990 and downward mobility increased somewhat. But by focusing only on younger males from 1972–1990, Hauser found a more significant slowdown in upward mobility and significant increase in downward mobility, including across the manual–nonmanual line.[12]

The failure by Blau and Duncan to explain the process of mobility stimulated much research. More was uncovered when researchers used such variables as educational and occupational aspirations, peer interaction, and the impact of significant others as ways to explain occupational (and income) status.[13] But rather than looking on all this as cumulative research leading to a grasp of objective reality, one has to ask (following today's interpretive epistemology), Was the stratification research tradition inaugurated by Blau and Duncan (the status-attainment approach) based on unassailable science or was it, like any human behavior, a sociohistorical artifact?

Social scientists are now much more aware of the inevitable sociopolitical nature of science than they were in the 1960s and 1970s. All science rests on assumptions that cannot be validated by science. Even the census of population, a one-by-one head count of the American people, is subject to wide variation depending on assumptions used (see Box 5–1).[14]

The first problem with the status-attainment approach was its focus on personal characteristics as attributes of individual human nature (the biopsychological explanation), thus confusing individualism (a product of capitalism and the class system) with the individual as human nature. This confusion takes many forms and has contaminated wide reaches of the social sciences. Under this assumption, grades in school, IQ, year of school completed, and so on are interpreted as "personal" mental or cognitive ability (and often characterized as the emergence of meritocracy). Under a different assumption, derived from the sociocultural approach, these alleged personal attributes are interpreted as social phenomena.

On a broader level, the Blau-Duncan approach was embedded in the liberal-functionalism that dominated sociology in the 1960s and 1970s. It should be noted that Blau and Duncan conducted a model scientific study as understood in their day and that criticisms of it should not be interpreted as a rejection of the quantitative method. The latter is one of the chief glories of Western civilization. It is the misuse of the quantitative method that is the issue, the failure to understand that all forms of empirical science are interpretive, in the last analysis, political acts. In some ways, Blau and Duncan sensed this—they early and clearly stated that interpretation is inescapable,

BOX 5–1 *The Political Nature of the Census*

> The constitutional requirement that a head count be taken every ten years to apportion representation in the House of Representative appears to be both nonpolitical and objective. But even this seemingly innocent activity is influenced by the struggle of power groups for advantage, and the results fall short of being objective. Historically, the census has been seriously inaccurate because enumerators fail to count everyone—the official figures for 1970 and 1980, for example, were anywhere from 5 million to 15 million persons short each time. The reasons for a short count are that enumerators are afraid to go into many urban neighborhoods and that many people hide from them anyway. Many poor families have to hide the fact that a father is present in order to collect welfare money. Others violate housing laws because of the desperate housing shortage. The count is also affected by the question of who to count (i.e., only citizens or illegal aliens as well?). Including all the poor and the illegal aliens in the population census could seriously affect apportionment to Congress and the distribution of large sums of federal monies. Thus a census can affect the distribution of political power (in Congress, between federal, state, and local governments) and the level of taxation. The big losers in the undercount are America's big cities and the Democratic party. In 1990, the Republican administration announced that no special efforts or allowances would be made to reduce the admitted undercount.

that the two authors have differing views, and that they do not intend to do stratification theory, but what they meant by all this was that they were trying as hard as possible to come up with an objective analysis that other scientists could validate or improve. And try as they might, they engaged in stratification theory in their concluding chapter, arguing that the American class system was not becoming more rigid despite the fact that some of the major factors favoring mobility in the past (the movement from agriculture to industry and large-scale immigration) were disappearing. They concluded that universalism was on the march and that new factors favorable to mobility and other American values would appear in due course. Later research would falsify their conclusions.

The early research on father-to-son mobility reflected the broad acceptance in sociology of the basic tenets of American liberalism (capitalism). From its beginnings until the 1960s and 1970s, American sociology envisioned the United States as an open society based on and progressively realizing universalistic principles. Universalism meant that science and achievement statuses were displacing nonscientific beliefs and statuses derived from ascription. Society was gradually developing objective criteria for evaluating people and positions. In time, all particularistic evaluations based on family, religion, race, and sex would be displaced by achievement criteria. Science, efficiency, rationality, and achievement would eventually triumph over any religious, philosophical, or humanistically derived beliefs and values that could not be empirically verified.

From Cooley to Parsons, and from Sumner to Davis-Moore, American sociologists had an image of society as a functional division of labor headed by natural elites as determined by competition, science, and achievement criteria. The United States was an open society, and whatever barriers to achievement remained were being dismantled. The occupational system already embodied the principle of merit as established in open-market competition. The occupational hierarchy was essentially a functional differentiation based on a growing consensus of what each occupation was worth. Already the rational division of labor had produced a large and growing middle-level mass.

The causes of progress were technology, education, urbanization, industrialization, and the growth of specialization and formal organizations. In the above, education had perhaps a special importance because one could actually observe the meritocratic process in action and understand how individuals were attaining their status in society.

This is the context in which early mobility studies were conducted.[15] Now known as the *status attainment* perspective, early mobility studies assumed that American society had already become a meritocracy (the theorists rejected the local community studies that had discovered deep nonmeritocratic class structures, claiming that they were not representative of the nation at large). Taking the United States at face value, status attainment theorists focused on individual characteristics, essentially asking: Who has the basic American values and how did they get them?

Status attainment analysts found a relation between class and success but did not evaluate this relation critically. They found personal characteristics and small-group experiences (related to class) that led to educational and occupational success, but again they did not disapprove. They found school systems that fostered success by those who came from the better classes, but again status attainment theorists did not interpret their findings, in effect endorsing them. The reason that status attainment analysts did not raise questions about what they found is that they assumed that the middle class (and above) represented the valid march of history, or rather the forces of science, rationality, and individual achievement. Thus it seemed right and proper that the middle class (and above) should produce sons who have the personal attributes that lead to success and that educational institutions should embody the universalistic values that were progressively enveloping all of society. The role of the objective, value-neutral researcher is simply to lay bare this objective, historical process.

During the 1970s the main creative currents in stratification research came out of the conflict tradition. In regard to mobility, conflict theorists criticized the status attainment model as narrow and biased, narrow because of its focus on occupation, and biased because of its focus on personal characteristics. Status attainment analysis, argued critics, was directly in line with mainstream liberalism and functionalism.[16] Its occupational categories were too broad, and important distinctions such as occupational power and complexity of skills were neglected. And fundamental structural forces in the economy and society central to mobility were also overlooked. Property relations are crucial in maintaining continuity among generations in the upper class and controlling the admission of new members. Property relations as economic concentration, and in static vs. dynamic sectors in the economy, are also central to mobility.[17] The actions of professional associations and trade unions in controlling labor flows, the actions of the government, the behavior of foreign countries, and so on are all important to how well each generation fares. All in all, the conflict perspective has made *structural* mobility central to how sociologists think of mobility and stratification.

The conflict tradition has also produced a different picture of education from the one found in mainstream American thinking and in status attainment research. Far from being a progressive force reflecting progressive middle-class values, the school is basically a class phenomenon, ensuring the success of the established classes and the failure of the lower classes. And to make matters worse, success in school cannot be linked to functional achievement in the outer society (for details, see Chapter 9).

Status-attainment scholars had worked hard to explain as much as they could about the overall national mobility process. Despite their efforts they acknowledged that there was much that remained a mystery, and they too increasingly looked to structural factors for explanations. Thanks to their pioneering efforts, both liberal and conflict researchers and theorists had something to work against. The distinctive emphasis of the conflict position now forms the heart of creative stratification analysis. Out of both liberal and radical conflict research and theory has come a redefinition of occupations (including the professions) and education, and a new emphasis on property, income, the overall economy, the role of the state, and the global economy.

BROADENING THE LIBERAL-FUNCTIONAL FOCUS: THE CONFLICT OUTLOOK ON CLASS VARIABLES

Despite an overlap between liberal-functionalism and the conflict position, the latter has some distinctive emphases. Conflict theorists do not take it on faith that the United States is an emerging meritocracy based on universalistic standards and practices. Conflict theories rejected this image as widely inconsistent with how the actual U.S. worked. American society, they argued, is best viewed as a creation of power groups, not as the release of human nature. It is a historical, sociocultural entity, not a natural, ahistorical system. All in all, the conflict position requires a change in basic assumptions, a change in how facts are interpreted, and an attention to overlooked facts.

The United States as a Land of Opportunity: Understanding Structural Mobility

Structural analysis means focusing on power, or rather on the groups that have the power to structure the lives of others. A structural view of social mobility focuses on the large-scale forces and power groups that generate movement or lack of it on the class ladder (technology, corporations, professional associations, voluntary groups, political action, educational and other sociological systems, government fiscal and monetary policies, overseas investment, foreign competition, civil rights, and so on). It means focusing on society as a self-explanatory structure in the spirit of Karl Marx, Max Weber, and Emile Durkheim.

The first thing to note is that the United States appears to have similar rates of overall mobility throughout its history and in comparison to other societies. It is not improving in this regard; actually recent decades have seen a decline in mobility. This means that it is a capitalist society, not that it has released human nature or based itself on universal meritocratic processes.

Second, the United States produces its rates of mobility, upward, downward, and stationary, in different ways and with some variation depending on the interplay of new and old causes. Even causes are not universal but themselves undergo change; for example, immigration helped upward mobility in the nineteenth and early twentieth centuries but immigration in the 1970s to 1990s is associated with declines in upward mobility. Technology had a positive impact in the nineteenth and early twentieth centuries, creating new and better jobs and forcing many Americans upward, but computer technology appears to be distinctive—it seems to be causing downward mobility. To take another example of this important point, the federal government was a positive force for economic mobility for most of American history, openly aiding economic development. In recent decades, however, it has not been able to do as much since the easy days of early industrialization are over (and the earlier beneficiaries of government are now opposed to government economic intervention).

What needs to be abandoned in studying stratification and mobility (or any other form of human behavior) is the assumption that one is studying an objective natural process. Even when persistent structures are uncovered, the causes of them over time may be different. What all this means is that the observer must be aware of old and new causes and be prepared to recommend changes in what is happening in order to achieve stated goals.

The United States has mobility rates that are distinctive in contrast to preindustrial societies, but they are not exceptional when compared to many developing societies or to all other industrial systems. As in other societies, these rates exhibit no trend toward universalism (growing rates of mobility through universal standards of achievement enforced by growing degrees of equal opportunity). The actual rates appear to be trendless—there is considerable immobility at the top and bottom and a great deal of mobility (more up than down) in the middle. The increase in downward mobility and decrease in upward mobility in recent decades may portend a significant departure from this pattern. In any case, the facts about mobility refute the essentials of American liberalism.

The ordinariness of the United States in this regard has long been asserted, but a recent synthesis has given the claim strong confirmation. Erikson and Goldthorpe have standardized and compared high-quality data from a large array of studies covering developing and developed European countries, plus the United States, Australia, and Japan (roughly from the 1920s through the early 1970s). Their conclusion is that no discernible trends exist toward steady upward mobility (the percent of male individuals who have class positions different from their fathers') or of relative rates (movement out of specified classes signifying greater fluidity or openness of the system). Developing countries have high rates of mobility, perhaps even higher than developed countries, but once industrialization occurs a trendless stability is established that has upward and downward mobility, but is still far from being an open, equal-opportunity class system. The Erikson-Goldthrope study has the added value of employing their data to evaluate both liberal and Marxist evolutionary theories. The data clearly indicate that both theories are wanting. Of these, they clearly tag American liberalism as ethnocentric and reject its claim that industrial societies are converging toward high and increasing rates of upward mobility based on expanding levels of equal opportunity and universalistic achievement standards.[18]

In evaluating mobility, it is important to understand that an entire society may be mobile. By *societal mobility* is meant the general upward absolute movement of the class system itself as measured by income (rising standard of living), occupation (more brainwork, less manual labor), and education (more literacy, more years of school completed). Seen in this way, the entire American population has experienced upward mobility during the last century (see Figure 5–1). Failure to note this aspect of mobility can cause confusion. What this means is that a family can experience a sizable improvement in its benefits over two or more generations and still remain in the same class.

Societal mobility is a form of structural mobility and leads to important insights. Much of America's mobility has resulted from movement into manual work followed by movement from manual to white-collar occupations. The first movement is now over and the shift to a nonmanual (or ser-

FIGURE 5–1 A Nonempirical Construct Depicting the Absolute Upward Movement of the American Class Structure and the Absence of Change in the Relative Distribution of Social Values Despite Upward, Downward, and Lack of Mobility

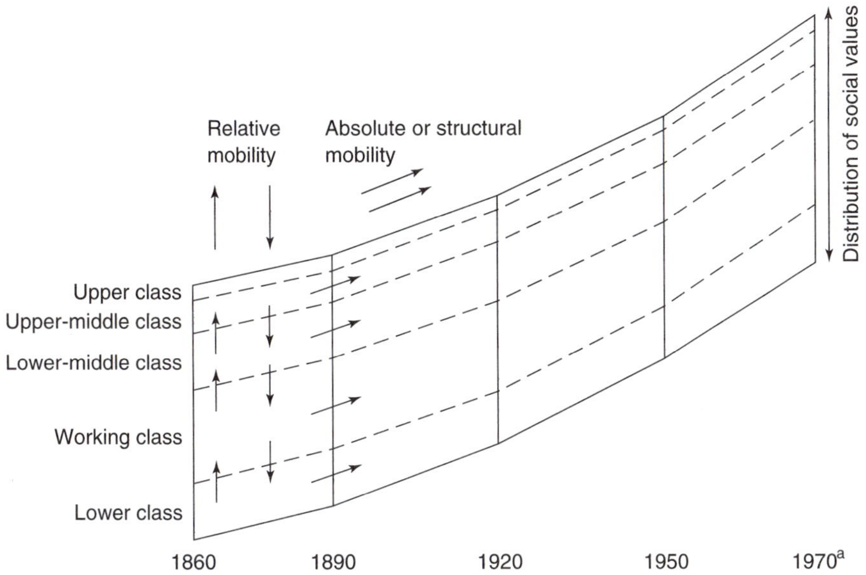

[a]The figure ends in 1970 because the upward movement of the American class structure may have ceased after that point (this possibility is a major theme in later chapters).

vice) economy may not necessarily be causing upward mobility (most white-collar jobs are not easy to distinguish from manual work either in conditions of work or income). Or stated differently, white-collar jobs have not resulted from an upgrading of work but have been caused by the concentration and bureaucratization of the American economy.

As a developing capitalist society and an advanced or corporate capitalism from 1850 to 1950, the United States first generated upward rates of mobility and then exhibited the same trendless levels exhibited by other capitalist societies. The flowering of corporate, world-market capitalism over the past few decades has undermined even these static trends. America's giant corporations, thanks largely to advanced forms of communication and transport, now have the ability to lower their professional, skilled, and unskilled labor costs by pitting Americans against the labor of the entire planet. Understandably, Americans have experienced less upward and more downward mobility in recent decades.

It is of the utmost importance in understanding all forms of mobility to avoid the liberal assumption that economic growth automatically promotes rising standards of living (including the elimination of poverty), equal opportunity and competition, more opportunity for all or even most, greater commitment to universal standards, and a reduction of distance among the several classes, in short, a progressive society with rising rates of upward mobility of all sorts.

The general slowdown in the standard of living since 1970 may have ushered in a new environment for mobility. Instead of a growing pie fostering a nonzero-sum game (a game that does not require losers), the distribution of America's growing pie has become a zero-sum game (one gains at the expense of others). Given changes in the American power structure, America's upper classes have been taking bigger slices of the pie for themselves. And once they have the bigger piece, they have resources to maintain and enlarge their shares, something that is happening aggressively in the 1990s.

The Myth of Equal Opportunity

Equal opportunity is a myth in two ways. One, it does not characterize the United States as some believe (and it fails, incidentally, by a wide margin). Two, equal opportunity cannot be established in the United States within existing institutions (power relations), no matter how hard we try.

Equal opportunity was analyzed in early mobility studies as *exchange* or *circulation* mobility though it is now probably best to use the Erikson-Goldthorpe term *relative mobility*. In any case, no society beyond hunter-gatherers can provide equal opportunity. The use of this term has contaminated American politics, public policy, and social science. Similarly, no society has yet provided equal justice or equality of political power. The use of the term *equal* is a key part of liberalism's mythology (mores). What capitalist societies provide are different kinds of opportunity that vary by class (and race, gender, age, disability, and sexual orientation). The term *equal opportunity* is really a way to put praise or blame on individuals, to allege that rewards are distributed by biopsychological factors, and to distract attention from power.

Professions and Occupations: Reappraising the Division of Labor

For most of its history, sociology has accepted the liberal view of the capitalist division of labor: occupations, spearheaded by the professions, are developing according to the imperatives of science, knowledge, and technology (universalism). From Saint Simon and Comte to Davis-Moore, Talcott Parsons, and Blau-Duncan, evolutionary liberalism celebrated the emergence of a rational division of labor—an occupational system, guided by science, technology, and the professions, progressively raising skill levels throughout the system.

In recent decades that view has largely been exploded. The facts had always been against that view, but by the 1980s the facts had become too obvious to deny. Some still believe in the ideology of convergence, the managerial revolution, postindustrialism, the information society, and so on, but it had become clear that most contemporary workers are unskilled or semiskilled and that the more skilled jobs, especially the professions, were far different than the idealizations of them. Even in Talcott Parsons's lifetime, a conflict view of the professions had emerged to cast serious doubts about the liberal view of them.[19]

The above analysis has deep negative implications for the liberal outlook—not only are occupations subject to power and arbitrary definitions, but this many-sided process has a deep impact on income, wealth, and education. What it means is that stratification analysis must always be a sociopolitical analysis using alternative definitions of everything, and it must frame its knowledge as a primer for action. To do otherwise in the postempirical (postpositive) age is to endorse the status quo.

Bringing the State Back In

Until recent decades, both liberal and Marxist theorists, along with sociology, tended to focus on economic factors alone and to neglect the role of the state in the economy. Separating economy and polity is a useful analytic convention, but taking the separation as empirical reality, as economics has done, for example, is fatal. Empirically, state and economy (as well as state and society) are joined at the hip. No understanding of the American class system is possible without keeping a steady eye on government fiscal and monetary policy and on numerous laws that impact on equality and inequality, for example, civil rights, affirmative action, student grants and loans, housing, and laws pertaining to the handicapped or gays and lesbians. Something as simple as a highway has positive and negative consequences for employment. Needless to say, wars and military expenditures also have a profound affect on the American class structure. The impact of the international economy on stratification deserves a special word.

The Globalization of the American Economy, or Who Is Us?

Economic relations among societies have been an important part of the life of society since the emergence of complex societies some 10,000 years ago. Students of history know the importance of trade in the life of ancient Greece and Rome. The emergence of trade routes within Europe and from Europe to the Middle and Far East was an indispensable adjunct to the rise of capitalism. And after 1450, the dynamic societies of Europe (and their offshoots like the United States) became even more dynamic through the exploitation of conquered territories. But even before the age of colonialism ended (in 1975 with the end of Portugal's African Empire), a new world market economy had emerged. This new world economy, based on trade among sovereign nations, represents a new form of imperialism. The basic trend in the world market economy has two features:

1. Foreign trade before World War II was a relatively small part of the economy of most capitalist economies (5 percent of the U.S. economy). World trade expanded enormously after World War II to become a much larger and even vitally important part of every economy, developed and developing (25 percent of the U.S. economy).

2. The second trend in the world market economy is the growth and transformation of multinational corporations. Starting in the nineteenth century, many large corporations began to operate in more than one country. This trend accelerated after World War II, spearheaded by American corporations. A new phenomenon replaced colonial imperialism: direct investment (that is, ownership of businesses) in other countries, developed and developing. This process has itself evolved into a new stage; whereas earlier, the multinational corporation had been *polycentric* (operating in a number of countries), it has now become *geocentric* (operating on a global basis).

The U.S. economy has always been somewhat dependent and always buoyed by the movement across national boundaries of raw materials, processed consumer goods, capital goods, and various kinds of labor (settlers, slaves, immigrants, illegal aliens, migratory labor). Today, the United States depends heavily on foreign trade to supply it with raw materials, inexpensive consumer goods, and capital goods. In turn, it needs foreign markets in which to sell the products that it is competitive in (food, lumber, tobacco, airplanes, computers, medical technology, arms, mass media, entertainment materials). On the whole, it has been buying more from abroad than it is selling, and its now chronic trade deficit has made it a debtor nation and become a serious drag on the American economy.

American economists and policy makers, unable to understand the international economy any more than they understand the domestic economy, simply espouse a free-trade philosophy (the counterpart on the international scene of domestic laissez-faire economics). And they have been even less able to understand the rapid evolution of geocentric corporations (also referred to as global or stateless corporations). In an astute analysis with an insightful title, Robert Reich has distinguished between American-owned companies that conduct much of their business abroad (including high-technology manufacturing and research and development) and foreign-owned companies in the United States that employ mostly Americans and do high-technology manufacturing and research and development in the United States. The latter corporation (for example, Philips and Thomson Electronics, Honda), says Reich, is better for America's economic competitiveness than the former (for example, IBM, Whirlpool, Texas Instruments).[20]

The new global corporation is difficult to regulate or tax. A Japanese plant in the United States exports to Europe and escapes European restrictions on Japanese cars. If a Japanese company manufactures VCR parts in Thailand, and assembles and exports them to the United States from Malaysia, the transaction does not show up in the United States–Japan trade accounts. Another headache for policy makers is to figure out how to make corporations that operate in many countries pay their legal taxes.

The international economy is important for the United States because the flow of capital abroad means fewer and poorer jobs at home. It means that American labor is pitted against cheaper labor in other countries. The global mobility of capital means it can avoid (and evade) taxes. Mobile companies can threaten to move when confronted by labor unions or environmental regulations. The mobility of capital means that governments cannot control or even keep track of the astronomical sums of money that flow across national boundaries every day.

The new global economy means that educated foreigners can come to work in the United States (the brain drain) or foreign students can study in the United States (approximately 20 percent of the students at MIT are foreigners). All this affects Americans struggling to advance themselves. The flow of legal and illegal immigrants, both skilled and unskilled, also affects Americans (the flow of illegal aliens continues unabated, indicating another loss of control over national boundaries). The large amount of drug traffic across national boundaries also seems uncontrollable.

Another way to see the impact of the global economy on our personal lives is that current American policies not only reduce the number of good jobs available to Americans, but make acquiring a home difficult. The process goes something like this: American corporations go abroad and export to the United States from Japan, Taiwan, Hong Kong, or Singapore, adding to our trade deficit. The United States also has been running a domestic deficit because such corporations and their wealthy American owners receive huge amounts of government welfare while paying low taxes. The twin American deficits means that the federal government must borrow huge sums, thus keeping interest rates high (so that the wealthy at home and abroad will lend the federal government money). This keeps mortgage interest rates high and makes buying a home difficult for Americans, even those who have fairly good-paying jobs.

The Underground Economy

Much of the foregoing implied that the real economy is different from our ideas about it. The economy has other dimensions that orthodox ideas do not capture. We have already said enough to show that government is an integral part of the economy. And so are schools, hospitals, churches, and voluntary organizations. Beyond all this lie informal behaviors of great variety, both within economic groups and outside them (legal and illegal self-help, do-it-yourself, family caring services, and both blue- and white-collar crime). Some of our failure in public policy reflects the lack of firm data about the informal economic sector, which can range anywhere from 5 to 20 percent of the total.[21] What is the significance of the drug trade for mobility? There are anywhere from 500,000 to 1,000,000 prostitutes in the United States uncounted by the official figures—one can argue that prostitution provides a greater opportunity for upward mobility for women than medicine or law.

Mobility Traps

An important idea for making sense of the American class system is Norbert Wiley's concept of a mobility trap.[22] A mobility trap is success within a class that does not lead to or blocks movement into another class. Wiley's focus is on the ethnic mobility trap but he lists four distinct types:

1. The "age-grade trap," or the tendency of age and sex groups to adopt prestige values that conflict with those of older age groups. Thus, popularity as a sports star or beauty queen in high school may well be a barrier to social mobility for those who cannot break into professional sports or the field of entertainment.
2. The "overspecialization trap," or lower-level, highly specialized administrative jobs from which one cannot be promoted.
3. The "localite trap," or the pursuit of local prestige at the expense of national standing. Certain occupations, such as social worker, planner, school superintendent, professor, and clergyman, increasingly allow for mobility only on a nationwide basis.
4. The "minority group trap," or advancement within a minority group in lieu of advancement into majority structures.

Bringing Stratification Analysis Abreast of Society and Creative Social Theory

Mainstream sociology, from Sumner and Ward through Cooley, W. I. Thomas, Talcott Parsons, and Blau-Duncan had little understanding of the basic dynamics and structure of corporate capitalism. Since the 1960s, the U.S. has become a hard-to-hide conflict society, a zero-sum rather than a positive-sum society, a transparent plutocracy. The "discovery" of poverty in the 1960s, the Vietnam War, huge military expenditures, the Civil Rights movement(s), foreign economic competition, and other factors have generated second thoughts in sociology about its value-neutral, nonpolitical, empiricism. As we saw in our discussion of liberal theories of stratification, creative sociologists such as Anthony Giddens, have stressed the embeddedness of social scientists in the society they are studying. Liberals have adopted a more historical, sociocultural view of society and have abandoned the assumptions of a naturally progressive, scientifically oriented social system. Neofunctionalism (Blau, Alexander) has worked to incorporate sociocultural and power variables into liberal-functionalism. Following the lead of Giddens, sociologists who would understand social stratification must think of themselves as in a never-ending interaction with their material, seeing what they assume, and changing what they assume when discoveries running counter to them are made. Interpretative sociology is all we have whether we know it or not and that means we are inherently political. Sociologists and stratification analysts must somehow become politically engaged as well as factually accurate and comprehensive. There are dangers in the new way of being scientific, but the old way of being a passive, detached specialist may be worse. Stratification analysis must come abreast of the main thrust of creative social science, the many-sided conflict perspective. Conflict theorists reject the assumption underlying objective empiricism (liberal functionalism), namely that a fixed and finished neutral observer can find the truth about a fixed and finished reality. Instead, radicals stress the historicity of both thinking and facts. They stress the need to develop new forms of thought in keeping with the movement of history. They stress the inevitable political-value nature of science.

Perhaps conflict thought can be summed up as an attempt to blend analysis and policy, the factual and the ideal, and scholarship and politics. Traditional liberals, on the other hand, feel obligated to don another hat when they advocate reform or pass judgment on what they find. Conflict thinkers assume that research and theory must be about the concrete experiences of people, especially the dominated, in concrete historical societies, and that it must have policy relevance for present day society (as opposed to mainstream liberalism, which seeks transhistorical knowledge about no society in particular).

Advances in understanding stratification have come from different quarters: old-fashioned demographers, conflict liberals, postindustrial and rational-choice liberals, Marxists, neo-Marxists, neofunctionalists, radical Weberians, human and cultural capital theorists, and African-American, feminist, and gay theorists. Even as we use these creative views to explore the American class system and other forms of inequality in the following chapters, we want to keep them separate. Mainstream social science is still embedded in modernism, or perhaps better said, in scientism, the search for objective truth through cumulative research by nonpolitical observers who believe they are anchored by a scientific method. For their part, Marxists, an important part of the conflict tradition, are also animated by the goal of objective truth and a transhistorical methodology. The postempirical world requires that the goal of objective truth be modified drastically. Analysts must always be aware of their basic organizing assumptions (what you see is what you assume). In canvassing the empirical materials of stratification and inequality in the following chapters, we will try to balance the liberal-functional and conflict perspectives against each other, and pit both against the complex and changing historical world of corporate, world-market capitalism.

SUMMARY

Stratification analysis in the U.S. has had to struggle to escape the powerful pull of American liberalism and its assumption that the United States is a free society with equal opportunity (or is on its way toward becoming one), and that inequality by birth has been or soon will be supplanted by an emerging hierarchy of natural ability (nonegalitarian classlessness).

The early study of stratification focused on small-town America. While small-town studies revealed deep inequality based on birth into economic classes and other ascriptive factors, the shift from entrepreneurial to corporate capitalism made it necessary to develop ways to understand the newly emerging national and international system of stratification.

The United States has had two distinct emphases in analyzing stratification and inequality: the liberal-functional and the conflict perspectives.

Liberal-functional theorists, exemplified by Talcott Parsons and Blau and Duncan (the status attainment perspective), while aware of ascriptive class factors, still thought in terms of an open, fluid, meritocratic society (nonegalitarian classlessness).

After the 1970s, a conflict perspective emerged (even among liberals) to spearhead creative advances in understanding class and other forms of inequality. By and large, conflict theorists focus on power, sociocultural causation, and the deep gulf between American beliefs and values and how the United States actually functions (and malfunctions).

Both liberal-functional and conflict theorists have used social mobility as a way to understand class and other forms of inequality. Social mobility refers to movement up or down between different class levels resulting in significant changes in material and symbolic benefits. Mobility of this kind must be distinguished from societal mobility or an increase in standard of living and other values without movement to another class.

Four different aspects of mobility have been distinguished:

1. Intragenerational mobility, or how individuals make out in the pursuit of their careers over their life cycle
2. Intergenerational mobility, or the analysis of the relation between parents' class position and their children's class position
3. Social origins mobility, or determining from what social class the occupants of various occupations have been recruited
4. Ascriptive barriers to mobility such as race, ethnicity, and gender

Liberal-functional analysis from Blau and Duncan to the present day has monitored social mobility using aggregate data supplied by the U.S. government and private surveys. What they have found is considerable up-and-down mobility in the middle and relative immobility at the top and bottom reaches of the class ladder. A significant new finding is that upward mobility has declined over recent decades, and downward mobility has increased.

Mobility and other studies have demonstrated that the basic tenets of the liberal-functional outlook are false. There is no movement toward more upward mobility, more equality of opportunity, a greater reliance on universalistic standards, or rising standard of living. The liberal emphasis on economic growth in the abstract as a way to achieve all of the above is a way to postpone indefinitely the political decisions that must be made if such goals are to be achieved.

Conflict theorists have supplemented the liberal-functional picture by explicitly framing their analysis in critical, conflict terms. Conflict theorists have gone beyond abstract, nonpolitical data about income, education, and occupation to include wealth and to stress the role of economic and political power, both domestic and international, in shaping the unequal distribution of all basic American values and behaviors.

A many-sided conflict perspective has come to the fore because American society itself has become openly conflict-ridden and Americans are now experiencing a zero-sum game of social mobility (rather than have many winners, the United States is now generating many, and perhaps increasing numbers, of losers).

Creative sociology has emphasized the interpretive nature of social science whether one is a liberal-functionalist or an explicit conflict theorist. Scientism, or the search for objective truth through cumulative research conducted by nonpolitical observers, is still powerful and must be resisted. Objective truth, whether searched for by liberals or Marxists, is certainly a desirable goal for the long term, but in the meantime the sure-footed scientist keeps the various perspectives separate and in fruitful interplay. American sociology has had to struggle to reach a position that Marx and Weber took for granted. A politically engaged scientist who is also factually accurate and comprehensive may be a difficult goal to attain, but the nonpolitical, objective positivist is worse because impossible.

NOTES

1. For a useful review of representative examples of this tradition between the 1920s and 1950s, see Milton M. Gordon, *Social Class in American Sociology* (Durham, NC: Duke University Press, 1958), chs. 3–5.

2. W. Lloyd Warner, Marcia Meeker, and Kenneth Eells, *Social Class in America: A Manual of Procedure for the Measurement of Social Status* (Chicago: Science Research Associates, 1949).
3. W. Lloyd Warner, the leading researcher associated with small-town studies, states this explicitly in the forward to *Democracy in Jonesville* (New York: Harper & Row, 1949), and implicitly in the titles of the first four volumes (of a total of five) of the Yankee City series: *The Social Life of a Modern Community and The Status System of a Modern Community,* both with Paul S. Lunt; *The Social System of American Ethnic Groups,* with Leo Srole; *The Social System of the Modern Factory,* with J. O. Low. The fifth volume is entitled *The Living and the Dead* (New Haven, CT: Yale University Press, 1941–1959).
4. August Hollingshead, *Elmstown's Youth* (New York: John Wiley & Sons, 1949).
5. For a full explanation, see August B. Hollingshead and Frederick C. Redlich, *Social Class and Mental Illness: A Community Study* (New York: John Wiley & Sons, 1958), Appendix 2.
6. Talcott Parsons, "An Analytical Approach to the Theory of Social Stratification," *American Journal of Sociology* 45, no. 6 (May 1940):841–862; "A Revised Analytical Approach to the Theory of Social Stratification," in Reinhard Bendix and Seymour M. Lipset, eds., *Class, Status and Power: A Reader in Social Stratification,* 1st ed. (New York: Free Press, 1953); and "Equality and Inequality in Modern Society, or Social Stratification Revisited," *Sociological Inquiry* 40 (Spring 1970):13–72.
7. Parsons, "Equality and Inequality," p. 24.
8. Talcott Parsons, "The Professions," in David H. Sills, ed., *International Encyclopedia of the Social Sciences* (New York: Free Press, 1968), vol. 12. Parsons is here an early advocate of what later came to be known as the concept of *postindustrial society.*
9. While such comparisons are difficult, there appears to have been no decrease in social class inequality since our colonial period. See Jackson T. Main, "The Class Structure of Revolutionary America," in Reinhard Bendix and Seymour M. Lipset, eds., *Class, Status, and Power: Social Stratification in Comparative Perspective,* 2nd ed. (New York: Free Press, 1966), pp. 111–121; Jackson T. Main, *The Social Structure of Revolutionary America* (Princeton, NJ: Princeton University Press, 1965); and Gary B. Nash, ed., *Class and Society in Early America* (Englewood Cliffs, NJ: Prentice-Hall, 1970). For an analysis of substantial social inequality during the second quarter of the nineteenth century, the so-called era of the common man, see Edward Pessen, *Riches, Class, and Power Before the Civil War* (Lexington, MA: D.C. Heath, 1973).

   Robert S. and Helen M. Lynd's classic community studies, *Middletown* (New York: Harcourt, Brace, 1929) and *Middletown in Transition* (New York: Harcourt, Brace, 1937), provide valuable material suggesting a growth in inequality by comparing three years in the history of Muncie, Indiana: 1890, 1924, 1935. An extremely valuable historical analysis of social stratification in New Haven and Connecticut that traces the changing bases of what it depicts as an unchanged relative structure of inequality may be found in August B. Hollingshead and Frederick C. Redlich, *Social Class and Mental Illness* (New York: John Wiley & Sons, 1958), ch. 3. Stephan Thernstrom, *Poverty and Progress: Social Mobility in a Nineteenth Century City* (Cambridge, MA: Harvard University Press, 1964, argues that Newburyport, Massachusetts (the same city analyzed by Lloyd Warner in his Yankee City series), is our best example of a typical American community of the nineteenth century and challenges the conclusion reached by Warner and the Lynds that upward mobility is becoming more difficult. It has always been difficult, he argues, no more so today than in the past.

10. New York: Wiley, 1967.
11. Horizontal movement refers to a change of occupation within a class: a sales manager becomes an advertising executive; a professor of geology becomes a government scientist; a milk-truck driver becomes a bus driver, and so on.
12. As reported by Dennis Gilbert and Joseph A. Kahl, *The American Class Structure: A New Synthesis,* 4th ed. (Belmont, CA: Wadsworth, 1993), Tables 6–5, 6–6.
13. William H. Sewell and Robert M. Hauser, *Education, Occupation, and Earnings.* (New York: Academic Press, 1975) and William H. Sewell and Robert M. Hauser, eds., *Schooling and Achievement in American Society* (New York: Academic Press, 1976).
14. For a fuller discussion, see Margo A. Conk, "The 1980 Census in Historical Perspective," in *The Politics of Numbers,* ed. William Alonso and Paul Starr (New York: Russell Sage Foundation, 1987), pp. 155–186.
15. For much of the above context, see J. David Knottnerus, "Status Attainment Research and Its Image of Society," *American Sociological Review* 52 (February 1987):113–121.
16. Patrick M. Horan, "Is Status Attainment Research Atheoretical?," *American Sociological Review* 43 (August 1978):534–541.
17. E. M. Beck, Patrick M. Horan, and Charles M. Tolbert II, "Stratification in a Dual Economy," *American Sociological Review* 43 (October 1978):704–720.
18. Robert Erikson and John H. Goldthorpe, *The Constant Flux: A Study of Class Mobility in Industrial Societies* (New York: Oxford University Press, 1992).
19. For a full discussion, see Chapter 6.
20. Robert B. Reich, "Who Is Us?" *Harvard Business Review* 90 (January–February 1990):53–64.
21. For pioneering studies, see Stuart Henry, ed., *Informal Institutions: Alternative Networks in the Corporate State* (New York: St. Martin's Press, 1981); Edgard L. Feige, ed., *The Underground Economies: Tax Evasion and Information Distortion* (New York: Cambridge University Press, 1989); Louis A. Ferman, "Participation in the Irregular Economy," in Kai Erikson and Steven Peter Vallas, eds., *The Nature of Work: Sociological Perspectives* (New Haven: Yale University Press, 1990), 119–40; and Bruce Wiegand, *Off the Books: A Theory and Critique of the Underground Economy* (Dix Hills, NY: General Hall, 1992).
22. "The Ethnic Mobility Trap and Stratification Theory," *Social Problems* 15 (Fall 1967):147–159.

6

Economic Classes, I: The American Occupational Hierarchy

◆ ◆ ◆ ◆

◆ ◆ ◆ ◆

Tonight, all over the United States, tens upon tens of thousands of Americans must find a place to sleep. These are not travelers or tourists, but America's homeless. Tomorrow, they must somehow find food and again wonder where they will sleep. More fortunate than America's homeless are the 35 million Americans who are poor. Most have a place to live, such as it is, and they have enough to eat, more or less, for the better part of the month. Far above, a few hundred thousand families live in comfort, security, and splendor.

In between these distant extremes are further contrasts. Some Americans face an interesting work day, but most labor at boring jobs. Millions more are not only bored at work, but are subject to disease, disability, and death from it because their workplace is unsafe. Most working Americans find it hard to make ends meet and their spouses have to work. The number of such Americans seems to be growing (as a percent of the whole), while the relative number of Americans in interesting, well-paid jobs appears to be declining. Some Americans work steadily at something from the age of twelve on, while millions work irregularly and never have a steady job. Some Americans who want and need work—for example, some black males—never even get a first job.

Analyzing the United States in terms of its contrasting social classes introduces us to a world not easily accessible through ordinary experience. Actually, it is social class itself that limits and shapes experience. It is not only that we acquire our personality and thus our ability to understand our experience from our class background, but we Americans are deeply segregated into class-based, homogeneous, residential, educational, and other enclaves. It is this that makes Americans think of themselves as average. It is this that makes it easy for them to continue believing that inequality emerges from individual competition and equal opportunity. Why don't Americans square these beliefs with the fact that major portions of the American economy are inherited? Americans also think that inequality comes directly from individuals and that it serves social needs. But don't humans acquire their personalities from their socialization experiences? Many argue that equality is opposed to efficiency. But how efficient is it to have an economy in which millions are idle? What right has government to take from some and give to others? How would Americans frame this question if they knew that government spending and taxation favored the upper classes?

Class analysis addresses these and other questions. Is equality increasing or decreasing? Is the United States still a land of opportunity? Is upward mobility through hard work a feasible dream for the majority of Americans? In short, we are back to our old question: Is the United States a legitimate structure of power and inequality—in other words, a meritocracy?

DEFINING AND CLASSIFYING OCCUPATIONS: USING INTERPRETIVE SCIENCE

This is a good place to remind ourselves that science achieves certainty only by employing arbitrary assumptions, not factual reality. We now know that it is our assumptions and how we ask questions that create facts and reality. As we see below, even the most skilled professionals must employ assumptions (stereotypes) to do their work. Awareness of the role of assumptions in science is nowhere more important than in trying to understand the American occupational system.

The American occupational system is highly specialized. The U.S. Department of Labor's *Dictionary of Occupational Titles*[1] lists over 20,000 occupations. From 1939 on, this dictionary has defined occupations in terms of the skills required in each job, attempting to capture changes in required skills as they occur. The dictionary is not directly relevant to stratification analysis, but unfortunately commentators over the years have used it to make statements about the U.S. division of labor. The most common mistake is to say that the upper nonmanual (professional) occupations have increased steadily, indicating America's progress toward a postindustrial, knowledge-based society. One need only note that the Department of Labor's category Professional, Technical, and Managerial Occupations covers architects, engineers, natural and social scientists, surgeons, pharmacists, registered nurses, dieticians, elementary school teachers, lawyers, judges, clergy, writers, artists, actors, athletes, and public relations and personnel specialists to see that data assembled under this heading do not tell us much. As we see, there are not only wide disparities in power, income, and education among the above occupations, but even within many of the occupations themselves.

The distorting power of assumptions is everywhere; for example, respondents to surveys give different answers about the same thing (in this case occupations) depending on region, small or large firm, and race and gender. It appears in the fact that inflated job titles abound and that the same job is given different names. The center of the problem for stratification analysis is that scientists, whether in government, private practice, or the social sciences, also distort through the use of assumptions. To cite two examples, there are somewhere between 500,000 and 1,000,000 prostitutes and a large but unknown number of professional criminals in the United States who do not figure in our official occupational tallies. Here we are not talking about mistakes but rather the inevitable use of assumptions. Today our unemployment rate makes sense only if it is understood to count only those who have neither a full nor a part-time job and are looking for work. This means that the large number of unemployed who have given up ("discouraged workers") are not considered unemployed, and that part-time temporaries are counted as employed; the 1.5 million Americans in prison are also not counted. Surveys that ask Americans if they want to work reveal an unemployment rate closer to 30 percent, much higher than the official rate of 6 percent.[2] Science, in other words, is not a matter of detached observers studying objective facts. Scientists do their work from a position in the structure of power and the assumptions they use are invariably selective and debatable, that is, essentially political. For our purposes, it is important to remember, therefore, that both the liberal-functional and the Marxist-functional perspectives are essentially clusters of interpretive assumptions: even when they look at the same facts, let alone different facts, they see them and interpret them differently.

Sociology's liberal-functional view of the division of labor has been exploded, but is still tenaciously held by some in sociology (rational choice theorists) and by many outside (for example, most economists). Liberals (both right and left) exaggerate the importance of knowledge and skills in the modern occupational hierarchy, relying on gross comparisons with the preindustrial era. Liberals also still believe that modern society, especially in the United States, is becoming increasingly more rational, that is, subject to universalistic criteria of efficiency and effectiveness. Even a nodding acquaintance with the facts reveals a very different picture.

In any case, creative social scientists are working hard to improve the accuracy and comprehensiveness of our quantitative indicators. Even more important is the growing recognition that knowledge must be usable, must actually serve as a prompter of personal and political action. Thus new indicators are being developed to help policy makers evaluate the effectiveness of their policies. A notable example in stratification analysis is the current effort to revise the poverty rate (see Chapter 7).

THE APEX OF CORPORATE CAPITALISM: OWNERS, EXECUTIVES, AND OFFICIALS

Bureaucracy: A Technology of Power Masquerading as Efficiency

Among capitalism's major technocratic creations is bureaucracy, which it brought to fruition in the nineteenth century. A bureaucracy (also known as a complex organization) is a group organized to ensure efficiency and responsibility. As described by Max Weber in ideal terms, a bureaucracy is an administrative structure in which a hierarchy of statuses, separated from other statuses, is given specified duties and rights. The statuses are occupied by employees selected by stated qualifications. Employees are expected to establish a career, that is, make a long-term commitment to the enterprise. The equipment and facilities that employees use to perform their duties belong to the group. Commands come from above and responsibility flows from bottom to top. As much business as possible is conducted in writing.

Actual bureaucracies deviate from this ideal. Behavior within corporations, schools, foundations, hospitals, law firms, the military, and government agencies varies considerably from the enterprise's official blueprint. While different theories of complex organizations abound, the key idea for making sense of them is power.[3] Bureaucracies belong to or are controlled by somebody, and represent not so much efficiency and responsibility as the power of property. Both private and public bureaucracies create an image of nonpartisan public service, but in the final analysis they represent the heart of corporate capitalism.

The Occupations that Obscure the Occupational Hierarchy

A long scholarly tradition, from Frederic Taylor in the early part of the century to present-day public administration, business administration, and organizational theory, has sought to perfect the science of management.[4] These efforts, however, have helped to cloak the deep trend toward economic and political centralization and concentration. This trend has also been hidden by analysts who argue that corporate capitalism has undergone a managerial revolution (well-educated managers have replaced property as the organizing principle of capitalism). Of course, managers are also property owners and share fundamental class interests with owners in any case. The trend toward a concentrated political economy is further obscured when it is called the End of Ideology, a Knowledge Society, a High-Information Society, a Postindustrial Society, the rise of Professional Society, or the End of History. Narrow, technical studies of organizations in a taken-for-granted world also obscure the trend toward and the reality of concentrated power.[5]

The basic managerial style in the United States stresses individual responsibility within a hierarchical structure. Orders come from on high, responsibility is from the bottom up. Within this ethic, the manager is free to hire and fire (subject to some controls and labor union contracts). The corporation is the stronghold of the managerial ethic, but it is also the model for managerial styles in government, the military, religion, education, health care, and voluntary groups.

Hierarchy and specialization have their uses, but also create problems. We now know that an efficient bureaucracy does not necessarily mean centralization and steep hierarchy. Workers must feel free to exercise skills and assume responsibilities. Cooperation among workers and worker participation in management yield better and more work. The excessive centralization, hierarchy, and specialization, characteristic of American administration, breed insecure workers, clog communication lines, and result in employees who "feather their nest" and carve out turfs.

In recent years, the managerial style of American corporations has been seen as the main barrier to corporate innovation, productivity, efficiency, and long-term investment. The American executive is an individual careerist who moves a great deal among different companies putting down few roots and developing only temporary loyalties, a practice that contrasts sharply with Japanese custom.[6] The American executive is subject to pressures to produce profits every quarter and thus cannot take the long view or argue for investments that will take years to pay off. Again this runs counter to Japanese practice. Centralized control around one dimension leads to inefficiency, and the hierarchical structure promotes social distance between adjacent levels and chasms between managers and workers. As a result, it is difficult to harness the experience and skills of those directly involved in creating products or providing services.[7]

Corporations strive to make their operations seem fair and just as well as efficient. Today the personnel director serves as the corporate conscience in this regard, in effect linking organizational behavior to broad concerns about social and individual justice in the outside world. Organizations have many features not directly linked to efficiency or work. But such things as company newsletters, inflated occupational titles, company bowling teams, and retirement parties are vital to fostering loyalty and commitment. And the pretense that ranks, income, and benefits can be determined through scientific assessment helps to give the organization legitimacy in the eyes of its members. Nevertheless, and despite the claims of "scientific management" and "scientific personnel work," the process of recruiting, testing, interviewing, hiring, and training new members of an organization is largely a legitimizing facade, not science.[8]

The science of management, like the social sciences, is not so much science as American science. Generated in a culture based on alleged universalistic secular principles and supported by a gigantic continental market, American symbolic culture stressed quantitative studies when it did research and universal principles when it reached conclusions. Flushed with victory in World War II, and able to take the functioning of society for granted, management science did the same thing as the social sciences in general—it concentrated on developing abstract, universalistic principles. This meant American phenomena were deemed somehow natural. The result in management science was to validate American practices that had little to do with America's economic success. The economic boom of the 1950s and 1960s, when management science came into its own as a profession, was largely due to the pent-up demand created by the Great Depression and World War II. It was also due to the fact that the other capitalist societies were either exhausted or in ruins; that is, America's economic success was an artifact of monopoly.

American management science has done little comparative work and has failed to see that American practices are culture-bound. Decades after many American companies have become global corporations and the American economy faces serious competition from abroad, American management science has still not engaged in comparative research to uncover other managerial styles and understand the cultures that spawn them.[9] This no doubt is part of the explanation for the poor showing by American employees abroad: between 16 to 40 percent return home early (each premature return costing $100,000) and approximately 30 to 50 percent who stay in their overseas assignments are considered ineffective or marginally effective by their firms.[10]

The deficiencies of management science are connected to deficiencies in business education.[11] In turn, business education is hampered by its reliance on mainstream economics.[12] Professionalized managers administer policies made by governing boards (or by policy-making committees, agencies, councils, and so on, depending on the type of activity). By and large, policy-making bodies have homogeneous memberships, often despite laws requiring diversification. For example, no progress has been made by the U.S. State Department in obeying the Foreign Service Act of 1980, which requires that America's diplomatic corps be representative of the American people. Corporate boards, university trustees, hospital boards, and presidential advisers[13] are still composed of like-minded individuals. The chances are high that up to 90 percent of the governing boards of American universities have had no training in education. Probably no one on the board or staff of a hospital understands where health comes from (good food, hygiene, exercise, rest, and meaningful work). And women, blue-collar workers, blacks, Hispanics, the handicapped, and gays are underrepresented on policy-making bodies throughout American society. Managers, therefore, are subject to policy groups of like-minded individuals who fail to generate the ideas needed for good decisions. And leaders in general are subject to a narrow pipeline of information guarded by a narrow circle of like-minded advisers. All in all, homogeneous policy bodies, mechanically organized one-dimensional bureaucracies, an obsolete managerial style,[14] and connections among power groups across the apexes of society[15] all go together to make up a major reason for America's economic, social, and political shortfalls.

Despite the trend toward all-purpose administrators, the field of administration is split up into business, public, hospital, welfare, recreational, and voluntary (nonprofit) administration. Of these, public administration is solidly established with a large association and a journal. Nonetheless, all forms of administration fail to measure up to what we know about complex organizations. A simple question about American bureaucracies (collectively, corporate capitalism) yields an important insight: Why does the United States use so many college graduates in its private and public administrative structures, including the military, in comparison with other developed capitalist societies? The only reason is that unnecessary educational requirements and unnecessary layers of personnel act as a buffer and camouflage to enable the top people to reap rewards far above those available to their counterparts in other developed capitalist countries. It is a telling fact about the large corporations that make up the heart of the American economy that their executives pay themselves and that there is no relation between income and the size and performance of the operation,[16] whether judged against other corporations or against similar bureaucracies in public utilities, government, or the military, either in the United States or in other developed capitalist societies.

ELITE POWER TO PRODUCE SCARCE, OVERPRICED LABOR AT THE TOP AND ABUNDANT, CHEAP LABOR AT THE BOTTOM

Initially, industrialization transforms a labor force away from *primary* occupations (agriculture, fishing, lumbering) and toward *secondary* occupations (manufacturing, mining, processing). Mature industrialization produces a further decline of primary occupations, a stabilization of secondary occupations, and a large growth in *tertiary* occupations (services, white-collar work, professions, semiprofessions). The trend toward service occupations is clear in all industrial countries.

Significantly, the American labor force is made up mostly of employees who work for bureaucratically organized corporations, schools, hospitals, voluntary organizations, churches, and governments. Americans no longer work for themselves and no longer work directly with or against nature. The intimate meshing of character, property, work, family, religion, and local community that was characteristic of rural, small-town America (entrepreneurial capitalism) has long disappeared. The contemporary economy separates the labor force from property ownership, family, and residential, religious, and political values and groups.

The United States makes little effort to manage its labor force. It tolerates considerable unemployment, on the average, more than other industrial countries (unemployment rates cannot be relied on for comparisons, since each country computes them differently). Some of its labor force is carefully trained, but most worker skill levels emerge haphazardly. Efforts to match the *quality* of man- or womanpower to the economy have failed totally. In the early 1980s, for example, as unemployment reached 10.5 percent, there were shortages of many types of skilled workers and professionals. Other mismatches exist between the economy and the labor force. There appears to be a growing dissatisfaction with work, especially among young workers, including the educated. And, ominously for young workers and today's college students, the economy seems no longer capable of generating large numbers of middle-level jobs; most of the new jobs are low-skilled, low-paid, and part-time.

The main reason for these mismatches and for the failure to develop overall employment-labor policies is America's deeply ingrained laissez-faire tradition and fierce resistance to economic planning by almost all professions and economic elites. Accordingly, the American labor force is characterized by chronic oversupply, especially at the lower levels. Among the professions and some skilled workers, there is considerable control over jobs (with a pronounced tendency to keep both good jobs and qualified people artificially scarce). The overall picture for the rest of the labor force is one of too many people chasing too few jobs. In recent years, some of the upper occupations have also been in oversupply; this is because laissez-faire means no explicit labor planning and because other power groups have more power (for example, the U.S. government stockpiles natural scientists and mathematicians, meaning that they are chronically in surplus even as we hear the need for more and better science education).

The most significant thing about the American labor force, therefore (excluding the professions and a small portion protected by trade unions), is that, except in wartime, it is always in oversupply. The lack of economic planning, along with immigration; illegal aliens; restrictive labor practices among the professions, semiprofessions, and skilled workers; the mobility of capital; and economic pressures that induce women, the young, and some of the old to join the labor force ensure a chronic oversupply of workers. The most important thing that can be said about the American economy, therefore, is that it rests on a very sandy foundation—the one-third or more of its labor force that is permanently unemployed, temporarily unemployed, underemployed, or poorly paid and insecure. Only 16 percent of the American labor force is organized in trade unions and the percentage is declining. Many workers in trade unions are poorly paid (for example, hospital workers), while some are highly paid (especially the unionized workers of the great oligarchic industrial corporations, which until recently had assured markets and could therefore buy labor peace and cooperation with high wage and fringe benefits).

The history of America's industrial labor-management relations is filled with violence and conflict. A relative peace occurred (strikes rather than violence) after the Wagner Act of 1935 legalized collective bargaining. One of the serious institutional inadequacies in the United States is the absence of a comprehensive labor relations law. While the federal government is acknowledged to have general jurisdiction over the economy (and can influence it in regard to taxation and monetary policy, labor-power policies, and immigration), it has no acknowledged authority over labor as such. State governments exert great influence over their labor forces, especially through boards that control entry into the professions and skilled labor. There can be little doubt that the ability of both the economic and the political spheres to perform their functions is seriously impaired by the lack of a workable national labor code.[17]

The general working class of the United States is not politically conscious or active. The middle and upper classes have hammered into the national consciousness a pervasive individualistic ethos. Schools, churches, mass media, voluntary organizations, government, and the law have all supported the entrepreneurial ethic. For most of American history, economic elites fiercely resisted all measures to improve the lot of workers, including the legalization of labor unions and elementary laborpower planning. The basic structure of power in the United States creates an oversupply of labor at the lower levels[18] not least by creating an artificial scarcity of labor at the top. As we see in Chapter 7, the freedom (power) given to the top (by the top) also means that they decide on their own income. As a result, the upper levels of the American occupational system, across all institutional sectors, get far more income than is warranted by their education, their work, or their performance.

The abstract right of property owners and professionals to use their property for profit affects American workers adversely. Elites are free to send capital to other parts of the country or abroad, weakening labor unions and leaving communities stranded.[19] The bias toward technology (supported by artificially high rates of depreciation in the tax code and government research and development funds) is a constant source of labor insecurity and labor-market softness. Chronic poverty and near poverty, along with underfunded social-service programs, force many into the labor market. Ineffective measures to prevent illegal immigration also work to depress some labor markets. The flood of aliens could not be stemmed as long as those who employed them were not held legally responsible (the new Immigration Law of 1987, which does hold employers responsible, has not had much effect). All of the above have created a large and relatively chronic supply of depressed labor. The structure of power outlined above has also produced another feature of depressed labor: it is disproportionately composed of minorities.[20]

CENTRALIZED LABOR CONTROL UNDER CORPORATE, WORLD-MARKET CAPITALISM

The Industrialization of Work

Economic (and other) processes have been transforming occupations for more than a century. Scholars are not agreed on what has happened, though data from recent years may bring more consensus. Essentially, the power of property ownership prevailed during the nineteenth century to transform independent craftspersons into, first, employees and then into standardized, less-skilled employees. All this occurred in the modern corporate structure shaped by the engineering mentality embodied by Frederick Taylor.[21] Essentially, property owners asserted control over the work process by blending standardized labor motions with the machine (thus reducing worker control of the work tempo and overall product), by piecework, by high wages, and by making it clear to all that dissenters would lose their jobs. By the late twentieth century, this overall process had produced a mass manufacturing and service economy that had large amounts of worker alienation and was producing (in comparison with other countries) overpriced, mediocre goods (such as steel and automobiles) and services (such as health care, justice, and education).

Work Inefficiencies: The Trust Gap

Careful studies of work in the 1970s revealed a considerable decline in worker satisfaction regardless of age, sex, race, or education. But this decline is only part of a many-sided problem associated with work in America. Dissatisfaction with work (largely a function of deep, degrading corporate controls over the work process), combined with the American individualistic success ethic, leads to a pronounced pattern of job hopping that has especially negative consequences when done by executives and professionals (unlike in Japan, those in upper-level jobs do not stay and identify with the group they work for, leading to a lack of commitment and responsibility).

Work, at all levels, from doctors and lawyers to police officers and nurses, is also associated with large amounts of stress and burnout, which in turn generate more incompetence on the job and enormous damage to human health (and, of course, increased health costs). All struggle to cope and find security (through golden parachutes, featherbedding, embezzlement, the big score, protectionist legislation for business, drugs and alcohol).

Until recent years, the United States had a large layer of unnecessary white-collar managers in business (and unnecessary officer staff in the military). The reason is that these act as a buffer between the owner-controllers and the working classes, allowing the upper classes to be routinely uncreative and enjoy unwarranted security and income. We know that these people are unnecessary (and thus costly and hardly satisfying to those forming the buffer) because other capitalist economies (and armies) do not have them. And when American industry had to compete against foreign economies, it fired huge numbers of middle managers to lower its costs and found no loss in efficiency.

The American workplace is also the source of many of our handicapped and causes many deaths. Laws on occupational safety are not enforced; the Workman's Compensation system, which pays small amounts to injured workers and denies them the right to sue their employers, undermines any incentive to make work safer.

Characteristically, business groups frame the question of improving our workforce by pointing a finger at our educational system and asking it to require more mathematics, language skills, and other elements of abstract literacy.

The structure of work can be summarized as a "trust gap."[22] Management, far removed from its workers, has no idea what workers want (respect, higher management ethics, recognition for employee contributions, honest communication between employees and senior management). Study after study finds worker morale low, and ebbing. Most managements do not survey their workers, and when they do, they do not follow through.

Messages from management are deeply discounted, if not ignored. Management goals and strategies are not spelled out. Workers are suspicious of the motives behind mergers and acquisitions. They do not understand or accept the widening gap between their pay and that of management. Top management is not only still mainly white, Protestant, and male, but its experiences are far removed from those of ordinary Americans. Not only is this a drag on overall productivity and morale, but there is overt sabotage by workers as well.

The Computer and the Electronic Sweatshop

Using an ad hoc collection of interviews, Barbara Garson has brilliantly captured a hidden trend in the general process of industrializing work, the use of the computer to deskill the American workforce.[23] Never claiming that hers is a full scientific study, Garson roams from the bottom to the top of the occupational ladder to show how owners are continuing to dominate workers through computers, not for efficiency and profit (Garson states she knows of no studies showing more efficiency through computerization) but for sheer control.

The thrust of the trend, says Garson, is to do to white-collar workers what has already been done to blue-collar workers: "Make them cheaper to train, easier to replace, less skilled, less expensive, and less special." And this trend does not merely affect lower-level workers. The computer controls not only how long McDonald's french fries must be cooked but the overall operation of the store. It specifies the kind of conversation airline reservations clerks should conduct, it automates the social worker (who becomes one of several low-paid specialties, such as financial assistance worker and eligibility technician), and it provides software systems to take over the work of professionals—not just automatic pilots for airlines but software that does some of the work of doctors, lawyers, psychologists, brokers, military officers, bank loan officers, federal probation officials, Workman's Compensation judges, and managers.

The computer, warns Garson, also yields a close monitoring of work both to control workers and to provide owners with precise information of their labor needs. Knowing how much labor is needed for time of day, and days of the week, month, and year has led to a huge increase of temporary and part-time, low-paid, no-benefits workers and even professionals.[24] The computer also reduces contact between human beings. And the computer is increasingly becoming normal, warns Garson, though it is not too late to prevent what happened in the past when the factory system, with its arbitrary features and severe drawbacks, eventually became part of the normal, taken-for-granted world.[25]

The computer also disperses labor so that central offices are no longer needed; for example, insurance salespeople now work out of their cars with a computer on their lap. Workers in other businesses now work at home, a trend that is sometimes good, but which also isolates workers and makes it difficult for them to organize as unions. And of course the computer is a control-and-command tool that allows a corporation to operate easily in dozens, even scores, of countries and is thus able to pit American workers and professionals-executives against the much cheaper labor of the rest of the world.

THE NEW ECONOMY AND ITS IDEOLOGY

The new economy of insecure, stressful occupations with stagnant or declining income for up to 80 percent of the population is well known. The characteristic response to this calamity has been twofold:

1. Both private and government sources have concocted a fanciful picture of a natural economy undergoing inevitable progress, increasingly requiring highly educated workers organized in cooperative work teams, turning out craft-customized products and services on a globally competitive basis, using computer-driven technology. While some of this is going on, it is a huge mischaracterization of the work experience of the vast bulk of Americans at all levels.[26]
2. Both private and official analysts have told the workers being whiplashed by the new economy that it is their responsibility to find work in this new world. Aside from yanking themselves up by their Protestant-bourgeois bootstraps, they are also being told that they are in trouble because they are poorly educated. The main way for America to cope with the progressive, knowledge-based new economy is to improve education.

This picture of the new economy is fantasy—most jobs are easy to do and skilled jobs are best learned on the job. Asking an abstract everybody to shape up is blaming the victim and protecting the capitalist economy. Nowhere is anyone stating the obvious: *Why isn't the economy being shaped to suit the needs of Americans?*

Focusing on what some are doing at the top (which is also misrepresented, but more on that later) is no way to discuss the bottom 80 percent of the occupational system. Other capitalist countries have clearly established tax-funded apprentice-worker training systems to service an economy guided by government. In the United States, corporations have relied on abundant, cheap labor for so long that they are finding it hard to change, especially since there is no prodding by government or labor unions. Thus the U.S. has approximately two million full-time workers workers who are below the poverty level. It has as many sweatshops as in the heyday of early industrialism (sweatshops of the soil as well as factory and office). To stay out of poverty, 7 percent of the labor force holds more than one job as breadwinner occupations continue to decline.

OUR OVERRATED PROFESSIONS

Understanding Consensus as Power

Americans unanimously agree on giving the professions high ratings (prestige) because they believe that they are performing society's most important functions (and because those in them have the most education and the highest incomes). By and large, this is also the view of liberal-functionalism, that is, how the professions themselves view themselves. A conflict approach would argue that the professions are overrated and over-rewarded, and that the unanimity with which they are regarded is a function of the success of the liberal power structure in transforming its power into authority relations, that is, power relations that are believed to be mutually beneficial and thus legitimate (moral). The more realistic view of the professions that has emerged in the past few decades is best started by seeing the unique way in which the American professions rose.

The Unique Rise and Unaccountability of the American Professions

As part of the liberal ideology of convergence, it was once thought that all professions went through a similar process of development. The rise of the professions, however, followed no uniform pattern, varying in terms of national socioeconomic development. Since national development shows marked differences among England, France, Germany, the Soviet Union, and the United States, marked differences in their professions also appeared. The professions have been studied extensively, especially in the major countries of the West,[27] in the former Soviet Union and in some of the former socialist countries of Eastern Europe,[28] and even in a developing country,[29] but no systematic comparative study exists.[30]

The most important difference among national professions is the one between the United States and all other countries. Outside the United States, in both the liberal and authoritarian capitalist countries, as well as in Russia and the Soviet Union, the state actively promoted the professions and employed them for public and elite purposes. Clearly associated with functions deemed important to national development, the state openly established schools to conduct research and train scientists and other professionals. The state also employed professionals in large numbers, either directly or indirectly through state welfare programs. Even in England, the country that most closely resembles the United States, the professions were part and parcel of England's aristocratic traditions: elitist, public-minded, ambivalent about working for money, all in all, corporatist in outlook. The English pattern influenced English-speaking Canada and the French pattern influenced French-speaking Canada.

The professions in the United States rose without explicit state sponsorship and without a clear identification with social functions. America's professions grew up in an entrepreneurial environment, in a society with an open, decentralized economy and a state with limited responsibilities for performing social functions. Accordingly, the professions sponsored themselves: they formed associations, helped establish schools and curricula, and engaged in politics to secure legal sanctions for the standards they were creating. Accordingly, the American professions were deeply geared toward securing income from private clients and private employers, especially schools.

In all this, the American professions participated in the national hypocrisy, along with business and farmers, of advocating competition while engaged in getting government subsidies and legal monopolies. Skillfully parlaying American mobility ideals and respect for knowledge with the cultivation of public anxieties, the American professions used their political power to elevate themselves both beyond ordinary people and state scrutiny. The overall pattern saw powerful groups denouncing politics and government while busily using both for their own ends—the net result was to deny the masses the ability to use government for their ends. Seen in another way, the American professions, along with business and farming, were given strong support by government, but with no explicit compact that the public would receive services in return. The ideology of laissez-faire made it unnecessary that the public's exchanges with private groups be of the same order as exchanges between private parties: an exchange of equivalences.

The New Liberal and Conflict Views of Professionalism

The early liberal-functional faith in science, technology, and knowledge took the form of professionalism. By the late nineteenth century, a large number of groups had emerged to claim jurisdiction over special fields of knowledge: Various disciplines and professions emerged, each with its own association, subject matter, credentials, research journals, and special methods (within the overall world of empirical science). Each claimed to have knowledge about a special area of behavior and a special cluster of problems; each sought to restrict entry through a system of credentials and licensing; and each struggled to obtain jurisdictional monopoly, high income and prestige, and autonomy from forces either to the side or below. From across the spectrum of professions came similar statements and claims: we are neutral, altruistic, objective searchers for and dispensers of knowledge; we can be judged only by our fellow professionals since we possess a high and difficult-to-obtain knowledge base; since knowledge is power and yields virtue, our activities will be service-oriented; whatever our deficiencies, we are the best guarantee of both knowledge and an improved society.

The study of the professions is fairly recent, but interest in them goes back to the very origins of modern social science. Actually, the academic (mainstream) study of the professions is continuous with the technocratic tradition found in Condorcet and Saint Simon and with the acceptance of the emerging capitalist division of labor by liberal sociologists such as Spencer, Durkheim, Sumner, Ward, and Cooley. In short, the study of the professions is itself part of the positive evaluation of science that dominates the West.

This positive outlook on knowledge is also characteristic of analysts in the sociology of knowledge tradition, most of whom assumed that the social source of knowledge was compatible with the idea of truth and progress. In American sociology, argues Fuhrman, the main formative figures (such as Sumner, Ward, Giddings, Small, Ross, and Cooley) all stressed the social nature of knowledge and its utility to society. These theorists were all squarely in the liberal tradition and their thought was conservative. They saw society as a plurality of causal agents, as something which moved slowly and whose outcomes, including knowledge, were progressive.[31] Fuhrman refers to the main sociological tradition in early American sociology as "social-technological" as opposed to a more political view of knowledge, which he calls "critical-emancipatory."

The study of the professions by mainstream academics has resulted in a considerable body of knowledge.[32] Early analysts had assumed that the professions had unique attributes and that they emerged in a distinct sequence. By the 1970s, research had revealed that professional claims to a unique knowledge base, autonomy, altruism, service, and self-monitoring were not true. In all cases, one found degrees of truth rather than absolutes. Also, analysts could find no discernible stages that marked the emergence of the professions; on the contrary, the professions displayed great historical and national variations. In addition, some academic analysts argued that the professions have been losing power to clients, other elites, or the state (deprofessionalization), while some claim that they are being proletarianized.

In recent decades, theorists have looked at the professions (to use Ritzer's and Walczak's word) in terms of "power." The professions openly seek to exclude others, work politically to get the state to give them monopolies, and engage in incessant turf battles. "Power" theorists have noticed that the professions grew concurrently with a corporate economy and the expanding rational-legal state.

"Power" theorists, however, still lack a theory of modern society. Implicit in the work of academic "power" analysts and of Ritzer's and Walczak's account of their work is the assumption that power in modern society is fluid, competitive, dynamic, and guided by science and liberal social and political norms. In short, "power" theorists accept the idea that modern society is what it says it is, a pluralistic system based on open, fair, competitive, meritocratic processes.

The academic perspective on the professions is similar to the way in which mainstream social science has seen modern society. Until recently, most social scientists took it for granted that progress was a law of history and that the West was simply leading humanity out of its dark past. More concretely, sociologists, perhaps the majority in the United States, saw the basic trend of the past six hundred years as a growth in the adaptive capacity of society. Mainstream sociologists (and social scientists) argued that modern society (by which they usually meant the capitalist democracies of the West) has or represents these elements:

1. Increased social differentiation toward functional specialization (a shift from diffused ascriptive statuses to specific, achievement statuses)
2. The emergence of abstract, disposable facilities (money, technology, rational law, abstract labor force, abstract electorate, abstract nature)—in short, a rational market economy, polity, and society
3. The emergence of a hierarchy of statuses known and accepted by most in which norm-role obligations are arranged in a structure of priority, thus providing predictability, stability, and direction
4. A growth of knowledge (provided by natural and social science)
5. The application and transmission of knowledge through the professions and education to yield higher living standards and social adaptation
6. The rise of rational organizations (bureaucracies) to ensure efficiency in the economy, professions, voluntary sector, and government

In recent years, sociologists have become less sure about where the overall trend of modern development is leading. Despite a revival of the evolutionary perspective, sociology (along with the other social sciences) is no longer so sure that economic and technological growth is automatically good for society. And it is not as optimistic as it once was about the ability of the professions, electorates, or markets to direct society and solve its problems. Accordingly, there is now a fairly wide difference of opinion about modernization in general. The liberal (capitalist) faith in the adaptive capacity of economic and political markets, aided and directed by professionalism, has been severely qualified (for the contrast between Parsons and Giddens, see Chapter 5). Beyond liberalism, radicals argue that modern society has long been bankrupt and is sustained only by imperialism and the victimization of many of its members.

In summary, the academic or functional view of the professions sees them as the outcome of the growth of knowledge and explains their proliferation since the nineteenth century as a response to social need and the imperatives of science. From this perspective, the professions result from objective, transhistorical, meritocratic processes. Functional analysts of the professions are themselves professionals and therefore speak the language of facts, function, and progress through scientific knowledge.

The current academic outlook on the professions, represented by theorists such as Freidson and Abbott,[33] depicts the professions as part of the political process. Gone is the assumption that professions have risen above the vulgar pursuit of power and dispense their various services altruistically in a nonpartisan manner. Instead, a new empirical realism has emerged about the professions. Large, conclusive abstractions about them, we are told, are not possible and there is no indication that research will eventually lead to a final understanding of them. There are endless qualifications that must be made to all statements about them. There is this nuance and that to be pursued. All is contingency, fluidity, and realignment. Nowhere does the new empirical realism embed the professions in any macrosocial structure (Freidson does give a valuable, nonpolitical analysis of the supports the professions received from the state). Nowhere are questions raised about the actual efficacy of the professions as among individuals, social classes, or society-at-large. Throughout, the impression is given of a rather messy but distinct upward thrust of knowledge through professionalization with an ensuing social betterment. Throughout there are conflicts, which in the lexicon of liberalism means competition to ensure the triumph of the most worthy.

When all is said, there is not much difference between the old and the new functionalism. The new functional perspective still assumes that modern society is institutionalizing knowledge via professionalism (compare the concepts of *postindustrial society, high-information society,* and *managerial revolution*) and that the professions emerge from and represent a meritocratic-based, pluralistic system of power.[34] The only difference is that the process of making society more rational is now messier and less linear than the old functionalism (note the similarity to Giddens's thought).

The radical conflict perspective rejects the assumption that the professions are objective creators and carriers of objective knowledge.[35] Intellectual-scientific work is always value-laden and entails subjective judgments about what is worth knowing. But the main reason for rejecting the liberal functional view of the professions is that the latter's accumulated belief and value decisions (made in service to an unacknowledged system of power) have led to a poor record of problem solving. The conflict perspective has come to the fore because it best accounts for strategic facts, especially the fact of widespread professional failure in solving social problems. Today, we know that both science and the professions are social phenomena and reflect the society in which they occur. In the capitalist world, the professions are best understood as forms of publicly sanctioned private property.[36] Seen from this perspective, the liberal professions, which for the sake of argument can include upper-level corporate managers and high civil, military, and elected officials (most of whom have received professional educations), belong to the upper classes of capitalist society.

The professions enjoy high income, the highest prestige, and great power in liberal (and socialist) society. Their historic achievements and their creative conflicts should not obscure the fact that they are the main beneficiaries of their own competence (and incompetence).

The occupational prestige studies of the past forty years have consistently shown that the American public accords the professions and disciplines top ratings. The high income of many professionals is well known. But as Bok has shown, the reward structure of the United States bears little relation to labor market theories. Not only is there no competitive labor market for talent in the United States, but, says Bok, American private-sector executives, doctors, and lawyers, not only make far more than ordinary workers compared to other nations, but these three occupations are also deeply stratified (beyond any measure of merit) with a few at the top making far more than their colleagues, again in comparison to other nations.[37] In broader context, these three occupations are part of a general pattern forming the dual labor market: managerial and professional workers, unionized workers, and workers in oligarchic industries or extremely large organizations are not subject to labor market competition as posited by mainstream economists.[38]

The radical conflict perspective focuses on the mutual support that the professions give each other as they operate at or near the apex of the state, corporations, hospitals, law firms, universities, and so on. The academic and applied professions, as seen by the conflict perspective, define their subject matter in narrow, artificial terms assuming that other factors are constant or inconsequential. Essentially, each divorces a slice of phenomena or a problem from the sociohistorical context that gave it birth. Each assumes consensus about the world outside its domain. Each assumes no need for priorities in knowledge—each can exist if it allows the others to exist and this implies no invidious distinctions among them. Thus, for example, natural scientists pursue what they feel are the frontiers of knowledge across a broad front, unaware that priorities are being set for them by corporations, governments, the military, churches, and so on.

Though the impression is created that all knowledge is useful and that seekers of knowledge are advancing on all fronts, the fact of the matter is that the entire enterprise is quite haphazard and many areas go uncovered (few knowledge seekers spend much time, for example, developing ways to guard against the harmful consequences of technology, pesticides, and drugs). Actually, the structured nature of the ignorance and ineffectiveness of the professions leads straight to the deepest level of concern about the professions: Are they organized to provide social adaptation and social self-determination? The answer is no. In keeping with the overall capitalist outlook on society, American elites deny the need for anyone, anybody, or any process to be in charge of society. In effect, those who set and fund priorities are unaware of what they are doing. Not only have the capitalist elites (especially in the United States) depoliticized society (which allegedly derives from the supernatural, human nature, and nature), but ominously they have depoliticized themselves.

Far from being detached respondents to evil, argue radical critics, the liberal professions provide biased definitions and explanations of problems, thereby setting up arbitrary parameters to how society responds to problems. Not only are their explanations and approaches faulty, but by actively exaggerating the complexity and dangers of problems, they help create the anxious, passive clients they need for their services. Born in the heyday of early industrialism, when society was in the throes of deep conflict, when massive social changes were upsetting social routines, the professions were an ideal way to create the impression that an abstract science (personified in the academic and applied professions) could handle the multiple new evils of industrialism, ideal because professionals were derived from and in the service of the property groups that were causing the problems.

Professionals, say critics, must stop thinking of themselves as value-free pursuers of knowledge and as value-free practitioners. The liberal professions share this value-free perspective with the overall liberal belief in a value-free market economy and objective electoral markets leading to nonpartisan government. The false belief by owners, managers, lawyers, accountants, engineers, doctors, soldiers, politicians, domestic and foreign policy experts, journalists, educators, economists, psychologists, and social scientists that they are nonpartisan goes a long way in explaining their formalism, failure, and unaccountability.

Professional thought and action not only have value consequences, but many of the consequences are negative. Critics argue that the professions must acknowledge that they are making value judgments and that much of their work is "political" in nature. But to acknowledge the value implications of their work would threaten elite authority, for who is able to claim expertise and objectivity about values? To acknowledge the importance of values would subject elites to the judgment of laypeople.

Regardless of how they are seen, the salient fact about the liberal professions is their universal lack of effectiveness in dealing with social problems (as opposed to their greater success in dealing with the problems of some individuals and groups, and in compiling formal, academic, socially sterile knowledge). The liberal professions are also characterized by basic procedures that are suspect (for example, peer review), by significant numbers of incapacitated practitioners, and by significant numbers of criminals (see Chapter 16 for a fuller discussion).

The accepted definition of what constitutes a professional is still a matter of considerable dispute.[39] The radical conflict or sociopolitical perspective argues that a profession is an occupation that has succeeded in keeping its numbers low in relation to need, or has devised other ways to guarantee itself high material benefits regardless of performance (primarily through state financing or state-granted monopolies). In short, the defining characteristic of contemporary professionals is that they provide support services, including ideological cover, for their respective societies (capitalist and socialist, fascist, liberal democratic, or authoritarian) and are rewarded by being exempt from the shortcomings of these various societies. In the United States, it is especially clear that professionals profit from a market society without being subject to all its workings. When ordinary labor is in surplus, unemployment occurs, but a surplus of surgeons consistently leads to huge numbers of unnecessary surgeries at high and rising prices. How efficient and how fair is it that the public finances research in technology, drugs, and agriculture, but receives no return either in royalties or lower consumer prices when the research becomes profitable? Why is it that the state finances much of the education of professionals and grants them a legal monopoly to practice, but is not permitted to set standards in regard to credentials or performance?

The radical view given so far is a composite of liberal and Marxist perspectives. In recent decades, new forms of radicalism have arisen from phenomenology, linguistic-literary studies, and feminism. An important source of this new radicalism is the thought of Michel Foucault, who has profoundly influenced social theory, literary criticism, feminism, critical legal studies, and specialists in sociology and psychology.[40] Foucault argues that knowledge comes from *discourse* and that there is no method, scientific or otherwise, that yields truth. Discourse is whatever it is possible to say under given historical power structures. The knowledge claims of modern natural and social science and its applied professions are arbitrary, argues Foucault, but appear objective because they have power behind them and can thus enforce consensus.

Foucault's analysis of the history of social-control agencies (prisons, asylums, schools, hospitals) has obvious implications for the professions and disciplines. To Foucault, modern control systems are arbitrary and do not deserve to be given metaphysical or so-called objective status. Traditional epistemology's claim to objective truth is really a disguised interpretive philosophy (we must use arbitrary assumptions in our empirical sciences). Further, the power/knowledge that an arbitrary science establishes gets imposed on people and this is what has happened in the fields of deviance (mental illness, crime), punishment, and sexuality. The social-control agencies of modern society and their professions are based on arbitrary notions of normality. They, along with the social sciences and humanities, are forms of power, and interpretive science gives us a way to resist domination by other people's alleged truths. Indeed, social-control structures violate the need of human beings to express their own forms of knowledge. Accordingly, Foucault invites resistance to the knowledge claims of power groups and their so-called rational or scientific control systems. As we see, Foucault has appealed to a wide variety of dissident groups.

Relying on a variety of perspectives, feminism has generated a rich body of criticism of the professions and disciplines. Dorothy E. Smith has rejected the objective, value-neutral, impersonal methodology of sociology as inherently biased against women.[41] Catherine A. MacKinnon has indicted the entire legal system as a masculine bias against women.[42] Sandra Harding has pointed to masculine bias in the natural sciences.[43] And feminist and nonfeminist writers have mounted a deep criticism of the literature profession for slanting the curriculum against women, African Americans, and all other minorities.[44]

Our survey of radical thought has not exhausted the indictments that have been made of the professions (for example, we have not discussed the criticism of the law and lawyers by the Critical Legal Studies movement and the deep criticisms that have been leveled at liberal journalism). But enough has been said to make it clear that regardless of whether they focus on social or natural science, or on the classics in literature and philosophy, radicals reject the assumption underlying objective empiricism, namely that a fixed and finished neutral observer can find the truth about a fixed and finished reality. Instead, radicals stress the historicity of both thinking and facts. They stress the need to develop new forms of thought in keeping with the movement of history. They stress the inevitable political-value nature of science.

STRATIFICATION WITHIN AND AMONG PROFESSIONS

Stratification Within Medicine, Law, and College Teaching

Professions are internally stratified by specialization leading to significant differences in power, prestige, and income. Surgeons and family practitioners are at very different levels, even though both are M.D.s. There is further differentiation based on medical school and hospital affiliation. Lawyers are also ranked by specialty, by ownership status in and by size of firm (with considerable segregation by race, ethnicity, and gender).

College professors are also stratified by specialty. Disciplines such as natural science, medicine, and law receive far more income than teachers in the social sciences or humanities. Here too there is prestige and income stratification by school.

Medicine, law, and college teaching all have well-established forms of exploited labor. In medicine, interns and foreign doctors fill undesirable positions in hospitals. Law has junior salaried staff who are overworked and discarded. Fully one-third of college teachers are temporaries with poor pay and no benefits. And beyond all of the above lie exploited nurses, orderlies, paralegals, secretaries, graduate students, and research assistants. (For further inequalities by race and gender within the professions and semiprofessions see Part Three.)

The Semiprofessions

Beneath the professions is a sizable contingent of semiprofessions: teachers, librarians, social workers, nurses, technicians, personnel officers, firefighters, police officers, and so on. Members of the semiprofessions behave toward their occupations in the same way as the incumbents of higher-level occupations. Turning an occupation into a profession requires control over entry, and the semiprofessions have sought to limit their numbers by emphasizing quality through education and professional training. As in the professions, *there is no discernible relation between amount and type of education and occupational performance.* (For a fuller discussion, see Chapter 9.) Unlike the professions, however, the semiprofessions have had only limited success in gaining control over their respective occupations.

The semiprofessions coordinate and control their interests as best they can through "professional" associations and "professional" journals. They work hard to achieve legal control over entry into their occupations. They seek certification and licensing by the state and endorse civil service examinations for entry to and promotion in public-service positions. The semiprofessions have also resorted to unionization. White-collar unions have been the most dynamic force in the trade union movement since World War II. The semiprofessions resist absorption into blue-collar unions though some are organized by the more traditional trade unions. For example, teachers have been organized by the American Federation of Teachers, which is affiliated with the CIO-AFL.

The economic autonomy of the semiprofessions is compromised by their inability to establish high-level educational credentials for entry and by the fact that many of them work for local, state, and federal governments and often do not have the right to strike. Many semiprofessions are made up mostly of women (for example, teachers, nurses, social workers, and librarians), which may have hampered solidarity and militancy. Subordination to the professionals above them and by their status as employees in bureaucratic groups have also undermined their power.

In and around the semiprofessions are occupations in flux: architects, accountants, pharmacists, and others that we need to know more about.

SUMMARY

Defining occupations raises the broader question of the role of assumptions in science: it is what we assume about facts, not facts, that tells us what we know. Thus all social indicators tell us things that are factual but also selective and ambiguous because of the assumptions underlying the assembly of facts (or data).

A bureaucracy is a hierarchy of occupations that ideally generates a responsible and efficient performance of tasks. All areas of society are now bureaucratized. Unfortunately, these bureaucracies are also command-and-control structures that give their owners enormous power; thus bureaucracies deviate from their ideals and they allow owners to funnel unearned rewards upward and to victimize those at the bottom.

Work has been industrialized on the soil, in the factory, and in the office.

Industrialized work has resulted in a trust gap between owners-controllers and workers. It has also led to growing work dissatisfaction (including among the educated), stress, injury, disability, burnout, and even death.

The computer has led to tight monitoring of work at all levels of the occupational hierarchy. In addition, it allows owners-controllers to use part-time and temporary workers and to pit the entire American labor force against the labor of the entire planet.

Both private and government sources have mischaracterized the real American economy, painting a fanciful picture of a cooperative, flexible, craftlike work made possible by the computer. It is up to workers to adjust to this inevitable world and the way in which public policy can help is to better educate Americans.

The above argument and its recommendation that what Americans need is Protestant-bourgeois pluck and more education in rank ideology. The vast bulk of jobs now and in the future are easy to perform and the best way to learn them is on the job. What this ideology does it to divert Americans from the main question about work: How should the economy be organized to be of most value to most Americans?

The American professions have also been misrepresented both by themselves and liberal-functional scholars. While the professions enjoy high income and prestige, there are a number of disquieting facts about them that conflict theorists have uncovered. The American professions are unique in the capitalist world in that they have demanded and received even more autonomy from public accountability than American business. The professions do not have the unique knowledge base they claim, they are not altruistic and nonpolitical, and they do poorly in performing social functions.

The professions are stratified themselves, something that can be seen most clearly in medicine, law, and college teaching. And the professions rest on lower levels of employees, many of whom are exploited (that is, they receive lower pay, benefits, and work authority than is necessary).

The semiprofessions are numerous and references to them in the abstract are one of the reasons why terms such as *white collar, nonmanual,* and *upper nonmanual* are often defective.

The semiprofessions have tried to enhance their class position using the same means as the professions. They too try to control entry with testing and unnecessary education. They too try to claim unique knowledge and public service. But on the whole, they have not been successful. On the contrary, many are public servants and have felt the squeeze as public budgets have contracted in recent decades.

NOTES

1. Revised fourth edition, 1991.
2. The use of valid assumptions giving an accurate account (always arbitrary and thus biased because the account is incomplete and must be given an interpretation) must be distinguished from invalid assumptions or mistakes in the scientific instrument (the Department of Labor admits it has undercounted unemployed women because it failed to revise its survey questions), which date back to 1967, to take into account the large influx of women into the work force since then. It has also seriously undercounted discouraged workers, again by the use of those questions.
3. Charles Perrow, *Complex Organizations: A Critical Essay*, 3rd ed. (New York: Random House, 1986).
4. For a critical history that claims that Taylorism is ideology, not science, and that it cannot bridge the gap between management and labor, see Stephen P. Waring, *Taylorism Transformed: Scientific Management Since 1945* (Chapel Hill: University of North Carolina Press, 1991).
5. The tiny group of owners (who also work hard) and the tiny upper level of top executives are discussed further in various places (see the index).
6. Japanese custom is changing under the pressures of world-market capitalism.
7. For a summary of the many studies showing that the American managerial style generates bad work and bad morale, see Alan Farnham, "The Trust Gap," *Fortune* 120, no. 14 (December 14, 1989):56–78.
8. Harrison M. Trice, James Belasco, and Joseph A. Alutto, "The Role of Ceremonials in Organizational Behavior," *Industrial and Labor Relations Review* 23 (October 1969):40–51.
9. For a valuable analysis showing the American roots of America's management science and the need for comparative analysis to develop a genuine universal science of administration, see Nakiye Avdan Boyacigiller and Nancy J. Adler, "The Parochial Dinosaur: Organization Science in a Global Context," *Academy of Management Review* 16, no. 2 (April 1991):262–290.
10. Stuart Black, Mark Mendenhall, and Gary Oddou, "Toward a Comprehensive Model of International Adjustment: An Integration of Multiple Theoretical Perspectives," *Academy of Management Review* 16, no. 2 (April 1991):291.
11. For an indictment of business education as excessively specialized and out of touch with business realities, including the new global economy, see Lyman W. Porter and Lawrence E. McKibbin, *Management Education and Development: Drift or Thrust into the 21st Century?* (New York: McGraw-Hill, 1988). For an interesting radical feminist criticism of this report as merely reasserting the patriarchal values and practices characteristic of business, see Marta B. Calas and Linda Smircich, "Thrusting Toward More of the Same with the Porter-McKibbin Report," *Academy of Management Review* 15, no. 4 (October 1990):698–705. Also see "Education's Failure to Perform Social Functions" in Chapter 9.

12. For a wide-ranging critique of the negative results from business education's alliance with mainstream economics, see Milton Leontiades, *Myth Management: An Examination of Corporation Diversification as Fact and Theory* (Oxford, England: Basil Blackwell, 1989).
13. In his study of the political leanings of White House staffs, John H. Kersel reports that the key advisers to President Reagan were extremely homogeneous, essentially Reagan clones; *New York Times*, August 27, 1983, p. 7G. William Domhoff, "Where Do Government Experts Come From?" in G. W. Domhoff and T. R. Dye, eds., *Power Elites and Organizations* (Beverly Hills, CA: Sage, 1987), ch. 10, shows that the President's Council of Economic Advisers is drawn from the corporate elite and a narrow spectrum of elite foundations, think tanks, research institutes, and private policy organizations.
14. For a discussion of the powerful impact of the engineering profession on management during the formative period of corporate capitalism, see David F. Noble, *America by Design: Science, Technology, and the Rise of Corporate Capitalism* (New York: Knopf, 1977).
15. Michael Useem, *The Inner Circle* (New York: Oxford University Press, 1984).
16. Articles criticizing excessive executive pay have appeared frequently in *Fortune*. CBS News reported (May 20, 1991) that chief executive officers in the United States are paid 85 times as much as average workers, whereas the ratio in Germany is 23 to 1, and in Japan 17 to 1.
17. Part-time workers have grown to 20 percent of the labor force but they are not covered by existing labor laws—for example, unemployment insurance.
18. The official unemployment rate (like any scientific statement) is based on assumptions about what facts count. It undercounts the unemployed because it omits those who have given up looking for work and includes as employed anyone who worked as little as one hour in the survey week. The unemployment rate of the 1990s would also be appreciably higher if adjusted for age—declining numbers of young people make the rate appear lower than in previous periods.
19. For a study showing that capital movement (plant closings and relocations) is related to the avoidance of labor unions, see David Jaffee, "The Political Economy of Job Loss in the United States, 1970–1980," *Social Problems* 33 (April 1986):297–318.
20. For two arguments that depressed minorities are integral parts of the capitalist economy, see Edna Bonacich, "Advanced Capitalism and Black/White Race Relations in the United States: A Split Labor Market Interpretation," *American Sociological Review* 41 (February 1976):34–51; and Albert Syzmanski, "Racism and Sexism as Functional Substitutes in the Labor Market," *Sociology Quarterly* 17 (Winter 1976):65–73.
21. For an analysis, see Robert A. Rothman, *Working: Sociological Perspectives* (Englewood Cliffs, NJ: Prentice-Hall, 1987).
22. See Alan Farnham, "The Trust Gap," *Fortune* 120, no. 14 (December 14, 1989): 56–78.
23. Barbara Garson, *The Electronic Sweatshop: How Computers Are Transforming the Office of the Future into the Factory of the Past* (New York: Simon and Schuster, 1988).
24. For background and data on the powerful push in American capitalism to lower labor costs, see Kevin Henson, *The Temp* (Philadelphia: Temple University Press, 1996), ch. 1. In the remaining chapters, Henson provides a fascinating,

Goffman-style, analysis of the "costs to labor" of the trend toward temporary labor.

25. Among the "costs to labor" of the bureaucratic controls over labor costs is the imposition of artificial personalities; see Arlie Russell Hochschild, *The Managed Heart: Commercialization of Human Feeling* (Berkeley: University of California Press, 1983).
26. For a prime example of this widely distorted picture of the world of work that Americans will face in the coming years, from combined private-official sources, printed on glossy, gold-trimmed pages, see Anthony Patrick Cornevale, *America and the New Economy* (Washington, DC: American Society for Training and Development, U.S. Department of Labor, 1991). Other variations on the same theme are Robert Reich, *The Work of Nations: Preparing Ourselves for 21st Century Capitalism* (New York: Knopf, 1991), and Lester Thurow, *The Coming Economic Battle Between Japan, Europe, and America* (New York: Morrow, 1992).
27. For England, see Harold Perkin, *The Rise of Professional Society: England Since 1880* (New York: Routledge, 1989). For France, no general work exists, but Stephen Crawford, *Technical Workers in an Advanced Society: The Work, Careers, and Politics of French Engineers* (New York: Cambridge University Press, 1989), provides some background beyond his focus on engineers. For Germany, see Charles E. McClelland, *The German Experience of Professionalization* (New York: Cambridge University Press, 1991).
28. Anthony Jones, ed., *Professions and the State: Expertise and Autonomy in the Soviet Union and Eastern Europe* (Philadelphia: Temple University Press, 1991).
29. Peter S. Cleaves *Professions and the State: The Mexican Case* (Tucson: University of Arizona Press, 1987).
30. Two short but valuable comparative analyses are Dietrich Rueschemeyer, "Contrasting Institutional Patterns of Professionalization," in his *Power and the Division of Labor* (Stanford, CA: Stanford University Press, 1986), pp. 118–124, and Elliott A. Krause, "United States, Western Europe, Eastern Europe: Comparative Issues," in Anthony Jones, ed., *Professionals and the State: Expertise and Autonomy in the Soviet Union and Eastern Europe* (Philadelphia: Temple University Press, 1991), pp. 35–39. Most studies of the professions in major countries and their indexes can be valuable in this regard. This is also true of Michael Burrage and Rolf Torstendahl, eds., *The Formation of Professions: Knowledge, State, and Strategy* (Newbury Park, CA: Sage, 1990), which has the added merit of containing valuable chapters on the professions in Sweden.
31. Ellsworth R. Fuhrman, *The Sociology of Knowledge in America, 1883–1915* (Charlottesville: University Press of Virginia, 1980).
32. The following relies heavily on George Ritzer and David Walczak, *Working: Conflict and Change*, 3rd ed. (Englewood Cliffs, NJ: Prentice-Hall, 1986), ch. 4.
33. Eliot Freidson, *Professional Powers: A Study of the Institutionalization of Formal Knowledge* (Chicago: University of Chicago Press, 1986); Andrew Abbott, *The System of Professions: An Essay on the Division of Expert Labor* (Chicago: University of Chicago Press, 1988).
34. Freidson, perhaps the leading academic (mainstream) analyst of the professions, has explicitly endorsed the present system of professionalism by stating it as an ideal worth fighting for politically; Eliot Freidson, "Professionalism as a Model and Ideology," in Robert L. Nelson et al., eds., *Lawyers' Ideals/Lawyers' Practices: Transformations in the American Legal Profession* (Ithaca, NY: Cornell University Press, 1992), ch. 6. Interestingly, Freidson's endorsement is not based

on an evaluation of all the criticisms of the liberal professions; he argues only that the present system is abstractly better than the two other possibilities, the free market approach and the approach that stresses order, efficiency, and comprehensive services. The present monopoly by experts is better than monopoly by capital or the state, he concludes. Why the professions cannot be thought of ideally as being embedded in a genuinely pluralistic power structure in which a democratic public holds them accountable for the performance of functions is not clear.

35. The radical conflict view presented here is a composite of ideas from numerous sources. It should be clear that the analysts discussed under the term *liberal-functional* have contributed many ideas useful to a more political, critical outlook here called *radical conflict,* for example, George Ritzer and David Walczak, *Working: Conflict and Change,* 3rd ed. (Englewood Cliffs, NJ: Prentice-Hall, 1986), pp. 79–85, and George Ritzer, "Professionalism, Bureaucratization, and Rationalization," *Social Forces* 53 (1975):627–634. Some important ingredients in the radical view of the professions may be found in T. J. Johnson, *Professions and Power* (London: Macmillan, 1972); T. J. Johnson, "The Professions in the Class Structure," in Richard Scase, ed., *Industrial Society: Class, Cleavage, and Control* (New York: St. Martin's Press, 1977), ch. 4; and Magali Sarfatti Larson, *The Rise of Professionalism* (Berkeley: University of California Press, 1977). Sources for some new radical outlooks on the professions are given later in the chapter.

36. Carolyn J. Touhy, "Private Government, Property, and Professionalism," *Canadian Journal of Political Science* 9 (December 1976):668–681.

37. Derek Bok, *The Cost of Talent: How Executives and Professionals Are Paid and How It Affects America* (New York: Free Press, 1993). It should be noted that while Bok's analysis has radical implications, he himself is a liberal. He accepts the myth that America is a meritocracy, or rather that it, including education, is generating talent despite the fact that income does not emerge from competitive forces. His analysis has little on the essentially class nature of education and little on whether or not executives and professionals are effective; his only concern is that American talent is poorly distributed in favor of an overpaid private sector and that professors, teachers, and federal civil servants are not paid enough.

38. For a recent study confirming dual labor market theory with a full bibliography of the relevant literature, see Arthur Sakamoto and Meicher D. Chen, "Inequality and Attainment in a Dual Labor Market," *American Sociological Review* 56 (June 1991):295–308.

39. Freidson's definition of a professional is someone who has higher education credentials. Freidson's reliance on the criterion of academic credentials is no accident. The study of the professions (which claim to be value-neutral possessors of skills and knowledge) has been done by value-neutral academics who are themselves part of the professional world.

40. Michel Foucault, *Madness and Civilization: A History of Insanity in the Age of Reason,* tr. Richard Howard (New York: Vintage, 1965); *The Order of Things: An Archaeology of the Human Sciences* (New York: Vintage, 1966); *The Archaeology of Knowledge and the Discourse on Language* (New York: Harper Colophon, 1969); *The Birth of the Clinic: An Archaeology of Medical Perception* (New York: Vintage, 1975); *Discipline and Punish: The Birth of the Prison,* tr. Alan Sheridan (New York: Vintage, 1979); *The History of Sexuality: An Introduction,* vol. 1 (New York: Vintage, 1980); *The History of Sexuality: The Uses of Pleasure,* vol. 2 (New York: Pantheon, 1985).

41. Dorothy E. Smith, *The Conceptual Practices of Power: A Feminist Sociology of Knowledge* (Boston: Northeastern University Press, 1990).
42. Catherine A. MacKinnon, *Toward a Feminist Theory of the State* (Cambridge, MA: Harvard University Press, 1989).
43. Sandra Harding, *Whose Science? Whose Knowledge? Thinking from Women's Lives* (Ithaca, NY: Cornell University Press, 1991).
44. Paul Lauter, "Race and Gender in the Shaping of the American Literary Canon: A Case Study from the Twenties," *Feminist Studies* 9 (Fall 1983):435–463.

7

Economic Classes, II: The Interplay of Wealth, Income, Poverty, Education, and Occupational Power

◆ ◆ ◆ ◆

◆ ◆ ◆ ◆

THE DISTRIBUTION OF WEALTH

Knowledge about wealth is important because it tells us who makes the investment decisions that determine how material and human resources will be used. Scholars in this field are generally agreed that the basic pattern in the distribution of wealth is high and relatively steady concentration.[1] Whether analyzed and measured in terms of liquid assets, personal property, real estate, business assets, bonds, stock ownership, ability to save, or income from property, the distribution of wealth in the United States is characterized by the same pronounced pattern of concentration. As we shall see, the concentration of wealth is even more pronounced than that of income.

James D. Smith's analysis of postwar trends in the distribution of wealth revealed a pronounced movement toward increased concentration between 1963 and 1983.[2] Our latest data reveal an accelerated pace of wealth concentration between 1983 and 1989. Using data supplied by the Federal Reserve Board and other sources, Edward N. Wolff has provided a compact, highly readable analysis of the distribution of wealth in American history and the unusual increase in inequality during the Reagan administration.[3] The net worth of the top 1 percent of owners increased from 34 to 39 percent of the total in these years. In the all-important category of financial wealth (basically ownership of the American economy, either directly or through loans), the top 1 percent went from 43 to 48 percent of the total. The top 20 percent went from 91 percent to 94 percent ownership! Data on ownership of the American economy is all-important because it locates those who make the basic investment decisions as to where and when factories, offices, and stores will be built or closed. Economic concentration in this area means that the economic fortunes of Americans are in the hands of a tiny minority. Understanding what happened in the 1980s is also important because the claim that releasing the business world from regulation and reducing its taxes would lead to a growth of opportunity and in standard of living for all did not happen. Actually, the results were the opposite. Despite the clear failure of right liberal (laissez faire) ideology, the 1990s have witnessed a further dismantling of America's already anemic ability to direct its affairs politically. Said differently, understanding wealth concentration is important because it translates into political-legal power.

The high concentration of wealth has persisted ever since colonial times. This does not mean that the same families have stayed rich since that time. It does mean, though, that the ownership of the American economy has remained in relatively few hands and that so far this pattern has been relatively immune to war, depressions, taxation, the expansion of suffrage, and the welfare state.

SOURCES OF WEALTH

To understand the causal processes that distribute material values one must go outside the American tradition, which attributes success and failure to personal attributes. Like everything else, the sources of wealth are social phenomena.

Concentration of Economic Power

Economic activity is not conducted by abstract capital or abstract individuals. The reality of economic behavior is *the group organized for economic action.* Profit-oriented groups, especially corporations, dominate the American economy. A corporation is a legal entity, administered bureaucratically, that allows large numbers of people to pool their resources and thus engage in a scale of economic behavior they could not do as solitary individuals. The result is a responsive chain of command that allows the owners or controllers of the corporation to amass and focus large amounts of capital to produce desired outcomes. The responsibilities and liabilities of corporations are spelled out in legal norms—one provision protects the owners' other property in case the corporation fails (law of bankruptcy). In addition, the corporation enjoys legal immortality and continues even though individual owners change hands or die.

The most striking feature of the American economy is the pronounced cleavage between dominant and weaker groups: a small number of corporations dominate all sectors of the economy and a small number of groups dominate economically related activities (professional associations, hospitals, universities, law firms, newspapers, and so on).

The size of dominant American corporations defies comprehension. A United States Senate study reports that the 122 largest corporations from all sectors of the American economy had 41 percent of the market value of all outstanding common stock in 1976.[4] The same study found that voting rights in large American corporations are concentrated among relatively few firms.[5]

A United States Senate study of 100 large corporations across the top of the business spectrum (banking and insurance, automotive industry, energy, telecommunications, information processing, office equipment, retailing, and twelve industry leaders) also found extensive economic concentration. The largest American companies each have concentrated ownerships and extensive participation in each other's governing boards (interlocking directorships).[6]

Concentration and the Ability to Save

Thrift is a virtue basic to capitalist society and is undoubtedly practiced by millions of Americans. Realistically speaking, however, the ability to save significant sums is restricted to relatively few people, basically those in high-income groups. To recognize this is to know a great deal about the basic class structure of American society. The fact that only high-income groups can save helps to explain the high concentration of wealth; conversely, the high concentration of wealth helps to explain high income. The ability of high-income groups to save creates extra income (dividends, interest, capital gains, stock appreciation), which in turn promotes the unequal ability to save, and so on. This has been called the Matthew Effect— "For to everyone who has will more be given" (Matthew 25:29, Revised Standard Version).

Further, the large majority of those who are wealthy either inherited their money or used an inheritance to make money. If we examine three factors—(1) the sources of income from property, (2) the ways in which such income is protected against taxation, and (3) the ways in which estate and inheritance taxes permit the transmission of wealth from one generation to the next—certain relationships become apparent that go far toward explaining the highly concentrated and highly stable distribution of America's material culture. A focus on the 400 richest individuals (*Forbes*) or on the 100 largest corporations (*Fortune*) obscures a fundamental fact if one is not careful. Rich individuals are parts of interconnected families, corporations are connected parts of a concentrated economy, and rich families are owners and directors of the concentrated economy. And the fact that the individuals and families who make up the rich and powerful are not always the same because of upward and downward mobility should not be allowed to obscure the reality of the processes that produce a high, stable, and often illegitimate structure of wealth in the United States.[7]

Power groups are invariably surrounded by myths, and the corporation is no exception. In the nineteenth century there developed the legal fiction that the corporation was a person and that its rights were absolute under the Constitution. Endorsed by the United States Supreme Court between 1865 and the 1930s, this myth facilitated the rise of the large corporation and the oligarchic economy. More recently, other myths have developed to camouflage the power of corporations. One such fiction is that the rise of labor unions has provided workers an effective check on managerial power. There is no evidence of any equalization of either income or wealth since the rise of trade unions in the 1930s.

Another myth is that the power of property has declined in favor of managerial power, and that the corporation, under the guidance of well-educated executives, has become socially responsible. This idea, which is similar to the myths of postindustrial and information society, implies that a basic change has taken place in capitalist society. Implicitly, and often explicitly, it is held that the prevailing elites have won their positions in open competition and can exercise power objectively because they are not tied to special interests, such as property. Many studies have cast doubt on the proposition that the power of property has declined and that occupation has supplanted it as the modal control force in the modern economy.[8] Actually, it is best to think of a mutuality of interests and motivations between property owners and managers. As Maurice Zeitlin reports,[9] there is no difference in profit orientation between family-controlled and manager-controlled businesses, and dollar profit and rate of return on equity are major determinants of executive compensation. Indeed, it is probably better to think of the ownership of corporate property as a chain linking many otherwise disparate groups to a capitalist order of society: Not only managers (who are important stockowners) but also labor unions, universities, churches, professional associations, and voluntary organizations of all kinds have their funds invested in corporate stocks.

Overseas Investment

Social classes do not begin and end at national boundaries. In their organized forms as corporations, trade unions, governments, churches, universities, foundations, and so on, their reach extends beyond national borders into other societies. The major economic units that carry on class relations beyond America's national boundaries are corporations engaged in manufacturing, agriculture, mining, timber, construction, and in various services such as banking, insurance, law, publishing, research, journalism, entertainment, and sports. Professional associations and labor unions also operate abroad in pursuit of class interests.

The United States was openly protectionist until the 1930s when the Great Depression forced it to liberalize its international trade in conjunction with other countries. At the end of World War II, from which it emerged with by far the world's strongest economy, the United States embarked on a philosophy of free trade. From the late 1950s on, American corporations began their spectacular surge of direct foreign investment. This unique historic process was part of the shift from empire imperialism to world-market imperialism: Instead of owning countries and then lending them money (the British Empire), the United States adopted the practice of direct foreign investment—the ownership and management of businesses in foreign countries.

Most international trade takes place among the developed capitalist countries and most of that is done by a small number of giant multinational corporations, many of them American. Significantly, the majority of American overseas trading has shifted to Asia in recent years. Another significant aspect of the growing internationalization of the United States' economy is an increase of direct investment in manufacturing in Third World countries. Still another significant development (representing movement away from entrepreneurial to corporate capitalism) is the gradual shift from ethnocentric and polycentric to geocentric organizations. Huge corporations, operating in as many as sixty nations, are each administered from a central command post thanks to advances in transportation and communication technology, especially the computer. These corporations are so large that the annual sales of each exceeds the gross domestic product of major nation-states.

Most international economic transactions are among the developed countries. However, underdeveloped nations attract considerable investment because they have important resources and cheap labor. The freedom of capital to move from Detroit, Cleveland, and other areas of the United States to utilize cheap labor in Taiwan, the Philippines, or South Korea is one of the reasons for unemployment and decay in America's midcentral and northeastern cities (and for a decline in good-paying, skilled jobs). Oftentimes capital movement is aided by tariff laws that allow American companies to send parts abroad for assembly, import the finished products to the United States, and pay a tariff on the "value added" overseas (which is very little when computed on the basis of the low wages paid abroad).

An important new development during the 1980s was the emergence of cooperation among the developed capitalist nations, actually a coordination of tax, interest, and spending policies so that international supply and demand could be put in better balance. Here was Keynesianism at the international level.

In 1993, the United States debated whether or not to pass the North America Free Trade Agreement (NAFTA). Americans were assured by both major political parties and by a nearly unanimous press that America would prosper and that there would be significant job expansion. By 1995–1996, it was clear that NAFTA had cost the United States a significant number of jobs as American corporations raced to take advantage of Mexico's cheap labor, nonexistent labor protections, and nonexistent environmental protections.

An important insight into the international context of the American class system is the fact that, while American incomes have declined and its social problems have risen, the share of the total world market held by American multinational corporations has held steady at significant levels.[10]

Wealth as a Source of Power Outside of Business: Foundations, Charities, Hospitals, Universities, Cultural Organizations

The wealthy are active managers of their economic wealth and they are active in a wide range of groups outside the economy. Businesspeople dominate the governing boards of foundations (conservative and liberal), charities, hospitals, universities, and museums, symphony orchestras, and other cultural groups (see Chapters 9, 10, and 13).

THE DISTRIBUTION OF INCOME

Absolute and Relative Income Levels

Distribution of income (and wealth) is roughly uniform in all developed capitalist countries. Despite variations owing to historical circumstances, political ideology, tax, defense, and welfare policies, the outstanding characteristic of the material culture of capitalist society—aside from the dramatic increase in the standard of living—is its radically unequal distribution. Of perhaps equal importance is the fact that this sharp inequality in the distribution of goods and services has been remarkably stable over the entire period for which we have reliable data. The inequality of income in the United States, for example, seems to be fixed over time and not to be affected by rising productivity, taxation, or the rise of the welfare state. No understanding of class (economic) stratification is possible, therefore, unless one guards against the popular equation of rising productivity, progressive tax schedules, and the inauguration of the welfare state with a growing equality of material conditions. As we have suggested, one must distinguish clearly between criteria that determine absolute levels of goods and services and criteria designed to establish relative shares of these benefits. It is especially important not to succumb to the popular ideology that equates rising productivity and income with a more egalitarian distribution of life chances.

To appreciate fully the fact that a rise in the absolute standard of living has not significantly affected the *relative share* of national income enjoyed by various income classes, one should think of modern structures of stratification as a fleet of ships in a harbor: an incoming tide—rising productivity and a rising standard of living—does not diminish the differences between rowboats, cabin cruisers, cargo vessels, and giant ocean liners.[11]

Comparative Income Distribution

All developed countries, capitalist and socialist alike, are very unequal and reveal no trend toward equality when looked at broadly. Under closer scrutiny, however, a number of variations appear. The developed capitalist countries that have had long-term socialist governments or sustained welfare states (for example, Sweden) have more income equality than the more market-oriented societies (for example, the United States). In addition, it is clear that capitalist countries with more income equality than the United States (because of their greater commitment to full employment and their more developed public-service sectors) have not suffered economically.

The latest available data on income inequality in the developed world (not including Japan) during the 1980s indicates that the United States is the most unequal capitalist country taking income from property, most government benefits, and taxes into account. The authors, Timothy M. Smeeding,

Lee Rainwater, and Anthony B. Atkinson, indicate strongly that their data also hold for the 1990s.[12]

INCOME DISTRIBUTION IN THE UNITED STATES

Income data from World War II on show that income in the United States is very unequal and that it has become more so in the past few decades (see Figure 7–1). The increase in income inequality can be computed as a ratio between the highest fifth and the lowest fifth (see Table 7–1). Another way to see income inequality trends is to note that the middle 60 percent of American households now makes less than the top fifth, 47.3 percent versus 49.1 percent respectively (see Figure 7–1).

Another way to see income trends is to distinguish between family, individual, and worker incomes. Income inequality has increased for all segments of the income hierarchy over the past twenty-five years with the top gaining at the expense of the rest. The loss has been greatest among the poor with a significant decline in the middle. The decline was greater in households with children as compared to childless households, greater among black and Hispanic households than white households, and greater among young as opposed to older heads of household.

FIGURE 7–1 Share of Total Household Income by Income Fifths, 1968–1994

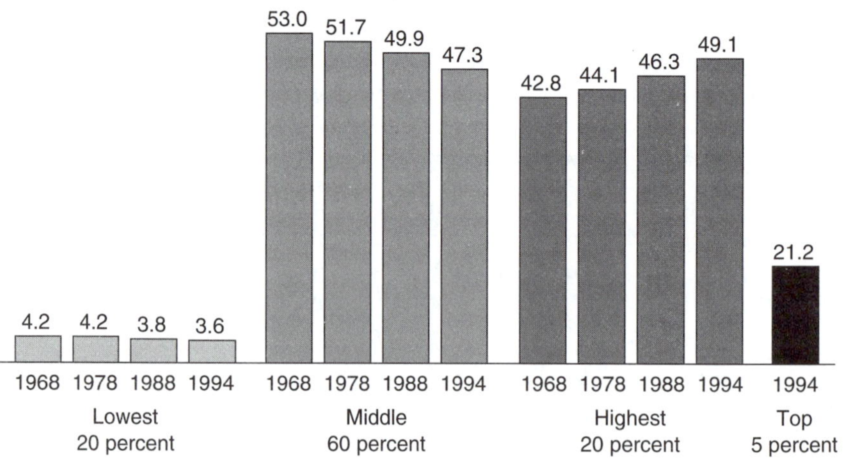

Source: U.S. Bureau of the Census, "Population Profile of the United States, 1995," *Current Population Reports,* P23-189 (Washington, DC: U.S. Government Printing Office, 1995), p. 41. For 1994 data, see Internet, http://www.census.gov/ftp/pub/hhes/www/img/shares.gif.

TABLE 7–1 The Trend of Growing Inequality Among Households, 1968 to 1994 as Measured by the Ratio Between the Highest and the Lowest Income Fifths

	INCOME SHARE HIGHEST FIFTH	INCOME SHARE LOWEST FIFTH	RATIO HIGHEST FIFTH TO LOWEST FIFTH
1994	49.1	3.6	13.6
1988	46.3	3.8	12.2
1978	44.1	4.2	10.5
1968	42.8	4.2	10.2

Source: See Figure 7–1

All workers have experienced declines in real wages, males experiencing the bulk of it. After a gain, women workers have begun to resemble the overall income distribution, namely, growing dispersion at the top and bottom. Growing inequality among workers is not explained by sex, education, or experience. It is as true of full-time workers as of part-time workers. Even college graduates have experienced stagnation in real income.[13] Data for 1994 reveal that the median household income continues its decades-old stagnation.[14]

It should be noted strongly that the Census Bureau's data on income are not completely accurate because they fail to consider nonmoney income, realized capital gains, and retained corporate earnings, and suffer from underreporting, especially in the areas of interest, rents, and dividends. On the whole, underreporting and the omission of certain kinds of income cause the Census Bureau to understate the degree of income inequality.

THE END OF A GROWING STANDARD OF LIVING?

The United States experienced a much higher growth in living standards in the 1950s and 1960s than in the period after 1970. The slowdown in economic growth can be seen in declining real wages, productivity, and personal savings. The medium household (not family) income declined from its high of $28,167 in 1973 to $23,580 in 1984. Seen in another way, the average 30-year-old male earned $25,580 in 1973 compared to $17,520 in 1983. And the same male had to pay 44 percent of gross earnings to buy a median-priced house in 1983 compared to 21 percent in 1973.[15] The percent of national income derived from property (rents, dividends, interest) has risen since the 1960s and the share going for wages and salaries has declined. Understandably, the amount of personal debt (as well as public and corporate debt) has risen to an all-time high as Americans find it hard to adjust their expectations to economic realities.

Another way of measuring standard of living is by median family income (the point at which 50 percent of families are above and 50 percent are below). Median family income grew strongly in the 1960s but remained fairly stationary after 1970. But different kinds of families fared quite differently. The Congressional Budget Office computed an Adjusted Family Income (using family size and a different inflation index) and found that elderly families and individuals had a strong growth (50 percent), families in general had a low growth of 14 percent, and single-mother families had an anemic 2 percent growth over the space of these sixteen years. Significantly, the Adjusted Family income of families varied by age. Families headed by sixty-five-year-olds rose 54 percent while young families under age twenty-five had a *drop* of 18 percent.[16]

Figure 7–2 provides a panoramic view of America's static standard of living between 1967 and 1992. The fortunes of various types of households were not the same, of course and whatever growth took place did not do so because of increased productivity or a better-run society. Growth occurred because some households had more workers as both spouses worked, because families grew smaller as the birth rate declined, and because the elderly received substantial sums of non-means-tested Social Security increases. And it grew because all sectors of the society (individuals, business, and state and federal governments) went deeply into debt.

FIGURE 7–2 Median Household Income 1967 to 1992

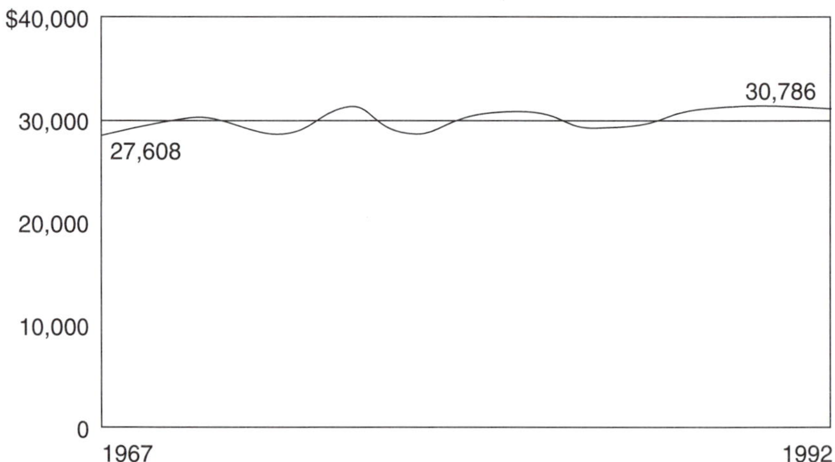

Source: U.S. Bureau of the Census, "Money Income of Households, Families, and Persons in the United States, 1992," *Current Population Reports,* P60–184 (Washington, DC: U.S. Government Printing Office, 1993), Figure 1.

POWER OVER INCOME

Recently stratification theory (often inspired by Karl Marx) has given much more attention to the tiny upper class that owns so much of the basic economy. From this perspective, the initial need was to go beyond individual income and occupation and focus on wealth and economic power, and this has been done clearly and persuasively by E. O. Wright and Luca Perrone, who argue that empirical research in sociology has neglected Marxian categories, especially the fundamental concept of owner vs. nonowner. Arguing directly against sociology's preoccupation with occupation, Wright and Perrone set out to learn whether being an owner has any bearing on income. Defining class as a position in the social relations of production, they use four criteria to place people:

1. The ownership of the means of production
2. The purchase of the labor power of others
3. The control of other people's labor power
4. The sale of one's own labor power

These criteria yield four classes: capitalists, managers, workers, and petite bourgeoisie. When income data are analyzed, owners (both capitalist and petite bourgeoisie) receive more income than do managers and workers *even when education, occupational status, age, and job tenure are held constant.* And managers, in turn, have more income than do workers even when education is held constant. Wright and Perrone argue that the high income of managers is largely a function of social control—here higher rewards induce rising executives to operate within the assumptions of a capitalist society, thus also providing a buffer between the upper class and workers.[17]

The power of wealth to generate income is also a characteristic of the professions. Here we are dealing with two forms of wealth: human capital and capital as ownership of commercial property. Given the unusual autonomy of the American professions, some of them make unusual incomes in relation to professions in other capitalist societies (doctors are a prime example). In addition, doctors, lawyers, and professors can turn their practices into lucrative businesses by setting up laboratories, law firms, and commercial ventures to exploit research findings. (No matter that human capital and research are largely financed by tax money).

In a rare analysis of a particular profession, lawyers, John Hagen identifies two stratifying relations—core sector, large firms (representing large businesses) versus peripheral firms (representing individuals and small businesses) and male versus female lawyers. Lawyers in core firms earn more than lawyers in peripheral firms with the owners of large firms making substantially more than their lawyer employees. Thus law is deeply stratified reflecting the stratification of the larger capitalist economy. In addition, female lawyers make substantially less regardless of where they practice.[18]

NEW INCOME TRENDS: A BIPOLAR AMERICA?

The 1970s saw a new trend in income distribution. Reversing its previous history, the United States appears no longer able to provide an expanding number of middle-income households. The American economy has continued to generate jobs but interpreting the number and quality of jobs is not easy.[19] One analyst argues that the United States continued to generate good middle-income jobs between 1973 and 1982 and that the middle class was alive and well.[20] Rosenthal may be right about middle-income jobs holding steady, but he confuses middle income with middle class[21] and individual with family income.[22] Others have argued that the United States is no longer generating good-paying jobs.[23]

Looking at high- vs. low-growth sectors of the economy reveals some disturbing trends. Many argue that service occupations (which have been setting the pace of the American economy) pay significantly less than do skilled manufacturing jobs. Blackburn and Bloom point out that the twenty fastest-growing businesses paid $100 a week less than the twenty fastest-declining businesses. Tracing the growth of family income between 1969 and 1983, Blackburn and Bloom found faster growth among lower and upper families as opposed to lower-middle and upper-middle families.[24] And in 1988, the Senate Budget Committee issued a report showing that jobs with middle-level wages had shrunk considerably and that the majority of newly created jobs were paying poverty wages (for a family of four).[25] Since then, there has been a steady growth of temporary and part-time workers who in addition to poor pay have no health or pension benefits.

The new household income structure is moving away from the big bulge in the middle that was once characteristic of the United States and toward a bipolar (hour glass, two-tier) shape (see Figure 7–3). The United States may or may not be generating as many good-paying jobs as in the past, but even assuming that it is, the crucial question to ask is: How are these jobs distributed by households? Double earners are now common at all levels, but better-paid individuals marry each other and this means that middle-income jobs are no longer held by single breadwinners. In addition, the lower classes have more single-income households largely because divorced mothers pile up at that level.

The structural reasons for the new distribution of household income are the surge toward service industries, the movement of capital to low-wage, nonunionized sections of the United States and abroad, the decline of trade unions, and active support of these trends by government (deregulation, the large tax cuts of 1981–1983, rapid depreciation for tax purposes, the

FIGURE 7–3 The Trend Toward a Bipolar Distribution of Household Income, 1960s–1990s

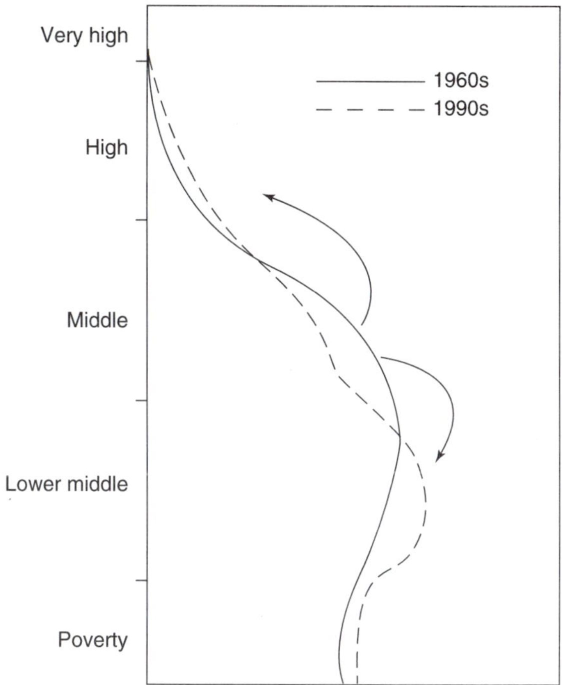

curtailment of public services and benefits, and anti-union rulings by a business-dominated National Labor Relations Board). The women's movement and the rising divorce rate also contributed to the new trend toward bipolar family incomes. The women's movement has opened up opportunities for the daughters and wives of the upper classes (see Box 19–3, Is Women's Liberation a Movement Favoring Only the Upper Classes?). But the general surge of civil rights, individualism (laissez-faire American liberalism), easier including no-fault divorce laws, and an erratic economy have also led to a high divorce rate—the major casualties of divorce, even in no-fault divorces, are women and thus the swollen ranks of lower-level, one-parent female households.

IS THE MIDDLE CLASS DISAPPEARING?

The American middle class has long since disappeared if middle class is defined as a moderate-sized property owner of a business or autonomous professional. Today, property is highly concentrated, and Americans, including professionals, are largely employees of large bureaucratic corporations, government, hospitals, foundations, voluntary groups, and churches.

The disappearance of the middle class was hidden from view by economic growth, especially from the late nineteenth to mid-twentieth century. Economic growth created a new middle class of salaried professionals and high-income semiprofessionals and blue-collar skilled workers. The new economy of abundance also homogenized a great deal of consumption, creating both a real and fictitious mass of middle-class consumers. And labor segmentation, the creation of meaningless gradations among occupations, also misled Americans into thinking that things were getting better.[26]

However defined, the new middle class that appeared in the twentieth century seems to be shrinking. In assessing trends in household income, it is important to distinguish between middle income and middle class. A middle income can be acquired in a household in which husband and wife both work in blue-collar or working-class jobs. Today middle income for most requires two workers. And both the nature of the work and family background make this a working-class family despite its middle-level of income. Middle class, on the other hand, means a certain level of income but from a source that promotes an independent, self-directed personality. It means awareness about and a desire to live in a certain way: owning a home with enough space for family members to have private lives, and enough appliances, including a second car, to service it. It means vacations as well as saving for the future. It means expectations for future advancement at work. And it means proper socialization of the young for future middle-class (or upper-middle-class) status, especially through a four-year college education.

In the 1970s and 1980s there were laments for the skilled workers in so-called smokestack industries. What few realized then was that during the same period millions of middle-level managers were laid off by hard-pressed corporations (many were "hard-pressed" by their own subsidiaries in cheap labor countries). And layoffs have continued through the 1990s, thus effectively curbing opportunities for the formation of middle-class households. From the 1980s on, it was clear that high-tech industries and upper-level occupations were also being exported to Third World countries.[27]

Trends in the ownership of productive property, household income, and occupation indicate an erosion in the size and power of the historic American middle class. And by the 1980s another change had taken place in the middle class—diversification. The middle class is now made up of singles, married childless couples, double-earners with children, divorced and remarried individuals, and older couples and singles.

The decline of the middle class and its fragmentation into many different subtypes has serious implications for American society. The broad, politically moderate middle class was the mainstay of American representative government. As we will see later, American political life has changed for the worse and this may well be due to the change in the American middle class.

STRUCTURAL POVERTY: THE OTHER SIDE OF THE COIN OF AFFLUENCE

Discarding the Liberal Myth of Universal Affluence

Structural poverty means that basic institutions and power relations are causing poverty. Specific causes are chronic socially created unemployment, unnecessary qualifications for occupations, poor management, the cultural bias toward technology and against labor, the movement of capital abroad, antifamily bias in welfare programs, the lack of public programs fostering birth control, the separation of work and residence, the irrelevance of education to work, and the absence of socioeconomic planning.

Growing inequality in the United States has hit the poor and children hardest. Other capitalist societies have antipoverty programs to keep their poverty rates lower than ours without hurting their economic growth rates. Incidentally, the poverty rate is not a result of how it is measured and arguments to that effect by conservatives have been a waste of time. Changes in how poverty is measured will concern us shortly; a proposed new way to compile the rate yields similar results, but has the enormous advantage of providing a way to evaluate the impact of public programs. All in all, the poverty rate from the 1960s on has varied somewhat but its chief significance is that it is always somewhere in the vicinity of 15 percent of the population.

Poverty in the United States and the other developed countries has persisted despite centuries of economic growth and numerous private and public efforts to curb it. To understand poverty one must jettison the idea that it is a temporary vestige of a previous world. Poverty is a result of basic capitalist institutions and it serves concrete social functions. The liberal myth of universal affluence must be discarded. Once this is done there are other myths to explore.

More Myths About The Poor

There are many persistent myths about the poor and programs to help them. Many Americans believe that the welfare rolls are filled with deadbeats and cheats, able-bodied individuals who don't want to work. They believe that welfare makes people dependent and that people don't want to get out of poverty. Many believe that welfare spending is the reason for their high taxes. Many Americans are afraid to provide help to the down-and-out because they think it will attract the poor to their city or state. The truth contradicts all these beliefs. People on welfare are mostly children, mothers, and the elderly. Most poor people are poor for a short time and most would work if work were available or possible. Able-bodied men cannot get welfare checks regardless of how poor they are (they can get food stamps). People do not move to get higher welfare. The amount of money spent on welfare for mothers with dependent children is very small and even the highest amounts represent a very low level of living. Food stamps make up a more sizable amount but this helps to dispose of surplus food that the federal government buys from farmers and which would rot if not given away. As for cheating and waste, experts agree that there is very little and that most of the waste and fraud is due to poorly researched laws, government confusion and incompetence, and corrupt administrators.

Leonard Beeghley, a leading expert on poverty, says we must distinguish between antipoverty programs and public assistance. The antipoverty programs of the 1960s and 1970s were designed to help the poor become self-reliant, productive members of society. These were far more successful than people realize, but because they threatened powerful business and professional groups and right-wing Republicans and racist Democrats, they were largely abandoned. Assistance for the poor, on the other hand, is basically institutionalized pauperism—one has to be destitute to receive aid, and aid levels are set at subsistence and sub-subsistence levels. In addition, the overall amount for public assistance is far lower than people think (and far lower than government benefits given to the middle and upper classes).[28]

The New Poor

The defeat by conservatives of programs developed during the 1960s and 1970s to empower the poor was conducted in the name of renewed economic growth through free-market economics. But the results of the new consensus on limiting the role of the central government in curbing poverty in favor of private markets has been a failure. All indicators of social pathology have risen since 1970.[29] The basic dynamics of an uncontrolled corporate capitalism have also generated persistent and perhaps growing levels of poverty.

The routine operation of the American political economy (power groups solving their own problems) generated a new mix of poor people even before the 1980s.[30] The picture became clearer during the 1980s and 1990s. The poor are still disproportionately made up of racial and ethnic minorities. But poverty is now made up of female-headed households and this means that children are disproportionately poor.[31] Twenty-two percent of America's children live in poverty.[32] There has also been a striking increase in full-time workers and their families that are poor (somewhere between 1 million to 2 million families). And there are large numbers of the nearly poor, families that must buy used clothing and cars, do without health insurance, live in substandard housing, and rarely travel. These working poor and nearly poor increased dramatically from the 1980s on. And then there are the poor of the poor, the homeless.

THE POLITICS OF POVERTY

Capitalist society generates significant rates of poverty (even though rates vary from country to country). Thanks to Herbert Gans, it is now much easier to understand the important role that poverty plays in maintaining capitalism. Gans argues that poverty is deeply connected to the structure of society.[33] The poor (by which Gans means mostly the historic poor of able-bodied workers, not the demoralized, apathetic underclass that has emerged recently) perform a number of functions for society. Their low wages, high relative taxation, and their work as servants directly subsidizes the well-to-do. The poor provide clients and customers for various businesses and professionals. They provide mobility for said businesses and professionals and allow the upper classes to gain prestige from sponsoring various charities. The poor built our cities and are dispossessed by urban renewal. The poor bore the costs of rural change as well. The poor are politically apathetic and their presence helps make possible a bland, noncompetitive political process.

Poverty, therefore, is a structural problem directly linked to the central institutions and power groups of American society. It is not a technical question to be solved by research and secondary reforms (such as welfare checks and food stamps). Gans argues that substitutes (functional equivalents) can be found for some of the functions served by the poor but most of the changes require a *change of power* and are a distinct and perceivable threat to the affluent. Though Gans may be overly optimistic about some aspects of his analysis, his overall conclusion appears sound: *Alternatives to poverty are dysfunctional to the nonpoor and thus cannot be changed without a reduction in the power of those who benefit from poverty.* Put differently, no inroads into poverty (or into many other social problems) appear to be possible unless American power groups accept economic and social planning, and put full (and meaningful) employment at the top of the political agenda.

The issue of poverty can be framed in stark political terms: the poor, along with others who have problems, result from the solutions that the upper classes have found for their own problems. The upper classes fight inflation with unemployment and bankruptcy. They favor technology over labor, oppose trade unions, and support immigration. Secure in their own identities and families, they stress individualism, thus making marriages and family life for those below them difficult. They oppose taxes for public services, helping to drive people into the labor market, creating yet another way to maintain labor surpluses. And they jealously guard their absolute right to control investment, including the right to use cheap labor overseas.

The evidence suggests that the disadvantaged are not a temporary phenomenon but appear to result from the *normal operation of American institutions.* The workings of the economy and the polity have disconnected large numbers from the American mainstream. This insight leads to more questions. Do civil rights laws and other minority-oriented legislation have any effect on economic inequality? The answer appears to be no. Should minorities make a greater effort in education? The answer appears to be no. Are the civil rights laws and programs mostly a way for corporate capitalism to modernize its labor force? Over the past 600 years capitalism has developed a labor force composed of legally free individuals. In the United States it also developed first a slave and then a segregated labor force. Are the civil rights laws merely a way to turn minorities into legally free individuals who can then be held responsible for failure?

All evidence points to systematic and stable injustice for large portions of the American population. The evidence again points not only to the failure of American society to live up to its norms and values but to what appears to be an inherent inability to do so. The evidence suggests that American society cannot hope to achieve its values as long as Americans, especially power groups, continue to take the basic structure of the economy for granted. Ineffective poverty programs, giving minorities their civil rights, and underfunded, unenforced laws to promote opportunity, may actually be more a process of legitimating exploitation than a real effort to help the American underclass. Little change can be expected until the working class and broad middle class realize that they too are forced to live in insecure and shrinking sectors of the American economy.

The Republican party's victory in the Congressional election of 1994 led to an onslaught on America's already poor system of social services. The ostensible reason was America's chronic deficit and the pressure it created to raise taxes or borrow. Under the cover of morality (the welfare system is fostering sloth and illegitimacy) and laissez-faire fantasy, the Republican party, with help from conservative Democrats, has proposed turning welfare for the poor from a human right (entitlement) into an annual budget allotment (the amount to be determined by the power of the contending budget parties), with provisions demanding that recipients (composed of mothers with small children and impoverished elderly) work (in an economy without jobs), and imposing strict limits on how long benefits will be given. The annual funds will be turned over to the states with no strings because they are closer to the people and will produce better programs.

Everyone knows that state governments in the United States are even less efficient and more corrupt than the federal government. Everyone knows that the amounts to serve the poor, already inadequate and the lowest in the capitalist world, will decline because the poor, being poor and diverse, are politically very weak. But so-called welfare reform serves to reduce the pressure to intervene in the affairs of the propertied, the only way to reduce poverty and alleviate its miseries. Perhaps the greatest boon of welfare reform to the powerful is that it eliminates a structuring at the bottom, that is, it lowers welfare benefits to keep them well below the declining wage levels of full-time workers, while simultaneously reinforcing the threatened work ethic.

CHANGING THE POVERTY INDEX TO AID PUBLIC POLICY

The current poverty level is based on criteria established in the early 1960s: families (adult couple, adult couple with two children) and unrelated individuals (singles, elderly) were assumed to be poor if their cash income before taxes did not cover a minimum diet multiplied by three to cover other expenses.

A new way to measure poverty has been purposed to take into account the diversity of poor households; noncash benefits such as food stamps, health care, subsidized housing, school lunches, and energy; tax credits; regional differences in the cost of living (especially housing), child care, and other work expenses; health care costs; and child support payments. The new poverty index does not change the overall number of poor from the old index but it has one great advantage: it allows legislatures, governments, and others to assess the impact of various public policies on the poor.[34]

The major advantage of the new index will not appeal to those who do not want evidence that government programs work. The antipoverty program of the 1960s was abolished precisely because it worked. The Republican party sabotaged President Clinton's legislative program in 1993–1994 and after their victory in 1994 they proposed eliminating one successful program after another. One of their motives was political strategy—successful government programs create supporters for the Democratic party. Another is that it justifies government intervention as a way to solve social programs. A third motive is that successful government programs run counter to the groups that are causing the problems, the main supporters of the Republican party.

ECONOMIC CLASSES AND THE DISTRIBUTION OF FORMAL EDUCATION

Education is America's all-purpose solver of problems including poverty. Education's inability to solve problems is now well documented, as outlined in Chapter 9. A word about education is necessary here to identify its role in providing legitimacy for America's dominant economic classes.

Formal education is a jealously guarded prerogative of most dominant strata, and until the nineteenth century only a tiny fraction of any given population could read and write. With the advent of industrialization, whether or not it was accompanied by political democracy, the requirements of occupation and citizenship made literate populations necessary. In the United States, as in other industrializing nations, a dramatic surge in education brought mass literacy into being.

Between 1900 and the 1930s the United States put almost all teenagers in high school. From the 1950s on the number going to college rose until approximately 50 percent of high school graduates were entering some form of higher education. If one looks at the formal distribution of education there is a steady increase in the number of Americans with high school, college, and graduate school diplomas and degrees. But the important thing about educational credentials is that they are still highly unequal. The dropout rates from high school and college are very high. Even as more Americans went to college, a degree from graduate school became ever more necessary for entry into the prized sectors of the occupational ladder. Educational inequality is heightened by the fact that the same degrees have different value depending on the school from which they are obtained.

The United States has promoted literacy beyond what people prior to the nineteenth century thought possible. But it still has millions who cannot read and millions more who are functional illiterates (that is, who cannot read well enough to understand application forms for a driver's license). Even when the lower classes or minorities show educational gains, even relative gains, it does not mean that the class system has opened up or is basing itself on merit. For one thing, the lower classes attend different kinds of schools and take different programs. And even when minorities make relative gains in education, education does not pay off for them as it does for white males. Mass education, therefore, has not equalized or homogenized Americans. Like the rise in income and occupational skill levels, therefore, it is best to think of the rise of educational attainment as resembling the rise of boats of unequal sizes on an incoming tide.

Most Americans, including the upper classes and our best educated, have false ideas about education. The class origins of students correlate strongly with achievement in school. And achievement in school, including elite schools, bears no independent, positive relation to performance in later occupational or citizenship roles! Education is essentially a status device to ensure the transmission of class status from one generation to the next. What is most worrisome about America's academic (abstract, value-neutral, nonpolitical) education is not merely that it results in an uncreative majority, but that it renders the upper classes uncreative as well.

Understanding the interplay between the class variables of income, wealth, occupation, and education over time is crucial to understanding the American class system. It is just as important not to misinterpret rising average years of schooling as it is not to misinterpret rising average income, wealth, or occupational levels. If better educated means an improvement in the ability to perform economic, political, and social roles, then Americans are not better educated today than in the past. Educational comparisons with the past based on years of schooling or degrees are meaningless. The essential criterion for judging education is whether it prepares one for performance in today's social statuses and for meeting today's problems. Seen from this perspective an illiterate frontiersperson may be better educated than today's typical college graduate (for a full discussion of education, see Chapter 9).

Not understanding the nature of education is one of the main deficiencies in stratification analysis. Both academics and students, having experienced the travails of achieving in school, find it easy to equate education with liberal mythology, especially the idea that it represents innate individual ability.

DECLINING MOBILITY, BIPOLARIZATION, AND STAGNANT LIVING STANDARDS: THE ADVENT OF STRUCTURAL CHANGE?

There have been ups and downs in rates of mobility in U.S. history, but something unique may now be occurring, not merely a decline but a chronic decline, that is, a change in the structural forces that control mobility. This decline has been obscured by continued American economic growth, double-breadwinner households, double job-holding, misleading government data, reforms such as affirmative action, and emphases on American ideology. Nonetheless, a large body of evidence points to lowered upward mobility, increased downward mobility, a stagnant (declining for many) standard of living, persistent poverty impervious to reform, increased income inequality, and a greater concentration of an already highly concentrated structure of wealth and economic power.

For over twenty-five years the relentless downsizing of American corporations has led to a distinct bipolar class system. Conservative business and religious interests have harnessed the insecurity and resentment of the American electorate to prevent government from being used except in their interests. One conclusion from the foregoing is that unless the United States moves to open economic and social planning, free enterprise will continue to be good for the upper classes and to provide gradations of insecurity and misery for the rest.

SUMMARY

Wealth in the United States is highly concentrated. The power of a small number to control investment decisions means that a politically unaccountable tiny minority has the power to determine how the vast majority of Americans live.

Inherited wealth is a central cause and feature of wealth concentration, starkly contradicting basic American beliefs and values. Wealth gives the wealthy considerable income unwarranted by education or work.

The wealthy use their power to generate auxiliary groups that also suck up illegitimate amounts of income.

Income in the United States is highly unequal and becoming more so as even the minor controls over the upper classes are relaxed.

A bipolar income distribution has emerged in the past few decades.

Despite mass education, the distribution of education is still highly unequal. Access to and achievement in education correlates strongly with class. The most important thing about education is that it appears to have no positive outcomes either for the economy or polity.

The interplay of wealth, income, poverty, education, and occupational power generates a hierarchy of households with vastly different resources to succeed from one generation to the next. These resources are used by the rich and well-to-do, not only to ensure the success of their children, but to create auxiliary private and public groups to uphold their interests and to maintain the capitalist system of social stratification.

It is clear from the data that economic values in the United States, and all industrial countries, are steeply and stably graded. Not only is the distribution of income, wealth, occupation, and education very unequal but there is no evidence that inequality has been reduced significantly either in comparison with past societies or since the inception of industrial society.

The functional view sees the United States as a society composed of voluntaristically propelled individuals competing for rewards in an open, fluid world of equal opportunity. Sociologists have increasingly abandoned this view for one that focuses on institutions and groups. This latter view reveals a power structure that shapes the world of rewards to suit itself.

After more than a century of economic growth *and* a rising standard of living, the United States has experienced what appears to be a historic reversal of momentous importance. There is increasing evidence that while slow economic growth has continued since 1970, it has more than been absorbed by a rising overhead of crime, pollution, military expenditure, support of idle people, and interest payments on debt (of which increasing amounts are going to foreigners).

The impact of economic slowdown on the American class system is significant:

1. The capitalist class has undergone considerable turmoil but, by and large, capitalism has remained an accepted part of the American scheme of things even as capital flows to cheap labor areas in the United States and abroad were causing considerable trouble for ordinary Americans.

The internationalization of the American economy has had a large impact on the American class system. Capital flows abroad have kept the American upper classes prosperous but have helped undermine the economic status of large portions of the rest of the population.

2. Economic slowdown and the exposure of the American economy to foreign competition have produced momentous changes in the American middle class. Defined as middle income, the American middle class is shrinking unless double-earners and smaller families are included. The middle class—defined as single-earner households or households headed by autonomous, self-propelled individuals who live in a certain way, who have hopes for advancement, and who raise their children to succeed—also appears to be shrinking. The middle class has been the mainstay of representative government, and its decline may help explain the declining performance of our political system.
3. Poverty appears to be a chronic outcome of American capitalism, by all evidence a necessary feature. There are many kinds of poor people: working poor, one-parent female households, the destitute and homeless, a disproportionate number of racial and ethnic minorities, and young white males. Poverty and near poverty stem from sectors of the economy that are faltering, and many Americans are disconnected from the economy altogether. The United States appears to have a permanent underclass. Significantly, 22 percent of American children live in poverty.

The most important conclusion to emerge from the foregoing analysis of economic values is that private property, economic competition, and economic growth have not brought about, and do not necessarily lead to, economic equality, equity, or universal achievement standards. The fundamental image that must be kept firmly in mind about liberal democracy, and industrial society in general, is of a deep, stable, and comprehensive system of stratification whose main differences with the past are not the degree, permanence, and extent of its inequality but rather its sources and forms.

NOTES

1. Jeffrey G. Williamson and Peter H. Lindert, *American Inequality: A Macroeconomic Analysis* (New York: Academic Press, 1979), and James D. Smith, ed., *Modeling the Distribution and Intergenerational Transmission of Wealth* (Chicago: University of Chicago Press, 1980).
2. James D. Smith, *The Distribution of Wealth* (Ann Arbor: Survey Research Center, University of Michigan, 1986), Tables 2 and 5.
3. Edward N. Wolff, *Top Heavy: A Study of the Increasing Inequality of Wealth in America* (New York: Twentieth Century Fund, 1995).
4. U.S. Senate Committee on Governmental Affairs, *Voting Rights in Major Corporations* (Washington, DC: U.S. Government Printing Office, 1978), p. 1; derived from *Forbes,* May 15, 1977.
5. Ibid., p. 1. As little as 5 to 10 percent ownership constitutes voting control since stockholders in general either do not vote or follow the lead of management.

6. U.S. Senate Committee on Governmental Affairs, *Structure of Corporate Concentration: Institutional Shareholders and Interlocking Directorates Among Major U.S. Corporations* (Washington, DC: U.S. Government Printing Office, 1980).
7. For a fascinating analysis of how wealth accumulates over the generations, complete with a vivid collection of case studies showing an almost feudalistic concern with family, see Michael Patrick Allen, *The Founding Fortunes: A New Anatomy of Super-Rich Families in America* (New York: E. P. Dutton, 1987). Also see *Forbes* magazine's special annual issue, "The Richest People in America" for vignettes illustrating the role of inheritance in the concentration of wealth.
8. For a careful analysis of the data that find a significant degree of family control in big business, see Philip H. Burch, Jr., *The Managerial Revolution Reassessed* (Lexington, MA: D.C. Heath, 1972). For a case study of an alliance or "interest group" formed by a number of wealthy families, see James C. Knowles, "The Rockefeller Finanical Group" (Andover, MA: Warner Modular Publications, module 343, 1973), pp. 1–59. For a review of the literature in this area that finds the alleged divorce of ownership and control highly problematic, see Maurice Zeitlin, "Corporate Ownership and Control: The Large Corporation and the Capitalist Class," *American Journal of Sociology* 79, no. 5 (March 1974): 1073–1119.
9. Zeitlin, "Corporate Ownership and Control," pp. 1094–1095.
10. Robert E. Lipsey and Irving B. Kravis, "Business Holds Its Own as America Slips," *New York Times*, January 18, 1987, p. F3.
11. Recent changes toward increased inequality are discussed below.
12. As reported by Keith Bradsher, *New York Times*, October 27, 1995, p. D2.
13. Lynn Karoly, "The Trend in Inequality Among Families, Individuals, and Workers in the U.S.: A Twenty-Five Year Perspective," Sheldon Danziger and Peter Gottschalk, eds., *Uneven Tides: Rising Inequality in America* (New York: Russell Sage, 1993).
14. Keith Bradsher, *New York Times*, October 6, 1995, p. A22.
15. Frank S. Levy and Richard C. Michel, "Economic Future of the Baby Boom," Report, Joint Economic Committee of Congress (Washington, DC: U.S. Government Printing Office, 1985).
16. "Trends in Family Income: 1970–1986," Congressional Budget Office (Washington, DC: U.S. Government Printing Office, 1988).
17. Erik Olin Wright and Luca Perrone, "Marxist Class Categories and Income Inequality," *American Sociological Review* 42 (February 1977):32–55.
18. John Hagen, "The Gender Stratification of Income Inequality Among Lawyers," *Social Forces* 68 (March 1990):835–855. For an analysis of gender inequality in law and other occupations, see Chapter 19.
19. It cannot be said too often that the unemployment rate is not a reliable indicator of how many people are out of work.
20. Neal H. Rosenthal, "The Shrinking Middle Class: Myth or Reality?," *Monthly Labor Review* 108 (March 1985):3–10.
21. For a fuller discussion of this distinction, see the section titled "Is The Middle Class Disappearing?" in this chapter.
22. For the need to go beyond individual income and for the complexities of determining family income, see Judith Treas, "U.S. Income Stratification: Bringing Families Back In," *Social Science Research* 66 (April 1985):231–251.

23. For two early warnings, see Paul Blumberg, *Inequality in an Age of Decline* (New York: Oxford University Press, 1980), and Lester Thurow, *The Zero-Sum Society* (New York: Basic Books, 1980).
24. McKinley L. Blackburn and David E. Bloom, "What Is Happening to the Middle Class?," *American Demographics* (1985):18–25.
25. Committee on the Budget, U.S. Senate, "Wages of American Workers in the 1980s" (Washington, DC: U.S. Government Printing Office, 1983).
26. David M. Gordon, Richard Edwards, and Michael Reich, *Segmented Work, Divided Workers: The Historical Transformation of Labor in the United States* (New York: Cambridge University Press, 1982).
27. For a fascinating picture of downward mobility in the American middle class (defined broadly to include managers and downward mobility by a blue-collar community), based on 150 in-depth interviews (not a random or representative sample), see Katherine S. Newman, *Falling From Grace: The Experience of Downward Mobility in the American Middle Class* (New York: Free Press, 1988).
28. For perhaps the best single book on poverty, see Leonard Beeghley, *Living Poorly in America* (New York: Praeger, 1983). For a valuable, ethnographic account of how poverty curbs occupational aspirations among both white and black youngsters and helps to reproduce the class system, see Jay MacLeod's follow-up to his 1987 study, *Aint No Making It: Aspirations and Attainment in a Low-Income Neighborhood* (Boulder, CO: Westview, 1995).
29. See Marc L. Miringoff, *The Index of Social Health* (Tarrytown, NY: Fordham Institute for Innovation in Social Policy, annual) for the worsening data on sixteen indicators of social pathology since 1970.
30. Michael Harrington, *The New American Poverty* (New York: Holt, Rinehart & Winston, 1984).
31. Ruth Sidel, *Women and Children Last: The Plight of Poor Women in Affluent America* (New York: Viking Press, 1986).
32. The gap between affluent households with children and poor households with children in the United States is the largest in the Western industrial world, according to data reported in the *New York Times,* August 14, 1995, p. A9.
33. Herbert J. Gans, "The Positive Functions of Poverty," *American Journal of Sociology* 78 (September 1972): 175–189; widely reprinted.
34. Constance F. Citro and Robert T. Michael, eds., *Measuring Poverty: A New Approach* (Washington, DC: National Academy Press, 1995).

8

Class, Marriage, Family, Personality, and Physical and Mental Health

◆ ◆ ◆ ◆

◆ ◆ ◆ ◆

The preceding chapters gave us a fairly complete picture of the unequal distribution of opportunity, wealth, income, occupation, and education in the United States. Our task in the chapters that follow is to analyze and evaluate the structure of benefits and behavior that make up the rest of the American class system.

Almost every conceivable form of behavior has been related to class position: methods of rearing children, types and amounts of interaction, sexual behavior and tastes, levels of information, perception, consciousness, marital styles, consumption, beauty contests, language skills, survival of disasters, combat survival, tolerance, voting, justice, sainthood, the sending of Christmas cards, nudism,[1] and so on.

In canvassing the available research material, our general strategy will be to increase our understanding of social class (individuals or groups that share a common location across the dimensions of class, prestige, and power) by identifying its constituent parts gradually. The family is an obvious starting point for analyzing the behavioral consequences of class position. For one thing, the class position of a breadwinner is by definition shared with all members of his or her family. Second, the family is the conduit by which the class system is transmitted from one generation to the next. Third, the structure of the family and the fortunes of its members are intimately affected by its class (economic) status.

CLASS, MARRIAGE, AND FAMILY

It is popularly thought that falling in love, acquiring a wife or husband, begetting children, and weathering the trials of marital and family life are attributable to body chemistry or drives (romantic love, sexual energy) and/or moral fiber (innate moral traits). There is evidence, however, pointing to the central role of class in such phenomena as sexual values, beliefs, and behavior; choice of marriage partner; marriage and family styles; number of children; styles of raising children; and family stability.

Class and Sexual Values and Practices

All societies distinguish between legitimate and illegitimate sexual activity, and legitimate sex, by and large, is synonymous with family institutions. The answers that society gives to such questions as how one acquires a mate, what mates are suitable, which births are legitimate, and what ties of kinship and descent exist make up the structure of its family life.

A nuclear family, which raises children to be individuals (independent, self-sufficient, adaptable), is obviously well suited to the needs of an economy that requires a mobile labor force—an economy, in other words, that is constantly generating new occupations. And with the emergence and institutionalization of the liberal political norms of liberty and equality, it is no wonder that arranged (instrumental) marriages were abandoned as fundamentally incompatible with the idea that all individuals are ends-in-themselves. It is the special function of romantic love to allow individuals to enter marriage as equals and to find their own class level irrespective of their family of origin.

Only in industrial society are love, marriage, reproduction, and child-raising combined into one basic relationship between a male and female. In the United States, this unique marital relationship is shaped by a fairly distinct definition of the nature and morality of human sexuality. The causes and legitimate forms and sexual behavior are defined by American society as follows (in general and without regard to such questions as who holds such views, with what degree of intensity, and with what consequences for behavior):

1. Sexual behavior springs from deep biological urges in human beings.
2. In some general way males are presumed to be more sexual than females.
3. Legitimate sexual relations are heterosexual in nature.
4. Sexual intercourse and reproduction are legitimate (normal and good) only within the confines of monogamous marriage based on love.
5. Certain individuals cannot marry each other, for reasons either of age or kinship.
6. Sexual relations are especially bad if one of the partners is a minor or if force is used.
7. Only certain sexual acts, out of the total range of possible sexual acts, are permissible.
8. The portrayal of nakedness and sexual intercourse in written and pictorial form for popular consumption is bad both morally and in terms of consequences.

The above code has undergone changes in recent decades in the direction of greater permissiveness and a greater similarity of attitudes among men and women. This change in attitudes has occurred at all class levels.[2] However, actual sexual behavior deviates from the above code and varies considerably by class. In a comparison of data compiled by Kinsey and his associates mostly during the 1940s with data collected in 1969–1970, Weinberg and Williams found that premarital sexual behavior still varies by social class (education). Less-educated males experienced sexual intercourse at an earlier age than better-educated males and had more sexual partners. The less-educated are now similar to the better-educated in the variety of sexual experiences but again engage in them earlier.

Kinsey found no difference among females by class in sexual behavior. Weinberg and Williams found a pronounced difference by class: Less-educated females were more likely to experience petting and especially coitus earlier and more frequently than better-educated females. Middle-class women also reported more positive feelings toward their various sexual experiences. On the whole, therefore, lower-class men and women had become more alike in their sexual behavior, the same was true of middle-class men and women, and the behavior of the two classes differed significantly from each other.[3]

Premarital sex is a violation of the American sexual code. Sex before marriage is partially sanctioned by the code itself, of course, in that men are presumed to be more sexual than women; it is accepted, therefore, for men in a partially acknowledged way. The double standard, however, seems to be on the decline within the middle class. The increase in premarital sex among college-educated females (starting past the age of twenty) is associated with courtship, affection, or love, eventual marriage, and a claim to equality. The growing sexual expressiveness of middle-class females is due, in part at least, to the increased education required for adult middle-class status, which has caused ever larger numbers of middle-class youth to attend coeducational colleges. Significantly, better-educated males engage in premarital sex with far fewer partners than do less-educated males, and presumably with females they intend to marry.

This deviation from the accepted sexual code on the part of the middle class is far more important than any deviation, however extreme, by the "lower class." As the custodian of American morals, the middle class is in a better position to legitimate its deviant practices. For example, pornography seems to be primarily a middle-class (male) phenomenon, and the general relaxation of legal prohibitions on it has a class base.

However, "lower-class" men (and women, where the reference is applicable) tend to accept middle-class definitions of sexual respectability. They distinguish between women one does and does not marry, are more likely to condemn deviations from the legitimate sexual code, are less likely to vary their sexual techniques than the middle class, and tend to accept the definitions of sexual and physical attractiveness of the classes above them. The double standard—the belief that men are more sexual and therefore should have more sexual freedom—is also more prevalent among the "lower class." Despite the more matter-of-fact attitude toward sex characteristic of the "lower class," its members tend to derive less satisfaction from sexual relations than do middle-class couples. Research has revealed considerable differences in how the middle and lower (working) classes view marital sex. James Henslin has summarized these differences, also asking us to note that middle-class males and females are more in agreement about sex than lower- (working)-class males and females.[4]

The illegitimacy rate in the United States varies inversely by social class with a particularly high rate among lower-class African Americans, a rate that reflects the unemployment plight of black males at this level. The number of abortions rose quickly after laws prohibiting them were struck down in 1973 reaching one and one-half million per year by 1980 and holding at that figure ever since. We have no data on how abortion varies by social class though we can assume that the further up the class ladder one goes, the more likely women are to abort unwanted pregnancies, especially since public funding for abortion has been drastically curtailed.

Class and Marriage

From the beginning of the twentieth century until the 1960s, Americans married at increasingly earlier ages. Since the 1960s this trend has reversed itself, largely in keeping with the growth of college attendance and economic hardship. These two causes have affected the classes differently: Greater college attendance by the middle class has delayed marriage for its members and economic hardship has delayed marriage for the lower classes. Nonetheless, age at marriage varies directly with class, the children of the upper classes marrying later largely because of the education required for adult economic roles. Another class-related aspect of marital behavior is that Americans tend to marry within their own class (as measured by residential closeness, education, occupation of breadwinner in family of origin, or occupation of spouses), and to marry within their own religion, ethnic group, and race.[5] The belief that American men marry women from a lower class than their own, and that women do the opposite, was questioned long ago.[6] Nevertheless, it would appear that the upper class has the fewest unmarried men and the most unmarried women while the lower class has the most unmarried men and the fewest unmarried women.

The hoary belief (found in many sociology textbooks) that marriages between individuals of different class backgrounds tend to be unstable appears to be an old wives' tale. In any case, one study found no empirical basis for this belief; indeed, it found limited evidence that marriages between low-origin males and high-origin females were remarkably free of divorce.[7]

Before the 1960s women acquired their adult status through marriage. This presented a problem for middle- and upper-class parents—their daughters had to marry someone of either superior or equal class status in order to avoid downward mobility. In a caste society, marriage is carefully confined within caste boundaries, but in a class society marriage can (theoretically) take place across ethnic and class lines. Thus, education is a threat to upper- and middle-class families in that it mixes the sexes across ethnic and class lines and creates the possibility that a female will marry outside such boundaries. A college campus, while a threat, also serves as an opportunity for middle-class girls to meet middle-class or upwardly mobile boys. It provides a means, in other words, to solve what John Finley Scott calls the "Brahman problem": the shortage of suitable marriage partners for high-status females and the competition they face from those in the classes below them. The college sorority, Scott argues, is an ascriptive mechanism by means of which parents can channel their daughters' attention away from males in the lower classes and into paths that lead to marriages suitable on both ethnic and class grounds.[8]

The importance of sororities has declined with the advent of contemporary feminism. Women are now striving for class status in their own right. Nonetheless, the channeling of behavior so that the right sort of people meet and marry still takes place through class-based educational (and other) structures.

Commentators on American marriage have identified several class-related variations in the basic structure of monogamous marriage:

1. The companion marriage—largely an upper-class phenomenon
2. The partner marriage—largely a middle-class phenomenon
3. The "husband-wife" or "working-class" marriage—largely a working- and lower-class phenomenon with a number of subvariations

LeMasters and Rubin have provided rich (and disturbing) portraits of working-class marriages, ranging from higher-skilled, better-paid, and more work-satisfied construction workers to lower-level, blue-collar workers and racial-ethnic minorities.[9] The lives of working-class spouses are differentiated by sex. Men lead their lives largely outside the home (at work and with male friends) while women lead their lives largely inside the home and with relatives. All this may be changing as more wives are forced into the labor market. Middle-class spouses may also lead differentiated lives, especially when only the husband works, but they have far more in common (about sex, raising children, planning for the future) than do working-class spouses. In another study, David Halle has provided a variation of working-class marriage. He too found much that LeMasters and Rubin had found. But because his study group consisted of well-paid workers at an automated chemical plant, the cleavage between the sexes and differences with white-collar workers were not as extreme as those found by LeMasters and Rubin.[10]

These class-based models are general in nature and one must be careful in using them. For example, the middle-class male has been found to be dominant vis-à-vis his wife in the selection of friends.[11] Males in the lower classes, though believing in and claiming authoritarian marital and family statuses, exercise less effective authority over their wives and children than men in the classes above them. By and large, it appears that the higher a man's position in the class system, the greater his dominance of the family (though a working wife curtails her husband's dominance at all class levels).[12]

The influx of women into the labor force has changed marital relations. The breadwinner ethic has declined and a number of class-based variations have appeared. Among the broad working classes, double breadwinners are an economic necessity. Marital stress here is still high because of sex-segregated lives and because women, in addition to working, are still saddled with housework and the raising of children. Working wives among the middle and upper middle classes have produced changes in the pattern found among early researchers. At one time middle-class wives were often "gainfully unemployed"—that is, the wife was often an adjunct to the husband's career. In a classic analysis, William H. Whyte outlined how the wives of business executives were incorporated into their husbands' companies. Wives were often interviewed when their husbands were being hired; they were expected to get along and to accept their spouses' long hours and frequent moves; and they were integrated into the company by such means as prizes, company socials, and norms governing breeding, deportment, and consumption, including place of residence. In effect, the wife became an "extra employee."[13] Women were also prominent in voluntary activities of all kinds, activities that closely correlated with class background.[14] The women's movement has brought important changes in this pattern. This movement, overwhelmingly middle and upper class in its goals and achievements, has produced the two-career marriage (for the middle-class nature of the women's movement, see Chapter 19).

Early studies indicated that marital satisfaction rose with class position. However, class differences in marital satisfaction have declined since the 1960s, largely because easy divorce has eliminated many unhappy marriages. Since the lower classes divorce more and the upper classes have higher expectations of marriage, one can still argue that marital satisfaction rises with class status, even when satisfaction scores are similar.[15]

Evidence shows that at all class levels the roles of husband and wife are deeply differentiated,[16] in effect making man-women and husband-wife relationships difficult. What data exist indicate that role segregation is deepest in working- and lower-class marriages, and suggest less strongly that there is significant role segregation by sex in upper-class families. By contrast, middle-class families tend toward the partnership type of marriage. All this seems to be changing, however. Davis and Robinson have uncovered a pronounced trend among all men and women, married and single, toward individualism.[17]

Class, Birthrates, and Birth Control

Birthrates are related inversely to social class (using family income and woman's education).[18] Class differentials also appear among black and Spanish-origin Americans.[19] There appears to be no deviation from national class-related patterns in fertility among religious groups.[20]

Class, Family, Socialization, and Personality

In 1958 Urie Bronfenbrenner published a paper that reconciled the serious contradictions that had appeared in research into class child-raising practices over a period of twenty-five years.[21] Bronfenbrenner showed that working-class mothers had been more permissive than middle-class mothers in the 1930s, but that after World War II this relationship was reversed: middle-class mothers became progressively more permissive, surpassing working-class mothers in this regard. The greater leniency of middle-class parents toward the expressed needs and desires of their children is accompanied by higher expectations of their children and the consistent use of reasoning and "love-oriented" techniques of discipline, techniques research has shown to be more effective than physical punishment in controlling and orienting children. Greater permissiveness, in other words, has not lessened the greater amount of normative social control exercised by middle-class parents.[22]

One way to illustrate the difference in "home atmosphere" between middle- and working-class families is to contrast their value orientations.

Using a representative national sample of all men employed in civilian occupations (that is, compared with samples drawn from Washington, D.C., and Turin, Italy), Melvin Kohn established the preeminent role of class (education and occupation) in developing the strikingly different value orientations of middle-class parents (independence) and working-class parents (conformity).[23] The single most important factor in this difference, according to Kohn, is that higher occupations (higher in the sense that they allow for greater independence) tend to emphasize self-direction whereas lower occupations tend to emphasize conformity to external authority. Kohn's findings, it should be emphasized, hold true regardless of age of children, sex, religion, race, region, or urban-rural location.

Class, Family, and the Transmission of Abilities and Values to Children

Studies show that parents socialize children differently by class. Do these differences result in different personalities and behaviors among children? In an early search for an answer to this question, Schneider and Lysgaard developed the concept of *deferred gratification pattern,* the tendency to postpone satisfactions and renounce impulses in favor of long-range benefits.[24] Youngsters who exhibit the deferred gratification pattern (or the Protestant-bourgeois ethic) would be less prone than others to physical violence, free sexual expression through intercourse, and free spending; they would be more likely to stay in school than go to work and to remain dependent on parents. In their analysis of a national sample of high school students, Schneider and Lysgaard found a strong relationship between student acceptance of the deferred gratification pattern and class origin—those further up the class ladder being more likely to accept it than those further down. Of special interest is a study done in Detroit, undertaken in the early 1950s, which suggested strongly that as the United States transforms itself from an entrepreneurial to a welfare bureaucratic society, a shift was taking place in its general pattern of child training. Evidence showed that those in "entrepreneurial" occupations continue to raise their children according to the deferred gratification pattern, but that families in "bureaucratic" occupations place less stress on strict impulse management. Because the American occupational structure was undergoing a shift toward bureaucratic forms of work, the authors concluded that this trend would be increasingly reflected in child training patterns.[25]

Basil Bernstein has provided an important analysis of personality differentials by studying ways in which the children of different classes develop linguistic skills. Bernstein distinguishes between *formal* (or elaborated) and *public* (or restricted) languages. Middle-class children acquire a language (less vocabulary than sentence organization) that facilitates comprehension of a wide range of symbolic and social relationships. The lower-class child, on the other hand, acquires a language with a lower order of conceptualization and causality and a greater emphasis on affective responses to immediate stimuli. Consequently, concludes Bernstein, the middle-class youngster who knows both languages is able to respond to and master a wider variety of symbolic and social situations than the youngster whose personality is environed, indeed constituted, by a public language.[26]

A follow-up of Bernstein's theory lends support to his supposition that the various classes impart different language codes to their children.[27] Using a sample of 163 black mothers and their four-year-old children drawn from four different class levels, this analysis focused on the communication process between mother and child. Judged in a number of different ways, the communication process was distinctly different in the various classes, the top classes providing their children with a greater range of linguistic skills than the lower classes. The relevance of this research to learning and education is obvious, and we will touch on it again later when we explore the relationship between class and education. Indeed, we will find class influence on personality reflected in a wide variety of phenomena: marital stability, mental health, IQ, values and beliefs in general, and political orientation.

In an important extension of his work on the relation between occupation and personality, Kohn and his collaborators have shown that occupational stratification not only affects parents' values and socialization practices, but that these are also clearly related to the personality and self-direction of children, especially as they pertain to education.[28] As we will see in Chapter 9, the ability of the upper classes to socialize their children for success in school is an important aspect of class power and perpetuation.

Class and Family Values

The extended family is a group of related nuclear families living and working together as a single structure in the performance of most social functions. It does not exist in this form in the United States, except in isolated instances. Cooperation among related nuclear families does exist, however. Within the upper class, for example, a "voluntary" sense of kinship among related nuclear families persists and is focused around the common ownership of large and varied forms of property. Among working- and lower-class families, it is often necessary for parents and young married couples, or aged parents and married couples, to live together. There is also a strong patriarchal preference among working-class males and among some Roman Catholic ethnic groups, although this tradition is not effective in practice. The matriarchal family common among poor blacks lacks normative support but has in practice helped blacks to prevail in slavery and postslavery class society. And, to further qualify the notion that the United States is made up of autonomous, isolated nuclear families, research has found considerable financial and other help, socializing, recreational and ceremonial activities, and positive kin feelings among related nuclear families.[29]

Our knowledge of the upper-class family is limited, but the partial studies that exist all point in the same direction.[30] Some upper-class families place value on the longevity of their family line, their accomplishments as a family line, and loyalty and cooperation among the various nuclear families that constitute a stem or general family line. Such families (old wealth, old family) must be distinguished from other upper-class families that have as much or even more money but lack a family tradition (*nouveau riche, parvenu* families). This distinction is expressed by the terms *upper-upper* and *lower-upper*, used by Warner. Upper-upper-class families have been found in one community after another, and the existence of an urban upper-upper class is attested to by *The Social Register*.[31] Such families enjoy financial security because of family trust funds, high income because of their occupations and savings, and high standards of consumption; they exercise close supervision over their children by means of servants, summer homes, private schools, and controlled socializing.

Middle-class and working-class families all exhibit significant amounts of interaction between relatives: visits, communication on ceremonial occasions, help with children, stabilization of broken families, and economic aid either bilaterally or between generations. The reasons for extended kin relations in an achievement society and for a possible increase in such relations have been advanced by Ira Reiss: about twenty years have been added to life expectancy during this century, increasing the number of families in which three generations are living simultaneously; the increased length of required education makes more young couples dependent on their parents; the undisputed primacy of the independent nuclear family makes it possible for kin (and related religious-ethnic) ties to exist without posing a threat to achievement-individualist values; and it may be that the nuclear family (the main focus of the individual's emotional life) yields such sparse psychic satisfaction that emotional need tends to enforce extended family relations. And a point made by Sussman and Burchinal should not be overlooked: modern means of transport and communication make it relatively easy for geographically separated nuclear families to maintain kinship relations.

The significance of extended kinship ties for class analysis has to be approached by means of indirect evidence. Extended family relations account for a much larger proportion of the total interaction of working-class families than other families. The classes above the working class, on the other hand, have significantly higher rates of participation in friendship groups and in formal voluntary associations.[32] The extended kin pattern in the working class has been documented in a number of studies and forms the basis for the belief in the existence of a distinct working-class subculture.

Class and Family Stability

Class is a good predictor of family stability. Overall, the higher in the class system a couple is, the better its chances are of avoiding family disruption through premature death, separation, or divorce. But the influx of women into the labor force after 1960 has changed the relation between class and family stability: women who can support themselves (that is, enter the class system as individuals) do not have to endure unhappy marriages. Nonetheless, divorce rates are still highest among the economically marginal classes.[33]

One of the more interesting attempts at a general explanation of marital failure, with important implications for class society, is Kirkpatrick's concept of *ethical inconsistency*.[34] Kirkpatrick argues that the United States has three general marital models, defined in terms of the wife's role: the wife-mother, partner, and companion types. Each is related to a specific class and each specifies a different set of rights and duties for the wife. But because all three types are well known beyond the confines of their classes of origin (and because of the society's general encouragement of self-interest), women tend to adopt aspects of each that are in their interest, whereas men select aspects in their interest. The result is that marriage at all levels is heavily burdened by contradictory role expectations. Men expect their wives to be hardworking drudges who are also responsible, efficient, pleasant to be with, and glamorous, while women expect credit and respect for household work, economic security, a say in family decisions, and certain forms of indulgence because they are women (romance, luxuries, courtesy). Too much should not be made of Kirkpatrick's limited study, but its theme is reminiscent of Merton's explanation of deviance, which helps to place marital instability in a broad social context and to bring it within the orbit of anomie theory.[35] In any case, America's universal encouragement of self-interest, together with its multiple class-related marriage models (widely known through the mass media), makes it highly unlikely that many married individuals at any class level will experience the stability and satisfactions of role complementarity in marriage.

Actually, a society based on competitive individualism is not conducive to a stable family life at any class level. The deeper reality of American individualism is the relative scarcity of prizes and rewards even in the best of times. Competition hides the fact that few win, most stand still, and many lose. These outcomes occur from the way in which economic activity is structured. When the economy slows down, as it did from the late 1960s on, the negative impact on the family increases.

The overall experience with the American economy during the post–World War II period has transformed the American family. Given our laissez-faire society (no economic planning, toleration of high unemployment, the absolute right of capital to move, and poor public services), the United States now has a highly stratified set of households diversified into stable and unstable families, two-parent and one-parent families, unrelated individuals, and the homeless. Along with these changes has come the feminization of poverty—the large increase in one-parent households run by women with inadequate income.

Seen from a different perspective, little evidence exists that the lower classes have adopted middle-class values and behaviors in marriage and family, any more than they have in other areas of life. In other words, the theory of convergence, the alleged movement toward classlessness, and the embourgeoisment thesis are wrong.

CLASS AND DIFFERENTIALS IN HEALTH, LIFE EXPECTANCY, AND MENTAL DISABILITY

The American Health-Care System

The United States has an abnormal health-care system compared to all other capitalist societies. The American health-care system began as and has remained a private-profit system providing different health care to the various classes and costing far more than any other developed capitalist society for health results that at best are the same.

The United States spends huge amounts of public money (and a larger percentage of its GDP than any other developed capitalist society) on its health-care system, but because there is no effective counterweight to the providers of services and products, prices, incomes, and profits are pretty much set by those who receive these funds. All in all, the medical establishment has succeeded in obtaining public financing without public supervision, direction, or control (actually, it decides on how public authorities behave). And to make matters worse there is no direct positive relation between money spent on curative medicine and better health.[36]

All other developed capitalist countries have national health insurance (private health care financed by comprehensive public insurance) or socialized medicine (free public health care), and costs are contained and standards maintained because the government acts as a monitor and negotiator on behalf of the public.[37]

The American health-care system (doctors, hospitals, drug companies, medical equipment suppliers, and various special services) absorbs 12 percent of the nation's annual output, about twice as much as any other developed capitalist society. What this means is that under the laissez-faire American political economy, the health-care system is an important part of the overall system of American-style capitalism, a system that channels large sums of money upward in violation of legitimizing norms. Assuming that 5 percent of health-care income is illegitimate, this means that 300 billion dollars (5 percent of our 6-trillion-dollar annual output) is being taken illegitimately, enough to balance the budget and provide health care for the uninsured.

Class, Health, and Life Expectancy

Many studies over the past decades have shown a relation between social class, on the one hand, and health and life expectancy on the other. Studies tend to refer to upper and lower classes, but all agree that the lower classes suffer more from all diseases (and have much higher rates of infant mortality). And the lower classes, whether judged by income, occupation, or education (or all together), live significantly fewer years than do the upper classes.[38]

The lower classes are also more likely to be uninsured and the uninsured do not utilize health services. By and large, the lower classes have poorer health and life expectancy because of their class status and not because they are not getting medical services (the absence of or inadequate health care merely aggravates their problems). The lower classes are more subject to work-related diseases, disabilities, and deaths. Their lives are more stressful, including the health-debilitating stress of unemployment.[39] And they know less about how to maintain health, and they suffer both from deprivation (hunger affects millions) and from the wrong foods and other style-of-life habits.[40]

Over and above all these factors is another factor that shapes the health-care system by social class—the health-care delivery system itself. As Dutton points out, the health-care delivery system is oriented toward the middle and upper classes, and barriers to using health-care facilities are an important part of the low use of health services by the poor.[41]

Class and Mental Illness

Research has discovered a direct correlation between class and amounts of mental illness, certain kinds of mental illness, and the type and effectiveness of professional treatment received. And it is also clear that the higher the class, the more sympathetic, positive, and tolerant the attitude toward mental disturbance and the greater the likelihood that deviant behavior will be attributed to mental illness.[42] The relation between social class and mental illness received little attention from social scientists until the pioneering community analysis undertaken by August B. Hollingshead and Frederick C. Redlich during the 1950s.[43] In their sophisticated empirical study of greater New Haven, Connecticut (at that time a metropolitan center of approximately 240,000), the authors posed five hypotheses:

1. The prevalence of treated mental illness is related significantly to an individual's position in the class structure.
2. The types of diagnosed psychiatric disorders are connected significantly to the class structure.
3. The kind of psychiatric treatment administered by psychiatrists is associated with the patient's position in the class structure.
4. Social and psychodynamic factors in the development of psychiatric disorders are correlative to an individual's position in the class structure.
5. Mobility in the class structure is associated with the development of psychiatric difficulties.

The data supported a clear affirmative answer to each hypothesis.[44] A follow-up study of the same patients ten years later showed that class is significantly related to the long-term outcome of treatment and to the adjustment of former patients in the community: the higher the class, the less likelihood that a patient would receive custodial hospital care and the greater likelihood that his or her adjustment to the community would be successful.[45]

The most ambitious investigation of mental health in American social science, a study of a midtown Manhattan residential area of 175,000 inhabitants, offers important corroborating evidence of an inverse relation between class and mental illness.[46] A number of other aspects of this study are of special interest: the authors suggest strongly that midtown Manhattan is typical of segments of other highly urbanized centers across the United States and that therefore their findings are not germane only to that locality. Second, the study attempts (by means of a questionnaire evaluated by psychiatrists) to diagnose the mental health of the entire population (and not to base its analysis on treated patients, as the New Haven study did). Third, the Midtown Manhattan Study distinguished between the class of the individuals studied and that of their parents, so that the impact of each on mental health could be studied.

While emphasizing that they are in no way implying that sociocultural processes account for all mental illnesses, the authors conclude (1) that class-of-origin and one's own class are both significantly related directly to mental health or, conversely, that both are inversely related to mental illness, with an especially high rate at the bottom levels; (2) that social mobility is associated with a higher level of mental health (which is directly at odds with the general belief that the opposite is true); (3) that there are no differences in the frequency of some forms of mental illness (schizophrenia, anxiety-tension, excessive intake) and intellectual, affective, somatic, characterological, and interpersonal disturbances; and (4) that the lower the class the less likely that those suffering from mental illness will receive treatment.[47]

Kessler compared eight mental studies from 1967 to 1976 and found a relation between socioeconomic status and psychological distress. Kessler made fine distinctions among such variables as income, occupational status, education, and job conditions, and concluded that we need to know more about these and other factors before we can decide between the selection explanation (individuals with psychological problems are selected out by the society and drift downward) and the social causation model (experiences at various class levels cause mental illness).[48] Kessler's distinction between individual and social factors is misleading. All human behavior is social, including "individuals with psychological problems."

Analysts of schizophrenia (inability to select relevant stimuli or to focus sustained attention on the important stimuli in given situations) have directly challenged the claim that the relation between low class status and schizophrenia (and mental illness in general) is because defective individuals sink in the class hierarchy. Though they caution that more work remains, these analysts found clear evidence that significant numbers of normal individuals in jobs characterized by noise, heat, cold, fumes, or physical hazards became schizophrenic.[49]

Mental health experts were disheartened by the failure to cure mental patients through hospitalization and were encouraged by evidence that what patients needed were structured social experiences. During the 1960s and 1970s hundreds of thousands of mental patients were released, presumably to go to community homes where they could learn to live productive lives. As these homes were never built, many of these patients ended up as America's homeless.

Preventing Mental Illness

The treatment of the mentally ill has not been marked by much success—indeed, suspicion has been cast on the basic ability of professionals to even identify the mentally ill. The most promising lead on how to treat the mentally ill and on how to prevent it in the first place is to construct a livable society. Instead of focusing on the best way to treat victims, research suggests that we should instead concentrate on eliminating social stress, false expectations, false promises, denied opportunities, and anomic groups and institutions.

Class and Mental Retardation

Researchers have established a link between class and mental retardation (organic impairment). Presumably, the extremely few naturally defective babies are randomly distributed on the class ladder. However, the bulk of all other defective human beings are products of an environment of poverty: the fetus is injured because the mother is in poor health, received an unskilled abortion, or is not under a doctor's care; or the child is organically impaired by illness, malnutrition, ingestion of lead paint, rat bites, or the like. Of some significance in understanding the class nature of mental retardation is the fact that its incidence in the United States is much higher than in England, Denmark, and Sweden, which have national maternal and child-care programs.[50]

Of perhaps greater significance is the growing suspicion that many of the mentally retarded are not organically impaired at all. Hurley has argued that at least 85 percent of those designated mentally retarded are simply poor people who have been damaged by their experience in a society with a strong propensity for using the middle class as the yardstick of normality and for labeling those who deviate from its norms as genetic defectives.[51]

In an interesting analysis, Farber has argued that modern society has restricted access to valuable social positions by progressively raising standards in all fields, thereby creating a surplus population (the mentally retarded, the unemployed, the mentally ill, the disabled, the criminal, the functionally illiterate, and so on), which he estimates at as high as 20 to 25 percent of the total population. Farber reports that the best estimate of the proportion of mentally retarded in the United States is between 2 and 3 percent (between 4 million and 6 million people).[52] Despite the vitality of the biopsychological tradition, which tends to stress a natural distribution of intelligence and ability in general, it appears that our mentally retarded are victims of the American class system.

The social creation of mental retardation has been demonstrated by Mercer in her analysis of the relation between mental retardation and education. Mercer suggests that her analysis is applicable to other social systems besides education: the family, the neighborhood, law enforcement, welfare, churches, and public institutions for the retarded. Mercer reports that empirical studies in California show that Spanish-speaking and black students tend to be assigned to special classes (thus beginning the process of becoming mental retardates) at significantly higher rates than English-speaking white students, *even white students with similar scores on intelligence tests.*[53] And in a full-scale study of Riverside, California, a city of 85,000, Mercer again documents the class-ethnic-racial basis of mental retardation. Of further value in this study is Mercer's argument that there is a sociocultural (middle class) bias in the evaluation of what is considered normal intelligence, and that this bias is deeply institutionalized in the individualistic clinical approach of professional diagnosticians and in the interlocking network of organizations that allegedly uncover and treat mental retardation—especially the public schools, public-welfare-vocational rehabilitation agencies, law enforcement agencies, medical facilities, the Department of Mental Hygiene, and private organizations concerned with mental retardation.[54]

Class and Learning Disability

The general class bias of American society applies to learning disability. James Carrier has shown that biased professional and political judgments create much of what is called *learning disability.* But Carrier goes much further. In a brilliant synthesis of existing research, he connects class bias about learning disability to similarly biased naturalistic arguments about a wide range of alleged deviations from normality: IQ, educational potential, mental retardation, mental illness, physical disabilities, sexual deviation, being gifted, and crime. And he also shows how professional judgments by psychologists, guidance counselors, medical researchers, teachers, and educators combine with economic and family interests to produce political pressure that results in the legalization of the alleged deviation from the normal. The overall result, Carrier argues, is class society, not nature, creating inequality and then reproducing itself.[55]

SUMMARY

The hierarchy of economic classes correlates with the distribution of family, personality, and health benefits.

Attitudes toward sex have grown more permissive in recent decades and do not vary much by class. However, sexual behavior does vary by class. Men and women in the middle classes (and above) are behaving similarly, but their first sexual experiences occur later than do those of working class males and females (who are also becoming more alike in their sexual behavior). Premarital sex among the middle (and upper) classes is more clearly associated with romance, commitment, and intention to marry than is true among the lower classes. Both upper and lower classes also have different orientations toward marital sex.

Lower classes have higher rates of illegitimacy than do the upper classes. The abortion controversy is related to class, with those opposed defending traditional marital family values while those in favor tending to be women (and men) in the middle and upper classes who want to combine career and motherhood.

Popular culture provides class-oriented views of sex, marriage, and family.

Americans are marrying later, but age of marriage varies by social class, with the middle and upper classes marrying later because of the need for longer years of schooling.

Americans marry within their own class, ethnic and religious group, and by race.

American marriages are sex-segregated at all class levels but more so at the lower levels.

Males in the upper classes are more effectively dominant in their marriages than males in the lower classes, but all power relations are equalized significantly if wives work.

Birthrates vary inversely by class but not as much as in the past.

The upper classes socialize their children for independence and provide them with the personality-cognitive skills·that ensure success in school.

Family values are important to Americans at all class levels, but the realization of these values varies somewhat by class. Important differences exist by class in marital stability, with the lower classes more unstable.

Economic change and the high divorce rate have diversified the American household.

All in all there is no convergence in sexual or family behavior among the various classes.

Physical health and life expectancy vary by social class, with the upper classes enjoying better health and longer life spans. Economic stress, dangerous workplaces, and poorer living styles are the main reasons for these differences.

Working- and lower-class women receive poorer health care and are also subject to sexist (inferior) medical care.

Mental retardation, mental illness, and learning disability are also related to class. The lower classes are physically impaired by poverty and they also suffer from being falsely defined as subnormal by the upper classes, who have a stake in keeping valued statuses scarce.

As with physical illness or disability, health-care treatment for those with personality problems varies by social class.

The pronounced relation between the hierarchy of economic class and the family, personality, and health benefits of households at each level is clear. This relation also means that parents in the upper classes are able to give their children important advantages in the struggle to join tomorrow's class system. The implications of this causal process for class power and perpetuation over the generations will become even clearer as we trace the relation between class and education.

NOTES

1. The relationships between class and sainthood, class and the sending of Christmas cards, and class and nudism will not be touched on here. For those who are interested in the upper-class bias in the selection of saints, see Katherine George and Charles H. George, "Roman Catholic Sainthood and Social Status," in Reinhard Bendix and Seymour M. Lipset, eds., *Class, Status, and Power: Social Stratification in Comparative Perspective,* 2nd ed. (New York: Free Press, 1966), pp. 394–401; for those who want some shrewd ideas and insights into the middle-class (and upper-class) basis and the upward mobility aspirations behind the practice of sending Christmas cards, see Sheila K. Johnson, "Sociology of Christmas Cards," in William Feigelman, ed., *Sociology Full Circle* (New York: Praeger, 1972), pp. 158–164; for those who are interested in the middle-class basis of nudism, see Fred Ilfeld, Jr., and Roger Lauer, *Social Nudism in America* (New Haven, CT: College and University Press, 1964), pp. 69–73.

2. Ira L. Reiss and Gary R. Lee, *Family Systems in America,* 4th ed. (Fort Worth, TX: Harcourt Brace, 1988), ch. 7.
3. Martin S. Weinberg and Colin J. Williams, "Sexual Embourgeoisment? Social Class and Sexual Activity: 1938–1970," *American Sociological Review* 45 (February 1980):33–48.
4. James M. Henslin, ed., *Marriage and Family in a Changing Society,* 2nd ed. (New York: Free Press, 1985), p. 346.
5. For a valuable review of the literature and a sophisticated analysis of cohorts in 1962 and 1973, who had been married 10 years or less, to determine the relative importance of class (father's occupation) and education when individuals marry, see Matthijs Kalmijn, "Status Homogamy in the United States," *American Journal of Sociology* 97 (September 1991):496–523. Kalmijn found that education and class were both important with education more important than class (with the latter fading somewhat over the two decades). Kalmijn's analysis, conducted in the status-attainment mode, would have been different if education had been defined as essentially a class phenomenon (see Chapter 9). The evidence uncovered would not then have been interpreted as the march of achievement over ascription.
6. Zick Rubin, "Do American Women Marry Up?," *American Sociological Review* 33 (October 1968):750–760.
7. Norval D. Glenn, Sue Keir Hoppe, and David Weirer, "Social Class Heterogamy and Marital Success: A Study of the Empirical Adequacy of a Textbook Generalization," *Social Problems* 24, no. 4 (April 1974):539–550.
8. John Finley Scott, "The American College Sorority: Its Role in Class and Ethnic Endogamy," *American Sociological Review* 30 (August 1965):514–527.
9. E. E. LeMasters, *Blue-Collar Aristocrats* (Madison: University of Wisconsin Press, 1975), and Lillian Breslow Rubin, *Worlds of Pain: Life in the Working Class Family* (New York: Basic Books, 1976), and *Families in the Fault Line: America's Working Class Speaks About the Family, the Economy, Race, and Ethnicity* (New York: HarperCollins, 1994).
10. David Halle, *America's Working Mass: Work, Home, and Politics Among Blue-Collar Property-Home-Owners* (Chicago: University of Chicago Press, 1984), ch. 3.
11. Nicholas Babchuk and Alan B. Bates, "The Primary Relations of Middle-Class Couples: A Study in Male Dominance," *American Sociological Review* 28 (June 1963):377–384.
12. For a summary of the literature, see Ira L. Reiss and Gary R. Lee, *Family Systems in America,* pp. 224–229.
13. William H. Whyte, Jr., "The Wives of Management," *Fortune* 44 (October 1951):86ff., and "The Corporation and the Wife," *Fortune* 44 (November 1951):109ff. Rosabeth Moss Kanter's case study of a large corporation, *Men and Women of the Corporation* (New York: Basic Bocks, 1977), reports (pp. 116–122) that the practice of making the wife a member of the corporation team is still prevalent. A claim that this practice has been curtailed by the women's movement may be found in *Fortune* (August 20, 1984), "The Uneasy Life of the Corporate Spouse," pp. 26–32.
14. For an analysis of the voluntary behavior of upper-class women, see G. William Domhoff, *The Higher Circles: The Governing Class in America* (New York: Random House, 1970), ch. 2, and Susan S. Ostrander, *Women of the Upper Class* (Philadelphia: Temple University Press, 1984).
15. Ira L. Reiss and Gary R. Lee, *Family Systems in America,* pp. 192–195.

16. For differences between the sexes in upper-middle-class American marriages (based on informal conversations), see John F. Cuber and Peggy B. Harrof, *The Significant Americans: A Study of Sexual Behavior Among the Affluent* (New York: Appleton-Century, 1965). The sharp separation between masculine and feminine roles among the working and lower class has been documented by, among others, E. E. LeMasters, *Blue Collar Aristocrats* (Madison: University of Wisconsin, 1975), and Lillian Breslow Rubin, *Worlds of Pain: Life in the Working Class Family* (New York: Basic Books, 1976).
17. Nancy J. Davis and Robert V. Robinson, "Class Identification of Men and Women in the 1970s and 1980s," *American Sociological Review* 53 (February 1988):103–112.
18. *Statistical Abstract of the United States, 1995,* Table 100.
19. Donald J. Bogue, assisted by George W. Rumsey, Odalia Ho, David Hartmann, and Albert Woolbright, *The Population of the United States: Historical Trends and Future Projections* (New York: Free Press, 1985), Table 6–23A.
20. Ibid., pp. 659–662.
21. "Socialization and Social Class Through Time and Space," in E. E. Maccoby, T. M. Newcomb, and E. L. Hartley, eds., *Readings in Social Psychology,* 3rd ed. (New York: Henry Holt, 1958); reprinted in Reinhard Bendix and Seymour M. Lipset, eds., *Class, Status and Power: Social Stratification in Comparative Perspective,* 2nd ed. (New York: Free Press, 1966), pp. 362–377.
22. E. E. LeMasters, *Blue-Collar Aristocrats* (Madison: University of Wisconsin Press, 1975), ch. 7, and L. B. Rubin, *Worlds of Pain* (New York: Basic Books, 1976), ch. 7 and *passim,* give rich details of parenting among both skilled and unskilled workers. For a review of the literature on socialization, see Viktor Gecas, "The Influence of Class on Socialization," in Wesley R. Burr, Reuben Hill, P. Ivan Nye, and Ira L. Reiss, eds., *Contemporary Theories About the Family* (New York: Free Press, 1979), pp. 365–404.
23. Melvin L. Kohn, *Class and Conformity: A Study in Values* (Homewood, IL: Dorsey Press, 1969). Kohn and his associates have reaffirmed the power of occupation, especially its complexity, over personality and cognitive outlook; for a variety of essays in this area, see Melvin L. Kohn and Carmi Schooler with the collaboration of Joanne Miller, Karen A. Miller, Carrie Schoenbach, and Ronald Schoenberg, *Work and Personality: An Inquiry Into the Impact of Social Stratification* (Norwood, NJ: Ablex, 1983). For a further discussion of Kohn's work into the relation between work and personality, see "Class, Personality, and World View" in Chapter 11 of this text.
24. Louis Schneider and Sverre Lysgaard, "The Deferred Gratification Pattern: A Preliminary Study," *American Sociological Review* 18 (April 1953):142–149.
25. Daniel R. Miller and Guy E. Swanson, *The Changing American Parent* (New York: John Wiley & Sons, 1958).
26. Basil Bernstein, "Social Class and Linguistic Development: A Theory of Social Learning," in A. H. Halsey, Jean Floud, and C. Arnold Anderson, eds., *Education, Economy, and Society* (New York: Free Press, 1961), pp. 288–314.
27. Robert D. Hess and Virginia C. Shipman, "Early Experience and the Socialization of Cognitive Modes in Children," *Child Development* 36 (December 1965):869–886.
28. Melvin L. Kohn, Kazimierz M. Slomczynski, and Carrie Schoenbach, "Social Stratification and the Transmission of Values in the Family: A Cross-National Assessment," *Sociological Forum* 1, no. 1 (Winter 1986):73–102.

29. For a review of the literature, see Ira L. Reiss, *Family Systems in America,* pp. 413–431.
30. For an invaluable summary of what we know about upper-class families, see Frederic Cople Jaher, *The Urban Establishment: Upper Strata in Boston, New York, Charleston, Chicago, and Los Angeles* (Urbana: University of Illinois Press, 1982).
31. Susan A. Ostrander's book, *Women of the Upper Class* (Philadelphia: Temple University Press, 1984), shows that the women of the upper class spend much time and energy in maintaining family tradition.
32. See Chapter 13.
33. For the nuances of the changing relation between class and family stability, see Ira L. Reiss and Gary R. Lee, *Family Systems in America,* pp. 291–295.
34. Clifford Kirkpatrick, "The Measurement of Ethical Consistency in Marriage," *International Journal of Ethics* 46 (July 1935):444–460.
35. For Merton's theory of anomie, see "Class, Universal Goals, and Deviant Behavior" in Chapter 16.
36. For a summary of research in this area, see John B. McKinlay and Sonja M. McKinlay, "Medical Measures and the Decline of Mortality" (1977), in Peter Conrad and Rochelle Kern, eds., *The Sociology of Health and Illness,* 4th ed. (New York: St. Martin's Press, 1994), pp. 10–23.
37. For an analysis of Canada's health-care system, which provides health outcomes equal to the United States at considerably less cost, see Theodore R. Marmor and Jerry L. Mashaw, "Canada's Health Insurance and Ours: The Real Lessons, the Big Choices," in Peter Conrad and Rochelle Kern, eds., *The Sociology of Health and Illness,* 4th ed. (New York: St. Martin's Press, 1994), pp. 470–480.
38. Some narrowing in the gap between the upper and lower classes occurred over much of the twentieth century but has now started to grow again, at least based on British data. See Richard G. Wilkinson, ed., *Class and Health: Research and Longitudinal Data* (London: Tavistock, 1986).
39. For a valuable analysis (by a leading authority on the blue-collar world) of stress at work among white blue-collar males, along with a picture of their physical and mental health and their fears about employment loss because of environmental protection, see Arthur B. Shostak, *Blue-Collar Stress* (Reading, MA: Addison-Wesley, 1980).
40. For a summary of the literature and a discussion, see S. Leonard Syme and Lisa F. Berkman, "Social Class, Susceptibility, and Sickness," and Karen David and Diane Rowland, "Uninsured and Underserved: Inequalities in Health Care in the United States," both in Peter Conrad and Rochelle Kern, eds., *The Sociology of Health and Illness: Critical Perspectives* (2nd ed.; New York: St. Martin's Press, 1986), Selections 2 and 22.
41. Diana B. Sutton, "Explaining the Low Use of Health Services by the Poor: Costs, Attitudes, or Delivery System?," *American Sociological Review* 43 (June 1978):348–368.
42. With regard to the latter point, see Judith Rabkin, "Public Attitudes Toward Mental Illness: A Review of the Literature," *Schizophrenia Bulletin* 10 (Fall 1974):21–22.
43. *Social Class and Mental Illness: A Community Study* (New York: John Wiley & Sons, 1958).
44. Data supporting the last two hypotheses are presented in Jerome K. Myers and

Bertram H. Roberts, *Family and Class Dynamics in Mental Illness* (New York: John Wiley & Sons, 1959).

45. Jerome K. Myers and Lee L. Bean, *A Decade Later: A Follow-up of Social Class and Mental Illness* (New York: John Wiley & Sons, 1968).
46. Leo Srole, Thomas S. Langner, Stanley T. Michael, Marvin K. Opler, and Thomas A. C. Rennie, *Mental Health in the Metropolis: The Midtown Manhattan Study* (New York: McGraw-Hill, 1962), ch. 11–13.
47. Our understanding of the nature of alcoholism and its relation to class is limited. We do know, however, that the diagnosis and treatment of alcoholism vary with class position and that this variation favors the upper classes (males); see Wolfgang Schmidt, Reginald G. Smart, and Marcia K. Moss, *Social Class and the Treatment of Alcoholism* (Toronto: University of Toronto Press, 1968).
48. Ronald C. Kessler, "A Disaggregation of the Relationship Between Socioeconomic Status and Psychological Distress," *American Sociological Review* 47 (December 1982):752–764.
49. Bruce G. Link, Bruce P. Dohrenwend, and Andrew E. Skodol, "Socioeconomic Status and Schizophrenia: Noisome Occupational Characteristics as a Risk Factor," *American Sociological Review* 51 (April 1986):242–258.
50. Rodger L. Hurley, ed., *Poverty and Mental Retardation: A Causal Relationship* (Trenton: New Jersey Department of Institutions and Agencies, 1968), especially ch. 2, Ronald Marlowe, "Poverty and Organic Impairment."
51. Ibid., introductory essay. *New York Times,* July 18, 1983, p. 1, reports that the number of newborns suffering from physical and mental disability doubled from the late 1950s to 1983.
52. Bernard Farber, *Mental Retardation: Its Social Context and Social Consequences* (Boston: Houghton Mifflin, 1968), ch. 1.
53. Jane R. Mercer, "Sociological Perspectives on Mild Mental Retardation," in H. Carl Haywood, ed., *Socio-Cultural Aspects of Mental Retardation* (New York: Appleton-Century-Crofts, 1970), pp. 378–391. This publication is an indispensable reference on mental retardation. The concluding summary by H. Carl Haywood is especially valuable.
54. Jane R. Mercer, *Labelling the Mentally Retarded* (Berkeley: University of California Press, 1973).
55. James G. Carrier, *Learning Disability: Social Class and the Construction of Inequality in American Education* (Westport, CT: Greenwood Press, 1986).

9
Class and Education

◆ ◆ ◆ ◆

◆ ◆ ◆ ◆

AMERICA'S FAITH IN EDUCATION: THE LIBERAL-FUNCTIONAL CONSENSUS

Thomas Jefferson wanted a society that allowed human nature's best to emerge and rise to the top as leaders. In Jefferson's time this idea was revolutionary just as a similar idea in Plato's *Republic* had been revolutionary. Both Jefferson and Plato thought of a society led by high-ability individuals recruited from all class levels. And both stressed the importance of education in developing a natural elite and thus a well-ordered society. Jefferson was as proud of his part in establishing the University of Virginia as he was of writing the Declaration of Independence.

Jefferson's faith in education as a way to reveal who was qualified to occupy positions in the division of labor was combined with a faith in free markets and free elections to become America's social philosophy of "non-egalitarian classlessness." For Americans, it is axiomatic that there should be no arbitrariness in the relation between social rewards and personal worth. Since the founding of their new Jerusalem, Americans have believed that they had found the way to realize nature's hierarchy of talent and to put unequal rewards on a just and natural basis. For Americans, the key to overcoming the artificial barriers of social condition, religion, ethnicity, and race and to revealing the true universe of individuals is equal opportunity and competition in the spheres of economics, politics, and education.

In this trinity of free markets, education holds a special place in American hearts. It is alleged to have great power to improve people and solve problems; nothing is more characteristic of an American faced with a problem than to attribute it to a lack of education. The power of education is thought to be enormous, largely because Americans attribute great power to ideas and knowledge. This faith in ideological causation—in the power of truth over ignorance and evil—along with the difficulty of running a regionally, racially, economically, and ethnically diverse society, has led the United States to assign a heavy burden of functions to education. And given their belief in biopsychological causation, Americans find it easy to equate the absence of formal barriers to education and the existence of free public schools with equality of opportunity.[1] For an American, an opportunity is something one seizes or makes use of; inequality in any field is simply the record of those who did and did not have it in them to profit from opportunities available to all.

THE CONFLICT POSITION ON EDUCATION

Most sociologists who analyze education differ profoundly from the basic beliefs of most educators, public officials, national leaders, and the lay public. Sociologists in the conflict tradition have reinterpreted past findings, and by using new assumptions have come up with a radically different view of education.

In fashioning their perspective, conflict sociologists built on the main tradition in stratification analysis. Earlier research going back to the Lynds' *Middletown* study of 1927 and Hollingshead's *Elmtown* study in the 1940s had established the class basis of education. Conflict sociologists were also inspired by an insight in the Coleman Report, namely, that education appears to have little independent power in its own right (this report will be discussed shortly). Running counter to basic American beliefs, conflict sociologists argue that education is merely a way to transmit class position from one generation to the next and to hide the fact that the basic power over occupation and income lies in the economy itself.

Early Research

The small-town focus of early stratification research (1925 to 1945) gave us a good portrayal of the mixed-class educational system that prevailed under the sway of this tradition of educational equality.[2] With some modifications, which will be noted, this system was probably characteristic of the United States from the advent of mass public education in the middle of the nineteenth century until close to the middle of the twentieth. Under this system the various classes throughout rural, small-town, and small-city America (probably) attended the same schools at every educational level through high school. Most of America's educational norms date from this period: free tax-supported compulsory education; a curriculum stressing literacy, abstract knowledge, patriotism, and the Protestant-bourgeois virtues; and a testing and grading system that supposedly revealed the hierarchy of talent ordained by nature. The fact that rich and poor often attended the same school, in combination with heavy educational expenditures, rising overall levels of education, and the great normative appeal of education, gave a semblance of reality to the norm of equal educational opportunity. However, Hollingshead's finding that Elmtown's schools were deeply biased in favor of its upper classes is much closer to the reality of American education, then and now.

Awareness of the relation between class and education has grown consistently in the twentieth century. In the early part of the century, progressive educators began to question the wisdom of imposing a uniform education on a student body composed of a mixture of social classes.[3] Though it took massive effort and caused deep controversy (and still does, for that matter), progressive educators managed somewhat to diversify the school to make it more suitable for a diverse student body. Accordingly, students were grouped into classes on the basis of their speed of learning; various types of programs (vocational, commercial, academic) were offered; and special schools (music and art, science, vocational) were made available for special students. The early efforts to adjust education to students' differing values and skills were motivated by a desire to overcome class differences, including ethnic and linguistic differences, and thereby to make equal education a reality. But progressive educators in the 1920s and 1930s, even when they advocated special programs and special schools, did not (and could not) envisage the trend that developed in the decades after World War II. The booming economy of the post-1945 period accelerated the process of urbanization and suburbanization, in effect segregating residential and political districts by social class throughout the United States. The inner city became blighted and black, and layers of white working, middle, and upper-middle-class suburbs grew up around the decaying core city. What makes this overall process important, of course, is that residential areas are also the economic and political units on which America's schools are based. Given the United States' powerful tradition of political decentralization, this class-structured hierarchy of local communities deeply affects its educational system; indeed, it particularizes education by class so deeply that it is probably a mistake to speak of an American *system* of education at all.

Class and Expenditure per Pupil

The amount of money spent on education in the United States varies enormously from state to state, and from one school district to another within any given state. The basic reason for these differences is that school expenditures are the responsibility of local communities: since there are enormous variations in the wealth of localities, there is enormous variation in the amount of money expended per pupil.

As part of the Civil Rights Act of 1964, Congress created a commission to study the "lack of availability of equal educational opportunities for individuals by reason of race, color, religion, or national origin in public educational institutions at all levels in the United States, its territories and possessions, and the District of Columbia."[4]

The Coleman Report found considerable variation in the nature of schools as measured by such factors as age of building, average number of pupils per classroom, textbooks, library, science and language laboratories, accreditation, specialized academic programs, teacher tenure, principal's salary, extracurricular activities, and the like. With due regard for the dangers inherent in the use of averages and for the marked regional disparities in the United States, it was found that African Americans had access to fewer of some of the facilities that seem to be related to academic achievement.[5] All in all, however, the report did not find as much disparity along these lines as many thought existed.[6]

The Coleman Report also found distinct differences in academic achievement between majority (white) students and ethnic-racial groups (Puerto Ricans, Native Americans, Mexican Americans, and blacks), and by implication between social classes. Variations in academic achievement by class will concern us again shortly, but are of particular interest here in connection with unequal educational expenditures. By holding socioeconomic status constant, the Coleman Report concluded that the quality of a school (library, curriculum, building, teachers' qualifications, and so on) has very little independent effect on the academic performance of students. (Minority students are affected somewhat more by the quality of a school than majority, or white, students.) The Coleman Report (p. 302) did find that students' aspirations and performance are strongly affected by the social composition of a school's student body; but this variable, it should be noted, is a function of class factors.

The Coleman Report (p. 325) summarizes its major finding in these words:

> Taking all these results together, one implication stands out above all: that schools bring little influence to bear on a child's achievement that is independent of his background and general social context; and that this very lack of an independent effect means that the inequalities imposed on children by their home, neighborhood, and peer environment are carried along to become the inequalities with which they confront adult life at the end of school. For equality of educational opportunity through the schools must imply a strong effect of schools that is independent of the child's immediate social environment, and that strong independent effect is not present in American schools.

The approach that emphasizes equalization of expenditures per pupil in order to equalize educational opportunity would appear to be futile. The difficulty of equalizing expenditures per pupil would itself be overwhelming, affecting as it would the deeply entrenched tradition of decentralized political control of schools. In any case, the strategy of focusing on educational expenditure as the key to equal opportunity is rendered suspect by the Coleman Report. One should not be surprised at this finding, since it is consonant with what is known about socialization. People learn from social relationships, not from buildings, libraries, cafeterias, or contact with curricula and teachers remote from and irrelevant to their previous (class) socialization. A well-educated teacher with middle-class beliefs and values in a plush school is likely to be ineffectual if the pupils come from lower-class families; indeed, such ineffectualness has a cumulative effect, making relations between the student and the school increasingly difficult. The same teacher in a run-down, ill-equipped school attended mostly by middle-class youngsters would probably be far more effective; the social environment of the school would mesh with and complement the values and beliefs acquired by the students at home. On any objective test the latter students would in all likelihood score higher than the former.

The error of relating equality of educational opportunity with equality of educational expenditure has a practical component: Virtually insurmountable political barriers confront those who want to equalize (or make more equitable) educational expenditures. But even if these barriers were overcome and an equal amount of money spent on each child in America, there would still be wide differentials in academic achievement—differentials best accounted for by the class structure.

Class and Educational Aspirations

The American commitment to education is well known: masses of people attend and service schools, great sums of money are spent on them, and the numbers rise every year. The high value Americans place on education must be qualified carefully, however, if we are to understand its social meaning. For one thing, Americans do not value education as an end in itself. Always, and often explicitly, it is a means to other ends. And of special significance is the fact that Americans value education unequally by class. Discussing the relation between class and personality, we pointed to sharp differences in the values of parents in the higher classes and those of parents in the lower classes. The relevance of these differences to education is apparent. Speaking broadly, families in the higher classes prepare and motivate their children for success in school, while families in the lower classes prepare and motivate their children for average academic performance or even failure.

Two things about aspirations should be kept in mind. One, the aspirations of the lower classes rise if they attend predominantly middle-class schools. Two, given the phenomenal growth of junior colleges, vocational training, and open admissions, aspirations to certain kinds of education appear to be strong at the lower levels of American society.

Class and Academic Achievement

Decades of research have yielded the same results again and again—namely, achievement in school correlates strongly with class origin. In addition to studies of small-town America, national and urban-studies conducted from the 1960s on all reached a similar conclusion: children's class origin is directly and strongly related to all forms of academic achievement, including IQ.[7]

Differentials in expenditure per pupil, educational aspirations, and academic achievement are not the only ways in which class influences education. While almost every aspect of education is implicitly embraced by these three categories, it should also be noted that pupil and teacher turnover, emotional health, regularity of attendance, regular promotion in grade, school-leaving rates, enrollment in college preparatory programs, participation in clubs, receipt of scholarships, parent participation in school activities, and school board composition are all directly related to class level. Surprisingly enough, even enriched and remedial classes and subsidized milk and food programs benefit middle- and upper-class youngsters more than those who come from the lower classes.[8]

Of no small importance in assessing the relation between class and education is the class position of the public school teacher. Recruited largely from middle-class backgrounds, teachers absorb the ethos of middle-class America, including the hunger for professional status, regardless of background.[9] As a result, they develop an image of the ideal student and an ideology of education highly inappropriate to many of the actual students and situations they face.[10] It has even been argued that teachers behave in such a way as to elicit from lower-class pupils the low achievement they expect.[11]

The class explanation of success or failure in school is part of the overall sociocultural approach to behavior. Though modern scholarship has tended in this direction, there persists a pronounced tendency to include biopsychic factors in explanations of educational and other behavior. And despite mountains of evidence to the contrary, many still rely on biopsychic variables, especially on the alleged existence of significant differences in inborn intelligence,[12] to explain educational behavior.

The false claim that the existing class system is caused by the inequality of innate intelligence (IQ) is centrally important to right liberals as witness the appearance of Richard J. Herrnstein and Charles Murray, *The Bell Curve: Intelligence and Class Structure in American Life.*[13] It is encouraging that the re-emergence of this position in 1994 was almost universally condemned as pseudo-science and as an effort to aid the political fortunes of those presiding over America's stagnant fortunes.[14]

LIFE IN CLASSROOMS: THE HIDDEN CURRICULUM

The classroom as a structure of interaction and power has been largely neglected by educators. But thanks to a pioneering work by Philip W. Jackson[15] we have begun to understand more about the classroom.

The typical classroom is affected by a number of factors that are not given much thought. Teachers routinely face classes that are too big even for the room let alone for the personal attention that each student needs. Often there are shortages of texts, other materials, and equipment. Students spend much time lining up to use facilities. The typical solution to crowding and scarce materials creates the classroom's basic power relation. Students are anchored at their desks and all proceed according to the same lesson plan. Teachers spend a great deal of time talking. Students must receive permission to talk or participate. Students are called on at random, producing fear and anxiety for students can never be sure they are prepared. Comments on their written or oral work are made by teachers and other students, thus exposing them to evaluation by others and often to humiliation and embarrassment. Many evaluations such as IQ scores remain secret.

The typical classroom wastes a great deal of time—students sit isolated and silent, and even when they try to listen their attention spans are short while teachers are long on wind. It is common practice for teachers to have students help them manage their classes. Standards for selecting students (and for evaluating class behavior) are arbitrary and lack balance. Teachers tend to favor character traits that suit the needs of managing large numbers: passivity, docility, conformity, silence until called on, and so on. There is a heavy reliance on textbooks, many of which are incomplete and biased (high school history texts, for example, were biased against labor and omitted two-thirds of what actually happened in American history, usually the disagreeable parts).[16] And typical texts have been found to be of little value to students.[17] The teacher also imparts nonideological skills that prepare students to fit in. The great emphasis on abstract reading and writing skills and on abstract science and mathematics shortchanges most of the middle classes as well as the lower classes.[18] In most respects education's stress on discipline, the passive learning of routine skills, and standardized testing all resemble the corporate economy and society that surround the school.

The school and the classroom have many of the characteristics of a total institution (prison, military, monastery). The school and classroom prepare students for life but not as we normally think of it. What the school most resembles is the factory and office, and it is preparation for subordinate roles in the economic division of labor that makes up the hidden curriculum for most students.

The average classroom does not awaken or nourish citizen skills—students are not introduced to the conflicts and shortfalls of American society, but are given, by and large, a bland, consensus picture of national achievement and progress. Instead of raising policy issues that bring national assumptions into question, the schools reinforce the ready-made world that students experience elsewhere. And the school fails to produce informed consumers—quite the contrary, the teacher tends to reinforce and extend the nonideological consumerism that students acquire at home and through the mass media.[19]

All in all, the power structure of the school and the hidden curriculum are part of the way in which schools reproduce the class system. Many studies have shown that schools have a pronounced bias in favor of the values, norms, and skills of the upper classes and that they either overlook or discriminate against the values and skills of the lower classes. Schools require character and cognitive skills (for example, punctuality, self-discipline, the ability to manipulate symbols) that are found in the middle and upper classes and are absent or lacking in the lower classes. Subject matter also favors the upper classes, and teachers and textbooks rarely discuss the world in conflict terms or from the standpoint of the lower classes. Instead, schools teach a complacent nonideological subject matter that suits children from the upper classes and ignores the conflicts and deficiencies in American life that children from the lower classes could relate to. Teachers also overlook assets and skills associated with the lower classes and frown on behavior and values that would be easy to include in the educational process. Students from the upper classes arrive in school already housebroken, and teachers can concentrate on academic work. In schools populated by the children of the lower classes much of the time is spent on fostering obedience to rules.

TRACKING AND CLASS REPRODUCTION

Most societies have explicit systems for separating students into academic and nonacademic groups to determine who will go on to higher education. In Great Britain children take tests at the age of eleven that decide who will go on to university training. Ralph Turner has called this *sponsored* mobility, a system in which students are selected from above (by the people who believe in the validity of tests) for sponsorship into higher achievement status. The United States, says Turner, relies on *contest* mobility, a system in which individuals compete to determine who goes on and who doesn't.[20]

The two systems, however, are not so different in their basic causes and outcomes. Education in both reflects social class and acts as a gatekeeper to elite positions. The ability to do well in school and on IQ and other tests correlates strongly with social class. The quality of schooling also varies by social class. One way to see education as a gatekeeper protecting class advantage is through the system of *tracking.*

The tracking system takes place in various ways. The tradition of community-based schools means that students often go to schools composed of similar income groups (this also leads to racial and ethnic segregation). Thus one form of tracking is when the lower classes do poorly in their own schools and the upper classes do well in their schools. Another form takes place *inside* a school. This occurs when students from various economic classes attend the same school. Here separate academic, business, and general streams or tracks emerge, a process affecting 85 percent of American students.

Explicit tracking would be sponsored mobility and would violate American norms and values. Rosenbaum has found that tracking takes place deceptively and that decisions by the school are made to appear as contest mobility and student choice.[21] Using class-based academic achievement from earlier grades, the high school separates students into two tracks, one for college and one for noncollege students. School records indicate a rigid tracking system in which students never attend mixed classes and the only crossover among programs is from college to noncollege tracks. A follow-up of the graduating class revealed that most college-track students attended four-year colleges and virtually all students in the noncollege track did not.

The school's grading system also made it virtually impossible for students in the noncollege track to shine. Teachers were stingier with good grades in the noncollege as opposed to the college track and the school discounted noncollege grades significantly when it came time to record them—an A in a noncollege course was considered a D. The net result was that noncollege students were not taking courses that prepared them for college admission and the grading system discriminated against them arbitrarily. Almost as if to make sure that these students would be refused admission to college, the school made it part of their record that they were in noncollege programs.

Throughout all this, noncollege students knew what track they were in but had no idea that they were in dead-end programs. Most of them in their senior year believed they were preparing for college. Throughout, the school and guidance counselors gave almost no information about the implications of choosing one course or program over another. Actually, there is evidence that the school encouraged misinformed choices. When asked, principals denied that their school had tracks.

Still another variation is gender segregation among the lower classes. While males and females among the lower classes are in nonacademic programs, they typically take gender-stereotyped courses—the males in industrial courses, the females in business courses.[22]

Whatever the form, tracking in elementary and secondary schools means that higher education is closed to large numbers of students who could profit from it. Those who don't go on are overwhelmingly from the lower classes, often despite good grades (the upper classes go on to college often despite poor grades and test scores). But even in higher education class-based tracking continues. Here it takes the form of offering students a wide variety of "choice" with most working- and lower-middle-class students going to community colleges while students from the middle and upper classes attend four-year colleges.

TRACKING AND ELITE PRIVATE SCHOOLS

Tracking also takes place through private schools. Elite private schools are of special importance because they provide the socialization necessary for wielding upper-class power and of course, for access to elite colleges. These schools arose originally as ways for old wealth to protect itself against the new rich, but as Levine points out, the elite private schools eventually assumed their true function—to blend old and new wealth into a cohesive national upper class.[23]

HIGHER EDUCATION: THE CAPSTONE OF CLASS EDUCATION

Through much of its history (approximately from 1500 to 1850), the nascent class society of the West required little formal training or education in the socialization process. By the mid-nineteenth century, the social need for literacy generated a system of mass public education, and at the end of the nineteenth century the free high school was on its way toward becoming a standard feature of American education. Between 1900 and 1940, enrollment in America's high schools rose from about 5 percent to over 90 percent of the relevant age group. But in the post-1945 period the terminal high school systems were asked to expand their college preparatory programs as the United States inaugurated a system of mass higher education. In 1940, only 15 percent of eighteen- to twenty-one-year-olds were enrolled in institutions of higher education; by 1970 this figure exceeded 50 percent. Since the 1960s, both graduate training and professional training have increasingly become the gateway to upper-level occupations.

American institutions of higher education developed in a decentralized fashion during the nineteenth century. As a result, a vast variety of "special-interest" colleges emerged: colleges for each of the many Protestant denominations; for Roman Catholics and for Jews; for men or women only; for whites or blacks; for farmers, engineers, or teachers; for inhabitants of a given town, city, or state; for adolescents or adults; and for the rich and not-so-rich.[24] While the composition of the governing boards of institutions of higher education was necessarily affected by this diversity, analysts agreed that, by and large, such boards exhibit a common trend: a decline in the power of clergy and a corresponding rise in the power of businesspeople and professionals. Though there are variations among institutions, it is clear that farmers, manual workers, lower white-collar workers, ethnic and "racial" groups, intellectuals, scientists, labor union officials, and artists (as well as women and young adults) are not represented on governing boards in proportion to their numbers or importance.[25]

Barrow provides a valuable Marxist analysis of higher education as an adjunct to corporate capitalism.[26] Assuming a collaboration between business and state to favor capital accumulation, Barrow sees the restructuring of American higher education between 1894 and 1928 as the incorporation of education into the political economy. Thus, education was increasingly viewed as a business, as amenable to efficiency measures, and as something that represents an investment that has to pay off.

Barrow argues that the incorporation of higher education into the capitalist political economy created tension with the traditional values and beliefs of intellectuals: one, that success in the knowledge field should rest on merit, and two, that intellectual work requires objectivity and autonomy. Both of these ideals conflict with the corporate ideal that education is a means for supplying business with the personnel and knowledge it needs for sustained capital accumulation. Barrow argues that business triumphed, by and large, but intellectuals (professors) did manage to get space for themselves and to maintain the ideal of open access to education and meritocracy. The freedom of academics, however limited, concludes Barrow, may become the basis for a more successful struggle against the dominant class in the future and help usher in a fuller democracy.

Barrow's optimism aside, the basic trend he outlined seems to have accelerated. Today, most major research universities and their faculties are in financial partnership with private corporations. The research facilities of higher education are subsidized by public money (with no provision for sharing gains with the public). And while this arrangement is alleged to help make America economically competitive, a large amount of the sale of American research knowledge goes to foreign corporations.[27]

It is of considerable interest that higher education can no longer claim to be an interconnected, multilevel meritocracy. It is what it has probably always been, a fragmented set of unrelated, noncompetitive clusters. High-quality, high-prestige institutions, both private and public, continue to emphasize elitist goals (pure research, liberal arts, preservation of the cultural heritage, an intellectual atmosphere of free inquiry). Such goals also further faculty members' professional careers and assign a low priority to teaching, especially at the undergraduate level. Lower-quality, lower-prestige institutions, usually public, appear to have given up trying to compete with front-ranking universities and have come to be characterized by different goals: vocational programs, applied research, teaching, service to the immediate community, and equality of opportunity.[28]

It should surprise no one to learn that higher education is deeply implicated in our class system.[29] But it is important to insist on viewing higher education as a class phenomenon and to resist the notion that colleges are attended exclusively by an elite of personal merit, and that such extraneous factors as race, ethnicity, religion, or class, though perhaps influential at the lower levels of schooling, have somehow been overcome or neutralized by the time students enter college. The student bodies of our colleges and universities not only do not include all the available academic talent, but are also havens of class privilege.

Class influence over entry to higher education takes a number of forms. First, local school districts are often homogeneous by income and are thus class-based. This means a vast difference in the amount of money spent on education from one district to another. But more important, it means that students entering school are already programmed either for success, mediocrity, or failure. This process is institutionalized by the high school tracking system in which students are assigned to programs by IQ or previous academic achievement, that is, essentially by class and gender.

All this leads to differential access to higher education with large numbers of youngsters with academic ability dropping out of high school or not going on (for the relation between family income and college attendance see Figure 9–1). And tracking continues in higher education because class again determines what quality of four-year school one attends and whether or not one attends a junior college.[30] In addition, class is also related to type of programs selected once in college. The conclusion reached by Bowles and Gintis for the United States and Bourdieu and Passeron for France—that education in capitalist society is a process of social reproduction—is difficult to avoid.[31]

FIGURE 9–1 Families by Full-Time Enrollment of Dependent Members 18–24 Years Old by Family Income, 1993[a]

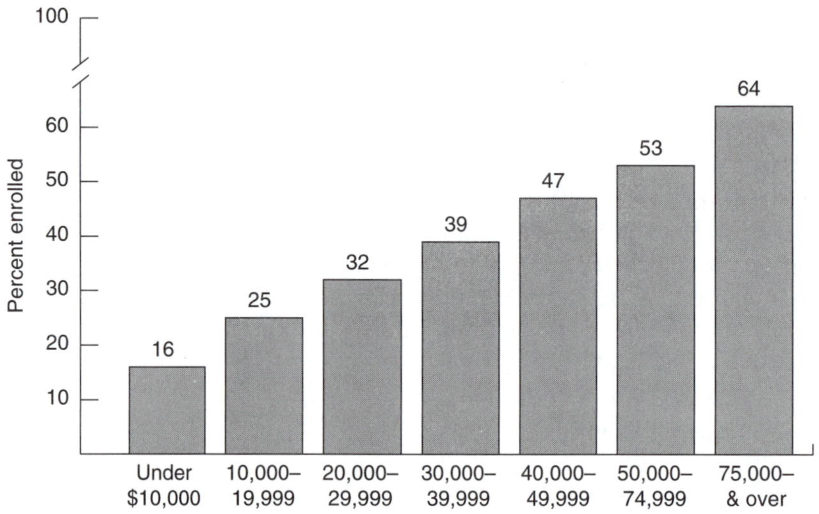

[a]College enrollment refers to junior as well as four-year colleges, and family income includes households with more than one wage earner. Class differences in college attendance would be far more pronounced if only four-year colleges were included.

Source: U.S. Bureau of the Census, Current Population Report, Series P-20, no. 479, "School Enrollment–Social and Economic Characteristics of Students, October, 1993" (Washington, DC: U.S. Government Printing Office, 1994), Table 16.

THE COOLING-OUT FUNCTION OF EDUCATION

Social mobility in the United States is thought to be, to use Ralph Turner's term, a contest between equals. Unlike the English system of "sponsored" mobility, in which members of the elite identify likely elite prospects in the classes below and consciously recruit them into the higher levels of society, American society regards upper status as a prize to be won by the worthiest individuals. The American contest system, says Turner, helps to solve a problem all societies face—maintaining loyalty to the system despite evident deficiencies. American education makes sense if seen in this light. American educational institutions avoid the formal separation (or *tracking*) of students, and the avenues from one program to another are kept open. Education is overtly viewed as a means to get ahead; it is avowedly vocational or practical; a great deal of effort is expended on keeping students in school as long as possible to insure a fair contest; much attention is paid to skills of "social adjustment," since the upward aspirant has no homogeneous elite on which to model his or her behavior and must not lose contact with the masses; and failure is due to individual deficiencies.

As noted earlier, however, behind the rhetoric and attempts to provide for equal opportunity and competition, the United States has a well-developed class-based tracking system. Actually, it appears that there is very little difference between the United States and England in continuity of social level from father to son, or in the relative importance of social origin and ability in the son's educational attainment. And while the two nations' educational systems differ greatly, the tracking of students into academic and nonacademic streams reflects class origin and ability almost identically. It appears, in other words, that the two countries use different mechanisms to produce the same results.[32]

Turner's classic analysis concentrates on the way in which education is used to institutionalize and legitimate upward mobility, or success. It ignores, except by implication, the way in which failure (or relative failure or only moderate success) is institutionalized. Addressing himself to the latter problem, Burton R. Clark has suggested that the junior college performs a "cooling-out" function.[33] The United States, says Clark, must somehow solve the problem created by the contradiction between its encouragement of all to succeed and the ability of the social structure to provide success only for a few—and a deeply graded structure of relative success and failure for the rest. Deliberately structured to diminish the enrollment pressure on colleges and universities, the junior college charges either low or no tuition and provides considerable choice among technical, commercial, and academic programs. But, says Clark, those who enroll in academic programs in the hope of eventually transferring to four-year colleges cannot all succeed, and a need exists to shift potential transfer students into terminal programs. Rather than allow for outright failure, says Clark, the junior college has developed an elaborate but disguised process for easing students into terminal programs and allowing all to save face. Among the features of this process are pre-entrance achievement tests, regular counseling interviews, a mandatory orientation course devoted to "realistic" vocational goals, an elaborate system of supervision in courses, and the routine use of probationary status.

It is important to recognize that standards of academic achievement (in all fields) are norms derived from the behavior in school of middle- and upper-class students. Departures from established academic norms are then labeled C or F students, low-IQ, "two years behind in reading," culturally deprived, dropouts, A^+ students, brilliant, "college material," and so on. Conformity to such upper- and middle-class norms is, by definition, harder for working- and lower-class youngsters, rendering the concept of equal educational opportunity (no matter how defined) highly problematic. What exists, in other words, is an unacknowledged tracking system or, actually, nonsystem, made up of noncompeting clusters heavily related to class. Any assumption or argument that the hierarchy of achievement produced by this interplay of class and education coincides with (or approximates) the structure of ability ordained by nature is thoroughly suspect. And, finally, it means that we have no way of knowing how good our best really are.

The nature of education is seen in quite a different light, of course, by lay persons and, I suspect, many professional educators and social scientists. IQ, achievement and aptitude tests, grades, prizes, diplomas, degrees, and the like are all commonly viewed as reflecting native ability and motivation. The wide diversity of types of education (the class-based tracking system) is seen both as a wise provision for tapping and developing differences in native ability and as a moral universe allowing choice and providing a redemptory process for "late bloomers." Scholarships, graduate school grants, and low or no tuition charges at quality colleges (which in reality represent a vast subsidy for middle and upper class students, since it is primarily they who meet admission requirements) are viewed as a contribution to equal educational opportunity.[34] And low or no tuition and low admission standards at good or poor institutions are also seen in this light, despite the fact that such opportunities are often accompanied by deliberately created high failure rates.

American education is through and through a class phenomenon, complete with mechanisms for mollifying average and marginal students. What the United States offers is educational opportunity, not equal opportunity; to fail to recognize this simple distinction, as well as the class nature of American education, is not to understand why and how American society produces shortage, waste, and privilege in the development of its woman- and manpower.

SMALL AND DIFFERENT WORLDS: THE ACADEMIC PROFESSION

The term *academic profession* has no referent; it is an abstraction left over from the early years of higher education when a small, homogeneous collection of colleges provided a tiny number of people with the then available amount of knowledge. Burton Clark has painted a disturbing picture of present-day higher education in which little unity can be found. There is mongrelization (my term) among types of school ranging from medical to hair-styling schools, from research universities to community colleges. There is mongrelization of subject matter ("It is virtually impossible," says Clark, "to name a subject that someone, somewhere, will not teach"). And subjects have splintered into subspecialities and beyond into topics, most with their own association and even journals. There is hierarchy and separation among the various departments within a school and all are separate from "the pieties of curricular integration."[35]

The teaching faculty of higher education has lost economic ground over the past decades (in addition, enormous disparity in income and teaching loads exist among the various schools and among disciplines). And while some instructors enjoy great autonomy, some have been put back under the control of trustees, and many are under the sway of clients (the student-driven bottom one-third to bottom one-half of institutions). Perhaps nothing is more telling than the fact that fully one-third of instructors in higher education are temporary and lack income, benefits, security, or career prospects. The academic profession is really (in Clark's words) one of small and different worlds. This exploitation of professional labor is matched by the exploitation of other educational labor (secretaries, clerical help, graduate and laboratory assistants), a pattern of exploitation that has its counterparts in all professions.

EDUCATION'S FAILURE TO PERFORM SOCIAL FUNCTIONS

Education is alleged to perform four distinct functions: (1) transmit the culture, (2) promote social solidarity, (3) provide for personal development and selection by merit, and (4) generate knowledge and update society. That it has failed and failed badly on all counts comes as no surprise. What is surprising is the continuing belief that education can and should perform these functions! To understand why (academic) education cannot perform any positive function, let us frame our beliefs about its role in society into two general purposes: one, to prepare (sift, train, and sort) the young for an ever-more demanding occupational hierarchy, and two, to prepare them for citizenship. As education was assigned ever-more explicit economic and social functions, Americans came to think of it as a natural or objective process for sorting out and training the talent manifested in each generation so that these functions could be served. This belief is now so universally accepted that it is almost impossible to raise questions about it. Of course, Americans have been openly critical of their educational institutions. They have spent and will no doubt continue to spend enormous amounts of time and energy debating their performance. What the empirical record suggests, however, is that America's fundamental premises about education are wrong; that is, a sizable amount of evidence indicates that *formal education bears no positive relation to economic behavior or to citizenship.* If anything, education is associated with negative economic and political consequences.

The Myth of Education as the Generator of Human Capital

Ivar Berg indicted education as a "great training robbery" as far back as 1970.[36] Summarizing the considerable evidence on the relation between formal education and work performance and satisfaction, as well as a study of his own, Berg found no relation between formal education and work productivity, low absenteeism, low turnover, work satisfaction, or promotion. If anything, he found an inverse relation between amount of formal education and occupational performance. While the studies reported by Berg varied with regard to the type and reliability of their data, the impression gained from reviewing data on blue-collar, white-collar, and engineer-scientist workers is that formal education plays one simple role: it determines where one enters the occupational system. What is crucial, in other words, is that employers *believe* that formal education makes better workers and therefore use it as a criterion for hiring. *But once hired, workers with more and less formal education exhibit no significant difference in work performance.* The only apparent difference is in income, because workers with more formal education enter the labor force at higher levels and change jobs more often.

Berg also found no relation between formal education and success in the military or the civil service. This was borne out in the early 1980s, in one highly demanding occupation (air traffic controller). When President Reagan fired striking air traffic controllers, the Federal Aviation Administration was forced to train new controllers quickly. Significantly, no differences in performance was found between high school and college graduates. To cite another example, the demand that teachers have undergraduate and even graduate degrees is associated with high turnover and departure from the profession. Thus Berg and others suggest that formal education is mostly a means of assigning credentials that control the supply of labor, and thus access to jobs and income. Given the close relationship between class and the acquisition of educational credentials, the American system of education is thus, as much as anything else, a way of transmitting class position from one generation to the next.

The association of formal education with positive economic outcomes has been exploded by Randall Collins's sophisticated and intensive analysis of this overall question. Reviewing the literature and the data on the increased schooling required for employment in the United States, Collins found that education is better understood as a status-conferring process by means of which dominant groups seek to control occupations by imposing irrelevant cultural requirements than as a reflection of the greater skills needed on the job due to technological change.[37]

School achievement does lead to higher occupations and income. But one need only look at the large difference in income between those with one to three years of college and those with four years to realize that employers honor credentials, not knowledge. In addition, those who do well in school cannot be shown to become better workers and citizens because of their schooling. Researchers have been unable to find a positive relation between grades or test scores, and success in later life.[38]

Our graduate and professional schools are no exception to the general ineffectiveness (lack of payoff for the general public) of American education. American graduate schools turn out professors who are untrained in education and teaching. Medical schools have faculties oriented mostly toward research and curricula that are overlong, technocratic introductions to a specialized medicine that neglects the patient as a whole person and is indifferent to health. Law schools teach students to memorize legal materials while neglecting almost all the things that real-life lawyers do (interviewing clients, negotiating, performing in a court of law). Business schools teach their MBAs to manipulate symbols and analyze financial statements while failing to stress that the world of business means negotiation, personnel evaluation, product development, labor relations, marketing, sales, and so on. And none of these graduate and professional programs has valid admission standards, and none has any evidence that graduates perform better for having attended its program.[39] What they all have in common is that they sharpen the minds of our professional elites by making them narrow; they do not sharpen them by discussing the important issues of the day: How do we generate full employment, how do we provide justice and health care for all, and how do we educate to attain these goals?

The absence of a positive relation between success in school and positive results for society is most easily understood by the fact that employers are not much interested in abstract cognitive achievement. When asked what kind of people they prefer, the world of business answers: individuals who hunger for work, can always give it all they have, can see a job through, and who have self-confidence, a zest for life, and a sense of direction in life. The business world's list of desired qualities does not even mention cognitive ability. That is probably why grades in school do not correlate with occupational success after school. The same is true of professional education—no study has ever validated a connection between grades in medical school, law school, business school, and so on with later professional success.

The idea that schools create human capital is understandable in a capitalist society and it is not surprising that it is supported in academe by mainstream economists. Economists are able to continue this myth because economics is largely a deductive science out of touch with the more empirical disciplines (more evidence of educational failure). Mainstream economists make a number of assumptions, long since contradicted by empirical research, that prevent them from questioning the relevance of higher education to economic growth.[40] They mistakenly equate the higher earnings of college graduates as proof that they are contributing to economic growth. They assume that the correlation of growth in education and economic growth is causal. But Randall Collins has shown that America's system of mass education came *after* the breakthrough into sustained economic growth. Also, the explosive growth of higher education from the 1950s on in the United States correlates with a *slowdown* in productivity. During the same time, Japan and Germany displayed substantial increases in productivity utilizing far fewer college graduates.

Economists, here as elsewhere, are basing their analysis on the master fallacy on which the discipline is based, that rational (efficient) markets are at work. It is important to dispel this myth because the same assumption informs how Americans-at-large look at their overall society, as one that allocates position and rewards through competitive meritocratic processes. How efficient is it, for example, to have over one-third of college graduates in jobs that high school graduates could fill? Economists and other analysts of the relation between education and productivity must investigate the matter empirically, being sure to distinguish between individuals being trained to do skilled work directly and broad aggregates enrolled in formal or academic education. But even here one must be careful not to assume that training for productivity is as difficult as we tend to think or as long as what we now require. And economists (and others) must also understand the significance, for example, of having too many surgeons performing millions of unnecessary operations, the cost of which is then registered as economic growth. Perhaps the best way for economists to disabuse themselves of their dubious assumptions about education is to remember the enormous cost to the economy and to government of training workers sent to them by our educational institutions. Or along the same lines, they might ponder why the United States has far higher numbers of supervisory white-collar staffs in all areas than other developed capitalist countries (and ponder the meaning of the fact that a large number of these college graduates were laid off from the 1980s on in order to *raise* productivity).

The Myth that Education Promotes Citizenship

The failure of education to provide positive outcomes also applies to the world of citizenship. In the nineteenth century, Americans believed that education in a common school would provide moral and intellectual cement to bind the nation together. Children would acquire a shared outlook and spirit by growing up together under adult supervision. The idea of a common curriculum in a common school was inspired by, or at least congruent with, the social experience of most Americans in the early nineteenth century. Most Americans had Protestantism, Newtonian cosmology, farming, and small-town life in common, which no doubt made it natural for them to think in terms of a common school. Later, the common school was also seen as a corrective to the increased diversity brought about by urbanization and immigration. Even when the school was diversified at the high school level, the faith persisted that educational homogenization was gradually taking place and that ever higher levels of education (years of schooling) were good for society.

Almost a century and a half after the advent of mass public education, Americans are probably no more united by common values and beliefs acquired through education than they were before public education. The public also displays ignorance about a large range of public matters as well as a lack of interest in politics.[41] Why Americans persist in thinking of education as a mechanism for promoting social integration through homogeneity cannot be explained with precision. Whatever its source, however, the ideology of homogeneity in education (equality of opportunity, objective-national norms, universalistic professional standards, national accreditation, national programs) helps to conceal an unfair contest for social position. In fact, beneath the rhetoric of homogeneity and universalism, American society has created wide diversification. It has diversified its high school system so much that even students who attend the same school receive different educations; it has created a highly diversified hierarchy of colleges, universities, and junior colleges; it has diversified its entire elementary and high school systems by class as a result of residential segregation and the tradition of the neighborhood school; and it has taken class diversification one step further to create severe racial isolation in all parts of the nation, creating more racial segregation in schools than existed in the 1960s. But educational diversification, disguised by the rhetoric of equality and competition, serves important latent functions. The truth of the matter is that the American educational nonsystem does create social stability, but in a manner extremely incongruous with normative ideology: the class-based educational system, in which youngsters start out and largely remain in separate tracks, protects those with power and legitimates the failure of those without power.

The lack of positive outcomes for higher education can also be seen in the fact that the United States has long had a surplus of college graduates. Unlike other capitalist societies, the United States uses college graduates in a large number of supervisory positions with no increase in productivity. The real purpose of these supervisory positions is to act as a buffer between the upper class and the working-lower classes and to disguise the unwarranted rewards of the upper classes (American executives, for example, have far higher incomes relative to their workers than executives in any other capitalist society).[42] Recently college graduates have noticeably begun to take over jobs that high school graduates have held[43] (earlier research established that one-third of college graduates reported that they were in jobs that did not require a college degree).

Education does not have positive outcomes because knowledge as such cannot be related to behavior in any one-to-one relation. People who *know* that AIDS is not easily transmitted continue to discriminate against AIDS victims. Individuals who *know* that condoms reduce the risk of acquiring AIDS nonetheless do not use them. Teenagers who take sex education courses do not avoid pregnancy any more than teenagers who do not take such courses. Doctors who take courses in nutrition do not incorporate knowledge about nutrition into their practices. Students who take language courses do not know more about foreign countries than students who do not take such courses. And so on. Actually, schools do not stress knowledge that can be used! Schools stress abstract skills presumably applicable to social policy or personal problem areas. But everything we know about learning tells us that humans behave in this way (know how to apply knowledge) only if they are trained to do so! In addition, the skills in abstraction that graduates have must be utilized in well-defined settings: for example, corporations, hospitals, law firms, schools, foundations, and public service bureaucracies.

Perhaps the easiest way to see and remember the failure of academic education is that businesses are training as many employees at all levels as there are students in all four-year colleges and graduate programs combined at a cost equal to all expenditures for the same schools.[44]

A recent massive (800 page) compilation of all available research on the impact of higher education on students confirms much of the above. The authors' main themes are that we do not have much research on the specific impact of higher education on students and that research in this area is declining. Second, what can be established points to an only modest impact of higher education on students. Though it is not possible to disentangle the characteristics of students, the aging process, and outside influences from the effects of education (because of how research has been designed), college seniors tend to have an array of cognitive skills that presumably they acquired in college. Changes in attitudes and values in the realms of politics and sex roles (presumably in the direction of enlightenment) are modest and may be declining. There is no evidence supporting higher education's claim that it enhances economic productivity (what evidence exists is negative), though there is evidence that a college degree leads to occupational advancement and yields a small amount of job satisfaction (largely, remember, because employers falsely believe that education enhances productivity and place college graduates in the better jobs). Pascarella and Terenzini also confirm that there is no evidence to support the belief that selective, prestigious colleges have a greater impact on students than less selective schools.[45]

The fact that higher education seems to promote cognitive skills does not mean that improving such skills should continue to be the main thrust of reform efforts. Quite the contrary, abstract cognitive skills have no direct payoff in better workers or citizens. And the same applies to higher education's success in promoting "better" attitudes about politics and gender: better attitudes about politics and gender are not the same thing as better behavior. College graduates pursue their own interests just as others do, deviating quite widely in their behavior from their attitudes and American ideals in general.

Why does a failed education endure? Or rather, how does it serve the interests of America's power groups? For one thing, it helps sustain the myth that the upper classes derive from meritocratic processes based on equal competition. Its prolonged and irrelevant system of credentials curbs labor flows into the good jobs, ensuring power groups control over the income, prestige, and power of upper-level occupations. A prolonged and irrelevant education also ensures the success of the children of the upper classes, thereby solving the problem of how to transmit class advantages to offspring without seeming to violate the achievement ethic.

Understanding the impotence of academic education goes a long way in understanding the performance shortfalls of both the disciplines and the professions. Ironically, as each profession and discipline confronts its shortfalls, it tends to reassert its dedication to the education that is the problem in the first place! The participation of the disciplines and professions in this failed system is thus sincere and not deliberate ideology. Beyond their understanding lie the latent functions of education for the knowledge elites. One, education's emphasis on mastering abstract symbols helps perpetuate the myth that society is under the guidance of knowledge elites. And two, education serves as a scapegoat: by blaming it for social problems and assigning it the responsibility for performing social functions that it clearly cannot perform, our elites deflect attention from the fact that they are the cause of problems and that they bear the responsibility for solving them.

Research clearly contradicts all our premises about education. Not only does education not have the power to perform the social functions assigned to it, but its lopsided stress on transhistorical objectivity (abstract, nonpartisan knowledge; abstract, all-purpose cognitive skills; abstract attitudes; objective, nonpolitical research) ensures failure. Or perhaps one should say, it ensures success of a different kind. The fact that evaluations of schools never focus on how much students and graduates, including managers, political officials, and professionals, actually know about the world they live in is extremely revealing. That would require challenging the many myths on which the power of the upper classes depends. Instead, American education continues to shape each oncoming generation into interchangeable nonpolitical units (certainly one outcome of our deep stress on abstract individualism), who can fit into a taken-for-granted world. That this process of depoliticization and standardization also applies to elites is the most ominous part of this latent social process.

THE RIGHT KIND OF EDUCATION

Abstract Literacy, Abstract Efficiency, and Other Tinkering

Since 1983 at least twenty education commissions and a half dozen authors have chanted the same tribal prayer: The community will be whole again and will prosper if students are made to achieve higher levels of abstract literacy (reading, writing, American history, mathematics, natural science, a foreign language), if they do this in common (that is, if it is achieved abstractly by all), and if they receive quantitative (that is, abstract) doses of these abstract subjects (a year of this, two years of that, one each from this and that).

This approach to national and educational problems recurs throughout American history. When schools were first started, they were called *common* schools. Early in this century, John Dewey said schools should provide "a common faith." Columbia University pioneered *general* education in the 1920s and the University of Chicago and St. John's University committed themselves to a *core* curriculum of Great Books. The Ivy League and similar schools developed the liberal arts philosophy (the all-around person, qualified to be a member of the governing classes, can be created by requiring students to take nonpractical courses in a variety of disciplines devoted to achieving abstract knowledge). Starting with the 1983 "A Nation at Risk" report, all high-level educational reports have stressed discipline in academic subjects and the need for a core curriculum. Allan Bloom's unreadable, incoherent, best-selling *The Closing of the American Mind* (1987), lamented the loss of absolute standards and a core curriculum complaining that students and teachers had too much freedom in picking and presenting educational elements. E. D. Hirsch, in a readable and coherent book, *Cultural Literacy* (1987), argued that our education suffers because it lacks a core vocabulary and then proceeded to supply the 5000 words and phrases that would make us culturally literate (and thus a better society).

What all of the above variations on the same theme have in common is the fallacy that society will improve if we impose a homogeneous universe of abstract skills and symbols on all young people. The utter insufficiency of thinking of education as the inculcation of a common set of abstract skills and symbols is apparent once common sense is given its head. Are not all the members of Congress, all the political appointees and high civil servants at Treasury, State, Commerce, and so on, all the owners and executives of our businesses, and all the members of all our professions well educated and could not they all pass a literacy test? But does being literate (or a graduate of our elite liberal arts schools) prevent billions of dollars from being taken criminally from the pockets of our citizens by the upper classes? Of course not. The millions of unnecessary operations every year are done by culturally literate surgeons. Does going to West Point, Annapolis, or the Air Force Academy (certainly examples of high-level, vigorous, disciplined academic training) prevent our military from squandering huge sums of money on useless weapons? Advocates of abstract literacy vary from traditionalists with their heads in the past to those who advocate scientific multiple-choice testing. The latter is used extensively to establish academic achievement (basic skills in fact acquisition and in reasoning) and to place the student in an alleged hierarchy of innate talent and achievement ability.

There is no evidence that good scores on IQ or SAT tests correlate with better work, economic success, or citizenship. Yet the demand from all sides continues that the schools establish a hierarchy of basic skills and incorporate them even more explicitly into the educational enterprise.

The other thrust of educational reform looks to making education more efficient. Currently, the schools are being flooded with advice (and earmarked money) from business leaders (who are concerned that America's future labor force needs are not being met) on how to run schools more efficiently. Nobody seems to be aware that the main criticisms of our economy is that it is poorly managed! The search for school efficiency has also led to proposals for a voucher system: giving parents vouchers that they can use to buy education. By subjecting schools to market economics, one will be assured that schools will shape up. No one seems to be aware that markets have failed to feed or house the American people, provide full employment, protect the environment, and so on.

There is no need to go on. Those who are busy trying to solve educational problems are themselves examples of how our well-educated people do not know how to perform in their own specialties. Their remedies for education are really ways to blame powerless African-American, Hispanic-American, and working-class students (and their teachers) for the incompetence of the powerful. Advocating high-level abstract subjects for all helps maintain the fiction of equal opportunity and guarantees that the upper classes will prevail because it is they who can endure the long years of learning useless knowledge. Thinking about education in terms of raising national levels of abstract literacy is worse than useless—it is really a way of allowing those who have excelled in abstract literacy to continue their blundering ways while blaming the not-yet-literate.

Instead, we should be asking our elite schools to examine the depoliticizing assumptions on which they are based: that education and knowledge are nonpartisan and value-neutral; that the United States is a democracy; that markets exist and therefore we do not need economic, family, housing, energy, health, or other policies; that the United States is God-favored; that the various social and natural sciences should be free to pursue research as they see fit, and so on. If we ask the Pentagon to make choices because we cannot afford every possible weapon, should we not also ask schools to make choices since we cannot afford every specialty and subspecialty? Here I am not talking about useful things like hygiene, driver's education, shop-cooking-plumbing classes, typing, and so on. Questions need to be raised about the excessive doses of the literature of England that are overloading the nervous system of our high school and college students and taking up valuable inner and outer space that could be devoted to more useful things. Does reading Chaucer, Shakespeare, and Thomas Hardy really help our country, or is all that window dressing, nonutilitarian conspicuous consumption to create the illusion that our elites are educated to the hilt and represent the best we can produce in the way of leaders. Why are we asking all students to study a foreign language when doing so does not lead to more knowledge about foreign countries. Certain foreign languages must be learned, but by whom, in what way, and which ones are the important questions.

The consensus on abstract literacy by all of our education experts is similar to our issueless presidential campaigns: Our society is so diverse that candidates cannot say anything concrete and relevant without crossing swords with some outraged group. An issueless campaign is a way out of this problem, just as pretending to be objective and value-neutral are ways out of the same problem for the natural and social sciences (and for that matter, journalism). Advocating abstract literacy gets our educational leaders off the hook of having to specify the concrete knowledge we need. Abstract literacy is part of the universalistic smog that envelops us all in the pretense that we are a functioning society.

The center of gravity in a curriculum should be the central intellectual, moral, and value problems we face *today.* Perhaps the central problem of the day is, How is the United States, the most poorly run of the developed capitalist countries, with the worst record in all social problem areas, going to cope with the dynamic capitalism represented by the emerging European Community and the dynamic Sino-based societies of the Asian Rim over the next quarter-century? Should not schools raise this question, give it priority over the million and one things they are now doing, and proceed to answer it. But they will get nowhere unless they disband those relics from the nineteenth century, our assorted artificial, specialized disciplines, which in recent decades, to their added disgrace, have splintered into incoherent subspecialities (can anyone say that the abstractions *education, economics, law, medicine, sociology,* and so on, really refer to coherent entities?). These disciplines cannot be made to work with fads and facades like accreditation, ethical codes, distribution requirements, competence tests for teachers, interdisciplinary studies, African-American studies, women's studies, environmental studies, and so on.

But education cannot turn out competent citizens and workers by itself because to do so runs counter to the interests of the top third of our society. One of the great insights in George Orwell's *1984* is that the monopolistic power structure of his nonimaginary society was attempting total control by depriving citizens of useful referents (for example, by abolishing history) and filling their heads with meaningless abstractions. A second insight in *1984* was that this effort was so successful in vacating and warping the consciousness of the masses that eventually even the Party Chief lost track of what was going on. Are not we doing much the same to our upper classes? Is not the definition of education as the acquisition of abstract doses of abstract subjects and abstract skills a sure prescription for a slow social death?

The defect in abstract literacy is the same defect in all of education: We humans have personalities acquired from social experience and the school not only does not mesh with experiences prior to or concurrent with it, but not subsequent to it either? Thus abstract literacy either cannot be acquired or, if acquired, fades from lack of use and reinforcement.

Education and the Ideology of Liberalism

Underlying the failure of academic education is the fallacy of the rational individual and its corollary, the laissez-faire society. Our education is still based on the nineteenth-century image of the rational individual who can synthesize inputs (experiences) and become an adaptive, forward-looking Jack- or Jill-of-all-trades. But everything we know about learning is that none of us is like that. Unless we are trained to synthesize and apply knowledge, we do not do so. We not only leave the special knowledge of specialized courses in separate compartments, but the formalism of that knowledge makes it fade quickly since it rarely has relevance for real life experience. And totally forgotten, in any case, is that our educated young, many saddled with large student loans and embarking on marriage and family life, must work in highly structured groups controlled by fifty- and sixty-year-olds.

Here I am not talking only of our misperception of student learning. The laissez-faire aspect of all education is quite apparent: if individuals are the integrators of all that counts, if the mistakes of the uneducated or specialized are nonetheless countered by the magical markets that keep society in balance (like gravity and other forces keep the solar system in perpetual equilibrium), then the various professionalized academic disciplines are all free to let abstract others see to social functions while they pursue their career-enhancing activities. It is this that makes it possible for the disciplines to devote themselves to excellence in the study of Chaucer, incest, subatomic physics, or inverse interest rates while ignoring the deterioration of American society. It is this outlook that necessitates adding separate environmental, African-American, or women's studies to the curriculum instead of asking all instructors to make these part of their courses (when schools attempt to upgrade their faculty—yes, faculty—as Stanford University has done in regard to its required humanities curriculum, all hell breaks out). The reliance on abstract others of laissez-faire capitalism makes it easy to generate specialized courses, disciplines, and subdisciplines (with journals to match), and specialized programs and schools. Given all this, it is easy to see why overeducation occurs and why the empty clichés of the liberal arts philosophy provide a convenient rationalization for making free riders of us all.

The United States experienced a number of setbacks from the 1960s on: defeat in Vietnam, political scandals, relative loss of power on the international scene, sluggish economic growth, stagnant living standards, and chronic deficits in both domestic and foreign accounts. Instead of focusing on its economic and political institutions and its elites as the cause of its problems, the United States (actually its leaders) placed most of the blame on education. Certainly they looked to education as the way to solve our economic, political, and social failures. Starting in 1983 and running through 1987, over a dozen national reports on lower and higher education appeared. Every report accepted blame for social failures on behalf of education, and, ignoring over fifty years of research, every report acted as if education could reform and thus improve American society.

The various commission reports all dealt with secondary problems, thus their proposed solutions were wide of the mark. Research has established that the best way to improve the functioning of American schools is to stabilize the homes from which students who do not do well come from. Beyond this, the critics of American schools have failed to identify the real problem—our elite high schools and colleges, which cannot show that they are producing better citizens or better professionals and leaders. And yet the heart of the commission reports stressed doing more of the same.

The surge of concern about education starting in 1983 has produced many proposals to strengthen academic programs. But the sociology of education prevents optimism. The large sums of money that are needed have not been forthcoming. Unless drastic changes are made, large segments of the working and lower classes will continue to flounder in middle-class schools. Above all, schools will continue to avoid political controversy and teach a consensus curriculum that favors the status quo. Bland, biased school texts will continue to be used. And the apolitical, politically conservative emphasis on abstract reading and writing skills will continue. Even if reform succeeds, the only result will be better scores on life-removed subjects and skills.

The fewest changes will take place where they are needed most—in our elite high schools and colleges. Abstract liberal arts will continue to dominate the curriculum and narrow and ineffective specialization will dominate the curriculum of graduate and professional schools. Since few realize that there is even a problem, there is little hope that American elites will give up the irrelevant education that favors them and their offspring. More science and mathematics will be taught but little will be said about the purposes of science or the threat to the environment posed by technology. Little will be said about the failure of economics to provide a better way to handle our economy. No realistic analysis of our stalemated political system will be forthcoming.[46]

The Republican administration of 1980–1992 stalled the federal programs developed from the 1960s on to improve education. The Republican Congress of 1994 openly cut federal education funds and was committed to abolishing the federal Department of Education. The Republican party is against all government efforts to direct society—that means less government on behalf of the lower classes and rigorous government promoting the ideal of laissez-faire and enforcing all laws only in that spirit.

Though federal government provides only 6 percent of all educational funds, its real threat is its continuous pressure on the class privilege of the classes that support the Republican party and their allies, conservative Democrats.

SUMMARY

The liberal-functional outlook dominates American thinking about education. Americans, including educators and mainstream social scientists, attribute great power to ideas and knowledge and assign important social functions to education: preserving traditions, promoting solidarity, revealing the hierarchy of innate ability, and generating new knowledge to ensure progress.

Conflict sociologists have rejected the liberal-functional position in its entirety. Study after study since the 1920s has revealed that education is a thoroughgoing class phenomenon and that its power to improve society is quite limited. No matter what type of behavior was investigated, research revealed the power of class: expenditure per pupil, attendance, educational aspirations, IQ and achievement tests, years completed, grades, diplomas, and degrees. The upper classes even benefit more from remedial courses. Of great importance was the finding that class determines who goes to college and to what type of college. By and large, attendance and completion of four-year colleges is a monopoly of the upper classes. What this also means is that the existing class system controls access to graduate and professional degrees.

Class interests are served by education (not consciously, of course) in various ways: through the establishment of high and rising (irrelevant) academic standards under the formalistic rallying cry of excellence, through deceptive tracking by providing a wide variety of class-related schools and programs (including a counseling process to mollify or cool-out victims), and tokenism (grants, scholarships, affirmative action) to create the illusion that recruits into the upper classes represent the best from the entire population.

Class education is not necessarily bad or illegitimate. What makes American education illegitimate with bad consequences is that it cannot be related to positive behavior outside the classroom, even on the part of those who succeed in it. Actually, education does not perform any positive social function and cannot, since it is itself a function of the outer hierarchy of social power.

The main (latent) function of education appears to be control of the flow of woman- and manpower into the economy; or, more exactly, its main function appears to be to ensure that the elite occupations are not oversupplied with qualified people. Academic education, in short, is primarily a means of maintaining and transmitting the existing class structure. But since it is not genuinely related to economic performance, academic education is really a prestige phenomenon masquerading as a personal achievement process, thus concealing the fact that entry into the valued levels of American society is primarily due to class birth. In addition, education serves as a convenient scapegoat for the power groups whose mistakes are the cause of social problems.

All evidence, in other words, points to education, at both the ideological and behavioral levels, as a prime legitimating process for an illegitimate system of privilege, waste, and incompetence.

NOTES

1. Equality of opportunity as an equal chance at the starting gate should not be confused with equal access to education of some sort or with proposals to provide different or more effective educational opportunities for diverse social classes.
2. The classic example is August Hollingshead, *Elmtown's Youth* (New York: John Wiley & Sons, 1949). This pattern, which suited the class system of rural–small-town and small-city America, did not prevail in the "caste" system of the South, which, after it began to provide education for black Americans, had a legally segregated system based on the doctrine of "separate but equal facilities" accepted as constitutional until 1954.
3. For an excellent history of Progressivism in education, see Lawrence A. Cremin, *The Transformation of the School* (New York: Alfred A. Knopf, 1961).
4. The formal title of the resulting study is *Equality of Educational Opportunity* (Washington, DC: U.S. Government Printing Office, 1966); its informal title is the Coleman Report. It should not go unnoticed that educational opportunity was placed in the context of civil rights and that while many of the factors that enter into social stratification were cited, class as such was ignored in the commission's terms of reference. The research team itself, though not ignoring class, consistently uses the euphemism "family background."
5. Ibid., pp. 8–15.
6. The Coleman Report is a broad abstract study of national and regional data, and caution should be exercised when its findings are cited. Shocking disparities between individual, black urban schools and upper-class suburban schools, for example, obviously exist.
7. In addition to the Coleman Report (1966), see Robert E. Herriott and Nancy Hoyt St. John, *Social Class and the Urban School* (New York: John Wiley & Sons, 1966); Patricia Cayo Sexton, *Education and Income* (New York: Viking Press, 1961); Robert J. Havighurst, Paul H. Bowman, Gordon P. Hiddle, Charles V. Matthews, and James V. Pierce, *Growing Up in River City* (New York: John Wiley & Sons, 1962); and Robert J. Havighurst, *The Public Schools of Chicago: A Survey Report* (Chicago: Board of Education, 1964). For general summaries, see Caroline Hodges Persell, *Education Inequality: A Theoretical and Empirical Synthesis* (New York: Free Press, 1977), and Richard H. de Lone, *Small Futures: Children, Inequal-*

ity, and the Limits of Liberal Reform, Report for the Carnegie Council on Children (New York: Harcourt Brace Jovanovich, 1979).

8. For a lucid and comprehensive presentation of data on all these areas from "Big City" (and from other studies), see Patricia Cayo Sexton, *Education and Income* (New York: Viking Press, 1961). For the first of a long line of research linking poverty, poor health, poor nutrition, and poor learning, see Herbert G. Birch and Joan Dye Gussow, *Disadvantaged Children: Health, Nutrition and School Failure* (New York: Harcourt Brace Jovanovich, 1970).
9. Robert E. Doherty, "Attitudes Toward Labor: When Blue Collar Children Become Teachers," *School Review* 71 (Spring 1963):87–96.
10. Howard S. Becker, "Social Class Variations in the Teacher-Pupil Relationship," *Journal of Educational Sociology* 25 (April 1952):451–465.
11. Ray C. Rist, "Student Social Class and Teacher Expectations: The Self-Fulfilling Prophecy in Ghetto Education," *Harvard Educational Review* 40 (August 1970):411–451.
12. For the radical genetic explanation, see Richard Herrnstein, *I.Q. in the Meritocracy* (Boston: Little, Brown, 1973). For the classic indictment of the IQ as a weapon of class domination, see Samuel Bowles and Herbert Gintis, "I.Q. in the U.S. Class Structure," *Social Policy* 3, nos. 4 and 5 (1972–1973):65–96; reprinted in Jerome Karabel and A. H. Halsey, eds., *Power and Ideology in Education* (New York: Oxford University Press, 1977), pp. 215–232.
13. Richard J. Herrnstein and Charles Murray, *The Bell Curve: Intelligence and Class Structure in American Life* (New York: Free Press, 1994).
14. In this connection, see Steven Fraser, ed., *The Bell Curve Wars: Race, Intelligence, and the Future of America* (New York: Basic Books, 1995). The two right liberals in this collection (Thomas Sowell, Nathan Glazer), while rejecting the claim in the Herrnstein-Murray book that African Americans are unequal in intelligence, nonetheless endorse the validity of the IQ.
15. *Life in Classrooms* (New York: Holt, Rinehart & Winston, 1968).
16. Jean Anyon, "Ideology and United States History Textbooks," *Harvard Educational Review* 49 (August 1979):361–386, and Frances Fitzgerald, *America Revised: History Textbooks in America* (Boston: Little, Brown, 1979).
17. *New York Times,* April 8, 1980, p. C 4.
18. For insight into how schools shortchange the middle classes, see Eleanor Smollett, "Schools and the Illusion of Choice: The Middle Class and the 'Open' Classroom," in George Mardell, ed., *The Politics of the Canadian Public School* (Toronto: James, Leurs, and Samuel, 1974). For a pioneering participant observation analysis of a community college, which reports that it fails to serve its lower-middle and working-class students, see Howard B. London, *The Culture of a Community College* (New York: Praeger, 1978). For the adverse effects of segregated all-black schools, see Ray C. Rist, *The Urban School: A Factory for Failure* (Cambridge, MA: MIT Press, 1973), and Helen Gouldner, with the assistance of Mary Symons Strong, *Teachers' Pet, Troublemakers, and Nobodies: Black Children in Elementary School* (Westport, CT: Greenwood Press, 1978).
19. For a long catalog of abuses, see Sheila Harty, *Hucksters in the Classroom: A Review of Industry Propaganda in the Schools* (Washington, DC: Center for the Study of Responsive Law, 1979). For examples of reforms and industry restraint, see ch. 8 of the Harty text.
20. Ralph Turner, "Sponsored and Contest Mobility and the School System," *American Sociological Review* 25 (December 1960):855–867.

21. The following discussion relies on James E. Rosenbaum, "The Structure of Opportunity in School," *Social Forces* 57 (September 1978):236–256; "Track Misperceptions and Frustrated College Plans: An Analysis of the Effects of Tracks and Track Perceptions in the National Longitudinal Survey," *Sociology of Education* 53 (April 1980):74–88.
22. For this overlooked aspect of tracking, see Jane Gaskell, "Course Enrollment in High School: The Perspective of Working-Class Females," *Sociology of Education* 58 (January 1985):48–59.
23. Steven B. Levine, "The Rise of American Boarding Schools and the Development of a National Upper Class," *Social Problems* 28 (October 1980):63–94. For a full-scale study of elite private schools, see Peter W. Cookson, Jr., and Caroline Hodges Persell, *Preparing for Power: America's Elite Boarding Schools* (New York: Basic Books, 1985).
24. Christopher Jencks and David Reisman, *The Academic Revolution* (Garden City, NY: Doubleday, 1968).
25. For a pioneering study of and still our most comprehensive body of empirical data on the composition and attitudes of governing boards, see Morton A. Rauh, *The Trusteeship of Colleges and Universities* (New York: McGraw-Hill, 1969).
26. Clyde W. Barrow, *Universities and the Capitalist State: Corporate Liberalism and the Reconstruction of American Higher Education, 1894–1928* (Madison, WI: University of Wisconsin Press, 1990).
27. For background on the absorption of natural science by industry (and the military), see David Dickson, *The New Politics of Science* (New York: Pantheon, 1984), and Sheila Slaughter, *The Higher Learning and High Technology: Dynamics of Education Policy Formation* (Albany: State University of New York Press, 1990). For a summary of recent developments (in the long-term transformation of higher education into an adjunct of corporate capitalism), see Russell Jacoby, "The Greening of the University: From Ivory Tower to Industrial Park," *Dissent* 38 (Spring 1991):286–292.
28. Burton R. Clark, *The Academic Life: Small Worlds, Different Worlds* (Princeton, NJ: Carnegie Foundation for the Advancement of Teaching, 1987).
29. The ability of the upper classes to get their children through college much more successfully than the lower classes has a long history of documentation by social stratification research. For the latest analysis, based on census and other data, tracing the relations between family income and college enrollment-and-graduation from 1970 to 1988, which clearly indicates "substantial stratification by income," especially in four-year colleges, see Charles F. Manski, "Income and Higher Education," *Focus* 14, no. 3 (Winter 1992–1993):14–19.
30. The increase in college attendance by the lower classes should not be misinterpreted. Postsecondary education for the lower classes takes place overwhelmingly at junior colleges, which now account for 36 percent of higher education enrollments. For a careful compilation of evidence showing the pronounced separation by class that exists at this level, see Jerome Karabel, "Community Colleges and Social Stratification: Submerged Class Conflict in American Higher Education," *Harvard Educational Review* 42 (November 1972):521–562; reprinted in part in Jerome Karabel and A. H. Halsey, ed. and intro., *Power and Ideology in Education* (New York: Basic Books, 1977), pp. 232–254.
31. Samuel Bowles and Herbert Gintis, *Schooling in Capitalist America* (New York: Basic Books, 1977), and Pierre Bourdieu and Jean-Claude Passeron, *Reproduction*

in Education, Society, and Culture, trans. Richard Nice (Newbury Park, CA: Sage, 1977).

32. For this comparison, see Alan C. Kerckoff, "Stratification Processes and Outcomes in England and the United States," *American Sociological Review* 39 (December 1974):789–801.
33. Burton R. Clark, "The 'Cooling-Out' Function in Higher Education," *American Journal of Sociology* 65, no. 6 (May 1960):569–576. The term *cooling-out* is taken from the work of Erving Goffman and refers to the management of disappointment. Goffman illustrates his argument by reference to the confidence game, which often features a means to mollify the victim and thus prevent him from alerting the police.
34. See Chapter 15 for an analysis of how public higher education redistributes income from the lower classes to the middle and upper classes.
35. Burton R. Clark, *The Academic Life: Small Worlds, Different Worlds* (Princeton, NJ: Carnegie Foundation for the Advancement of Teaching, 1987). Clark's careful, comprehensive, and elegantly written analysis stays inside higher education, assuming it to be a knowledge-driven, self-contained entity that is generating its own deficiencies. One feels the absence of any discussion of the socioeconomic basis of education as well as the failure to note that higher education is not performing the functions attributed to it. A comparative analysis, Philip G. Altbach, ed., *Comparative Perspectives on the Academic Profession* (New York: Praeger, 1977), also stresses the diversity and drift of the academic profession across developed and developing countries as it comes under pressure from the outside to do more and more for business, government, and clients, both old and new (to the middle and upper classes have been added the working class and those who have hitherto been excluded from the benefits of higher education because of race, ethnicity, sex, age, or disability). A useful discussion of the academic disciplines as each having its own "culture" (different views of method, goal of research, national versus international focus, education, and so on) is provided by Henry Bauer under the heading "The Antithesis," *Social Epistemology* 4, no. 2 (1990):215–227.
36. Ivar Berg, assisted by Sherry Gorelick, *Education and Jobs: The Great Training Robbery* (New York: Praeger, 1970).
37. Randall Collins, *The Credential Society* (New York: Academic Press, 1979). For a pioneering study that discovered that high-quality colleges have relatively little impact on the future occupations of their students, since the type of student they recruit more adequately explains future success, see Duane F. Alwin, "College Effects on Educational and Occupational Attainment," *American Sociological Review* 39 (April 1974):210–223.
38. Michael R. Olneck and James Crouse, "The IQ Meritocracy Reconsidered: Cognitive Skill and Adult Success in the United States," *American Journal of Education* 88 (November 1979):1–31; Michael Useem and S. M. Miller, "The Upper Class in Higher Education," *Social Policy* 7 (January–February 1977):28–31.
39. For the lack of positive results from professional programs for doctors, lawyers, and business executives, see Andrew Hacker, "The Shame of Professional Schools," *Harper's* 263 (October 1981):22–28.
40. For example, William E. Becker and Darrell R. Lewis, eds., *Higher Education and Economic Growth* (Boston: Kluwer, 1993).
41. Norval D. Glenn, "The Distribution of Political Knowledge in the United States," in Dan D. Vimmo and Charles M. Bonjean, eds., *Political Attitudes and*

Public Opinion (New York: Longman, 1972). Astonishingly, there has been no followup of Glenn's pioneering study, with one recent exception; for survey evidence of a decline of interest and knowledge about politics among young adults, see *New York Times,* June 28, 1990, p. 1. For the failure of high school history texts to even take on the function of preparing students for democratic citizenship, see Paul Gagnon, "Why Study History," *Atlantic Monthly* 262 (November 1988):43–66.

42. Eric Olin Wright and Bill Martin, "The Transformation of the American Class Structure, 1960–1980," *American Journal of Sociology* 93 (July 1987):1–29. Wright and Martin also argue that owners and managers receive more income than is warranted, even holding education, occupational status, and job tenure constant.
43. *New York Times,* June 18, 1990, p. 1.
44. Nell P. Eurich, *Corporate Classrooms* (Princeton: Carnegie Foundation for the Advancement of Teaching, 1985). The cost to business (ultimately to taxpayers and consumers) is much higher if employee wages and benefits are included. The education by governments of their employees would raise the figures for both costs and the number of students still more.
45. Ernest T. Pascarella and Patrick T. Terenzini, *How College Affects Students: Findings and Insights from Twenty Years of Research* (San Francisco: Jossey-Bass, 1991).
46. For a more detailed indictment of the higher education reports, see Daniel W. Rossides, "Knee-Jerk Formalism: The Higher Education Reports," *Journal of Higher Education* 58, no. 4 (July–August 1987):404–429.

10
The Legitimation of Class Inequality: America's Hegemonic Culture

◆ ◆ ◆ ◆

◆ ◆ ◆ ◆

THE CONCEPT OF LEGITIMIZATION

To legitimate is to make something moral, right, normal. A sexual union and the resulting offspring are considered legitimate if the couple is married. A government is legitimate if established by accepted norms, for example, divine right or elections. Once established, legitimate behavior is taken for granted and becomes the nonconscious presupposition of daily life, in effect, part of the mores.

Cultures differ profoundly in what they consider legitimate and this means that we are dealing with social power. Things and practices became legitimate because power groups have succeeded in institutionalizing their definitions. Once culture is understood as a historical creation, it opens up choices and fertilizes politics. Unfortunately, Americans have not yet realized that the economy and its class system are the historical creation of power groups. We have seen, however, that at least in stratification analysis, the near monopoly of functionalism from the 1920s to 1960s has been shattered by the rise of a many-sided conflict perspective.

Majority and minority Americans believe that rewards should be distributed by personal merit and by one's contributions to the social good. In their personal lives, Americans have a lively sense of what constitutes fair play and equal justice. But these beliefs and values do not carry into life beyond the personal level. There are no clear criteria for establishing personal merit or social contribution and, in any case, professionals and educators regard these as value questions and ignore them. The result is that the American public gets very little systematic education either in school or through the mass media in sociopolitical analysis. Americans would be shocked, for example, to learn that in comparison to other capitalist countries, the upper classes receive much higher rewards for their efforts and that their efforts do not lead to a better society; if anything, the United States compares poorly with other developed nations. Actually, American education, objective, nonpolitical social science and journalism, and other areas of American life form a depoliticizing process that legitimates the status quo. That this occurs unintentionally for the most part makes it all the more effective and dangerous.

Like all societies, the United States gets its essential identity from well-established boundaries. Despite noisy disagreements, even those who disagree agree on a great deal that they are not aware of. African Americans, for example, disagree with whites on many issues, but most agree that the ideal United States is possible. Mainstream women's groups disagree with conservatives on many issues, but they too think that the ideal United States is possible. (The ideal America, of course, expressed in stratification terms, means nonegalitarian classlessness.) The deep unconscious agreements that make up the structure of legitimacy has found expression in the concept *hegemonic culture.*

THE CONCEPT OF HEGEMONIC CULTURE

The concept of a hegemonic culture is associated with the Italian Marxist Antonio Gramsci (1928–1971). Gramsci's concept of *hegemony* asks us to stop thinking of dominance only in terms of universal values, political control, and propaganda-ideology. The process of domination, argued Gramsci, is a pervasive and enduring part of our entire experience: at home, in school, in church, at work, at leisure, attending festivals, as well as politics and government. But hegemony, he argued, is always problematic—elites and masses are always in a process of negotiating the terms of domination.

A hegemonic culture has its roots in the basic economy from whence causes flow to embrace the polity, the voluntary sector, and personal and family life. Explaining the hegemony of culture consists both of showing relative unanimity among those at the top and how the masses are absorbed into elite thought forms. Herbert Marcuse and C. Wright Mills led the way in the 1950s and 1960s in elaborating the concept of a hegemonic culture by pointing to economic concentration and the absorption of the masses through ideology, fear, and consumerism. Both also indict the mainstream social sciences for having helped to construct America's hegemonic (liberal) culture.

LEGITIMIZING THE LIBERAL UNIVERSE

The liberal universe was no natural flowering, but a construction by power groups, who used specific means at specific times, and who effectively blocked other ways of looking at things.

The Commercialization of Land, Labor, Knowledge, Religion, Time, Place, and Power

The essential thrust of the American economy was to turn nature into a source of private profit. Indeed, the main thrust of American beliefs, values, practices, and technology (at least until the environmental movement of the 1960s) was to *exploit* nature: canal building and river travel, the railroad, wagon technology, federal cavalry, the Homestead Act, mining, smelting, manufacturing, give-away programs of federal lands, and the right by law to use private property as one saw fit.

Labor was also commercialized as the practice of buying individual labor time became the norm. Knowledge was commercialized in the sense that newspapers, books, and researchers assembled it and dispersed it for money. The social sciences provided the ideology of laissez-faire and American exceptionalism. Organized religion, as well as popular and civil religion, supported capitalism (actually American-style capitalism) by claiming that it was sanctioned by God, nature, and human nature. (For more on religion, see below.)

Communication technology changed the way in which time and space were defined. Both were rationalized and turned into controllable abstractions, helping to create the timeless, placeless world of ahistorical liberalism. The railroad played a key role in severing Americans from the rhythms of nature and the uniqueness of times and places.[1]

The commercialization of political power also occurred. Universalisms such as liberty, equality, and happiness for all posed a threat to property and professional groups. The history of American politics is essentially the story of how the American upper classes prevented democracy, without most—including many at the top—realizing it. The commercialization and depoliticization of power took many forms:

1. Property qualification for voting up to the 1850s
2. The need for organizational skills and money to run for political office
3. The need to pay for political messages by which to influence voters
4. The use of money from Washington's day to the present to bribe, support, or rent the services of legislators, judges, and government officials

Providing a Common Faith and Natural Leaders: Education

The United States has enormous faith in the power of education to generate a meritocracy and to improve society. By providing all with equal opportunity in education, Americans believe that educational markets, along with similar competitive processes in the economy and polity, will reveal a natural hierarchy and a legitimate set of leaders.

Equal opportunity in education means equal exposure to a similar curriculum, something that should help homogenize the population as well as make for an equal race to the top. Despite the development of highly specialized schools and programs, the idea of a common standard for judging students has continued strong. That standard consists of measuring how well students do in abstract subjects and how skillfully they can read, write, and compute. It also means exposing them to deeply biased history textbooks.

The result of imposing a common nonpolitical curriculum on all, leading to an apex made up of abstract (liberal arts) subjects and skills, has been to legitimate the American class system. As we saw in Chapter 9, study after study has confirmed the dominance of social class in all forms of educational achievement. The dominance of class over education is not surprising. What is surprising is the near absolute failure of education to produce better workers-managers-professionals or better citizens. Note that this means that even when education succeeds in achieving its academic goals (our elite high schools and colleges), it fails in achieving social goals. It is not surprising that whenever the upper classes are confronted with the deficiencies of the American economy, they refer the American people to education as the solution.

The Separation of Elite and Mass: Professionalism

In a brilliant study that provides the indispensable historical background to American professionalism, Burton Bledstein has pointed to the pervasive influence of science on nineteenth-century American life and to the way in which it contributed to and helped legitimate unequal power relations.[2] The emerging culture of nineteenth-century America was everywhere animated by the rationalizing tendencies of American capitalism. By 1870, the surge of American industrialization and its diversifying occupational system had everywhere presented opportunities for a more efficient way to conduct business and conquer or contain evil. Efficiency appeared in the mass distribution of books through subscription and rationalized marketing techniques. The important lecturing business was rationalized. Spectator sports were professionalized with the first professional baseball team appearing in 1869. Even college sports were professionalized by the development of varsity sports guided by expert staffs. During the last decades of the century, professional associations appeared in a wide variety of fields (for example, the first national professional association in law was established in 1878). A wide variety of professional schools appeared: dentistry in 1867, architecture and pharmacy in 1868, schoolteaching and veterinary medicine in 1879, accounting and business in 1881.

Enrollments in professional schools rose rapidly as did their length and specialization (led by medicine). By the end of the century, a huge array of associations and learned societies had appeared. Of special interest is the appearance of associations for historians (1884), economists (1885), and political scientists (1889). And in all areas there appeared a piece of paper, issued either by the state or private groups, signifying that an individual had the competence and the legal right to practice an occupation.

The essence of the new professionalism, continues Bledstein, is the mastery of nature's principles so as to acquire a mastery over the chaos of experience. Theoretical and applied knowledge (over specialized parts of worldly phenomena) gave the professional the ability to identify and control the seen and unseen factors in areas as diverse as mining, constructing bridges or skyscrapers, commercial farming, curing diseases in all parts of the body, obtaining justice, coping with poverty, establishing rational management in business and government, rationalizing politics, and even in areas such as diet, hygiene, sex, dress, and recreation.[3]

Armed with knowledge, the professional was a truly free, independent, autonomous individual and thus in harmony with a central theme of American culture. But, says Bledstein, the freedom of the professional had deep conservative consequences. Professional claims to competence, augmented by rituals, costumes, technology, and physical settings, resulted in the marked dependence of the professional's clients. In all of life's spheres, the public was told that it faced one evil after another: crime, strikes, political uprisings, foreign threats, diseased bodies and minds, financial losses, legal calamities, and so on. Professionals preyed on and cultivated the insecurities and fears of the public. In the larger context, industry, technology, and science were upsetting the world while also offering themselves as the solution to the world's problems. In particular contexts, Allan Pinkerton in 1870 was extolling the virtues of the professional private detective in the war against the professional criminal; journalists were warning the public about the menaces in their lives and claiming that they had an objective view of them; reformers were rationalizing politics and the labor movement; and even the struggle against poverty was professionalized (a national association of social work appeared in 1874). The net result was to make ordinary persons dependent and accept on trust that their betters knew better.

The emergence and establishment of this power relation in business, in private professional practice, and in the polity (politics, government, and law), then led, says Bledstein, to the emergence of professionalism as an orderly lifetime career. The role of higher education in all this was to persuade the public that those in high places were competent and thus trustworthy. By standardizing admissions and prescribing formal courses of study, by giving examinations, and conferring degrees, higher education proclaimed that the intelligent were rising to the top and that the country had a way to overcome family inheritance, political favoritism, and subjectivism. The ideology of professionalism meant that the power and profit of an unsupervised and unaccountable set of class-based professions were legitimate. To the extent that professionalism pervades the entire apex of corporate capitalism, it is a potent part of the liberal legitimating process.

Technocratic Liberalism and Corporate Capitalism

By the closing quarter of the nineteenth century, the essentials of the American industrial system were in place and the liberal professions and disciplines arose to do two things:

First, the applied professions emerged to grapple with the practical problems of the everyday world on a pragmatic basis: Each problem was taken at face value and efforts to solve it were undertaken without relating that problem to anything much beyond itself. A prime example is applied psychology, which began in World War I when psychologists introduced testing to help the military evaluate individuals and place them in the niches for which they were best suited. During the 1920s, applied psychology expanded and began to advise corporations, schools, universities, and government on how to evaluate individuals and fit them into otherwise unproblematic hierarchies. They also began to advise parents on how to raise children and to advise individuals on how to solve personal problems. All in all, they became "architects of adjustment" who simply took society for granted, ignored workers, women, and minorities, and using Darwinian ideas, thought of the human psyche as something that should adjust to its environment.[4]

Second, the theoretical disciplines arose to provide the metaphysical legitimacy that all power systems seem to need. By the last quarter of the century, the American economy had been separated from any controllable or accountable connection to social functions, and economics and administration emerged as professions to tell us that economic behavior reflected a law of nature and that administering corporations was a science. The American political and legal systems were in place and political science, public administration, and jurisprudence arose to formalize them. Political theory was on its way toward being a philosophical discussion of political issues (often referred to as perennial issues) in abstraction from an unproblematic civil society. Psychology emerged to provide the human nature underpinnings for an economic system that needed a more cerebral approach to economic and other social tasks. Its supreme achievement was the IQ examination, or rather its distorted adaptation of the intelligence test that France had developed to evaluate its educational system. All in all, academic psychology, testing specialists, educational psychologists, school boards, teachers, and university admissions officials all foisted a highly arbitrary test on the American people, giving an enormous advantage to the upper classes in the scramble for scarce benefits.[5]

In fact, all of America's mainstream knowledge elites took the legitimacy of the United States for granted. Mainstream social scientists from 1900 to the 1960s assumed complacently that American society was a naturally adaptive system and that the function of social research and thought was to learn more about society's natural processes in order to help it along. Along with other segments of mainstream social science, and together with other professions and elites, sociology and functional stratification analysis became part of the technocratic elitism that would help America get rid of the vestiges from the prescientific past. As Ross has shown so brilliantly, all the anxieties generated by an industrial-urban system, beset by one problem after another, helped feed a commitment to scientism, the faith that a professionalized science would lead America out of the temporary wilderness it had found itself in.[6]

Sustaining Myths: The Garden of Eden and the Frontier

Lester Kurtz argues that complex myths, such as the Garden of Eden myth, can both manage conflict and help forge a new boundary or identity among conflicting groups.[7] The Garden of Eden story contains two contrary images: a humanity free of social and physical constraints (freedom) and a fallen humanity punished by the need to work and subject to the authority of God. Kurtz shows how groups in Jewish, early Christian, and early American history have used different aspects of this myth to promote their legitimacy, manage conflict, and establish new identities.

The Garden of Eden myth focuses on ultimate identity and downplays class, gender, political, and other issues. The myth helped to reduce internal divisions and establish the Jewish identity vis à vis the surrounding Gentiles as well as quell the factionalism of the early Christians. In American history, Edenic imagery worked to increase—not reduce—conflicts and was used in an effort to emancipate Americans from the Old World as well as from Calvinism and the corruptions of urbanism. The Eden myth was framed in agrarian terms by eastern literary figures and combined with the frontier myth to create an image of a bright future of independent, free individuals. The Calvinist clergy fought this interpretation by emphasizing the Fall and the need to submit to the authority of God. But the first half of the nineteenth century was a period of intense industrial activity and all parties debated the great question—where is industrial capitalism taking America?—in terms of this familiar myth. By and large, left liberals saw politics and government as a way to realize the freedom implied in Edenic imagery while right liberals tended to emphasize that government's role is to maintain order and punish deviants. But regardless of emphasis, the religious imagery of a Garden of Eden played an important role in the creation of America's master myth that it is a revealed society based on a pristine human nature.

Richard Slotkin has also made a valuable contribution to understanding America's legitimation process. Slotkin is a cultural historian who assumes that the beliefs and values (ideology) of a culture emanate from historical experience, not from mental archetypes or the biases of language. These beliefs and values are sometimes stated openly as creeds or constitutional declarations, but they also receive mythological expression. A myth is a highly compressed, emotion-laden story accepted by a population as somehow given and natural, a story that evokes a rich store of associations. Myths arise from the historical experiences and salient concerns of a population. As instruments for coping with experience, they must bear some relation to reality and if circumstances change, the myths must be updated. They are not updated in the abstract, says Slotkin, but are framed by particular classes of people, who use them to mobilize a population in support of society's dominant ideology.

Slotkin's three-volume study of America's "oldest and most characteristic myth," the myth of the frontier, traces the use of this master metaphor through the colonial period ("the white settler-state or colonial outpost of the European metropolis," roughly 1600–1820), the period of rapid economic growth (1815–1870), and the period since the 1890s.[8] These periods experienced modernization difficulties and the frontier myth helped cope with the unique features of each period. The frontier myth of the colonial period emphasized the menace to civilization of the "savage" (Native Americans) and the need to defeat another outsider, the unjust authoritarian regime in England. The frontier came to signify separation, regression, and renewal through redemptive violence. The boundaries between evil and good were sharp and the stakes were total victory or total defeat. The ability to project the survival and progress of the white colonial settlements outward was also to project the internal conflicts among the white settlers outward and avert class warfare.

The frontier myth was updated to reflect the needs of the rapid and novel economic growth from 1815 to 1870. As we saw with the Garden of Eden myth, complex societies generate complex mythologies that can be used to support different political positions. The Jeffersonian ideal of a nation of free-holding farmers was supported both by the idea and the opportunity of westward expansion and "bonanza" economics. But the major use of the myth was by those who wanted to wed the resources of the West to the industrial East without interference from the masses. The reality of westward expansion was a corporate capitalism able to amass the capital, technology, and organizational skills to link the factories of the East and Midwest to the natural resources of the rest of the continent.

The frontier myth allowed all this to take place without contradicting the myth of democracy. The frontier did more than beckon all to new opportunities—what it did was to take the serious economic and political problems that had arisen by the 1870s, many of which revolved around freed slaves, immigrant workers, and Native Americans. These latter groups were resisting incorporation into the discipline of the corporation. Instead of open discussion and negotiation among equals and a link between progress and a wide dissemination of property, American elites invented a "savage war" against a combined set of lower-order beings: freed slaves, immigrant labor, and Native Americans. Combined with the ideology of social Darwinism, the new frontier myth became a central part of the legitimating ideology of corporate capitalism.

Advertising and the Construction of National Markets

Advertising one's wares and services is inherent in a market economy and polity. It represents communication between sellers and buyers and candidates and voters who are strangers. American advertising goes back to pre-Revolutionary days, with significant advances in forms and techniques occurring during the eighteenth century. Its fortunes have followed the contours of American capitalism. By the second half of the nineteenth century, advertising consisted of both words and art and appeared in many forms:

outdoor signs, newspapers, directories, magazines. Between 1850 and the 1920s, advertising as we know it emerged in tandem with the onrush of the corporate economy. Major corporations used advertising to establish their names and products on a national level, thus helping to undermine localism. The major vehicle for this was the emergence of national magazines, such as *Harper's* and the *Saturday Evening Post*, and mail-order catalogs from such companies as Montgomery Ward and Sears, Roebuck. Needless to say, the U.S. Postal Service (along with the railroad) played an important role in tying the nation together, not least through the delivery of catalogs and goods representing the thrust of manufacturers oriented to a continental market.

By the opening decades of the twentieth century, advertising, augmented by radio, was a fully established adjunct of corporate capitalism. By the 1920s, in conjunction with the mass-produced automobile, it was ready to do its part to inaugurate the era of mass consumption using what are now familiar techniques:

- Identification of unique qualities of given products (even if there are none)
- Repetition to establish brand names
- Association of a product with values other than that of the product

By the 1920s advertising had clearly gone beyond being informative and was now associating capitalist production and consumption with happiness and the rest of America's values.[9] And it was during the 1920s that advertising was harnessed to new functions—the need by a hugely productive capitalism to sell products and services that went far beyond the necessaries of life. The 1920s pioneered the substitution of images that satisfy (at least for the moment up to purchase) for the actual satisfaction of the products and services themselves. It also helped to legitimate the connection of income with consumption and the legitimacy of widely different levels of class consumption (for a full discussion, see Chapter 12).

Organized, Civil, and Popular Religions

The rationale for establishing American society (the liberal nation-state) was supplied, to a large extent, by Protestantism. Setting up a society based on the free individual was not an appealing prospect. Individuals are likely to choose self-interest over the social good, likely to quarrel rather than work in harmony. Protestantism reconciled the public good with the free individual by assuming that individuals were in the service of God. It declared the New World the Promised Land and Protestant New Englanders the Chosen People, and society was at once a covenant among believers and between believers and God. The affinity between the Protestant world view and the liberalism of Jefferson and Madison is apparent. In the years after the American Revolution, the Puritan image of society was secularized or, perhaps better said, liberalism was sacralized. The tension between religion and secular society remained, but was transmuted, by and large, into the service of liberalism, providing what one author calls a "Christian industrialism."[10] Eventually, the free individual was reconciled with social order and the welfare of society, not only by Providence but by the providential market.

The intertwining of religion and liberalism eventually became what Robert Bellah has called a *civil religion*, the celebration of Americanism using vague religious terminology.[11] Through its civil religion, the United States seeks to identify itself with both the natural and the supernatural worlds. Through civil religion much about the United States passes beyond conscious thought into the taken-for-granted world.

Civil religion has a number of sources. Christianity supplied the concept of a single God with special plans for the United States. The early secular leaders of the republic turned this into deism and evoked the concept of a concerned God to buttress the American social order. The Civil War spurred the development of civil religiosity. Memorial Day, Arlington and local cemeteries, and a variety of public monuments imparted sacredness to the Civil War effort. Today, Washington's and Lincoln's birthdays, Veteran's Day, the Fourth of July, and Memorial Day celebrate America and promote solidarity. American exceptionalism rests in large part on Americans' belief that God has specially favored them and their way of life.

Civil religion is a pervasive auxiliary to secular institutions, a celebration and reinforcement of the American way of life, a legitimating process of the first importance. Public bodies and artifacts (for example, legislatures, courtrooms, coins) and public occasions of all sorts from presidential inaugurals to baseball games evoke the sanction of the divine. In effect, American institutions are made divine by clothing them in vague, nondenominational religious terminology. Americans are the most religious of all the industrial nations if judged by church attendance and beliefs in God and an afterlife, but it is clear that Americans do not take religion seriously enough to let it interfere much with the pursuit of liberal (secular) values. What Americans worship, in short, is Americanism.

Organized religion also provides a legitimation for American institutions by putting them in a supernatural context. It deflects attention from the present, like liberalism, by projecting a better life into the future. Like liberalism, it explains success and failure in terms of attributes directly in human beings. All in all, American society is identified with God's purposes in a straightforward manner. Less straightforward is "popular" religion. Popular religion is when worship, faith, and miracles occur, and participants are not aware they are in church. Popular religion is when religious themes permeate secular life clothed in secular terms. The social sciences have long had a religious dimension. The concept of Providence was smuggled into economics during the eighteenth century to become the magical market. The concept of a golden age (the Garden of Eden), the idea of heaven, and the idea of the Second Coming were transformed by the French Enlightenment into the liberal (capitalist) concepts of perfectibility and progress.[12] Popular religion is also found in America's family-centered holidays in which a diffused religiosity celebrates and supports family life (see the next section). The mass (and elite) media are saturated with religious themes in secular garb. Recent decades have seen more than the usual number of supernatural thrillers, science-fiction morality plays, and disaster films in which inexplicable evil is overcome by individuals displaying faith and courage against great odds.

Peter Williams argues that there is a religious dimension throughout American culture.[13] Religious figures have achieved celebrity status through television propagating a "middle-class common sense" and an "ecumenical moralism." The advice given by religious broadcasts is very similar to the advice given by "Dear Abby" and similar columns. Mass circulation tabloids such as the *National Enquirer* have recurring "religion" motifs: miracle cures, astrology and predictions about the future, lottery winners, and the worship of celebrities, individuals who "seem to live in a world of their own in which the rules that govern and restrict mortals are suspended." Popular religion has a powerful voice in the *Reader's Digest*. Williams finds a continuity between the *Digest* and the McGuffey *Readers* that were so influential in nineteenth-century education. In each, "a system of values derived from implicit religious assumptions is disseminated as an unspoken frame of reference which underlies all of the other aspects of culture and society that are dealt with explicitly." And both are linked to the inspirational literature that has had such phenomenal success in the United States.

The *Reader's Digest* is obsessed with order, according to Wayne Elzey.[14] It affirms the ordinary and accepts the social order, asking only that individuals adjust so that they can fit in. In the *Digest*, an idealized social order is squared with its contradictions, not through intellectual analysis but through inspirational anecdotes or, to use the biblical term, parables. Medicine, science, and technology are good; failures are due to defective or evil individuals; anyone who wants to can work. The police and the FBI are good because they uphold the law and order but the IRS and welfare programs, along with labor unions, communist and socialist countries, and a vague something called "Asia" are outside the normal and natural. And the *Digest*'s "unforgettable characters" turn out to be ordinary people who always manage to summon up the inner strength needed to prevail against adversity. Beyond that, the *Digest* always has stories in which "the elements of violence, defeat, death, and persecution are blended in such a way that they become occasions for recollecting the timeless values and reaffirming the providential logic of history." Overall, concludes Elzey, "the presence of the invisible (and visible) Hand of Providence in the 'world's most popular magazine' marks it as a work of Scripture, second only to the Bible in sales and influence. It is a religious text because it markets a distinctive and alluring picture of the logic of American life."

National Events, Holidays, Monuments, and Artifacts

The enhanced communication capability of the nineteenth century helped complete the creation of nation states and gave added fire and focus to nationalism. Everywhere governing elites sought, with varying success, to identify the masses with a piece of geography, with sacred myths about peoplehood, and with the economic and political institutions they had created. These emotions and beliefs were distinctive and invariably defined in opposition to other national identities, making communication among peoples difficult.

The creation of nation-states and the development of emotions and beliefs about society as a special cluster of cosmic values ensconced on a special piece of geography occurred at many levels and involved the family, religion, local government, voluntary groups, and public education as well as national political parties and government.

All the countries of the West developed a host of symbolic justifications and rituals for promoting social cohesion and institutional legitimacy during the late nineteenth century.[15] Buildings and monuments of state power and pride appeared everywhere. Like other countries, the United States developed many civic ceremonies, national holidays, and public monuments to celebrate itself. Great events in the emergence of society were recorded and celebrated, and a host of physical entities were created to memorialize them. In the United States, the main events are wars, especially the Revolutionary and Civil wars. The physical entities that communicate meanings are the flag, coins, currency, and public buildings and monuments. The use of such things to promote and protect social hierarchies even as they allow viewers to interpret them differently is argued by Murray Edelman[16] (see Box 10–1).

The legitimating power of the national state has been extended during the twentieth century, much of it consisting of efforts to support the family and business interests. Along with industrialization, the growing movement by women into the labor force, and perceived threats to family stability, the United States has developed an elaborate cycle of family celebrations. Mother's Day was deliberately created, along with Father's Day and more recently Grandparents' Day. Significantly, many of our religious and national holidays have been transformed into family celebrations with special reference to the role of women as mothers and wives. Religious holydays such as Easter, Halloween, and Christmas, and national holidays such as Washington's birthday, Memorial Day, Independence Day, Veterans

BOX 10–1 *How Meaning-Infused Buildings, Monuments, and Spaces Communicate and Reinforce Social Hierarchies*

The governing classes of complex society use buildings, monuments, and defined spaces to objectify their subjective definitions of the world. Palaces, temples, tombs, statues, and public arenas and plazas are the more obvious ways in which meanings about power, hierarchy, justice, and legitimacy are established and reinforced on a daily basis. No less obvious are towering corporation headquarters, market places, residential areas, museums, theaters, and the like.

Edelman has used this idea to provide insights into contemporary complex society. The Capitol, White House, and Supreme Court building and all their inner trappings evoke a common political heritage, while the F.B.I. building and the Pentagon are massive monumental structures that denote defiance of disorder. Edelman also calls attention to the plush offices experienced by the upper classes when they deal with government and the squalid welfare and unemployment offices experienced by the lower classes.

Edelman emphasizes that buildings and spaces have no intrinsice meaning—their significance must be given to them. He also emphasizes that meanings are often sufficiently ambiguous to allow different groups and classes to read different meanings into them. For liberals, physical entities mean pluralism and freedom, while for Marxists (and others) the same entities can mean false consciousness.

Day, and Thanksgiving have all been transformed into family-centered holidays.[17] Needless to say, most of these holidays are also occasions for heightened commercial activity.

Nationalism received added force with the advent of radio and film. Television has now made it possible for the public to participate directly in events of national importance. In a fascinating study of "media events," Daniel Dayan and Elihu Katz identify the positive functions of the "live broadcasting of history."[18] In a frankly neo-Durkheimian spirit, Dayan and Katz argue that broadcasting events such as Anwar el-Sadat's journey to Jerusalem, the Olympics or the Superbowl, presidential debates, John F. Kennedy's funeral, the Pope's visit to Poland, royal weddings and coronations, and the Watergate hearings serve multiple functions: they promote "mechanical solidarity" by giving all a shared experience, they define society in ideal terms by highlighting one or some of its central values, and they (perhaps) promote pluralism (the liberal world of equality, achievement, and rule of law).

The scripts of these events, they argue, fall into three categories, all exemplifying "turning points" in the career of a hero: the first serves to "qualify" the hero (Contest), the second "shows the hero reaching beyond human limits" (Conquest), and the third recognizes and glorifies the hero (Coronation). The authors suggest that these events "can be considered enactments of Max Weber's traditional, rational-legal, and charismatic forms of legitimating authority" (see also "The Culture Hero as an Index to Prestige" in Chapter 11).

The authors acknowledge that their argument about the positive effects of the live broadcasting of history is not based on empirical research and ask us to consider their work as a set of hypotheses (an appendix carefully situates their analysis in the tradition of communication research). Carefully and elegantly written, and filled with insights, the study's main defect is that it somehow manages to depoliticize what it knows to be highly political events. Their functional analysis of live media events contrasts sharply with the conflict account by David Chaney of three major events in Great Britain: the Victory Parade of 1946, the Festival of Britain in 1951, and the Coronation of 1952. Chaney argues that all three events ignored the history-making victory of the Labor party that had taken place at the same time, a victory that had established a socialist government with a clear mandate to restructure British society.[19] Media events undoubtedly do what Dayan and Katz say, but how much different their study would have been had Weber (or Marx), not Durkheim, been their guiding spirit. It might have become a sociopolitical analysis that asks: How do media events legitimate illegitimate (obsolete, contradictory, inept) power structures?

LEGITIMATION AND RITUAL ELECTIONS

America's Plutocratic Polity

American politics is energized by money, and those with the most money have the greatest amount of political power. To understand American elections one must also keep in mind that the two major political parties represent competing sectors of the American upper classes (reaching down, of course, for support from below). Each party has the same three objectives: to favor the property-professional groups they represent, to co-opt active political groups, and to mobilize the masses in their favor.

The backdrop for today's politics is the extension of the suffrage, first to white males from the 1850s on, and then to all during the twentieth century. The American upper classes faced a new problem with universal suffrage. While apathy (socially induced) represented one solution, they still have to gain a majority of the 50 percent who vote. The nonpolitical, antipolitical nature of the American electorate gives added power to politically active minorities. A very small, extremely conservative group, for example, dominates the Republican party.

The extreme diversity of America's interests has always generated weak political parties. But direct financing of individual candidates (PACS) has weakened them still further.

The Capitalist Campaign: A Case Study

The capitalist campaign means that elections in the United States are purchased. It means that they are conducted by paid professionals. It means that candidates concentrate on techniques and avoid substance. It means that they are rituals upholding the idea of popular government, but not the reality.

Communication technology plays a central role in constructing a campaign. Present practices are a continuation of the past. Newspapers and magazines became important political forces during the nineteenth century. In the 1930s, President Roosevelt used the radio to galvanize the American people and help overcome the Great Depression. Communication technology's impact on politics has continued in the age of television. The advent of television (along with other technology) may actually have introduced new and dangerous levels of control over American political life. For one thing, the dominance of television has turned politics away from written to oral discourse. No sane businessperson or professional would dream of conducting business primarily through oral discourse. But radio and now television have steered the American political world away from writing to audiovisual interaction. The new audiovisual technology, in combination with other technology, actually makes it possible for people to see and believe in things that do not really exist. The carefully arranged studio settings, the live shots in shopping malls and residential areas, and the staff of advertising experts, media consultants, pollsters, and psychologists allow political elites to package and *sell* a candidate.[20] What is sold is an image, an individual larger than life, one who corresponds to the public's hunger for a leader of heroic, unblemished stature. With careful editing, the leader always has a word of wisdom to offer. There is no fumbling or hesitation. With careful attention to props, the leader is associated with God, flag, children, books, fireplace, and the current fashion in dress. The leader is against evil, is generous to the needy, and verbalizes society's highest values. The result is not politics, but a civil religious ceremony.

The mobilization of opinion and voters takes place through political commercials and films that present an abstract political point of view. The selling of the candidate is supported by film shots of the candidates on the campaign trail. These are supplied free to the news bureaus of television stations. But the clips are carefully edited so that the candidate's mistakes and hesitations are omitted. Editing allows candidates to appear with famous people—even when the famous people do not support them—and the large adoring crowds; sparsely attended rallies and opposition heckling are carefully edited out. Film clips are carefully geared to play on regional biases. Not only are commercials and news clips indistinguishable from one another, but seeing is no longer believing. Technology and its owners have created a vivid, plausible, but false reality.

LEGITIMATION THROUGH JOURNALISM

Covering (Hiding) the World at Large[21]

Like professionals in medicine, law, and the social sciences, journalism bases itself on the ideals of objectivity and nonpartisanship. But here, as in other areas of professional life, a new realism has emerged. Analysts have shown that the news media are distinctly ethnocentric and provide a false picture of the world at large, especially the Third World.[22] The two American international news agencies (Britain and France have one each and the former USSR had one) routinely support United States and Western interests in their news reporting. Philip Elliott and Peter Golding have found that the British news media have created a typical image of developing nations (they imply that the same is true of news media in all capitalist countries):

1. Developing countries are depicted only in terms of political, military, or economic crisis.
2. Direct British interests are highlighted in any news from a developing country.
3. Events are invariably framed in an East–West Cold War perspective.
4. The structure of the developing country is simplified—countries are seen in terms of their national leader and conflicts are reduced to tribal or religious disputes. National, regional, and racial stereotypes are also widespread.
5. Foreign news stories are framed within a narrow range of story cycles which limit the possibilities open to the developing country.

Western news media assume that it is normal for a developing country to strive to meet Western standards. Because of their reliance on Western agencies and journalism training, Third World countries devote more attention to the developed world than to other Third World countries, and as is done in the West, they focus mostly on political leaders, defining political action as that done by elites and equating official diplomacy with the substance of international politics and conflict.[23]

Framing the News

Domestically, the press is an integral part of the American power structure[24] transmitting the news from the standpoint of the upper-middle class and from a distinctively American value standpoint.[25] By and large, the press depoliticizes social problems even as it promotes a corporate liberalism at the national level and an entrepreneurial liberalism at the local and regional level. Journalism depoliticizes by alleging that it is objective. We now know that objectivity is a fiction invented by elites to protect themselves against each other. We know that journalism has neither the time nor the money to cover the news fully or carefully (and still remain profitable). We know that journalists lack the expertise and experience needed to get beneath the surface of substantive issues. We know that journalists become dependent on their sources, most of whom are powerful groups and individuals. We know that journalists work in bureaucratic settings in a highly concentrated business. During the 1990s the communication world has experienced an enormous consolidation as giant corporations such as Disney and Time-Warner have bought into all aspects of entertainment, sports, music, publishing, and news. The result is to further diminish the importance of news as it becomes a less and less significant part of giant organizations. Perhaps more important is the fact that these giant corporations have other interests and distinct relations with government, thus creating difficulties for journalists who want to criticize what they see.

In his classic analysis of the day-to-day routine of journalists on a small-city newspaper, framed in terms of the "reality construction perspective," Mark Fishman shows how deeply constrained news reporters were by the logic of a profit-oriented, bureaucratically run newspaper. With the organization spelling out the where, what, when, who, and why of news reporting, with private and governmental groups and individuals supplying the majority of their facts and interpretations, and with their corresponding American way of looking at things, journalists *create* a highly selective body of news. News is really a way of not knowing, a highly ideological way to create reality.[26]

We are aware, in other words, that the news is a socially created reality that supports the status quo and (this may be especially true of television news) creates dependency and undermines reflexivity (the ability to see oneself as an active participant in the formation and control of social reality[27]). TV news does not encourage viewers to understand and explain their problems in terms of the larger socioeconomic world. And it does not present alternative public or private policies for viewers to choose from. Instead, it presents viewers with a taken-for-granted world, a fixed "objective" world in which people are acted upon. In this world, action takes place in terms of unquestioned cultural a priori about the family, government, capital, labor unions, the legitimacy of experts, and other countries.[28] The basic causes in the world are different types of individuals, fixed impersonal institutions, and sinister or unstable foreigners. In this sense, TV news is part of the overall symbolic world that constitutes the basic outlook of all the theoretical and applied sciences and all the professions. As part of the larger culture, TV news does not control by imposing itself on viewers; perhaps more important is its ability to connect with the already fashioned personality of its viewers and to engage and involve them completely in a mythical world common to both.[29]

Newscasts pretend to have an authoritative picture of what is going on in the world. They consist of fragmented bits of information in vivid word and picture. They appear omniscient because of their technical ability to conquer space and time. But all this undermines understanding and promotes passivity. Broadcast journalism rarely encourages action by its audience or works to empower it by locating personal troubles in public and private institutions. And it never provides historical background so that the audience can learn from the past and locate itself in an ongoing process of social creation.

As we saw with medicine, law, and other professionals, both broadcast and print journalists work for large profit-seeking organizations. Steven Brint argues that journalism and other professions have suffered a loss of autonomy as markets have stripped away some of the protection that they once had against such forces.[30] Brint's analysis is framed in terms of his overall thesis, that the once nonpolitical, nonprofit professions, motivated by a service-scholarship ethic, have become experts for hire, experts who are oriented toward markets and income. Brint's thesis is a common one that surfaces continuously in the individual professions and is based on the dubious assumption that the professions were once separate from and above the capitalist economy. It is closer to historical reality to see the professions as essentially capitalist actors who invented ideals of service, objectivity, and so on to enhance their market capabilities. What Brint and others are observing is change within an unchanging capitalist world. This change has led, in journalism as elsewhere, to corporate world-market capitalism. News organizations are not merely dependent on advertisers—they are big businesses in their own right, whether in newscasting, newsprint, or as parts of giant, often global, multimedia corporations. In any case, there is little doubt that the news media exhibit a strong trend toward monopoly.[31]

Organizational dependence is not the only constraint on journalists. They are also extremely dependent on their sources, who often are people in power—that is, those who make news. Given this overall context, it is not surprising that journalism often falsifies by accepting the facts as presented by politicians and representatives of interest groups. It collaborates with political figures and police departments at budget time to create false crime waves.[32] It falsifies by omitting facts; for example, in reporting on elections in El Salvador in 1984, it hailed the large turnout as a victory for moderation, forgetting to note that voting in El Salvador is compulsory. Journalism falsifies by discussing a limited range of reform proposals as the only choice open to Americans. It falsifies by faithfully reporting what government officials have to say. And there is evidence that journalists who report on science have consistently portrayed it as humanity's best hope and have failed to raise critical issues about it.

In an important empirical study of the impact of TV newscasts on public opinion, Shanto Anger found that the *episodic* framing of the bulk of newscasting (the depiction of particular acts by individuals, particular events, individual perpetrators, or victims) as opposed to *thematic* format (putting the episodes in an explanatory context) reduced the public's attribution of acts and events to societal factors and to the actions of elected officials.[33] Hundreds of acts of terrorism, for example, were reported during the 1980s, but there were virtually no reports on their socioeconomic or political antecedents. In addition to terrorism, crime and poverty were reported episodically, racial inequality featured both episodic and thematic reports, and unemployment was primarily thematic. With the exception of unemployment, the public was sensitive to the format employed. The influence of the format used by TV news is resisted by other variables (for example, party affiliation and political ideology, but not level of education). Nonetheless, depending on the format it uses, TV news has the power to raise or lower the public's ability to hold political officials accountable. Anger's conclusion is that it lowers the public's ability to hold elected officials and social factors responsible for social problems, not least because it prevents the public from seeing the interconnections among "episodes," for example, unemployment and crime.

Another careful study, this time of the personality of elite journalists (in the context of the national media), reports that elite journalists are fairly homogeneous in origin (upper-middle class, eastern, urban, nonchurchgoing) and in personality (they are politically liberal and alienated from traditional norms and institutions, to the left on social issues such as abortion, gay rights, and affirmative action, and would like to strip power from traditional holders and empower black leaders, consumer groups, intellectuals, and the media).[34] All this leads them to give the news a left liberal slant as judged by long-term coverage of nuclear safety, busing, and energy issues. The slant given to these questions (which occurs on all issues, say the authors) can be seen in two ways: American executives consistently see all issues differently than journalists (on tests), and the journalists veer toward the left in comparison with experts on nuclear safety, busing, and energy.

The authors tend to conclude that journalists cannot be objective (that is, they do not make the mistake of criticizing them for not being objective). But their study creates the impression that executives have sounder judgment than journalists, and assumes that the experts they consulted are objective. Instead of realizing that executives and experts are no different than journalists (one or another form of liberal bias), the authors' purpose seems to be to discredit journalists, not so much for displaying bias, but for being biased on the liberal left. Somehow journalists are biased because personality tests reveal that they are anti-authority and their need for power is stronger than their need for achievement. The authors would have also been wise to be suspicious of experts in testing.

Public confidence in newspaper and television news has dropped significantly in the past decade or so (part of a general loss of confidence by the American people in their institutions and professions). In a paper to the American Political Science Association's annual meeting, Kathleen Hall Jamieson argues that journalism's standing has suffered because it focuses on the maneuvering of public participants and their attacks on one another and fails to report on the substantive content of policy proposals.[35]

Jay Rosen has emphasized the many subtle assumptions underlying the practice of journalism. He too names the tendency by journalists to focus on the strategy of public actors and to connect public life to the wider American value of winning. And by claiming to be objective, journalism tags those who do not share this ideal as subjective. All in all, concludes Rosen, the desire to be objective is really a desire "to be free of the results of what you do."[36]

Journalism, perhaps especially TV news, is politically biased despite—or perhaps because of—its strenuous effort to be objective and nonpartisan. To achieve objectivity, it searches out and affirms the broadest area of agreement. By focusing on social consensus, it neglects conflict, special points of view, and the possibilities for change. The world it creates is seen as unchanging and unchangeable. Investigative journalism (for example, *60 Minutes*) focuses on rotten apples and ignores the barrel (the institutions of capitalism). In-depth coverage of issues (the news documentary) has all but disappeared from television: the prime-time public is not interested, it represents a loss of profit, and it only causes controversy. The demise of the Fairness Doctrine (the requirement that different positions on issues be given) means that the discussion of public issues will be subject to the power of money. And journalism, again especially television news, has become an integral part of the new politics, the ability of candidates to create a false world through a careful management of symbols: privately produced film that is presented as news and staged news events and photo opportunities at which little of substantive value is said.[37]

THE COMMERCIALIZATION OF CULTURE

Culture, Inc.

In an application of the concept hegemonic culture, Herbert Schiller has pointed to the commercialization of culture as an ominous development. His analysis rests on the assumption that the prime cause in modern society is the concentrated economy, and its auxiliary, the polity. Here Schiller is continuing the radical conflict tradition in American life that stretches from Veblen through Mills and Marcuse. Schiller's contribution to this tradition is to call attention to the new trends in knowledge generation and transmission made possible by twentieth-century communication technology. Schiller's basic thesis is that the corporate economy, and its helpmate, the polity, has reached out to commercialize knowledge, indeed, all of culture, both at the macro and micro-levels of society. The means by which this is done are part of the economy itself, the culture industries. These include "publishing, the press, film, radio, television, photography, recording, advertising, sports, and more recently, the many components that make up the information industry (data-base creation, production of software for computers, and various forms of saleable information)." The culture industries include "museums, art galleries, amusement parks (Disneyland, Sea World . . .), shopping malls, and corporate 'public' spaces." In addition, Schiller claims, the entire range of the creative arts such as dance, drama, music, and the visual and plastic arts have been separated from their group and community origins and turned into commodities.[38]

Schiller's focus on the direct buying and selling of symbols directs him away from the disguised manner in which symbols protecting and furthering corporate interests are generated and transmitted by education, research institutes, foundations, charities, and churches. Nonetheless, he provides many new insights into the deeper meaning of some well-known trends. In the corporate world itself, says Schiller, knowledge comes from the top and trickles down the hierarchy on a need-to-know basis, hardly an experience conducive to the development of democratic personalities. Schiller (along with others) has also sounded the alarm at the strong trend toward the privatization of knowledge.

In recent decades, a more explicit trend toward the privatization and commercialization of knowledge (as information) has occurred as private information businesses have multiplied and the federal government has shaped its data-gathering operations to accommodate them. The basic pattern that has emerged is that the government pays to amass data, reduces its free distribution, and allows private companies to use its data free of charge as a profitable commodity. Congress and the courts have helped in privatizing symbol creativity by extending the types of knowledge that are patentable[39] and the U.S. Supreme Court has given the sanction of law to corporate power by protecting its right to speech both through advertising and contributing to political campaigns.[40]

The computer has made selling data profitable and today a thriving business has developed providing information on the private lives of individuals. Computer searches of tax, bankruptcy, lawsuit, asset, lien, and other records are valuable to many businesses as they check potential employees or try to identify credit risks and markets. Market research has long used survey methods, but few realize that polling on public issues is also a private business that tends to ask only the questions elites are interested in.[41]

Schiller is also insightful in pointing to the public mall as an extension of the power of private property (its owners can prevent political and intellectual expression even as they immerse citizens in commerce).[42] Sports, and many cultural activities, including theater, parades, and festivals in parks and streets, along with public television, are now thoroughly encased in advertising and corporate sponsorship. By and large, the nonpartisan sponsorship of sports, art, and public television does more than provide corporate visibility and recognition, and does more than make the corporate world appear altruistic—it tends to create the false impression that these reaches of human expression have no social base and no politics.

In a related argument, but focused on intellectuals, Philip Elliott argues that we are witnessing a "shift away from involving people as political citizens of nation states toward involving them as consumption units in a corporate [global] world." The result is to curb two-way interaction, restrict the public sphere, and undermine the power of politically aware intellectuals. [43]

The Globalization of Corporate Expression

Schiller (along with others) has also called attention to the outward thrust of America's (and other countries') transnational corporations, not only to establish a free flow of capital and labor (and goods and services), but a free flow of information.[44] With the help of the American government, corporate capitalism mounted an onslaught against all nationalized systems of communication (including the well-regulated, quasi-public monopoly AT&T in the United States) in both developed and developing countries. And it worked hard to curb anyone who defended the need to have communication systems under public supervision, whether at home, in other countries, or at the United Nations. Along with the transfer of communication technology and systems into private hands has come an elaboration of "intellectual property" law and its application to all countries and their interchanges.

At the end of World War II, the United States pushed hard to break the British monopoly on global communications. It emphasized the "free flow of information," which had a democratic appeal, but which was largely a way to provide the information networks needed by giant American corporations. The ability to transmit data about all the things that are vital to corporations (taxes, currency rates, personnel and inventory records, technical designs, and so on) effectively makes capital mobile, ready to move wherever costs are low and profits highest. It also means that Third World countries will have little to say about how they will develop.[45] By the mid-1990s the United States had not only effectively blocked Third World efforts to gain some power over the world's communication networks, but it had succeeded in getting information transfer defined as a trade service. Included in the new GATT treaty of 1995, global information was now in the service of global capitalism.

Far more is involved than the free flow of economic data. News, advertising, and entertainment are now also "free." The capture of corporate capitalism of communication around the globe means not only that all messages running counter to capitalism are reduced (often through misinformation, or the deliberate creation of false realities), but the marketing messages of consumerism now blanket the world. And the messages are not merely transmitted formally by voice, picture, or print, but are found permeating the atmosphere at international sporting events from the Olympics to auto racing. In addition, the international nature of scientific knowledge creation and exchange, whereby knowledge is assembled in global corporations, privatized, and wedded to profit, was seen in the example of plant science. This process of appropriating the culture of others is far more extensive than is commonly understood.[46]

LEGITIMATION AND PUBLIC INTEREST GROUPS

To see the ideolological nature of public-interest groups is difficult because the very idea sounds like a contradiction in terms, like saying "married bachelor." But the term *public interest,* signifying being above partisanship, is part of the legitimating mythology of American culture.[47]

Health Charities and the Disease Establishment

The unmonitored nature of America's power groups extends to the area of charities with the same dire results. In a superb summary of research, focused on the giants of the health charities—the American Cancer Society, the American Heart Association, and the American Lung Association, with a case study of the scandal-ridden United Way—James Bennett and Thomas DiLorenzo have identified numerous abuses amounting to a gigantic scam perpetrated on the American people.[48]

The health charities solicit donations from the public ostensibly to fight diseases and to serve patients. In reality, they provide few services, their research grants subsidize traditional health professionals, and as organizations are poorly managed. In addition, their executives give themselves lavish salaries, pensions, and benefits, and they also benefit by building up the assets (plush facilities) of the organizations they work for. These charities also emphasize treatments that are profitable to allied business (exaggerating their value) and are hostile to nonpatented, alternative treatments.

Bennett and DiLorenzo also connect these charities to allegedly nonprofit health insurance groups (Blue Cross–Blue Shield) and nonprofit hospitals. In all cases, surplus revenues do not go into enhanced services or patient care, but into the pockets of executives and health professionals.

The boards of these groups are dominated by health professionals, ensuring a medical approach to disease and disability. The latent function of a medical approach is to distract attention from the social causes of disease and disability and to avoid demands for a better environment, diet, and style of living. Actually, there is a deep tie-in between the health charities (and United Way) and the corporate world, with both working through Congress and the National Institutes of Health to maintain the medicalization of disease and disability and distract attention from their causes. (For a fuller discussion of one of these charities, see Box 13–1.) The health and other charities, therefore, are not only a way of funneling the money of ordinary people into the pockets of professionals and the well-to-do, but a way to legitimate a disease- and disability-causing capitalist economy. These twin processes are found in all institutional areas.

The Ideology of Voluntarism

The philosophy of voluntarism enunciates a nonexistent world of homogeneous individuals and asks a nonexistent everyperson to shoulder social burdens. As an example, the Advertising Council, an organization financed by the powerful business and professional groups that constitute the real America, sponsors public service announcements emphasizing the responsibility of all Americans to stop pollution, curb forest fires, and so on. The American Cancer Society stresses individual responsibility for preventing cancer. The United Way, supported by corporations and other private organizations, dispenses charity to the victims of an ineptly run society; the Republican party, many editorials, and many political commentators emphasize the need for private organizations to tackle social needs. The philosophy of volunteerism, of course, is a depoliticizing political stance that diverts attention from the power groups that are causing our problems and from needed political action to solve them—all in all, a legitimating facade for a malfunctioning class society.

LEGITIMATION THROUGH MASS MEDIA ENTERTAINMENT AND SPORTS

The Class Nature of Popular (and Elite) Culture

The class nature of all culture is an all-important feature of human history ever since post–hunting and gathering society. The symbols of society and the explanation of where humans come from and where they are going have always reflected the problems and interests of the upper classes. This is as true of the rational culture of the West, including today's myths and universalisms, as it is of feudal-authoritarianism.

Differences in culture during the modern period can be discerned. The culture of the upper and lower classes was probably more differentiated prior to the twentieth century, especially before World War II. The upper classes consumed culture differently by going to school for longer periods. They went to churches that were more theologically oriented than the churches of the lower classes. They attended lectures, concerts, and operas;

read more demanding books, magazines and newspapers; and were the most active in the politics of their day.

The upper classes have always translated their wealth into artistic and ideological supports for their way of life. The prestige dimension identified by Max Weber includes a large number of subdimensions that simultaneously exhibit the difficult-to-acquire refinements of the upper class of old wealth and make it difficult for those with mere money to enter their ranks (see Chapters 11–13).

The new technology of manufacturing made it possible to produce larger volumes of cultural products as far back as the nineteenth century. The volume of products has accelerated, reaching flood-tide in the second half of the twentieth century. Today, old class distinctions still hold, though certain changes are also apparent. The upper classes are now diverse and highly professionalized. Despite broad differences in cultural intake, the era of mass communication has also tended to homogenize what both the upper and lower classes experience, especially in entertainment. Nonetheless, the era of mass culture is still a class structure, that is, it upholds the worldview of the upper classes. From one perspective, the pervasive themes of liberalism in the media hold the working and lower classes in place and continue to help socialize them to accept the world as it is. From another perspective, the pervasive participation of all classes in mass culture means that the middle and upper classes are also being depoliticized and thus rendered unable to govern effectively. From the standpoint of stratification analysis, the themes of mass culture, both advertising and content, are ways to absorb the population and lock them into an illegitimate and malfunctioning class system.

The themes that constitute popular culture are easily converted to the language of social class. Individualism is the central theme of both popular-elite culture and the ideology of nonegalitarian classlessness. Individualism is everywhere a way to hide social structure as well as class structure. Everywhere superior individuals, often adept at using technology (gun, scalpel, space ship, and so on), are busily solving problems and protecting the taken-for-granted Edenic community (a marriage, a family, a ranching community, an urban center, the United States). Individualism also hides social structure by having individuals generate both good and evil, thus making it impossible for viewers to understand that social structures (and history) are responsible for both.

The mass media, both as entertainment and journalism, uphold a class-based society by not focusing on social class as such. Classes are portrayed, of course, but in a manner that denies their existence. The middle and lower classes are extensively portrayed but they become Everyperson. The problems of small business or semiprofessionals are not discussed as such (except in elite newspapers or magazines). Neither are the problems of the working classes or the poor. All are depicted as ordinary people coping with life through humor and improvisation. Or they are depicted as people with problems or as the cause of problems—in both cases, there is a need for professionals to come to their aid or to thwart them.

Soap operas are perhaps the best example of how class is asserted so pervasively that it is denied: working-class people are never seen, but solid upper-middle-class executives and professionals are everywhere and they interact easily with the very rich. Also present is the Edenic theme that permeates American culture and politics: soap operas are usually set in small-town communities, an ideal marital-family world is always assumed, and both community and family life are disrupted by some evildoer.

Roseanne: Workers Without a Class

The television program *Roseanne,* centering on a working-class family, might seem to contradict the claim that the mass media neglects the working class. *Roseanne* touches on every problem faced by the working classes: lack of educational credentials, lack of employment skills, sporadic employment, cash flow problems, and children who are consumers beyond their means, who engage in premarital sex, who make bad marriages, and who go on to school through happenstance. The generational inheritance of class troubles is also fully outlined. Roseanne and Dan, who had unsatisfactory parents, are also depicted as parents who cannot provide their children with firm guidance. *Roseanne* raises all these problems only to have them seem like the universal problems of Everyfamily, problems solvable by humor, cynicism, and ad hoc coping. Even Roseanne's small success running a fast-food store occurs only because of inherited money (from one of the despised parents).

The Latent Class Functions of *Playboy* Magazine

On the surface, *Playboy* magazine appears to be an incitement to sexual passion. Its latent functions, however, are far different. *Playboy* must be put in the context of America's pervasive commercialization of sex (advertising, hard- and soft-core pornography), and like the overall pattern, serves to devalue family values (mutual commitment to marriage and children). Beyond the commercialization of sex is the main theme of popular culture itself, the celebration of the individual achievement ethic (nonegalitarian classlessness), which often explicitly devalues love and commitment. Complex societies need achievers (heroes) who can solve problems, especially those that lie beyond the confines of the home. In popular culture, a common theme depicts an individual (invariably male, often young) who must transcend family values in order to achieve. Young males must leave home, adult males must forgo romance or sex or leave wives behind. Popular culture, from Superman comics to Walt Disney, from Doc Savage adventure stories to *Playboy* magazine, tend to have a common theme: sexual renunciation by males and segmentation between males and females. Men are either indifferent to women or under siege by them. Even *Playboy,* as Robert Jewett and John Shelton Lawrence argue, is part of this pattern. Its focus on sex and nudity has nothing to do with love and commitment. Instead, it creates a uniform world of cool, faceless men and an image of lustful women imploring men to satisfy their needs.[49] Like popular culture in general, it makes clear that love and commitment between the sexes must not interfere with masculine achievements, all of which lie beyond home and hearth.

As Jewett and Lawrence (and others) point out, *Playboy* is antisensual, amounting to a rejection of commitment to enduring sexual relations. *Playboy* separates the sexes, making women appear to want men, while the latter pick and choose like calculating consumers. Here one can also identify perhaps the major latent function of *Playboy*, as a guide to consumption for upwardly mobile males (or those with disposable income) in the realms of cars, stereo equipment, clothing, dining, and reading.

Playboy magazine can also be placed in the context of structural trends in the American economy and class system. Barbara Ehrenreich has argued that the post–World War II period witnessed a flight from commitment by men.[50] From the 1950s on, the breadwinner ethic, the idea that men work for others, has declined. Men still want to work hard but not for others. There are various signs of this: the new psychology of personal growth, the criticisms of life in the corporate world, and warnings about the adverse health effects produced by the economic rat race. But, argues Ehrenreich, the publication of *Playboy* magazine in 1953, with its open rejection of marriage and family, is perhaps the best way to understand the male "liberation" from commitment. *Playboy* is primarily a guide to upper-middle-class consumption and its attitude toward women and sex continues the tradition that sees them as a barrier to the achievement of male values. Far from heralding the sexual revolution, *Playboy* divorces sex from sexuality, commitment, reciprocity, and procreation. As Ehrenreich suggests, the antifeminist backlash of the 1970s and 1980s is really against the decline of the breadwinner ethic. Few understand, says Ehrenreich, that the decline has occurred because the economy is no longer generating single-breadwinner jobs.

Gail Dines has spotted the consumerism of *Playboy* while also stressing its meaning for gender inequality. She has also shown that *Playboy*, with 5000 employees and $200 million in sales by the 1970s, has successfully mainstreamed itself. Its role in maintaining gender and class relations has been achieved, in Dines's words, by its success in "commodifying sex and sexualizing commodities."[51]

The Adventure Story

The adventure stories in television programs, films, and publications stress male achievement through skill, heroism, luck, and technology. (They now have token minority members sprinkled among the achievers, all thoroughly assimilated into liberal culture.) The major latent function of such stories is to focus on personal behavior while neglecting structural themes, in effect promoting a taken-for-natural attitude toward all forms of inequality. In common with journalism, it promotes a rotten-apple approach to evil and injustice.

The basic adventure stories celebrate technology and use the frontier myth to promise progress against deviance and foreign enemies. The present is also sanctified by setting stories in a mythical past (King Arthur, Robin Hood, the American West) or a mythical future (*Star Trek* and its many sequels, science fiction in general). The adventure story relies on exotic locales to identify national enemies and often to justify American or Western intervention in Third World countries (in the case of *Star Trek*, intervention by a superior culture anywhere in the galaxy).

The adventure story also resolves the contradiction between absolute self-interest and the common good. Self-interest must always conform to acceptable means for success. Those who use immoral or illegal means (the villain) are depicted in deeply negative terms and die violently. This theme is central to the Western film, as is the definition of the hero as an outsider and the depiction of ordinary citizens and government officials and politicians as weak, cowardly, or corrupt (see below for a fuller discussion of the Western). The antidemocratic bias of popular culture is especially apparent in the adventure story.

The film *Jaws* (1975) illustrates not merely the pervasive use of social class in popular culture, but the way in which class myths remain invisible even as they suck audiences into the story. A prosperous resort (Eden) is shaken by a nonsocial disaster—a huge shark has eaten a young woman. The small-business people (America's entrepreneurial past) are frightened and unable to act except to keep the beach open. After another victim falls to the shark, they offer a reward (capitalist material incentive), and the ocean front becomes a madhouse of bungling amateurs (the people are incompetent). An experienced fisherman (another small businessperson but with a skilled manual trade) combines the reward with motives of revenge (sharks ate many of his navy comrades during the war). He fails as befits someone with unworthy (material and moral) motives. To the rescue come a professional police officer and a rich Ph.D. fish expert (he owns a large boat with scientific equipment). Their motives are pure: duty and a disinterested search for knowledge. But even technology, knowledge, skill, and bravery are not enough—in the last analysis they need luck (society cannot solve its problems through ordinary people, the middle class, the upper class, or professionals).

All genres of contemporary popular culture have built-in ambiguities and token representation of minorities so that today's audiences can be reached. Until well into the post–World War II period, American popular culture used racist and sexist stereotypes openly as ways to build audience-receptive stories. Open racist-sexist stereotypes are no longer acceptable in the United States, and given the importance of the foreign market to American producers of popular culture, not acceptable there either. By avoiding open bias, by sprinkling minority individuals among both the heroes and the villains, and by leaving a certain amount of inclusiveness in the story lines (though white males and liberal norms and values predominate), today's popular culture lends itself to various interpretations and allows various groups to find satisfaction in the same offering.[52]

Crime, Law, and Medical Stories

Crime, law, and medical stories could have been included in the adventure genre, but have distinctive ideological aspects that need to be identified. Crime and mystery stories can no longer follow the structure found in Sherlock Holmes or Hercule Poirot stories: a crime is solved because a settled, highly predictable society makes it possible to find clues and identify villains. Crimes today are not easy to solve and have many ambiguous and conflicting features reflecting contemporary society. But one function remains: those who violate the Protestant-bourgeois ethic are deviants who deserve damnation and doom.

Law and medical stories also feature the white male achiever, technology, and problem solving in a world of rotten apples. Law and medical stories also have token representation of assimilated nonwhites and women. What is distinctive about these stories is that many of the problems encountered by achiever-heroes are caused by ordinary citizens involved in everyday life. The overall impression created by the display of deviance up and down the class ladder is that problem behavior comes from a hard-to-control human nature.

The latent function of crime, law, and medical stories goes beyond the legitimation of American professionalism (also a function of adventure stories). These stories, along with the mass media and journalism in general, protect the American economy and polity from scrutiny. They prevent Americans from asking: Is our unsatisfactory economy the cause of America's crime rate, the highest in the industrial world? Why doesn't the United States have a national health-care system like the rest of the capitalist world, to get the same results at half the cost? Exactly what is required to construct a judicial system that generates equal as opposed to class justice?

Targetting the Audience

The nature of the audience is much better known to those who devise programs to reach it (because they do market research) than it is to social science. The latter has studied the content of popular (and elite) culture and speculated about its ideology and its effects on audiences, but exact research on the class, age, sex, and racial-ethnic composition of audiences is missing—largely because it is taken for granted that there is a match between type of offering and type of audience.

Herbert Gans's classic analysis of elite and popular culture (which identified five taste cultures, all deserving of equal respect) took it for granted that these taste cultures corresponded largely to class background.[53] In his highly detailed *Commercial Culture: The Media System and the Public Interest*,[54] Leo Bogart has much to say about audiences, but reports little empirical research about them. Audiences reflect the daily rhythm of social life rather than conscious decisions about content. They reflect media opportunities that are richer in urban than rural areas. They reflect geography, sex, race, age, and class. The upper classes read more, the lower classes prefer television. Newspaper readership has declined, not only with the decline in the number of newspapers, but because of competition by television (radio news has almost disappeared with deregulation). By and large, says Bogart, the American audience is both homogenized by the media and fragmented by them with specialized publics.

The creation of audiences through market research is important; the producers of culture create their markets just as the producers create soap, automobiles, and so on. In a sense, the concept of a public (a politically active citizenry) has been replaced by the audience (a depoliticized, skilled receiver of elite messages). The ability to track and reach audiences is now technologically highly advanced.[55]

Not surprisingly, audiences prefer programs and printed material in ways that correspond to class, gender, race, age, and ethnicity. A good example is Radway's study of readers of romance novels, which provides evidence of class-based, gender-based, and age-based consumption of popular culture: readers tend to be working, lower-middle-class females between twenty-five and fifty (for details see the section "Romance Novels," in Chapter 19). Taste in popular music, television programs, and films also varies by age.

The interpretation of the same material also varies by class, gender, age, and context.[56] Many approved of Archie Bunker despite the program's intent to ridicule him. And of course different cultures will interpret the same program differently (for example, *Dallas*).

Commentators have found opportunities in popular culture for resistance to social power. Soap operas, *Roseanne,* and romance novels could foster female resistance to patriarchy, although no evidence of this effect has been discovered. There is a long history of dissidents using communication ideology to mount criticisms of oppressive conditions, even oppressive regimes.[57] Nonetheless, perhaps the most important thing about the class nature of mass media is that it supports, often on an unconscious basis, the basic foundations of American capitalism. Sari Thomas argues that it is a mistake to think of television as mere entertainment around which advertisers target their audiences. Television programs show us how the world at all levels works; it has more to do with everyday life than formal schooling. The idea that individuals interpret what they see is individualistic ideology—variations correspond to sociodemographic differences rather than to unique individuals. The selling of products through advertising presupposes an audience housebroken to capitalist behavior. Entertainment programs help to provide acceptance of the general process of capitalism. All this is done almost invisibly, as part of background: spending is taken for granted, excess money is to be spent, saving is deviance, celebration is a material event, spending cures depression, big spenders get better treatment, being cheap is vulgar, hard work is the way to get money, and honest work is its own reward.

Television entertainment, Thomas points out, also has myths about social mobility: its focus on a world of middle- to upper-class people makes it appear that there is plenty of room at the top (contrary to the facts). Linked to this myth is the myth that anyone can achieve (most of the better-off on television come from humble origins). On the other hand, those at the top have lots of trouble, while poorer families enjoy love and harmony, and have minor problems solvable in half an hour. In short, if you want success, be hopeful, but also be grateful you don't have to pay its price.[58]

Sport: The Triumph of Class Ideology

The world of sport is constituted by norms and values that reflect the American class system: giving your all in a win-lose competitive struggle, being a good loser and gracious winner, playing fair, exhibiting personal discipline and hard work, engaging in group discipline and obedience, and not giving up. These values are openly espoused and openly declared to be good for people and society.

Sport also reflects the rationalizing and professionalizing processes that characterize American capitalism. The educational system openly fosters elitist sports programs (varsity teams) while neglecting participation by all. The corruption of college sports is pervasive and has defied all reform efforts. Colleges and universities are essentially part of the "farm" systems of professional teams. Television provides many hours of sports, further helping to turn the United States into a nation of flabby spectators. And sports are full partners in American corruption and hypocrisy, from the pervasive corruption of college sports to creative bookkeeping by sports owners and huge, hidden subsidies given to owners by public bodies.

Sport has followed the contours of capitalist development. The professionalization of sport started in the nineteenth century along with the general growth of professionalism, developed slowly, and accelerated after 1950. During this period, the strong tradition of amateurism declined steadily and today is no more. Amateurism had a two-fold connection to precorporate capitalism. Agrarian elites stressed versatility and participation in high culture and sport as leisure activities, and shunned activities based on earning income directly from work. Early capitalist elites, who emulated feudal elites far more than we care to acknowledge, also stressed amateurism in sports and versatility in participation in high culture as a way to gain prestige and hide the way they earned their money. Amateurism was also related to the form that individualism took under early capitalism: democratic and egalitarian, early individualism stressed the all-around, versatile, nonspecialized personality.

The movement to corporate capitalism diversified America's concept of individualism by stressing the value of specialization and expertise. Understandably, sport also changed in keeping with the change from entrepreneurial to corporate capitalism (for example, as Stanley Eitzen points out, baseball, based on the versatile individual, was superseded by football, based on the specialized individual embedded in a tightly coordinated group[59]—to be discussed further shortly). Football was originally played without rules. The emergence of rules for football at the turn of the century (on the initiative of Yale University and Teddy Roosevelt) bespeaks the transformation of a Darwinian laissez-faire economy to the managed economy of corporate capitalism. Sport became a big business in its own right after World War II.

Sport is now hard work, conducted according to all the imperatives of the economic world: special training, discipline, scheduling, standardization, technology. The hard work (rather than play) starts early with Little League, junior high, and high school.

Sport uniquely supports the status quo—any status quo—simply by virtue of the fact that it emphasizes abstract character traits and alleges that rewards reflect innate human nature in a world of innate scarcity. In this way, sport blends easily with different power structures. American sports reflect American capitalism: they are competitive, aggressive, impersonal, methodical, specialized, professionalized, and profitable. Sports are designed to yield a small elite, as are the economy, the other professions, the polity, and education. Sports also reflect changes in American society: women and minorities are now more prominent in sport; sport has diversified to accommodate all age groups; and there is no longer one national pastime—baseball must now share the spotlight with football and basketball and to a lesser extent with auto racing, hockey, tennis, and golf.[60]

Sport depoliticizes by allowing all to participate in the reenactment of American values as if they had no contradictions or bad consequences. It depoliticizes by being nationalistic.[61] It depoliticizes by creating the impression that society, like it, is based on equal opportunity, promotes mobility, and has clear winners and losers emerging from a fair, refereed contest.

Sport also depoliticizes by providing variations on basic American values. Individualism, for example, is a highly ambiguous value, the source of much social conflict. Sport mediates such conflict by providing successful examples of individualism in a wide variety of contexts by a wide variety of individuals. America's two major sports (baseball and football) for example, provide different versions of individualism. As Eitzen points out, baseball is a nineteenth-century sport (entrepreneurial capitalism): leisurely, not bound by rigid time schedules, equalitarian, and unspecialized. In baseball, players come in all sizes and shapes, play both offense and defense, and are judged as a composite of abilities (the all-around versatile individual). Football (a distinctively American game) is a game more appropriate for twentieth-century corporate capitalism. Here individuals are incorporated into a highly specialized corporate (team) effort. A militarylike discipline spells out what is required under any and all circumstances. Players not only play only on offense or defense, but some only placekick, some only punt, some play only on kickoffs or third downs. Here is the specialized, nonpolitical worker who turns a bolt, handles only kidney diseases, or teaches Chaucer, microeconomics, American politics, or social problems.

Michael Real argues that the Super Bowl (which decides annually which football team is number one) has become the central mythic spectacle of American capitalism. Here Americans collectively celebrate a game that is openly aggressive, violent, and male-dominated; a game committed to seizing territory through force, guile, and technology (a way to legitimate imperialism?); a game that is profitable big business with ties to the corporate world and the polity; a game that openly associates itself with patriotism and the American way of life.[62] The Super Bowl may even have surpassed the World Series to become our central mythic spectacle. Perhaps more important, however, is the way football and baseball monopolize the meaning of individualism within a common American-style capitalism.

Professional sport as a mass opiate should not obscure the similarities and mutual supports that exist between sport and the rest of the American political economy. Elitism in sport has yielded world-class athletes and a flabby, overweight population. The U.S. Supreme Court gave baseball an exemption from antitrust laws and Congress has given professional sports generous tax subsidies. Local governments subsidize stadiums and arenas for professional sports at very high levels.[63] Professionalism in sport has yielded monopoly profits for many owners,[64] high incomes for athletes, modest incomes for auxiliary personnel, and dead-ends for the hundreds of thousands of youngsters who fail to make big-time sport teams. Sports organizations, athletes, and television networks combine to sponsor public service announcements extolling the United Way (a charity) as a solution for unemployment, poverty, and disability. Professionalism in sport receives massive support from the voluntary groups who sponsor Little League teams; from high schools and colleges; from cities, states, and the federal government, which provide massive subsidies through outright grants and the tax laws; and from newspapers and television stations, which celebrate professionalism as a given way of life. The similarities with professionalism in all other sectors of society is apparent, forming a seamless political economy that is as powerful as it is invisible. Perhaps its most insidious disservice is to support the myth that talent in all areas of life is scarce as all sectors funnel undeserved income and wealth upward.

DISPUTED SECTORS OF LEGITIMACY

American history is fulled with disputes about many issues, even fundamentals. Farmers, labor, racial supremacists, socialists, and others have voiced their disagreement with how America was and is being run. Currently, African Americans, Hispanics, women, the handicapped, environmentalists, and gays and lesbians are voicing serious discontent over the terms of their membership in American society. All this reminds us that much of the liberal consensus up to 1940 contained huge doses of racism, sexism, and homophobia, all legitimated with well-reasoned if empty abstractions.

From the Great Depression of the 1930s to the Great Society programs of the 1960s, the United States developed a welfare-interventionist state whose goals were to help the poor, the elderly, and minorities, and to protect workers, consumers, and the environment. A working consensus also emerged on another role for government—to help farmers and distressed businesses, and to manage the ups and downs of the business cycle through its tax, spending, and credit policies. These programs and new functions for government were opposed by right liberals even though astute observers were pointing out that the welfare-interventionist state was protecting, not challenging capitalism.

In the 1970s, right-wing forces, under severe competetive pressures from other capitalist countries, especially Japan and Germany, mobilized a head-on attack on the left-liberal welfare-interventionist state. Armed with a highly formalistic philosophy of laissez-faire, and supported by conservative Democrats and some well-organized, Old-Testament Christians, they attacked both the legitimacy and the programs of the left-liberal state. From 1980 on, and with renewed vigor in the 1990s, this reactionary coalition worked openly to dismantle core elements in the programs that protect the poor, the elderly, minorities, and the environment. Having defeated labor unions earlier, this collection of power groups broadened its assault on the welfare state in the mid-90s. Seen differently, it is clear that to construct a society in which all Americans can participate in a meaningful way requires a severe curtailment of the power and privileges of the upper classes. It is also clear that America's upper classes intend to use their formidable (largely illegitimate and dysfunctional) power, not only to maintain it, but to increase it. (For a discussion of studies indicating a steady erosion in the legitimacy of America's groups and institutions, see Chapter 14.)

SUMMARY

The concept *legitimation* refers to the way in which power groups define supernature, nature, and human nature to create a power structure that is difficult to see or criticize because it has been given plausible origins and purposes, declared to be true and moral, and has been lodged in the nonconscious layers of the personality.

The concept *hegemonic culture* refers to the dominating influence of elite values and beliefs at all levels of society. Elite values and beliefs are expressed formally throughout the various disciplines, voluntary groups, churches, interest groups, and political parties, but are also found in everyday family life and leisure activities.

Usage varies among liberals and radicals, but the concept *hegemonic culture* appears to make the most sense when used to refer to the absorption of both elites and masses into a culture that has a comprehensive answer to all problems, including the ability to excuse or hide the failures of the powerful by referring to human nature, nature, or supernature.

The history and present structure of the United States can be told in terms of the success of American elites in legitimating their interests, beliefs, and values.

The surging capitalist economy of the nineteenth century effectively commercialized land, labor, knowledge, religion, time, place, and power.

From its origins until today, education has imposed an abstract, depoliticized curriculum on students, thus both protecting the status quo and disguising its generation of a class-based professionalism.

Professionals reap rewards far beyond their ability to perform and mask oligarchic practices throughout American society.

American leaders use the Garden of Eden and the Frontier Myths to evoke a common identity and forestall conflict among classes, also freeing the upper classes to pursue their interests in the name of the common good.

Advertising plays an important role in fostering the legitimacy of class consumption and reinforcing capitalist values.

Organized, civil, and popular religions impart a sacredness to America's capitalist institutions, helping to hide the fact that these institutions are human creations and deeply deficient.

Like other nation-states, the United States developed a variety of nationalistic symbols and practices to legitimize itself. It identified America with God, history, human nature, motherhood, and a special piece of geography. It celebrated and symbolized the abstract nation (and state power) through buildings, monuments, artifacts, and song. It created monuments and holidays to celebrate its heroes and veterans. Ever mindful of the needs of business, it has even moved holidays to Monday to lessen the disruptions of the work week and to create long weekends useful for the tourist business.

The power of the state is used largely to benefit the upper classes, but its legitimation comes from an elaborate set of electoral rituals. Firmly in the hands of the upper classes (who supply the money and the personnel), elections give the United States what all complex societies from ancient Egypt to fascist and communist dictatorships have claimed for state power—an origin in the people.

Objective, nonpolitical journalism joins with the same tradition in social science to provide a legitimating cover for American society.

Thanks in good measure to the phenomenal growth of communication technology, the culture industries have grown exponentially. Advertising, public relations, and the transformation of knowledge into private property have transformed huge areas of public space into commercial space, that is, a private world that is not perceived as such.

Public interest groups and assorted nonprofit health and other charities, nonprofit insurance organizations, and nonprofit hospitals, all legitimate the status quo by restricting the alternatives available to Americans. The nonprofit organizations do not use their surplus revenues to benefit patients, consumers, or the needy as they claim, but put them into the pockets of executives and allied professionals.

Individualism, defined largely in technocratic liberal terms, is the central theme of popular culture. Individuals tend to be superior masculine types. While youthful males predominate, individualism is now portrayed by individuals from all demographic groups making it appear that we are seeing human nature in action.

Popular culture also hides society by using individualism to portray good and evil—in effect, hiding the structure of social power as the cause of both.

Recent decades have seen a trend toward professional, nonpolitical heroes adept in the use of nonpolitical technology. Love, marriage, and family join the political as secondary to heroic professionalism.

The mass media uphold and reinforce the class system in a number of ways. One, their focus on individual achievement, their diverse personalities, their emphasis on the unique attributes of singers, athletes, models, and so on, are all forms of nonegalitarian classlessness, expressions of the biopsychological explanation of inequality. Two, the mass media ignore the lower classes even as they are widely portrayed. The lower classes are portrayed either as ordinary citizens improvising and joking their way through life, as citizens who cannot cope, or as troublemakers (in the latter cases as deviants who must be helped or thwarted by the upper classes).

The mass media promote the class system through advertising. This was illustrated by the example of *Playboy* magazine whose major (latent) function is to guide the consumption of young males with discretionary income.

The class nature of popular and elite culture is also found in the fact that the various classes consume the culture differently.

Sports are the classic case of nonegalitarian classlessness. Sports promote the assumption that there is a hierarchy of innate talent based on refereed competition, implicitly suggesting that it should be possible to perfect the rest of society and base it on talent only, too. But the world of sports is not what it appears to be. Access to sports is class-based and many Americans do not compete. In addition, sports are racist and sexist. Perhaps the important thing about sports, with implications for the rest of society, is that there is considerable evidence that almost all can become top athletes provided they are given systemic training.

Popular culture has grown and now appears to form a larger part of the population's daily existence. The various ways in which popular culture upholds the class system were outlined here, especially its focus on individualistic behavior and explanations, professionalism, and its pervasive depiction of the upper and neglect of the lower classes.

All in all, the culture industries and its elites are a vast depoliticizing process that takes its place alongside the other professions and elites to render American society difficult to see and difficult to democratize.

Everywhere we see organized groups enunciating and updating the liberal worldview ever alert to challenges. Education, religion, nationalism, ritual elections, journalism, public-interest groups, and the mass media all uphold the legitimacy of class inequality by implicitly and explicitly claiming that it emanates from human nature, nature, and supernature.

Despite the best efforts of the various groups that make up the American power structure, American society has been malfunctioning, and disputes have arisen about aspects of the American consensus: race, gender, disability, sexual orientation, and the environment. Despite the efforts by both left and right-wing liberals to revitalize America, an ominous decline in legitimacy has occurred over the past decades.

Though right and left liberals lament America's rising tide of social problems and its decaying consensus, no challenge to liberalism per se has arisen. Actually, the mid-1990s have seen another concerted attempt by the Republican party and conservative Democrats (the bulk of the governing classes) to revitalize America by stressing the very institutions that are the cause of our problems. No better proof of the power of America's hegemonic liberalism is possible.

NOTES

1. For an insightful sociology of the railroad, see Wolfgang Schivelbusch, *The Railway Journey: The Industrialization of Time and Space in the 19th Century* (Berkeley: University of California Press, 1986; originally published in 1977).
2. Burton J. Bledstein, *The Culture of Professionalism: The Middle Class and the Development of Higher Education in America* (New York: Norton, 1976).

3. One can add parenting to the things that were professionalized in the nineteenth century. A wide array of self-improvement manuals also appeared, followed by self-therapy manuals in the twentieth century.
4. Donald S. Napoli, *Architects of Adjustment: The History of the Psychological Profession in the United States* (Port Washington, NY: Kennikat Press, 1981), esp. ch. 2. Also see Michael M. Sokal, "James McKeen Cattell and American Psychology in the 1920s," in Josef Brozek, ed., *Explorations in the History of Psychology in the United States* (Lewisburg, PA: Bucknell University Press, 1984), pp. 273–323. Loren Baritz, *The Servants of Power: A History of the Use of Social Science in Industry* (Middletown, CT: Wesleyan University Press, 1960), focuses on how industrial psychologists served the interests of corporations.
5. For background on the professions, see Daniel W. Rossides, "A Sociopolitical Critique of the Liberal Professions," *Social Epistemology* 4, no. 2 (1990):229–258.
6. Dorothy Ross, *The Social Origins of American Social Science* (New York: Cambridge University Press, 1991), ch. 10.
7. Lester R. Kurtz, "Freedom and Domination: The Garden of Eden and Social Order," *Social Forces,* 58 (December 1979):443–465.
8. Richard Slotkin, *Regeneration Through Violence: The Mythology of the American Frontier, 1600–1860* (Middletown, CT: Wesleyan University Press, 1973); *The Fatal Environment: The Myth of the Frontier in the Age of Industrialization* (New York: Atheneum, 1985); and *Gunfighter Nation: The Myth of the Frontier in Twentieth-Century America* (New York: Atheneum, 1992).
9. James D. Norris, *Advertising and the Transformation of American Society, 1865–1920* (New York: Greenwood Press, 1990).
10. For a fascinating picture of the organization of an early industrial town in Pennsylvania and the role of Christianity in helping the propertied classes fight socialism and in providing religious support for the expansion and consolidation of American capitalism, see Anthony F. C. Wallace, *Rockdale* (New York: Knopf, 1978).
11. Robert N. Bellah, "Civil Religion in America," *Daedalus* 96 (Winter 1967):1–27.
12. Marxism has its own version of these themes, but that requires a separate treatment.
13. Much of the following is indebted to Peter W. Williams, *Popular Religion in America: Symbolic Change and the Modernization Process in Historical Perspective* (Englewood Cliffs, NJ: Prentice-Hall, 1980), esp. ch. 4.
14. Wayne Elzey, "The Most Unforgettable Magazine I've Ever Read: Religion and Social Hygiene in *The Reader's Digest,*" *Journal of Popular Culture* 10 (Summer 1976):181–190.
15. Eric Hobsbawn, "Mass Producing Traditions: Europe, 1870–1914," in Eric Hobsbawn and Terence Ranger, eds. *The Invention of Tradition* (New York: Cambridge University Press, 1983), ch. 7.
16. Murray Edelman, "Space and Social Order," (Madison: University of Wisconsin Institute for Research on Poverty, 1978).
17. For an interesting discussion, see Theodore Caplow et al., *Middletown Families: Fifty Years of Change and Continuity* (Minneapolis: University of Minnesota Press, 1982), ch. 10.
18. Daniel Dayan and Elihu Katz, *Media Events: The Live Broadcasting of History* (Cambridge, MA: Harvard University Press, 1992).
19. David Chaney, "A Symbolic Mirror of Ourselves: Civil Ritual in Mass Society,"

in Richard Collins et al., eds., *Media, Culture, and Society: A Critical Reader* (Newbury Park, CA: Sage, 1986), pp. 247–263.

20. For a classic analysis of the 1968 presidential campaign on behalf of Richard Nixon, see John McInniss, *The Selling of the President, 1968* (New York: Trident, 1969).
21. This play on words is borrowed from the title and theme of Edward Said's book *Covering Islam* (New York: Pantheon, 1981).
22. Oliver Boyd-Barrett, "Media Imperialism: Towards an International Framework for the Analysis of Media Systems," in James Curran et al., eds., *Mass Communications and Society* (London: Edward Arnold, 1977), pp. 116–135; William Steif, "On the 'Objective' Press," *Progressive* 43 (January, 1979):23–25; Edward W. Said, *Covering Islam* (New York: Pantheon, 1981); Soheir Morsy, "Politicalization through the Mass Information Media: American Images of the Arabs," *Journal of Popular Culture* 17 (Winter 1983):91–97. The enormously influential *National Geographic* invariably leaves out conflict, exploitation, civil war, and imperialism in its portraits of developing countries; see Herbert I. Schiller, "The *National Geographic:* Nonideological Geography," *The Mind Managers* (Boston: Beacon Press, 1973), pp. 86–94.
23. Philip Elliot and Peter Golding, "Mass Communication and Social Change: The Imagery of Development and the Development of Imagery," in Emanuel DeKadt and Gavin Williams, eds., *Sociology and Development* (London: Tavistock, 1974), p. 230.
24. Peter Dreier, "The Position of the Press in the U.S. Power Structure," *Social Problems* 29 (February 1982):298–310; Ben H. Bagdikian, *The Media Monopoly,* 4th ed. (Boston: Beacon Press, 1993).
25. Herbert J. Gans, *Deciding What's News: A Study of CBS Evening News, NBC Nightly News, Newsweek, and Time* (New York: Pantheon, 1979).
26. Mark Fishman, *Manufacturing the News* (Austin: University of Texas Press, 1980).
27. Peter Dahlgren, "TV News and the Suppression of Reflexivity," in Elihu Katz and Tamas Szecsko, eds., *Mass Media and Social Change* (Beverly Hills, CA: Sage, 1981), pp. 101–113.
28. For a fully developed analysis of journalism as part of the world it is reporting on and thus unable to avoid distorting the facts to suit American assumptions, see Alan Rachlin, *News as Hegemonic Reality: American Political Culture and the Framing of News Accounts* (New York: Praeger, 1988). To substantiate his argument, Rachlin provides case studies of bias in the way American journalism handled the downing of the Korean airliner in 1983 by a Soviety fighter plane (Canadian accounts were quite different and more objective), and in its coverage of labor unions at home and abroad (strikes at home are unwelcome interruptions, threats to society and its proper functioning, whereas the Polish trade union movement, Solidarity, was a welcome development in communist Poland).
29. Herbert I. Schiller, *The Mind Managers* (Boston: Beacon Press, 1973), ch. 1.
30. Steven Brint, *In an Age of Experts: The Changing Role of Professionals in Politics and Public Life* (Princeton, NJ: Princeton University Press, 1994), pp. 123–126.
31. Ben H. Bagdikian, 4th ed., *The Media Monopoly* (Boston: Beacon Press, 1993).
32. Mark Fishman, "Crime Waves as Ideology," *Social Problems* 25 (June 1978):531–543. For a fuller discussion, see Kevin N. Wright, *The Great American Crime Myth* (Westport, CT: Greenwood Press, 1985). The false crime wave is part of the widespread pattern in American professional and business life of

identifying and exaggerating the dangers faced by the public, all the more to make them dependent on existing power structures, who are rarely identified as the cause of these dangers.

33. Shanto Anger, *Is Anyone Responsible? How Television Frames Political Issues* (Chicago: University of Chicago Press, 1991).
34. S. Robert Lichter, Stanley Rothman, and Linda S. Lichter, *The Media Elite* (Bethesda, MD: Adler and Adler, 1986).
35. *Wall Street Journal,* August 31, 1994, p. A14.
36. Interview in the *New York Times,* December 12, 1994, p. D7.
37. For a picture of bias in the news media stemming from a variety of sources, see Peter Golding, "The Missing Dimensions: New Media and the Management of Social Change," in Elihu Katz and Tamas Szecsko, eds., *Mass Media and Social Change* (Beverly Hills, CA: Sage, 1981), pp. 63–81.
38. Herbert I. Schiller, *Culture, Inc: The Corporate Takeover of Public Expression* (New York: Oxford University Press, 1989), pp. 30–31.
39. For a discussion of this process in plant science and biotechnology, see Jack Ralph Kloppenberg, Jr., *First the Seed: The Political Economy of Plant Technology, 1492–2000* (New York: Cambridge University Press, 1988), and Martin Kennedy, *Biotechnology: The University-Industrial Complex* (New Haven: Yale University Press, 1986).
40. Schiller, *Culture, Inc.,* ch. 3.
41. Herbert I. Schiller, *The Mind Managers* (Boston: Beacon, 1973), ch. 5. A full-scaled analysis of polling also shows that results (public opinion) emerge from the way questions are asked, their location in the interview, and the class and racial characteristics of the interviewer; see David W. Moore, *The Superpollsters: How They Measure and Manipulate Public Opinon in America* (New York: Four Walls, Eight Windows, 1992). The title of Moore's book is more radical than the book, which concentrates on the evolving science and profession of polling and its relative success in "monitoring the pulse of democracy."
42. A few states (for example, New Jersey) have extended free speech protection to shopping malls.
43. Philip Elliott, "Intellectuals, the 'Information Society,' and the Disappearance of the Public Sphere," in Richard Collins et al., eds., *Media, Culture, and Society: A Critical Reader* (Newbury Park, CA: Sage, 1986), pp. 105–115.
44. Schiller, *Culture, Inc.,* ch. 6.
45. Eileen Mahoney, "American Empire and Global Communication," in Ian Angus and Sut Jhally, eds., *Cultural Politics in Contemporary America* (New York: Routledge, 1989), pp. 37–50.
46. For a fascinating collection of essays on the transformation of Third World folk wisdom, knowledge about plants, the plants themselves, art, songs, and artifacts into the private property of Westerners, including examples of and suggestions for a more equitable distribution of benefits, see the special issue "Intellectual Property Rights: The Politics of Ownership," *Cultural Survival* 15, no. 3 (Summer 1991).
47. For the class nature of foundations and public-policy think tanks, see the section "Political Parties and Interest Groups" in Chapter 14.
48. James T. Bennett and Thomas J. DiLorenzo, *Unhealthy Charities: Hazardous to Your Health and Wealth* (New York: Basic Books, 1994).
49. Robert Jewett and John Shelton Lawrence, "Playboy's Gospel: Better Wings

than Horns," in Robert Jewett and John Shelton Lawrence, eds., *The American Monomyth,* 2nd ed., (Lanham, MD: University Press of America, 1988), ch. 4.

50. *The Hearts of Men: American Dreams and the Flight from Commitment* (Garden City, NY: Doubleday, 1983).
51. Gail Dines, "'I Buy It for the Articles': *Playboy* Magazine and the Sexualization of Consumerism," in Gail Dines and Jean M. Humez, eds., *Gender, Race, and Class in Media: A Text-Reader* (Thousand Oaks, CA: Sage, 1995), pp. 254–262.
52. For a good introduction to the adventure story, see Gina Marchetti, "Action-Adventure as Ideology," in Ian Angus and Sut Jhally, eds., *Cultural Politics in Contemporary America* (New York: Routledge, 1989), pp. 182–197.
53. Herbert Gans, *Popular Culture and High Culture* (New York: Basic Books, 1974).
54. Leo Bogart (New York, Oxford University Press, 1995).
55. Oscar H. Gandy, Jr., "Tracking the Audience," in John Downing, Ali Mohammadi, and Annabelle Sreberny-Mohammadi, eds., *Questioning the Media: A Critical Introduction* (Thousand Oaks, CA: Sage, 1990), pp. 166–179.
56. Jen Ang, "The Nature of the Audience," in ibid., pp. 180–191.
57. John Downing, "Alternative Media and the Boston Tea Party," in ibid., pp. 180–191.
58. Sari Thomas, "Myths in and about Television," in ibid., pp. 330–344.
59. For a good introduction to the sociology of sport, see D. Stanley Eitzen, ed., 4th ed., *Sport in Contemporary Society: An Anthology* (New York: St. Martin's Press, 1993).
60. Fascist and communist dictatorships, past and present, have fully recognized the political value of sport.
61. Individuals and teams from various countries now play on a year-round basis in almost all sports. The Olympic Games are especially nationalistic. The staged wrestling matches that are so popular on television also have a blatant xenophobic flavor.
62. Michael R. Real, "The Super Bowl: Mythic Spectacle," in M. R. Real, *Mass-Mediated Culture* (Englewood Cliffs, NJ: Prentice-Hall, 1977), ch. 6.
63. James Quirk and Rodney D. Fort, *Pay Dirt: The Business of Professional Team Sports* (Princeton, NJ: Princeton University Press, 1992), chs. 3, 4.
64. The average total return (profit) of baseball, football, basketball, and hockey owners in the early 1990s was 27 percent, with half of the owners above 30 percent. This is well above the return of the 500 largest industrial corporations and can be considered a monopoly rate of profit; for the data see Gerald W. Scully, *The Market Structure of Sports* (Chicago: University of Chicago Press, 1995), ch. 6.

11

The Prestige Dimension: How Americans Regard Themselves

◆ ◆ ◆ ◆

◆ ◆ ◆ ◆

The class order is a hierarchy of families and unrelated individuals (embedded in economic groups such as business enterprises, professional and trade associations, public service occupations and associations, and labor unions) ranked on the basis of ability to prevail in various economic markets. In our discussions of income distribution, wealth, occupation, education, family stability, family values, basic personality structure, health, and education, we identified the salient features of the United States' class hierarchy. The American population is composed of a hierarchy of families and unrelated individuals separated into levels on the basis of worth in various economic markets. Different levels are characterized by significant differences in family values and stability, life expectancy, and mental health, and by pronounced differences in the ability to put children through school successfully, an overall structure and process that tends to produce a static class system over time (as measured by the distribution of the above class values) and a considerable amount of class perpetuation (ascriptively based achievement and nonachievement).

Our task now is to consider the class dimension as a hierarchy of families and unrelated individuals who not only face economic markets, but who also behave as moral agents acting to maintain and enjoy various levels of psychic and social existence (the prestige dimension). In analyzing prestige, we will again deal with some of the phenomena we encountered in the analysis of class. This time, however, we will focus more explicitly on group formation and structure and on the development and distribution of psychic resources and satisfactions. To this end, prestige phenomena have been put into three major categories: how Americans regard themselves (discussed later in this chapter), how Americans consume "material" and "symbolic" culture (Chapter 12), and how Americans associate, or the structure of prestige groups (Chapter 13).

THE REALM OF EVALUATION

The classic analysis of prestige is Max Weber's. Weber identified status or prestige stratification as a realm separate from, though related to, class stratification. Stratification by status, he argued, is based on the distribution of honor (or prestige) and can take a number of forms:

> The term of "social status" is applied to a typically effective claim to positive or negative privilege with respect to social prestige so far as it rests on one or more of the following bases:
> a. mode of living,
> b. a formal process of education which may consist in empirical or rational training and the acquisition of the corresponding modes of life, or
> c. on the prestige of birth, or of an occupation.[1]

According to Weber, prestige differentials stem from usurpation, but their long-range stability and effectiveness require successful conventionalization and often require added support from the legal order (privilege). Though the bases of prestige can be as varied as birth (into a religious, family, ethnic, or racial status), breeding, property, occupation, education, or some mixture of these, the prestige hierarchy is always opposed to the free play of market (class) forces. Prestige stratification thrives, says Weber, when the distribution of economic power is stable. It reaches its highest development when a prestige group(s) succeeds in embedding property and occupations in a hierarchy of prestige values, thus making them immune to the play of economic forces, and is able to monopolize education and other opportunities for subjective development. Impersonal economic forces threaten prestige stratification because they cannot be relied on to honor the special prestige status of persons, property, or occupations. Dynamic economies undermine and transform prestige hierarchies beyond recognition. In short, Weber argued that class and prestige inequality are different though related and that, in a broad sense, classes stemmed from the production of goods and services, while prestige groups were derived from the consumption of ideal and material values.

Weber directed his analysis of prestige against Marx's argument that class is the universal basis of social stratification. But Weber never meant to replace class with prestige as the universal source of stratification; he was simply against the use of metaphysical generalizations. And he would no doubt have interpreted prestige phenomena *within* class society in economic terms. Today, the economic basis of prestige is commonly acknowledged. But it is still necessary to distinguish between the economic and evaluative realms. Perhaps the best way to understand this distinction is to cite some examples. When an individual buys a house to shelter his or her family, we can associate this event with class by calling it a real estate transaction, relating it to income distribution, using it to determine whether the demand for housing is elastic or nonelastic, and so on. But when an individual buys a house (especially one he or she cannot quite afford) because it or the neighborhood has prestige, or when someone acts to prevent those who can afford the same house from buying it because they are black or *nouveau riche,* the event involves the special moral realm of prestige (style of life, status evaluation, snobbery, deference, exclusiveness, social etiquette, values, consciousness, honor, breeding, taste, racism, and the like).

Other examples of prestige-related behavior come readily to mind. When an employer hires a less qualified individual for a position in preference to a better qualified Jew, Roman Catholic, black, or Protestant, this act also inhabits the realm of moral appraisal (prestige). If we assume that there are ten, twenty, or fifty colleges that provide educations equivalent or even superior to that of, say, Harvard College, the higher cash or occupational value of a Harvard degree is attributable to an unwarranted academic reputation (prestige). Prestige (or status) considerations are paramount when an upper-class woman cannot be seen shopping for food or carrying packages, or when a widow cannot work because work is considered demeaning in her "class." Every culture has its own peculiar prestige-related associations and taboos. There is an interesting story of an African student at a midwestern American university who reported a faculty member as an impostor because he saw the man washing his car, something no faculty member would ever do in the student's country.

In the history of social stratification, free economic markets are scarce; in fact, free markets are analytical fictions created by economists. Whatever their origin, prestige groups exert moral pressure on economic behavior and on the uses to which economic goods and resources are put. In some societies, families withdraw homes, land, and labor from economic markets—

by means, for example, of entail and primogeniture or of family trust funds—in effect lodging these "economic" values in a structure of familistic values. In preindustrial societies occupations tend to be assigned on the basis of family or religious status at birth. And industrial societies have powerful prestige forces as well. The United States may think of itself as a rationalist business civilization, but its economy is and has always been massively distored by racial, ethnic, religious, and gender biases, as well as superfluous consumption of all sorts.

High-prestige groups can bias the uses to which a society's economic resources are put by monopolizing the use of some goods and benefits (for example, forbidding lower-prestige groups to own land, hunt, or wear fur); by creating and supporting a demand for luxuries; by demanding abstention from work on the Sabbath and/or holidays; or by abstaining from work in favor of conspicuous leisure. The prestige order can also affect consumption-related behavior by, for example, requiring segregated facilities on railroads or segregated barbershops and restaurants. It can also—and this is of considerable importance in the United States—promote the value of residence in one-family houses in the suburbs, a phenomenon that entails a specific pattern of allocating economic resources (land, labor, building materials, automobiles, highways).

The various hierarchies of prestige are based on standards defined as moral, decent, civilized, beautiful, or tasteful across a wide range of behavior and personal attributes. Prestige groups use their economic and political power to establish their standards. As we see, these standards are often used to maintain the economic status quo.

ACHIEVED AND ASCRIBED PRESTIGE

The distinction between achieved and ascribed prestige is found by asking whether a given prestige status is achievable or not—that is, by asking whether it is accessible to individuals and their families on the basis of training and competition or is assigned to them by criteria deemed important and unalterable.

The major source of achieved prestige in industrial society is occupation. Given its ultimate value-idea that mastery of the world is possible through science and human effort, industrial society accords the major share of prestige to occupations directly related to control of the social and natural environments. Ascriptive barriers to occupational achievement, therefore, not only deny individuals and groups the benefits of class but prevent them from acquiring prestige as well. Achieved prestige can also be found in education, in the realms of taste and consumption, and among members and participants in nonprofit, professional, fraternal, philanthropic, civic, sports, and cultural groups. Achieved rankings in these areas again presume individuals or families to be qualified (or unqualified) for inclusion according to an achievable criterion: for example, achieving an A average or good grooming; being a volunteer at a shelter for battered women; or being interested in opera or heart research. When a fixed attribute such as race, religion, ethnicity, family, or sex is used to withhold prestige or to deny membership in prestige-giving organizations or activities, regardless of an individual's performance vis-à-vis the relevant achievement standards, one is dealing with an ascribed form of prestige.

The areas of ascriptive evaluation in the United States that are fully contradictory of the achievement ethic are age, sex, and especially race: Native Americans, Hawaiians, Chinese, Japanese, dark-skinned groups, and especially African Americans have at one time or another all been categorized as permanent outsiders unfit to participate in the full range of available social statuses. Sexual ranking does not figure directly in social stratification, since females who are wives (or daughters) generally receive the class position of their husbands (or fathers). It is germane to the case of many working females, who are subject to deep ascriptive discrimination in pay and employment. However, the tradition of sexual inequality in America has never had the sustained ideological and political-legal base of racist inequality, and while women have not always been treated well they have never suffered the overt systematic degradation visited on nonwhite racial groups, especially African Americans.

MORAL (OR PRESTIGE) EQUALITY

Stratification analysis does not always give due recognition to America's deep commitment to moral equality. Many of the definitive components of moral equality have been standard features of Western society since the ancient Greeks and Hebrews. Until the modern liberal period, however, moral equality in the West simply meant that all individuals were subject to universalistic moral norms, such as the Ten Commandments, and that all should aspire to certain universalistic ethical goals, such as love and brotherhood. While this tradition helped to prevent the development of a caste system in the West, it was perfectly compatible with an estate system of inequality (feudal Christendom). With the rise of liberal society, this moral tradition blended with the economic and political needs of capitalism to give rise to a more comprehensive definition of moral equality. It is not sufficiently understood that moral equality is an indispensable feature of industrialization. Prestige differentials based on birth invariably subsume and ultimately rigidify economic behavior, and are therefore the deadly enemy of economic expansion. The modern tradition of moral equality should also be understood, in other words, as a means of inviting all to participate in the new economy of capitalism or, in effect, as a moral sanction for dissolving feudal ties and developing an abstract labor force. Though the principle of moral equality emerged differently in the various countries of the West, it has come to mean, speaking ideally, that all individuals either are or have the right to become persons—that is, self-propelled, responsible actors in and of the society in which they live. As a result, modern society affirms and promotes (at least as an ideal and often in practice) the equal right of all citizens to influence the state and to participate in social life.

The American version of moral equality is unique, given the absence of a feudal tradition. The American state is unrivaled, except by France, in its formal acceptance of the almost absolute reality and rights of individuals. This atomistic-egalitarian definition of political-legal relations is matched by a widespread egalitarianism in social matters. Speaking broadly, Americans expect their leaders to be folksy, and they resent titles, uniforms, and badges denoting supersubordination.

On the whole, prestige forces tend to make populations unequal. In the West, however, an important prestige force stemming from the Judaic-Christian tradition, democratic ideology, and secular humanism emphasizes the equal worth of individuals as moral-spiritual entities. In the United States, this realm underlies the widespread institutionalization of peer relations, "democratic manners", and political-legal egalitarianism.

THE NEW "FREE" TIME (LEISURE)

Many of the most important forms of prestige behavior take place outside of work during noneconomic or "free" time. There is a widespread belief that people today have more "free" time than their forebears, and that modern populations are being gradually emancipated from the compulsions of work. It is widely believed that as an economy grows it relaxes its grip on the personality and allows people to develop and elaborate morally valuable prestige pursuits. Americans have long believed that economic growth leads to an increase in goods and services (discretionary income) and an increase in freedom from work (discretionary time), which in turn lead to an enhanced morality, higher culture, and personal fulfillment. That industrialization has brought about a growth in goods and services and an increase in time spent away from work cannot be denied. But as we shall see in examining consumption (of both "material" and "symbolic" culture), it is not at all clear that there have been increases in discretionary income and time, if by *discretion* one means the capacity to choose freely from a meaningful set of alternatives.

It is undeniable that industrial society has brought about changes in the amount of "free" time as well as in the way in which time away from work is spent. Preindustrial societies are characterized by aristocracies with little interest in economic activities and a penchant for lavish consumption.

Industrial society has obviously foreclosed the possibility of the dominant stratum being a leisured, nonworking group of this sort. Indeed, as we will emphasize, to understand contemporary society it is necessary to explore the fact that the powerful middle classes, and probably the upper class as well, are work-oriented.

Exactly what developments have taken place, then, in "free" time? Over time (between 1850 and the 1960s) the American economy has reduced the percentage of the labor force engaged in hard physical labor and produced a dramatic increase in the standard of living. There has also been a well-known decrease in the average work week. But the consequences of these changes have been badly misinterpreted. Many have come to the erroneous conclusion that affluence and the reduced work week have produced a style of life (consumption, use of time) that reflects a dissolution of classes. Just as we saw little evidence of the growth of a middle class mass in our analyses of income, wealth, occupation, education, and family and related behavior, we will find little evidence that the classes are converging in the area of prestige. It is important, therefore, that the deeply ingrained belief that economic growth leads directly to moral growth (the dissolution of classes, growing participation in and harmony between groups, a rise in the levels of personal fulfillment and social service) must be carefully qualified if we are to understand prestige phenomena. For one thing, it is not at all certain that modern society has made more free time available. In a pioneering analysis, Wilensky has pointed out that the work week lengthened from the Middle Ages through the nineteenth century.[2] Preindustrial societies are characterized by a great deal of what in modern terms we would call unemployment and underemployment. Modern society, on the other hand has sought to employ its labor force more fully. To appreciate the high level of work in modern society, one must include housework, work devoted to personal maintenance, and work devoted to the maintenance of consumption goods.

In an insightful analysis, Staffen Linder has argued that time has become increasingly scarce.[3] Linder argues that people experience the modern shortage of time in many ways: as a sense of being endlessly busy, a hectic tempo, compulsive punctuality, a yearning for simpler times, and a constant need to calculate the highest yield for any unit of time (either at work or during "free" time). This shortage of time stems from a class-based definition of time. In thinking about this and other aspects of "free" time in industrial society, a number of considerations should be kept in mind. First, the reduction of the work week appears to have ended during the post-1945 period; second, "free" time is distributed very unevenly; third, the use of "free" time differs qualitatively by class; and fourth, the basic uses of "free" time (prestige) are deeply embedded in and difficult to distinguish from "unfree" time (economic behavior and values).

More will be said about these various aspects of "free" time in subsequent chapters on prestige. At this point, we need clarify only one of the many misconceptions in this area, the tendency to assume that the work week has declined significantly for all and that it will continue to do so. It is undeniable that the work week itself has declined: During the nineteenth century it was well over sixty hours, in 1909 fifty-one hours, and by 1929 it had declined to forty-four hours. Since 1945, however, the work week has remained at about forty hours, which represents not only no decrease but also not much of a change since 1929. Averages (which include part-time work) are misleading and so are comparisons with the past, when more people worked in agriculture. Also, the legal work week should not be confused with the actual work week, since many workers put in overtime (much of it compulsory) and approximately 5 percent of the employed labor force holds two or more jobs. Though data in this area tend to be crude, Linder's general conclusion seems justified: the reduction in the work week ceased after 1945.[4]

Wilensky has also argued against the popular notion of increasing leisure, claiming that the decline in the work week during the last century or so is vastly misunderstood. Basically, he argues, upper occupational groups work very long hours, and much of the apparent new leisure is actually involuntary under- or unemployment among the lower classes. The more favored occupations and classes, concludes Wilensky, "have what they have always had—the right to choose work as well as leisure."[5]

Wilensky's general theme is borne out by retirement studies showing that the upper classes tend to retire later than the lower classes, but that they also anticipate and plan more for retirement and experience less of a loss in self-esteem and, of course, income than the lower classes.[6]

THE PRIMACY OF CLASS

The power of prestige vis-à-vis class in industrial society must not be exaggerated. Weber reminds us that the market is no respecter of persons. Once unleashed, economic forces can upset even the most deeply rooted prestige structures, such as when colonial powers promote extraction, commerce, and industry and thereby undermine the authority of tribal elders and the family; or when considerations of efficiency hasten the absorption of blacks into the labor force and weaken commitment to racially segregated waiting rooms and toilets; or when businesspeople endow universities, receive honorary degrees, and eventually come to dominate their governing boards.

The rise of capitalism represents a major transformation in the relationship between prestige and class (and power). The basic thrust of liberalism in the past five hundred years has been to free land, labor, and prices—and values and beliefs in general—from their subordination to moral, religious, and ascriptive-feudal standards. For this reason one must not exaggerate the autonomy of prestige within liberal society.[7]

In the rest of this chapter and the two that follow we will explore a large and diverse body of prestige data. In exploring this highly complex material, our basic orientation will be to view the dimension of prestige in terms of the logic of a class system of stratification, being careful, however, not to assume that economic institutions are always at odds with ascription or that prestige phenomena are always easy to relate to class.

CLASS AND HOW AMERICANS REGARD THEMSELVES

In the remainder of this chapter we examine how Americans regard themselves and explore some of their basic attitudes about the world they live in. This aspect of stratification analysis has a rich history and has yielded important data not only about inequality, but also about the congruities and incongruities between economic life (class) and the world of subjectivity (prestige). Perhaps the most important form of prestige inequality is that attributed to occupational status, a subjective hierarchy that correlates highly with income and education (though there are some exceptions).

THE HIERARCHY OF OCCUPATIONAL PRESTIGE

The first scientifically reliable national study of the prestige of occupations was conducted by the National Opinion Research Center (NORC) in 1947.[8] Americans were asked to rate ninety occupations as "excellent," "good," "average," "somewhat below average," "poor," or "don't know where to place." Their answers, though they contained few surprises, composed a valuable profile of occupational prestige in the United States. Highest prestige was consistently accorded to occupations characterized by highly specialized training and high responsibility for the public welfare. The occupations of United States Supreme Court justice, physician, state governor, member of the federal cabinet, diplomat in the United States Foreign Service, mayor of a large city, college professor, and scientist headed the list, and were followed by other professions. Then came skilled and unskilled workers, with garbage collector, street sweeper, and shoe shiner at the bottom of the list.

In 1963 the NORC conducted another study of occupational prestige, reproducing its original study as closely as possible in order to see what changes, if any, had occurred in the intervening period. The results revealed a remarkable overall stability in Americans' views of occupations. Though there was some shifting of ranks, the hierarchy of occupational prestige scores in 1963 remained essentially the same as in the earlier study.[9]

The lastest NORC survey, despite some changes in how the study was conducted, has confirmed the constancy of this hierarchy in public opinion (see Table 11–1). Of perhaps greater importance than the stability of occupational prestige is the striking consensus Americans display about the relative worth of occupations. The fact that a sample representing the American population are in substantial agreement time and again on how to rate occupations is of enormous significance because it means that those in low-rated occupations voted that their own occupations deserved low prestige. This finding dramatically illustrates why social inequality is rarely a matter of physical coercion, resting instead on "moral coercion," or, social power (or politely put, socialization). The significance of the American social achievement in this regard is enhanced if one remembers that work is the central source of identity in modern society and that the United States also has a deep commitment to egalitarian values. Perhaps nothing in the annals of functional role specialization equals the way in which Americans combine a commitment to moral and political-legal equality with a consensus on the radically unequal worth of occupations.

The stability and consensus about occupational ratings in the United States should not be interpreted as a fundamental of social structure or that we live in a meritocracy. This mistaken view of occupation can be found in a comparative study of occupational prestige in sixty countries by Donald Treiman, who argues that occupational prestige is similar in countries representing complex feudal and industrial societies. This similarity means that we are dealing with a fixed feature of social organization and that functional imperatives see to it that similar occupational hierarchies arise everywhere. These hierarchies reflect ability and training and result in differentials in income and authority.[10]

Critics have questioned the reliability of Treiman's data from developing countries where occupational titles are different and where there is a tendency to rely on urban, better-educated respondents. The strong similarities among developed countries can be accepted, however—but here another, more serious objection to Treiman's functionalism arises. Far from being a functional imperative, occupational prestige, as well as differentials in income and authority, all result from social power—they do not reflect either human ability or functional necessity. If it were more widely known, as we discovered in our analysis of the American economy and professions, that America's upper occupational groups do not serve social functions as is thought, then occupational prestige differences would certainly decline. Or one could criticize occupational rankings by noting that the socially important "occupation" of parent is not even listed.

Nothing in American society matches the importance of occupation for influencing the images people have of themselves and each other. Changing their position in the occupational structure is vital, for example, to enhancing the image and power of minority groups. But for minority and majority groups alike, there is a problem that transcends discrimination and prejudice: the problem posed by an economy that not only cannot provide jobs for all, but also contains a great many jobs with negative prestige.

TABLE 11–1 The American Occupational Prestige Hierarchy Illustrated by Selected Occupations, 1989

OCCUPATION	PRESTIGE SCORE	OCCUPATION	PRESTIGE SCORE
Physician	86	Public transp. attendants	42
Lawyer	75	Data-entry keyers	41
Postsecondary teachers	74	Auto. mechanics	40
Dentist	72	Receptionists	39
High govt. officials	70	Brick/stone mason	36
Clergy	69	Hairdresser	36
Civil engineer	69	Sales counter clerks	34
Registered nurse	66	Bulldozer operators	34
Accountant and auditor	65	Bus driver	32
Air traffic controller	65	Billing clerks	31
Elem. school teacher	64	Truck driver	30
Airline pilot	61	Cashier	29
Police and detectives	60	Taxi driver/chauffeur	28
Dietician	56	Waiter/waitresses	28
Firefighter	53	Garbage collector	28
Social worker	52	Bartender	25
Dental hygenist	52	Farm workers	23
Managers, administrators	51	Household servants/cleaners	23
Electrician	51	Janitors and cleaners	22
Computer operators	50	Garage, service sta. occup.	21
Funeral director	49		
Machinist	47		
Mail carrier	47		
Secretary	46		
Insurance sales	45		

Source: Adapted from James A. Davis and Tom W. Smith, *General Social Surveys, 1972–1994: Cumulative Codebook* (Chicago: National Opinion Research Center, 1994), Appendix F. Used by permission.

OCCUPATIONAL STRUCTURE AND THE LACK OF PRESTIGE

The United States (its powerful corporations and its property-oriented legislatures) tolerates significant amounts of unemployment. America's insensitivity to unemployment not only causes physical but also psychic hardship for millions of Americans. In addition, there are many occupations (out of a total of approximately 20,000 job titles in the United States) that afford little if any prestige and often burden their occupants with negative prestige. Thus, while there is a hierarchy of occupational prestige, it must be visualized as characterized by sharp breaks: an upper range of high-prestige occupations that coincide, by and large, with high position in all other hierarchies; a middle range of heterogeneous occupations difficult to define easily; a lower middle range of occupations with little or no prestige; a still lower group of negatively evaluated jobs, and beneath them the underemployed and unemployed. Those who occupy these lower occupations, or are chronically out of work or only partially employed, also occupy the lower rungs of other stratification ladders.

The importance of the occupational prestige dimension for unifying and legitimizing the hierarchies of class, prestige, and power is difficult to exaggerate. Those at the top receive the moral blessing of society by virtue of their occupations, which helps to legitimate their activities, benefits, and leadership in other areas; those at the bottom are morally evaluated in a negative way, which tends to legitimate both their economic failure and their overall position at the bottom of society.

Occupations that provide little prestige are invariably associated with close supervision, confining routines, punching a time-clock, and wearing a uniform (though some upper-level occupations, such as admirals and archbishops, also involve uniforms). Perhaps the ultimate prestige difficulty is to be without work. Because the problem of job prestige shades off into other problems, such as work satisfaction, pay, and personal identity, the following remarks have been framed in general terms. There are, first of all, the well-known disastrous consequences to personality and family life of unemployment.[11] There is the tendency to invent ego-inflating occupational titles (such as "sanitary engineer" for janitor) and to provide name plates and other prestige-associated items in the work situation. Workers set informal production quotas to prevent their identities from merging with the incentive-oriented, impersonalized factory system. The "protection of the inept" appears to be widespread as society struggles to find places for average people and noneconomic values.[12] Featherbedding occurs as workers violate achievement norms rather than face the humiliation of unemployment. Low-level and dissatisfied workers retire early when given the choice, and mass-production automobile workers, responding overwhelmingly to early retirement plans, expressed great enjoyment of the freedom of retirement.[13] The demand for high wages is probably largely understandable as a compensation for psychologically unrewarding occupations and, in some cases, an overt substitute for social mobility. Some workers with good jobs have a prestige problem because their work is difficult to describe and understand, and is therefore not readily converted into prestige; examples are legislative committee staffers and systems analysts. And some jobs present particularly onerous prestige problems—for example, servant, garbage collector, and so forth.

Stratification Within Classes and Occupations

Social classes tend to be roughly uniform in prestige, income, occupation, and power. But a social class can also contain economic statuses that differ in significant ways. For example, within the upper-middle class, doctors and professors enjoy comparable prestige but have very different incomes. The same thing is true of ministers, psychologists, and airline pilots.

A similar form of hierarchy is the hierarchy within a given occupation. Thus, some doctors earn more and are accorded more prestige than other doctors, and a similar pattern is apparent in many other occupations. With a few exceptions, stratification within occupations is not well documented.[14] We do know, in a general way, that the world of the corporate executive is permeated with prestige gradations and distinctions. The executive washroom is a well-known example and symbol of the numerous occupationally based benefits that have prestige significance; size and location of office, type of desk, furnishings, and the like make for deep prestige differentiation among members of the same occupation.

The world of government (the legislature, the judiciary, and the executive, including the civil service and the military) also contains obvious hierarchies within occupations. For example, a member of the United States Senate has far more prestige than a senator in the Maine legislature. A judge is only an abstraction until we know whether he or she works at the municipal, state, or federal level.

The growth of professionalism has undoubtedly led to greater internal stratification in business, government, and other occupations, including the world of sports. Perhaps the best way to conceptualize stratification within occupations is to note two characteristics of occupations: (1) occupations (especially organized occupations) try to maintain and promote the overall social class level of their members, and (2) occupations tend to be stratified internally. Perhaps the best-known example of stratification within an occupation involves lawyers. We know that lawyers enjoy high national prestige when ranked in the abstract. They also have high incomes and exercise great power. In fact, one of the interesting features of the legal profession is its close alliance with the modern corporation as well as with the exercise of political power. No other profession enjoys such enviable access to high stratification benefits in both the class and power dimensions. Straddling the upper reaches of all three dimensions of stratification, lawyers are a strategic link in the structure of social power. However, despite their high abstract class position, lawyers are not a narrowly homogeneous group. Jerome Carlin's empirical study[15] of a substantial number of the lawyers in New York City (who are probably representative of lawyers in most urban areas of the nation) reveals a distinct hierarchy *within* the legal profession. According to Carlin's evidence, the bar of New York City is "a highly stratified professional community" based on a hierarchy of law firms (or business enterprises). The large firms tend to have more respectable clients and to deal with the upper levels of the court and governmental systems. Their members come from the established classes and the more prestigious colleges and law schools, and tend to be Protestant. The cleavage between the elite firms and those below them tends to maintain itself over time, suggesting an organized pattern of recruitment and retention. Mobility between the various levels is rare and tends to favor those with elite backgrounds. Contact between the levels is also rare, and their separation is formalized by the existence of two separate bar associations. Violations of professional norms occur mostly at the lower levels of this hierarchy. And, finally, the overall organization of the profession results in a decided class pattern in the distribution of legal services. The upper classes are well served by the elite firms, the poor are not served at all, and the rest are served by the nonelite firms.

Within an occupation, prestige tends to be highest among those who work for national and international enterprises (corporations, governments), size tending to reflect importance and competence. A similar set of standards operates in other occupations: colleges, universities, and professional schools, for example, are ranked according to national (and international) standards, and professors' prestige in the academic world as well as among the general public is a function of the prestige of the school they work for. Occupations also derive prestige from the clients they serve. Federal politicians and civil servants work for "the people," while local politicians work for the town, city, or state. Research doctors work for humanity, while medical practitioners work for individual patients; doctors with rich patients have more prestige than doctors with poor patients. Professors with well-to-do students gain prestige, while professors at plebian schools lose prestige. Prostitutes with uppermiddle class clients enjoy more prestige than streetwalkers. And lawyers associated with corporate or public power enjoy more prestige than those whose activities are confined to divorce and criminal cases.

These well-structured hierarchies of prestige within occupations may forestall a number of prestige problems. (We have no direct evidence on this question.) To the extent that people are oriented toward prestige within occupations, for example, the social system is spared the task of judging the absolute or relative worth of the various occupations. Secondly, the focus on prestige *within* occupations probably leads to absorption with the economic issues pertinent to specific occupations, which may in turn reduce concern about differences in the economic worth of occupations. And, finally, preoccupation with prestige (and economic) status within occupations may make it possible for a social system to avoid having to make precise correlations between standings in the realms of class and prestige (and power). Though this is all mostly conjecture, it is probably no exaggeration to say that "status communities" based on occupation can reveal a great deal about how modern society remains stable and integrated. And they can probably tell us a lot about the unethical conduct, incompetence, and outright exploitation that are such significant and chronic features of our economic system.

The existence of stratification within various occupational statuses raises an important problem for class analysis. Because many economic enterprises and occupations are internally stratified, one cannot automatically assign all members of a given economic status to the same class. This is of special importance when analyzing the middle classes. In other words, individual farmers, businesspeople, lawyers, doctors, professors, and so on do not have uniform economic statuses; by and large, it appears that some are upper, some upper-middle, and some lower-middle class.

CLASS SELF-IDENTIFICATION

If Americans are asked what class they belong to, or whether they are upper, middle, or lower class, their overwhelming response is to select the middle class. In his pioneering study based on 1945 data, Richard Centers gave white (male) Americans the choice of these three classes and the working class. As a result of the extra option, he elicited a different response than did previous surveys; 40 percent of his respondents identified with the middle class and slightly more than half identified with the working class.[16]

A needed distinction between upper middle class and middle class appeared in surveys soon after. In a study of 1975 data, Mary and Robert Jackman found that 1 percent of Americans put themselves in the upper class, 8 percent in the upper middle class, 43 percent in the middle class, 37 percent in the working class, and 8 percent in the poor class.[17]

Studies that fail to distinguish an upper middle from a middle class and which fail to indicate similarities between manual and nonmanual work in their survey questions do not help respondents make relevant identifications. The Jackmans' assessment remains our best. Americans are very much aware of classes and use basic variables such as income, occupation, and education to define them. According to the Jackmans, Americans perceive classes as a graded series of social communities (people should and do associate, live, and marry according to class). The Jackmans found no cleavage between blue- and white-collar workers or between the propertied and nonpropertied. Americans also failed to carry their awareness of class into the arena of politics. This is not surprising, says the Jackmans, because American political institutions, including our political parties, consistently deny the existence of class-based interests.

The Jackmans also found that women used their husband's class position as their own. Davis and Robinson report that this changed from the 1970s to 1980s because of the growth in the participation of women in the labor force.[18] In the 1980s, and presumably since, employed women used their own and their husband's economic characteristics to identify their class position (giving somewhat more weight to their own). Davis and Robinson also found that men became even more pronounced in the use of their own economic status (despite having a working wife) and both single men and women also adopted a self-oriented class identity (as opposed to borrowing one from their father).

THE CULTURE HERO AS AN INDEX TO PRESTIGE

The Culture Hero in America

Culture heroes personify some of the core values and beliefs of a society, and therefore illustrate the processes that elevate some individuals above others. In the United States, the culture hero *par excellence* is the individual who is his or her own person and who overcomes adversity by drawing on his or her own resources. American culture heroes are easy to name: George Washington is an obvious choice, as are some of our other presidents, most notably, Thomas Jefferson, Abraham Lincoln, Theodore Roosevelt, and Franklin Roosevelt. Of all our culture heroes perhaps none has achieved the stature of Lincoln, a man who personified all that Americans value: humble origins, hard work amid adversity, intellectual striving, moral strength, and a common touch.

The United States, like most nations, has a rich complement of heroic figures, real and mythical, who serve as models or reference "groups" for its population. As Dixon Wector[19] has pointed out, Americans love character more than brains; earthy secular personalities more than saints; lowbrow more than highbrow types; and men of simple, decent, and honorable traits who are forgiven bad means if the cause is noble. It is noteworthy that our major heroes are Anglo-Saxon and Protestant; that women have rarely been chosen as heroic models; that artists, doctors, and lawyers are bypassed; and that invariably the soldier, the explorer, and especially the wartime leader has been cast as a hero.[20]

Our understanding of the relation between heroes and social stratification has been furthered by Theodore Greene's use of magazine biographies to gauge changes in America's images of its heroes.[21] Greene distinguishes three periods in American history, each characterized by a distinctive type of popular hero, as judged by magazine biographies. Between 1787 and 1820 America worshipped "The Idols of Order"; in Greene's terms, the "hero emerges as a Patriot, a Gentleman, and a Scholar in magazines of gentlemen, by gentlemen, and for gentlemen." Between 1894 and 1913 America worshipped "The Idols of Power and of Justice"; according to Greene, the "hero has become the Master of His Environment and gains national stature in new magazines of the people, by business entrepreneurs, for profit." During the latter part of this period the "hero dons some social garments to protect his individualistic frame in magazines at the peak of their power." And finally, from 1914 to 1918 (and presumably since), America worshipped "The Idols of Organization"; as Greene says, the "hero becomes a Manager of Massive Organizations portrayed in magazines for the masses."

The Celebrity

Twentieth-century communication technology has produced a new type of culture hero, the celebrity. What is the significance of celebrities and what images of life are portrayed through them by the mass media? Does their advent represent a significant change in the models held up for Americans to emulate? In the absence of rigorous empirical research, one can only speculate about these and other questions. Does the cult of the celebrity provide vicarious meaning and satisfaction to millions of otherwise drab lives? As C. Wright Mills has suggested, the phenomenon of the celebrity may serve as a distraction from other problems and is probably influential in diverting attention from the shortcomings of society.[22] Exactly how "mass culture" works to distract the masses and distort their image of the world cannot as yet be said scientifically. But questions are easily raised. What is the significance of the theme of violence and aggression in America mass media (the cowboy, the gangster, the private detective, the football star and team)? Does violence, for example, help the audience to discharge in fantasy its resentment of bosses, or competitors, or economic forces? Do the mass media portray a world of clean-cut morality and easy solutions, thus disguising the role of power groups and compounding the ambiguities and conflicts in the workday world? What is the significance of the heroes who use unsavory or illegal means to achieve their ends?

It is possible that the rise of the celebrity signifies a shift from a world of achievement to a world of ascription. Celebrity status is difficult to achieve—after all, an unusual voice, face, figure, height, or agility is inborn. And the cult of the celebrity tends to associate success with luck and inborn traits rather than with hard methodical work. The rags-to-riches theme is prevalent in the world of the celebrity, but the celebrity's success is often attributed to good fortune rather than intelligence, frugality, or work. Nonetheless, the phenomenon of the celebrity may serve to keep the American Dream alive among the disadvantaged and oppressed: black youth may derive vicarious satisfaction from seeing Bill Cosby, Michael Jordan, and Whitney Houston make it big. There are many analogues for other minorities and for whites as well.

The celebrity may also signify a shift from a production-oriented society to one in which consumption must be stimulated and managed. Celebrities are often connoisseurs of consumption, and are used extensively in advertising to encourage and guide others in their consumption. In so doing, celebrities lend their prestige to the world of business and help to develop and legitimate the ethic of consumption. And one must not forget that the various spheres of entertainment in which celebrities perform are big business in their own right. Celebrities also involve themselves in politics and in the sphere of voluntary action (for example, United Way). They support various political parties, run for office, and are occasionally elected. And celebrities lend the magic of their names and presences to many forms of moral uplift (boys' clubs, neighborhood programs, ghetto youth activities). And, finally, the celebrity signifies the professionalization and commercialization of sports and entertainment, processes related to basic developments in other areas of modern society. Indeed, the realms of sports and entertainment may reveal more clearly than other areas the emergence of a spectator society, a basic cleavage between elite and mass, and the failure of the early liberal ideal of the versatile individual in a participatory society.

The relationship between public and celebrity is a national phenomenon, a true nationwide prestige currency. But, as C. Wright Mills reminds us, prestige relationships based on the worship, admiration, and envy of celebrities are difficult to institutionalize, and thus provide no easy way for the economic, political, and "social" elites to legitimate themselves. The celebrity's fame is too personal and ephemeral to serve as a basis for the long-range legitimation of positions acquired by other means. For that reason, says Mills, the cult of the celebrity is primarily a distraction and only an indirect way of enhancing and sanctioning high class and high political power.

CLASS, PERSONALITY, AND WORLDVIEW

The most influential and best-known analysis of class and personality is in the work of Karl Marx. Marx had a profound influence on social science by treating not only conventional behavior but also thoughts and emotions (personality) as reflections of class position. Marx, it will be remembered, held that the key to the nature of classes is the modal technology of the period, and that ownership and nonownership of the means of production is the basic factor in the composition of social classes. However, classes can also be identified by their thoughts and values, according to Marx. Each class, he argued, has a distinctive subjective existence that emanates from its relation to the means of production. Marx's sociology of knowledge—the relation between social experience on the one hand, and values and ideas, subjective existence, and personality on the other—was capped by his concept of ideology. According to Marx, when a class is riding the crest of a new mode of technology, its thoughts and values are rational, valid, and progressive. In time, however, technological change renders these ideas and values obsolete, thereby turning them into ideology, or the symbolic defense of an outmoded social system.

While enormously influential, Marx's ideas about the relation between class and personality are not easy to verify empirically. For one thing, the means of production are now enormously complex. For another, it is difficult to establish a relation between the ownership of productive property and the occupational system. Despite these difficulties, however, the fundamental thrust of Marx's thought was sound: classes emerge from economic institutions and can be identified by their distinctive world views.

In his pioneering cross-national study, Melvin L. Kohn found a profound cleavage in the basic perception of self and reality between higher and lower classes, as distinguished by occupation. Analyzing data from

Turin, Italy; Washington, D.C.; and a national sample of the United States representing all men in civilian occupations, Kohn concludes that the intrinsic nature of work is the most important determinant of a worker's values. A self-directed personality and the feeling that one lives in a "benign" society are associated with jobs that are not closely supervised; entail complex work involving data or people, rather than things; and are intricately organized. Workers whose jobs are closely supervised, simply organized, and involve things are likely to be conformists and feel that they live in an "indifferent or threatening" society.

The variable of occupational self-direction was found to be more important in determining world view than family structure, race, religion, national background, income, or subjective class identification. Other variables of occupation, such as bureaucratic or entrepreneurial settings; governmental, profit-making, or nonprofit employers; degree of time pressure; job satisfaction; ownership of the means of production; and job rights and protections (union contracts, seniority, grievance procedures, tenure, civil service, and such) were also less consequential. The self-directed personality, says Kohn—though related to education, which is itself closely related to occupation—is basically a function of occupational self-direction.[23]

Evidence from other sources indicates that class tends to override other allegiances. For example, it is known that Protestants, Roman Catholics, and Jews, as well as whites and nonwhites, who are members of the same class, share similar values and beliefs and develop similar personalities. Indeed, the cultural assimilation of immigrants and acculturation across religious-ethnic-racial lines by class is widespread.

CLASS AND CLASS CONSCIOUSNESS

Are Americans Conscious of Stratification by Class?

Karl Marx saw class consciousness as the awakening of the working classes (the great majority of the population) to their exploitation by a small group of big property owners. Marx felt that class consciousness was a natural by-product of class struggle in which first the middle class rises against the feudal lord (in the name of liberty, equality, and representative government) and then the working class rises against the now obsolete middle class (in the name of humanity and the classless society).

Are Americans class conscious in the Marxian sense? Are they conscious of social classes and class exploitation in any sense? Are they aware that the American class system has many illegitimate elements? Are they aware that their society has a deeply rooted system of advantage and disadvantage based on family birth?

By and large, the answer to these questions is no. Americans are not very conscious of class and do not consciously frame their lives in class terms. Invariably, they interpret differential striving and differential success in individual terms (as functional competition between individuals of different innate ability). Of course, Americans are aware of the existence of inequality, even radical inequality, but they do not characteristically think of it in class terms—that is, they do not explain inequality in terms of economic and social variables. Class consciousness is awareness that one's social level derives from an economic and social environment one shares with those in similar circumstances and that social level has little to do with natural forces, human or otherwise. Class consciousness, in other words, is awareness that basic forms of inequality are historical in nature—that is, changeable, with those at the top of society usually interested in preventing change and those at the bottom (who are class conscious) wanting a restructuring of economy and social power.

Americans are aware, naturally, that some people are rich and others are poor, that some are advantaged and others disadvantaged, that some have easy jobs while others have difficult jobs, and that some individuals inherit considerable sums of money while others inherit little or nothing. By and large, though, Americans believe that a person's position in society is the result of work, brains, drive, or even luck or connections; only rarely do they see the distribution of benefits as the reflection of a class system. What consciousness of class does exist is found mostly among the upper classes. Probably the closest approximation of class thinking among Americans is the view that the lower classes face barriers to achievement because of inadequate opportunity. They have little awareness, however, of a comprehensive social system that determines the distribution of opportunities and other social benefits. Americans are not aware, in other words, of the highly organized system of social power connecting the economy, the professions, education, family, health, consumption, interaction in primary and secondary groups, politics, government, and law.

Americans are conscious of inequities in their society, but they regard them as correctable defects of a fundamentally sound society—sound because it works the way people say it works and because it is flexible and reformable. Invariably, reform is directed at making functional competition between individuals more equal. Despite persistent criticism and occasional denunciations of middle-class society, very few have questioned the ability of capitalist society to reform itself and become what it is supposed to be: a system based on equality of opportunity leading to legitimate inequality.

Why the Lack of Awareness About Class Stratification?

Marxists argue that the lack of class consciousness and the belief that capitalist society is either already classless or can become so are manifestations of "false consciousness." But one need not be a Marxist to understand the social processes that have prevented Americans from becoming class conscious:

1. Economic expansion has diversified the economic interests of Americans, often giving them contradictory and cross-cutting interests. Economic growth has provided economic mobility for many and has raised living standards (remember that a general rise of living standards is not the same thing as social mobility or movement across class lines, but it can easily be misinterpreted as such).
2. Immigration and migration (along with the aftermath of racial slavery) have diversified economic classes on ethnic, religious, and racial grounds, making it difficult for those in similar economic positions to develop an awareness of their common class identity.
3. Sexual inequality has also contributed to diversity among those in similar economic statuses and has also made it difficult to think in terms of common class interests and grievances.
4. The steady extension of legal and political rights encouraged Americans to feel that equal, individual competition was either a reality or could become one. However, American political institutions have always reflected the interests of property and professional groups—not surprisingly, political parties and the politically powerful rarely present the problems of American society in class terms.
5. American popular and intellectual culture, including the social sciences and religion, have a pronounced tendency to formulate goals and to explain success and failure in individualistic (biopsychological) terms and to assume that social problems are temporary and correctable (evolutionary liberalism). By and large, the American ethos of individualism prevents Americans from seeing their world as an organized structure of institutions and power groups. By and large, American popular culture, religion, social science, and intellectual culture have depoliticized American society by claiming that it derives from supernature, nature, and human nature.

All evidence points to the chronic nature of American inequality, including massive amounts that are illegitimate (by American norms). That most Americans, regardless of class, continue to believe that America works or can be made to work with minor reform is understandable. Their immersion in American institutions and legitimation processes effectively hides American society and thus prevents the reforms needed to make it work as it says it should.

SUMMARY

In this chapter we examined the vast and complex world of prestige (subjectivity) and looked at one aspect of this world—how Americans regard themselves and each other. The inner world of human beings is not always easy to characterize or interpret. It seems clear, however, that class position is the controlling variable in explaining how people think about themselves and the world they live in. Two extremely important subjective phenomena, occupational prestige and basic personality (self-direction versus conformism), are directly related to class (those in unsupervised occupations involving complex work tend to have self-directed personalities who feel at home in society; those in highly supervised occupations doing simple work tend to be conformist and uncomfortable with society).

Occupational prestige is highly graded and has been stable for the almost three-quarters of a century that it has been studied. Of great significance is the fact that Americans with the lower-ranking jobs also give them lower prestige. Functionalists see the stability and universality of occupational prestige as natural to society; conflict theorists see them as the result of social power masking incompetence and privilege.

Americans rank themselves in terms of a wide assortment of achieved statuses. But the use of ascribed statuses (birth into racial, ethnic-religious, and sexual statuses) is also widespread. An achieved status is something that individuals can become—an ascribed status is unalterable and is not compatible with the Achievement Ethic.

Class self-identification corresponds roughly to data on the hierarchy of wealth, income, occupation, and education. Working married women no longer identify themselves by borrowing their husband's economic status but use a combination of their own and their husband's economic characteristics. This change is part of a deeper trend on the part of men and women, married or single, toward using their individual economic characteristics to identify themselves.

Americans value heroes from humble backgrounds who achieve against adversity, and who display moral strength and a common touch. But sports and entertainment celebrities have become prominent, which is a significant development because celebrities in many respects use inborn traits in pursuits that have limited social value.

We also found that Americans are not class conscious (the ability to see the macro class order as a powerful but alterable structure controlling their lives and generating their problems). Nevertheless, it is justifiable to explain our findings in class terms: the class dimension and related areas are so complex and inconsistent that they have diffused and blurred subjective awareness of class. In addition, a general process of legitimation (see Chapter 10) also makes it difficult for Americans to think in terms of social class.

NOTES

1. *Max Weber: The Theory of Social and Economic Organization,* tr. A. M. Henderson and Talcott Parsons, ed. with an intro. by Talcott Parsons (New York: Oxford

University Press, 1947), p. 428. For Weber's major discussion of prestige, see Max Weber, "Class, Status, Party," *From Max Weber: Essays in Sociology*, tr., ed., and with an intro. by H. H. Gerth and C. Wright Mills (New York: Oxford University Press, 1946), ch. 7.

2. Harold L. Wilensky, "The Uneven Distribution of Leisure: The Impact of Economic Growth on 'Free' Time," *Social Problems* 9 (Summer 1961):32–56.
3. Staffan Burenstam Linder, *The Harried Leisure Class* (New York: Columbia University Press, 1970), chs. 1–5.
4. Ibid., pp. 135–137.
5. Wilensky, "The Uneven Distribution of Leisure," p. 56.
6. Frances M. Carp, ed., *Retirement* (New York: Behavioral Publications. 1972), pp. 176f., 251f., and Malcolm H. Morrison, ed., *Economics of Aging: The Future of Retirement* (New York: Van Nostrand Reinhold, 1982), pp. 120–122.
7. On the other hand, it is of some significance that Christianity provided much of the moral lubrication needed to bring about the free interaction of entire populations, a freedom indispensable to a dynamic economy. Thus, Christians (unlike Hindus, for example) regarded themselves as well as non-Christians as human beings capable of having social relations; in this connection see, for example, St. Paul's *Epistle to the Romans.* In recent American history, Christianity has played a similar role in bringing blacks into American life. Though framed in terms of morality and civil rights, the drive for black equality (often spearheaded by black churches) can also be seen as an effort to incorporate a despised rural labor force ("caste") into America's abstract, mobile, industrial labor force (class).
8. C. C. North and P. K. Hatt, "Jobs and Occupations: A Popular Evaluation," *Opinion News* 9 (1 September 1947):3–13.
9. For this study and for additional materials showing stability in the distribution of occupational prestige between 1925 and 1963, see R. W. Hodge, P. M. Siegel, and P. H. Rossi, "Occupational Prestige in the United States, 1925–63," *American Journal of Sociology* 70, no. 3 (November 1964):286–302.
10. Donald J. Treiman, *Occupational Prestige in Comparative Perspective* (New York: Academic Press, 1977).
11. The classic pioneering empirical study in this area is Mirra Komarovsky, *The Unemployed Man and His Family* (New York: Octagon Books, 1971; originally published in 1940).
12. See William J. Goode, "The Protection of the Inept," *American Sociological Review* 32 (February 1967):5–19.
13. Richard Barfield and James N. Morgan, *Early Retirement: The Decision and the Experience* (Ann Arbor, Mich.: Institute for Social Research, 1970), pp. 1–7.
14. An interesting and unexplored avenue to information in this area is analysis of the proliferating Halls of Fame in such areas as sports, aviation, agriculture, the franchise industry, and the like, and among songwriters, actors, cowboys, ethnic groups, and the like, and of the wide variety of achievement awards in such fields as moviemaking, the recording industry, the theater, writing, sports, industry, government, and so on.
15. Jerome Carlin, *Lawyers' Ethics: A Survey of the New York City Bar* (New York: Russell Sage Foundation, 1966). For similar results in Chicago, see John Heinz and Edward Laumann, *Chicago Lawyers* (New York: Russell Sage Foundation, 1982).

16. Richard Centers, *The Psychology of Social Classes* (Princeton, NJ: Princeton University Press, 1949), Table 18, p. 77.
17. Mary R. and Robert W. Jackman, *Class Awareness in the United States* (Berkeley: University of California press, 1983), Table 2.1.
18. Nancy J. Davis and Robert V. Robinson, "Class Identification of Men and Women in the 1970s and 1980s," *American Sociological Review* 53 (February 1988): 103–112.
19. Dixon Wector, *The Hero in America* (New York: Charles Scribner's Sons, 1941), ch. 18.
20. Religious-ethnic and racial groups have their own heroes (Malcolm X and Martin Luther King, Jr., for example, among African Americans). It would be interesting to know more about the heroes who serve as models for minority groups, and to know whether there is variation in hero worship by class among both majority and minority groups.
21. Theodore P. Greene, *America's Heroes: The Changing Models of Success in American Magazines* (New York: Oxford University Press, 1970).
22. For these points and for a valuable general discussion of prestige, see C. Wright Mills, *The Power Elite* (New York: Oxford University Press. 1956), ch. 4.
23. Melvin L. Kohn, *Class and Conformity: A Study in Values* (Homewood, IL: Dorsey Press, 1969). For follow-up studies in the same vein, see Melvin L. Kohn and Carmi Schooler with Joanne Miller, *Work and Personality: An Inquiry into the Impact of Social Stratification* (Norwood, NJ: Ablex, 1983).

12
Class and Style of Life: Consumption

◆ ◆ ◆ ◆

◆ ◆ ◆ ◆

Households at various class levels spend their money differently, yielding not merely different levels of material well-being, but a hierarchy of consumption prestige as well. In this chapter, therefore, we are interested in understanding another of the ways in which "economic income" is turned into "psychic income." While our analysis distinguishes between material and symbolic culture, this distinction is adopted for expository purposes only. All human artifacts are infused with symbols or meanings of the most varied sort. The purchase of clothing or a dwelling is no mere material or economic act; it has important symbolic-value overtones—overtones relevant in the present context to prestige stratification.

Analysis of the noneconomic or honorific aspects of economic behavior was pioneered by Thorstein Veblen (1857–1929),[1] whose penetrating insights into the ways in which honor is acquired through material accumulation and consumption are the source of much of our present-day understanding of prestige behavior (though, as we will see, his ideas have to be updated somewhat). It was Veblen who focused attention on the fact that men and women above the level of subsistence engage in what he called *pecuniary emulation*. In the past, according to Veblen, men and women created invidious distinctions by accumulating more property than they could use, because to do so gave them prestige and thus made them morally worthier than their neighbors. Modern society makes pecuniary emulation difficult, however: property must be conspicuous if it is to enhance prestige, and much of modern property is inconspicuous because of residential segregation, or because it takes the form of factories, office buildings, and the like, or has no tangible form other than pieces of paper.

Veblen also pointed to conspicuous leisure—careful avoidance of work and cultivation of noneconomic activities and skills—as a way in which high economic position is advertised. Acquiring prestige in this way is difficult in industrial society because of its high valuation of work and utilitarian activity. A final means Veblen identified of translating economic or class position into prestige is conspicuous consumption. It is this phenomenon that has particular relevance to prestige stratification in industrial society, especially if one defines it in combination with pecuniary emulation and conspicuous leisure as the display of all manner of economic assets on a scale and with a flair that has known prestige meaning.

HONORIFIC POSSESSIONS, CONSUMPTION, AND ACTIVITIES

The concept of conspicuous consumption is probably best introduced by noting Veblen's synonym for it, conspicuous waste. Perhaps the most dramatic example of this form of prestige is provided by Ruth Benedict's portrayal of the value system of the Kwakiutl Indians.[2] Native to the northwest coast of North America, the Kwakiutl enjoyed an economy of abundance. The sea provided ample food for slight labor, which allowed for their absorption in self-glorification at the expense of rivals. The specific form their ego rivalry took was the potlatch, a social convention based on the distribution and/or destruction of property. Noneconomic, nonmaterial property such as names, titles, myths, songs, privileges, and pieces of copper were combined with other forms of property such as fish oil, blankets, and canoes to serve as the means of personal rivalry. The object of the potlatch was to enhance personal prestige by shaming a rival, either by giving him property he could not return with the required heavy interest or by destroying one's property in amounts he could not match.

Veblen employed the term *waste* neutrally to signify economic behavior with no immediate or obvious economic utility. Something is done or used because it is expensive either of material or of time; because it is aesthetically novel, moral, or true; or because it combines certain of these features. The individual engaged in conspicuous waste can be either aware or unaware of what he or she is doing. Quite often, the compulsions of class position make conspicuous consumption (waste) a necessary aspect of one's standard of living, part of the minimum level of decency in dress, housing, equipment, and services required to maintain class standing.

Veblen provided an enormous catalogue of prestige pursuits whose consequences, intended or not, were to create invidious distinctions between economic classes: acquired wealth; inherited wealth; abstention from productive labor (by a man, by his wife, and sometimes by both, often accompanied by the employment of slaves, servants, or mechanical devices); the cultivation of nonutilitarian pursuits and skills such as (in Veblen's words) quasi-scholarly, quasi-artistic accomplishments like languages, correct spelling and syntax, domestic music; the latest proprieties of dress, furniture, and equipage; games, sports, and fancy-bred animals; and manners and breeding, polite usage, decorum, and formal and ceremonial observances in general.[3]

NONUTILITARIAN BEHAVIOR IN INDUSTRIAL SOCIETY

While Veblen's work contains many insights into the manifest and latent functions of consumption, his analysis is not a complete guide to present-day consumption. Veblen was primarily concerned with identifying vestiges of feudal and barbarian prestige in an emerging industrial civilization. To analyze the prestige patterns developed by a maturing industrial class system, therefore, requires an updating and refocusing of Veblen's ideas. His insights into preindustrial forms of prestige (property accumulation, leisure as avoidance of work, waste, canons of taste that emphasize expense over utility, and the cultivation of a wide assortment of nonutilitarian values and skills) are still pertinent, since consumption is still linked strongly to class, but must be supplemented.

To understand prestige consumption in advanced capitalism, one must start by noting that America's upper classes are gainfully employed. This appears to be true even of the very rich, though there are no exact studies of how members of this class are employed by sex and age. Members of the upper class of industrial society are undoubtedly different from other classes in their ability to choose not to work and to choose their work from a wide variety of options (though in this respect they are probably similar to the upper middle class). Nevertheless, the upper class of industrial society appears to be neither a leisure nor a *rentier* class, and it certainly does not specialize in religious, governmental, and military occupations. All available indications are that the upper class is actively engaged in a wide variety of (economic) occupations, chief among which, undoubtedly, is the management and supervision of property interests. The significance of all this is that it is work, not property, that legitimates consumption in industrial society, a phenomenon that makes it difficult to uphold cultivated idleness as a prime social value.[4] In the United States, free time is the mark of the half-citizen: the young, the old, the retired, women, the infirm and disabled, and the unemployed. One enjoys leisure in a positively valued sense only after one's work is done: after five o'clock, after fifty weeks, or after age sixty-five. Given the heavy emphasis on work and on such related values as thrift, economic growth, and technical efficiency, it is also difficult both to uphold waste as a positive value and to place supreme or even high value on nonutilitarian activities such as art, music, classical learning, religion, and exotic hobbies. Activities of this sort exist and even flourish, but by and large run counter to the main thrust of American culture.[5]

The United States never developed deep ascriptive limitations on consumption. The African American, of course, was forced to consume in segregated stores and to use segregated facilities, a tradition that represents the most serious contradiction of pure class consumption in American history. And women have been segregated with regard to certain forms of consumption; examples are the need to have an escort in order to use certain facilities, and moral strictures against smoking and drinking. By and large, however, such ascriptive forces have been overcome by the power of class. The central point about consumption in the United States is that it is legitimate for all to be interested—indeed, very interested—in material consumption. One of the major changes in twentieth-century life is the growing respectability of consumption and the apparent decline of Protestant-bourgeois asceticism. The major reason for this development, of course, is the emergence of a mass-production economy and the consequent economic need to make consumption a major public virtue. In the process, consumption has become a semiofficial way of establishing prestige and, from a broader standpoint, of establishing and maintaining class position.

The ways in which consumption is promoted are also of considerable importance. Our mass media, for example, do much to support and inculcate consumption values, in terms of both program content and advertising. The mass media cater both to class and prestige mobility aspirations and undoubtedly contribute heavily to creating them in the first place. Consumption prestige is also promoted by the power dimension. The rise of the Keynesian state parallels the rise of a mass-production economy. Under Keynesianism, government acts to maintain effective economic demand either by acting as a consumer itself or by cutting taxes or interest rates.[6] Tax laws favoring the upper classes permit a wide range of luxury consumption. By declaring holidays, the power dimension specifies the values to be celebrated and preserved; and the legal fiction that the birthdays of some of our national heroes take place on Mondays is partly due to the fact that three-day weekends are good for tourist and recreational businesses and thus of more prestige value to those with the money to travel on such mini-vacations.[7] The state also regulates the work week and vacations; subsidizes postal rates for magazines, newspapers, and books, publications which help to promote many other prestige activities; and grants tax deductions for expense accounts (more stringent under the Tax Reform Act of 1986 but still a large source of differential prestige through club membership, dining, entertainment, and travel).

The federal government also subsidizes the arts, humanities, and public television, following the lead of municipal and state governments. The power dimension also supports professional sports in a number of ways: by not holding them strictly accountable to the antitrust laws; by granting money to build sports facilities or by backing their bond issues with public credit; and by building the highways that make it possible to locate such facilities in the suburbs (thus making them accessible to some income groups and not to others). The government also subsidizes differential recreation through its system of national parks, which are used mostly by the middle and upper classes, and it has even paid for public works which have resulted in lakes and recreation areas becoming the preserves of private residential communities.

The blurring of the private (prestige) and public (power) spheres of behavior has occurred on another front as well. Public regulation of the airways lends an aura of legitimacy to private enterprises in radio and television, though the public's control over program content and advertising is minimal. Public regulations on land use, building materials, house and plot size, and the like (zoning) are often tantamount to class and racial segregation; and, of course, public highways make it possible for certain income and racial groups to enjoy the prestige of nonurban living.

In studying the oftentimes bewildering array of consumption behaviors and analyzing the relation of prestige consumption to class, there is a general pattern that helps to structure understanding: Some consumption behaviors are based on differences while others, especially in industrial society, result in broad and significant similarities.

DIFFERENTIAL CONSUMPTION: INDUSTRIAL POTLATCHING

Despite our many ideas about the relation between class and consumption, little research exists in this area. To organize what is known about the distribution of consumption prestige, we will examine six all-important areas of consumption: residence, dress, servants and services, commodities, the consumption of time and "symbolic" culture, and the donation of time and money.[8]

Residence

The importance of residence for identifying and certifying class position needs little emphasis. The significance of residence is apparent in such stratification-related images as "the wrong side of the tracks," the Gold Coast, a slum, Nob Hill, the East Side, and so on. Type of house and dwelling area are so important to class position that one early school of stratification analysis used both to construct an index of class position.[9] Prestige stems from one's residence in a number of ways: for example, from its size, architectural style, location, size of plot, and exterior decoration and maintenance. Obviously, one's residence, especially a single-family house, is an important way to display income and/or wealth. But it is also a way to advertise lineage and good taste. Thus, the Early American style in the Northeast suggests continuity of descent as well as good taste; its counterparts are Greek Revival in the South, Spanish in the Southwest and California, and Victorian in the Midwest. Actually, a house affords many ways of displaying values (furnishings, a separate dining room, a private bedroom for each child, a music room). Geographical location (high ground, distance from commerce and industry), size of plot, and landscaping are all important to the prestige (as well as economic) value of a house. In other words, one's address is often a quick and easy way to know who one is.

A rise in class position usually calls for a change of residence. In fact, it is one of the functions of differential consumption in general to help to establish people who have moved up (or down) in the class hierarchy. Residence is also an index of low prestige (and power) and low class position.

To move from the palatial residences of the rich to the comfortable homes and apartments of the upper middle class and from there to the modest homes of the lower middle and working classes on to the squalid dwellings of the lower class is to take a quick trip through the American class system. Residence does not signify social class in a mechanical fashion, of course. There is evidence that working-class people are not overly conscious of residence as a mark of class, and people are not always as mobile as they might be because of ethnic and other ties to their old neighborhoods. A further complication is the shortage of housing: Many people who might have moved have not done so because of the almost chronic undersupply of housing in the United States. In recent years the gap between income distribution and the affordability of housing has widened because of slow, erratic economic growth and the stagnation—even decline in many cases—of real wages since 1970. During the 1980s this gap produced a significant number of homeless people, including large numbers of homeless families (including many with full-time workers). One interesting pattern in American housing is the significant number of second homes. In 1993 there were 1,925,000 vacation homes.[10] (For a fuller discussion of housing, see the section "Class and Housing" in Chapter 15.)

Dress

In addition to providing warmth and helping to promote and uphold the sense of modesty, clothing is an important advertisement of class status. The terms *white-collar* and *blue-collar*, for example, signify distinct stratification worlds. Many occupations entail special costumes, the function of which is to identify those who wield authority and to provide for the mutual recognition necessary to efficient work, communication, and exchange of services—for example, judges, soldiers, prostitutes, police officers, airline attendants, doctors, and clergy.

A discerning observer can usually identify a man's class by looking at his clothing, even when he is not wearing a conventional occupational uniform. This may be even truer of his wife, since women are strongly encouraged to advertise class status through dress. Female participation in the full length of the occupational hierarchy has resulted in a widening array of work clothes ranging from the "power" suits of women in the upper occupations to the distinctive clothing of those in the pink ghetto. All in all, the norms of dress, or fashion, are widely used to identify those with good taste, money, and exemptions from labor, as well as type of labor.

Servants and Services

The days when the wealthy had many servants maintaining palatial homes are apparently over. But the upper classes still have servants and enjoy many services that others have to perform for themselves. There is little research here and thus we will do no more than list some of the labor that money can buy to perform personal services: nannies or child care services, chauffeurs or transport services, gardeners or gardening services, caterers, and personal shoppers and secretaries. All these and other forms of hiring labor for personal life not only provide escape from burdensome activities, but free one's own labor and time for economic, political, and prestige pursuits.

Commodities

There are many types of goods associated with class that lend prestige to their owners. At the advent of the automobile age, only the wealthy could afford to own cars. Mass production caused car ownership to spread, but until recently the type of car one owned was still an indicator of one's class. Now that the same car is owned by members of many different income groups, mere ownership is no longer an easy guide to class. Ownership of two or more cars, however, still indicates the class to which the owner belongs as does ownership of extremely expensive or exotic cars.

Many other types of commodities are still strongly associated with class. Though ownership of some commodities, such as television sets, loses its strong association with class over time, possession of many major appliances, such as clothes dryers and dishwashers, is still a class phenomenon.

The Consumption of Time and "Symbolic" Culture

The expenditure of "free" time can be thought of as a form of consumption, and there are evident differences in the ways in which the various classes spend their time away from work. A great many studies have shown that blue-collar workers differ from middle-class individuals in that they read less; attend fewer movies, concerts, lectures, and theaters; travel less; display less interest in artistic and musical pusuits; and participate far less in formal associations. Working-class individuals spend more time than their middle-class counterparts working around the house, watching television, working on their automobiles, taking automobile rides, playing cards, fishing, informally interacting with relatives and friends, and tavern-visiting.[11] There is also little doubt that significant differences in the use of "free" time characterize the poor and the middle class.

Differences in the use of time can also be represented as differences in modes of consuming "symbolic" culture. The term *symbolic culture* is a roomy construct into which we can deposit whatever evidence we have about differential participation in the moral, aesthetic, and intellectual life of society. We have already analyzed the most important form of symbolic consumption in modern society, formal schooling. No conclusion in the realm of education is more important for understanding contemporary inequality and differentials in subjective development and enjoyment than the fact that formal schooling and professional training are largely middle- and upper-class monopolies. An important variation on this theme is that rising levels of education have led neither to greater homogeneity nor to a greater consensus of values and outlooks. Actually, effective participation in American society is severely limited for many people by functional illiteracy.

Participation in "symbolic" culture can also take the form of participation in voluntary groups, especially those devoted to religion, reform, and politics. We discuss this form of participation further in Chapter 13 but here again there is little doubt that the stimulation and prestige afforded by associational activity correspond to a general pattern of middle- and upper-class dominance.

Participation in "symbolic" culture also takes the form of differential class consumption in the aesthetic and intellectual-moral sphere.[12] And perhaps of even greater significance is the fact that "symbolic" culture is now in an advanced industrial stage of production and consumption. In other words, organizations engaged in creating and distributing aesthetic, intellectual, and moral values are managed in much the same way as is the economy; they are characterized by narrow upper class "ownership" and control, professional staffs who manage day-to-day operations, and benefits bestowed according to class.

A case in point is Edward Arian's analysis of the Philadelphia (Symphony) Orchestra.[13] Suggesting that the forces at work in Philadelphia are found throughout the United States, Arian argues that the Philadelphia Orchestra Association is dominated through its board of directors by upper class (old-rich) families, and that they and the upper classes are its chief beneficiaries. To combat mounting costs, the board has instituted a rigidly bureaucractic, efficiency-minded mode of operations; this innovation has enabled the board to retain control, since the orchestra's budget can still be financed by private wealth. One of the interesting by-products of this process is that the orchestra does not play before a wide spectrum of community audiences and performs little modern or experimental music.

Middle- and upper-class dominance in the general area of aesthetic-intellectual-moral values makes for differences in the amount and type of enjoyment available to the various classes. Furthermore, control of prestigious forms of cultural activity by the upper classes strengthens and supports the general system of stratification by class. To the extent that high culture is thought to bear a special relationship to the integrity of society, the upper and middle classes are seen as its patrons and preservers. To the extent that the aesthetic-intellectual-moral realm has a bearing on social problems and issues, it is the upper classes that control its operations and compose its audiences, thereby deeply influencing the way in which issues and problems are formulated and solved. And, finally, it is the upper and middle classes whose sensibilities are stimulated and wits sharpened by offerings in the worlds of music, theater, painting, dance, sculpture, and quality publications, outcomes that are valuable in their own right and that have applications in the areas of class and power.

The relation between voluntary organizations in the field of "symbolic" culture and government (power) is of growing importance and deserves much greater study. In addition to its growing influence on higher education, the federal government now supports an extensive television network (the Corporation for Public Broadcasting and Public Broadcasting System) and has made large sums of money available to the arts and humanities (through the National Arts Endowment and the National Humanities Endowment). Framed in the image of the independent regulatory commissions, these public bodies resemble their predecessors: ostensibly nonpartisan, objective and aloof from politics in practice, they dispense public monies and public prestige in a manner that coincides with the basic structure of class and political power.

An interesting review of some empirical findings on the mass media suggests that because the logic of economic life, and especially its technology, impels the mass media to try to attract mass audiences, very little of their content is specialized according to class.[14] While blue-collar and white-collar families clearly tend to have different tastes and preferences in broadcast programs and print media (the former preferring more entertainment and less information), the interesting thing, according to Leo Bogart, is that the differences are so small. What the mass media represent, Bogart suggests, is a powerful instrument for inducing working-class conformity to a middle-class society.[15]

Pressure to conform is one thing; actual homogeneity of outlook and values is another. Despite the mass media, significant differences exist between the symbolic interests and skills of white- and blue-collar Americans. This is not surprising given differences in the amount and type of reading (books, magazines, newspapers), formal education, socialization, travel, community participation, and occupational experience engaged in by the two groups.

The Donation of Money and Time

One of the ways to convert money into prestige is to give it away. Donating money enhances one's reputation among those who benefit from such generosity and among those who are impressed that one can afford to give money away. It also helps to make people forget how one earned one's money. (The classic case is the Rockefeller family, which has succeeded in living down the image of John D. Rockefeller as a robber baron.) Thus, individuals give money to hospitals, settlement houses, adoption agencies, colleges, museums, symphony orchestras, and the like, and in return often gain fame and social immortality through the buildings, scholarships, or endowed chairs that memorialize their names.

Another way to gain prestige is to give time to community service. Despite constant complaints that they are overly busy, upper- and middle-class men often serve on committees or boards associated with the full range of voluntary organizations.[16] Their high class status and skills are useful to voluntary organizations (even if they merely lend their names) and, in turn, the moral prestige of such groups rubs off on volunteers. The wives of such men are also deeply involved in community work, the donation of time in their case also signifying freedom from the need to work.[17] Such women are so secure economically that they can afford to give their time away. They too lend their prestige (actually, the prestige of their families and/or husbands), time, skills, and money to such enterprises, and in return they and their families gain prestige by being associated with projects and organizations dedicated to moral and civic betterment.

The linkage between the upper classes and voluntary organizations involves far more than prestige. Voluntary groups, whether called nonprofit or not, generate large revenues and surpluses that must be considered as profits. The economic nature of much of the voluntary world is now more openly recognized and challenges have been mounted in Congress and local governments on the tax exemptions given to the economic activities of schools, churches, hospitals, charities, and service organizations such as the AARP and NRA.

Interestingly enough, membership on the boards that control voluntary associations appears to be remarkably homogeneous.[18] One can assume that charitable and social service agencies are hampered in their purposes by the exclusion from membership of the people they serve. And, obviously, the absence and exclusion of many professions, ordinary workers, lower-level businesspeople, the semiprofessions, and minorities from the governing boards of voluntary associations also hamper their operation and represents a serious loss of prestige and power for such groups.

Finally, an important means of acquiring prestige through the sacrifice of economic assets is public service. Upper-class individuals contribute their time to public commissions of all kinds and accept public positions at considerable sacrifice of income. Ambassadors are perhaps the best examples of the latter, but there are many high-income businesspeople and professionals who accept government positions or run for public office at some (temporary) economic sacrifice. Obviously, the prestige of such individuals is enhanced, and so is that of upper occupational and income-wealth groups in general. Above all, this process helps to create and maintain the impression that middle- and upper-class interests and values are identical with the public interest, an impression fostered by the entire range of voluntary behavior.

COMMON CONSUMPTION

The Logic of Mass Production

An outstanding feature of consumption in the United States is that large portions of the American population consume the same items and services. The inherent tendency of an industrial economy is to create a national (and international) market for products and services and to transform all citizens into equivalent consumers. A mass-production economy is obviously at odds with norms and values that seek to restrict or differentiate consumption according to social position. Unlike industrial social systems, agrarian societies often develop *sumptuary laws,* or laws that lend the power of the "state" to moral and religious norms governing consumption. Such laws establish differential consumption by, for example, stipulating that only aristocrats can wear fur or silk. In caste, multireligious, or multiethnic societies, there develop strong normative traditions that define appropriate forms of consumption for each level or segment of society, especially in the areas of food, drink, and clothing. But the United States, like other industrial societies, has successfully established the primacy of class position with regard to consumption. One's income, and thus one's relation to the commodity market, is the main legitimate restriction on consumption.[19]

Common consumption does not, it should be noted, mean equivalent expenditures. The various classes obviously spend different amounts in their overall consumption. What is of interest here is that sharp differences in consumption, and resulting sharp differences in prestige, do not exist in the United States in an easily recognizable way. The major reason for this is that the majority of the population consumes a wide range of similar products, often brand-name goods with national prestige: food (staples as well as nonstaples); beverages (milk, soft drinks, beer); household products (soap, polishes, waxes, detergents); household appliances (refrigerators, vacuum cleaners, television); clothing (quality ready-made clothing of all sorts, such as suits, dresses, shoes, underwear); and such other items as cigarettes, entertainment products, and sporting goods. The crucial point is that vast portions of the public consume these goods in common regardless of income. In addition, sizable segments of various classes can afford to consume in common even such expensive goods as automobiles, washing machines, air conditioners, and personal computers.

The meaning of common consumption, and other common behavior, is not self-evident. As Gerald Handel and Lee Rainwater emphasized in a classic study, there is only a superficial similarity between the working and middle classes even when they seem to be saying or doing identical things. For example, both classes have positive attitudes toward education and home ownership, but the meanings they attach to these values are quite different. The working class views education quite instrumentally, while the middle class also sees it as a process of refinement, a foundation for later learning, a means to enjoy life more, and a way to learn how to get along with people. Similarly, the working class sees home ownership as a way to escape from the landlord while the middle class tends to see it as a "validation of status." In addition, the working class tends to purchase durable goods in common with the middle class, but not such services as meals in restaurants, vacations, home and automobile repairs, clothing, and education.[20]

In his empirical test of the thesis of the *embourgeoisement* of the working class, Gavin Mackenzie also found that the various classes (in Providence, Rhode Island) do not attach the same meanings to similar consumption. It is clear, for example, that skilled blue-collar workers attach a different meaning to home ownership than do white-collar workers, especially managers. Mackenzie's conclusion is the same as Handel's and Rainwater's finding about stable working class families: basically, skilled workers see home ownership as a way to escape accountability to landlords, an urge analogous to their desire to escape their bosses. For their part, members of the lower and especially the upper middle classes, though they also stress privacy and freedom, cite the economic advantages and prestige of owning a home.[21]

Public Accommodations and Facilities

Another category of common consumption is "public" accommodations and facilities, both those that are privately owned—such as restaurants, housing, hotels, movie theaters, and stadiums—and those that are usually run by government—national, state, and local parks, transit systems, highways, beaches, swimming pools, recreation centers, golf courses, hospitals, colleges, libraries, theaters, stadiums, and museums. The United States has a long history of regarding such services and facilities as less than totally public; their use, for example, was deeply affected by racial segregation in the American South.[22] This situation was changed by law during the 1960s. The Civil Rights Act of 1964 forbade discrimination on the basis of race, religion, or national origin in such "public" facilities as private hotels, motels, restaurants, lunch counters, movie houses, gasoline stations, theaters, stadiums, barbershops and taverns located in hotels, restaurants located in department stores, and facilities that receive federal funds (hospitals, schools for the deaf and blind, colleges and universities). A fundamental feature of this act is that it voids on constitutional grounds state laws requiring segregation in private facilities not engaged in interstate commerce, but cannot forbid private discrimination in them.[23] The Housing Act of 1965 also asserted the public nature of most privately owned housing and forbade discrimination in the sale or rental of most of the nation's housing stock.

On the whole, there is now full formal access to most such facilities and accommodations. Speaking broadly, use and nonuse is now based on class rather than "caste" for all Americans. In practice, however, there are glaring exceptions to pure class consumption, the most important of which is housing. It appears that, in relative terms, no significant progress has been made in providing African Americans with more, better, or integrated housing. Though systematic data are lacking, the same is probably true of hospital use and a host of public services such as police and fire protection, garbage removal, and the like. And, of course, the ghettoization of African Americans and other minorities means that effective access to many free or low-cost public facilities is severely reduced.[24]

The amount and type of use made of "public" accommodations and facilities is also related to class, but no exact picture can be drawn due to lack of research. Many "public" accommodations (hotels, restaurants, lunch counters, housing) are geared to income, and often psychologically deter people who could otherwise afford them. Many rich and many poor people do not use low-cost public facilities such as subways, buslines, and golf courses, or use them less than do the middle-rich and near-poor. The poor probably do not use public facilities such as highways, libraries, and museums much, speaking both in absolute terms and in relation to higher income groups. And while hospitals are ostensibly open to all, their use depends on money. They are thus segregated internally by class—the poor who use hospitals are identified as charity cases—and little common consumption can be said to take place in this area.

Both the rich and the poor, therefore, are exceptions to the pattern of common consumption of public accommodations and facilities. But while the rich consume privately and out of the public eye (though aided extensively by the power dimension which, for example, protects their privacy, property, and income through favorable and discriminatory zoning and taxation), the poor face important prestige disabilities because they consume minimally and are objects of private and public charity. The prestige implications of poverty in the midst of plenty are difficult to gauge. Earlier in our history, the poor were subject to private charity, which allowed the upper classes to acquire prestige by displaying their concern and generosity. During the twentieth century responsibility for solving the problems of the poor has shifted from private markets and private organizations to government. In any case, the poor continue to suffer from low prestige because of low consumption, but in new ways, and perhaps more severely, now that they are acknowledged to be wards of the state.

In sum, the impact of "public" accommodations and "public" facilities on the American class system cannot be gauged with precision. It is clear that such accommodations and facilities could not exist under caste or estate systems of stratification. It is also clear that in a society oriented toward private life, many undoubtedly take governmental services for granted, others resent them as unearned gifts to the poor, still others do not use them, and many lack access because rights are not enforced or because equal services are not provided. On the whole, it cannot be said that the common consumption of class society is as egalitarian as a cursory comparison with caste and estate systems might suggest, nor that any significant reduction of inequality can be said to result from it. The formal right to use "public" accommodations and facilities does, however, create the illusion that an important form of common (and thus equal) consumption is taking place. And, like the illusion of equality of opportunity to consume education, this illusion serves to legitimate and stabilize the American class system.

CLASS, CONSUMPTION, AND THE LEGITIMATION OF INEQUALITY

The evidence about consumption indicates that rising absolute income (and a shorter work week) has not led to the homogenization of the American population into one great middle class bounded at the top by the very rich and at the bottom by the very poor. The American working class, including highly skilled workers and their families, has not translated its income into middle-class levels of prestige. Even if the idea of cultural consumption is broadened to subsume any use of time or money, or to refer to the intake of intellectual, aesthetic, and civic values in general, no middle-class homogenization of the American population is discernible.

Consumption patterns undoubtedly play a role in reducing social stress and producing social stability. Large amounts of common consumption (and the illusion of still more) are undeniable. Patterns of common consumption have a moral effect: They tend to create and uphold belief in moral (prestige) equality. It is not unimportant in this respect that various income groups, Protestants, Roman Catholics, Jews, Republicans, Democrats, whites, blacks, and other "racial" groups all use or are free to use the "same" soap, drink the "same" water, eat the "same" food, and wear the "same" clothes.

Perhaps more important to social integration than common consumption is differential consumption. To understand the American class system fully, it is essential to recognize that, by and large, the culture of capitalism has successfully established the legitimacy of differential styles of class consumption and resulting styles of differential prestige. Americans at all levels accept the principle of a hierarchy of consumption, which is in keeping with their acceptance of the differential worth of occupations and the legitimacy of a hierarchy of income and wealth. Those who consume well or even lavishly deserve to do so, it is thought, because of their economic accomplishments. As long as differential consumption does not lead to rigid categories of prestige affecting the moral or political-legal worth of individuals, there is little public resentment of differential income classes and differential prestige through consumption.[25] In other words, American society has successfully compartmentalized the forces of liberty and success (inequality) and the forces of equality. Nothing signifies the stability of American society so completely as the fact that its disgruntled groups do not draw on the tradition of equality to question the overall class structure. Immersed thoroughly in laissez-faire liberalism, Americans draw on the tradition of equality to demand equal opportunity, not to question whether American capitalism is capable of providing it. Similarly, Americans may ask for help in housing but they do not question what is apparent to many observers—the chronic inability of American capitalism of providing adequate housing for all. Americans have been socialized to accept differential consumption, including homelessness, hunger, no health insurance, and illiteracy, because they believe falsely that consumption is related to what individuals earn and what they earn is due to innate worth.

COUNTERFEIT AND COMPENSATORY CONSUMPTION

C. Wright Mills has suggested that white-collar people in lower-middle class occupations engage in a "status cycle" to alleviate "status panic."[26] The secretary who skips lunches to save money for a wardrobe and a two-week vacation in a plush resort is one example. Many other means of enjoying prestige above one's class level are available to Americans because of the anonymity of modern life: after-hour clothing, a splurge on theater tickets, a new hairdo, inexpensive travel tours, and the like. Again, as is true of so much consumption behavior, we have little data and can only speculate on the extent to which Americans rely on a "status cycle" to alleviate prestige anxieties.

Another way of counterfeiting prestige is to live beyond one's income, either by endangering one's economic position (by, for example, failing to save for retirement, or to own life or medical insurance) or through credit. Installment credit and mortgages do allow an unknown number of Americans to live on future earnings, a practice that often entails serious psychic and family costs. The role of the state in making credit and mortgage money available (and allowing the interest paid as an income tax deduction) is an indispensable aspect of our prestige system. Expense-account living, also subsidized by the state, is another form of counterfeit consumption; how many engage in it cannot be said with certainty. The role of the state in enforcing one-sided contracts and credit terms also allows for a form of high-cost "compensatory consumption" among the poor. The function of this type of consumption is to provide consumer goods to high-risk customers and thus promote self-respect among the poor.[27] As we have suggested, the integrative function performed by consumption at this level—maintaining loyalty to the system among the poor—is performed by various forms of consumption (common, differential, counterfeit) at various class levels.

CONSUMPTION EXTREMES

Commentators on American society have tended to stress the decline of ostentatious display by the rich, in terms both of the long-term historical transition from feudal society and of developments within industrial society during the twentieth century. (The White House, says Talcott Parsons, is not the Palace of Versailles.) This overall perspective on consumption is sound enough, though some of the conclusions drawn from it are not.[28] Comparisons between modern society and feudal systems, as we have pointed out, are monumentally difficult to make and a source of endless confusion and distortion. For example, most of the French aristocracy during the heyday of Versailles led lives of relatively deep impoverishment and were incapable of flaunting luxurious consumption. It is also true that there has been a decline of splendor in private residences—in the use of gold plumbing, large servant staffs, and the like—simultaneous with the decline of "High Society." The reasons generally adduced for this decline are the income tax (a much-exaggerated cause), the competition for and cost of servant labor, the growth of a democratic spirit, and the decline of a leisure class of nonworking very rich.

Of central significance in understanding consumption extremes is the phenomenon of relative deprivation. Industrial populations are now highly urbanized and subject to high levels of stimulation—for example, through the mass media—which among other things make known to them higher and often unattainable levels of consumption. And it is no longer possible to comfort most Americans with the promise of a better life in the next world, or to persuade them that their poverty is due to original sin. The fact remains that an upper-class man or woman may routinely spend on clothing an amount that millions of Americans must live on for an entire year. In short, large numbers at the upper levels enjoy multiple dwellings, expensive hobbies, and private boats and planes while significant numbers go hungry, lack plumbing, and suffer from lack of medical care.

TRICKLE-DOWN IDEOLOGY: THE CONSERVATIVE ATTEMPT TO REVITALIZE AMERICA

The American social system depends a great deal on motivating people to work hard in order to acquire tangible consumption goods and services. The period since 1970 has witnessed a slow or erratic economy, a decline in real wages, and demands by racial and ethnic groups, women, the handicapped, and gays and lesbians for a share in the economic pie. In addition, large amounts of the pie have been going into military preparedness, preventing pollution, fighting crime, and welfare (for all class levels). The net result has been serious discontent and discord among Americans because of the disparity between their expectations and their rewards.

Conservative sectors of the American upper classes mounted a concerted political challenge to the mass-oriented Keynesian-welfare state in response to the economic slowdown of the 1970s (for details on the latter, see Chapters 6 and 7). They succeeded in electing a conservative (right-liberal) administration that lasted from 1980 to 1992. Their economic ideology was an elite-oriented Keynesianism, or cuts in spending on the masses and tax cuts to help property groups, a public policy that right liberals claimed would lead to economic growth and a trickle-down effect that would benefit the public at large. The first occurred to some extent but the latter not at all—actually, a large majority of the American people saw either a stagnation or a decline in their fortunes.

Conservative Republicans captured both Houses of Congress in 1994 and again proceeded to build an elite-Keynesian legislative program. Openly slashing programs for the poor, the elderly, and middle-income groups, the Republican party, with the help of conservative Democrats, also attacked environmental laws and a host of social service programs such as support for the arts and public broadcasting. One can assume that the logic behind these actions was to use economic deprivation to drive people into the labor force (thereby lowering the price of labor) and to reduce the social overhead (thereby making it possible to lower taxes). Their other purpose in reducing government was of course to undermine the power of the Democratic party.

SUMMARY

The use of property, money, and time has prestige implications, and a wide variety of prestige differences has appeared in industrial society. The hierarchy of class is accompanied by a hierarchy of differential consumption that leads to sharp and enduring differences in prestige. Unlike agrarian societies, however, industrial society is characterized by a sphere of common consumption and promotes expectations of increased consumption at all levels. Given an expanding economy, and thus rising consumption, Americans accept prestige differences in consumption despite the fact that such differences are at odds with their moral and political-legal egalitarianism. There is little evidence of the development of a great middle mass of consumers. If anything the middle-income sector has shrunk in recent years. In sum, the area of consumption prestige reflects the nature of the capitalist economy and its steeply and stably graded class system and constitutes an important support of both legitimate and illegitimate elements in the latter.

NOTES

1. Much of the following is indebted to Veblen's classic, *The Theory of the Leisure Class* (New York: New American Library, 1953; originally published in 1899).
2. *Patterns of Culture* (Boston: Houghton Mifflin, 1959; originally published in 1934), ch. 6.
3. Veblen, *The Theory of the Leisure Class,* p. 47.
4. Though the rich undoubtedly enjoy their property and its income as much as they do their income from work, it cannot be said that the ownership of property as such has ever established itself in the normative culture of America in the same way that work has.
5. Nonetheless, prestige skills and values in these areas are acquired only after considerable nonutilitarian effort, and Veblen's central concept of waste behavior is still relevant in this respect.
6. For a fuller discussion of Keynesianism, see the section on "Public Economic Policies" in Chapter 15.
7. Travel, both in general and in terms of specific categories (visits to friends and relations, business trips and conventions, outdoor recreation, sightseeing and entertainment, weekend travel, and vacation travel), is distinctly class-related. (The relation between class and visits to friends and relatives is not pronounced.) For the way in which higher income, occupation, and education are related to more travel, see U.S. Bureau of the Census, Census of Transportation, 1982, *National Travel Survey: Travel During 1982* TC72-N3 (Washington, DC: U.S. Government Printing Office, 1983), chart 4.

8. Even death does not end the search for prestige. One need only think of the tombs of the Pharoahs, the state funerals of the mighty, segregated cemeteries, and the class-oriented appeals of undertakers and cemeteries to appreciate the varied ways in which the lower classes are denied even the democracy of death. For a marvelously insightful analysis and critique of funeral practices in America and the economic groups behind them, see Jessica Mitford, *The American Way of Death* (New York: Simon & Schuster, 1963).
9. See W. Lloyd Warner, Marcia Meeker, and Kenneth Eells, *Social Class in America* (New York: Harper & Row, 1960; first published in 1949), pp. 39–42.
10. U.S. Bureau of the Census, "Current Housing Reports," H151/93-1 (Washington, DC: U.S. Government Printing Office, 1996), Table 1-6.
11. For an interpretive study that identifies various levels of "culture" in America and their relations to class, see Herbert J. Gans, *Popular Culture and High Culture: An Analysis and Evaluation of Taste* (New York: Basic Books, 1974). For dominance by the upper classes in the consumption of high art, see Paul DiMaggio and Michael Useem, "Cultural Democracy in a Period of Cultural Expansion: The Social Composition of Arts Audiences in the United States," *Social Problems* 26 (December 1978):179–197. For a general survey of research in this area with considerable reference to the United States, see Stanley Parker, *Leisure and Work* (London: George Allen and Unwin, 1983).
12. Two Marxist scholars who have achieved fame exploring the general relation between society (class) and aesthetic life are Georg Lukacs, especially his *The Historical Novel* (London: Merlin Press, 1962) and *Studies in European Realism* (New York: Grosset & Dunlap, 1964), and Arnold Hauser, *The Social History of Art*, 4 vols. (London: Routledge and Kegan Paul, 1962; originally published in 1951). For a valuable historical analysis of the class basis of various forms of art, see Vytautas Kavolis, *Artistic Expression: A Sociological Analysis* (Ithaca, NY: Cornell University Press, 1968).
13. Edward Arian, *Bach, Beethoven, and Bureaucracy: The Case of the Philadelphia Orchestra* (Tuscaloosa: University of Alabama Press, 1971).
14. The growth of publicly supported television has produced significant diversification of television programming. As is true of the other subsidized arts, public educational television represents stimulation for the middle and upper classes.
15. Leo Bogart, "The Mass Media and the Blue-Collar Worker," in Arthur B. Shostak and William Gomberg, eds., *Blue-Collar World: Studies of the American Worker* (Englewood Cliffs, NJ: Prentice-Hall, 1964), pp. 416–428.
16. Participation in voluntary organizations is in general a middle- and upper-class phenomenon; see Chapter 13.
17. This has changed since the late 1970s and voluntary groups are experiencing a shortage of volunteers at all levels since many women in the middle and upper middle classes are now working.
18. The basic analogue is corporate ownership and control. The reader should also remember the homogeneity found to characterize the boards of institutions of higher education, especially private ones.
19. There are, of course, laws prohibiting certain kinds of consumption (such as consumption of drugs), but these laws are applicable to all.
20. Gerald Handel and Lee Rainwater, "Persistence and Change in Working-Class Life Style," in Arthur B. Shostak and William Gomberg, eds., *Blue-Collar World: Studies of the American Worker* (Englewood Cliffs, NJ: Prentice-Hall, 1964), pp. 36–41.

21. Gavin Mackenzie, *The Aristocracy of Labor: The Position of Skilled Craftsmen in the American Class Structure* (London and New York: Cambridge University Press, 1973), pp. 74–77.
22. At one time, Oklahoma even had segregated telephone booths.
23. Many states outside the South have their own laws prohibiting discrimination.
24. Minority groups have in recent years asked for access to the public airwaves (radio and television channels). While this demand has not been met as often or as fully as minority groups would like, it has served to raise the question of how such public facilities denigrate or neglect minorities.
25. This does not mean that Americans do not complain about inequities and inadequacies in living standards and public services.
26. C. Wright Mills, *White Collar: The American Middle Classes* (New York: Oxford University Press, 1953), ch. 11.
27. David Caplovitz, *The Poor Pay More: Consumer Practices of Low Income Families* (New York: Free Press, 1963), ch. 2.
28. Actually, the American presidency is embellished by impressive facilities, ceremonies, and protocols, and has been referred to as the imperial presidency.

13

Class and How Americans Associate: The Structure of Prestige Groups

◆ ◆ ◆ ◆

◆ ◆ ◆ ◆

PRIMARY AND SECONDARY PRESTIGE GROUPS: THE VOLUNTARY SECTOR

The analysis of prestige groups is central to understanding the American class system. In analyzing prestige groups, we will maintain our society-wide focus, making few references to prestige structures in local communities (despite the fact that small-town America is still a stronghold of mutually accepted prestige claims). As the nation has urbanized and suburbanized, a pronounced trend toward the segregation of class and prestige groups by residence and political community occurred and the small-town hierarchy of prestige groups is not an accurate model of contemporary national prestige behavior.

Many of the terms traditionally used to differentiate prestige from class behavior are ambiguous and misleading. The distinction between private and public is not overly useful. For example, private clubs are prestige groups, but so are publicly supported museums, schools and universities, and charity organizations. Some prefer to think of the area of prestige as social space particularly amenable to individual choice; indeed, it is often referred to as the *voluntary sector.*

Voluntary behavior can be both primary and secondary in nature: its focus can be intimate, as is true of love, family, friendship, and some clubs, or it can be reformist, humanitarian, or charitable, like the League of Women Voters, political parties, the Red Cross, and the Salvation Army. We speak of this realm in terms of the rights of free speech, free association, and petition. But despite such traditional phrases and the appearance of behavior in this area as natural and spontaneous, it would be a mistake to think of prestige as the domain of human nature and of freely chosen behavior. Choices in the realm of prestige are still social choices tied closely to class (and power), and the alternatives that are considered normal effectively rule out many other feasible courses of action.

There are two perspectives that can guide us through the maze of prestige phenomena as they express themselves in America's associational life. First, voluntary behavior exerts an influence beyond itself to counteract or modify the inequalities and inequities of class and power. A vital tradition of moral egalitarianism, derived largely from Christianity and secular humanism, and especially from the liberal democratic tradition, permeates the voluntary sector and supports its autonomy from the rigid frameworks and compulsions of work and law. It is in this realm that Americans relax and rest, undertake new activities, pursue old interests and values, criticize themselves and their institutions, and launch movements of reform and regeneration. The voluntary realm has seen a significant historical increase in the number of people eligible to participate in important institutional sectors and to consume hitherto restricted goods and symbols. And it is in the voluntary realm that commentators from Tocqueville on have found the essential explanation of America's freedom, equality, and democracy: here, theorists argue, we find a pluralistic, decentralized group structure responsive to both personal and public need.

The other perspective that will guide us through the sector of prestige or voluntary groups is equally important, if not more so. As we will see, all available evidence points to a steeply graded, sharply segregated, and highly stable stratification of benefits derived from memberships in prestige groups. Not only are such benefits distributed unevenly, but there is also a far-reaching interpenetration of class, prestige, and power structures. The prestige realm, for example, is subject to the same inexorable growth of rational organization (bureaucracy) as the realms of class and power. The United States has an incredible number of formally organized, private associations.[1] Beneath this multiform associational life there is a basic trend toward bigness and concentration. Churches; universities and colleges; fraternal and charitable groups; research institutes; foundations; the mass media and entertainment businesses (radio, movies, television, recording, sports); businesses devoted to hobbies and recreation; publishers of magazines, newspapers, and books; and the world of "high" culture (symphony orchestras, ballet groups, museums) are all characterized by large-scale organization and increased concentration. A shift from preindustrial to industrial modes of operation is clearly discernible in the fields of entertainment, religion, "high" culture, philanthropy, education, medicine, and the professions in general. Services formerly provided on the basis of individual need are beginning to be offered in large-scale standardized ways to families, neighborhoods, cities, states, regions, the nation, and even other countries. In other words, private organizations in these areas are in step with the major trend evident in our economy and government, concentration and bureaucratization.

PRESTIGE, DIVERSITY, AND STRUGGLE

American history is filled with rivalries between prestige-seeking groups: whites have oppressed nonwhites; the well-bred have struggled to maintain ascendancy over those they consider their social inferiors; native-born American whites have looked down on immigrants and native nonwhites alike; people of property and/or education have expected deference from the poor; unlettered rural people have railed against the city; and so on. The winners of these various struggles are not always easy to determine. It is important to the development of American prestige patterns, however, that the United States has never had to dislodge a powerful set of feudal families from the upper levels of its economic, religious, educational, and political life. But while it was spared this problem, the United States has witnessed many attempts to translate old wealth and lengthy pedigrees into a prestige (and even power) factor.

Analysts have found deep prestige divisions based on "family lineage" in every community they have studied. This is not to say that Americans assert the superiority of particular family bloodlines (except when families are differentiated according to "race"). Americans believe in biopsychic differences between individuals, which is quite different from the feudal principle of a hierarchy of hereditary families. Where families come to believe themselves superior (or inferior), their prestige claims (or shame) are based on achievable factors such as income, wealth, expensive residence, breeding and good taste, philanthropy, leisure pursuits, or some mixture of these.[2] The American social system encourages and accords achievement prestige in a wide variety of areas: business, science, education, the arts, charity, reform movements, and in such areas of taste as dress, speech, home furnishings, music, and art. By and large, therefore, when prestige distinctions seem at odds with class, they are really at odds with *newly acquired* class position; thus the distinction between the old rich and the new rich.

The identification of prestige differentials as the basis of social stratification is best exemplified by the Warner school. Their own research and that of others led W. Lloyd Warner and his associates to identify six class levels in the more established regions of the country (New England and the Deep South) and five levels in the Midwest and Far West.[3] The essence of Warner's scheme was to assert the independent force of prestige differences based on old wealth, tasteful consumption, superior breeding, and public service. Critics have pointed out, however, that while these hierarchical prestige differences exist, they are not only lodged in economic status (as Warner is not unaware) but must be seen in historical context: prestige phenomena are not the essence of social class but manifestations of economic positions consolidated over generations.

THE UPPER CLASS AS A PRESTIGE GROUP

An important feature of the American class system is that no prestige group has ever been able to establish itself on a nationwide basis. For such a thing to happen one group would need to combine prestige assets with either class or power assets, or both, to form a dominant stratum. On a regional basis, the plantation aristocracy of the old South can be considered such a stratum. And one can interpret the prestige aspirations of the "Four Hundred" at the end of the nineteenth century as an abortive attempt to become a national prestige group. But while that attempt to establish a high society failed, the American upper class—composed essentially of families of old wealth—has developed a unique and powerful prestige position. Though it lacks public acceptance, the upper class's prestige pursuits and achievements are in keeping with its high class and power position and serve many important functions.

The identification of this class through its prestige practices is primarily the work of E. Digby Baltzell. In his study of the upper class in Philadelphia[4] and subsequent historical study of the upper class on a national scale,[5] Baltzell has traced the parallel fortunes of an emerging national political economy and a national upper class, defined as possessing a common cultural tradition, a sense of solidarity resulting from regular interaction, and a consciousness of itself as a distinct social class.

Though his account of the upper class is badly marred by the assumption that the United States has (and has always had) open class and power dimensions that allow individuals of ability to rise in the economic and political-legal systems, and though he fails to understand that prestige exclusiveness buttresses class and power interests and privileges, Baltzell nevertheless draws a fascinating and insightful picture of what he calls America's "caste-ridden" prestige dimension. Primarily as a response to large-scale immigration but also, Baltzell suggests, as patrician protective devices against populism, progressivism, urban blight, and trust-busting, the WASP upper class began in the 1880s to develop a series of exclusive prestige groups and practices:[6]

1. The trend toward exclusive summer resort communities was ratified when President Eliot of Harvard built a summer cottage at Northeast Harbor, Maine, in 1881.

2. The trend toward exclusive country clubs was initiated by the founding of The Country Club at Brookline, Massachusetts, in 1882.
3. The patrician search for family roots and the craze for genealogy gave rise to the founding of the Sons of the Revolution in 1883, followed by the Colonial Dames in 1890, the Daughters of the American Revolution in 1890, and the Society of Mayflower Descendants in 1894.
4. That important institution for socialization, the exclusive country day school and boarding school, experienced its most rapid growth in the last two decades of the nineteenth century. Andover and Exeter, established in the eighteenth century, and St. Paul's, established before the Civil War, experienced their greatest growth in these decades. They were joined by Groton in 1884, Taft in 1890, Hotchkiss in 1892, Choate in 1896, and approximately seventy other similar schools. Among the exclusive suburban day schools established at the same time are Browne and Nichols (1883) in Cambridge, Massachusetts, and Haverford (1884) and Chestnut Hill (1895) in Philadelphia.
5. The development of exclusive suburban residential areas, initiated by the opening of Tuxedo Park, New York, in 1886, ushered in a flight from the city on the part of the upper class.
6. Graduates of the exclusive lower schools attended high-prestige universities (Yale, Princeton, and Harvard) of, in those decades, somewhat indifferent quality. We must add that there is now a circuit of high- (and medium-) quality liberal arts colleges and universities, primarily in the northeastern United States, to complete the educational careers of upper-class men and women.
7. *The Social Register,* first published in 1887 in New York City, soon added listings for many of America's major cities. This widely imitated register, sold by a profit-making publisher, adheres to no established rules for rejection or ejection. It simply lists details about old wealthy families who stay out of trouble and receive no adverse publicity.[7] *The Social Register* probably contributes considerably to facilitating social events and intercity mobility on the part of the upper class.
8. The metropolitan men's club emerged as a potent adjunct to corporate power during the latter part of the nineteenth century. Baltzell, who makes much of the anti-Semitism and anti-Catholicism of all upper-class prestige activities, points out that Jews were excluded from clubs (and some Jewish members expelled) at this time. He fails to note, though, that this was probably necessary because Jews were also being systematically excluded from the upper reaches of the business world.

The development of these prestige groups and practices, says Baltzell, helped to unify the upper class both locally and throughout the metropolitan United States, and in time produced a national upper class. The unity of this upper class results from common socialization; intermarriage; frequent interaction in clubs and resorts, and at parties; and trusteeships of such prestige organizations as schools, clubs, resort associations, and the like. The possibility that the upper class is or could become a dominant stratum does not concern Baltzell, who believes that every society needs a "representative establishment," or an elite that is also an aristocracy—that is, an establishment that represents talent in the spheres of class and power, and expresses a society's highest values in the prestige realm. Assuming that class and power are open elite systems, Baltzell's main concern is that the upper class practices ethnic-religious and racial exclusion and therefore violates in the prestige dimension the moral universalism that should accompany the open merit system of the class and power dimensions. Baltzell is hopeful, given leadership by elite elements of the upper class, that these practices will be abandoned, the upper class will again become a representative establishment, and the United States will cease being a "caste-ridden, open class" system.

Baltzell's evolutionary liberalism pervades his work, and is particularly evident in his failure to see deep connections between the castelike nature of upper class prestige patterns and the protection of class and power interests and privileges. This is not the case with two theorists who have benefited from Baltzell's analysis of upper class prestige practices and have incorporated it into their radical analyses of the American class system. C. Wright Mills treats the foregoing prestige practices as devices to unify the elites who control the apexes of the economic, political, and military orders. As such, these prestige practices are integral features of the United States' power elite, the tiny group of men and families Mills believes to control the nation's basic decisions.[8]

G. William Domhoff, pursuing the approach established by Mills and others, developed a set of social indicators to more positively identify members of the upper class (and has thereby helped to update Baltzell's prestige analysis). According to Domhoff, a male can be considered to belong to the upper class:

1. If he is listed in an edition of *The Social Register* or one of its counterparts
2. If he, his father, brothers, or father-in-law attended an exclusive prep school
3. If he, his father, brothers, or father-in-law belongs to an exclusive club
4. If his sister, wife, mother, or mother-in-law attended an exclusive school or belongs to an exclusive club
5. If his or his wife's father was a millionaire entrepreneur or $100,000-a-year corporation executive or corporation lawyer *and* if he or she attended any of several private schools or belongs to certain clubs.[9]

Domhoff also offers an interesting analysis of the socialization of upper-class women and their leadership of voluntary and reform groups—groups that help to stabilize society and enhance the prestige of the upper class.[10] In addition, he analyzes upper-class control of prestigious research and public-interest organizations and their impact on foreign and domestic policymaking.[11]

Mills's view that the United States is dominated by a power elite (and Domhoff's view that we are dominated by a ruling class) will concern us again later. The evidence, however, makes one thing certain: the various elites at the apex of a centralized economy and state have developed prestige groups that provide them with a common psychology and a means to coordinate and protect their interests, values, and privileges. In sum, while the American upper class has not been able to elicit national consensus on its prestige superiority, it has managed in practice to establish formidable prestige barriers between itself and the general public. These barriers support a set of benefits that are enjoyed in their own right, are aped by and thus help to divide and co-opt the classes below them, and above all, protect the economic and political power of this class from being diluted by the free play of economic and political forces. Whether or not the upper class is the dominant stratum in America, these prestige values and practices are essential to the formation and maintenance of its extraordinary wealth and power.

CLASS AND PRIMARY BEHAVIOR

Primary relations (groups) are forms of interaction that usually occur face to face, have diffused emotional-moral content, and involve the entire personality in an enduring web of obligations and rights. Friendship, love, marriage, family, neighborhood interaction, as well as dining and certain other forms of socializing, all belong in this category. The fact that primary relations seem normal and spontaneous should not mislead us about their social nature or their relation to the prevailing system of stratification. Class society, no less than estate and caste societies, is characterized by class-related prestige groups that control the basic forms of primary interaction. We know that class factors play an important role in determining marriage and eating partners, as well as place of residence and membership in clubs.

Though many stratification analysts have long been intrigued by the role of clubs in stratification inequality, no systematic study has been done. Of all the classic empirical studies, perhaps the most systematic, and certainly the most informative, is August B. Hollingshead's *Elmtown's Youth.* Hollingshead found distinctive types of clubs and club affiliations for each of Elmtown's five classes.[12] For their part, Baltzell and Domhoff have examined upper-class clubs.[13] Though much about the class nature of clubs is known, much has to be conjectured. It would not be amiss, however, to assume that the exclusive urban men's clubs offer basic psychic benefits in their own right and are important adjuncts of the business world as well. The simplest and most direct clue to the latter relation is that it is common practice for businesses to pay the club dues of their executives.[14] High-prestige clubs of all types often have annual fees and dues that amount to thousands of dollars, and as such obviously represent an exclusiveness based on price (class). There is also an obvious and fairly specific class factor (old wealth) in the membership of exclusive men's clubs: Duquesne (Pittsburgh), Detroit (Detroit), Union, Knickerbocker, Brook, Racquet and Tennis, Century, Union League, Metropolitan, and University (New York), and so on. There are also elite women's clubs such as Colony (New York),

Friday (Chicago), Chilton (Boston), and Acorn (Philadelphia). Patriotic-historical-genealogical societies are by definition limited to members of old families (often possessing old wealth).

Class content is also obvious in the membership of country clubs and resorts, some of which are restricted to old wealth, some to wealth, and others of which cater to the middle classes at large. Service clubs such as the Kiwanis and Rotary are anchored in the world of business and the professions, while fraternal orders and lodges and veterans' groups, such as the Elks, Shriners, and American Legion, appear to be largely lower middle and working class in composition. An interesting new form of primary interaction (in a commercial setting) is the singles club and bar, and the singles weekend at resorts. Though little researched, it is highly likely that this is a primarily middle class activity. In sum, primary relations have a pronounced class basis: Fundamentally, only class peers engage in primary or intimate forms of interaction.

One must add that there also exists a relatively sharp qualitative discontinuity by class in the *kind* of primary relations Americans enter into. Working-class Americans tend to have fewer friends, entertain less, and belong less to clubs and other organizations devoted to entertainment and companionship than the classes above.[15] And working-class marriages and family life provide fewer and lower-quality satisfactions than characterize those of the classes above. And below the working class is an underclass that experiences deep social isolation, since members of this class do not engage much in either primary or secondary behavior.

Primary relations are also affected by forms of consumption: Since consumption skills and interests can vary within a given class, individuals and families having similar class positions may enjoy different levels and types of primary interaction. The best-known distinction is between the old rich and the new rich, but such distinctions are applicable at all class levels. However, while style of life (consumption) can be independent of class, it invariably succumbs to class; in other words, given time, a household with a given economic position can and does acquire the prestige credentials needed for inclusion in primary prestige groups. It was inevitable, in other words, that Mrs. Astor (old real estate wealth) would call on Mrs. Vanderbilt (new railroad wealth). And, of course, primary relations between families and individuals with similar class positions are strongly differentiated by religion, ethnicity, and "race"—but this issue is best discussed separately.

CLASS AND SECONDARY BEHAVIOR

Secondary interaction involves only a portion of an individual's personality and tends to be functionally specific and emotionally neutral: seeing a doctor, getting on a bus, going to school, working in an office or factory, going to church, voting, being on trial, serving on a committee, joining an interest group, going to the park or a ball game or a restaurant or a movie, and joining a trade union or professional association are all examples of secondary interaction.

Research has revealed a pronounced class-related pattern to participation in secondary (voluntary) organizations. The upper classes, identified by occupation, income, and education (either separately or combined), have higher rates of membership, active participation, and leadership in secondary groups, especially in general-interest, career-related business and professional, community-and-service-oriented, educational, cultural, and political-pressure groups. The working class tends to concentrate its membership in churches, unions, fraternal groups, and sports clubs. By and large, the overall rate of participation in important power groups is low among the working class and almost nonexistent among the lower class.[16]

The low rate of participation by ordinary citizens in voluntary organizations is far from the full story. Participation in policy-making and in the management of voluntary organizations is restricted to very small numbers drawn almost exclusively from the upper middle and upper classes. No effective or meaningful popular participation takes place in such groups as hospitals, colleges and universities, charities, public-policy research institutes and foundations, and cultural groups. An analysis of Scouting and the Young Men's Christian Association (YMCA) has shown biases derived from the upper classes in even these seemingly nonpartisan groups.[17]

Indeed, the working and lower classes engage in so little voluntary secondary behavior that one must conclude that qualitatively different life experiences divide these two segments of American society. Not only is the United States not a nation of joiners—excluding trade unions and churches, it is doubtful that even half of the adult American population belongs to a secondary organization—but the evidence clearly indicates that the American social system tends to restrict and routinize the experience of its working and lower classes.[18]

Foreign commentators—for example, Tocqueville and Max Weber—were impressed by how much American society relies on voluntary behavior to handle social functions. European societies also experienced a growth of voluntarism but less so than the United States. The reasons are relatively clear—Europe had established churches and governments to perform many of the functions and to tackle many of the problems that arose with industrialization. Given the conditions of the New World, Americans were forced to do for themselves. Today, organized as private groups, Americans initiate reforms across a wide front and take on social problems such as disease, homelessness, distressed families, alcoholism, battered wives, and unmarried pregnant women. The voluntary sector is also responsible for a good deal of American education (and private schools provide a model for much of public education). It also conducts a great deal of American research and is responsible for much of what goes on in the world of the arts.

Right liberals favor a voluntary solution to most social problems. The Reagan-Bush administration of 1980–1992 stressed a return to voluntarism to justify cuts in public services. Left liberals support voluntarism but are much more likely to view it as a way to test ideas so that the good ones can be implemented by government. Radicals argue that voluntarism is an ideology to keep social problems out of the political arena and thus prevent the public from evaluating how property and professional groups behave. In addition, voluntarism protects income and wealth groups from paying taxes (the United States, remember, is the least taxed of all industrial nations except Japan).

Radical critics specifically charge that:

1. The absence of public participation in cultural groups means that only the art of the upper classes is available.
2. The boards of hospitals and universities are effectively dominated by business and professional interests and many alternatives to present-day health and educational policies are ruled out.
3. The United Way tends to support only traditional, respectable charities and discriminates against consumer advocacy, political reform, tenants, feminist, gay rights, and other groups.
4. The voluntary approach to research and development means that many dubious projects are undertaken and that the interests of power groups are served under the cover of academic freedom and objective research (for an example of bias in research that favors the upper classes, see Box 15–1, "The Tomato Harvester: How Education Serves the Corporate Economy").

Participation in secondary prestige groups is a well-known way in which the upper classes exert influence over important activities (outside of class and power) and an important source of moral, intellectual, and aesthetic prestige. It is also a way in which upwardly mobile families establish their claims to full inclusion in a higher social stratum. Large business firms routinely use fund drives to test the abilities of young executives; and they are quite aware that their participation in such drives is a means to acquire a favorable public image. The ties between the upper levels of the business and professional worlds and institutions of higher education are well documented. We also have considerable documentation of the upper and upper-middle class base of foundations, prestigious research institutes, hospitals, cultural groups, and voluntary organizations in general.

While secondary organizations are primarily middle and upper class groups, the class composition of particular organizations varies. Though data are scarce and often impressionistic, it is clear, for example, that cultural groups like museum or symphony orchestra boards have different class memberships than parent-teachers associations, and that various shades of upper- and middle-class membership characterize the Rotary, the

Kiwanis, the Elks, the Masons, the Young Men's Christian Association, the Democratic and Republican parties, the Red Cross, the American Cancer Society, the American Bar Association, the American Sociological Association, and so on. There is also wide variation by class in type of church and church membership; this matter is best discussed separately, since it touches on differences based on religion and ethnicity.

Any sharp distinction between the dimensions of prestige and power must be fallacious, for the traditional distinction between the private and public sectors has been badly blurred by the dynamics of mature industrialization. Actually, the separation of these spheres was never as complete as we sometimes imagine. For example, the property and income of religious, charitable, and educational organizations have traditionally been exempt from taxation. This practice indicates a broad consensus on the value of such activities, and the exemption from taxation of our churches, foundations, and institutions of higher education is contingent on their political neutrality.

One of the more portentous aspects of the relation between government and the private sector of voluntary organizations is the growth of government by grant and contract. In recent decades, federal, state, and local governments have sought to achieve a host of purposes by contracting with established private groups such as the National Urban League or the Young Men's Christian Association or financing new organizations to render intellectual and scientific services at home and abroad. ("Not-for-profit corporations" provide advisory and technical services to the military, the Atomic Energy Commission, the Department of State, the Central Intelligence Agency, and so on.) This trend has made many traditional voluntary organizations dependent on government for financing, creating a new type of quasi-voluntary group. As critics point out, the trend toward government by contract and grant has important implications for the autonomy of private bodies and poses problems of accountability.[19]

In addition, the federal government has begun large-scale funding of medical, scientific, and educational undertakings, often funneling public monies through "nonpolitical" conduits like the National Science Foundation. In the case of education, institutions of higher education (including private and religious schools) have received direct governmental grants for construction, special programs, research, and (since the Higher Education Act of 1972) normal operation.

The trend toward public institutions of higher education also represents a way in which power is explicitly engaged in serving class values in the realm of prestige.[20] This process also characterizes the many areas in which power endorses the right of private or "public" organizations to certify individuals for high-level occupations and to enforce regulations controlling the behavior of their members (for example, the American Medical Association, the National Association of Securities Dealers, the American Bar Association).

Still another way to examine the interrelatedness of our class-prestige-power systems is to trace the pattern of overlapping personnel and policies in the areas of research, reform, and public policy formation. Presidential and congressional commissions are composed of high-level representatives of various segments of the economy and the professions; and private foundations, associations, and institutes (such as the Committee on Economic Development, the Rockefeller and Ford Foundations, the Brookings Institution, the Council on Foreign Relations, and the Twentieth Century Fund) cultivate images of public disinterestedness and develop highly influential policy proposals in the realms of business, education, population, foreign policy, medicine, the arts, race relations, and the like.[21]

One of the more interesting examples of a partisan political stance with partisan consequences by an ostensibly nonpartisan research-charitable group is the American Cancer Society. With very little input from the public, the American Cancer Society helps to channel huge resources (far more than can be efficiently or honestly absorbed) into a search for a cancer cure while diverting resources and attention away from the most promising way to curb cancer—direct public action to create healthy natural and social environments. Unable to ignore a rising tide of knowledge connecting cancer to unhealthy habits (for example, smoking, sunbathing), unhealthy diet (for example, the excessive intake of animal fat), and unhealthy air, water, and workplaces, threatened business and professional groups now advocate prevention—not prevention through direct public action but through *voluntary* changes in personal life style (see Box 13–1, "The Cancer Establishment"[22]). Here is an example of how high-minded reform is mostly a way to depoliticize a problem and to protect the status quo (the capitalist economy that is causing the problem).

In sum, it is clear that the entire realm of secondary prestige groups (along with consumption and primary group behavior) represents an adjunct to economic and political power. It is through various secondary prestige activities that a vital moral and intellectual cement is applied to the overall structure of American inequality. And secondary prestige groups are as narrowly based, unresponsive, and backward in their procedures and policies as corporate and governmental bureaucracies. The function, largely latent, of secondary prestige groups can perhaps be stated more simply: By deflecting attention away from the class (and power) basis of America's social problems, such groups help to preserve the status quo.

SUMMARY

The United States has an enormously varied array of both primary and secondary prestige groups. There is a distinct class basis to both types of pres-

BOX 13–1 *The Cancer Establishment*

The powerful and rich have a large stake in finding a cure for cancer. For one thing, no matter how much money they have they can't buy a cure. But more important, they have an economy to protect.

For over fifty years powerful individuals and groups have defined cancer as a medical problem that is somehow in the genes of individuals (individual human nature at fault). Though we know that there are many different kinds of cancer and that there is no magic bullet to cure it, the basic approach remains the same as in dealing with other diseases. Some medical progress has been made in treating cancer through surgery, drugs, and radiation. Survival rates have risen. But the limits of a medical-scientific approach are also known and yet not acted on. Why? The fear of cancer (its unpredictable and mysterious nature) gives power and rewards to those who have any knowledge about it (medical specialists, biology researchers, drug companies, medical technology manufacturers). Given the dominance of professionalism (only experts should be allowed to solve problems), what could be more plausible than medicalizing cancer?

However, the basic causes of cancer are in the American economy and this makes it more of a political than a medical problem. Research has established that tobacco, asbestos, and certain chemicals, industrial processes, foods, drugs, and energy sources (including the sun) are cancer causing. Prevention requires that Americans be protected from exposure to these agents. But cancer prevention is a direct threat to much of the American economy. It is no accident that a cancer establishment, linking the basic economy, voluntary groups, the mass media,* cancer treatment and research centers in hospitals and universities, and the federal government (National Cancer Institute, Federal Drug Administration) has developed across the apex of American society to promote *one* approach to cancer. For many years this approach was narrowly medical—treat cancer patients and find a cure. In recent years this medical approach has been widened to include advice to the public to adopt voluntarily healthier life-styles. What the voluntary approach does, of course, is to undercut efforts to reap the large gains in health that would result if the natural and social environments were directly cleansed of disease-causing agents. Whether the problem of cancer (and all the other problems affecting the health of the American people) can be kept depoliticized by a glamourized, high-technology medical approach combined with voluntaristic ideology remains to be seen.

*Juanne N. Clarke reports that between 1961 and 1980 six general-interest magazines discussed cancer in images of war and combat and only 5 percent of the articles referred to social causes (such as industrial pollution) in a political context; reported in *The Chronicle of Higher Education*, September 4, 1985, p. 20.

tige behavior. The major function of prestige behavior appears to be to maintain existing class (and political-legal) inequalities.

The major patterns in prestige group activity (which can be defined broadly to include forms of consumption, education, and use of leisure in general) provides strong integration and reciprocal support among class, prestige, and power for the upper, upper-middle, and lower-middle classes, and a general pattern of less prestige and support from prestige activities in the working and lower classes.

The wide diversity in types of prestige that is such a salient feature of class society, as opposed to the tightly meshed and all-encompassing ascriptive prestige systems of caste and estate societies, has important consequences for the functioning of American society. On the one hand, it leads to struggle and conflict, since those with low ascribed prestige can combat their prestige "superiors" with prestige values the latter accept, like accomplishments in science or warfare, the Bill of Rights, and Christian brotherhood.

But prestige diversity can also prevent struggle, since individuals and families have access to a wide variety of traditional and new opportunities to acquire prestige. In this sense, prestige phenomena can be likened to the American economy: both undergo continuous expansion and diversification, thereby avoiding to a considerable extent the *subzero* type of competition in which one person's or group's gain is another's loss.

Despite their functional importance, the autonomy and power of prestige processes and structures should not be exaggerated. The evidence points overwhelmingly to the power of class and power over prestige. Class and power forces determine the boundaries and cleavages in prestige differentiation, and more often than not prestige phenomena are blatantly economic or political-legal in nature. Direct links between class and prestige are abundantly evident, as are the links between power and prestige. For one thing, many prestige activities—including music, art, sports, books, magazines, and consumption in general—are now dominated by profit-making organizations. For another, the staffs of profit and nonprofit organizations in the realm of prestige have similar qualifications, which also makes them interchangeable with personnel in the realms of class and power. It is also well known that many voluntary organizations, such as museums, hospitals, symphony orchestras, universities, and charities, rely heavily on business and professional people and their spouses for policy-making and financial support. An additional link between class and prestige is the investment of the endowment funds of churches, universities, foundations, and other voluntary organizations in the major corporations of our economy. Studies of university and hospital boards reveal that the upper classes exercise strong control over the budgets of voluntary-prestige groups, and thus over the allocation of community resources.

The dependence of prestige groups on the power dimension is also pronounced. Government supports prestige groups in many ways, and thereby endorses private solutions to public problems.

It charters private education and allocates tax money to an enormous range of class-oriented educational services. It subsidizes cultural activities and research, and its tax laws exempt a wide range of charitable, religious, and educational groups. Government also has enormous impact, often inadvertent, on the prestige realm through postal rates, highway and recreational programs, mortgage policies, and the celebration of holidays.

The consolidation of the existing class system appears to be the major function of the prestige dimension. Perhaps this point can be stated differently. The possibility that class, prestige, and power differentials will lead to social friction is ever-present in a formally egalitarian society, and the specific prestige processes that serve to minimize this danger are of more than passing interest.

Thus is it not unimportant that primary prestige groups exist in relative isolation from each other (or are insulated from each other). By and large, each class level develops distinctive primary prestige groups, and the various classes do not participate in each other's primary forms of interaction. Just as important is the fact that membership in secondary prestige groups, while formally open to all according to achievement criteria, tends to be relatively homogeneous by class. And where membership is heterogeneous, prestige problems are minimized by the segmentalization of interaction; that is, people do not interact as members of a class but as individuals with a common specialized interest, such as birdwatching, stamp collecting, or helping retarded children.

Because of these processes, there is no need for class society to develop a society-wide consensus about all prestige values. The isolation and insulation of primary prestige groups makes it possible for people who would not dream of eating together, let alone intermarrying, to regard themselves as moral, political, and legal equals. Class society avoids, in other words, the general supersubordination by an upper prestige stratum (aristocrat) of a lower prestige stratum (serf). When Americans of different prestige interact, it is invariably in a functionally specific situation (such as at work, in a voluntary group, in a court of law, as a patient).

Thus, the American prestige system avoids the spread of one form of prestige into other areas (diffused, categorical-ascriptive prestige) and inhibits the development of behavior that expresses and continuously reinforces the general superiority of one collection of families over another, a prestige system characteristic of caste and estate societies. The operation of its particularistic prestige processes allows the United States to avoid tension between its universalistic moral (and political-legal) system and the requirements of a class structure of stratification. And these isolating and insulating prestige processes help to moderate the deep tension between, on the one hand, the tradition of moral equality and achievement and, on the other, the United States' ascriptive values in ethnicity, religion, and especially race relations.

NOTES

1. *Encyclopedia of Associations,* 30th ed. (Detroit: Gale Research Company, 1996). Volume 1, "National Organizations of the United States," lists more than 22,000 trade associations, professional societies, labor unions, fraternal and patriotic organizations, and other types of groups consisting of voluntary members.
2. For a history of prestige phenomena in the United States, such as democratic politics, books of etiquette, blue books and *The Social Register,* clubs, the society page, the American search for feudal splendor, and prestige sports, see Dixon Wecter, *The Saga of American Society: A Record of Social Aspiration, 1607–1937* (New York: Charles Schribner's Sons, 1937). Other accounts of the American plutocracy's concern with establishing "society" are Cleveland Amory, *The Last Resorts* (New York: Harper and Brothers, 1948), and *Who Killed Society?* (New York: Harper and Brothers, 1960); and Lucy Kavaler, *The Private World of High Society* (New York: David McKay, 1960).
3. W. Lloyd Warner, Marchia Meeker, and Kenneth Eells, *Social Class in America: The Evaluation of Status* (New York: Harper & Row, 1960), pp. 11–24; originally published in 1949 without chs. 16 and 17, which have been substituted for the original appendix.
4. E. Digby Baltzell, *Philadelphia Gentlemen: The Making of a National Upper Class* (New York: Free Press, 1958).
5. E. Digby Baltzell, *The Protestant Establishment: Aristocracy and Caste in America* (New York: Random House, 1964).
6. Ibid., ch. 5.
7. Baltzell's analysis of *The Social Register* and comparison of it with *Who's Who in America* may be found in his *Philadelphia Gentlemen,* ch. 2.
8. This is the theme of Mills's discussion of prestige in *The Power Elite* (New York: Oxford University Press, 1956), ch. 3.
9. G. William Domhoff, *The Higher Circles: The Governing Class in America* (New York: Random House, 1970), ch. 1.
10. Ibid., ch. 2.
11. Ibid., chs. 5 and 6. This aspect of Domhoff's analysis has been updated in his *Who Rules America Now? A View for the '80s* (Englewood Cliffs, NJ: Prentice-Hall, 1983).
12. August B. Hollingshead, *Elmtown's Youth: The Impact of Social Classes on Adolescents* (New York: Wiley & Sons, 1949), ch. 5.
13. Baltzell, *The Protestant Establishment,* ch. 16; G. William Domhoff, *Who Rules America?* (Englewood Cliffs, NJ: Prentice-Hall, 1967), ch. 1; *The Higher Circles: The Governing Class in America* (New York: Random House, 1970), chs. 1 and 4; and *Bohemian Grove and Other Retreats: A Study in Ruling Class Cohesiveness* (New York: Harper & Row, 1974).
14. Courts have begun to recognize this and have begun to enforce civil rights laws against single-sex clubs and service organizations.

15. For an old but excellent review of the literature in this area within the context of role theory, see the article by Alan F. Blum, "Social Structure, Social Class and Participation in Primary Relationships," in Arthur B. Shostak and William Gomberg, eds., *Blue-Collar World: Studies of the American Worker* (Englewood Cliffs, NJ: Prentice-Hall, 1964), pp. 195–207.

    For a valuable start toward understanding primary associational structures in our urban-suburban life, see Edward O. Laumann, *Prestige and Association in an Urban Community: An Analysis of an Urban Stratification System* (Indianapolis: Bobbs-Merrill, 1966). Laumann, who used both old and new empirical techniques to study Cambridge and Belmont in the Boston metropolitan area, found a considerable relation between occupation and intimate (primary) relationships, especially friendship, and a more pronounced relation at the top and bottom levels. The world of the upper and lower working classes has been studied more recently by, respectively, E. E. LeMasters, *Blue-Collar Aristocrats: Life Styles at a Working Class Tavern* (Madison: University of Wisconsin Press, 1975), and Lillian B. Rubin, *Worlds of Pain: Life in Working Class Families* (New York: Basic Books, 1976).
16. For a comprehensive guide to voluntary behavior, see David Horton Smith and Jacqueline Macauley, eds., *Participation in Social and Political Activities: A Comprehensive Analysis of Political Involvement, Expressive Leisure Time, and Helping Behavior* (San Francisco: Jossey-Bass, 1980).
17. David I. MacLeod, *Building Character in the American Boy: The Boy Scouts, YMCA, and Their Forerunners, 1870–1920* (Madison: University of Wisconsin Press, 1983).
18. There is also evidence that, in addition to relying on family and friends for most of its interaction experience, the working class does not travel as widely as the classes above it, and that its participation in the thought-life of the nation is qualitatively lower than the classes above it. The amount and quality of moral, intellectual, and artistic enrichment is even lower among the lower class.
19. For an indictment of the federal government's use of advisory bodies and private consultants, see Daniel Guttman and Barry Willner, *The Shadow Government: The Government's Multi-Billion-Dollar Giveaway of Its Decision-Making Powers to Private Management Consultants, 'Experts,' and Think Tanks* (New York: Pantheon, 1976).
20. For a discussion of the way in which public institutions of higher education subsidize the middle and upper classes, see Chapter 15.
21. For further discussion, see the section "Political Parties and Interest Groups" in Chapter 14.
22. For much of this discussion, see Ralph W. Moss, "The Cancer Establishment: Whose Side Are They On?" *The Progressive* 44 (February 14, 1980):14–18.

14

The Dimension of Power: Class, Political Participation, and Access to State Power

◆ ◆ ◆ ◆

◆ ◆ ◆ ◆

Power is one of the most ambiguous terms in social science. Using it in stratification analysis, care should be taken, first of all, to distinguish between *social* power (the combined effects of class, prestige, and power) and *political-legal* power alone. Following Max Weber's usage, *political-legal power* refers to only one form of social power, the state, or the political-legal forces that promote or reduce social inequality.[1]

All societies, and particularly the more complex, develop some form of politics to handle conflicts, enforce norms, and legitimate the general structure of supersubordination. Political institutions, Weber says, can reflect class or status (prestige) groups, or a mixture of both. The purpose of political action is to influence or control a specific category of norms, law. Law is said to exist, according to Weber, when a staff can obtain conformity to norms (or punish those who violate them) by either physical or psychic means. When such a staff and such a body of norms are accompanied by accepted procedures for controlling the staff and for legislating law, one can speak of the state (power). Politics, in other words, means access to and influence over the state—that is, the tax collector, the courts, the police, the military, and so on. *Stratified politics* means that the various levels of society have differential access to and differential control over the state.

Our major purpose in this and the following two chapters is to analyze the stratification of politics in America, or, in other words, to find out how the hierarchy of class (and prestige) is related to the hierarchy of power (politics, government, and law). Our strategy will be to relate class (the hierarchy of individuals and families defined in terms of economic market assets and liabilities) and prestige (the hierarchy of individuals and families defined in terms of psychic and interactional or, roughly, moral assets and liabilities) on the one hand, to the structure of state power on the other hand. To portray a full-fledged social class, in other words, one must examine political-legal power in combination with economic and prestige power. *Formally defined, a social class (or social stratum) is the composite of assets and liabilities that characterizes aggregates of individuals and families (and other groups and collectivities) in the economic realm, the social (or prestige) realm, and in the realm of politics, government, and law.*

POLITICAL-LEGAL (POWER) STRATIFICATION IN THEORY: THE ALLEGED SEPARATION OF STATE AND SOCIETY

Much of our thinking about politics (and society) is formal in nature—that is, concerned with appearance, words, and ideals, rather than substance and operational reality. Indeed, so prevalent is formal thinking in American life that it seems best to begin by articulating the conventional or formal view of politics, so that we can devote ourselves fully to examining its validity. To put the matter bluntly, whenever the word *formal* is encountered, the reader should be on notice that the reality of the phenomenon being discussed will be challenged.

During the seventeenth and eighteenth centuries, and even into the nineteenth, the leading liberal societies (England, France, and the United States), each in its own time and way, struggled to separate the state from society. Liberal theorists assisted this process by asserting individual rights that the state could not violate and by claiming that citizens deserved equal access to and equal treatment by the state. The process of distinguishing the state from society reached its climax in the characteristic liberal separation of law (the state) from morality (freedom of speech, association, worship, and so on), a separation that seeks to limit the discretionary power of the state by specifying in precise legal norms what it is authorized to do and what it cannot do.

The separation of state and society and equal access to and treatment by the state are far from being operational realities. And laissez-faire theory, one of the main devices with which liberal theorists have tried to separate state and society, is also an empty formality. As we will see in abundant detail, it is far more realistic to think in terms of the *intertwining* of state and society—an intertwining that represents a coordination, if not a merger, of the hierarchies of class, prestige, and power. In contradiction to the alleged existence of common rights and equality before the law and the alleged separation of state and society, therefore, we will speak of a corporate state or a political economy.

LATE LIBERAL (CORPORATE CAPITALIST) SOCIETY: SOME BASIC TRENDS

The Bureaucratization of Politics

Bureaucratization in one form or another has come to characterize all spheres of life. Though the tendency to associate bureaucratization only with governmental administration is unfortunate, there is little doubt that the power and effectiveness of public bureaucracies have grown steadily. The growth of government has occurred to service the economy and because private actions and economic markets are unable to supply employment, food, housing, education, health care, research, statistical information, clean air and water, and many other things. The overall political system has become more important and more difficult to operate because the growing complexity of mature industrialization has generated an unprecedented diversity of narrowly focused, insecure, and dependent interest groups ever on the prowl for political support. The very movement of these ever growing numbers and types of interest groups into the political arena has also enhanced the importance of politics and government and has led to difficult-to-reconcile conflicts.

The conflicts and stalemates in American politics has also led to the relative growth in power of governmental bureaucracies vis-à-vis legislatures. Given the highly decentralized structure of American political life (federalism, states' rights) and the complex issues and interests that arise routinely in an advanced industrial system, it is difficult for political parties to forge detailed, coherent programs of action. As a result, the United States' two national parties are loose coalitions of diverse interest groups and classes held together by vague rhetoric and improvised policies. Thus, legislatures are not controlled by disciplined parties with coherent mandates; instead, they tend to reflect rather accurately the enormous variety of articulate social interests and thus tend toward stalemate, inaction, or inappropriate action.

One of the significant effects of the professionalization of political life is the relative decline of the political entrepreneur, or political boss. In his classic discussion of the power dimension,[2] Max Weber referred to the boss as a central figure at the advent of representative government—that is, during the initial stage of politics based on mass suffrage. Political bosses had no personal economic base and enjoyed little prestige. Their strength was derived from their ability to mobilize and control voters, and thus candidates and legislators—in reality, the ability to dispense public jobs, and to pass legislation and obtain state concessions for clients. The rise of a merit-based civil service, municipal reform, and the welfare state combined to undermine the power of bosses (and, of course, that of political machines and the masses in general).[3]

With the advent of a dynamic, complex national and international politics, the state has come to mean a merit-based civil service, an administered, expert, nonpolitical government, expert legislation through professional staffs, professional party managers and staffs, and professional political intellectuals and image makers.

Our Three Welfare States

The term *welfare state* is ambiguous and hinders political analysis. It is sometimes used to refer to the interventionist state that developed in the United States after 1890. The growth of the welfare state was significantly advanced in the 1930s when the United States Supreme Court abandoned its tenacious sixty-year-old opposition to governmental intervention in economic matters and allowed the federal government to take measures against the worst depression in the nation's history. The term *welfare state,* however, is also used in a narrower and derogatory sense to mean state action to serve the needs of workers (the legal recognition of trade unions, unemployment insurance, social security, minimum wage, and the improvement of working conditions), as well as the working and dependent poor (poorly paid workers, broken families with dependent children, the aged, the blind, and the disabled and sick).

The denunciation of state activity—especially by the Republican party in the name of self-reliance, individual responsibility, and competition—stigmatized efforts to do for workers and the poor what has been done on a much larger scale for other segments of American society. Antigovernmental rhetoric, which stems primarily from small business but also suits the interests of big business and professional groups, obscures the fundamental reality of American political history: the state has been used actively and extensively by the upper and middle classes to serve their many and varied interests. Actually, the main impetus to an enlarged sphere of activity on the part of government has come from business and upper occupational groups of various kinds: bankers, farmers, transportation businesses, large and small manufacturers, retailers, doctors, and so on. Only during the Great Depression did workers and the needy come to be acknowledged as legitimate recipients of state support (largely because there existed a depressed and badly hurt middle class). It is important to recognize that, by and large, the lower classes have had things done to them and for them (paternalism). Unlike the classes above them, the poor and even the working class (labor unions notwithstanding) neither set the pace nor prevail in American politics.

There is little doubt that *in practice* Americans do not believe in the theory of laissez-faire; and if one judges beliefs by behavior, they have never believed in it. American economic and other interest groups have never hesitated to use political means, including organized violence, to obtain their ends. American history is filled with examples of state action on behalf of interest groups: bank charters, laws protecting slavery, subsidies for canals, land grants for railroads, policies to dispossess Native Americans, territorial annexation, land grants for education, tariffs, gunboat diplomacy, cheap credit, aid to farmers, subsidies for industry, the use of troops to break strikes, antitrust legislation, collective bargaining legislation, the protection of consumers, and so on. And, judging from contemporary public opinion polls, the majority of the American people believes the government should be more active with regard to practical bread-and-butter issues. Beneath the formalities of political life, it is clear that the main functions of political-legal institutions are to reduce economic and other conflicts, to stabilize or restore economic relations, and to enhance and promote opportunities within an expanding industrial society.

Among the many myths about government, it is popularly thought that the federal government has grown bigger and stronger during the twentieth century. Measured in absolute terms, the activities of the federal government have undoubtedly grown, whether judged by expenditures, revenues, number of employees, or functions. But measured in more meaningful terms—such as relative to the growth of the American economy, the labor force, or state and local governments—a very different picture emerges. Using a constant dollar and excepting the special military and international obligations of the federal government and such unusual domestic crises as the Great Depression, there has been an amazing stability in federal domestic expenditures, tax revenues, and numbers of civilian employees, and a steady and sizable decline in the national debt when computed as a fraction of the gross domestic product.[4]

The federal deficit, which has figured so large in the politics of the 1990s, is also a myth derived from yet another false way of compiling social data and indicators. No capitalist enterprise or household would dream of conducting its affairs without distinguishing between expenditures that represent capital investment and expenditures that represent dead, overhead expenses, but that is exactly how the federal budget is put together and evaluated. The federal deficit disappears if federal spending for such things as education, worker training, health, research, and transportation are counted as investments. And connected to the above myths about the federal government is the myth that better government will occur if federal programs are returned to the states. No matter how the federal government is evaluated, almost all political scientists would agree that state governments are more corrupt, inefficient, and unaccountable than it is. It is not well known, for example, that most federal programs and funds are administered by state and local governments, which goes a long way toward explaining why the purposes of federal legislation are so often thwarted.

The use of the derogatory term *welfare state* and the exaggeration of the benefits given to workers and the poor hide the enormous benefits the middle and upper classes receive from the state. The cost of government-subsidized loans to college students is roughly equal to the total federal expenditure for poor mothers and their children. Benefits to corporations far exceed welfare for the poor. Far more money per capita is spent on the education of the upper classes than the lower. Unnecessary credentials for professionals amount to a huge subsidy for the upper classes, as do deductions for mortgage interest. And so on.

In addition, these benefits prevent the upper classes from seeing that the problems of workers and the needy are often attributable to governmental policies that aid the middle and upper classes. For example, lavish governmental aid for research leads to technological displacement; urban renewal and highway grants deprive the poor of homes and isolate them from jobs and public services. But perhaps the most harmful aspect of this charade is that the two huge welfare states for the upper classes—disguised by such euphemisms as progress, public interest, national defense, and excellence—prevents Americans from realizing that the laissez-faire market economy and society is and has always been a myth.

AMERICA'S UNIQUE CLASS POLITICS

Before addressing the intricacies of political behavior, we need a more explicit framework for understanding the class basis of politics. Specifically, we must look beyond the fairly well-established idea that economic interests are the basis of most political behavior. We need to see economic interests in class terms, which is, ironically enough, difficult to do if we rely exclusively on Marx's conception of politics and government. Marx's conception of class focuses on just one form of class action: the labor market, or the struggle between the buyers and sellers of labor. While this class relationship (which became prominent during the nineteenth century) is of great importance, it is but one of a number of forms of class action.

For Weber, a class is any group sharing a "class situation," a "typical chance for a supply of goods, external living conditions, and personal life experiences, in so far as this chance is determined by the amount and kind of power, or lack of such, to dispose of goods or skills for the sake of income in a given economic order." For Weber, as for Marx, the basic polar determinants of class situation are "property" and "lack of property"—but between these poles a great many class situations must be distinguished. Class situations, says Weber, lead to class protest or struggle only when it is widely recognized that the distribution of life chances is due to a given distribution of property or to the structure of a concrete economic order. Such recognition depends on the general nature of society but especially on "communalization," a process that takes place, according to Weber, when there is interaction between members of *different* classes (and not, as Marx said, when there is interaction between members of the *same* class). The history of class struggle, Weber suggests, is roughly a sequence of the three basic forms of class action and rivalry: the credit market, the commodity market, and the labor market.[5]

The "transparency" of class interest is obscured by general sociocultural conditions, and a number of unusual political consequences flow from the vagaries of class experience. Direct competition between buyers and sellers of labor, for example, is usually bitter while the "unearned" income of the *rentier,* shareholder, and banker go unchallenged. Thus, a full understanding of American political life in class terms is impossible if one relies on Marx's exclusive emphasis on the struggle over the price of labor. Even Weber's suggestion that an evolution has taken place in the modal type of class action is somewhat misleading. But, as Norbert Wiley points out, Weber's theory of class does contain the conceptual elements needed for framing American political behavior in class terms. The United States should be thought of, Wiley says, as a rich mixture of all three basic forms of class situations, a mixture that gives it a unique class politics. The three basic market relationships are:

1. The labor market (occupational versus property-owning groups)
2. The credit or money market (debtors versus creditors)
3. The commodity market (buyers versus sellers; tenants versus landlords)

One can distinguish, says Wiley, groups that have consistent, inconsistent, and highly inconsistent class interests in their total market or class relationships. An individual with consistent class attributes is one who is an employer-creditor-seller (propertied) or is an employee-debtor-buyer (non-propertied). But many have inconsistent and contradictory class attributes, making it difficult for them to unite with groups holding similar class interests in some respects.[6]

An examination, provided by Wiley, of class-related political behavior in American history is instructive. The most radical political group in American history has been the farmers, whose economic class interests focus on the prices they pay for money (credit), equipment and services (such as railroad transport) on the one hand, and the prices of the products they sell (basically, food), on the other. When the allegedly rational markets in these areas did not perform as expected, American farmers turned to politics to protect and enhance their class interests—interests they defined as cheap money and manufactured goods, and high price supports for farm products. In their political and economic struggles, farmers could not readily identify with labor, another class underdog, whose class interests lay in the high price of labor, the high price of manufactured commodities, and the low price of food.

Class analysis is also revealing when applied to other economic groups. Small businesspeople are both buyers and sellers of products; they are often in debt and are small-scale buyers of labor. Thus they are a classic mixed type who find it difficult to identify with either big business or labor. As an economic group whose class interests are highly inconsistent, small businesspeople are also radical politically, though on the right wing. Others who suffer from high inconsistency in their class positions are workers with property or side income, retired people on small incomes, and white-collar workers. The difficulties experienced by individuals with high (class) inconsistency stem from ambivalence, or, in other words, from the inability to identify a coherent class enemy. All in all, Wiley concludes, the United States has not experienced generalized class warfare because of its rich and inconsistent class structure.

Individuals subject to cross-pressures, along with those who are powerless and economically insecure, see the world as capricious and arbitrary. When these class pressures reflect on personal worth (the prestige dimension), there emerges America's deep streak of paranoid politics. America's individualism and its metaphysical underpinnings channel many of its disaffected into a world of simple certainties. Recent decades have seen an increase in economic pressures on wide reaches of the American public, with a subsequent flowering of paranoid politics harnessed largely by the Republican party.

In the remainder of this chapter we will inquire into the relation between the many forms of political participation and class-prestige standing. Thought of in broad historical terms, we want to find out if the growth of representative government marks an increase in the power of the general populace. To put the matter bluntly, has formal political equality resulted in any appreciable measure of actual political equality and has it reduced economic and social inequality?

THE SEGREGATION OF CLASSES BY POLITICAL JURISDICTION

A basic and increasingly prevalent pattern in America's political system is the segregation of class-prestige groups by political jurisdiction. This is perhaps the most ominous political development of the twentieth century, amounting as it does to a decline in political jurisdictions with mixed constituencies. Much of the vigor of liberal democracy—indeed, perhaps, its very existence as a form of government—is attributable to the fact that it has forced those who would exercise political power to persuade a majority of a mixed group of articulate interests (either groups or voters) to support them. The need to search for common interests stimulates and develops the political creativity of candidates and parties. And, once elected, officials and parties are more likely to be independent and broad in their outlooks when their mandates are from mixed rather than homogeneous constituencies.

The pattern of class-based political constituencies has resulted from the class-driven growth of homogeneous suburban and urban areas. The problem of class-based political jurisdictions has been aggravated by a further problem, the lags and imbalances that characterize the American system of political representation.

CLASS AND POLITICAL REPRESENTATION

The American population has been badly represented in state and national legislatures, in terms of both numbers and social composition (economic, ethnic, and racial differences), during the entire period for which we have reliable records. Until the 1960s, this malrepresentation had steadily worsened to the point that it is not amiss to characterize it as a "rotten borough" system. Numerically smaller portions of the population enjoyed significantly more political power than larger portions, and rural–small-town populations (often synonymous with the smaller portions) were more heavily represented in legislatures than urban populations.

Aside from the dynamics of industrialization and urbanization, two basic processes created these imbalances: (1) legislatures that had the power and often the constitutional obligation to reapportion did not do so (or did not reapportion strictly on the basis of numbers); and (2) legislatures practiced gerrymandering. The first of these causes of representational imbalance was struck down by the United States Supreme Court in a series of decisions between 1962 and 1964. After having declined jurisdiction in this area, the Supreme Court changed its mind and in a landmark decision[7] gave individuals the right to sue to protect their voting rights, thus making voting rights a constitutional rather than a political issue. The Court did not define the kind of representation required by the Constitution in this decision, but in a later case it held that "the fundamental principle of representative government in this country is one of equal representation for equal numbers of people, without regard to race, sex, economic status, or place of residence within a state."[8] As a result of this and other cases, the basic doctrine of "one person, one vote" was upheld for primaries, and for elections to the House of Representatives and to both houses of state legislatures.

But while the Supreme Court has clearly spelled out the doctrine of equal representation, even full application of the principle of "one person, one vote" will not correct the imbalance in the American system of representation as long as legislators are free to gerrymander—that is, to concentrate voters for the opposing party (usually identified in terms of class-prestige factors) in selected constituencies where votes will be wasted in overwhelming victories, and to allot supporters so as to achieve narrow victories in as many constituencies as possible. Since congressional districts (which are reapportioned on the basis of census figures) are drawn by state legislatures, the national House of Representatives is also gerrymandered, and thus represents neither quantitatively nor qualitatively the nature of the American population. The significance of the gerrymander for the student of social stratification is that it allows obsolete or declining class and prestige groups (racists, farmers, small town businesspeople, and professionals) to entrench themselves politically. The United States Supreme Court dodged a gerrymander case in 1986, in effect endorsing the practice. In 1995, it outlawed the use of the gerrymander that had been used to ensure the election of African Americans but did so on racial grounds, again avoiding the principle behind the gerrymander.

The segregation of classes and ethnic-racial groups by political jurisdiction goes a long way in explaining the politics of recent decades. The freedom of capital to move as it pleases, the failure to integrate minorities, the decline of public services, the failure to keep up public investment in highways, bridges, and the like, the decay of cities and many suburbs, and the persistence of poverty can be attributed in part to this interplay of class, prestige, and power forces. It is of special interest that the process of suburbanization, which has done so much to segregate the United States' political jurisdictions by class and prestige, has become an important component of this broad alignment of political forces. High-income suburbs, which pay heavy local taxes to support high-quality schools and other public services for their own families, are reluctant to pay taxes to support similar public services in the big cities and in working class suburbs. The fact that high income groups often earn their livings in these cities does not prevent them from taking advantage of their political power.[9] In any case, the *ad hoc* growth of local governments (towns, cities, suburbs) characterized by a tangle of overlapping jurisdictions, duplication of services, and unresponsiveness to public complaint and need signifies the power over political life exercised by the hierarchies of class and prestige and explains most of what has gone wrong with public policies over recent decades.

CLASS AND POLITICAL CAREERS

Elected and Appointed Officials

Considerable evidence shows that individuals elected to public office at the federal level come largely from the middle and upper classes: professionals, proprietors and officials, and farmers tend to account for the overwhelming majority of those elected to the presidency, vice-presidency, the Senate, and the House of Representatives. The upper levels of prestige hierarchies based on race, ethnic origin, and religion are also overrepresented among elected federal officials.[10] Those elected to state legislatures are considerably higher in class position (as measured by income, education, and occupation) than their constituents.[11] And delegates to both Democratic and Republican presidential conventions have incomes far in excess of the average American's.

The influence of socioeconomic status in the recruitment of high federal civilian and military officials is pronounced throughout American history. In an analysis of intellectuals who served the Roosevelt administration during the Great Depression, it was found that most of them came from the middle and upper classes, especially the upper middle class. A study of the occupations of fathers of high federal civilian and military personnel found that the offspring of business executives, owners of large businesses, and professionals were heavily overrepresented, especially in the military.[12] A study of high civil servants in California revealed an overrepresentation of the middle and upper middle class at the state level, which is almost identical with Lloyd Warner's findings at the federal level.[13]

In his study of military leaders, Morris Janowitz found that while they have become more representative of the general population over the years, military leaders are still drawn from white Protestant professional and business backgrounds.[14] It is also important to note that schoolteachers, a large and influential group of public employees, appear to come from the upper third of the socioeconomic scale, and not primarily from lower-middle-class backgrounds, as is popularly thought.[15]

Interchangeable Class and Political Statuses

Men, and increasingly women, from high-class positions find it easy to move into high elected and especially appointed office. The traffic among the upper echelons of industry, finance, commerce, law, medicine, university teaching, research, natural science, and the upper reaches of government is pronounced. Though we do not have sufficient data to answer this question conclusively, there is sizable if unsystematic evidence of considerable traffic among, on the one hand, banks, law firms, universities, and businesses (especially large corporations) engaged in agriculture, transportation, mining, communication, military manufacturing, and the like, and on the other, the various departments (civilian and military) and regulatory commissions of the federal government.[16] Career interchangeability is limited, however, by professional ethics, conflict-of-interest laws, and technical occupational requirements.

Many political leaders on the federal level, both elected and appointed, do not rise through the ranks of state and local politics and thus must learn their jobs after acquiring them. The practice of ignoring experience and proven worth is perhaps most conspicuous in appointments to ambassadorships (many of which are actually sold), but it is common practice to appoint amateurs at the apex of the federal government. One of the more damaging results of the practice of filling the more than two thousand high administrative positions at the federal level on a patronage basis is that it has helped to prevent the development of a strong civil service tradition at the upper levels of the federal bureaucracy. One can even conjecture that the prevalence of amateurs at the upper levels of the federal government makes it easier for their predecessors in office, who are now pursuing business and professional careers, to outmaneuver them. And, of course, this practice helps to insure the general control of public policy by the upper classes.

POLITICAL PARTIES AND INTEREST GROUPS

The capitalist societies of the West are characterized by a specialized, changing division of labor openly driven by self-interest. Some fantasize that such a system would be harmonious and self-governing if left alone (laissez-faire or anarchistic liberalism). But the truth is that Western societies routinely generate conflicts and problems that require explicit attention. The basic way these conflicts and problems are both generated and addressed is through political parties and interest groups.

Political parties' financial and voting support, as well as their staff recruitment (both professional and volunteer), are deeply related to class and prestige. And the major interest groups in contemporary society are also related to the hierarchies of class and prestige and tend to develop ideologies in keeping with their location in the class system. Politically relevant interest groups include learned societies, civic betterment associations, reform movements, groups concerned with particular problems (such as taxation, foreign affairs, or veterans' affairs), professional associations, and, of course, the entire range of pressure groups. Most pressure groups emanate from the American economy, but they also include governmental units themselves, associations of civil service employees, and even associations of elected officials.

Despite the highly visible organizations that represent workers and racial and ethnic minorities, interest groups with direct relevance for political life are overwhelmingly middle and upper class in character. Whether measured by rates of participation by members, income, occupation, the credentials of staff members, mode of operation, or consequences for society, pressure groups basically reflect the interests and power of the middle and upper classes (as do almost all voluntary groups).

Americans have traditionally been uneasy about concentrated power, whether public or private. Helping to minimize uneasiness about the political and social impact of private interest groups are various laws, regulations, and ethical codes that seek to limit the influence of those with too much money or too few scruples, or both.

Thus various laws (especially the Corrupt Practices Act of 1925, the Hatch Act of 1940, and the Taft-Hartley Act of 1947) ostensibly prevent the financing (and thus control) of political parties by private wealth and private groups. These acts forbid corporations and labor unions to contribute to political parties, and limits have been set on the amounts that individuals can contribute to political parties and the amounts that can be spent on political campaigns. Lobbyists are required by the Federal Regulation of Lobbying Act of 1946 to register and to list their employers, salaries, and activities, and there are conflict-of-interest codes for political appointees and civil servants. In 1972 another effort to limit campaign spending and political contributions occurred but to no avail. In 1974 the Federal Elections Campaign Act was passed, strengthening the effort to control the power of private wealth in public elections. Contributions by individuals and groups have been limited, matching tax funds are available for campaigns for presidential nominations, tax funds help pay for presidential elections, strict limits have been placed on presidential and congressional campaign spending and enforcement machinery has been created. But apparently through an oversight no real control over the political power of wealth appeared because political action committees (PACs), or direct contributions to individual candidates are legal. In 1995 Senator Bob Packwood was forced to resign from the U.S. Senate because of sexual harassment and other charges. In the process, Packwood had to make his diary public, revealing rare details about the connections between moneyed-corporate interests and how a legislator negotiates to get money and personal favors in return for legislative favors.[17]

Lobbies still flourish and continue to pressure legislators, parties, and public opinion,[18] but now also deal directly and on a large scale with governmental bureaucracies. The result is a massive intertwining of interest groups and government, or, more exactly, of particular interest groups and particular governmental agencies, bureaus, and commissions.[19] One of the interesting and not necessarily beneficial consequences of direct interest group involvement in government is that it has probably strengthened the trend toward objective, expert, and nonpolitical government. As we have pointed out, the professionalization of our class-prestige system has a parallel in the professionalization of our political institutions. Though it is difficult to be certain, the trend toward nonpolitical boards, commissions, and authorities, and the direct cooperation of interest groups and governmental bodies of all kinds appears to be a significant corollary of the modernization of our class system. However, both the neutrality and the accountability of these bodies are highly questionable. Furthermore, the legal status of many such bodies is hazy, and the scope and volume of their economic activities are very great.

Lobbying also occurs by a large array of "nonpolitical" think tanks and foundations (such as the Carnegie Foundation, Council on Foreign Relations, Rand Corporation, Committee for Economic Development, Twentieth Century Fund, American Enterprise Institute, Heritage Foundation, and Brookings Institution) that are far from being nonpartisan.[20] These groups are characterized by a narrow class composition, direct ties to specific business and professional interests, and great influence over domestic and foreign policies.[21]

In recent years, we have learned more about these allegedly neutral groups. A study of the Carnegie Corporation, for example, has shown how it steered policy making away from economic and political issues and reforms, favoring an approach that stressed science, education, and elite culture. And within science and education, it favored certain approaches and fields of knowledge, thus helping to define the knowledge-producing elites (not just knowledge areas but also racial, gender, and class attributes of the knowledge elites). The high-minded reforms promoted by the Carnegie Corporation should not blind us to the fact that corporate liberalism is merely one of alternative approaches to policy problems.[22]

It is worth noting that five of the most important think tanks, or public policy institutes, self-consciously adopted a conflict approach from the 1970s on, seeing the major conflict between a dynamic, rational capitalism and a meddling, wrongheaded, wasteful democracy as the major barrier to America's revitalization.[23]

CLASS, VOTING, AND OTHER FORMS OF POLITICAL PARTICIPATION

Class and Voting Participation

The act of voting per se is clearly related to class position (and, as we see, to such prestige factors as race and ethnicity). Those at the upper levels of the class system vote at far higher rates than do those lowest in the class hierarchy. Measured in terms of education, it is clear that those with four or more years of college vote at significantly higher rates even than high-school graduates (see Figure 14–1). The same pattern holds true for the other dimensions of class, occupation and income. The higher occupations vote at much higher rates than the lower, and there is also a substantial difference between the 32.4 percent voting rate of those with incomes under $5000 and the 79.9 percent rate of those with incomes of $50,000 or more.[24]

Political apathy and political involvement are outcomes of class experience. Those low on the class structure tend not to lead lives that emphasize active self-direction, and nonvoting is consistent with such experience. The upper classes, on the other hand, enjoy a socioeconomic experience that prepares them for and predisposes them toward political involvement. Typically, members of the upper and upper-middle classes have had considerable formal education and are familiar with the concepts and skills needed to organize politically relevant information. They work in occupations that are, on the whole, more mental than manual. They participate in voluntary-interest groups that focus and reinforce their class-prestige interests, and their participation in voluntary groups in general gives them experience in the verbal and written analysis of public issues. They absorb "higher" levels

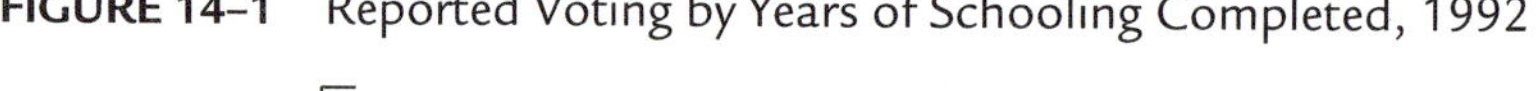

FIGURE 14–1 Reported Voting by Years of Schooling Completed, 1992

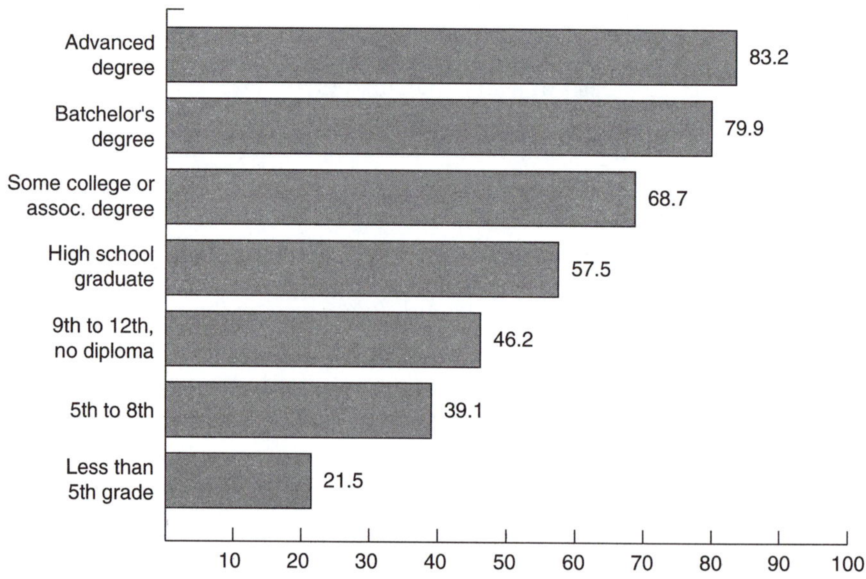

Source: U.S. Bureau of the Census, Current Population Reports, Series P-20, no. 466, "Voting and Registration in the Election of 1992" (Washington, DC: U.S. Government Printing Office, 1993), Table 8.

of stimuli through reading, viewing, listening, and traveling. They are more secure in their finances and in their personalities. And they are quick to perceive political threats to their interests, and to counter them with both symbolic and overt political action. In other words, the typical member of the upper and upper middle classes is, in contrast to a typical member of the working and lower classes, much more of a self-propelled, conscious decision-maker across a broad range of activities. Thus, higher rates of voting participation reflect and reinforce higher rates of involvement in the upper reaches of the hierarchies of class and prestige.

Class and Voting Preference

Like voting participation, voting preference correlates with the hierarchy of class-prestige (though there is little class consciousness in this regard in the United States). High- and middle-class-prestige individuals (professionals, managers, proprietors and other white-collar workers, college graduates, and individuals with high incomes) largely support the Republican party, while members of the working class and those with low prestige status regardless of class (manual workers, laborers, African Americans, Roman Catholics, Jews) have tended to support the Democratic party, a division that corresponds roughly to the difference between laissez-faire and interventionist views on the economic responsibilities of government.

It has long been taken for granted that the upper classes are more liberal on social issues: the rights of women and African Americans, personal freedom (abortion, birth control, divorce, premarital sex, homosexuality), and law and order (wiretapping, capital punishment, gun control). John Zipp, however, has found no differences on such issues when economic classes are compared by only economic status (owner, income, type of occupation). What differences appear are due to education (which Zipp prefers to call a *nonclass* variable), with the better educated exhibiting more liberalism in their attitudes.[25] If education is included in the definition of class, then class and attitudes toward social issues are directly related—the higher the class, the more liberal one's attitudes. Remember, however, that attitudes and behavior are not the same.

The amount of class voting in the United States appears low in comparison to other countries—for example, Great Britain and Australia. However, this should not obscure the class basis of racial, ethnic, and regional factors in American politics. "Racial" divisions stem from plantation capitalism; ethnic and religious diversity stem from immigration promoted by industry in order to acquire cheap labor. All in all, the American economy has grown so fast, and become so large and so diversified, that it is not surprising that its various elements do not fit readily into static homogeneous class categories. But one need only recall Wiley's argument about the unique class basis of American politics to see that American political behavior is not as unrelated to class as it appears. Americans, in other words, are subject to cross-pressures and inconsistencies *within* the class dimension unparalleled in other societies. There are also the effects of economic mobility: many white-collar persons who do not vote for the Republican party are not violating the class behavior expected of them, since many white-collar workers are really working class both by origin and by function. And when a blue-collar male fails to vote for the Democratic party, it may be that his wife works and that their combined income has led to property and rental income; or his wife and daughter may be working in white-collar jobs, thus introducing diversity and cross-pressures into an otherwise blue-collar family. At both the apex and the bottom of the various class hierarchies (commodity, credit, and labor) cross-pressures make it difficult for those in similar economic circumstances to develop a common consciousness (something that is much more difficult to achieve at the bottom). And, of course, differences *within* the class dimension are magnified by ethnic, religious, and "racial" differences.

All in all, the class interests of the mass of the American people appear to be distorted and deflected from political expression by a number of factors from the past, including the pervasive ideology of individualism that stems from early capitalist experience. Fundamentally, the upper and upper middle classes dominate American politics and provide little political choice for the remainder of the American people. William Gamson has proposed an alternative to the pluralist model of political participation. Though pluralist theory tends to emphasize the openness of the American political system and its responsiveness to public need and changing times, Gamson argues that a model he calls *stable unrepresentation* may be more accurate. He hypothesizes that

> the American political system normally functions to (1) keep unrepresented groups from developing solidarity and politically organizing, and (2) discourage their effective entry into the competitive establishment if and as they become organized. The competitive establishment is boundary-maintaining and the boundary-maintaining process involves various kinds of social control.[26]

The evidence of recent decades indicates that Gamson's concept of stable unrepresentation is deeply embedded in the political dynamics of the American class system.

WHY DOES THE UNITED STATES HAVE SUCH LOW POLITICAL PARTICIPATION?

Low and Declining Levels of Political Participation

Creative politics requires high levels of political participation by diverse groups. Creative politics derives from a many-sided interaction in which participants have to juggle and reconcile many points of view other than their own, in effect forcing them to recognize the many conflicts and gaps between self and public interest. It is obvious, therefore, that the structure of political participation is fundamental to the adaptive capacity of society. Any exclusion of the mass of the population from meaningful political participation means that the upper classes will have that much less trouble equating their interests with the social interest. Research reveals that the United States has low levels of political participation and that its political system is marked by widespread apathy (and alienation). The rate of electoral participation in America is among the lowest in the liberal democracies and has been declining steadily in the post–World War II period. In recent decades only 35 to 40 percent of the electorate has turned out for congressional elections and only 50 to 55 percent for presidential elections.

Political participation takes other forms besides voting: campaigning, contacting government officials, contributing money, attending rallies, and the like. In an early survey, Sidney Verba and Norman Nie found that upper socioeconomic status levels (based on an average of income, occupation, and education scores) dominate all forms of political participation.[27] These two researchers also found that the policy preferences of both Democratic and Republican participants were much more conservative than those of the general population. They conclude that

> the relationship of social status to participation as well as the relationship of political ideology to participation push in the same direction: the creation of a participant population different from the population as a whole. Our data show that participants are less aware of serious welfare problems than the population as a whole, less concerned about the income gap between rich and poor, less interested in government support for welfare programs, and less concerned with equal opportunities for black Americans.[28]

In a later cross-national analysis, Verba, Nie, and Jae-On Kim found low participation in all countries. Interestingly enough, the United States' rate of political participation was the lowest in the industrial West (that is, the one that offered least obstacles to political domination by a small number of affluent political activists).[29]

Not surprisingly, the American polity does not reflect the wishes of the American people.[30] Political parties and politically relevant elite groups that control the definition of issues and the forms of participation consistently thwart policies that the majority of the population endorse. Specifically, the will of the population is thwarted by gerrymandering, by high-level foundation reports that co-opt policy discussion, by the mass media, by the trend toward professionalized objective, expert government, and by the tradition of nonpartisanship.[31]

Political participation is also hampered by the antigovernment ideology that is peculiar to right-wing American liberalism. The decline of the political party has severed an important link between elites and masses. Political participation is hamstrung by a chaotic tangle of political jurisdictions (the federal system) and by a jungle of regulatory agencies, advisory and executive committees and boards, commissions, and special government districts and authorities. In comparing their 1967 survey of political participation with American electoral behavior compiled by the Survey Research Center at the University of Michigan, Verba and Nie concluded that low participation rates had been stable for two decades. More recent data suggest a decline. In addition, the alienation of the American people from politics and government is fairly large and appears to be growing.

Low political participation by broad segments of the American citizenry has important implications. In recent presidential elections only about half of eligible voters participated. It is clear that the legitimacy of the American political system is seriously threatened—the authority of legislatures and government (that is, the felt sense that those in power are looking after the interests of those not in power) becomes questionable.[32]

Analysts have noted a rise in the political organization and effectiveness of American business, especially the corporate elite. Their profits threatened by the stagflation of the 1970s and by foreign competition, America's upper classes mobilized during the 1970s and succeeded in getting the public policy they wanted with the Reagan-Bush administration of 1980–1992. Essentially, this policy consisted of an attack on public spending (except for defense), a relaxation of environmental and other public regulation, and an anti-labor stance by government. The strong leadership by business was essentially an attempt to return society to the laissez-faire philosophy of the nineteenth century.[33]

In 1994 the Republican party gained control of both houses of Congress and immediately proposed the dismantling of a wide variety of federal programs to protect the poor, the elderly, consumers, and the environment. The party had won 20 percent of the 39 percent of the eligible voters who had turned out but still claimed that they had a mandate from the people. They also claimed that voters had endorsed their legislative agenda (Contract with America) even though polls showed that few voters had heard of it. Here is another consequence of voter apathy (a consequence, remember, of depoliticization and ritual elections—see Chapter 10).

The American pattern of empty political discourse and oligarchic action will be difficult to break: a weak and fragmented public leads to a cry for strong leadership. Strong leadership cannot solve social problems but comes up with half-solutions (often those that are causing the weak community in the first place). The lack of solutions perpetuates the weak community, fosters apathy, and the pattern continues. *The American political process and its assorted professionals (candidates, party officials, party jobholders, pollsters, media and advertising specialists) are part of the broad separation of material and human capital from social functions that appears to be taking place across the apex of all institutional sectors.*

Our Alienated Electorate

Most analysts agree that significant portions of the American electorate find the political realm alien and beyond control. One response is mass political apathy both at the ballot box and in civic organizations. Another is to use the vote to punish political figures who look as if they are agents of the status quo. Much of the difficulty that political experts and pollsters have had in recent years in predicting political behavior is due to their failure to take into account the alienation of many sectors of the electorate.

Functional theorists explain alienation in terms of the decline of intermediate organizations such as local political parties, neighborhood associations, newspapers, racial and ethnic associations, and reform groups. These groups are needed, say functionalists, because they involve and inform citizens and create the feeling and the reality of power for ordinary citizens.

Conflict theorists tend to agree, but point to the growth of corporate capitalism as the problem. Economic and political concentration (engendered by technology, rationalization, and bureaucratization), they argue, is the main reason why local groups have declined. If we are to understand our alienated electorate, we must see its roots in remote national and multinational corporations, national business and professional associations, large-scale churches, charities, foundations, research, and reform groups, and nationwide film, publishing, newspaper, and television corporations.

The general explanation of why the United States has such low political participation and is so alienated is relatively easy. Despite the fact that Americans have a strong inclination to participate, they are subject to a comprehensive process of depoliticization. Elites across the apexes of institutional areas (economics, journalism, law, politics, religion, education, and popular culture) insist that the United States is a society based on human nature, nature, and the supernatural and that, therefore, politics and collective action are somehow against the national consensus.

The American population appears to be uniquely negative—even cynical—about politics. This attitude is found at all levels and reflects the overall depolitization process. By and large, Americans affirm their faith in democracy even as they withdraw their faith in politicians.[34]

Knowledge about politics and public issues is extremely limited among the American people. From 60 to 80 percent of the American people do not know the name of their representative in Congress (and state legislature), what their representatives think about issues, including burning issues of the day, or how they vote on them. More than a third do not even know if their representative is a Democrat or Republican. Females tend to have less knowledge about politics than males, younger people less knowledge than older ones, and residents of small towns, rural areas, and larger urban centers less than intermediate cities. Of even greater interest is the fact that there appears to be *no increase in political knowledge during the period when surveys have been conducted, the 1940s to the 1970s.* And this occurred during a period when the American people became better educated, had more money, more leisure from work, and when politics became more explicitly connected with all other aspects of American life.[35]

Declining Legitimacy?

A society rests on faith that its norms are fair and effective. There is considerable evidence that this faith has eroded in the United States. The United States has a huge underground economy made up of many respectable people. In this chapter we found considerable political apathy. Ominously, tax evasion is on the rise and seems to be feeding on itself.

In 1979 a Peter D. Hart and Associates poll revealed that half of the American people did not believe that they would ever collect their Social Security benefits. A Yankelovich poll in 1981 revealed that 83 percent of Americans agreed that rule breakers are rewarded while rule observers go empty-handed. The use of deception by the F.B.I., local police, journalists, and a wide variety of government agencies is often in a good cause but, nonetheless, the sense of trust that underlies authority relations is eroded.

Another index into disenchantment with public authority is the growth of direct-action groups, not only self-help programs, neighborhood organizations, communes, public-interest firms, and malpractice suits (by individuals) against a wide range of professionals, but direct-action groups aimed at corporations and other private groups. Many of these direct-action groups are political, but there appears to be less of a trust in government and legislature than in the past and more emphasis on self-reliance and direct action.

The trend toward an *alienated* public appears to be paralleling the rise of a stalemated society. Public opinion polls have shown a steady loss of confidence by the American people in their leaders. Americans from all income levels and in all other social categories are disenchanted with the elites who serve them. On a scale measuring powerlessness, cynicism, and alienation (disenchantment), Americans registered 55 percent in 1973, up from 29 percent in 1966. Americans felt that the quality of life in the United States had declined and, on average, only 33 percent of the American people expressed confidence in its leadership (only two functional areas still enjoy majority support: medicine and local trash collection). All areas fell in public confidence except for television news and the press.

The American elite (as represented by public officials) disagreed sharply with these views and expressed considerable satisfaction in American achievements as well as confidence in the future. Particularly striking was the cleavage between the people and public officials over television news and the press—public officials were far more critical of the news media than the general public.

The Survey Research Center and the Center for Political Studies (of the Institute for Social Research at the University of Michigan) studied the attitude of trust in government for over two decades. Trust in government showed significant declines beginning in the early 1960s and plunged during the 1970s. In tracing this development, Arthur N. Miller concluded that "analysis conclusively demonstrates that the current, widespread political distrust of government is rooted in attitudes that are more generic than evaluations of the incumbents."[36] In short, American distrust of leaders is so profound that it seems to be undermining their faith in *institutions.* Widespread apathy toward elections can certainly be interpreted in this way. Trends in confidence toward institutional leadership rise slightly from time to time as presidents are elected or if the economy improves. But the long-term trend from the 1960s to 1982 clearly indicates a decline in confidence by the American people in its leadership. As such, this poses a distinct threat to the legitimacy of American institutions.[37]

Polls since the 1980s have continued to show declining levels of public confidence in American institutions and groups. Polls indicate a growing loss of confidence through 1990 in political leaders, parties, and officials.[38] And by 1994, small business was the only sector of American society that was able to muster a (bare) majority of Americans who expressed "a great deal" or "quite a lot" of confidence in it.[39]

The cleavage between elite and people extends to policy matters. The American people clearly want a strong federal government to solve the problems of war and peace, the economy, and quality of life. Nine out of ten Americans believe that the federal government is responsible for seeing to it that no one goes hungry and that every person achieves a minimum standard of living. Americans clearly express a preference for wage and price controls to fight inflation, and they support a woman's right to an abortion and favor a curb on handguns. Seventy-five percent of the American people express a clear preference for jobs as the best way to curb crime, a preference that runs counter to elite beliefs.[40] Moreover, the American people express clear support for national health insurance. Their attitudes toward nuclear arms and foreign policy were also at variance with those of American elites during the Cold War, with most preferring a nuclear freeze and a less belligerent foreign policy.

The elites of the United States, with some minor exceptions, tend to ignore the public's wishes. There is a tendency among elites, including public officials, to regard the ordinary citizen as uninformed and self-contradictory. American elites, including sociologists, have a longstanding tendency of blaming and ignoring the masses, largely by regarding them as uneducated, selfish, and undisciplined.

The decline in legitimacy can be expressed in different terms. American behavior exhibits a strong trend toward self-centered individualism. Over the past few decades, Americans have participated less across almost the entire spectrum of political and voluntary life. Robert Putnam has compiled the evidence for this decline, calling attention to its implications: a decline in voluntary and political participation, or what he calls "civic engagement," means a reduction in the generation of social capital, "the networks, norms, and trust that enable participants to act together more effectively to pursue shared objectives.[41] In our terms, this means that as faith in the legitimacy of institutions declines, people withdraw from sociopolitical life and thus fail to generate the faith in institutions that is needed to participate in the first place. As social capital declines, Americans participate less, and so on. Conflict sociologists in an earlier generation had referred to the above process as mass society atomizing its members and making them feel powerless and paranoid. Their warning that such a population is extremely vulnerable to political manipulation has had considerable confirmation in recent years.

Putnam blames television for the decline in civic engagement, but it seems best to focus on the class basis of civic participation, the class-based way in which Americans experienced the economic ups and downs of recent decades, and the class-based ways in which Americans interpret America's norms and values. The decline of political and voluntary participation is best explained by the following:

1. Intensified competition for business success and for upper-level occupations from the 1970s on meant that males in the upper classes devoted more time and energy to work and less to civic participation.
2. Women in the upper classes, an important source of voluntary labor, devoted far more time and energy to careers and far less to civic participation.
3. The economic insecurity and squeeze experienced by both men and women in the lower classes led to a reduction in their already low level of civic participation.
4. The mobilization of business and its antigovernment, antipolitics stance from the 1970s on meant an intensification of the American legitimation process (see Chapter 10) in right-liberal terms, an interpretation of American norms and values that denigrates collective action and throws people back on themselves as individuals for identity and solutions.

The decline in legitimacy appears real. By and large, it stems from the deep cleavage between the interests and values of American elites and those of the American people. In another sense, it reflects a decline in the adaptive ability of American elites. Again, the master problem seems to be a social system whose basic institutions separate elites from direct experience with the problems of ordinary people. Elites are separated from ordinary people because institutions allow them to solve their own problems under the false faith that by doing so they are also serving the public.

SUMMARY

It is widely believed that the emergence of representative government marks a significant advance in equality, but the realities of political participation are otherwise. It is more accurate to say that elections and other forms of political participation are means to translate economic and prestige power into political power and vice versa. It is clear from the evidence, in other words, that class and prestige control all forms of political participation and that the middle and upper classes dominate political life.

The dominance of the upper classes has made the solution of social problems difficult since they are the causes of most problems. As a result, there is a clear trend toward an alienated public and loss of faith in the legitimacy of America's leaders (and to some extent of American institutions). As legitimacy declines, Americans participate less in both political and voluntary life, thus further eroding legitimacy (they fail to generate social capital through sociopolitical participation). This leads to less participation, and so on, a process that generates feelings of powerlessness and paranoia among Americans making them vulnerable to political manipulation.

We have warned against the uncritical acceptance of a formal definition of political behavior. Over the centuries, a heady mixture of both right- and left-liberal rhetoric has created the impression that invoking the ideas of equal rights and equal treatment by government is the same thing as actually realizing these ideals. In reality, politics and government have a pronounced class base. While class forces in the United States are exceedingly complex and lead to a unique form of class politics, there is little doubt that the upper levels of the class structure have more direct access to, exert more influence over, and receive far more benefits from the state than their fellow citizens in the classes below.

The shortfalls of representative government go far beyond the matters of electoral and campaign financing reform. Representative government in the United States was established to forestall both authoritarianism and democracy. It is based on the principle of property (class) and only the modification of that principle can reverse the oligarchy of property that governs the United States.

NOTES

1. For Weber's discussion of law and politics in relation to social stratification, see his "Class, Status, Party," in H. H. Gerth and C. Wright Mills, ed. and tr., *From Max Weber: Essays in Sociology* (New York: Oxford University Press, 1946), ch. 7, sect. 1, 10.
2. "Politics as a Vocation," in ibid., ch. 6.
3. It was already clear to Max Weber that civil service reform meant a curtailment of the power of the masses in favor of the educated (and thus the propertied); see his essay "Bureaucracy," ch. 8, sect. 14.
4. The national debt grew enormously from 1980 on largely because of tax cuts and large military expenditures initiated by the Reagan administration. Today it stands at about 60 percent of what the nation produces each year.
5. Max Weber, "Class, Status, Party" in Gerth and Mills, *From Max Weber*, ch. 7, sect. 2–4; the above quotation is from p. 181.

6. Norbert Wiley, "America's Unique Class Politics: The Interplay of the Labor, Credit and Commodity Markets," *American Sociological Review* 32 (August 1967):529–541.
7. *Baker v. Carr,* 363 U.S. 186 (1962).
8. *Reynolds v. Sims,* 377 U.S. 533 (1964).
9. The suburbs are very diverse and have grown so much (while big cities have stagnated or even declined in size) that they too are now underrepresented in state and national legislatures.
10. John Nagle, *Systems and Succession: The Social Bases of Political Elite Recruitment* (Austin: University of Texas Press, 1977).
11. Harmon Zeigler and Michael A. Baer, "The Recruitment of Lobbyists and Legislators," *Midwest Journal of Political Science* 12, no. 4 (November 1968):493–513; reprinted in Donald P. Sprengel, ed., *Comparative State Politics: A Reader* (Columbus, Ohio: Charles E. Merrill, 1971), pp. 187–206.
12. For evidence concerning the social origins of New Deal intellectuals, see Thomas A. Krueger and William Glidden, "The New Deal Intellectual Elite: A Collective Portrait," in Frederic C. Jaher, ed., *The Rich, the Well Born, and the Powerful: Elites and Upper Classes in History* (Urbana: University of Illinois Press, 1973), pp. 338–374. For the social origins of high federal and military personnel, see W. Lloyd Warner, Paul P. Van Riper, Norman H. Martin, and Orvis F. Collins, *The American Federal Executive: A Study of Social and Personal Characteristics of the Civilian and Military Leaders of the United States Federal Government* (New Haven: Yale University Press, 1963), ch. 2; Beth Mintz, "The President's Cabinet, 1897–1972," *Insurgent Sociologist* 5, no. 3 (1975):131–149; and Philip H. Burch, *Elites in American History: The New Deal to the Carter Administration* (New York: Holmes & Meier, 1980).
13. Bruce M. Hackett, *Higher Civil Servants in California: A Social and Political Portrait* (Berkeley: University of California Press, 1967), ch. 2.
14. Morris Janowitz, *The Professional Soldier: A Social and Political Portrait* (New York: Free Press, 1960), ch. 5.
15. For data to this effect from Wisconsin, see Ronald M. Pavalko, "Recruitment to Teaching: Patterns of Selection and Retention," in Ronald M. Pavalko, ed., *Sociological Perspectives on Occupations* (Itasca, IL: F. E. Peacock, 1972), pp. 239–249; reprinted from *Sociology of Education* 43 (Summer 1970):340–353.
16. The interchangeability of careers leads to conflicts of interest; thus there are extensive tie-ins between members of Congress and professional (especially law) firms and businesses of all kinds. Some tightening up to prevent conflict of interest among legislators has appeared in recent years but whether abuses will stop remains to be seen.

    Though not strictly their careers, note should be made of the middle- and upper-class individuals who serve on presidential or congressional commissions and advisory groups or as special appointees to the United Nations and other bodies. This general type of activity is now so widespread and routine that it should be considered "public office"; and some individuals serve in these capacities so often that such service should be considered part of their careers.
17. *New York Times,* September 10, 1995, p. 1.
18. Actually, legislators do not have to be pressured to abandon independence and objectivity. Legislators are elected because they agree with the views of this or that constellation of pressure or interest groups. Pressure on legislators should

thus be regarded as a means of reinforcing prior commitments. Two general discussions of lobbying are Ronald J. Hrebener and Ruth K. Scott, *Interest Group Politics in America* (Englewood Cliffs, NJ: Prentice-Hall, 1982), and Congressional Research Service, "Congress and Pressure Groups: Lobbying in a Modern Democracy" (Washington, DC: U.S. Government Printing Office, 1986). Other important books in this area are Mark Green, *Who Runs Congress?*, 3rd ed. (New York: Bantam Books, 1979); Gordon Adams, *The Iron Triangle: The Politics of Defense Contracting* (New York: Council on Economic Priorities, 1981); and Sar A. Levitan and Martha R. Cooper, *Business Lobbies: The Public Good and the Bottom Line* (Baltimore: Johns Hopkins University Press, 1984).

19. All books on lobbying emphasize this point. For a general survey, see Samuel Krislov and David H. Rosenbloom, *Representative Bureaucracy and the American Political System* (New York: Praeger, 1981).
20. For a pioneering set of essays on the political nature (corporate liberalism) of foundations, see Robert F. Arnove, ed., *Philanthropy and Cultural Imperialism: The Foundations at Home and Abroad* (Bloomington: Indiana University Press, 1980). For a focus on the foreign policy impact (corporate liberalism) of three powerful foundations, see Edward H. Berman, *The Influence of the Carnegie, Ford, and Rockefeller Foundations on American Foreign Policy: The Ideology of Philanthropy* (Albany: State University of New York Press, 1983).
21. William Domhoff has studied the latter phenomenon closely as part of his argument that the United States is ruled by a small upper class; see his *The Higher Circles: The Governing Class in America* (New York: Vintage, 1971), esp. chs. 5 and 6. Also see Thomas R. Dye, "Oligarchic Tendencies in National Policy-Making: The Role of the Private Policy-Planning Organizations," *Journal of Politics* 40 (1978):309–331. More recently, Domhoff has written "Where Do Government Experts Come From? The Council of Economic Advisers and the Policy-Planning Network," and Dye has written "Organizing Power For Policy Planning: The View from the Brookings Institution," both in G. W. Domhoff and T. R. Dye, eds., *Power Elites and Organizations* (Beverly Hills, CA: Sage, 1987). Two studies have clearly established that the right-liberal and moderate-conservative think tanks are funded by a national corporate elite: J. Craig Jenkins and Teri Shumate, "Cowboy Capitalists and the Rise of the 'New Right': An Analysis of Contributors to Conservative Policy Formation Organizations," *Social Problems* 33 (December, 1985): 130–145, and David Stoesz, "Packaging the Conservative Revolution," *Social Epistemology* 2, no. 2 (1988):145–153.
22. For a full analysis of the Carnegie Corporation, see Ellen Condliffe Lagemann, *The Politics of Knowledge: The Carnegie Corporation, Philanthropy and Public Policy* (Middletown, CT: Wesleyan University Press, 1989).
23. For a sophisticated, critical analysis of the attempt to revitalize American society by the Brookings Institution, the Trilateral Commission, the American Enterprise Institute, the Heritage Foundation, and the Institute for Contemporary Studies, see Joseph G. Peschek, *Policy-Planning Organizations: Elite Agendas and America's Rightward Turn* (Philadelphia: Temple University Press, 1987).
24. U.S. Bureau of the Census, Current Population Reports, Series P-20, no. 466, "Voting and Registration in the Election of 1992" (Washington, DC: U.S. Government Printing Office, 1993), Tables 11, 12.
25. John F. Zipp, "Social Class and Social Liberalism," *Sociological Forum* 1 (Spring 1986):301–329.
26. William Gamson, "Stable Unrepresentation in American Society," *American Behavioral Scientist* 12 (November–December 1968):19f.

27. Sidney Verba and Norman H. Nie, *Participation in America: Political Democracy and Social Equality* (New York: Harper & Row, 1972).
28. Ibid., p. 298.
29. Sidney Verba, Norman H. Nie, and Jae-On Kim, *Participation and Political Equality: A Seven Nation Comparison* (New York: Cambridge University Press, 1978).
30. For a summary analysis of the cleavage in a wide variety of policy matters between American elites and ordinary people, see the section "Declining Legitimacy?" below.
31. For a comprehensive study that concludes that nonpartisan elections at the municipal level favor the upper classes, see Willis D. Hawley, *Nonpartisan Elections and the Case for Party Politics* (New York: John Wiley & Sons, 1973).
32. For a fuller discussion, see the section "Declining Legitimacy?" later in this chapter.
33. For one analysis showing the mobilization of American business under the leadership of the corporate elite, see Michael Useem, *The Inner Circle: Large Corporations and the Rise of Political Activity in the U.S. and U.K.* (New York: Oxford University Press, 1984).
34. For a valuable empirical study of negative political attitudes, combined with faith in American democracy, among well-paid blue-collar workers, see David Halle, *America's Working Man: Work, Home, and Politics Among Blue-Collar Property/Home/Owners* (Chicago: University of Chicago Press, 1984), pts. 4 and 5.
35. For a perceptive analysis, see Norval D. Glenn, "The Distribution of Political Knowledge in the United States," in *Political Attitudes and Public Opinion,* eds. Dan D. Vimmo and Charles M. Bonjean (New York: Longman, 1972). Eric R. A. Smith, *The Unchanging American Voter* (Berkeley: University of California Press, 1989), argues that there was no increase in the low level of political knowledge in the American electorate even during the political ferment of the 1960s. For evidence of a *decline* in interest and knowledge about public affairs among the young, see *New York Times,* June 28, 1990, p. 1.
36. Arthur H. Miller, "The Institutional Focus of Political Distrust" (paper delivered at the 1979 Annual Meeting of the American Political Science Association), p. 46.
37. For a comprehensive review of the many polls tapping public confidence, and an analysis of the relation between declining confidence and the legitimacy of American society, see Seymour Martin Lipset and William Schneider, *The Confidence Gap: Business, Labor, and Government in the Public Mind* (New York: Free Press, 1983).
38. Michael Oreskes, "Alienation From Government Grows, Poll Shows," *New York Times,* September 19, 1990, p. A26. The same lack of interest and distrust of government appears regularly in polls of college students.
39. U.S. Bureau of the Census, *Statistical Abstract of the United States: 1995* (Washington, DC: U.S. Government Printing Office, 1995), Table 457.
40. As reported by Elliott Currie, "Fighting Crime," *Working Papers* 9 (July–August 1982):22.
41. Robert D. Putnam, "Tuning In, Tuning Out: The Strange Disappearance of Social Capital in America," *PS: Political Science and Politics* 28, no. 24 (December 1995):664–683. For an abbreviated version, see *The American Prospect,* no. 24 (Winter 1996) or the Internet, http://epn.org/prospect/24/24putn.html.

15
Class, Legislation, and Government

◆ ◆ ◆ ◆

◆ ◆ ◆ ◆

The power of the upper classes that we saw in analyzing political participation and access to political power is also reflected in legislation and government.

CLASS AND TAXATION

Despite a strong verbal tradition affirming "ability to pay" as the underlying principle of taxation, and despite an equally strong commitment to reward work and achievement—and, by implication, not to reward idleness or inherited wealth—the American tax system violates these American values and beliefs.[1]

Many believe erroneously that estate and inheritance taxes reduce inequality. Many also believe erroneously that taxes reduce work incentives.[2] Also erroneous is the belief that income taxes equalize income. The U.S. Bureau of the Census reports that federal and state income taxes have little effect on income inequality. Government benefits (cash, food stamps, health care, school lunches), especially nonmeans-tested Social Security pensions and health care, on the other hand, do equalize incomes somewhat.[3]

The analysis of taxation indicates clearly that a political system based on universal suffrage, which ignores income and wealth by giving each individual one vote, does not lead to a redistribution of income and wealth despite the fact that lower income-wealth groups (the lower middle class and below) form a numerical majority. Nowhere is the contradiction between the ideal of equal opportunity and the class system so vividly apparent as in taxation: the American tax code not only reflects the power and privilege of the class-prestige structure, but also facilitates and legitimates the accumulation of power and privilege over time.

The Republican majority in Congress that appeared in 1994, aided by conservative Democrats, emphasized the need to cut taxes further, something that required deep cuts in government spending. The main beneficiaries of the tax cuts would be the upper classes and the main losers of the spending cuts would be the poor.[4] The fantasy behind these proposals is the anarchistic theory of laissez-faire—let everyone do what they want with their property and all will be better off.

CLASS AND PUBLIC SUBSIDIES (WELFARE) FOR PROPERTY AND PROFESSIONAL GROUPS

By *not* taxing income and property, Congress and state legislatures are making what analysts call *tax expenditures.* It is doubtful if the thousand and one tax loopholes could stand scrutiny as a direct expenditure in the budget. Accordingly, property and professional groups receive favored treatment, most of it unwarranted by standards of public interest and often obtained secretly, through the tax code. The welfare for the well-to-do and rich represented by tax expenditures exceeds many times over the direct expenditures for the poor.

The decision not to tax state and local taxes, mortgage interest, pensions, and medical insurance premiums, and to lower taxes on profits from the sale of property, represents enormous subsidies to the upper classes. In concrete terms, allowing interest and property taxes to be deducted means that the upper classes save 40 to 50 percent on their expenditures for housing and local schools and services. This is also good for builders of luxury homes and for the children of the well-to-do who go to well-supported public schools.

Direct outlays include farm subsidies ($7.9 billion), medical research ($3.7 billion), energy research ($3.4 billion), soil conservation ($1.9 billion), technology research ($1.8 billion), export-import credit and insurance for overseas investment, depreciation on capital expenditures (that exceed cost), excessive military equipment for the Pentagon, and education expenditures.

The above programs were enacted and maintained by both Democratic and Republican administrations and were left largely intact by the great tax reform proposals of 1995–1996.

CLASS AND PUBLIC SUBSIDIES (WELFARE) FOR THE POOR AND ELDERLY

Most subsidies for the poor and elderly result from the Social Security Act of 1935, amended many times. The Social Security system is a contributory insurance system to assist the retired and a public assistance program for those who cannot help themselves. Its components are as follows:

1. Old Age, Survivors', and Disability Insurance (OASDI), a system of benefits financed by a tax paid by workers and employers. Benefits go to retired individuals, disabled workers, and the widows and orphans of employees.
2. Old Age Assistance (OAA) and Aid to Families with Dependent Children (AFDC), a system of welfare benefits paid to the needy aged and to families with dependent children. This is a noncontributory program paid for largely through general federal revenues and administered by the states.
3. Health insurance for the elderly (Medicare), financed by employees' and employers' compulsory contributions.

The social insurance portion of this legislation has a number of features that need to be much better understood. Financed by a flat tax rate on only a portion of individual income, with no allowances for dependents or for deductions, it is a highly regressive tax. The funds collected under this system are then paid out to retirees in terms of the amounts they have paid in, rather than on the basis of need. Actually, lowest-income retirees receive proportionately more than they paid in than do higher-income retirees, but the minimum pensions are extremely small; it cannot be said that income is significantly redistributed, or that this feature alters the regressive nature of the social insurance system.

Furthermore, the amounts collected represent very large sums, amounting in effect to a major tax (running a close second to the personal income tax) and a considerable burden on most white-collar and working-class incomes. Also, many jobs held by the lower classes were not covered between roughly 1936 and the late 1960s and early 1970s, and the retirement age of sixty-five discriminates against the lower classes; whole-life expectancy only began to reach that level in the 1980s (the average African-

American male was still not living to age sixty-five as of 1985 when the retirement age began to rise). The lower classes do benefit most from the provisions for widows and for disability, since they die earlier and are disabled more frequently, but child support through college favors middle-class families. Incidentally, the original Social Security tax was based on extremely conservative actuarial estimates, and from the beginning the monies collected have been put in trust funds earning minimum interest (that is, the federal government lends the money to itself at interest rates lower than when it borrows from private sources). Unlike other countries, Social Security funds cannot be used as instruments of governmental fiscal and monetary policy or to provide capital for housing and other needs. If Social Security funds had been invested in the American economy like the pension systems of state government, their size would have grown enormously, making it possible to keep the Social Security tax much less burdensome than it now is. But investing Social Security funds in concrete areas of public interest or in a balanced portfolio of stocks and bonds would have made the federal government an owner of the American economy, a competitor of private capital, and presumably given it power to influence directly the direction of capital investment. For government to play a direct role in the economy is common in all other capitalist societies but fiercely resisted in the United States.

Payments to the needy from general tax revenues are designed to alleviate hardship, and they are ostensibly distributed according to need. But welfare programs are administered by the states, and there is wide variation in levels of payment, criteria used to establish need, and methods of administration. This portion of the Social Security system is still considered a "handout," an attitude that, along with a mode of administering payments that humiliates and stigmatizes recipients, tends to create a pariah group of public dependents. Not only does the administration of this program tend to invade the rights and privacy of the poor, but as Frances Fox Piven and Richard Cloward argued as far back as 1971, its latent function is to support and legitimize the social system that creates this form of poverty. Piven and Cloward's argument is that poor relief rises with economic downturns in order to curb civil disorder and falls when conditions are right in order to enforce work norms among the marginal labor force. In an up-dated 1993 analysis Piven and Cloward present evidence that the period after the 1960s has witnessed an unrelenting assault on public assistance by the upper classes (Republican party and conservative Democrats).[5] This time they offer a valuable added insight. The American upper classes' have been obsessed with curbing poor relief over the past two decades and have employed a wide variety of legal and illegal means to do so. They have made applying as difficult and humiliating as possible, they have seen to it that recipients have lost ground by not adjusting payments for inflation, and in some cases they have simply dropped people from the rolls illegally (stopped in the courts on occasion). Conservatives have also mounted huge publicity campaigns denouncing welfare dependency and idleness and insisting that recipients be made to work, knowing full well that there is no work. Why this obsession on the part of the upper classes? Why have they been willing to risk embarrassment with illegal behavior and sophomoric arguments—the amounts of money involved are not large, and those being denounced are mothers and children? The reason, say Piven and Cloward, is that welfare threatens their ability to lower the incomes of the general labor force—what they are really interested in is maintaining the work ethic for the low-income occupations that have been proliferating over the past two decades. By lowering welfare income and by creating a despised, outsider group, conservatives are creating a hell worse than the hell of employment at the lower levels of American capitalism.

CLASS AND HOUSING

Housing legislation in the United States is a preeminent illustration of class politics.[6] Various stages of public concern about and action on housing can be distinguished from the beginning of the century to the present. But all such legislation and action failed to provide housing for the poor: Every piece of legislation and every form of implementation has been heavily biased in favor of those that Lawrence Friedman calls "the submerged and potential middle class" and against the poor. What Friedman does not stress, because of his focus on the poor, is that housing is in chronically short supply for many who are not poor.[7]

Over the years the federal government has developed a variety of ad hoc housing programs but has never developed a coherent housing policy. The many piecemeal programs, however, manifest a rather distinct pattern, the trickle-down strategy—concentration on quality construction and subsidies, by far the largest of which is income tax deductions for homeowners (which of course favors the middle, upper middle, and upper income brackets), a strategy that benefits the poor only in that older homes eventually become available to them.[8]

The federal government acted to protect homeowners during the 1930s and it fostered low-income housing largely as an economic stimulus. During the 1950s and 1960s, the federal government undertook a gigantic support program for middle- and upper-class housing (through credit, tax, and highway programs). Throughout the 1930s to the 1960s the federal government actually cooperated with local governments to create a racially dual housing market. Little changed after the Fair Housing Law of 1968 because the federal government failed to develop a set of implementing regulations. After 1980 things actually got worse as the Reagan administration actively curtailed legal safeguards for minorities and curbed the already inadequate funds for low-income housing.[9] During the 1980s a new housing phenomenon appeared: homelessness. Throughout the United States, to its disgrace, anywhere from five hundred thousand to three million Americans are presently forced to sleep in alleyways, bus stations, huddled over gratings, or in their automobiles. The homeless are a diverse lot, consisting of the mentally ill who were released from mental institutions but who did not get the promised community-based shelters that were to serve as transition homes on the way back to normal life; the poor who used to find shelter in single-room occupancy hotels now torn down to make room for office buildings and other alleged improvements; the alcoholic; and the new poor made up of families either unemployed or whose income does not buy housing.

Many stereotypes prevent an accurate perception of political facts and keep observers from seeing the structure of power and the real and often ironic consequences of political-legal action. For example, it is well known that public authorities evict tenants whose incomes have risen above the maximum level of eligibility for public housing. Initially, one is likely to assume that this is a means of protecting the class interests of the poor. However, such an assumption overlooks the fact that public housing legislation was explicitly formulated to ensure that public housing would not compete with private housing. In other words, the eviction requirement is intended to protect the private housing market by guaranteeing that the nonpoor buy their housing from private owners! The net result is that the moral, economic, and political power of the state is used to make housing a private-profit field. Indeed, one of the latent functions of public housing itself is to divert attention from the failure of our economic institutions to house our population adequately, and from the possibility that this is a condition chronic to American-style capitalism.[10]

America's chronic housing shortage results from a disparity between the price of housing and the American income structure. This disparity grew worse from 1970 on. A thirty-year-old person in 1970 paid 21 percent of gross earnings to buy a medium-priced house—by 1983 that same individual had to pay 44 percent. A full explanation of this disparity must acknowledge the formidable class-prestige-power forces that stand between Americans and adequate housing. Private credit policies; monopolistic craft unions; outmoded building codes; snob zoning; local tax policies; planning practices; the compliance of real estate boards with snob and racial practices; and the transportation, credit, tax, and housing policies of the federal government[11] all function to mesh the availability, type, and location of housing with the income-wealth and prestige structure of the United States. In sum, there is little doubt that the power dimension at the federal, state, and local levels is deeply implicated in the processes that keep housing scarce and segregated along class-prestige lines.[12]

CLASS AND EDUCATION

Elementary and High School Education

Given the control of local, state, and federal governments by the upper classes, it is easy to understand why the distribution of educational resources conforms to class lines. The *Serrano-Priest* decision (1971), in which the California Supreme Court ruled unequal expenditures on education unconstitutional, stimulated an effort to make school expenditures more equal. However, in 1973 the United States Supreme Court ruled that unequal educational expenditures are not unconstitutional and spending more on the education of the well-to-do is now a taken-for-granted fact of American life. But even equal expenditures will do little to equalize educational opportunity, since (as we saw in Chapter 9) the school itself has negligible impact on differentials in academic achievement.

Historically, Congress and the federal government have exerted considerable influence on education, largely through deliberate neglect. Though fought for in the name of equal opportunity, the flow of federal money to the schools, which began in 1958, has not changed the class character of American education. All that can be said is that federal aid may have provided better education for all, but without changing relative differences. Even when federal money is earmarked for the poor it does not reach them because states spend the money on all, leaving relative differences intact.

Higher Education

Public policy in the realm of higher education also reflects and reinforces the American class system. As we have seen, higher education conforms to the basic pattern of class-structured education.[13] None of this is surprising, given (1) colleges' and universities' ideals of detachment from society (objective scholarship, political neutrality, and cloistered campuses); (2) their actual deep dependence on and involvement in society (control of their governing boards by businesspeople, professionals, churches, and state legislatures, the involvement of universities and professors in governmental research and consulting, and the dispensation of knowledge in terms of unconsciously held cultural postulates); (3) the fact that presidents, deans, and faculty enjoy upper- and upper-middle-class status; (4) and the fact that faculty and administrators are almost without exception innocent of any systematic training in education and up-to-date social science.

Basically, neither the infusion of public money into higher education nor the establishment and expansion of public institutions of higher education have equalized educational opportunity. For example, the free education made available to all veterans of World War II and subsequent wars represents an unparalleled educational opportunity for Americans—but making education available to all is not to make it equal. For one thing, not all veterans availed themselves of their educational rights. While precise data do not exist, it is safe to assume that a larger percentage of the well-to-do than of the poor did so. Second, one can assume that rich and poor attend different colleges and schools and pursue different academic programs. And third, the rich are thus enabled to invest the money they would otherwise have spent on education. The net result of the United States' generous support of education for veterans, therefore, was probably to widen the gap between rich and poor (as well as to help many individuals from the lower classes to succeed via education).[14]

The federal low-cost insured loan program for college students (a provision of the Higher Education Act of 1965) is a more recent example of the differential impact of allegedly nonpartisan equal opportunity programs. Designed to lower economic barriers to higher education, this program provides low-cost loans to college students. Students can borrow money with no interest during four years or more of school and then pay it back over ten years at subsidized rates. Though income limits were set in the early 1980s, effectively only the very wealthy are ineligible. Thus, the middle and upper classes can invest the money they would otherwise have paid for their children's education. By the mid-1980s it was costing the federal government $3 billion annually to generate $9 billion worth of guaranteed student loans.[15] That this program theoretically covers the poor and the general working class is of very little practical consequence. The children of the various classes acquire the motivation and skills necessary for college at different rates, attend college at unequal rates, choose different types of colleges, take different programs, earn different academic records, and complete different amounts of higher education. Thus, a formally equal opportunity is far from constituting equality of opportunity or equality of competition in practice. Nor do such programs even necessarily promote a higher level of ability among college populations. It is well known, for example, that there is class bias in the distribution of financial aid by institutions of higher education.[16] Students who can profit from higher education are turned down while students of equal ability who can afford to pay are given public aid, all in the name of equal opportunity (not to mention the unaccomplished well-to-do who feed at the public trough).

Colleges and universities are demonstrably subject to business, religious, and local political control, and one finds higher education explicitly implicated in serving social ends other than detached scholarship and the preservation and transmission of high culture. Higher education is part of a far-flung, intertwined network of economic, professional, and political interests. It engages in research for the military, for industry, and for government. This is not necessarily bad, but there are many suspicions that partisan interests are being served (for an example, see Box 15–1, "The Tomato Harvester: How Education Serves the Corporate Economy").

BOX 15–1 *The Tomato Harvester: How Education Serves the Corporate Economy*

The University of California at Davis is the biggest agricultural research station in the country. Out of its efforts has come a large-wheeled vehicle that can pick tomatoes. The picker is ungainly and unattractive, but it works. As a result, the backbreaking work of picking tomatoes is now done by a nonsweating, nonsuffering machine. Not only is an undesirable type of work being replaced but presumably productivity will increase. Seen from this perspective, all is to the good. But critics charge that there is far more to the story.

What happens to farm workers? Predictably, the introduction of machinery was accelerated after the victory of the Cesar Chávez–led farm workers union in getting better wages and working conditions. Jobs picking tomatoes have shrunk drastically in recent years. And this is not a question of the right of private property owners to manage their businesses any way they want. The tomato harvester was developed at a tax-supported state institution that also uses federal tax dollars for research. Critics charge that the University of California looks favorably on research that favors large agribusiness and chemical companies. This bias is furthered by private research grants to the university, which however small a fraction of the total, set the general direction of research. The bias is also explained by the fact that the university's governing boards have members with direct ties to farm, chemical, and other economic interests. In addition, say critics, the university neglects nutrition research, research that would benefit small farmers, and does little research into nonchemical ways to control pests. Characteristically, no provisions are made in research grants that would require its beneficiaries to help displaced workers develop new skills and find new jobs.

The tomato harvester cost $80,000 when it was introduced in the late 1970s. As only large farms could afford it or found it economical to use, it benefitted them most. Its use gave them a competitive edge over the small farmer and thus helped to accelerate the trend in farming in which more and more land goes into fewer hands. To make matters worse, big farm owners pay for the harvester with money borrowed from federal agencies (which were originally set up to help needy small farmers) and they used publicly paid-for irrigation water illegally (the open violation for fifty years of a law restricting such water to small farmers of 600 acres or less was rectified by changing the law!).

To compound the injury a tomato must be bred to withstand mechanical picking—again, the University of California helped by developing a thick-skinned tomato. And the price of tomatoes has risen disproportionally, argue critics, despite claims that science and technology increase productivity. All in all, the deep bias toward technology, energy-intensive, chemically dependent, cash-crop farming in the United States causes human suffering, threatens the soil, and leads to concentration in farming and interlocks between agribusiness, concentrated industry, scientists, and educators.

Our awareness of the class nature of public higher education is based on more than insight and hypothesis. Thanks to a study of the California system of public higher education,[17] we are now on firm ground when talking about the educational role played by the power dimension. As is well known, California has an extensive system of post–high-school public education, financed by public funds and characterized by low tuition and entrance and retention on academic merit. In their analysis of this system and its relation to class, Hansen and Weistrod conclude that public higher education in California is a system for redistributing income from lower to higher income groups. The authors add that California's reinforcement and aggravation of existing inequality by means of substantial subsidies to middle-class and upper-class students through "public" higher education is probably even more characteristic of the other forty-nine states.[18] Given what we know about public education at all levels, these findings are not surprising.[19] It is difficult not to conclude that the power dimension (local, state, and federal governments and political institutions), as it focuses on education, is an integral part of the American system of stratification. In performing its role in the American system of class, the power structure does more than certify the existing class system; it actually widens differential advantages while labeling its efforts "equality of opportunity," thus creating the impression that it is a neutral promoter of classlessness.

CLASS AND ECONOMICS POLICIES OF THE FEDERAL GOVERNMENT

Antitrust Policy

The United States has a long history of concern about monopolistic economic power, much of it framed in terms of a theoretical ideal of free market competition. Free markets based on equal competition exist only in the minds of theorists. Why this utopian image of economic competition persists is unclear: It may relieve anxiety about failure for some; it may serve others as a rationalization for easy success; and it may be a convenient facade behind which powerful groups can hide. In any case, the American public and the federal government have accepted bigness—or, perhaps more precisely, they tend to assume that the trend toward bigness is compatible with competition, efficiency, individualism, and democracy.

Americans see no contradiction in valuing both competition and bigness, perhaps because they believe that each promotes efficiency. One thing is certain, however: in the United States competition is honored more in ideology than in actual behavior, especially if behavior is measured against the classic ideal of competition among a large number of equals. In the name of this imaginary world, the Reagan administration noticeably relaxed even the weak restraints on monopoly that had existed up to 1980. By 1996 it was apparent that economic concentration was occurring in one field after another (for example, communications, health care, and banking) under the fiction of market competition.

The role of the power dimension in promoting concentrated market power or oligarchic competition is apparent. The federal government is not, on the whole, a trust-busting agency. Its regulatory policies; its granting of patents, franchises, and licenses to engage in various businesses, including the production of atomic energy; and its import and production quotas clearly promote bigness and noncompetition.

The government's policies with regard to its own purchases of goods and services also contribute heavily to economic concentration, and thus to the redistribution of income and wealth through oligarchic control of markets. The Defense Department, the Nuclear Regulatory Commission, and the National Aeronautics and Space Administration clearly prefer to purchase goods and services from a small number of large contractors.

Regulatory Policy

Beginning in the late nineteenth century, Congress began to regulate certain forms of economic activity in the public interest: Almost all observers are agreed that government's various regulations and programs are biased in favor of the industry or profession being regulated. Workman's compensation, for example, was hailed as a gain for workers but what it did was to safeguard the unsafe world of work—workers got something for being injured on the job but they had to give up the right to sue the employer. In the meantime, occupational health and safety laws go unenforced. Other regulations help to rationalize markets for those in them, thus providing a legal facade for oligarchic markets. We Americans are such innocents about government that during the crucial formative decades of nuclear energy policy we put both its promotion and regulation in the hands of the same agency. And despite much posturing in the health-care field there is little effective monitoring of either its costs or results. Deregulation was the watchword from the late 1970s on, and by the 1980s deregulation has led to new forms of concentration (the airline and railroad industries are prime examples).

Public Economic Policies

From the early nineteenth century until 1929, Americans developed a great faith that theirs was an economy based on natural principles. They believed that if left alone (laissez-faire economic theory), an economy inherently seeks equilibrium and brings about the most rational use of human and material resources. This faith was shattered by the Great Depression of the 1930s, which left 25 percent of the American labor force unemployed and devastated farmers and businesses. It also broke the consensus among property owners and professionals about the existence of a natural economy.

During the 1930s Americans looked to government to help them. Much of what government did was hit-and-miss, for government had had no direct experience in managing the economy. Gradually, however, a theory developed by the English economist John Maynard Keynes was adopted. Keynes argued that the economy is not governed by an inherent process of equilibrium. The economy contains no principles that will produce full employment (the full use of material and human resources). Economic groups, especially business firms but also labor unions, professions, and so on, seek security and control, not competition. Thus, the economy as a whole lacks the flexibility (markets) that ensures adaptation to new conditions. Over time, there is disequilibrium; for example, savings do not all go into productive investment, demand can falter and snowball into recession and depression as business cuts back production. Thus, argued Keynes, the government has a continuous and legitimate role to play in directing the economy. Though never clear on how the government was to do this, Keynes suggested three policy options—government can keep the economy growing in a balanced manner (full employment with price stability) by acting as a consumer itself (government spending for housing or public works, etc.), by cutting taxes to give private consumers or producers more money to spend (even if it means a public deficit), and by adjusting interest rates (the price of credit) to either stimulate or slow down consumption and investment.

The Democratic and the Republican parties have both adopted Keynesianism but interpret it differently. Democrats emphasize government spending and giving tax cuts to individual consumers to stimulate the economy (demand-side economics) whereas Republicans reject government spending and emphasize giving tax cuts to business to stimulate economic growth (supply-side economics). However, our experience with a *mixed economy* (a private economy dependent in important ways on government activity) is not overly positive. Democratic administrations have had some success in stimulating the economy by enhancing consumer demand but have been unable to control inflation.[20] The Reagan administration of the 1980s inaugurated an approach emphasizing tax cuts for producers. Almost all analysts agree that Reagonomics did not succeed in producing more capital investment and that economic growth in the 1980s resulted from private and public debt.

Actually, investment declined during the early 1980s because the tax cuts were not targeted to produce productive investment. In 1981, the industrial sector of the American economy (for example, the steel industry) showed evidence of decay and decline, and home construction was far below needed levels. Deep tax cuts had been made to stimulate investment, but the United States Steel Company, rather than modernize its plants, bought an oil company, Coca-Cola purchased a movie studio, and Holiday Inn announced a program to build luxury hotels. The improved economy after 1982 was led by consumers (who went heavily into debt), by cheap imports (which led to trade deficits and debt to foreigners), and by government buoyed by debt.

Public economic policies tolerate a large amount of unused economic capacity. America's powerful groups fear inflation more than idle capacity because it erodes the value of wealth, especially that of creditors. And governmental economic policies can be judged from still another perspective. An enormous backlog of needs has developed in the public sector: sewers and sewage treatment plants, garbage disposal facilities, schools, housing, park and recreational facilities, and mass transportation. By and large, federal tax and credit policies and direct governmental expenditures can be characterized as *reactionary Keynesianism*—the lopsided emphasis in public economic policy on stimulating private consumption and economic activity in the early liberal faith that "free" private markets rationalize an economy and promote the general well-being. The net result has been to starve public programs for mass transit, housing, waste treatment, and so on, and encourage, in John Kenneth Galbraith's words, "private luxury and public squalor."

Finally, despite a highly unsatisfactory employment record, little progress has been made in rationalizing our labor market (such as through job training programs). Ironically, unemployment and underemployment caused by recession, bankruptcies, technological displacement, foreign competition, and the flow of capital overseas eventually create an underclass of welfare recipients who are denounced as shiftless and made dependent wards of the state. To compound the hypocrisy, both parties support made-to-work rules knowing full well that there are no jobs.

All in all, it is apparent that federal economic policies do not run counter to the general structure of economic power, and that federal tax, spending, and monetary policies simply reflect and reinforce the American class-prestige hierarchy.

CLASS AND FOREIGN POLICY

The Ideology of Free Trade

By and large, post–World War II American governments have pursued a policy of free trade in international economic affairs. This philosophy is identical to domestic laissez-faire ideology—all should compete by doing what they do best (the doctrine of comparative advantage) and the result will be a rational domestic and international division of labor. This no more works on the international level than it does on the domestic. The doctrine of free enterprise hides a great many class-related phenomena. First, a huge amount of American capital went overseas from 1945 on, thus contributing to enormous problems for American workers, small farmers, small businesspeople, and older cities. By and large, American multinational corporations prospered on a global basis even though the American economy has suffered in terms of job losses, loss of good jobs, and declining competitiveness.[21] Second, there is a vast network of protectionism beneath the rhetoric of free trade. Corporations, farmers (especially industrial farmers or agribusiness), and workers have benefitted from protectionism depending on the strength of the affected industries—textiles, farm products, shoes, steel, automobiles, computer chips, and so on. The voluntary agreement by Japan to limit its exports of automobiles was really a way for American manufacturers to raise the price of their cars by roughly $1,000 to $1,500 each.

The United States is massively dependent upon foreign resources to run its industrial economy, and it needs overseas markets for its goods, capital, services, and surplus food and staples. Like all modern societies, the United States cannot exist without relatively continuous economic growth, and economic growth is not possible unless its access to world markets is unhampered. In short, it is vital to American society that international trade is unhampered, that sea lanes are kept open, and that many diverse societies remain friendly and compliant to its wishes.

The most dramatic examples of the class basis of the policies of the United States government are its efforts (often secretive and illegal) to influence the internal politics of friendly countries (for example, the U.S. Central Intelligence Agency has a long history of contributing money to Italy's capitalist political parties), or to prevent the establishment of socialist and communist societies, as witness its actions in Russia (1917), China, Cuba, and Chile.[22] Less well known and often misunderstood are the elaborate tax and tariff laws that facilitate the penetration of American capital abroad, and the foreign aid programs that tie other countries to American technology and services. Very little of American foreign aid is given away as a gift, though there is a widespread impression that this is so. American foreign aid is primarily a subsidy to American business and professions (the impact on labor is mixed because jobs are won and lost through foreign aid) and a way for American capital to trade and invest abroad. Foreign aid invariably stipulates that foreign countries must buy American products and use American services such as engineering firms. This not only promotes sales on a long-term basis, since replacement parts must come from the United States, but prevents recipient countries from developing their own engineering and other skills.

Foreign aid also consists of providing money for various international lending agencies. The United States government participates in and is a preponderant influence in a number of international agencies such as the World Bank, the International Monetary Fund, and the Asian Development Bank. Essentially capitalist institutions, these agencies promote development along capitalist lines in Third-World nations by lending money primarily to finance the construction of ports, electric power plants, highways, and other facilities essential to trade and investment.

The United States also encourages exports—for example, through low-cost government loans (Export-Import Bank), government insurance against investment loss, and through its tax laws. Aid to investment abroad is explicit American policy. An empirical analysis has largely substantiated the radical claim that private investment by American companies and economic and military aid by the American government have a common feature: The recipient countries have compliant right-wing governments.[23] The United States has also developed some (small) payment and retraining programs to cushion American workers against the loss of jobs due to foreign competition. It also protects a large number of American industries not so much through tariffs but through voluntary agreements, in effect, allowing private corporations in foreign countries and the United States to divide up markets, raise prices, and keep the gains at the expense of American consumers.

American Leadership in Linking Class Interests Within the Capitalist World

From the beginning of the century to the 1970s, the United States gradually assumed the leadership of the capitalist world. Foremost among its objectives was to further the interests of American banks and manufacturers. The Marshall Plan, which brought Europe to its feet after World War II, was part of this process. By the 1960s the European powers were able to assert some independence, and the United States began to lose its clear dominance.[24]

In a related analysis, Michael Useem has shown the extensive cooperation that exists between core elements in American and British capitalism and their successful efforts to maintain profit margins against the demands of their respective populations for greater public spending on mass welfare (the Thatcher and Reagan governments of the 1980s).[25]

CLASS AND CULTURAL IMPERIALISM: EDUCATION, CHURCHES, FOUNDATIONS, AND MASS AND ELITE MEDIA

Class action is rarely suspected in the activities of educational groups, churches, foundations, philanthropies, news media, and so on because such groups are generally regarded as nonpartisan. Critics have argued, however, that the extension of American (or Western) educational principles to other societies amounts to neocolonialism.[26] Colonial nations such as England and France have a long tradition of educating at home the leaders of their colonies. Today the United States educates large numbers of foreigners; in 1993–1994, it had 449,750 foreign students, a large majority coming from the developing world.[27]

Cultural imperialism takes many forms. The role of missionaries, technical-aid teams, exchange programs, foundations, philanthropies, and the news, publishing, and entertainment media are undoubtedly supportive of class values but their impact has not been studied systematically. There is little question that the United States has a large impact abroad through its entertainers, films and other mass-media materials, novelists, and athletes, and that it dominates global trade (outside the socialist countries) in television programs, films, books, magazines, and scholarly journals.[28] The content of American books, films, and television programs is often nationalistic and racist but such biases have declined as foreign sales have become more important to media producers. American publishers, however, continue to print books in languages and about subjects that correspond to the interests of privileged native elites.[29]

Cultural imperialism takes place in unsuspected ways. Textbooks and the media distort our image of foreign nations and people. Western literature has promoted ethnocentrism in the West and has created myths about the white man's burden.[30] American best-sellers about Asia in the twentieth century have given Americans a twisted view of all Asian peoples and societies.[31] The Western scholarly tradition has also biased the West's perception of other peoples, and, in turn, its perception of itself. Anthropology supplied information that furthered the ends of colonial administrators.[32] The West's main scholarly tradition, especially in England, France, and the United States (claims Edward Said), also created a fictitious Oriental world (encompassing the Middle East, parts of Africa, and all of Asia), which served largely to further the ends of colonialism.[33] The late nineteenth century also witnessed the spread of ethnocentrism to the general public through the medium of ethnographic exhibits,[34] the spread of mass education, and the rise of the yellow press. Even today, argues Edward Said, the mass media have a narrow and biased view of the world, as witness their handling of the Iranian crisis, especially from 1979 to 1981.[35]

The Rockefeller Foundation's sponsorship of agricultural research to spur food production in Third World countries illustrates how "objective" research sponsored by "public interest" foundations can create more problems than it solves. The Rockefeller Foundation's agricultural research centers developed high-yield hybrid plants, the basis of the Green Revolution in the developing countries. High-yield plants require fertilizer, irrigation, and considerable technology; as a result the Green Revolution has everywhere led to high land concentration, the displacement of millions of families, massive Third-World unemployment, hunger, and dependence.[36]

As noted earlier (Chapter 14), a number of private voluntary groups exercise considerable influence in foreign affairs: the Council on Foreign Relations, the Committee for Economic Development, and a number of research corporations and institutes. All are basically financed by large corporations, their membership is drawn exclusively from the world of big business along with a few lawyers and university presidents, their members have often served in government foreign policy posts, they recruit candidates for government service, and their research reports and research grants play an important role in shaping public policy.[37]

SUMMARY

In *The Federalist Papers,* number 10, James Madison argued that individuals are unequal by nature, that natural inequality leads to economic inequality, that economic inequality leads to conflict, and that the proper province of government is to mediate and regulate (not change or eliminate) economic differences and disputes. Our own view is that explaining inequality by invoking human nature is a dubious enterprise. Nonetheless, American society is not only based on this view but has institutionalized Madison's political prescription for coping with inequality. Our analysis of federal legislation and its administration indicates that Madison's view, however dubious from the standpoint of science, accurately describes the performance of American political institutions. Government acts to soften and update inequality, not to curtail it and certainly not to eradicate it. In a sense, of course, government can only reflect the society that spawned it. But the American power dimension is charged with high moral purpose, often expressed in dynamic language. We are constantly led to believe, in other words, that government can and does change things; thus, it is important to note that it does not and probably cannot do this unless major changes are made in the American political system.

In assessing the relation between class-prestige forces and legislation, therefore, we must be careful not to overestimate the independence or power of the power dimension. During the course of American history, political institutions appear to have done little to change the positions of the various groups in the hierarchies of class and prestige. Basic changes and displacements have come about largely as results of economic expansion and inadvertent governmental action. (For example, the government helped to open up the West by subsidizing canals and railroads and by granting homesteads.) In point of fact, our political institutions either register changes in class or prestige or operate to forestall change. (For example, the economic decline of farmers has been arrested by their political strength.) Thus, it is especially important to exercise caution with regard to the role of the federal government vis-à-vis class and prestige forces.

In examining federal legislation in the areas of taxation, Social Security, housing, education, and economic policy, the conclusions are inescapable that government changes very little and that politics, legislation, and government are the handmaidens of the class-prestige hierarchy. Actually, an examination of other areas can only support the conclusion that the power dimension is an auxiliary of the American class and prestige hierarchies. Highway legislation, urban renewal, support for the humanities and arts, funds for pre- and postdoctoral faculty research in science, funds for medicine and mental health, disaster aid, small business loans, the enforcement of safety regulations, antipollution standards, labor legislation, and minimum wage laws are all heavily slanted in favor of the upper classes. And nothing at the local and state levels runs counter to this pattern; if anything, the class-prestige nature of government is even more pronounced and apparent at these lower levels.

America's foreign economic, political-military, and cultural policies have also all furthered the interests and values of the American upper classes.

NOTES

1. For two classic studies, see Joseph A. Pechman, *The Rich, the Poor, and the Taxes They Pay* (Boulder, CO: Westview Press, 1986) and Michael Patrick Allen, *The Founding Fortunes: A New Anatomy of Super-Rich Families in America* (New York: E.P. Dutton, 1987). For a fascinating analysis naming the individuals, corporations, and various interest groups that the American tax system favors over ordinary Americans, see Donald L. Barlett and James B. Steele, *America: Who Really Pays the Taxes?* (New York: Simon and Schuster, 1994).
2. For our only full-scale study, see Robin Barlow, Harvey E. Brazer, and James N. Morgan, *Economic Behavior of the Affluent* (Washington, DC: Brookings Institution, 1966).
3. U.S. Bureau of the Census, "Measuring the Effect of Benefits and Taxes on Income and Poverty: 1992," *Current Population Reports* P60–186 RD (Washington, DC: U.S. Government Printing Office, 1993), pp. x–xiv.
4. There were also deep cuts and attempts to eliminate a wide variety of successful government programs; for the significance of policies to undermine successful programs, see below.
5. Frances Fox Piven and Richard A. Cloward, *Regulating the Poor: The Functions of Welfare,* updated ed. (New York: Random House, 1993).
6. For a brilliant summary and analysis of housing legislation and action in American history, with valuable insights into the politics of class, see Lawrence M. Friedman, *Government and Slum Housing* (Chicago: Rand McNally, 1968).
7. As Friedman points out, housing for the elderly has received substantial support, partly because the middle-class nuclear family is not geared to accommodate aged parents.

8. Henry J. Aaron, *Shelter and Subsidies: Who Benefits from Federal Housing Policies* (Washington, DC: Brookings Institution, 1972). The use of the tax code to subsidize housing favors the upper classes because they can reduce their property tax and interest payments by approximately 40 to 50 percent, whereas the lower classes can reduce theirs only by their much lower rates.
9. For full background, see Citizens' Commission on Civil Rights, *A Decent Home: A Report on the Continuing Failure of the Federal Government to Provide Equal Housing Opportunity* (Washington, DC: Center for National Policy Review, Catholic University, 1983).
10. Public housing projects (our "penthouse prisons") also have the well-known effects of segregating the residences of white and black Americans and keeping the poor of both races out of the neighborhoods of the nonpoor.
11. The Reagan administration made drastic cuts between 1981 and 1987 in the federal government's already inadequate housing programs.
12. For a radical indictment of American housing presenting valuable data and insights from successful policies abroad, see Rachel G. Bratt, Chester Hartman, and Ann Meyerson, eds., *Critical Perspectives on Housing* (Philadelphia: Temple University Press, 1986).
13. See "Higher Education: The Capstone of Class Education" in Chapter 9.
14. Veterans of the Vietnam War were treated less well than their predecessors for a number of reasons, not the least of which is the pronounced class bias in the system of drafting men to fight in Vietnam. In contrast to veterans of previous wars, Vietnam veterans include proportionately far more of the poor and minorities, and thus had less appeal for Congress and other public officials than did veterans of former wars.
15. *The Chronicle of Higher Education* 33 (April 15, 1987), p. 1.
16. George A. Schlekat, "Do Financial Aid Programs Have a Conscience?," *College Board Review* 69 (Fall 1968):15–20.
17. W. Lee Hansen and Burton A. Weistrod, *Benefits, Cost, and Finance of Public Higher Education* (Chicago: Markham, 1969).
18. The authors demonstrate that this is the case for Wisconsin, a state famous for its system of public higher education; see W. Lee Hansen and Burton A. Weistrod, *A New Approach to Higher Education Finance* (Madison: Institute for Research on Poverty, University of Wisconsin, 1970). For a study of public higher education in Florida, which corroborates the above findings, see Douglas M. Windham, *Education, Equality, and Income Redistribution: A Study of Public Higher Education* (Lexington, MA: D.C. Heath, 1970).
19. It should be noted that public institutions enroll 75 percent of all college students.
20. John E. Schwarz, *America's Hidden Success* (New York: W.W. Norton, 1983), argues that the Democratic party's consumer-targeted Keynesianism (during the 1960s and into the 1970s) was far more successful than we have been allowed to believe.
21. Robert E. Lipsey and Irving B. Kravis, "Business Holds Its Own as America Slips," *New York Times,* January 18, 1987, p. F3.
22. For the actions of the United States government (in conjunction with major American corporations) that helped to overthrow socialism in Chile, see James Petras and Morris Moreley, *The United States and Chile: Imperialism and the Allende Government* (New York: Monthly Review Press, 1975).

23. Steven J. Rosen, "The Open Door Imperative and U.S. Foreign Policy," in Steven J. Rosen and James R. Kurth, eds., *Testing Theories of Economic Imperialism* (Lexington, MA: Lexington Books, 1974), ch. 6.
24. For background details on this overall process, see Kees Van der Pijl, *The Making of an Atlantic Ruling Class* (London: Verso, 1984).
25. Michael Useem, *The Inner Circle: Large Corporations and the Rise of Business Political Activity in the U.S. and U.K.* (New York: Oxford University Press, 1984).
26. For general background, see Martin Carnoy, *Education as Cultural Imperialism* (New York: David McKay, 1974), and Ali A. Mazrin, "The African University as a Multinational Corporation: Problems of Penetration and Dependency," *Harvard Educational Review* 45 (May 1975):191–210. For a history of the Ford, Rockefeller, and Carnegie foundations' educational policies toward Africa and a charge that they furthered American corporate rather than African interests, see Edward H. Berman, "Foundations, United States Foreign Policy, and African Education, 1945–1975," *Harvard Educational Review* 49 (May 1979):145–179 (with brief but vigorous responses from foundation officials—pp. 180–184).
27. *The Chronicle of Higher Education* 38 (November 23, 1994):A39.
28. Richard P. Nielsen, "International Trade and Policy in Mass Media Materials: Television Programs, Films, Books, and Magazines," *Culture* 3, no. 3, pp. 196–205 (UNESCO, 1976).
29. Philip G. Altbach, "Literary Colonialism: Books in the Third World," *Harvard Educational Review* 45 (May 1975):226–236.
30. Jonah Raskin, *The Mythology of Imperialism: Kipling, Conrad, Forster, Lawrence, Carey* (New York: Random House, 1971).
31. Daniel B. Ramsdell, "Asia Askew: U.S. Best-Sellers on Asia, 1931–1980," *Bulletin of Concerned Asia Scholars* 15 (October–December 1983):2–25.
32. Talal Asad, ed., *Anthropology and the Colonial Encounter* (New York: Humanities Press, 1973); Roy F. Ellen, "The Development of Anthropology and Colonial Policy in the Netherlands: 1800–1960," *Journal of the History of the Behavioral Sciences* 12 (1976):303–324; and Gerrit Huizer and Bruce Mannheim, eds., *The Politics of Anthropology: From Colonialism and Sexism Toward a View from Below* (The Hague: Mouton, 1979).
33. Edward W. Said, *Orientalism* (New York: Pantheon, 1978).
34. William Schneider, "Race and Empire: The Rise of Popular Ethnography in the Late Nineteenth Century," *Journal of Popular Culture* 11 (Summer 1977):98–109, and "Colonies at the 1900 World Fair," *History Today* 31 (May 1981):31–36.
35. Edward W. Said, *Covering Islam* (New York: Pantheon, 1981).
36. For background on the widespread misery produced by Western, especially American, agricultural aid, and for a critical analysis of the rationalizations that cover American policies, see Susan George, *How the Other Half Dies* (Montclair, NJ: Allan Held and Osmun, 1977). George shrewdly notes the connection between fertilizer and the Rockefeller oil interests. For a radical but balanced critique of the Green Revolution and for alternative strategies, see Bernhard Glaeser, ed., *The Green Revolution Revised* (London: Allen and Unwin, 1987).
37. For an analysis from a conflict perspective, see G. William Domhoff, *Who Rules America Now?* (Englewood Cliffs, NJ: Prentice-Hall, 1983), ch. 4.

16
Class, Law, and Deviance

◆ ◆ ◆ ◆

◆ ◆ ◆ ◆

In this chapter, we want to determine whether obedience and disobedience to the law have anything to do with social class. We also want to know whether the state—represented by police officers, prosecutors, juries, defense attorneys, judges, court officials, professional auxiliaries, and prison officials—treats individuals equally or in keeping with their positions in the class and prestige hierarchies. In other words, are the agencies of power that specialize in maintaining the law impartial in their treatment of the American people? In short, is there equality before the law? We begin our analysis of the relation between law and class society with a brief depiction of the

American legal system and a discussion of the functional and the conflict views of the law.

THE AMERICAN LEGAL SYSTEM

Americans have great respect for the law and associate it with fundamental values such as personal liberty, social unity, orderly change, and social adaptation. To serve these important values the American legal system employs a number of basic premises. One, Americans distinguish between ordinary laws and constitutional law with the former subject to the latter. Two, all laws can be changed should the need arise. And three, conscience and intellect are respected against law in that individuals can speak against laws they don't like and are protected against self-incrimination or arbitrary acts by the state.

The American legal system has a number of other distinguishing features. The United States has far more lawyers per capita and far more of them employed in private practice than in other countries. American law is subject to the power of money probably far more than any other developed society (shown dramatically by the O. J. Simpson trial of 1994–1995). Private groups with money exert a powerful influence on the creation of law by legislatures and government officials. The services of lawyers must be purchased, which means that those with money get more and better legal services. And while Americans respect the law in the abstract, they are also great lawbreakers and dispute the law in great numbers both in and out of courtrooms.

All of the above is understandable given the main thrust of America's social development:

1. An unprecedented commitment to individual rights
2. An unprecedented incitement to material gain through competition
3. A dynamic economic development that quickly outgrew custom and religion as sources of dispute resolution
4. Slavery and immigration, which diversified the American population and further undermined customary sources of social control and conflict resolution
5. The inexpensiveness of law (the loser pays nothing in court or legal fees)
6. Lofty, expansive constitutional ideals and a difficult and expensive-to-influence political system have prompted Americans to turn economic and political grievances into legal issues

THE LIBERAL-FUNCTIONAL VIEW OF LAW

Elites uniformly regard law as the product of a society based on consensus. Law, they argue, reflects the considered judgment of the community and is thus binding on the community. Functionalist sociologists tend to agree, emphasizing the contribution of law to social stability, justice, and adjustment. Despite faults, law embodies our highest moral values and seeks goals that most agree on. Law as a set of procedures guarantees everyone a fair hearing and protects us against arbitrary state action. When law breaks new ground it does so in terms of values that people accept. True, there are many conflicting opinions about laws and the judicial process, but this is because law is in the thick of things busy solving problems and helping individuals, groups, and society adapt to new conditions. The law may lag behind society but that is not necessarily bad since it forces people to think before they act. The established classes and most lawyers accept this view of law.

THE CONFLICT VIEW OF LAW

Conflict theorists agree that the law is a stabilizing, integrative force, but, they argue, this serves to protect both the good and the bad in the status quo. Law is always and everywhere primarily an instrument for legitimating and supporting existing power groups be they priesthoods, landed aristocracies, businesspeople and professionals, or dictatorships. The development of American law during the late colonial and early republican period (to cite one conflict legal theorist) clearly reflected the interests and needs of America's emerging commercial and industrial classes. American law has been intimately associated with their interests ever since (see Box 16–1, "The Partisan Nature of Objective Law").

Americans break the law in large numbers and engage in litigation far more than other people, argue conflict theorists, precisely because the law does *not* rest on consensus. Legislatures enact ambiguous, vague, and contradictory laws, not because legislatures cannot write clearly but because legislatures themselves do not rest on consensus. Law, argue conflict theorists, is an expression of power. While it may sometimes express the common interest, law mostly expresses the interests of the strong and neglects the interests of the weak.

All this leads to poor law enforcement. Laws expressing a consensus often lack enforcement teeth (for example, fair employment and occupational safety laws). Though there is consensus on the need for law and order, the most important forms of criminal behavior cannot be controlled because they are being done by powerful business and professional groups often in conjunction with public officials.

Many of the deficiencies of the American legal system have been summarized by Derek C. Bok.[1] Bok charges that American law (for example, labor law, antitrust law, workplace safety regulations) cannot be related to the public interest (to verifiable results in each specific area). Legal scholars

BOX 16–1 *The Partisan Nature of Objective Law*

Legal historians and philosophers have portrayed American law as an objective, apolitical, and autonomous code of norms. Despite disagreements, say between Roscoe Pound and Oliver Wendell Holmes, American jurisprudence has argued that the development of American law is marked by consensus and that its outcome serves the common good. Even when legal analysts have seen the law in relation to economic and political developments, they have tended to adopt a functional and consensus approach in their interpretations. However, a minority of legal historians has argued that law is better seen from a conflict perspective. M. J. Horwitz,* for example, argues that American law was drastically altered during the formative years of the Republic primarily through judicial interpretations. The eighteenth century regarded law as stemming from community customs derived from natural law. Property meant the absolute right to enjoy something and to be able to prevent others from interfering with that enjoyment. From 1780 to 1860, argues Horwitz, the legal conception of property was drastically altered to mean that one had the right to develop and use property *regardless of injuries to others.*

Not surprisingly, argues Horwitz, the changed meaning of property was accompanied by a change in the meaning of a contract. In the eighteenth century a contract had to be fair and could be set aside if it wasn't. By the mid-nineteenth century, a contract was enforceable *even if its provisions were patently unfair.* The law was simply reflecting a fact of economic life: strong commercial and industrial interests were using their competitive advantages to exploit smaller businesses, consumers, and workers, and they legalized their exploitation by putting it in the form of a contract. They also protected their economic power by getting the courts to reduce their responsibility for damages (in keeping with the new dictum that the central meaning of property was the right to develop it), and juries gradually had the power to make judgments and award damages on the basis of fairness curtailed. Once all this had been accomplished, legal philosophers who earlier had argued in the name of utility and progress then obscured the resulting changes by arguing that law is neutral, objective, and apolitical.

Why was all this permitted by a people who thought of themselves as living in a democracy? For one thing, the United States did not introduce universal male suffrage until the 1850s, that is, until *after* the new legal structures had been established. But perhaps the best explanation lies in the fact that the law was being shaped to benefit the dynamic property groups in the American economy. It suited the needs of an industrial capitalism and it was difficult to argue against the seemingly plausible assumption that economic growth was good for everyone. And those for whom it wasn't good—small manufacturers, small retailers, small farmers, consumers, and workers—were too weak and disorganized to do much about it.

*M.J. Horwitz, *The Transformation of American Law, 1780–1860* (Cambridge, MA: Harvard University Press, 1977).

do little research into the legal system as such. The legal field, like medicine, is succumbing to bigness. The United States, says Bok, has far more lawyers than any other industrialized society, not only channelling huge numbers of able people away from fields in which they are needed, but once in place these lawyers (like surplus surgeons) create work whether needed or not. The legal system caters to the rich and powerful and neglects the interests of the middle class and the poor. Law schools have done little to counter all this—legal education, or learning how to think like a lawyer, means memorizing unique cases and knowing how to find variations in detail. Teaching students to think like lawyers, argues Bok, "has helped to produce a legal system that is among the most expensive and least efficient in the world." Ironically, concludes Bok, "the blunt inexcusable fact is that this nation, which prides itself on its efficiency and justice, has developed a legal system that is the most expensive in the world, yet cannot manage to protect the rights of most its citizens."

Though one must be careful to balance conflict and functional perspectives when assessing the law, it is probably best to assume that the main consequence of law is to uphold the status quo. This is especially important for Americans to remember because their legal tradition tends to depict law as the cutting edge of freedom, progress, and reform. Most Americans and certainly most upper-level Americans have an image of American society as an arena of free behavior bounded by a framework of impartial, commonly accepted legal rules. However, in recent years the most creative work in the sociology of law has been to view law and legal behavior from a conflict rather than a functional perspective. Perhaps the best way to understand the conflict perspective is to assume that legal rights are often empty formalities and that legal reform is more likely to modernize power relations than to change them.

MIDDLE-CLASS VALUES AND DEVIANCE

Class, Universal Goals, and Deviant Behavior

Sociologists have long recognized that a great deal, if not most, of deviant (abnormal) behavior is caused by the normal demands society places on its members. Conforming or trying to conform to social norms is, in other words, the prime cause of nonconformity. Perhaps the most ironic characteristic of American society is the way in which its rationalistic culture produces nonrational and irrational behavior. The American achievement ethic monopolizes the definition of identity (economic success) and stipulates the means to achieve it (the Protestant-bourgeois virtues).[2] When this moral universalism is promulgated within a deeply structured class system, which by definition cannot allow all to be successful, there are generated social pressures for individuals to acquire success illegitimately (innovation, basically crime) or to compensate for the lack of success (ritualism and retreatism). Robert Merton's depiction of the five ways in which people can respond to cultural goals and the institutional means for achieving them is illustrated in Table 16–1.

Society's response to deviant behavior (categories II–V in Table 16–1) is to pass laws, often of a type that make the deviance criminal. Innovation and rebellion are heavily criminalized, and if one thinks of some forms of vagrancy, gambling, and drugtaking as retreatism, it too has been criminalized. (Ritualism is heavily stigmatized and ridiculed morally by means of such epithets as *parasite, hack, bureaucrat, pencil-pusher,* and the like.) In sum, the deviant American is no aberration of human nature but an outcome of identifiable social variables.

Middle-Class Morality and the Creation of Crime

As we have suggested, middle-class morality and its legalization is a prime source of crime. To understand this process, one must view crime as a socially defined act, rather than as an intrinsic thing-in-itself. Illustrations of the sociocultural context of crime are easy to cite. In ancient Athens, Socrates' free thinking was judged criminal; in the United States freedom of thought is a constitutional right. A prime example of the creation of crime through the legalization of a moral position is Prohibition. A rural-religious

TABLE 16–1 The Five Modes of Adjustment in a Class-Stratified Society to a Universal Success Goal[a]

		UNIVERSAL GOAL OF SUCCESS	ACCEPTABLE METHODS OF ACHIEVING SUCCESS	PREDICTABLE RESPONSES IN A STRATIFIED SOCIETY
I	Conformity	+	+	Diligent, law-abiding citizens, dynamic Protestant-bourgeois achievers
II	Innovation	+	–	White- & blue-collar criminals
III	Ritualist	–	+	Formalism among elites, uncreative majority
IV	Retreatist	–	–	Dropping out, alcoholism, mental illness, suicide
V	Rebellion	±	±	Revolutionary middle class in past, socialist today

[a]Symbol equivalents are: (+) signifies acceptance, (–) signifies elimination, and (±) signifies rejection and substitution of new goals and standards.

Source: Adapted from Robert K. Merton, "Social Structure and Anomie," *American Sociological Review* 3 (October 1938): 676. Examples of predictable responses are mine.

middle-class movement, whose morality differed from that of the urban middle class, the lower classes, and even the upper class, succeeded in outlawing the use of alcoholic beverages, and during the 1920s the United States experienced a great deal of crime as Americans in large numbers circumvented Prohibition.

Middle-class morality—heavily influenced by biopsychic explanations, agrarian values, nationalism, and religion—has at one time or another come to view a large assortment of behavior as immoral, and consequently made it illegal. Middle-class sexual morality, for example, has in combination with other forces made abortion, birth control, and various sexual values and practices (homosexuality, pornography, prostitution) criminal offenses. Middle-class morality's emphasis on work and productivity also gave rise to vagrancy laws, which defined certain forms of idleness and poverty as criminal offenses. The liberal emphasis on self-control and belief in a rational, predictable universe led to laws that treat gambling, alcoholism, and drug use as criminal offenses.

The need to lengthen the period of youth and to keep the statuses of young people abstract, so that they can be kept abreast of new knowledge and prepared for new and more demanding occupations, has enhanced the potential for deviant behavior among the male young in industrial society. Anthony M. Platt has charged that upper-middle-class reformers (mostly women) invented the concept of *juvenile delinquency* and the judicial process that regulates it largely to protect their own values. According to Platt, many forms of youthful behavior have been labeled delinquent that are innocent enough and unindictable when engaged in by adults. Furthermore, this reform movement helped to consolidate the paternalistic and dependent legal status from which youth still suffer.[3]

Thus, it is difficult to escape the conclusion that crime is largely a product of society and its power groups, a view attested to by the history of criminal law. A good example of the way in which power groups translate their interests and values into law is the English law of vagrancy. In 1349 the first vagrancy statute made it a crime for any citizen to give charity to the unemployed and for unemployed persons to refuse to work for anyone who requested their labor. Quite clearly, this law was passed on behalf of landowners who were losing their supply of cheap labor to competition from a growing commercial and manufacturing town economy; in short, it was intended as a substitute for serfdom. When no longer needed, the law became dormant, only to be revived after 1500 in an effort to control the growing crime problem. The association of idleness (lack of employment) with crime persisted into modern times in both Great Britain and the United States.[4]

The image of society as an arena of free behavior bounded by a static framework of impartial legal rules is a serious error. The law is always biased in favor of power groups, and all behavior is bounded, molded, and defined by law. A society that encourages self-interest, defines identity in terms of middle-class ideals, stigmatizes old ways of doing things, and constantly creates new opportunities to get ahead, often at the expense of others—in short, a dynamic industrial-urban society that separates the individual from control by the family, neighborhood, church, or work group—must rely increasingly on explicit legal norms and specialized structures (police, courts, prisons, regulatory commissions, schools) to ensure social control. And this reliance on law results in overcriminalization, which enhances the power of law-related professions and organizations, both public and private, and creates vested interests in legal solutions to social problems.

WHITE-COLLAR CRIME: BUSINESSPEOPLE

Sociologically speaking, a crime is any violation of a legal norm punishable by the state. But such a definition raises numerous problems. Why are some violations of law not punished? Why is it that some violations of the law are punished but not considered crimes by the lawbreaker, his or her peers, or the general public? Why are various types of crime and of lawbreakers dealt with quite differently by law enforcement agencies? As we will see, the answers to these questions require an understanding of social class.

In a classic study, Edwin H. Sutherland drew attention to a major form of crime that had escaped the label of crime. Sutherland called this form of illegal behavior "white-collar crime," and defined it approximately "as a crime committed by a person of respectability and high social status in the course of his occupation."[5] He focused his discussion of overlooked crime on corporate business, saying little about the professions. Though the concept of white-collar crime initially evoked considerable controversy, it has achieved widespread general acceptance among criminologists and related professions.[6] Sutherland's conclusions (paraphrased below) about the nature of big business criminality—which is only one aspect of white-collar crime—are quite interesting:

1. Criminality among corporations is persistent; repeaters are as common here as in ordinary crime.
2. Illegal behavior at this level is much more extensive than is indicated by complaints and prosecutions.
3. Businesspersons who violate the law do not lose status among their associates, since a violation of the legal code is not a violation of the business code.[7]
4. Crime by businesspeople is organized crime, entered into deliberately and in skillful cooperation with others. Criminal businesspeople are also like other criminals (for example, the professional thief) in that they are contemptuous of law, government, and government personnel. Such businesspeople, however, do not look upon themselves as criminals (here they differ from the profes-

sional thief), nor are they looked upon as such by the general public. Businesspeople accept the designation "law violator" but on the whole their policy is to profess adherence to law publicly and to make defections from it in secret. While the professional thief must hide his identity, the white-collar criminal must hide the fact of crime. Secrecy is possible under the umbrella provided by lawyers, deceptive corporate structures and practices (especially against a divided, weak public), and public relations experts.[8]

Sutherland's insights can help us to answer the questions we raised earlier, which can now be rephrased as follows: Why are there such variations in the views on crime of members of the same society? Or, in other words, why was it possible for Sutherland to make a genuinely creative contribution to criminology by pointing out that members of the upper classes who break the law should be called criminals?

Ordinary or lower-class crime is more visible and more easily translated into personal terms than white-collar crime. It involves personal loss and violence, which makes it memorable and emotionally evocative. But ordinary crime does not cost as much as white-collar crime; in fact, the money costs of white-collar crime are infinitely higher. And the differential in moral costs is just as large: white-collar crime invariably involves a violation of trust, and if prestige is bestowed on crime by middle-class individuals (and eventually on lawbreaking in general), the bases of social respectability and authority could be undermined.

Conceivably, the illegal behavior of people in positions of prestige and authority could be defined as crime, and their reputations and positions could become tarnished. The reasons why this has not happened should be clear. While Sutherland's demand that lawbreaking by the high and mighty be called crime has been heeded by criminologists and some related professions, society-at-large has ignored his commonsense judgment. The illegal behavior of people in high social positions is still not seen as identical to the illegal behavior of those in inferior social positions. Robert K. Merton has outlined the nature of this moral hypocrisy in his essay "The Self-Fulfilling Prophecy,"[9] and one of his illustrations is particularly apt: a Jew who studies hard is labeled a grind and a grade-grubber, but a non-Jew who exhibits the same behavior is regarded as intelligent, studious, and ambitious. Similarly, when doctors control the supply of people who go into medicine, they are a professional association; when manual workers do the same thing, they are engaged in a restrictive labor practice. When wealthy, politically influential, and respectable people receive public money, it takes the forms of price supports, grants, tax benefits, or low-cost interest rates; when the lowly and despised receive public money it is called welfare, a handout, or something for nothing. The relevance of this point to the definition of criminal behavior is clear. Behavior has no meaning until society (its power groups) defines it. It is clear that our class-prestige structure, while not strong enough to prevent the passage of laws detrimental to the interests of the upper classes, has managed to keep the lawbreaking of the upper classes from being associated with that of the lower classes. Crime, in other words, has been successfully defined as something the lower classes do. There is no more dramatic example of the pervasive and powerful influence of the American class system.[10]

The double standard is partly explained by the fact that the various classes commit different types of crime. Compared to middle-class youth, for example, youngsters from the lower classes seem to engage more in gainful crime and to be more violent and destructive.[11] Similarly, working-class and lower-class adult criminals commit different types of crime and use different techniques than do their middle-class counterparts. But neither these differences nor differences in the rates of crime and arrest at various class levels are sufficient to explain why we do not equate lawbreaking behavior with criminal behavior at all levels of society. They do not explain why we tend to define the teenage middle-class lawbreaker as a "problem child" and the teenage lower-class lawbreaker as a delinquent. The only satisfactory explanation is the power of class over our perception of reality, a power to which the universality and majesty of both reason and law are subject.[12]

WHITE-COLLAR DEVIANCE: THE PROFESSIONS

Failure to Perform: The Deviance of Unnecessary Incompetence

The professions deviate considerably from their norms and values of competence and service. A simple way to see this is to note that doctors whose education is subsidized by the public then refuse to abide by their agreement to serve in communities that lack doctors. Another example, drawn from the academic disciplines, is deviation in the practice of peer review and journal reviewing (considerable fraud in the form of falsified data escapes detection by reviewers; reviewers are biased against young scholars with nonestablishment views, and many reviews are shoddily done).

The medical profession has a large number of nonperforming doctors and a large number of errors by overworked doctors. Doctors also fail to keep up with effective new remedies, are rendered incompetent by specialization, and employ common American biases in their diagnoses. The legal profession requires excessive education and yet fails to train lawyers to do many of the things that lawyers do. Excessive doses of the wrong kind of education and the failure to train students in the necessaries of their respective lines of work is also characteristic of all Ph.D. and M.B.A. programs.

Fallows and Luttwak report enormous departures from both professionalism and common sense by the military.[13] Admission to higher educational institutions (from undergraduate to graduate and professional schools) is quite removed from the idea of academic merit and achievement. Ninety percent of American institutions of higher education are noncompetitive and the remaining schools make many exceptions to favor alumni and athletes, and to accommodate minorities.

Unnecessary incompetence is also present in the case of educators who persist, despite mountains of evidence to the contrary, in trying to reform education from the inside using traditional ideals. Unnecessary incompetence is also characteristic of the academic disciplines, especially those that have had ample opportunity to show what they can do, for example, economics and psychology. Deviance here is both by individuals and aggregates and by the professional organizations that have accepted the responsibility for service and performance.

Unnecessary incompetence can be approached in terms of professional stereotyping that continues despite having known harmful effects. David Sudnow was one of the first to expose public defenders, lawyers who employ negative stereotypes about their clients from the lower classes, use typical crimes to categorize defendants, and who then negotiate convictions on this basis. In return for more lenient sentencing, the public defender does not criticize the law enforcement system for violating rights, breaking the law, or ignoring the interests of the wider community.[14]

Thomas J. Scheff extended Sudnow's finding that public defenders rely on typical or normal cases to define individual defendants to other problem areas: disease, welfare, probation and parole, divorce, adoption, police handling of juveniles, and mental health.[15] Scheff argues that the more numerous the stereotypes the more likely that they will fit the individuals experiencing problems. The validity of stereotyping declines when the clients are members of marginal classes or racial and ethnic groups (patients that have money can negotiate about their diagnosis).

Since these promising beginnings a great deal has been learned about professional stereotyping, though there has been no systematic research. We know that the sighted have used false definitions of blindness, thus denying the blind opportunities to lead far fuller lives.[16] We know that doctors use different images of health for men and women, on the one hand, and overlook distinctive female medical problems by *not* being biased in the direction of their distinctive biological processes and medical histories. One of the most flagrant examples of professional ineffectiveness is in mental health. And it is only recently that we have begun to understand that universalism in professional practice and the *absence* of ethnic and racial stereotyping may *retard* professional performance in medicine, psychological therapy, law, and social work.[17]

The expression "unnecessary incompetence" implies that professionals are making mistakes through inadvertence, habit, and deficiencies in their education. Even the large number of biases in the various academic disciplines (with the exception of fraud) can be thought of as accumulation of unintentional mistakes over time. One could interpret incompetence in the professions as a need to reform their educations or improve their practices. But incompetence is so pervasive and persistent that one cannot but suspect that professional incompetence is institutional and systematic, that is, a result of illegitimate power. This can be seen clearly in the way in which American power groups create false realities.

The Systematic Creation of False Realities

Earlier we reported on false crime waves that appear at budget and election time. We also reported that politically biased information (for example, from government) is routinely reported by journalists as objective fact (for both, see "Framing the News" in Chapter 10). Persistent failure in foreign policy does not produce changes in policy.[18] A continuous stream of reports citing basic flaws in the Department of Defense's procurement practices produces no reforms. Systematic and persistent exaggeration of Soviet strength created a false reality that was transparent to many knowledgeable analysts. The U.S. Corps of Engineers has a long history of unrealistic cost estimates based on obviously unreal interest rates. The Federal Bureau of Investigation collects crime data and reports to Congress in a way that puts the Bureau in the best light and makes it impossible for Congress to monitor its activities.[19] Advertising and public relations specialists, along with political consultants, form a cluster of professionals who systematically create and maintain false realities.

Creating false realities is not an isolated act by rotten apples, nor is it merely typical of the various professions (which it is). Each of the above examples benefits other groups besides the creative deviant. Congress and defense contractors were part of the wasteful system of military procurement and the exaggeration of Soviet strength. Local and state governments, along with farmers and real estate developers, are quite willing to go along with unrealistic cost estimates by the U.S. Corps of Engineers. Many in Congress and outside were more than willing to give the FBI a free hand. Creating false realities, therefore, is not a random collection of discrete acts easily rooted out or amenable to long range forces like science and education.

To understand the process of creating false realities fully, however, one must see not only that they produce results (crime-fighting budgets rise, products sell), but that the false becomes true (we arm because we believe the USSR is strong, causing it to arm, causing us to arm further, and so on). Education affords striking examples of how false realities emerge from a deeply entrenched, self-perpetuating power relation that remains invisible partly because its falsehoods become empirically true. Educators, along with most of the upper classes, believe that education can identify the talented through IQ tests, grades, and diplomas, and that the best educated will make corresponding contributions to the economy and polity. As we saw in Chapter 9, however, behavior in school (by aggregates) has no positive relation to behavior outside school. Why do myths persist? As long ago as 1970, Ivar Berg, summarizing research in this area, found no positive relation between education and various aspects of work behavior, including productivity.[20] In a major work, Samuel Bowles and Herbert Gintis[21] also pointed out that education did not have a positive relation to economic behavior, a fact (anomaly) that since has been substantiated many times over. Yet the belief that education is a potent problem solver continues undiminished. Why?

Bowles and Gintis supplied a possible answer—they argued that false beliefs are part of a class society reproducing itself. Simply put, employers hire those with good academic records falsely believing that they make better workers, thus making it appear that education has positive results for the economy. Those who succeed then send their children to school, where they succeed academically, and the progress repeats itself. The fact that this process continues despite being repeatedly exploded by empirical research means that we are dealing with a fundamental part of the American power structure.

Remember in all this that we are dealing with a variety of power groups: the state (public schools), the voluntary sector (state-certified private schools), employers, and the politically potent families of the upper classes. The creation of false realities goes far beyond merely distinguishing between inferior and superior students. Mercer has shown that schools actually create inferior students with help by other state agencies. And Carrier has shown that biased professional and political judgments create much of what is called *learning disability*.[22]

Betraying Clients: Crimes by Professionals (and Other Elites) Against Individuals, Groups, and the Public

Deviance by the professions also consists of violations of law, the commission of white-collar crime. White-collar crime is many-sided and can refer to pilferage by employees of retail stores, or to crimes by small businesses (for example, arson to collect insurance). But its most important form, both in money and impact on public morality, is crime by highly placed executives and professionals who steal from their businesses (embezzlement), use business to defraud the public (price fixing, adulterated or counterfeited products), steal from clients (securities fraud), defraud the government (doctors and Medicare-Medicaid, the Pentagon and defense contractors), or steal from other businesses (industrial espionage, patent fraud, stealing fashion designs, kickbacks, bribery, payoffs in the construction business).

An interesting background note on crime by elites is that much of it is committed by those that set their own incomes. Executives of large corporations and doctors are two prime examples. This practice bespeaks a larger autonomy that is fertile ground for crime. Doctors engage in a wide variety of questionable practices. Some own testing and pharmaceutical companies and thus stand to benefit from overtesting and overreliance on drugs. Doctors break the law and their service oath by not reporting diseases and disabilities caused by the corporations they work for. Doctors fail to report cases of child and spouse abuse.

The medical profession (a small number of doctors) also defrauds the government, insurance companies, and patients of very large sums of money—more than all the money stolen by the lower classes put together.[23] Lawyers (again, not all of them or even most) also violate canons of trust in a variety of ways. Accountants are guilty of giving false audits to benefit themselves and client firms. Accountants, lawyers, and financial planners, who advise clients on investments, sometimes accept fees from those who are selling investment instruments, a fertile field for collusion. Professionals who are entrusted with the finances of others also engage in large-scale embezzlement from individuals (the elderly, widows, heirs, and ordinary investors) and from organizations (pension funds, corporations, banks, and so on).

Brokers and brokerage firms "churn" their accounts (excessive buying and selling) to earn unwarranted fees. They also engage in insider trading, the use of information garnered from one side of their professional role used to benefit themselves and others in another side of their role.[24]

Interesting cases of betrayal of public trust arise in government. The Atomic Energy Commission, now called the Nuclear Regulatory Commission, was commissioned to both promote and regulate nuclear energy. Its history is one of promoting nuclear energy and neglecting nuclear safety.

The U.S. Department of the Treasury is the trustee of Social Security funds and is also a large-scale borrower. The Department consistently lends itself Social Security funds at the lowest interest rates (making the government look better, protecting the taxpayer, but also favoring private investors and neglecting its pension obligations).

The betrayal of trust is widespread in government, as discussed in the next section, which analyzes cooperation among the powerful to betray the public.

COLLUSION AMONG THE POWERFUL AND NEAR-POWERFUL

Many white-collar crimes represent criminal alliances among powerful groups; for example, kickbacks, bribery, and payoffs in the construction business often involve the architect, contractor, labor unions, workers, government inspectors, and the owners of the building. White-collar crime connects with street crime as banks launder ill-gotten gains from drug sales and other crimes. White-collar criminals keep abreast of the latest technology; for example, they use the computer to steal money from banks or information from whoever has it. White-collar crime involves the failure to enforce antitrust laws, banking laws, environmental laws, and civil rights laws. It means government officials biasing decisions in favor of companies they will eventually work for. It means criminal networks involving city and state officials, businesses, professions, and police and law enforcement officials.

White-collar crime occurs on a wide scale because the United States relies heavily on voluntary adherence to legal, ethical, and moral norms by powerful groups, or rather, it has been persuaded by these groups, who hide behind fictional notions of pluralism and competition, that this is the way society should be run. When capitalism arose, it developed extensive relations among strangers and these relations have continued to grow. Relations among strangers require new social-control techniques, including laws, ethical codes, and personalized morality. But the most important of these, law, has lagged badly as enterprising economic and professional groups commit new crimes out of developing opportunities much faster than the politically organized public can keep up with. Even when laws appear, they are not enforced because government represents the powerful, not the American people. Much of that representation (our executive, judicial, and legislative branches of government) is itself a result of crime and other deviant behavior.

White-collar crime by elites takes place in all developed capitalist societies, but evidence points to the United States as the leader. Insight into this unique status can be gleaned by noting that the United States provides huge subsidies to the upper classes, including the professions and disciplines, but unlike other capitalist societies, there is little monitoring by government to see to it that elites use subsidies for the purposes intended. (For the contrast between how the professions arose in the United States and all other societies, see "The Unique Rise and Unaccountability of the American Professions," in Chapter 6.)

Perhaps the greatest weakness in the American control system, therefore, is the widespread use of fiduciary or trust norms, the almost universal reliance on voluntary compliance to law, ethics, and professional codes. This, of course, is the other side of the laissez-faire coin (or reliance on abstract markets) to achieve social goals, including the control of powerful groups. What makes this a structurally defective system can be seen most clearly by remembering the enormous encouragement of self-interest.

Reliance on voluntarism and unmonitored trust relations is like hiring foxes to protect the chicken house. Reliance on abstract markets and the good behavior of the powerful represent an admission that we have given up trying to figure out how to run an industrial society that yields multiple values. Rather than tackling the trade-offs that should be made about conflicting values, American power groups have opted for anomie, that is, an abstract commitment to one value (economic growth and success) and a faith in abstract markets.

So far are we from recognizing this structural flaw that we have actually reenergized our commitment to it. The Carter administration began a process of deregulation in the late 1970s and this was accelerated by the Reagan administration, which acted legally and illegally (that is, it was itself a deviant, perhaps the most deviant federal government in U.S. history) to reduce government oversight of one basic sector of the economy after another. One result was the most colossal scandal in American history, the savings and loan bank debacle in which hundreds of billions of dollars were lost to fraud and deviance from accepted norms of prudent banking. The scandal is much larger if one includes the huge losses in the commercial banking and insurance business. What all these deviant businesses have in common is the use of other people's money on trust, combined with lax government supervision. It is not enough to refer to this as being somehow connected to finance capitalism or to blame the Reagan administration. The mid-1990s saw another strong drive by the Republican party, in collaboration with conservative Democrats, to enfeeble the federal government's ability to protect workers, consumers, and the environment.

The culture of American-style capitalism obscures the danger of allowing powerful groups to go unchecked; it does this by depoliticizing power relations and by relying on hollow control processes (markets, voluntarism, capitalist governments, that is, governments derived, for one thing, from elections that reflect money). A naive reliance on voluntary compliance to law is pervasive throughout the economy (for example, oil industry, safety laws, hospitals, Medicare, airline manufacturers, drug companies), and fiduciary relations are fundamental to the professions. Not only do large portions of each of these groups fail to abide by laws, but they often cooperate to provide the multiple skills needed to defraud and otherwise harm the public. For example, the savings and loan scandal required collusion among bank owners, accountants, lawyers, appraisers, architects, real estate developers, investment brokers, bank examiners, and elected officials.[25]

Relying on nonexistent abstract forces to safeguard society is characteristic of all complex societies. From the emergence of universalistic beliefs and norms in feudal-authoritarian society to the present, elites protect themselves, not society, with empty concepts. Perhaps the easiest deviant-producing policy to see and avoid is the type that emerged when the Reagan administration evoked a nonexistent force, the market, to provide housing. Reducing government grants (which were there to make up for the mismatch between the income of large numbers of Americans and the cost of housing) was supposed to spur housing construction, but did the opposite. And by reducing government grants precipitously, misguided policy makers promoted huge amounts of corruption as well. Government grants were in place because construction companies, real-estate developers, banks, architects, and realtors needed them. These businesses and professions were threatened when the grants slumped and fierce competition for the dwindling grants occurred. Faced with bankruptcy by an anomic world constructed out of empty concepts by policy makers, businesses and professions predictably resorted to bribery and other forms of corruption to stay afloat.

White-collar crime is huge and difficult to deal with because it is committed by the powerful and respectable. Combating it requires new laws, the enforcement of old laws, and the training of lawyers and law enforcement officials to deal with both old and new forms of white-collar crime. Above all, it requires a better-run economy and society. In any event, the focus on deviance by middle- and upper-level individuals and by the organizations they head is the most important development in criminology in recent years.

It is not always easy to distinguish between criminal behavior and incompetence. Behind the terrible record of the U.S. Department of Energy's handling of nuclear production for the military, the horrendous hemorrhaging of public funds in the savings and loan debacle, and other shortfalls involving professionals is secrecy and preferential access by power groups to governmental and legislative officials.[26]

Violation of Anti-Trust, Consumer, and Environmental Laws

Perhaps the most important white-collar crime is violation of antitrust law, something that requires the help of legislators and government officials. Corporations engage in collusive price-fixing and this finds its counterpart in the restrictive labor practices of the various professions and disciplines (organized as professional associations, these groups fix the price of labor by requiring unnecessary education for entry into their respective fields).

Businesses and professions also violate laws protecting consumers, a violation that is systematic and requires the collaboration of government. There is also widespread violation of environmental laws, which also requires help from the government. An interesting and neglected aspect of collusion by the powerful to violate law and the environment is the long history of competition between the U.S. Corps of Engineers and the U.S. Reclamation Service to see which could do the most to upset the way nature wanted water distributed in the western United States (not to mention their mistakes and illegalities elsewhere). In a word, the entire social structure of California and much of the rest of the West and Southwest is based on water distribution by dams or pumped from a giant aquifer (a natural underground reservoir accumulated over tens of thousands of years) underlying seven states. The dams have a limited life expectancy (because of silting) and the aquifer is being exhausted. Much of the long history of building dams and encouraging development is premised on a long-term supply of water that is probably not forthcoming. The government agencies involved have not been controllable by law, largely because their interests coincide with the interests of private business (farmers, ranchers, real estate developers, industry) and publicly elected and appointed public officials.[27]

Collusion in Defense Contracting

A varied group of professionals (military specialists, accountants, lawyers, engineers, researchers, Congressional policy analysts, and intelligence specialists) collaborate in an intricate process of defense contracting. The interrelations among the Department of Defense, Congress, and giant defense contractors has been called an *iron triangle.*[28] Gordon Adams's case study of eight of these contractors reveals a world in which the federal government and Congress enjoy a tight, often secretive relation with each other and with military contractors in violation of basic American norms and values (including the violation of legal norms). Defense contracts are noncompetitive, and in addition to their wasteful cost-plus basis, they include many hidden subsidies. There is a revolving door of personnel from the Pentagon to defense contractors and vice-versa. There is a questionable emphasis on high-technology weapon systems and a neglect of conventional weapons and combat readiness. And the general public is excluded from participation in the formulation of defense policy. The iron triangle caused a huge drain on national resources and contributed to America's economic woes of the past decades.

Of special interest in assessing the power of this network of groups and professionals is that it has successfully survived numerous reports severely critical of its practices and demanding reforms. Even the end of the Cold War in 1990 did not bring an end to this power complex. In 1995–1996, defense spending remained at levels far higher than anything required by national security.

Collusion in Education

Public programs to support higher education are ways for legislators and elected officials to curry favor with important constituencies (the parents of students, administrators, academic and applied sciences in all areas, and so on). But support is given in abstract terms (education is a good thing), with few questions asked about results. As happens in all problem areas, instead of defining the problem accurately, new "professionals" and new agencies are developed to create the facade of problem solving: for example, financial aid officers (complete with an association and journal) and agencies specializing in student loans.

Federal aid to local government to support education in poor districts appeared in the 1960s but never worked as intended. Clearly earmarked by Congress for poor districts, state legislators and government used the funds to aid all districts, thus keeping relative positions intact.

The widespread fraud and failure to produce is most apparent in the for-profit vocational schools. Many studies going back many years have reported the same dreary message to no avail. Banks make publicly guaranteed and subsidized loans without evaluating the schools that students will attend. Vocational schools are accredited by agencies that receive their income from the schools being accredited. Federal and state governments, despite one critical report after the other, continue to subsidize flagrant fraud and utter ineffectiveness.

THE CLASS NATURE OF LAW ENFORCEMENT

There is a vast difference between the ways in which the law is enforced against the white-collar criminal and against the ordinary criminal.[29] One need only compare the treatment of antitrust violators with the way in which law is enforced in a black ghetto to appreciate this point. White-collar criminals have fewer dealings with the police than do ordinary criminals; they are arrested less often; and, if arrested, they are rarely subject to pretrial detention.

Another such variation is the selective manner in which laws are enforced, which seems to be related to class. A classic example is urban renewal legislation, all the provisions of which are eagerly obeyed save the requirement that dispossessed families be relocated. Strenuous efforts are made to combat ordinary crime, but the development and enforcement of laws to protect the consumer and to stimulate competition are less than enthusiastic. It is well known that better police protection and public services are usually available in middle- and upper-class neighborhoods than in working- and lower-class areas. But the strong are protected in other ways too. Embezzlement laws, which protect the powerful against the weak, were quickly and easily passed when this form of theft first made its appearance. And the Securities and Exchange Commission is, despite its many failings, perhaps the most effective fiduciary structure among the various regulatory commissions. Also striking is the lack of enthusiasm with which the constitutional rights of black Americans are enforced against lawbreaking southern officials and safety laws are enforced against industries and business.[30]

Until recently, public programs of consumer protection were largely ineffective.[31] Consumer problems obviously vary with class level: the lower classes are affected more by the price of food than by the prices of swimming pools or single-family residences. Similarly, the lower classes are affected less by laws designed to protect wilderness areas or establish national parks than the classes above them. Even the routine operation of our courts tends to be biased against the lower classes. For example, members of the lower classes are systematically cheated by an assortment of white-collar criminals and subjected to deceptive advertising, defective goods, tricky contracts, and shoddy services. Not only do they have little chance of legal redress, but the law is actually used against them to enforce tricky contracts, garnishee wages, and collect debts.[32]

THE CLASS NATURE OF LEGAL SERVICES AND THE ADMINISTRATION OF JUSTICE

The Anglo-American legal system reflects the core values of society-at-large. The liberal presumption of the inherent validity of individual action is paralleled by the legal assumption that an individual is innocent until the state proves otherwise. The liberal dichotomy between the individual and society is echoed throughout the judicial process, most dramatically in the standard phrase "The People v. the Defendant." That court proceedings are competitive is obviously related to the liberal belief that competition is good for society. Under the Anglo-Saxon adversary system, it is assumed that justice (like better mousetraps and cheaper pig iron) will result if lawyers engage in combat under the eye of a referee, the judge. Another parallel is that justice must be purchased in much the same way as are food and clothing; thus, lawyers must be hired and court expenses and fees paid for before justice is done.[33] The reliability of the accused is also gauged by money (the bail system), and punishment is quite often monetary (the payment of a fine). And the law still assumes, despite modifications, that individuals cause their own behavior. The law is also still centered on the pleasure-pain principle of early liberal psychology in which it is assumed that clear-cut rewards (probation, parole, trustee positions, TV and exercise privileges) and punishments (imprisonment, execution, withdrawal of privileges, solitary confinement) serve as effective incentives and deterrents.

It is not surprising that the parallel between our judicial system and liberal society extends to the relation between law and the class system as well. Indeed, the emphasis on money produces a deep class bias throughout the judicial system. Legal services are performed primarily on behalf of the middle and upper classes, and especially of their most wealthy and powerful elements.[34] Many types of contract favor the rich and powerful, the myth of voluntary equal bargaining notwithstanding.[35] Those with money do not, as we have said, suffer pretrial detention, and if convicted are often given the option of sacrificing money rather than freedom. Class also determines what a life is worth legally (see Box 16–2). And even the jury system

BOX 16–2 *What is a Life Worth? It Depends on Who You Work For*

The lawyers for Philip D. Estridge want Delta Air Lines to pay his estate $25 million for an accident that took his life. Delta acknowledged responsibility but disputed the amount of compensation. Lawyers produced witnesses saying that Mr. Estridge, forty-seven, had many productive and lucrative years ahead of him as a high-ranking executive for IBM. The chances are that the Estridge estate will get a sum somewhere in the vicinity of $25 million while most of the other victims in the plane crash will get less than 5 percent of that sum. Incidentally, the Estridge lawyers also wanted $5 million for Mrs. Estridge's estate, but it was not clear why her life was worth that amount.

reflects class forces—for one thing, the jury system is shunned by defendants from the lower classes, suggesting that they regard a trial by their peers as unobtainable. We know very little about the class composition of juries, but prodding by the United States Supreme Court has prompted efforts to curtail the use of flagrantly unrepresentative juries. However, even juries chosen at random and representing a cross-section of the class structure do not guarantee that deliberations will be conducted by equals. One of the rare studies of a jury system that has relevance for class analysis found that jurors of higher occupational status were selected more as foremen, participated more in discussion, had more influence, derived more satisfaction, and were perceived as more qualified for jury duty than jurors from lower occupations.[36]

In general, acquittals, favorable sentences, and commutations of sentence are contingent on the skill of one's lawyer, which is in turn contingent on money. Mere representation by a lawyer does not ensure equal justice. One study has shown that among those convicted of murder, especially African Americans, defendants with court-appointed counsel were less likely to have their executions commuted. Among blacks, those with private counsel were more likely to have their executions commuted. And sentencing itself varies in regard to identical offenses: drunkenness is a classic instance where social position is a strong determinant of differential sentencing.[37] Where upper- and lower-class juveniles commit identical offenses, differential treatment and sentencing also appear. And restitution for a wrongful death is explicitly based on the decedent's class position; damages are computed on the basis of his or her projected lifetime income. But type of crime in general is so geared to class that it is difficult to establish class bias in sentencing. Data showing that the indigent plead guilty more, are convicted more often, receive probation less often, and so on, while suggestive, do not automatically add up to class bias; the various classes commit different crimes, are involved in crime at different rates, and present a different problem for sentencing and rehabilitation.

The Supreme Court's guarantee of due process to all, especially its controversial *Gideon, Escobedo,* and *Miranda* decisions, has done little to change the class character of justice.[38] Formally, due process means among other things that accused individuals are entitled to free lawyers, trials, and appeals if they are too poor to pay their own expenses, and to the right to remain silent and have a lawyer present at all stages of their dealings with the state. This new interpretation of due process, and the Court's determination to invalidate confessions and other evidence obtained illegally, has been hailed by some as rebalancing the relation between the individual and the state and condemned by others as contributing to the breakdown of law and order. But the real significance of these rulings seems to be to affirm the validity of our traditional adversary system of justice and reassert the traditional liberal view that the individual and the government are enemies. The general power of class over justice is not curtailed; an economic floor has simply been placed under the class system of justice to prevent the poor from being bypassed altogether.

There is no doubt that these rulings curtail shoddy and illegal behavior on the part of some law enforcement officials. But the administration of criminal justice differs markedly from the images conjured by these rulings and by those who applaud or condemn them. Despite these rulings, most crime in the United States will continue to go undetected and unpunished, rates of arrests will not change, rates of confession will continue at previous levels, and the overwhelming majority of defendants (mostly individuals from the lower classes) will continue to plead guilty. In other words, the reality of criminal justice is not the adversary system (or competition between legal entrepreneurs), abstract rights, or solemn pronouncements. The key to understanding criminal justice is the expression "the administration of justice." There exists a vast system of "bargain justice" in which judges, prosecutors, and private and public defense attorneys negotiate punishment to avoid trials. As Donald J. Newman argues, the idea of bargaining is at odds with a legal process based on facts and rules of evidence, favors the experienced criminal over the first offender, and promotes a general disrespect for law.[39] This assembly-line system of justice is a jerry-built construct created by judges, court officials, probation officers, court psychiatrists, prosecutors, and defense lawyers. As Abraham S. Blumberg points out, the Supreme Court's rulings upholding the rights of the accused have had the ironic result of enriching the resources of this existing organizational and professional arrangement by providing for a more efficient way of eliciting guilty pleas from defendants.[40]

The administration of justice in the realm of civil law is also heavily weighted against the lower classes. In general, members of the lower classes rarely use the machinery of the law on their own behalf, though they have many legal problems (and legal rights). Our legal institutions assume middle-class status: to benefit from the law in practice, one must be educated, informed about one's rights, comfortable in a world of specialization and impersonality, able to take initiative, and, of course, affluent. Members of the lower classes are thus by definition beyond the scope of law as an operational right.

But the law by no means ignores the lower classes, and its impact is not limited to differential treatment by the police and courts in criminal cases. It is no exaggeration to say that the power dimension supplies one set of legal procedures and even of laws for the lower classes and another set of procedures and laws for the upper classes. Three distinct types of differential treatment of the upper and lower classes in substantive and procedural law have been identified: favored parties, dual law (*de jure* denial of equal protection), and *de facto* denial of equal protection.[41] The law favors landlords over tenants and lenders over borrowers; of course, the favored parties in such cases tend to enjoy higher class status than their adversaries. Dual law for the lower and upper classes characterizes the realms of family law and welfare law.[42] When they concern the lower classes, divorce, property settlements, and support relations are handled as public matters to ensure the smallest cost to the public; when they concern the upper classes, such cases are treated as civil matters pertaining to private individuals. Law and legal philosophy also differ with regard to government benefits for the lower classes (public assistance, unemployment insurance, public housing) and the upper classes (licenses, loans, subsidies, contracts). *De facto* bias means that equal application of law works to the detriment of the lower classes. Impartially applied restrictive abortion and divorce laws actually favor the upper classes; acceptance of common law market precepts ("let the buyer beware") works to the disadvantage of the lower classes in economic transactions. The draft law burdens the lower classes inequitably, since they are less likely to have exempt occupations or to be college students. In general, Jerome E. Carlin, Jan Howard, and Sheldon L. Messinger observe, "the law itself serves to define and maintain the position of the poor."[43]

Implicit in these substantive differences between the law of the upper classes and the law of the lower classes are sharp differences in legal procedure. The assembly-line system of justice routinizes, standardizes, and processes a vast percentage of all legal cases involving the lower classes. There is a pronounced tendency to employ criminal proceedings in welfare and family cases involving the lower classes. And the lower classes are treated as wards of the state on the presumption that they are incompetent and that the interests of the state are in harmony with their interests.

The courts that deal with the lower classes tend to dispense with procedural safeguards: they do not give notice; they fail to observe rules of evidence; they are characterized by a lack of genuine adversariness; and they tend to delegate decisions to such nonlegal personnel as probation officers, psychiatrists, and social workers, which results in confusion and diffusion of responsibility. Carlin, Howard, and Messinger also note that the courts for the lower classes are characterized by grossly inadequate resources and least adequately trained and experienced judges and other personnel.

Of course, the net result of this system of mass-production justice is to help create the type of individual the law presumes. The law of the lower classes, in other words, is a self-fulfilling prophecy to the extent that it assumes that people in the lower classes are untrustworthy and incompetent and treats them as such. It is not surprising that, under a regime that deprives them of the opportunity to act as persons, the lower classes see the state and the law as remote and alien phenomena, are suspicious and cynical of its justice, and seem childish and confused. Their experience with the law is consistent with their dealings with authority at home, in schools, at the doctor's or dentist's office, in church, at work, at the unemployment or welfare bureau, and at the employment agency.

The intentions of the state are not in question. That the state "individualizes" justice for juvenile delinquents and the lower classes in an effort to treat all fairly can be taken for granted.[44] But the treatment of some (the upper classes) according to what they do and have and of others (the lower classes) according to who they are is a flagrant violation of the legal theory of the liberal state and contributes heavily to the serious identity problem of the lower classes. According to Carlin, Howard, and Messinger, the ultimate denial of identity by the legal system is that the lower classes are not allowed to mean what they say. Thus, if there is only one possible legal identity—broadly speaking, middle class in nature—those who cannot achieve it must do without a legal identity. (This status rounds out their nonidentity in other areas.) Or, perhaps, to pursue a suggestion by Garfinkel, the successful degradation of the deviant requires the treatment we now give defendants from the lower classes.[45] Whatever the reason for their present treatment, the American legal system would be far different were there equal treatment under law for the upper and lower classes.

THE OBSOLETE DISPUTES ABOUT THE CAUSES OF CRIME

The social causation of crime (and deviance in general) is now accepted by most sociologists.[46] But some sociologists have argued that there is no relation between class and crime because it is widespread at all levels of society.[47] The denial of class-based behavior is widespread in the United States and must be confronted here as elsewhere. The lay public is also aware of lawlessness at all levels of society. Particularly striking are mass media accounts that report that the middle classes (both adults and juveniles) break the law and deviate in other ways in large numbers.

In a careful examination of the literature, John Braithwaite has shown that the empirical evidence clearly establishes a relation between class and crime. The "lower" class (essentially the marginal blue-collar class) commit considerably more juvenile and adult (blue-collar) crime than do the upper classes. One source of confusion in analyzing the class-crime relationship is the failure to distinguish between the crimes of the lower and upper classes. When crimes involving abuse of power and trust (price-fixing, embezzlement, consumer fraud, violation of professional norms, and so on) are analyzed, the class-crime relation also appears in a different form: the upper classes are clearly more criminal than the lower classes.[48]

The denial of a relation between class and crime extends to a denial of unemployment as a cause of crime. In a careful analysis of the data, Theodore Chiricos found a positive relation.[49] And in a finely textured analysis, Allan and Steffensmier found a heavy relation between property-crime arrest rates among male juveniles and young adults and labor market conditions (unemployment, underemployment, and poor job quality).[50]

COMPARATIVE CRIME RATES: THE UNITED STATES AS WORLD LEADER IN CRIME

No comparative data on crime by the upper classes exist, and most intersocietal comparisons have been about blue-collar crime. It is clear that the "lower" class (not poverty class) commits more direct property crime and more violent crime (murder, rape, robbery, assault).[51] As Braithwaite reports, the higher crime rate for these offenses among the lower class also holds for developing and for developed countries outside the United States.

Our most important comparative analysis of crime reveals that the United States has a much higher overall crime rate (2.8 times as high) than do all industrialized countries in the period 1970 to 1975. On a per capita basis, individual crimes are committed approximately three times more frequently in the United States than in other industrialized countries with robbery committed 5.7 times as much. While robbery (an amalgam of property and violent crime) is much more frequent, the overall amount of violent crime is not higher in the United States than elsewhere. The higher crime rate in the United States is largely a post-1945 phenomenon. The United States and other industrializing countries experienced an initial rise in crime, especially violent crime, during the early phase of industrialization and then crime, including violent crime, declined for all. But after following the pattern of other countries for a century, the United States experienced a rapid growth of crime after 1945 to become an international anomaly.[52]

THE OBSOLETE DISPUTES ABOUT CONTROLLING BLUE-COLLAR CRIME

Almost all the disputes about how to deal with crime tend to be about blue-collar crime. Conservatives (right liberals) argue that criminals deserve to be punished, and that swift and stern punishment will deter people from crime. Left liberals argue that punishment has always failed both to deter crime and to reform criminals. During the 1960s significant efforts were made to rehabilitate inmates through job training and other activities. There was also a focus on school and community programs to help the disadvantaged. The judicial system was put on notice to respect the rights of suspects and defendants. But all this failed miserably—the tide of crime rose ever higher. Since the 1970s, right liberals have dominated the discussion of crime. The federal government supplied huge amounts of money for crime-fighting technology and for the development of national and even international cooperation among law enforcement officials. The cry for "law and order" meant more people in jail for longer periods. Various neighborhood watch programs were instituted. Police and schools cracked down on trouble spots and repeat offenders. But stern law-and-order methods also failed—crime continued to rise. By 1994, the United States had the largest number of prison inmates per capita than any other country—a staggering one and one half million, representing a huge overhead expense.

Law enforcement is a complex of many activities, none very successful. As a penal system the failure is well-nigh absolute.[53] Prison doesn't just brutalize inmates (or make them skillful, hardened criminals), it also brutalizes the guards.[54] In its other forms, law enforcement is badly hampered by institutions and socioeconomic policies that create resentment, frustration, and suffering. Law enforcement doesn't work because it is expensive and taxpayers don't want to pay for prisons, prison guards, or even police and the judicial system. One result of the conflict between wanting criminals caught and the refusal to pay for law enforcement is the widespread use of pleabargaining (reduced sentences to save the expense of trials and imprisonment). Law enforcement doesn't work because many law enforcement officials are corrupt and are themselves criminals, often in collaboration with other criminals. Law enforcement doesn't work because it represents a threat to the affluent—strict law enforcement would quickly turn many among the well-to-do and powerful into defendants.[55] And it doesn't work, argues Reiman, because its very design protects not only the criminals in the upper classes but the basic system of capitalism.[56]

Sociologists vary in how they would deal with the fact of crime. Their approaches range from those who advocate prison reform, better-trained police, and an attack on poverty and slums to those who argue that crime can be controlled only by changing the fundamental capitalist system. Most sociologists, however, agree that crime by the lower classes stems from recession, poverty, unemployment, and broken homes, and most would agree that the best approach to controlling crime would be economic policies oriented toward providing meaningful jobs for all.[57] But public leaders resist despite an awareness that all other developed countries have far less crime than the United States. Conservatives argue that human nature needs restraints and that the breakdown of traditional morality has led to crime (as well as other social problems). Conservatives oppose government intervention in the economy by arguing that government cannot succeed and should focus on curbing crime by dealing firmly and directly with criminals. For some reason conservatives are oblivious to government intervention in the form of taxation, transportation, energy, and other policies, which support an economy that disrupts communities and contains, on average, more unemployment than is present in other industrial countries (readers will remember that the official American rate counts part-time workers as employed and does not count the large number who have been out of work for one year or more).

Left-wing reformers are once again talking of the need to go beyond law and prison reform. Other countries intervene directly to provide better levels of employment, family support, and more stable communities. These are known ways to bring down the crime rate—but power groups resist and (blue-collar) crime in America flourishes.[58]

SUMMARY

The nature of law is directly related to the American class system. In general, law follows the interests of powerful property and professional groups.

Deviance, especially criminal deviance, is also directly related to the class-prestige system. Though the lower classes commit the most numerous and easily understood forms of crime, the main criminals in the United States are middle- and upper-level individuals and organizations, both private and public.

Businesspeople, businesses, voluntary groups, government officials, and the professions commit enormous amounts of white-collar crime. The amounts of money illegally taken and the violations of trust are so large that they threaten the legitimacy and viability of American society.

Our perception of crime also reflects the class system. For a long time the upper classes succeeded in associating crime with the lower classes. However, white-collar crime is now so prevalent that this may be changing.

Law enforcement also reflects the class-prestige system. Crime is defined differently depending on the class of the lawbreaker; law enforcement agencies treat lawbreakers from the various classes differently; legal services are more readily available to the upper classes than the lower classes;

and legal reform rarely affects the essential inequality before the law characteristic of class society.

By and large, the working and lower classes enjoy substantially fewer legal rights, inferior legal services, and less justice than the classes above them.

The United States is the world leader in blue-collar crime (no studies exist but in all likelihood it is the world leader in white-collar crime too).

Though crime is a social phenomenon, resulting from the way in which economic and political power relations are structured, American elites continue to blame it on human nature (rotten apples) and waste huge sums of money and moral effort in a vain attempt to suppress it with police, courts, and prisons.

The main way to curb blue-collar crime is through full employment and integrated communities. Adopting such a social program would also mean harnessing the upper classes to social functions and thus would curb our most important form of crime, that committed by the upper classes.

NOTES

1. Derek C. Bok, "A Flawed System," *Harvard Magazine* (May–June 1983):38 ff. Bok is a former dean of Harvard Law School.
2. This is a reference, of course, to Robert K. Merton's classic analysis, "Social Structure and Anomie," *American Sociological Review* 3 (October 1938):672–682.
3. Anthony M. Platt, *The Child Savers: The Invention of Delinquency* (Chicago: University of Chicago Press, 1969).
4. William J. Chambliss, "A Sociological Analysis of the Law of Vagrancy," *Social Problems* 12 (Summer 1964):67–77; reprinted in Delos H. Kelly, ed., *Deviant Behavior,* 4th ed. (New York: St. Martin's Press, 1993), pp. 151–163.
5. Edwin H. Sutherland, *White Collar Crime* (New York: Holt, Rinehart & Winston, 1949), p. 9.
6. There are obvious difficulties inherent in the term *white-collar crime* if one restricts its use to crimes by those of high social status, and primarily to the crimes of big businesspeople. The term *white-collar crime* should be also used (or refined or dropped) to account for the crimes of professionals and semiprofessionals, such as doctors, lawyers, advertising people, police officers, and inspectors; skilled workers in television repair, watch repair, automobile repair, and plumbing; and assorted small and intermediate businesspeople, such as slumlords, manufacturers of misrepresented or misgraded products, butchers who shortweight, fuel companies and gas stations that shortcount, and sales personnel who pilfer ("inventory shrinkage"). From the standpoint of class analysis, it is probably best to think of a hierarchy of types of crime associated with basic class attributes (income, property, education, occupation).
7. There is an interesting parallel here with youth gangs.
8. Sutherland, *White Collar Crime,* ch. 13.
9. *Antioch Review* 8 (June 1948):193–210; reprinted in Robert K. Merton, *Social Theory and Social Structure,* rev. ed. (New York: Free Press, 1968), ch. 13.

10. For a fact-filled, radical indictment of our criminal justice system, which argues that its failure to control crime is a mark of success because it diverts attention from the crimes of the upper to those of the lower classes, see Jeffrey H. Reiman, *The Rich Get Richer and the Poor Get Prison: Ideology, Class, and Criminal Justice,* 4th ed. (Boston: Allyn & Bacon, 1995).
11. For a comprehensive review of what we know about the class background of juvenile delinquents, see Don C. Gibbons and Marvin Krohn, *Delinquent Behavior,* 5th ed. (Englewood Cliffs, NJ: Prentice-Hall, 1991).
12. It has been suggested by an experiment that unskilled workers who have criminal records are punished further by loss of employment opportunities, and that unskilled workers who have been *acquitted* of criminal charges are also discriminated against by prospective employers. By contrast, doctors who have been either convicted or acquitted of malpractice suffer almost no ill effects in their subsequent careers; see Richard D. Schwartz and Jerome H. Skolnick, "Two Studies of Legal Stigma," *Social Problems* 10 (Fall 1962):133–142; reprinted in Delos H. Kelley, ed., *Deviant Behavior,* 2nd ed. (New York: St. Martin's Press, 1984), pp. 497–509.
13. James Fallows, *National Defense* (New York: Vintage, 1981), and Edward N. Luttwak, *The Pentagon and the Art of War* (New York: Simon and Schuster, 1984).
14. David Sudnow, "Normal Crimes: Sociological Features of the Penal Code in a Public Defender's Office," *Social Problems* 12, no. 3 (Winter 1965):255–276.
15. Thomas J. Scheff, "Typification in the Diagnostic Practices of Rehabilitation Agencies," in Marvin B. Sussman, ed., *Sociology and Rehabilitation* (Washington, DC: American Sociological Association, 1965).
16. Robert A. Scott, *The Making of Blind Men: A Study of Adult Socialization* (New York: Russell Sage Foundation, 1969).
17. For the need to pay special attention to ethnic and racial cultural differences in these areas of professional work, see Monica McGoldrick, John K. Pearce, and Joseph Giordono, eds., *Ethnicity and Family Therapy* (New York: Guilford, 1982); Stanley Sue and James K. Morishima, *The Mental Health of Asian Americans* (San Francisco: Jossey-Bass, 1982); Jay C. Chunn II, Patricia J. Dunston, and Fariyal Ross-Sheriff, eds., *Mental Health and People of Color: Curriculum Development and Change* (Washington, DC: Howard University Press, 1983); and Man Keung Ho, *Family Therapy with Ethnic Minorities* (Newbury Park, CA: Sage, 1987).
18. Lloyd S. Etheredge, *Can Governments Learn? American Foreign Policy and Central American Revolutions* (New York: Pergamon, 1985).
19. James Q. Wilson, *The Investigators: Managing FBI and Narcotics Agents* (New York: Basic Books, 1978), pp. 97–100, 143–147, 172–174.
20. Ivar Berg, assisted by Sherry Gorelick, *Education and Jobs: The Great Training Robbery* (New York: Praeger, 1970).
21. Samuel Bowles and Herbert Gintis, *Schooling in Capitalist America: Educational Reform and the Contradictions of Economic Life* (New York: Basic Books, 1977).
22. For a discussion, see the sections "Class and Mental Retardation" and "Class and Learning Disability" in Chapter 8.
23. For an analysis, which also argues that the organization of public health subsidies through Medicare and Medicaid invites fraud, see Henry N. Pontell, Paul D. Jesilow, and Gilbert Geis, "Policing Physicians: Practitioner Fraud and Abuse in a Government Medical Program," *Social Problems* 30 (October 1982):117–125.
24. For the classic analysis of these and other status-role conflicts of the stockbroker, and for attempted safeguards against deviance in this area, see William M.

Evan and Ezra G. Levin, "Status-Set and Role-Set Conflicts of the Stockbroker: A Problem in the Sociology of Law," *Social Forces* 45, no. 1 (1966): 73–83.

25. For a valuable reading suitable for undergraduate students that captures the relation between the banking scandal and politics, see Lenny Glynn, "Who Really Made the S. and L. Mess?" *Dissent* 38 (Spring 1991):195–201. For a detailed analysis that calls attention to the shift to finance capitalism as the generator of new opportunities for white-collar crime, see Kitty Calavita and Henry N. Pontell, "'Other People's Money' Revisited: Collective Embezzlement in the Savings and Loan and Insurance Industries," *Social Problems* 38 (February 1991):94–112. The term *collective embezzlement* might have served better, however, had it referred to America's extreme version of laissez-faire capitalism and its collusive network of deviant elite groups rather than to "the siphoning off of company funds for personal use by top management."
26. For one account, see Robert Nelson, *A World of Preference: Business Access to Reagan's Regulators* (New York: Democracy Project, 1983).
27. Marc Reisner, *Cadillac Desert: The American West and its Disappearing Water* (New York: Viking, 1986).
28. Gordon Adams, *The Iron Triangle: The Politics of Defense Contracting* (New York: Council on Economic Priorities, 1981).
29. It should be noted that many white-collar criminals, such as small retailers, small service businesses, and landlords, are subject to conventional treatment by law enforcement officials.
30. Public protection measures in such areas as civil rights, fair employment, consumer protection, and factory safety are framed in terms of much-publicized goals, but invariably lack the provisions for enforcement necessary to make them effective. Thus, goals are not met and the authority of law and government is diluted.
31. For an early but still useful analysis of the consumer problems of the poor, which refers to the way in which law is used to exploit poor consumers, see David Caplovitz, *The Poor Pay More: Consumer Practices of Low-Income Families* (New York: Free Press, 1963).
32. Small claims courts, which are now used as collection agencies, were originally established to allow ordinary individuals to adjudicate small disputes with a minimum of fuss and expense.
33. Of course, the salaries of police officers, prosecutors, judges, court officials and, where clients are indigent, defense lawyers and court fees are paid out of public funds. In spite of this, the judicial process has a pronounced market flavor—the most important cases are handled by private law firms organized as profit-making businesses. And, as we will see, the provision of free justice for the poor has cheapened rather than guaranteed it.
34. John P. Heinz and Edward O. Laumann, *Chicago Lawyers: The Social Structure of the Bar* (New York: Russell Sage and American Bar Association, 1982); Robert L. Nelson, *Partners With Power: The Social Transformation of the Large Law Firm* (Berkeley: University of California Press, 1988); and Richard L. Abel, *American Lawyer* (New York: Oxford University Press, 1989).
35. Friedrich Kessler, "Contracts and Power in America," in Donald Black and Maureen Mileski, eds., *The Social Organization of Law* (New York: Seminar Press, 1973), ch. 10; reprinted from *Columbia Law Review* 43 (1943):629–642.
36. Fred L. Strodtbeck, Rita M. James, and Charles Hawkins, "Social Status in Jury Deliberations," *American Sociological Review* 22 (December 1957):713–719.

37. For differences in commutation of execution sentences, see Marvin E. Wolfgang, Arlene Kelly, and Hans C. Nolde, "Comparisons of the Executed and the Commuted Among Admissions to Death Row," in Richard Quinney, ed., *Crime and Justice in Society* (Boston: Little, Brown, 1969). For different sentencing among those convicted of drunkenness, see Jacqueline P. Wiseman, *Stations of the Lost: The Treatment of Skid Row Alcoholics* (Englewood Cliffs, NJ: Prentice-Hall 1970), pp. 90–94.
38. The definition of due process has evolved slowly through a considerable number of Supreme Court decisions. The basic elements of due process are specified in three famous decisions: *Gideon* v. *Wainwright,* 372 U.S. 335 (1963); *Escobedo* v. *Illinois,* 378 U.S. 478 (1964); and *Miranda* v. *Arizona* 384 U.S. 436 (1966).
39. Donald J. Newman, *Conviction: The Determination of Guilt or Innocence Without Trial* (Boston: Little, Brown, 1966).
40. Abraham S. Blumberg, "The Practice of Law as Confidence Game: Organizational Cooptation of a Profession," *Law and Society Review* 1 (June 1967):15–39.
41. Jerome E. Carlin, Jan Howard, and Sheldon L. Messinger, *Civil Justice and the Poor: Issues for Sociological Research* (New York: Russell Sage Foundation, 1967). Though the authors use the terms *rich* and *poor* throughout, it is clear that they are referring broadly to the upper and lower classes.
42. Jacobus tenBroek, *Family Law and the Poor* (Westport, CT: Greenwood Press, 1971), and "The Two Nations: Differential Values in Welfare Law and Administration," in M. Levitt and B. Rubenstein eds., *Orthopsychiatry and the Law* (Detroit: Wayne State University Press, 1968).
43. Carlin, Howard, and Messinger, *Civil Justice and the Poor,* p. 21.
44. In fact, however, true individualized justice is restricted to the nonpoor, who can hire good lawyers to particularize and devote attention to their unique legal problems.
45. Harold Garfinkel, "Conditions of Successful Degradation Ceremonies," *American Journal of Sociology* 61, no. 5 (March 1956):420–424.
46. For a well-known political scientist and a psychologist who still think crime comes from human nature (psychological predispositions mediated by social factors), see James Q. Wilson and Richard J. Herrnstein, *Crime and Human Nature* (New York: Touchstone, 1985).
47. C. R. Tittle, W. J. Villemez, and D. A. Smith, "The Myth of Social Class and Criminality: An Empirical Assessment of the Empirical Evidence," *American Sociological Review* 43 (October 1978):643–656.
48. John Braithwaite, "The Myth of Social Class and Criminality Reconsidered," *American Sociological Review* 46 (February 1981):36–57.
49. Theodore G. Chiricos, "Rates of Crime and Unemployment: An Analysis of the Aggregate Research Evidence," *Social Problems* 34 (April 1987):187–212.
50. Emilie Andersen Allan and Darrell J. Steffensmier, "Youth, Underemployment, and Property Crime: Differential Effects of Job Availability and Job Quality on Juvenile and Young Adult Arrest Rates," *American Sociological Review* 54 (February, 1989):107–112.
51. For the latter, see Judith R. Blau and Peter M. Blau, "The Cost of Inequality: Metropolitan Structure and Violent Crime," *American Sociological Review* 47 (February 1982):114–129. Both whites and blacks who suffer from economic inequality (not poverty) commit significantly more violent crime. Ascriptive inequality (racist inequality) adds somewhat to the black rate.

52. Louise I. Shelley, "American Crime: An International Anomaly?," *Comparative Social Research* 8 (1985):81–95.
53. For an unsurpassed discussion, see Jessica Mitford, *Kind and Usual Punishment: The Prison Business* (New York: Random House, 1974).
54. For a classic experiment in which college students played at being guards and then became guards with a vengeance, see Philip G. Zimbardo, "Pathology of Imprisonment," *Society* 9 (April 1972):4–8.
55. Richard Neeley, "The Politics of Crime," *Atlantic Monthly* 250 (August 1982):27–31.
56. Reiman, *The Rich Get Richer and the Poor Get Prison.*
57. We do know that public assistance has a significant negative effect on crime rates; see James DeFronzo, "Economic Assistance to Impoverished Americans: Relation to Incidence of Crime," *Criminology* 21 (February 1983):119–136. We also know that modest transfer payments to ex-prisoners can reduce arrests for both property and nonproperty crime; see Richard A. Berk and Kenneth J. Lenihan, "Crime and Poverty: Some Experimental Evidence from Ex-offenders," *American Sociological Review* 45 (October 1980):766–786.
58. For a brilliant summary of what is known about crime, for a judicious presentation of the flaws in the positions and practices of both left and right reformers, and for a focus on full employment and integrated communities as the best way to tackle (blue-collar) crime, see Elliott Currie, *Confronting Crime: An American Challenge* (New York: Pantheon, 1985).

17

The Class Position of America's Racial Minorities: African Americans

◆ ◆ ◆ ◆

◆ ◆ ◆ ◆

The term *minority* was first used in the peace treaties of World War I to refer to ethnic groups in Eastern Europe that needed protection against dominant ethnic groups. Today the term refers to a wide variety of groups and aggregates that want a change in power relations: ethnic, racial, and religious groups as well as such aggregates as women, the aged, youth, the handicapped, the overweight, and homosexuals (who prefer to be called gays and lesbians).

ETHNICITY AND RACE IN COMPARATIVE PERSPECTIVE

Science tells us that human beings have the same mental and moral capacity regardless of skin color, sex, or other physical features. The fact that all must learn to behave is of the greatest importance in establishing human equality. Most observable differences among human beings are due to *what* they experience (learn), and differences become pronounced if human beings in different classes, different ethnic groups, or different cultures are compared.

In the great agrarian empires of the past, different ethnic groups lived together as separate societies within a larger imperial whole. The relations of these groups were sometimes peaceful, sometimes turbulent, but there was no effort to mingle or assimilate the various ethnic or racial groups in a greater whoie. All this was changed by the rise of capitalism. The dynamic capitalist economy moves people around to suit the needs of commerce and industry, and this tends to bring ethnic groups into contact with each other. The capitalist economy is powered by cheap labor, and capitalist societies import labor often diversifying their ethnic and racial makeup. The United States imported a large number of slaves to toil on the cash-crop plantations of the American South. It imported 40 million immigrants during the nineteenth century to work in its cities and factories. Also important in the development of the United States is the wide use of female labor outside the home. One consequence of all this was the emergence of ideologies of ethnic, racial, and sexual inequality. Often these themes took on the force of law and well-established practice.

In the twentieth century, the United States has admitted many more immigrants than it did in the nineteenth century. In addition it has been unable to stop the flow of illegal immigrants. Americans have responded to these newcomers with the same racist-ethnic biases as in the past. And recently, efforts have been mounted to cut off both legal and illegal immigrants from social benefits. Thought of in broader terms, American capitalism wants the cheap labor immigrants provide, but it doesn't want to include them in its national life.

Capitalism also had a counter current. As it developed in England, France, and the United States, it declared all people eligible for participation in the main benefits and positions in society. The rising middle classes argued that all human beings had the right and the duty to develop their brains, morals, and tastes. This could best be done by participating in a free and rational division of labor. In keeping with this argument, capitalist society transformed its members into a legally free, all-purpose labor force (possessive individualism, or the doctrine that individuals own themselves and are free to work for themselves or sell their labor to others). All this runs counter to racial and ethnic beliefs and practices that keep people ignorant, idle, and apart.

The clash of these two traditions is at the heart of America's majority-minority relations. To state the conflict concretely: early (entrepreneurial) capitalism developed racist-ethnic-sexist norms and values to justify the cheap labor it needed, but it also established values declaring all humans eligible for full membership and participation in the life of society. When beliefs that ethnic newcomers, nonwhites, females, and others were innately inferior crumbled in the face of experience and science, and when economic need required a more fluid, flexible (efficient) use of labor, a later (corporate) capitalism changed the legal and political statuses of minorities in an effort to create an abstract labor force, that is, a labor force made up of all members of society. In recent decades, however, the economic squeeze on middle- and working-class Americans has led them to blame (falsely) America's recent immigrants for their economic troubles.

ETHNIC AND RACIAL MINORITIES IN THE UNITED STATES

The United States has had a continuous wave of newcomers from different ethnic and racial backgrounds.[1] Though some came willingly and others by force, newcomers were largely thought of and treated as inferiors. The groups that have fared the worst are racial groups. Race, as such, has no scientific standing since no causal relationship between behavior and skin color (or hair texture, eyelids, or other such physical attributes) has ever been established. But to its enduring shame, white America has been openly racist in its treatment of all nonwhites and, at one time or another, has made African Americans, native American Indians, Hawaiians, Aleutians, Chinese, Japanese, and Filipinos into distinctly depressed racial minorities.[2]

ETHNIC AND RACIAL DEMOGRAPHICS

Minority groups vary considerably in size (see Table 17–1). African Americans are the largest minority group, forming 12 percent of the total population. Latin or Hispanics, most of whom are Mexican American, are the next largest at 10 percent. Ethnic and racial minorities are younger than dominant groups. Their birthrates are higher and they have a shorter life expectancy than majority Americans. And they have a higher dependency ratio (the number of those not likely to work in relation to those that are).

MAJORITY MALES VERSUS ALL OTHERS

The federal government did not collect meaningful and useful data about American minorities until well after World War II. Its growth in data-gathering capability about minorities was climaxed by the 1978 publication of the United States Commission on Civil Rights, *Social Indicators of Equality*

TABLE 17–1 Racial and Ethnic Minorities in the United States

			PERCENT
Total American Population	260,000,000 (1994)		
African Americans	31,192,000 (1994)		12.0%
Hispanic Origin	26,077,000 (1994)		10.0%
Mexican	14,628,000 (1993)		
Puerto Rican	2,402,000 (1993)		
Cuban	1,071,000 (1993)		
Central and South American	3,052,000 (1993)		
Other Hispanic	1,598,000 (1993)		
American Indian, Eskimo, Aleut	1,907,000 (1994)		0.7%
Asian and Pacific Islander	8,438,000 (1994)		3.0%
Asian and Pacific Islander	7,274,000	1990	
Chinese	1,645,000	1990	
Filipino	1,407,000	1990	
Japanese	848,000	1990	
Asian Indian	815,000	1990	
Korean	799,000	1990	
Vietnamese	615,000	1990	
Laotian	149,000	1990	
Cambodian	147,000	1990	
Hawaiian	211,000	1990	
Samoan	63,000	1990	
Guamanian	49,000	1990	

Source: U.S. Bureau of the Census, *Statistical Abstract of the United States, 1995* (Washington, DC: U.S. Government Printing Office, 1995), Tables 19, 31, 51, 53.

for Minorities and Women.[3] The commission's report is particularly valuable because it contains data on both large and small minorities: women, African Americans, American Indians, Alaskan natives, Mexican Americans, Japanese Americans, Chinese Americans, Filipino Americans, and Puerto Ricans.

The commission addresses the following concerns of minorities and women:

1. Underdevelopment of human skills through delayed enrollment, nonenrollment in secondary education, and nonparticipation in higher education
2. Lack of equivalent returns for educational achievement in terms of occupational opportunities and earnings
3. Discrepancies in access to jobs, particularly those having greater-than-average stability, prestige, and monetary returns
4. Inequality of income, relatively lower earnings for equal work, and diminished chances for salary and wage increases
5. A high likelihood of being in poverty
6. A proportionately higher expenditure for housing, less desirable housing conditions, restricted freedom of choice in selecting locations in which to live, and greater difficulty in attaining homeownership[4]

The thrust of its analysis is to establish equality ratios between majority males and minorities over time. Assembling data from 1960, 1970, and 1976, the Commission's findings are clear and unequivocal—minorities and women are grossly unequal (even when achievement is held constant) in twenty-one measures in the above areas. Even more important, their position had not improved since 1960, and in some areas had not even kept pace with majority males!

AFRICAN AMERICANS

Historical Background

The class position (income, occupation, education) of African Americans changed dramatically for the better between the late nineteenth century and the 1950s as a result of migration from southern farms to northern and western cities.[5] Thanks largely to technological displacement from agriculture, a burgeoning industrial economy, and wartime labor shortages, African Americans also made class gains relative to whites during this period. Most of these gains came from the quickened economic pace and subsequent boom produced by World War II. Between 1939 and 1954, black median annual income jumped from 37 to 56 percent of white income. The movement out of agriculture and into the lower reaches of the urban industrial labor force also represented a significant upgrading of occupational status for African Americans. And gains both absolute and relative were made in education.

The 1950s on tell a different story. Despite the greatest and longest period of prosperity in American history, the economic status of African Americans grew more slowly after the 1950s and in some ways stagnated and even worsened. Though blacks made steady gains, their gains came mostly from continued migration out of agriculture, the Vietnam War, and because black families tend to have multiple wage earners more often than whites. Thus, black *family* income improved during the 1960s and 1970s in relation to white family income. But the economic slowdown of the 1970s and the recession of the early 1980s hit blacks harder than whites and black gains have receded. The same period saw a much larger increase in one-parent black households than white, and black poverty levels today are higher than they were in the 1960s.

Wealth and Income

The median net worth of African-American households in 1993 was only 10 percent of the net worth of white households,[6] a ratio that has remained constant since net worth by race was first studied in the early 1980s. Not only do African Americans find it hard to save but the lack of assets means psychological insecurity and, of course, lack of economic power.

Table 17–2 shows the disparity in income between blacks and whites in 1993. Table 17–3 highlights the lack of progress in closing this gap since 1969, that is, after decades of economic growth, civil rights, and affirmative action. Black married couple families did make relative progress in income, however, and so did male and female workers if earnings as opposed to income are compared. These latter comparisons focus on younger, better educated groups and also reflect the stagnation of white earnings in this period.

The lack of progress among *all* blacks and *all* whites is because of the larger decline in the percentage of married couple families among blacks. Poverty ratios for all ages and types of households remain 3 to 4 times higher for blacks (see Table 17–4). Poverty figures become more ominous if one remembers that an enormous percentage of black children (39.3%) live in poverty as compared to 11.6% of white, non-Hispanic children.

Occupational Status

African-American employment status has also remained highly unequal to that of whites. Black unemployment has been double that of whites for the entire postwar period (regardless of education or occupation). Among black teenagers, unemployment is chronically of crisis proportions and more than twice the rate for white teenagers. Despite gains, blacks are still heavily underrepresented in top occupations. Whether blacks can consolidate and extend their small relative gains remains to be seen.

By and large, African-American gains in occupational status reflect structural changes in the American economy. The rise in the overall eco-

(*text continues on page 402*)

TABLE 17–2 Income of Persons and Families by Race, Sex, and Age in 1993

NUMBERS IN THOUSANDS	BLACK	WHITE
INCOME OF PERSONS IN 1993		
Males with income	8,947	77,650
$1 to $4,999 or loss	18.6	11.0
$5,000 to $9,999	18.0	11.3
$10,000 to $19,999	26.8	23.0
$20,000 to $29,999	16.7	18.1
$30,000 and over	19.9	36.6
Median income (dollars)	14,605	21,981
Females with income	11,267	79,484
$1 to $4,999 or loss	26.5	24.6
$5,000 to $9,999	25.3	21.0
$10,000 to $19,999	24.8	25.2
$20,000 to $29,999	12.8	14.5
$30,000 and over	10.6	14.7
Median income (dollars)	9,508	11,266
PER CAPITA INCOME IN 1993		
Per capita income (dollars)	9,863	16,800
INCOME OF FAMILIES IN 1993		
Total families	7,989	57,870
Under $10,000	25.8	7.3
$10,000 to $24,999	30.0	21.7
$25,000 to $34,999	13.7	15.1
$35,000 to $49,999	13.0	18.8
$50,000 and over	17.6	37.2
Median income (dollars)	21,548	39,308
POVERTY STATUS OF FAMILIES WITH HOUSEHOLDER 55 YEARS OLD AND OVER		
All families	1,788	17,915
Percent below poverty level	22.1	5.6
Married couple	1,078	15,351
Percent below poverty level	16.6	4.7
Female householder, no spouse present	636	2,015
Percent below poverty level	31.2	11.1
Male householder, no spouse present	73	550
Percent below poverty level	23.8	9.5

Source: U.S. Bureau of the Census, Current Population Reports, P20-480, *"The Black Population in the United States: March 1994 and 1993"* (Washington, DC: U.S. Government Printing Office, 1995), Table 2.

TABLE 17–3 Income of Households, Families, and Persons, by Sex and Race: 1993 and 1969

	1993				1969		
INCOME AND EARNINGS	BLACK	WHITE	WHITE, NOT HISPANIC	RATIO: BLACK TO WHITE	BLACK	WHITE	RATIO: BLACK TO WHITE
MEDIAN INCOME							
Households (dollars)	19,533	32,960	34,173	0.59	19,408	32,109	0.60
Families (dollars)	21,548	39,308	41,114	0.55	22,001	35,920	0.61
Persons-							
Male (dollars)	14,605	21,981	23,171	0.66	14,432	24,811	0.58
Female (dollars)	9,508	11,266	11,599	0.84	6,748	8,003	0.84
MEDIAN INCOME BY TYPE OF FAMILY							
Married couple (dollars)	35,228	43,683	45,241	0.81	26,879	37,559	0.72
Female householder, no spouse present (dollars)	11,905	20,003	21,649	0.60	12,253	20,171	0.61

Male householder, no spouse present (dollars)	19,476	28,274	30,168	0.69	22,823	32,340	0.71
MEDIAN EARNINGS OF PERSONS							
Male (dollars)	16,753	23,670	25,299	0.71	15,902	26,241	0.61
Female (dollars)	12,534	14,041	14,561	0.89	7,280	9,704	0.75
MEDIAN EARNINGS OF YEAR-ROUND, FULL-TIME WORKERS							
Male (dollars)	23,019	31,090	31,971	0.74	21,565	32,040	0.67
Female (dollars)	19,816	22,023	22,383	0.90	14,703	18,623	0.79
PER CAPITA MONEY INCOME							
Per capital income (dollars)	9,863	16,800	15,777	0.59	6,462	11,641	0.56

Source: U.S. Bureau of the Census, Current Population Reports, P20–480, *"The Black Population in the United States: March 1994 and 1993"* (Washington, DC: U.S. Government Printing Office, 1995), Table M.

TABLE 17–4 Selected Characteristics of Families and Persons Below the Poverty Level by Race, Sex, and Age: 1993, 1979, and 1974

[Numbers in thousands. Families as of March of the following year]

	1993			1979		1974	
CHARACTERISTIC	BLACK	WHITE	WHITE, NOT HISPANIC	BLACK	WHITE	BLACK	WHITE
TYPE OF FAMILY							
All families	7,993	57,881	52,470	6,184	52,243	5,491	49,440
Percent below poverty level	31.3	9.4	7.6	27.8	6.9	26.9	6.8
Married couple	3,715	47,452	43,745	3,433	44,751	3,357	43,049
Percent below poverty level	12.3	5.8	4.7	13.2	4.7	13.0	4.6
Female householder, no spouse present	3,828	8,131	6,798	2,495	6,052	1,934	5,208
Percent below poverty level	49.9	29.2	25.0	49.4	22.3	52.2	24.8
Male householder, no spouse present	450	2,298	1,927	256	1,441	200	1,182
Percent below poverty level	29.4	13.9	12.9	13.7	9.2	17.4	7.3
Families with related children under 18 years	5,525	29,234	25,477	4,297	27,329	3,915	26,890
Percent below poverty level	39.3	14.5	11.6	33.5	9.2	33.0	9.0
Married couple	2,147	22,670	20,166	2,095	22,878	2,187	(NA)
Percent below poverty level	13.9	8.2	6.3	13.7	5.3	14.5	(NA)
Female householder, no spouse present	3,084	5,361	4,330	2,063	3,866	1,623	3,244

Percent below poverty level	57.7	39.6	34.8	54.7	31.3	58.5	36.4
Male householder, no spouse present	295	1,203	981	139	584	105	(NA)
Percent below poverty level	31.5	19.6	18.1	18.4	14.1	26.2	(NA)
Householder 65 years old and over	944	10,054	9,584	807	8,107	641	7,319
Percent below poverty level	22.6	5.2	4.6	26.4	7.4	27.7	7.7
PERSONS							
All persons	32,910	214,899	190,843	25,944	191,742	23,699	182,376
Percent below poverty level	33.1	12.2	9.9	31.0	9.0	30.3	8.6
Persons 65 years and over	2,510	27,580	26,272	2,040	21,898	1,721	19,206
Percent below poverty level	28.0	10.7	10.1	36.2	13.3	34.3	12.8
RELATED CHILDREN UNDER 18 YEARS IN FAMILIES							
All families	10,969	53,614	45,322	9,172	51,687	9,384	55,320
Percent below poverty level	45.9	17.0	12.8	40.8	11.4	39.6	11.0
Families with a female householder, no spouse present	6,230	8,988	6,762	4,574	6,808	4,078	6,254
Percent below poverty level	65.9	45.6	39.0	63.1	38.6	65.0	42.9
All other families	4,739	44,626	38,560	4,598	44,879	5,310	49,217
Percent below poverty level	19.5	11.3	8.3	13.7	7.3	20.0	6.9

Source: U.S. Bureau of the Census, Current Population Reports, P20–480, *"The Black Population in the United States: March 1994 and 1993"* (Washington, DC: U.S. Government Printing Office, 1995), Tables N and O.

nomic status of blacks (and whites) is largely due to the drastic displacement of agriculture from the center of the American economy and the emergence of a manufacturing and white-collar economy. Situated in marginal occupations, and thus subject to technological change and cutbacks during recessions, African Americans are displaced more often than whites, which goes far toward explaining their higher level of unemployment. However, they also find jobs at higher skill levels, thus their occupational upgrading, however slow. All in all, African Americans have not made any breakthrough into the white-collar ranks despite their presence in the urban-industrial scene for at least three generations. Not only are they heavily overrepresented in blue-collar occupations but perhaps chronically so. A closer look at white-collar data also reveals that African Americans are concentrated at the lower reaches of the white-collar world, epecially with regard to managerial positions, and they tend to practice their professions in a segregated context. Among blue-collar workers, African Americans are highly underrepresented in elite trade unions and have had little success in expanding their representation. And in recent years blacks have faced considerable competition from the influx of white women into the labor force.

Empirical studies confirm the difficulties that black males have had in recent years. Ernest R. House and William Madura argue that structural changes in the economy have been especially harmful to black males and the major cause of their plight; they also cite competition from women. Marshal J. Pomer found little upward mobility among prime-age men (white or black) in low-paying occupations from 1962 to 1973, a period of economic expansion. But black mobility was far less than white mobility, and black males who advanced did not go nearly as far as did whites.[7] And Daniel Lichter found that while underemployment (a more important indicator of economic status than unemployment alone) increased among both white and black urban males between 1970 and 1982, black underemployment increased far more.[8]

Table 17–5 shows the disparity between black and white workers in March 1994. The census category Managerial and Professional Specialty does not distinguish between upper and lower levels, it should be remembered. Note should also be taken of the higher rate of black workers who work for governments, which also means that they are vulnerable to the cuts in government programs that America's politically mobilized upper classes inaugurated in 1995–96.

Education

In education, African Americans have made significant absolute and relative gains against formidable odds. African Americans aged 25 to 34 reached parity with whites in achieving high school diplomas between 1980 and 1994.[9] But the story in the important area of higher education is differ-

TABLE 17–5 Black and White Americans in the Labor Force, March 1994
[Numbers in thousands.]

CHARACTERISTIC	BLACK	WHITE
LABOR FORCE STATUS		
Both sexes, 16 years and over	22,770	165,176
In civilian labor force	14,160	109,667
Percent in civilian labor force	62.2	66.4
Percent unemployed	13.0	6.2
Males, 16 years and over	10,203	79,845
In civilian labor force	6,782	59,818
Percent in civilian labor force	66.5	74.9
Percent unemployed	14.0	6.7
Females, 16 years and over	12,568	85,331
In civilian labor force	7,379	49,849
Percent in civilian labor force	58.7	58.4
Percent unemployed	12.1	5.5
OCCUPATION		
Employed males, 16 years and over	5,836	55,786
Percent	100.0	100.0
Managerial and professional specialty	14.7	27.5
Technical, sales, and administrative support	17.6	20.6
Service	20.0	9.8
Farming, forestry, and fishing	2.0	4.3
Precision production, craft, and repair	15.0	18.5
Operators, fabricators, and laborers	30.7	19.3
Employed females, 16 years and over	6,487	47,094
Percent	100.0	100.0
Managerial and professional specialty	20.1	29.9
Technical, sales, and administrative support	39.4	43.2
Service	26.9	16.8
Farming, forestry, and fishing	0.2	1.2
Precision production, craft, and repair	2.5	2.1
Operators, fabricators, and laborers	10.8	6.8
CLASS OF WORKER		
Employed persons, 16 years and over	12,322	102,880
Percent	100.0	100.0
Private wage and salary workers	72.9	76.1
Federal government workers	5.6	2.5
State government workers	6.4	4.0
Local government workers	11.1	7.9
Self-employed workers	3.9	9.3

Source: U.S. Bureau of the Census, Current Population Reports, P20–480, *"The Black Population in the United States: March 1994 and 1993"* (Washington, DC: U.S. Government Printing Office, 1995), Table 2.

ent. Black gains in achieving a bachelor's degree or more were offset by white gains and no relative progress occurred between 1980 and 1994. Two things about black education should be noted, one, black women are outdistancing black males in acquiring college degrees, and two, black and white graduate and professional education, and the quality of higher education received by blacks and whites, both important determinants of who gets the top jobs, remain very unequal.

The African-American Family

Black families are significantly less stable than majority families:

1. Black males are more passive at home than whites and share tasks less with their wives.
2. The male is absent more in black homes than in white homes.
3. There is deeper estrangement between the sexes before and after marriage among blacks than among whites.
4. Lower income and greater size place greater financial strains on the black family.
5. Rates of family disruption due to desertion, separation, divorce, and death are much higher among blacks than among whites.

All these data are characterized by marked variations in class. Black family life ranges from matriarchal-extended forms among poor blacks in both rural and urban areas to the nuclear family among working- and middle-class blacks. While much attention has been given to the pathology of the lower-class black family, the adaptive mechanisms developed by blacks to cope with a hostile social environment have been neglected. Given the harsh reality of slavery and segregation, migration and economic marginality, it is not surprising that the black family has experienced severe instability and malfunctioning. The industrial nuclear family needs considerable support: steady employment for the breadwinner(s); a congenial neighborhood of stable families; a compatible, supportive school system, and so on. All these supports were denied large portions of the black population as it struggled to overcome the legacy of slavery and segregation.[10]

Data comparing 1994 and 1980 reveal that never-married rates among African Americans are considerably higher (43 percent) than white rates (25 percent) and have widened since 1980, a reflection of the drastically deteriorating employment prospects of black males (many of whom are in prison). And there are far more single-parent (female) families among blacks (48 percent) than white single-parent (female) household (13 percent), which also means that a large and growing number of African-American children are growing up in marginal one-parent homes.[11]

African-American Health and Health Care

Wornie Reed's comprehensive analysis of African-American health and health care exposes the enormously adverse health consequences of low socioeconomic status.[12] African Americans suffer higher rates of all important diseases. In consequence, blacks live shorter lives, black males about 7 years less than white males and black females five years less than white females in 1988 (after paying into the Social Security system since 1936, black males reached an average life expectancy of 65 only a few times during the 1980s and have barely been able to stay at 65 since. Since the retirement age will rise gradually over the coming years and health care for the poor is likely to decline after 1996, the average black male may never qualify for a Social Security pension).

Infant mortality rates and birth complications are shamefully high in the U.S. and especially prevalent among low income, ummarried teenagers, and thus more prevalent among black Americans. Successful federal programs, such as Maternal and Child Care (MCH) and Maternal and Infant Care (MIC), have been either reduced and turned over to the states or are not available to all because of inadequate funding and outreach. These will both become less adequate under the health care "reforms" of the Republican Congress of 1995–1996.

Lead poisoning is an enormously important health hazard and derives from lead paint in old buildings, old industrial sites, and of course from gasoline before lead was removed. These sites are found largely where blacks live and it explains why black lead poisoning rates are much higher than white rates. The impact of lead on the body impairs cognitive functioning and causes a wide variety of serious diseases. Cleaning such sites has low priority for public officials. Smoking, alcohol and drug misuse, AIDS and other sexually transmitted diseases, and homicide are further scourges among African Americans.

Health care for African Americans is uniformly inferior, largely a case of money, less insurance, less useful insurance, few health services and personnel serving African-American areas, and a severe shortage of African-American health-care professionals and auxiliary personnel. While shortages of personnel exist for all American racial and ethnic minorities, the shortages are especially acute for African Americans. These shortages will be aggravated if recent proposals to cut back on medical school enrollments are enacted.

African Americans, Crime, and the Law

African Americans are subject to arrest and imprisonment in much larger numbers than whites. They are also mistreated by the police and legal system and black neighborhoods are subject to open, heavy patrol. The discussion of African-American crime and differential treatment by the police and the judicial system centers around race. But in a classic study, Edward Green concluded that African-American crime rates are identical to white *once class is held constant.*[13]

It is probably best, therefore, to think in terms of class rather than race—law enforcement agencies deal illegally and harshly, and are more openly antagonistic to all members of the lower classes regardless of race, religion, or ethnicity. Basically, law enforcement agencies deal illegally with, and display excessive zeal and force against, all members of the lower classes, whether white, black, yellow, red, Anglo, Mexican American, Protestant, Jewish, or Roman Catholic. In short, the main purpose of law enforcement agencies, like all branches of government, is to defend the existing system of stratification.

Upper-income groups consistently express higher evaluations of the police than do lower-income groups (though support in general is high). However, African Americans are negative toward the police regardless of income. Generally speaking, they dislike the police and suspect them of singling them out for mistreatment. Thus, one of the (largely latent) ways in which the police defend the existing order of things is to displace the lower classes' resentments toward themselves and away from the class system. In other words, to the extent that African Americans interpret their relation to the police and the law in racial terms, they are overlooking the class system, which is the prime source of their problems.

Coramae Richey Mann has provided an invaluable, detailed picture of the relation between African Americans and the law focused on race.[14] But Mann's focus on race often broadens to interpret racism as an integral part of the American economic system and is thus compatible with an explanation based on social class.

According to Michael Tonry, the issue of race and crime is so inflammatory that scholars have shied away from research in this area.[15] Though he does not use the language of social class, Tonry argues that race, however important, is not at the center of the relation between African Americans and the law—rather, African Americans commit different amounts and types of crime because of their social location and experience. The law weighs heavily on African Americans because they commit the offenses that the law seeks to protect society against. Instead of race as the explanation, suggests Tonry, we should focus on unjust laws in an unjust society. More concretely, says Tonry, the crackdown by the Reagan-Bush administrations on crime and drugs was a predictable failure—it not only resulted in the imprisonment of large numbers of unimportant black drug dealers but it diverted attention away from the only way possible to curb crime, by changing the social environment in which so many African Americans grow up in.

The African-American Middle Class and Prospects for the Future

Prospects for improving their overall position in American society can also be analyzed in terms of the strengths and weaknesses of the black middle class. The black professional-managerial class has been and continues to be small relative to whites. Within it there is a lopsided emphasis on medicine, law, the ministry, and teaching, at the expense of business administration and the natural sciences. The situation is similar with regard to black business people: They are few in number relative to whites and their number has been shrinking as desegregation has undermined their protected markets. And within black business there is a significant pattern of specialization in small business. Of the few black-owned businesses, most tend to be eating and drinking establishments, grocery stores, personal services (barbershops, beauty salons), and insurance companies.

The American systems of racial and class stratification have produced what appears to be a deeply institutionalized pattern of inequality for African Americans. Improvement in blacks' legal status, income, occupation, and education since their migration to the North are best interpreted as a change in position from bottom "racial caste" to the bottom levels of class society. Of course, their concurrent rise in absolute social benefits, especially since World War II, is real and has no doubt eased the physical hardships of many black Americans. But the *relative* position of blacks in American society has not changed. When blacks and whites are compared in the aggregate, blacks are still concentrated at the bottom of every index used to measure the benefits of American life.

The reforms of recent years do not appear to have produced much change in blacks' overall position. *In other words, black gains (with some minor exceptions) are offset by corresponding white gains.* Without attributing any conscious design to the overall process that has transformed blacks from a rural to an urban labor group, we must acknowledge that the result has not been the gradual integration of blacks into white society. (We are defining *integration* to mean the random distribution of African Americans throughout the occupational, income, educational, residential, and associational structures of the country, in effect producing a salt-and-pepper society.) The history of blacks since the Civil War—including the reforms of recent years—is best seen as the incorporation of a black (and white) rural labor force into the lower reaches of an urban-industrial system.

African Americans are not predominantly situated in the lower class, although they make up a disproportionate percentage of that class. The large majority of blacks are members of fairly stable working-class families. But the improvement in blacks' class position should not be misinterpreted: Black entry into skilled occupations has been very slow; the black middle class (defined in terms of the income of one earner) is still small and vulnerable; and black income and employment rates are distinctly lower than white rates, regardless of education. And given their economic weakness, even black gains are not secure. Many black advances, including entry into the middle class, are due to public employment and public service programs, leaving them vulnerable to cutbacks (as has happened from the Reagan administration of 1980 on). In addition many blacks who hold "managerial" positions tend to be in public relations and affirmative action positions even when they have professional qualifications in other fields.[16] Given the recessions of 1979–1983 and 1989–1992 and the continuing pressure of having to compete with all types of labor in the developing world, African Americans are even in danger of losing the gains they made between 1875 and 1950.[17]

African-American Poverty

During the 1960s the persistence of black poverty gave rise to the "culture of poverty" explanation. Blacks were poor, said this theory, because once the middle and working classes left the city, the way of life (culture) of poor blacks led to assorted forms of pathology and failure. Essentially, black traits, perhaps those brought to the North from sharecropper experience in the South, were to blame for black poverty and immobility. This theory is still strong and should be resisted because it blames the victim rather than structural forces and the actions of power groups. The economy moved out of the older industrial cities during the 1960s and 1970s aided and abetted by public policies (taxes, highways, FHA mortgages). Given this process, cities were emptied of working-class and middle-class families, leaving the poor behind. Poor blacks no longer had role models on how to behave and aspire and, perhaps more important, they had no local job or other opportunities. By the 1980s, large portions of the American population (white and black) had been disconnected from the mainstream economy by structural forces in the economy and polity.[18] The onset of America's greatly increased participation in the world economy also added to the mobility of capital, a trend that will if anything grow stronger in the coming decades to the detriment of American workers, perhaps especially minorities.

Housing: Severe Racial Segregation

African Americans experienced a significant improvement in their housing during the 1950s and 1960s as whites vacated urban centers. They were also aided by actions of the federal government. But things after the 1970s worsened for African Americans as builders focused on higher priced homes and federal subsidies and protections declined.[19]

Overcrowding, lack of plumbing, stagnant rates of ownership, and severe segregation are now the lot of African Americans. Residential segregation by race does not come about by accident, due to the play of impersonal market forces, or as a result of attitudes. The people and organizations that create and perpetuate residential racial segregation are identifiable: real estate brokers, real estate firms, real estate boards, banking and other lending agencies, and local residential communities themselves, including property and tenant organizations and local governments.

Residential segregation does not affect African Americans alone. Many other minorities are segregated residentially (though none with such thoroughness and seeming permanence). Native Americans on reservations and in urban enclaves, Chinese Americans restricted to Chinatowns and widely excluded from suburban housing developments, white ethnic groups, and Mexican Americans in *barrios* and in rural isolation have all been hemmed in by geographical boundaries. And, of course, geographical boundaries mean social boundaries. The effects of residential segregation, in addition to the loss of comfort and convenience, are to deny some members of minority groups the prestige their class position calls for and to make it difficult for the rest to change their class position (for example, by restricting educational and employment opportunities).[20]

Though we have emphasized the roles of private forces in producing residential segregation, the power of the state is used to the same effect. Though discrimination in most housing sales and rentals is now illegal, an extremely important form of legal protection for property is the widespread use of zoning, a device that serves to segregate minority groups and the poor in general and to make housing scarce for both groups and for others further up the social ladder. In addition, government credit, mortgage, tax, transportation, and general housing policies all work to perpetuate the class-prestige hierarchy of housing (see also the section on housing in Chapter 15).[21]

Associational Segregation by Race, Religion, and Ethnicity

Americans from all ethnic and racial backgrounds have, by and large, been acculturated—that is, they accept America's economic and political beliefs, and much of its diet, dress, manners, and language (Spanish-speaking groups are an important exception to the latter). But the various racial, ethnic, and religious groups do not associate freely. The United States is characterized by multiple associational systems divided by race, ethnicity, and religion. In turn, class divisions are found among the various racial, ethnic, and religious groups to create what Milton Gordon calls *ethclasses*.[22]

At first, prestige differentiation and discrimination in the United States, along with the facts of economic and political life, created clusters of "ethnic communities": separate churches, social clubs, philanthropic organizations, residential areas, and schools; ethnic cultural activities; foreign-language newspapers; and specialized forms of economic life were salient characteristics of first-generation ethnic groups. But the virtual institutional self-sufficiency of ethnic communities gradually disintegrated. In response to the impact of public education and economic mobility, ethnic groups severed ties with the past (illustrated by the decline of foreign-language newspapers), and began to exhibit class differentials among themselves. Thus, to the extent that Irish Americans are rich, middle rich, and poor, and high, middle, and low on the occupational and educational ladders (class differences), they are less likely than before to live together, intermarry, and belong to the same clubs or other voluntary organizations.

African-American Primary Behavior

It seems best to treat class and "racial" forms of primary behavior separately. Despite the strength of religious-ethnic values and beliefs among whites, there is still enough social and moral elbow-room for members of various religious-ethnic groups to mix (or even to "pass") to make it necessary to distinguish this form of segregation from racial segregation. In the aggregate, American whites and blacks (and Indians, Orientals, and other groups whose skin color is not white) simply do not mix on a primary, or even a secondary, basis.[23] Thus residence, intermarriage, friendship, and socializing at home, in clubs, or at church (even within a given religion) are all sharply bounded by lines based on color and impervious to equality in class.[24] Primary relations among African Americans do not compare favorably with the primary relations of the rest of the population, primarily because of the historic disorganization of the black family. As we have pointed out, the economically marginal black male has historically played a passive role in his family; he is often entirely estranged. There also appears to be a sharper estrangement between the sexes among blacks, though this is not uncommon in American, and especially in working class, life. The relation between parents and children in economically marginal or depressed black families differs markedly from that of stable families. The absence of adult role models makes for a different form of socialization and means that black children at this level are highly subject to peer control, often in the form of street gangs. And because of their historically depressed economic position, blacks have been unable to develop kinship networks or communal groups to help them face their problems or to provide capital for economic needs and endeavors.[25]

African-American primary relations are also differentiated internally by class. As is true of whites, upper-level blacks enjoy more stable family lives (though not as stable as those of whites at similar class levels), belong to more clubs, and participate in a greater variety of social events than lower-level blacks.[26]

African-American Secondary Behavior

Despite some weakening of the rigid barriers between the white and nonwhite "races," it is still best to discuss racial segregation in secondary groups separately from religious-ethnic segregation. African Americans do not as a rule belong to white secondary organizations, largely because of class factors—membership in secondary organizations is a middle- and upper-class phenomenon, and few blacks enjoy such class status (due, it must always be remembered, to centuries of oppression). Racist exclusion has also prevailed in many areas, forcing African Americans to found their own organizations. Furthermore, blacks have probably believed that their interests would be submerged and their power dissipated if they joined white organizations. Thus, parallel to white secondary organizations there exist all-black clubs, charities, veterans groups, labor unions, and associations of manufacturers, lawyers, doctors, psychiatrists, ministers, bridge players, cowboys, businesspeople, executives, and the like. Of great importance in the history of black Americans is the all-black religious organization. The racially segregated church is as much a part of the history of blacks and whites as the segregated school or waiting room. So too, the all-black college has played a considerable role in the ability of blacks to survive, though all indications point to its relative decline in the near future.

The best-known black organizations are those dedicated to civil rights and politics: the National Association for the Advancement of Colored People (founded in 1909 as an interracial group but now predominantly black), the Southern Christian Leadership Conference, the Student Nonviolent Coordinating Committee, and the Congress of Racial Equality (founded in 1942 as an interracial group but soon thereafter predominantly black). Also well-known is the National Urban League (1910), which works mostly to advance the cause of blacks in the economy and in the field of housing.

The secondary behavior of African Americans is not too well researched, though the class basis of black business and occupational groups is obvious. Class is also associated with residential distinctions among blacks, and there are black upper class "society" organizations and events and magazines devoted to reporting black class achievements (for example, *Ebony*). In short, the concept of ethclass encompasses both primary and secondary behavior among blacks.

Changing Attitudes Toward African Americans

The belief that some people are unalterably different from and inferior to others is a widespread feature of both the internal and external histories of societies. Essentially, such views are promoted by dominant power groups to support their economic exploitation and political control of their own or subject peoples. This relationship is somewhat obscured in the United States, where the dominant ethos proclaims the moral equality of all human beings and the upper classes tend to voice more tolerant views than the lower classes. Attitude studies, however, should probably be discounted somewhat: The upper groups have greater verbal facility and are conscious of the bad publicity that attends expressed prejudices; in other words, their more tolerant views may contain a certain measure of hypocrisy and rationalization. And perhaps more importantly, attitudes are not the same as behavior. Upper, intermediate, and even lower (nonminority) groups can voice egalitarian views while practicing and benefiting from discrimination. *Formally expressed opinions, in other words, do not necessarily represent people's actual behavior in other contexts.* Therefore, while attitudes are important indices of stratification, they should not be confused or equated with actual behavior. Lofty thoughts and noble emotions expressed in the abstract are often ineffective when they conflict with contradictory thoughts and values in concrete situations.[27] And lofty thoughts and sentiments often serve to camouflage power relations and important social processes.[28] In the following analyses of attitudes toward black, Jewish, and Mexican Americans, we will see two patterns: the expression of prejudice is related to class, and the growing tolerance and acceptance of these minorities does not mean that they are entering an era of achievement, equality of opportunity, and nondiscrimination.

White Americans develop a dramatically more favorable view of the capabilities and rights of black Americans from the 1930s to the 1980s. White Americans expressed a clear acceptance of the idea that blacks have the same intelligence as whites; of the African Americans' formal right to equality of opportunity in education, employment, and housing; and of the need to desegregate schools and transportation. Nonetheless, Americans continued to be prejudiced about African Americans, though less so among the young and the better educated.[29]

These trends, it should be repeated, indicate nothing more than a change in attitudes, which cannot necessarily be equated with other forms of behavior. Nevertheless, while majority Americans are still capable of discrimination (and prejudice), they are less and less willing to justify their actions with words.

The Burden of Moral Equality

The modern belief in the moral (including political-legal) equality of human beings is not an unmixed blessing, and it should not be assumed that this tradition rejects all forms of social inequality. It is unquestionable that the concept of moral equality is deeply incompatible with caste and estate forms of stratification. But it is wrong to believe that moral equality conflicts with class stratification; it actually meshes with and reinforces the class hierarchy. One need only remember that the liberal tradition of moral equality is often posited on the assumption that individuals as individuals are responsible actors to appreciate the way in which this tradition harmonizes with the liberal explanation of social stratification, "nonegalitarian classlessness." Given equality of opportunity, according to this explanation, all social inequality is natural and just since it reflects the innate capabilities of the individual.

One of the best illustrations of the irony contained in the American tradition of moral equality is apparent in the pattern of white attitudes toward blacks. Remember that a comparison of public opinion polls from 1939 on found a dramatic decrease in the percentage of white Americans who believe that whites are racially (morally and intellectually) superior to blacks. But when asked in the late 1960s the cause of the depressed social position of Negroes, a majority of whites answered "Negroes themselves." In other words, acceptance of the African-American as an equal entails acceptance of the liberal belief that human beings are free to determine their own destinies and therefore responsible for their own lives.[30] Stated another way, Americans have little understanding of behavior as a function of institutions, and the fact that white Americans are discarding racist beliefs does not mean that they have adopted a sociocultural explanation of inequality. What they have done in discarding racist views, it appears, is to explain black behavior in the same way that they explain white behavior, as emanating from forces in individuals themselves.

The ability of the class system to protect itself is enhanced, therefore, by the widespread prestige phenomenon called moral equality. Obviously, the tradition of moral equality is also helpful to minorities in combating inequality; indeed, it is a continuing source of tension in American society. Our purpose here, however, is to stress the latent consequences of this tradition: to point out that insofar as it rests on the assumption that individuals are free to determine their own destinies, the tradition of moral equality is a burden to those who seek redress for inequities through the reform or restructuring of society.

When the tradition of moral equality is manifested in public policy as equal treatment and equal opportunity, the results are just as mixed. Obviously, it is a gain for minority groups no longer to be discriminated against, but to be treated uniformly does not have the positive consequences our tradition of equality implies. When African Americans, Mexican Americans, Puerto Ricans, or Native Americans in the aggregate are allowed to compete in school and for jobs, fellowships, and so on, the outcome is predictable: they will lose because their social experience has shaped them for failure. Special efforts to offer realistic opportunities to minorities are another matter. But even here no change in the relative position of minorities in the aggregate (as opposed to individuals) should be expected to follow automatically.

African Americans and Voting

In the presidential election of 1992, 54.1 percent of African Americans voted as opposed to 64.9 percent of white Americans. By and large, African-American participation in elections is consistent with their class position—

the lower classes vote less than the upper classes. African-American voting participation increases with income as does white voting, though lower black income groups vote more than white, while upper black income groups vote less than their white counterparts.[31] It should be noted that African-American electoral power is diluted by more than their class position—their political strength is weakened by gerrymandering, multimember districting, at-large elections, and in other ways.[32]

African Americans are employed in federal civil service occupations at higher rates than whites, and they have made significant gains in winning elective office in recent years, especially at the local level. However, African Americans are still far from holding a proportionate share of important public positions, at either the elected or the appointed level.

Government and African Americans

The liberal universe is obviously deeply at odds with American traditions that categorize human beings in ascriptive terms (race, sex, religion, ethnicity, and age). It is undeniable that the tradition of class (liberalism) has made inroads into the "caste" structure of the United States. And there is little doubt that its primary victim, the African-American, has at least begun a transition from ascriptive inequality to achievement inequality. The explicit use of power to deny blacks the vote or to segregate them socially is now illegal and in growing disuse. The basic landmarks in the abolition of "caste" boundaries are well known: armed forces integration, fair employment laws, school desegregation, and civil rights acts, especially those relating to voting and the use of public accommodations and facilities. Implementation of these decisions has, however, lagged badly. Regardless of political party, all national administrations up to the 1960s failed to carry out their clear statutory and constitutional obligation to eradicate "caste" inequality. The inaccuracy of the popular belief that the federal government is an equalizing force is readily apparent if one examines the historic role of the federal government in fostering "caste" stratification in the United States. Of course, it was state governments, reflecting the values and wishes of white power groups, that institutionalized racial segregation as a way of life in the American South. State electoral laws systematically disenfranchised African Americans, and state and local laws decreed and enforced segregation in social life.[33] But Congress and the federal government looked the other way; indeed, the federal government actually fostered segregation in the armed forces and in federally assisted housing. Meanwhile, the U.S. Supreme Court accepted and legitimized racial segregation in one decision after the other, not merely before the Civil War but also between 1865 and the 1930s. (The Court issued no major attack on segregation until *Brown* vs. *Board of Education* in 1954).

The class bias that characterizes even the most high-minded legislation, ensuring that the upper classes gain more from political life than the lower classes, is readily apparent if one examines the impact of legislation on blacks. To use an example we have already discussed, the military conscription laws and practices in effect during the Vietnam War discriminated against those who were not in college—that is, against blacks, the poor, and the working class in general. Social Security taxes and minimum ages of eligibility burden blacks unequally because they start work earlier than whites, receive incomes mostly from wages (the only taxable income) and mostly within the taxable maximum, and have larger families (thus being burdened more by the Social Security tax's lack of exemptions). Also, the life spans of blacks are shorter than the classes above them, and thus they do not collect Social Security for as long a time or, in the case of the average black male, not at all (until 1986).

The federal and state trickle-down policy in housing tends to provide housing for blacks only when it is overage; subsidized housing tends to segregate blacks (often far from jobs); and urban renewal is often tantamount to black removal. Governmental policies to stimulate the economy through subsidies, tax depreciation, and low interest rates are another version of the trickle-down philosophy, which can be expressed as "what's good for the upper classes is bound eventually to be good for the lower classes." However, such policies never seem to have much impact on black unemployment. Furthermore, governmental policies that tolerate inflation burden the poor hardest, as do policies to fight inflation, which invariably amount to socially created increases in unemployment. And the substitute for meaningful employment, the welfare system, has provided only an inadequate level of goods and services and a heavy dose of social stigma.

Fair employment laws have never contained provisions for enforcement, and their ability to create a wider range of opportunities for blacks has thus been minimal. In the 1970s, however, as an aftermath (along with sexual equality laws) of the strong civil rights laws of the mid-1960s, the government and the courts began to strike down discriminatory hiring, retention, promotion, and pay practices. The impact of these initiatives has been small, but it represents a significant departure from the hypocrisy of the past.

And, finally, to explore one area in a little more depth, governmental efforts to desegregate schools have had very mixed results. Essentially, the causes of unequal education for blacks are increasingly located beyond the jurisdiction of explicit public policy and in the realm of private life (class position). The pattern of segregation by residence (class) is quite pronounced and no changes are in sight. Black children are just as effectively segregated in public schools, despite equality before the law and equality of opportunity, as they were in the segregated schools of the southern "caste" system. And it is unlikely that the pervasive pattern of class segregation will be modified by the power dimension at the federal, state, or local levels. Not surprisingly, there is evidence that while *de jure* segregation (the overt use of power to segregate schools) has declined in the South, *de facto* educational segregation (based on class forces that segregate the races by income, occupation, and residence) has become well entrenched.

It is interesting that education is the only sector of the class dimension in which African Americans seem to have made gains relative to whites during the post-1950 period.[34] But because education seems not to be related to economic advancement for blacks in the way it is for whites, African Americans are probably expending a disproportionate amount of effort in this area. It is clear, for example, that a given amount of schooling benefits blacks much less than whites: It affords significantly less income and is no protection against the greater unemployment rates prevalent among blacks, even for college graduates. It is also significant that relative gains in education by blacks have been confined mostly to the level of high school. Ironically, the worth of a high school diploma began to decline in 1945 (about the same time that blacks began to achieve in this area) with the advent of mass higher education. And, to compound the irony, blacks are now exerting themselves against great odds at the level of undergraduate education just as the bachelor's degree is undergoing a relative decline in value and postgraduate degrees have begun to be the educational credential for acquiring positions in the upper classes.

POPULAR CULTURE AND RACE[35]

Historical Trends

The early content of the mass media (radio, film, and television) expressed America's racism fully and openly: African Americans were either invisible or depicted as lazy, stupid, incompetent, objects of comic ridicule, and always in menial occupations. From the 1960s into the 1970s, changes occurred and African Americans were portrayed in a more positive light. This change corresponded to a major shift in American (white) attitudes toward African Americans during the post–World War II period and to the realities of the civil rights movement. The changed depiction of African Americans has its own shortcomings, however, and a new, more subtle racist stereotyping has appeared: the more "realistic" all-black shows are characterized by "irresponsible and absent black males, esteem given to bad, flashy characters, and a general lack of positive attributes in the Black community." Research since indicates that the media are still in this stage.[36]

Head Counts, Types of Roles, and Black-White Interaction

This is a good place to remind ourselves that experience is not always a good guide to reality. Whatever the appearances, research reveals that white males and females have increased their representation in television character roles in recent years, while black males and females are below their population percentages, with black females far below. As far as other racial minorities are concerned, America has none if television is our guide. Native Americans, Hawaiians, Pacific Islanders, or Asian Americans are virtually nonexistent as far as the mass media are concerned. (Print media does have occasional stories about Native Americans and gambling casinos, and Asian-American complaints against affirmative action.)

As for types of roles, black males lost ground in both major and supporting roles and black females lost even more ground. Another major pattern on television is segregation. Whites and nonwhites do not interact much on friendly, respectful terms in mixed-race shows, and the bulk of African-American representation on television is on all-black shows. Incidentally, there is also a strong tendency for whites and blacks to watch like-race shows. In one poll of top ten shows watched by black and white audiences, there was not one overlapping show!

Journalism and African Americans

Newspaper coverage of African Americans increased from 1960 on, but by and large, the coverage focused on crime, celebrities, and black politicians with little coverage of or explanation of black protests about their problems. Of special interest was the tendency to depict black politicians in negative terms as special interest pleaders, as opposed to white politicians, who are seen as spokespersons for the general interest.

The Republican party's onslaught against the federal welfare system and affirmative action in 1995, matters of considerable concern to African Americans and other minorities, was discussed in the media largely by white males. Of particular interest is the implicit indictment of African Americans as innately immoral because of their illegitimacy rates. Throughout, nary a journalist—or sociologist, for that matter—pointed out that marriage presupposes a structured world with a sound economic base and material assets (or character traits that will lead to material assets) that are worth passing on to heirs, things missing in large parts of the African-American population and, for that matter, among nonblack Americans, who also have significant illegitimacy rates.

Advertising

Male and female African Americans are also either absent or buried in a sea of faces or other style of presentation in the field of advertising. Incidentally, the underuse of African Americans in both print and television advertising bears no relation to white audience preferences, which indicate no negativity to the use of black models.

Children's Programs

Children's programs tend to have fewer African Americans and to depict them as inadequately as programs for adults. Interestingly, audiences here, especially blacks, also identified strongly with same-race shows. It is noteworthy that public television has a much more positive portrayal of African Americans on children's programs than does private television.

The Mass Media and African Americans

Researchers report that Americans who watch entertainment programs believe that African Americans are much better off than they are, while those who watch television news programs think they are worse off than they are. Both here and elsewhere, an important reform in improving the depiction of African Americans is to have more black reporters, commentators, and executives in the various media, where they are very underrepresented. A striking example of racial bias by commentators is from sports: in a 1977 study, white commentators gave white players "more play-related praise and more favorable comments on aggressive plays, while blacks were more the subject of unfavorable comparisons to other players, and all eleven negative references to nonprofessional past behaviors were to black players."[37] The recent influx of black commentators into the broadcast booth has not been studied to see if improvements have occurred, but one can guess that they have.

Changes in the depiction of African Americans since the 1950s can be interpreted in terms of unintended consequences. African Americans are no longer uniformly depicted as inferiors and there are many examples of blacks in high achievement positions. But the special barriers to black achievement are rarely discussed and they are uniformly depicted as assimilated, a normal outcome of a progressive society that is what it claims to be. This way of endorsing the status quo leads to a second way in which the media legitimate the present order of things and people. Because blacks are shown in a positive light, the media cannot be accused of racism when they concentrate on African Americans as dangerous deviants. Since neither depiction is accompanied with explanations based on history and socioeconomic causes, viewers are confined to status quo interpretations: racist explanations or right liberal explanations (all individuals are what they are by nature).

Sport and Racial Inequality

African Americans are prominent in many professional sports (basketball, baseball, and football, but not hockey, tennis, golf, auto racing, or horse racing). African Americans succeed in sports that are accessible to them, in other words, in terms of class position. In addition, African-American success in professional sports belies their lack of success in American society. Perhaps the most bitter irony is that the success of a tiny handful of African Americans on the playing field took place at the same time that the American economy was moving away from muscular labor toward cerebral labor (1950s on). The civil rights movement and the integration of sports allowed professional sports teams to expand dramatically in the South and Southwest from the 1960s on, but they also allowed northern and midwestern corporations to move to the cheap labor of the nonunionized South and Southwest. One result was to leave many African Americans high and dry in decaying, older industrial, urban centers.

On a concrete level, stacking (positional segregation by race and ethnicity) is still prevalent. In addition, African Americans have not been able to move into managerial positions in sports. Basketball has a better record than baseball and football in recruiting African Americans into coaching and front office jobs, but progress in all areas stalled in 1991.[38]

THE DECLINING SIGNIFICANCE OF RACE?

William Julius Wilson has argued that race has given way to class as the major determinant of the life chances of blacks. The United States, argues Wilson, has gone through three stages of race relations: the plantation economy of racial-caste oppression in the pre–Civil War South; the period of industrial expansion, class conflict, and racial oppression between 1875 and the 1930s; and the period of progressive transition from race inequalities to class inequalities after 1945. Race relations, says Wilson, have been shaped by the systems of production characteristic of each period and by the laws and policies of the state.

Today, says Wilson, blacks are more differentiated and somewhat resemble the white class structure. Young educated blacks, especially males, are entering the middle classes at rates exceeding those of whites. Blacks are going to college in huge numbers, their percent of college students even exceeding their percent of the population (and most are going to white colleges). But, says Wilson, there is a huge black underclass that is subject to "class subordination" and unable to enter the American mainstream. The dislocations of the modern industrial society affect many whites and other minorities as well. What are needed, Wilson concludes, are broad public policy programs to attack inequality on a broad class front.

Charles V. Willie has criticized Wilson for using social class theory, a theory preferred by the affluent because they can argue that poverty is a function of individual capacities, not institutions. But after this promising beginning, Willie argues that blacks have not progressed as far as Wilson claims and that the reason is still discrimination by race (and sex). Black income, education, occupational status, and residence are still far less satisfactory than whites, show no great improvement, and still lend themselves to racist rather than achievement explanations. And, concludes Willie, the black middle class today is still very much concerned, even obsessed, by race.[39]

Perhaps Wilson and Willie are both wide of the mark. Combining Wilson's focus on class and Willie's realism about race, a conflict sociologist might argue as follows: Wilson's class explanation is on the right track but incomplete. To understand the present position and prospects of black Americans, Wilson must realize that racism has been a function of class interest throughout American history, first as slavery, then as racist segregation and discrimination to favor both the white property and working classes, and now as a theory of equal opportunity and competition through civil rights, busing, and affirmative action. In the present period, blacks are still subordinated by the system of production. The black middle class is very small and has made its gains through employment, not business ownership. And a substantial part of the gains in black employment has been in the public sector. Here again there is status without power—the mobilization of business since the 1970s and its success in cutting public services and its anti-urban policies have hurt the black middle class as well as the black poor. Wilson must be asked, therefore, whether abstract talk about economic growth and the abandonment of concrete policies to help the underclass is really the answer. The corporate capitalist society that he identifies is highly concentrated, generates large amounts of unskilled jobs, and appears inherently unable to achieve full employment. And the belief that economic growth will trickle down to add the lower classes and minorities was suspect as early as the 1960s. By the mid-90s, it is clear that America's corporate economy, now thoroughly enmeshed in the world market and its cheaper resources and labor, is operating directly counter to the interests of minorities, and by all accounts, counter to the interests of white workers and even professionals. If Willie cannot use the overt racism of the pre–World War II era to characterize black-white relations, then neither can Wilson use mainstream optimism and incrementalism.

AFRICAN-AMERICAN SOCIAL THEORY[40]

African-American Liberal (Assimiliationist) Thought: From Booker T. Washington to William Julius Wilson

African-American assimilationist views are well-known and need no emphasis. Prominent black leaders from Booker T. Washington (1865–1915) to Martin Luther King, Jr., and Shirley Chisholm; some black organizations, like the NAACP; and some scholars, like Charles Hamilton and William Julius Wilson, have all supported a liberal (assimiliationist) perspective. The underlying assumption of assimilationist thought is that the essential structure of liberal democracy in America is sound and that black people should work hard, with or without allies, to turn America into a truly democratic and racially integrated social system. Essential to their vision is a federal government that is capable of acting to promote racial justice.

African-American Socialist Thought: From W.E.B. DuBois to Manning Marable

A radical strand of African-American socialist thought, from W.E.B. DuBois (1868–1963) to Manning Marable, denies that American society, as presently constituted, can integrate its racial minorities. They also argue that whites are oppressed and that liberation for blacks can come only through the liberation of all, something that can be achieved only through socialism.

The leading contemporary African-American Marxist socialist is Manning Marable, who teaches at Columbia University. Marable acknowledges W.E.B. DuBois as the source of his work, along with other scholars.[41] In typical Marxian fashion, Marable's analysis is both an attempt to find a pattern in the facts of history and to inspire action leading to human liberation. The essential pattern for Marable is found in the dynamics of capital formation and social stratification. These interrelated processes are the key to unlocking the diverse forms of inequality and oppression that burden humans everywhere regardess of skin color or gender.

Though he is consistent about the need to keep all humans in mind, Marable depicts the struggle for freedom largely through the eyes and actions of blacks, both male and female, both in the United States and the Third World. His work is a fascinating, occasionally horrifying, chronicle of how blacks, both males and females, have suffered under various capitalist and precapitalist regimes and how they resisted oppression in whatever ways were available to them.

Marable's attention to the special problems of black women continues the work of Federick Douglass and W.E.B. DuBois, and, of course, continues the work on gender of Engels. Marable is also at pains to cite black males and white females, including suffragists, as additional sources of trouble for black females beyond those imposed by white males.

Marable's analysis is also noteworthy because he links the fate of oppressed people in all societies to each other. He sees the struggle against capitalism as both a domestic and an international matter. In pursuing this perspective, Marable provides fascinating analyses of black resistance to a wide variety of colonial regimes and connects them to black struggles in the United States.

Though Marable's prediction of when a new democratic order will emerge is vague (as with Marx, one must wait until things and souls are ready), he does provide motivation to resist oppression in whatever contexts one finds oneself. Perhaps his most important contribution to the morale of those who might feel overpowered is his focus on the logic of capitalism: to keep up the level of capital formation and profit, capitalists must do things that often stir oppositional consciousness on the part of noncapitalists. At some point the logic of capitalism will destroy capitalism and its various forms of oppression. In an analysis of the Reagan presidency of 1980 (written in 1983), Marable saw it as a response to a crisis in American capitalism, to wit, faltering capitalist accumulation and a falling rate of profit. The Reagan emphasis on tax cuts, cuts in social services, military buildup, support for capital over labor, and increased law enforcement against the lower classes is bad for majority whites, says Marable, but worse for blacks—it is destroying the institutions that blacks have worked so hard to build in order to protect and emancipate themselves. Whether the logic of capitalism in this instance will galvanize the oppressed to action, Marable does not say.

For over three-quarters of a century, from DuBois to Marable, African-American socialism has argued that oppression is a necessary feature of American capitalism. Its position contradicts the American belief that the United States has the adaptive capacity to integrate its minorities. It also reminds white Americans that a large portion of the white population is not yet integrated. But even its position on African Americans is quite different from mainstream scholarship. The latter takes it for granted that the real America is the America of ideals, and that assimilation will take place incrementally, somehow, sometime. An example is the massive four-year study by a wide variety of foundations and quasi-public bodies, which provides an empirical analysis of the status of African Americans that neither DeBois nor Marable would find much to argue with.[42] What they would argue with is the study's continual references to vague explanations such as *negative* cause (for example, "slowdown in economic growth," "technological change, national and international economic developments, and large population movements") and as *redemptory* cause (for example, scattered appeals to an abstract reader that reforms are necessary in all areas of African-American life).

African-American Separatist Thought: From Marcus Garvey to Muhammad and Baraka

A second strand of radical African-American thought seeks liberation for blacks through separation from the contamination of white society. Marcus Garvey (1887–1940) argued for a return to Africa, while black Muslim leader Elijah Muhammad (1898–1975) argued that blacks must build their own world within territorial America. The latter's vision of the good society is separate institutions run by blacks united by Islamic religion.

There are two other variations on black separatism. Imamu Baraka has argued that a separate black society must be based on black culture, and that a black political party, emerging out of black communities, is the means by which blacks can build their own nation. Imari Obadele I advocated immediate action to achieve black freedom starting with a Republic of New Africa on land in Mississippi. In a (failed) appeal to the United Nations, Obadele I hoped to force the United States to hold a plebiscite giving blacks options of various kinds. Obadele I was not opposed to using violence and included a military strategy in his proposals for building black communities.

African-American Feminist Thought

African Americans exhibit a split between radical and socialist theories on the one hand (whether or not these theories pay attention to the problems of black women or not) and theorists who insist on a distinctive black feminist outlook (we find a similar split between liberal and socialist theories and [white] feminist theory). Frederick Douglass, W.E.B. DuBois, and Manning Marable paid considerable attention to African-American women. Nonetheless, black women have asserted the right to speak for themselves and to claim a distinctive black feminist outlook.

Black feminist thought is unique in that there is no Irish, Italian, Jewish, or Greek feminist thought, though there may be a Chicano feminist voice. The reason is that white ethnic women can identify with mainstream (middle-class) feminism and focus on gender issues. Black women, however, must contend with three powerful negatives in the lives: race and class as well as gender.

Patricia Hill Collins has provided a valuable description and analysis of what African-American women have thought throughout American history in an effort to identify a tradition of black feminist thought.[43] Black women, she argues, have special angles of vision because they are (undefeated) outsiders to mainstream academic life, male black social theory (and organizations), and white, middle-class feminist theory. They also benefit from their "outsider-within" status doing domestic work for white families, where they clearly see gender inequality of white-on-white.

Collins concludes her enormously valuable substantive analysis by extracting an epistemology from the black feminist tradition that is similar to that of Dorothy E. Smith (see Chapter 19). Black women, this tradition argues, should avoid the masculine world of objectivity and impersonality. They must cultivate subjectivity, caring, dialogue, and empathy with others, put themselves in contact with all other special perspectives, and be ready to form coalitions with others in the name of humanism, all this while resisting domination in the various spheres of race, gender, and class.

Collins does not raise the danger that black women (who are currently doing better than black males in higher education) may be handicapping themselves by not also being proficient in mainstream epistemology. The issue of not resisting negative gender relations with black males, for fear of undermining the already vulnerable position of black males, is also not raised. And she does not ask if educated black women with successful marriages and careers can empathize with black women in the lower classes who are still being oppressed by being at the wrong end of race, gender, and class relations.

SUMMARY

Racial and ethnic minorities live separately as miniature "societies" in agrarian society. Capitalism establishes an abstract labor market pulling all out of their racial and ethnic worlds to compete for positions in the abstract division of labor. In the United States the powerful forces of discrimination are offset somewhat by the achievement ethic.

Racial and ethnic minorities make up approximately 25 percent of the American population. African Americans at 12 percent are the largest group, followed by Hispanics at 10 percent and Asian Americans at 2–3 percent.

African Americans made relative gains in the American class system from the late nineteenth century until the 1950s. They were helped by movement to northern industrial areas during a stage in American economic development when unskilled and semiskilled labor was in demand. Since the 1950s and despite civil rights and affirmative action, African Americans have found it difficult to make relative advances or even to hang on to previous advances.

Most African Americans beong to the working class and lower middle class, with a small number of upper-middle-class households. An out-of-proportion number belong to the lower class.

African Americans have achieved a great deal in all areas of American life, despite the harrowing barrier of racism and having to start their climb from a deeply disadvantaged position. At present, they appear stalled on every index that measures social class: wealth, occupation, education, income, family stability, health, housing, associational life, politics, and relation to government and law.

The civil rights movement has helped in some regards but it has also burdened African Americans with the American ideology that individuals are responsible for what happens to them. The same ironic consequence emerges from the dramatic decline in the number of white Americans who believe that blacks are innately inferior.

Popular culture (entertainment, including sports, and journalism) does little to enhance the image of African Americans, even though the demeaning images of the pre-1960s era no longer appear.

African Americans have developed liberal (assimiliationist), separatist, socialist, and distinctive feminist outlooks. They have also debated whether racism or class disadvantage is their major burden. If racism is seen as an ideology derived from the caste-slave system of the Old South and carried into the era of class stratification and the corporate capitalist world market economy, then disadvantaged class position is the major burden of African Americans; that is, African Americans, along with other minorities, are bearing the largest sacrifices of the American population so that the upper classes can compete in the global economy and maintain their levels of comfort and security.

NOTES

1. For a comprehensive reference book with good thematic essays on American ethnic and racial groups, see Stephen Thernstrom, ed., *Harvard Encyclopedia of American Ethnic Groups* (Cambridge, MA: Harvard University Press, 1980).
2. Prentice-Hall's Ethnic Groups in American Life Series, edited by Milton M. Gordon, provides excellent case studies of major ethnic and racial minorities, including a study of white Protestant Americans. Harry H. L. Kitano and Roger Daniels, *Asian Americans: Emerging Minorities,* 2nd ed. (Englewood Cliffs, NJ: Prentice-Hall, 1995) updates our picture of Chinese and Japanese Americans and provides a valuable picture of other Asian Americans as well as Pacific Islanders.
3. United States Civil Rights Commission, Washington, DC 20425.
4. *Social Indicators of Equality for Minorities and Women 1978,* p. 3. The commission notes that a lack of data prevents it from inquiring into such areas as the working order of housing facilities, criminal victimization, health service utilization, and hidden unemployment. It should be noted that the commission has faced deep hostility by the Republican party, aided by conservative Democrats, and has been unable to continue its work of documenting the sorry state of America's minorities.
5. Good general sources of information about African Americans are W. Augustus Low and Vergil A. Clift, eds., *Encyclopedia of Black America* (New York: McGraw-Hill, 1981), the National Urban League's annual report *The State of Black America,* and the U.S. Bureau of the Census, *Current Population Reports,* "The Social and Economic Status of the Black Population in the United States, 1970–1978," Series P-23, no. 80 (Washington, DC: U.S. Government Printing Office, 1979). Two books with background on the class position of blacks, which also include a refreshing emphasis on policy analysis, are Harrell R. Rodger, Jr., ed., *Racism and Inequality: The Policy Alternatives* (San Francisco: W.H. Freeman, 1975) and Dou-

glas G. Glascow, *The Black Underclass: Poverty, Unemployment, and Entrapment of Ghetto Youth* (San Francisco: Jossey-Bass, 1980).

6. U.S. Bureau of the Census, "Asset Ownership of Households: 1993," *Current Population Reports* P70-47 (Washington, DC: U.S. Government Printing Office, 1995), Table F.
7. Ernest R. House and William Madura, "Race, Gender, and Jobs: Losing Ground on Employment," *Policy Sciences* 21 (1988):351–382; Marshall J. Pomer, "Labor Market Structure, Intragenerational Mobility, and Discrimination: Black Male Advancement Out of Low-Paying Occupations, 1962–1973," *American Sociological Review* 51 (October 1986):650–659.
8. Daniel T. Lichter, "Racial Differences in Underemployment in American Cities," *American Journal of Sociology* 93 (January 1988):771–792.
9. U.S. Bureau of the Census, Current Population Reports, P20-480, "The Black Population in the United States: March 1994 and 1993" (Washington DC: U.S. Government Printing Office, 1995), Table E.
10. For a comprehensive sociological analysis of the African-American family, see Robert Staples and Leanor Boulin Johnson, *Black Families at the Crossroads* (San Francisco: Jossey-Bass, 1993). For a collection of up-to-date readings, see Robert Staples, ed., *The Black Family*, 5th ed. (Belmont, CA: Wadsworth, 1994).
11. U.S. Bureau of the Census, "The Black Population in the United States: March 1994 and 1993," *Current Population Reports,* P20-480 (Washington, DC: U.S. Government Printing Office, 1995), Tables E, F.
12. Wornie L. Reed with William Darity, Sr., and Noma L. Roberson, *Health and Medical Care of African Americans* (Westport, Conn.: Auburn House, 1993).
13. Edward Green, "Race, Social Status, and Criminal Arrest," *American Sociological Review* 35 (June 1970):476–490.
14. Coramae Richey Mann, *Unequal Justice: A Question of Color* (Bloomington: Indiana University Press, 1993). Mann's study is also invaluable and unique because she provides detailed pictures of the relations of Native Americans, Asian Americans, and Hispanic Americans to the law.
15. Michael Tonry, *Malign Neglect—Race, Crime, and Punishment in America* (New York: Oxford University Press, 1995).
16. Sharon M. Collins, "The Making of Black Middle Class," *Social Problems* 30 (April 1983):369–392, and "The Marginalization of Black Executives," *Social Problems* 36 (October 1989):317–331.
17. For a full-length treatment of the black middle class, which agrees largely with the above (but which defines the black middle class as households that include white-collar workers, firefighters, police officers, and which therefore has a rosier picture of black success), see Bart Landry, *The New Black Middle Class* (Berkeley: University of California Press, 1987).
18. For a structural explanation of the underclass (the routine operations of capitalist investment aided by government) as opposed to racial discrimination or the characteristics of blacks, see William Julius Wilson, *The Truly Disadvantaged: The Inner City, The Underclass, and Public Policy* (Chicago: University of Chicago Press, 1987).
19. Frank Harold Wilson, "Housing and Black Americans: The Persistence of Race," in William Velez, ed., *Race and Ethnicity in the United States* (Dix Hills, NY: General Hall, 1995).
20. Nancy A. Denton and Douglas S. Massey, in their "Residential Segregation of Blacks, Hispanics, and Asians By Socioeconomic Status and Generation," *Social*

Science Quarterly 69 (December 1988):797–817, argue that blacks are still heavily segregated residentially through all socioeconomic levels and that they are the only minority that has been unable to integrate with a rise in class status. Marta Tienda and Ding-Tzann Lii, in their "Minority Concentration and Earnings Inequality: Blacks, Hispanics, and Asians Compared," *American Journal of Sociology* 93 (July 1987):141–165, argue that the three minorities they studied all suffered earnings losses because of residential and labor market concentration, but blacks, and especially college-educated blacks, suffered the greatest losses (thus benefiting white college graduates).

21. The pattern of residential segregation by class (and by minority status) has far-reaching political implications. Essentially, it makes possible the neutralization of the numerical strength of the lower classes through the gerrymander (employed in a variety of ways); for a discussion, see Chapter 14.
22. Milton M. Gordon, *Assimilation in American Life: The Role of Race, Religion, and National Origin* (New York: Oxford University Press, 1964).
23. Even death does not unite the "races"—cemeteries have traditionally been segregated, though the practice is now being modified by legislation and court decisions.
24. Upper-class blacks and other "races" tend to mix more with whites than their counterparts lower on the class ladder.
25. For an analysis of the weak primary group development of blacks relative to economic development contrasted with the strong development of economically relevant primary behavior among Japanese and Chinese immigrants, see Ivan H. Light, *Ethnic Enterprise in America: Business and Welfare Among Chinese, Japanese, and Blacks* (Berkeley: University of California Press, 1972).
26. The primary relations of upper-level blacks depicted in E. Franklin Frazier, *Black Bourgeoisie* (New York: Free Press, 1957), ch. 9 can be contrasted fruitfully with the primary relations among lower-level blacks depicted in Elliot Liebow, *Tally's Corner: A Study of Negro Streetcorner Men* (Boston: Little, Brown, 1967).
27. For example, individuals who sincerely believe in human equality may, because they also believe in protecting or enhancing their own property, resist low-income housing in their community.
28. For example, the civil rights movement is as much a class process (a way of transforming rural labor into an urban-industrial labor force) as it is a political-legal-moral movement.
29. Howard Schuman, Charlotte Steeh, and Lawrence Bobo, *Racial Attitudes in America: Trends and Interpretations* (Cambridge, MA: Harvard University Press, 1985), and *Public Opinion* 10 (July–August 1987), Special Issue on Prejudice.
30. For the development of this point by means of a comparison of these two sets of data, see the article by Howard Schuman, "Free Will and Determinism in Public Beliefs About Race," *Transaction* 7 (December 1969):44–48.
31. U.S. Bureau of the Census, *Current Population Reports*, Series P-20, No. 466, "Voting and Registration in the Election of November, 1992" (Washington, DC: U.S. Government Office, 1993), Table 13.
32. Chandler Davidson, ed., *Minority Vote Dilution* (Washington, DC: Howard University Press, 1989).
33. Among the prime stereotypes that distort our perception of power is the false belief that "local" government is more democratic, more personal, and more responsive than the national government.

34. Relative gains *within* the class system should not be confused with progress in overcoming "caste" barriers blocking blacks' entry *into* the class system.
35. The following relies on the superb summary of research on minorities and the media by Bradley S. Greenberg and Jeffrey E. Brand, "Minorities and the Mass Media: 1970s to 1990s," in Jennings Bryant and Dolf Zillmann, eds., *Media Effects: Advances in Theory and Research* (Hillsdale, NJ: Lawrence Erlbaum Associates, 1994), pp. 273–314.
36. As depicted in television programs, especially soap operas, African-American characters who achieve are thoroughly assimilated into white society.
37. Bradley S. Greenberg and Jeffrey E. Brand, "Minorities and the Mass Media: 1970s to 1990s," Jennings Bryant and Dolf Zillmann, eds., *Media Effects: Advances in Theory and Research* (Hillsdale, NJ: Lawrence Erlbaum Associates, 1994), p. 289.
38. Richard E. Lapchick with David Stuckney, "Professional Sports: The Racial Report Card," D. Stanley Eitzen, ed., *Sport in Contemporary Society: An Anthology*, 4th ed. (New York: St. Martin's Press, 1993), pp. 355–371.
39. Wilson's argument may be found in William Julius Wilson, *The Declining Significance of Race: Blacks and Changing American Institutions* (Chicago: University of Chicago Press, 1978), and *The Truly Disadvantaged: The Inner City, The Underclass, and Public Policy* (Chicago: University of Chicago Press, 1987). An exchange between Wilson and Willie may be found in W. J. Wilson, "The Declining Significance of Race," *Society* 15 (January–February 1978):56–62; Charles V. Willie, "The Inclining Significance of Race," *Society* 15 (July–August 1978):10ff.; and W. J. Wilson, "The Declining Significance of Race—Revisited but Not Revised," *Society* 15 (July–August 1978):11ff.
40. A full analysis of black political and social thought, eminently suitable for undergraduates, may be found in John T. McCartney, *Black Power Ideologies: An Essay in African-American Political Thought* (Philadelphia: Temple University Press, 1992).
41. Marable's basic position may be found in *How Capitalism Underdeveloped Black America* (Boston: South End Press, 1983), and *Black American Politics: From the Washington Marches to Jesse Jackson* (London: Verso, 1985). Marable's writings have also been published as pamphlets on select topics (fourteen in all), making his ideas even more accessible to undergraduates.
42. Gerald David Jaynes and Robin M. Williams, Jr., eds., *A Common Destiny: Blacks and American Society* (Washington, DC: National Academy Press, 1989).
43. Patricia Hill Collins, *Black Feminist Thought: Knowledge, Consciousness, and the Politics of Empowerment* (New York: Routledge, 1991).

18

The Class Position of America's Hispanic Minorities: Mexican, Puerto Rican, and Cuban Americans

◆ ◆ ◆ ◆

MEXICAN AMERICANS
- Historical Background
- Occupation, Income, and Education
- The Mexican-American Family
- Voluntary Associations
- Voting and Political Participation
- Government and Mexican Americans
- Mexican Americans and the Law
- Hispanics and the Mass Media
- Current Prospects and Problems

PUERTO RICAN AMERICANS
- Historical Background
- From Empire to World-Market Imperialism
- Occupation, Income, and Education
- Current Prospects and Problems

CUBAN AMERICANS
- The Cuban Exodus: U.S. Imperialism and Cuban Americans
- Wealth, Occupation, Income, and Education
- Current Prospects and Problems

HISPANIC-AMERICAN ATTITUDES: MORE AMERICAN THAN HISPANIC

SUMMARY

NOTES

◆ ◆ ◆ ◆

MEXICAN AMERICANS

Historical Background

Mexican Americans are the largest ethnic minority in the United States, but reliable data about them have appeared only in recent years. The Census Bureau has also changed its way of counting Mexican Americans, making comparisons over time difficult. Further, Mexicans make up the bulk of the millions of illegal aliens in the United States, thus further clouding our picture of the Mexican-American population.

Mexican Americans numbered 14.6 million in 1993 making up about 60 percent of Hispanic Americans and about 6 percent of the total American population (see Table 17–1). Their history is unique in a number of ways. Some are from families that have been living in what is now the United States from before the Pilgrims landed at Plymouth Rock. When the United States expanded into the Southwest, the native inhabitants, both Mexicans and Indians, were treated as subject peoples.[1] Mexican Americans are also unique in that they are the only minority in American history (excepting the American Indian) that failed to make significant economic and other gains from one generation to the other prior to 1950.[2]

Occupation, Income, and Education

Mexican Americans have made gains since 1950, especially in urban areas, but gains have been slow and their income, occupational, and educational levels are still low. Table 18–1 shows the distribution of Mexican Americans in the occupational structure of the United States. Note the difference when compared to the Not Hispanic column. In addition, the Mexican-American unemployment rate is chronically about twice the rate of the Not Hispanic population (similar to the unemployment rate of African Americans). In 1994, after two years of good economic growth it stood at 11.2 percent versus 6.6 percent for Not Hispanic—see Table 18–2.

As Table 18–3 shows, Mexican-American family income remains substantially below that of the Not Hispanic population. And Table 18–4 reveals that the Mexican-American poverty rate is substantially higher than the Not Hispanic population—almost one-third of Mexican Americans live in poverty (the comparable figure for Not Hispanic is 13.4 percent).

The educational status of Mexican Americans chronically lags well behind the Not Hispanic population. Table 18–5 reveals this lag in the all-important area of higher education. All in all, the economic class status of Mexican Americans is poor and their relative position has not changed for as far back as records go. In addition, a sizable portion of Mexican Americans is economically depressed and, with portions of other minorities (and whites), forms what must be called a *permanent underclass.*

TABLE 18–1 The Occupation of Hispanic Americans, 1994

		HISPANIC ORIGIN				
	TOTAL	HISPANIC	NOT HISPANIC	MEXICAN	PUERTO RICAN	CUBAN
Total	100.0	100.0	100.0	100.0	100.0	100.0
Occupation:						
Managerial and Professional	27.5	13.0	28.9	10.9	18.5	21.7
Technical, Sales, and Admin. Support	30.7	24.5	31.2	22.7	31.5	33.1
Service	14.2	21.1	13.6	20.0	21.0	17.2
Precision Production, Craft and Repair	10.7	12.8	10.5	13.9	10.1	8.2
Operators, Fabricators, and Laborers	14.3	23.5	13.4	25.2	17.9	18.8
Farming, Forestry, and Fishing	2.7	5.1	2.1	7.3	1.0	1.0

Source: U.S. Bureau of the Census, Internet, http://www.census.gov/ftp/pub/population/socdemo/hispanic/occ94.txt.

The Mexican-American Family

Mexican Americans' high birth rate has changed their population composition from that of the wider American population. The Mexican-American family is large, even larger than the black or Puerto Rican family. Given their marginal economic status, their high birth rate has created an unfavorable dependency ratio (those of working age in relation to those not likely to work). Mexican Americans are also unusual in that there are more males than females (except among the old).

Though Mexican-American family troubles are not as severe as those of black Americans, Mexican Americans have more family problems than majority Americans. The image of the warm, caring, extended Mexican-

TABLE 18–2 The Unemployment Rate of Hispanic Americans, 1994

		HISPANIC ORIGIN				
	TOTAL	HISPANIC	NOT HISPANIC	MEXICAN	PUERTO RICAN	CUBAN
Employed:						
Yes	93.0	88.9	93.4	88.8	85.8	93.2
No	7.0	11.1	6.6	11.2	14.2	6.8

Source: U.S. Bureau of the Census, Internet, http://www.census.gov/ftp/pub/population/socdemo/hispanic/lfs94.txt.

TABLE 18–3 The Family Income of Hispanic Americans, 1993–1994

		HISPANIC ORIGIN				
	TOTAL	HISPANIC	NOT HISPANIC	MEXICAN	PUERTO RICAN	CUBAN
Total	100.0	100.0	100.0	100.0	100.0	100.0
Family Income						
Loss or < $10,000	9.6	17.9	8.8	16.2	28.5	13.5
$10,000 to $24,999	22.8	34.6	21.6	36.9	30.2	31.4
$25,000 to $49,999	32.8	30.6	33.0	31.3	26.6	28.0
$50,000 Plus	34.9	16.9	36.6	15.5	14.7	27.1

Source: U.S. Bureau of the Census, Internet, http://www.census.gov/ftp/pub/population/socdemo/hispanic/finc94.txt.

American family directed by male authority is a romantic myth. Mexican Americans clearly prefer the nuclear family. Many Mexican-American children lack two parents (especially fathers) and the percent of such families increased between 1982 and 1988 from 26 to 30 percent. While the norm of male dominance is maintained in theory, in practice women exercise considerable power. The use of contraceptives is high, especially among women, attesting both to their independence and to their lack of desire for large families (the acceptance of birth control is higher among higher income groups). And Mexican-American families exhibit high rates of pathology in all areas: divorce and separation, domestic violence, trouble between parents and children, and so on.[3]

Voluntary Associations

For most of their history, Mexican Americans were unable to develop a network of supportive voluntary organizations due to both private and official coercion, poverty, and rural isolation. This pattern has changed somewhat since the 1960s, when Mexican Americans began to shed the apathy

TABLE 18–4 The Rate of Poverty Among Hispanic Americans, 1994

		HISPANIC ORIGIN				
	TOTAL	HISPANIC	NOT HISPANIC	MEXICAN	PUERTO RICAN	CUBAN
Total	100.0	100.0	100.0	100.0	100.0	100.0
Poverty Status						
Poor	15.1	30.6	13.4	31.6	38.4	19.9
Not Poor	84.9	69.4	86.6	68.4	61.6	80.1

Source: U.S. Bureau of the Census, Internet, http://www.census.gov/ftp/pub/population/socdemo/hispanic/ppov94.txt.

TABLE 18–5 Educational Attainment Level by Ethnicity Population Age 25 and Over, 1994

		HISPANIC ORIGIN				
	TOTAL	HISPANIC	NOT HISPANIC	MEXICAN	PUERTO RICAN	CUBAN
Total	100.0	100.0	100.0	100.0	100.0	100.0
Educational Attainment						
No college	53.5	72.9	51.7	77.4	72.2	62.0
Some college	17.4	13.3	17.7	12.3	13.5	14.6
AA degree	7.0	4.7	7.2	4.0	4.5	7.2
Bachelor's degree	14.7	6.2	15.5	4.4	6.9	9.0
Advanced degree	7.5	2.9	7.9	1.9	2.8	7.2

Source: U.S. Bureau of the Census, Internet, http://www.census.gov/ftp/pub/population/socdemo/hispanic/ed94.txt.

induced by poverty and oppression and to take steps toward determining their own future. Nonetheless, a recent poll indicates that over 90 percent of Mexican Americans do not belong to any ethnic organization and do not engage in any political activity organized around ethnicity.[4]

Voting and Political Participation

Mexican Americans have a low rate of voting and political participation. Their unusually low voting rates are attributable to such barriers as the requirement to register, often in unaccessible places; literacy tests, conducted in English; poll taxes; a low rate of naturalization; gerrymandering; and the cooptation of Mexican-American leaders by Anglo groups. However, when Mexican Americans in San Antonio are compared with their ethnic counterparts in Los Angeles, it is apparent that Mexican American political behavior begins to approach that of other Americans in the freer and more inviting political atmosphere of Los Angeles: their rate of participation is higher, and upper-level Mexican Americans participate more than do those in lower levels.

On the whole, Mexican Americans are quite ambivalent about politics, tend to have little confidence in government, and overwhelmingly reject any alliance with black Americans. Viewed nationally, the Mexican-American voting rate is unusually low. Using the more general term, Hispanic-Origin Americans (of whom Mexican Americans are the majority), their reported voting rate in the 1992 presidential election was 28.5 percent, 36 percent below white and 25 percent below African-American rates.[5]

The above evidence notwithstanding, Mexican Americans—and Hispanics in general—are no longer marginal to American political life. Mexican Americans have become significantly more politically aware in recent decades, and their political power, based on numbers and organization, has increased. By and large, Mexican Americans—and Hispanics in general—are now a significant force in American politics.[6]

Government and Mexican Americans

Much of what has been said about African Americans' relations to legislation and government also holds true for Mexican Americans. Therefore, after briefly noting these similarities, we will turn our attention to novel features in the Mexican American's relation to public law and authority.

Mexican Americans, like all others at the lower levels of society, are not affected equitably by laws passed and administered by those who dominate the political process. Laws passed for the benefit of typical Americans (such as the Social Security Act) affect those who are below typical levels differently, and usually unequally. National economic policies designed either to stimulate or restrain the economy affect Mexican Americans adversely since they, like all working and lower class people, bear the brunt of economic stagnation and inflation.

Furthermore, Mexican Americans have borne (and still bear) a series of hardships, ranging from minor embarrassment to physical brutality, peculiar to their unique status in American society.[7] As an aggregate, Mexican Americans' legal status as citizens has been continuously challenged and/or ignored by the federal government (Border Patrol), local law enforcement agencies, and even welfare departments. American citizens of Mexican descent are indiscriminately lumped together with Mexicans who have entered the United States illegally, and they are constantly required to prove their legal status. During the 1930s, welfare departments throughout the country even helped to "repatriate" thousands of American citizens of Mexican origin who were on welfare, making no attempt to distinguish between citizen and noncitizen.

Governmental agencies tend to have poor relations with working-class and lower-class people because of the incompatibility of the impersonality and better education of civil servants and the greater personalism and ignorance of the lower classes. This relation is aggravated in the case of Mexican Americans because of a language barrier and because government in general, never having helped them—indeed, having mistreated them—is viewed with suspicion, hostility, and withdrawal.

Mexican Americans have a great deal of trouble with government, partly because laws are passed that ignore them, partly because laws are not enforced, and partly because laws designed to protect American citizens are broken or ignored in their case. To take an important example, some Mexican Americans earn their living grazing sheep; when laws are passed establishing national parks and regulating the use of park land, recreation and aesthetic pleasure for the upper classes are purchased at the expense of Mexican Americans. State employment bureaus typically think of themselves as agents of employers, and even break laws regulating minimum wages. And local law enforcement agencies, from vigilante groups to the Texas Rangers to the Los Angeles Police Department, have long histories of unconstitutional behavior toward Mexican Americans, including violence and brutality. Law enforcement officials have a long history of siding in economic matters with property owners against Mexican-American workers, even when it means breaking or ignoring the law.

The United States Commission on Civil Rights has documented the United States' drastically unequal and discriminatory educational policies toward Mexican-American children. Mexican-American children go to schools that are ethnically unbalanced, and do less well in their studies and drop out more than do majority students. Schools not only do not welcome or reinforce the language and culture of Mexican Americans but Spanish is actively suppressed, and little effort is made to recognize the language barrier in dealing with children or parents.[8] Indeed, the Mexican-American community is ignored by the schools when involving parents in education, setting up advisory boards, and hiring consultants. And Mexican Americans are deeply discriminated against in the financing of schools; much less is spent on Mexican-American children; Mexican-American communities bear a heavier tax burden for education; and Mexican-Americans are not represented on school boards in proportion to their numbers, even in predominantly Mexican-American communities.[9]

Some modifications in Mexican-American education have occurred in recent years, mostly bilingual pilot projects (the attempt to use Spanish in school in order to facilitate the learning of English). But so far no great improvements can be noted. And given a dismal record at the lower levels, American higher education is also remarkably unattended or understaffed by Mexican Americans.

The Mexican-American has been virtually ignored by the federal government (except the Border Patrol). During the unrest of the 1960s, Mexican Americans came to the attention of Congress and the executive branch for the first time. (So ignorant was Congress that an early report on "Mexican American Affairs" was sent to the Foreign Affairs Committee.) The Mexican American's difficulty in gaining attention and help from government was changed somewhat by the antipoverty efforts of the 1960s. Under the Community Action Program, federal money was granted directly to Mexican-American organizations—that is, to groups aware of the special needs of a distinct linguistic-ethnic group. For the first time, Mexican Americans had the opportunity to act on their own behalf and to develop the skills to help themselves and to deal with government. For the first time, they had become a constituency for federal legislators and administrators, which is an important prerequisite to acquiring political power and thus governmental attention and assistance. The political consciousness and power of Mexican Americans has grown, and by the late 1980s they had become a force to be reckoned with in both local and national politics (for current developments in the politics of Mexican Americans, Cuban Americans, and Puerto Ricans, see Garcia, *Latinos and the Political System*).

Mexican Americans and the Law

Mexican Americans' relation to law enforcement agencies, as to government in general, has been thoroughly unsatisfactory.[10] In 1970, the United States Commission on Civil Rights found considerable discrimination against Mexican Americans on the part of law enforcement agencies. The police used excessive zeal and force against American citizens of Mexican descent, were disrespectful of their persons and their rights, and interfered illegally with Mexican-American organizations. Adequate remedies against such abuse did not exist and the police retaliated against complainants. Furthermore, Mexican Americans were vastly underrepresented on juries, subject to bail when Anglos are not, inadequately represented by counsel, and greatly underrepresented in law enforcement agencies in general. And they have been mistreated by federal customs and immigration officials.[11]

A recent and comprehensive picture of the relation between Mexican Americans (and Puerto Ricans) and the law shows that little has changed. Coramae Richey Mann's analysis focuses on race as the basis of American's unequal treatment of minorities. But by embedding America's racism in the economy and an overall unjust society, her analysis goes beyond merely criticizing racism in an otherwise sound law enforcement system.[12] In any case, our view is that the relation between the law and America's racial-ethnic minorities should be viewed as a stratification phenomenon, a legacy partly of "caste" status and partly of class. Of course, law enforcement officials find it relatively easy to treat distinctive groups such as blacks and Mexican Americans differently. But it is crucial to keep in mind that all types of groupings in the lower classes are mistreated by law enforcement officials. The fact that mistreatment takes on a racial or ethnic flavor helps to divide groups with common grievances and interests. In other words, one of the latent functions of the mistreatment of blacks and Mexican Americans by law enforcement agencies is to foster racial and ethnic defensiveness among those mistreated. To the extent that it does so, the affected parties are unlikely to recognize the class factor common to their shared mistreatment.

Hispanics and the Mass Media

Ethnicity is still presented stereotypically in the mass media, though not as blatantly as in the past when Irish, Italian, Jewish Americans, and other of the earlier immigrants to America were openly denigrated. These former minorities are no longer economically depressed or segregated and have organizations to protect their image.

The new consciousness about minorities has also improved the way other ethnic minorities, such as Hispanics, are depicted, though some are still occasionally portrayed in negative terms. But the most important thing about ethnic minorities is their virtual absence from the mass media.[13]

Current Prospects and Problems

Mexican Americans have not only not made relative gains in the overall class structure in recent years but have actually lost ground. The basic reason is the same one we have emphasized in regard to other groups and classes—the restructuring of the American economy to allow property groups to maintain their profits in the world-market economy.[14] This restructuring has already tipped the scales of power against the American labor force and especially the poor. And the prospects for the future are grim since the American upper classes are now fully mobilized to employ the state to achieve their ends.

A concrete list of negatives and positives exhibits far more of the former than the latter. In addition to growing inequality of income and stagnation in the labor market, Mexican Americans have lost ground in college education. Another negative is the current wave of anti-immigrant fervor; incidentally, Mexican Americans themselves believe that there is too much immigration.

The anti-immigration fervor has been prompted by the negative economic experience of Americans and could lead to some positive economic gains for some—the United States has been importing significant numbers of skilled and professional labor, thus hurting some of its own citizens. A reformed immigration policy could be part of a more comprehensive effort at economic and educational planning. But this is not what is on the mind of right-wing legislators; their efforts are directed at lower-level immigrants and their main goal is to reduce public-service programs for political reasons—to curry favor with conservative-ignorant voters who don't know (as the polls indicate) that immigrants contribute more in work and taxes than they get in public services. Another incentive is that curbing public programs reduces the number of supporters for the Democratic party.

Mexican Americans are still highly segregated residentially—even beyond their class standing, it should be strongly noted—and this makes access to jobs and better schooling difficult.[15]

Mexican Americans will also suffer if the current effort to curb, even abolish, affirmative action succeeds. They will also suffer from the "reform" of the welfare system proposed by Congress in 1995 because there will be less money, and state governments, with their history of indifference to the lower classes, will be in charge of it.

Mexican Americans will continue to suffer from a variety of health problems because of the nature of their work, income, and education, and from their powerlessness. In a study of Anglos, Mexican Americans, and Mexicans living in the companion cities of El Paso, Texas, and Juarez, Mexico, John Mirowsky and Catherine E. Ross found paranoia clearly associated with low socioeconomic status (and with Mexican heritage, and being female). A sense of having enemies who are plotting against one is related to a sense of being powerless. The association of paranoia with low-class position confirms previous studies.[16] Mexican Americans, along with racial and ethnic groups in general, will benefit if mental health professionals continue their efforts to understand nonmajority patients in terms of their distinctive subcultural experience.[17]

On the positive side, Mexican Americans, together with other Hispanics, especially Puerto Ricans, both by improved class status and awareness and by sheer numbers, are somewhat more able today than in the past to use their political strength to protect and improve their economic status. There is also evidence that their attitudes are mainstream (not necessarily altogether a positive)[18] and that majority Americans changed their attitude toward Mexican Americans between 1947 and 1987 and now have a more positive view of Hispanics.[19]

PUERTO RICAN AMERICANS

Historical Background

The Caribbean island of Puerto Rico (current population about 3.5 million) was taken from Spain in the Spanish-American War of 1898 and became first a colony and then a Commonwealth (internal self-government subject to U.S. approval). Since 1917, Puerto Ricans have been citizens of the United States (though they have no voting rights in presidential or congressional elections) and this has made movement back and forth from island to the mainland relatively easy.

The people of Puerto Rico have struggled to free themselves from U.S. rule and to improve their domestic situation. They succeeded in establishing self-rule and replacing mandatory English in schools with Spanish. Efforts to achieve independence and statehood have so far been defeated at the ballot box.

From Empire to World-Market Imperialism

The United States has had an imperialist relation with all its Hispanic neighbors (Mexico, Puerto Rico, Cuba, and Central America).[20] As we saw earlier, the United States conquered Mexico's northern provinces (now forming much of the southwestern United States) and validated it by the

Mexican War of 1845–1848. U.S. imperialism simply made areas of Mexico part of the United States and Mexicans became a subject people (similar to what happened to Native Americans, Aleuts, and Hawaiians). The imperial relation to Puerto Rico is different, and clearly illustrative, first of an imperialism of empire, and then a world-market imperialism.[21]

Puerto Rico became an American colony when the United States defeated Spain in the Spanish-American War. As a colony (1898 to roughly 1948–1952 when commonwealth status was established), Puerto Rico was transformed from a diversified farming-based society with the vast majority of land owned by Puerto Ricans into a dependent mono-crop (sugar) economy owned by absentee landlords (Puerto Rico even had to import food). Then, under commonwealth status (which provided a facade of autonomy), Puerto Rico granted long-term tax exemptions to American manufacturers who enjoyed a bonanza using native cheap labor. Eventually, the exemptions ran out, companies moved to other cheap labor areas, recessions occurred because neither the United States nor Puerto Rico plan their economies, and Puerto Rico's labor force was devastated.

Occupation, Income, and Education

Puerto Ricans are the poorest among American minorities (excepting Native Americans). They were squeezed out of Puerto Rico during the colonial period and entered the urban areas of the mainland northeast from the 1920s on but could not prosper because of the Great Depression of the 1930s and because of World War II. A huge influx from the late 1940s into the 1970s found them entering an urban America in full decline (for data on their occupation, unemployment, income, poverty, and education, see Tables 18–1 through 18–5).

Earlier immigrants (Irish, Italians, Jews, Greeks) had been able to use America's booming urban world to establish an economic base so that later generations could qualify for better occupations. Not so for Puerto Ricans. Earlier immigrants faced discrimination, but not the combined racist-ethnic discrimination of Puerto Ricans. Their ability to go back and forth between the mainland and Puerto Rico also worked against them by making it difficult to establish family, community, or educational continuity. It also made it easier for them to maintain the Spanish language, thus making it harder for both children and adults to succeed in an English-speaking world. But the main reason why Puerto Rican Americans have been unable to move up in the American class system is that they entered a political economy where good jobs were scarce even for better-educated, English-speaking Americans and where urban centers could only offer dead-end, poor-paying jobs. The scarcity of good jobs, in a larger context, meant that Puerto Ricans were being subjected along with the rest of the American population to the full force of world-market imperialism—they and all Americans have become part of the enormous global labor pool.

Current Prospects and Problems

The Puerto Rican portion of the Hispanic-American population has become somewhat better organized—it can at least make itself heard at various political levels. Segregated close to African Americans and subject to similar racist discrimination, it is more prone to cooperate with blacks than other Hispanics. But the future does not look good because it is lodged in a stagnant sector of the American economy and it faces a political economy dominated for at least the next few years and probably longer by ascendant right-wing forces.

CUBAN AMERICANS

The Cuban Exodus: U.S. Imperialism and Cuban Americans

Cuba is a large island nation-state 90 miles south of the United States with a stable population of about 10 million. From 1511 to 1898, it was a colony of Spain. The United States occupied Cuba from 1898 to 1902, turned it into a protectorate (1902–1934), and allowed it a nominal independence from 1934 to 1958. Throughout, the Cuban economy was shaped to rely on sugar, and the small middle class and tiny upper class were oriented to the United States. The propertied and professional classes had shallow roots in Cuba and both they and the United States relied on a repressive dictatorship to keep things going. The socialist revolution of 1958–1959, led by Fidel Castro, succeeded easily and the Cuban upper classes left for the United States. This is the background of the unusual minority called Cuban Americans.

Wealth, Occupation, Income, and Education

Unlike immigrants from other countries, the initial contingent of Cubans who fled Cuba in 1959 were from the propertied-professional classes, that is, they arrived with both material and human capital assets.[22] Their initial status in Miami was well below the one they held in Cuba. For various reasons, including the fact that they established a critical social density by all settling and staying in the same place, they quickly improved their class status. Unlike Puerto Ricans, who arrived in decaying northeastern cities, unskilled and uneducated, Cubans settled in a city that enjoyed a boom as the trading and financial capital of American–South American trade.

The solidarity of the Cuban-American community derived from a strong desire to undo the revolution that had deprived them of their privileged place in Cuba. In this they were strongly helped by the American government, which gave them special support (whereas other Hispanics were actively opposed or poorly served by officials). The American government's motive was also to undo the revolution and return American property to its former owners.[23] Undoing the revolution was important because the last thing the United States wants is an example of a successful socialist regime in its backyard.

Later currents of Cuban refugees were unskilled and they have lowered the socioeconomic status of Cubans somewhat. But as Tables 18–1 through 18–5 attest, Cuban-Americans are distinctly better off than other Hispanics and are even on a par in some respects with the Not Hispanic population.

Current Prospects and Problems

The Cuban regime continues strong today as an authoritarian socialist society. After almost forty years, the revolution has put down deep roots. Without Soviet help, the Cuban economy floundered after 1990 and Cuba has opened its economy to foreign investment. The United States, with Cuban-American help, and the Republican party and conservative Democrats (especially members of both parties from Florida and the South) has a strict trade embargo on Cuba. This of course plays into Castro's hands (the Yankee bully is still at it), especially since Cuba has developed a wide array of trade-investments with other countries, including Mexico and South America.

American business has quietly pressured the federal government to drop the embargo because they are losing out economically to rivals from other capitalist countries. The Clinton administration has taken a few steps to normalize relations but it must go slowly. Things will ease gradually as older Cubans die, since it is clear that younger Cuban Americans are not interested in returning to Cuba. Indeed, judging from a recent poll of attitudes, they are almost identical in outlook to Mexican Americans, Puerto Rican Americans, and majority Americans.

HISPANIC-AMERICAN ATTITUDES: MORE AMERICAN THAN HISPANIC

Hispanic Americans have maintained their language far longer than other newcomers to America. The main reasons for this is that some were a conquered people; they were even less welcome than other immigrants; they did not benefit from America's economic expansion; and, chronically segregated, marginalized, and infused with the newcomers, they relied on their common language to build whatever community they could. It was also easier for them to maintain their language than earlier immigrants because of the radio and television stations that present distinctive Hispanic music and entertainment programs. All these signs of apartness, however, should not mislead us. An important poll has revealed that Hispanic Americans (Mexican, Puerto Rican, and Cuban Americans, making up 80 percent of Spanish-origin Americans) have views about a number of questions (including the need to learn English) that are identical to majority Americans.[24]

SUMMARY

All Hispanic Americans, except those from Cuba, occupy the lower rungs of the American class system. The prospects for Mexican Americans and Puerto Rican Americans (and other Hispanics from Central America and the Caribbean) are not good. Unlike immigrants from Europe and Canada, most Hispanics were unable to take advantage of America's economic boom between 1820 and 1960 led by manufacturing. After 1960, their depressed, marginalized class position made it difficult for them to participate in the economic growth induced by service industries. Actually, most Hispanic Americans have been affected negatively over the past few decades by the American-led world-market corporate economy. On the other hand, Cuban Americans were affected positively by the growth of foreign trade and, having arrived better off, have continued to be better off than other Hispanics. But regardless of their socioeconomic status and history, the story of all Hispanic Americans is the story of U.S. imperialism.

NOTES

1. For a careful, detailed Marxist analysis of the history and sociology of Mexican Americans with valuable comparisons with African Americans, see Mario Barrera, *Race and Class in the Southwest: A Theory of Racial Inequality* (Notre Dame, IN: University of Notre Dame Press, 1979).
2. Though the time periods are different, Hawaiians and Puerto Ricans have also been unable to enter mainstream America.
3. For an early empirical study of Mexican-American families in San Antonio and Los Angeles, see Leo Grebler, Joan W. Moore, and Ralph Guzman, *The Mexican-American People: The Nation's Second Largest Minority* (New York: Free Press, 1970), ch. 15. For our most recent analysis, see Joan Moore and Harry Pachon, *Hispanics in the United States* (Englewood Cliffs, NJ: Prentice-Hall, 1985).
4. *New York Times,* December 15, 1992, p. A20.
5. U.S. Bureau of the Census, *Current Population Reports,* Series P-20, No. 466, "Voting and Registration in the Election of November, 1992" (Washington, DC: U.S. Government Printing Office, 1993), Table 13. For general background on the political experience of Mexican (and Spanish-Origin) Americans, see Leo Grebler et al., *The Mexican-American People: The Nation's Second Largest Minority* (New York: Free Press, 1970), ch. 23; F. Chris Garcia and Rudolph O. de la Garza, *The Chicano Political Experience: Three Perspectives* (North Scituate, MA: Duxbury Press, 1977); and Joan Moore and Harry Pachon, *Hispanics in the United States* (Englewood Cliffs, NJ: Prentice-Hall, 1985), ch. 8–12.

6. For the growth of Mexican American and Hispanic political consciousness and power, see Joan Moore with Harry Pachon, *Mexican-Americans* (Englewood Cliffs, NJ: Prentice-Hall, 1976), ch. 8, and Joan Moore and Harry Pachon, *Hispanics in the United States* (Englewood Cliffs, NJ: Prentice-Hall, 1985), ch. 10. For a valuable contrast among pluralist, elitist, and internal colonialism interpretations of the political (power) relations of Mexican Americans to their outer society, see F. Chris Garcia and Rudolph O. de la Garza, *The Chicano Political Experience.* For a valuable collection of essays in a more conventional political science mode focused on the politics of Mexican Americans, Cuban Americans, and Puerto Ricans, see F. Chris Garcia, ed., *Latinos and the Political System* (Notre Dame, IN: University of Notre Dame Press, 1988).
7. For much of the following, see Leo Grebler et al., *The Mexican-American People: The Nation's Second Largest Minority* (New York: Free Press, 1970), ch. 21; Joan Moore with Harry Pachon, 2nd ed., *Mexican-Americans* (Englewood Cliffs, NJ: Prentice-Hall, 1976), ch. 8; and Joan Moore and Harry Pachon, *Hispanics in the United States* (Englewood Cliffs, NJ: Prentice-Hall, 1985), ch. 10.
8. A recent poll indicates that 93 percent of Mexican Americans agreed that citizens and residents should learn English; *New York Times,* December 15, 1992, p. A20.
9. U.S. Civil Rights Commission, *Mexican American Educational Series,* "Report I. Ethnic Isolation of Mexican Americans in the Public Schools of the Southwest" (April 1971); "Report II. The Unfinished Education: Outcomes for Minorities in Five Southwestern States" (October 1971); "Report III. The Excluded Student: Educational Practices Affecting Mexican Americans in the Southwest" (May 1972); "Report IV. Mexican American Education in Texas—A Function of Wealth" (August 1972). All are available from the U.S. Government Printing Office, Washington, DC.
10. For a good review, see Leo Grebler, Joan W. Moore, Ralph C. Guzman and others, *The Mexican-American People: The Nation's Second Largest Minority* (New York: Free Press, 1970), ch. 21, and Joan Moore and Harry Pachon, *Hispanics in the United States* (Englewood Cliffs, NJ: Prentice-Hall, 1985), pp. 164–168.
11. U.S. Commission on Civil Rights, *Mexican Americans and the Administration of Justice in the Southwest* (Washington, DC: U.S. Government Printing Office, 1970).
12. Coramae Richey Mann, *Unequal Justice: A Question of Color* (Bloomington: Indiana University Press, 1993).
13. For the larger context, see the section "Popular Culture and Race" in Chapter 17.
14. For a focus on restructuring in regard to Hispanic Americans, see Rebecca Morales and Frank Bonilla, eds., *Latinos in a Changing U.S. Economy* (Newbury Park, CA: Sage, 1993).
15. Marta Tienda and Ding-Tzann Lii, "Minority Concentration and Earnings Inequality: Blacks, Hispanics, and Asians Compared," *American Journal of Sociology 93* (July 1987):141–165, argue that the three minorities they studied all suffered earnings losses because of residential and labor market concentration, thus benefiting white college graduates. See also Nancy A. Denton and Douglas S. Massey, "Residential Segregation of Blacks, Hispanics, and Asians by Socioeconomic Status and Generations," *Social Science Quarterly 69* (December 1988): 797–817. For an analysis showing that Mexican Americans have a significantly lower level of home ownership than majority whites even when income is held constant, see Lauren J. Krivo, "Home Ownership Differences Between Hispan-

ics and Anglos in the United States," *Social Problems 33* (April 1986):319–334. One reason may be discrimination in advancing credit by banks; see *New York Times,* September 26, 1991, p. A18, and October 28, 1991, p. D1.

16. John Mirowsky and Catherine E. Ross, "Paranoia and the Structure of Powerlessness," *American Sociological Review 48* (April 1983):228–239.
17. For an earlier discussion, see "Failure to Perform: The Deviance of Unnecessary Incompetence" in Chapter 16.
18. See the section below "Hispanic-American Attitudes: More American than Hispanic."
19. *Public Opinion* 10 (July–August 1987), Special Issue on Prejudice.
20. The same is true of Filipino, Hawaiian, and Koreans, and of course, Native Americans and Aleuts.
21. Here the similarity is with the Philippines. For an earlier discussion of types of imperialism, see Chapter 3. Central America and other Caribbean societies such as Panama, Nicaragua, Guatemala, El Salvador, and the Dominican Republic were de facto colonies though officially part of the world-market political economy. For a case study of El Salvador, see Chapter 3.
22. Though different, there is a similarity with the flight of wealthy Chinese from Hong Kong during the 1990s.
23. And of course to thwart the Soviet Union, which was a strong supporter of Cuba from 1959 to 1990.
24. *New York Times,* December 15, 1992, p. A20.

19

Gender Inequality: The Interplay of Class, Gender, and Race

◆ ◆ ◆ ◆

◆ ◆ ◆ ◆

COMPARATIVE GENDER RELATIONS

Men and women seem to be unequal in almost all societies. Even among the Arapesh peoples, in which men and women both have nurturing personalities, men have more privileges and authority.[1] But the inequality of females, even though universal, varies considerably depending on the type of society. One need only compare women among the Tiwi[2] (where they are essentially the property of older men) to middle-class and upper-class women in the United States (who have considerable independence and who have achievements in a variety of fields) to appreciate the sociocultural basis of gender identity. Women and men are unequal in hunting and gathering societies but, on the whole, are far more equal than in any of the complex societies. The most sexual inequality occurs in agrarian societies where most of the ideology about women's innate inferiority was developed as part of the great universal, patriarchal religions. The basic variable associated with more equality for women, argues Rae Lesser Blumberg (on the basis of the anthropological-historical evidence), is not work or economic participation but control over produce property and its surplus.[3] Marvin Harris argues that male supremacy stems from warfare and the male monopoly over weapons.[4] Though social scientists continue to disagree about causes, most have discarded human-nature explanations as the reasons for sexual inequality.

Comparisons among contemporary countries (developed and developing) do not reveal any real break with the pervasive pattern of sexual inequality. Developing socialist societies bring about dramatic changes in the position of women but seem only to incorporate them into more up-to-date, male-dominated family, educational, and political-economic institutions. Women in some countries are better off in some ways because of local policies (for example, better maternity or child-care facilities) or they may be more equal to men because the entire society is more equal (for example, Sweden, a highly unequal capitalist society, has more overall equality for all people, including women, than does the United States). On the whole, however, women in industrial societies are very unequal to men regardless of the ideology of their respective societies and regardless of whether they live in capitalist or socialist societies.[5]

CONCEPTUALIZING WOMEN AS A MINORITY

Racial and ethnic groups can be radically stratified because they are composed of households. Female inequality (along with age inequality) must be conceptualized differently since females (and different ages) are found in most households high or low in the ladder of social class—thus women in the upper classes have a very different level of existence than do women in the lower classes. And quite apart from class, women have fewer benefits and opportunities than do men, holding class constant.

MAJORITY WOMEN, MINORITY WOMEN

Women are considered a minority but there are also minorities *within* the female minority. Women as a whole have unequal economic statuses (occupations and earnings) in relation to majority males, but inequality *among* females is also significant. In education, American Indian, Alaskan Native, African-American, Mexican-American, and Puerto Rican females do less well than majority females, Japanese-American, Chinese-American, and Filipino-American females, and they are much more likely to be poor. There are other minorities within the minority. Homosexual women face a double burden. Handicapped, deformed, or disfigured women probably suffer more than men in similar straits. And the same is probably true of women who are overweight, mentally ill, or "overaged." It goes without saying that all of the above burdens can be made heavier or lighter by adding race, ethnicity, social class, or age to any given category.

FEMINIST THEORY

Left-Liberal Feminism: Miriam Johnson and Janet Saltzman Chafetz

A concern for women and feminine (domestic) values has a long history in Western society. In social terms, this concern was expressed mostly by men, largely in terms of prevailing male values.[6] Modern society has broadened the concern for women and feminine (domestic) values since the nineteenth century and social theorists have voiced that concern in two distinct vocabularies: liberal and radical feminism. Perhaps the most noteworthy thing about today's feminism is that the major voices are female.

Strong criticism about the condition of women in the United States was made before the Women's Movement of the 1960s. Most of the basic ideas used by today's feminists are the product of the past or of nonfeminists. Nonetheless, women's issues tended not to have priority with male scholars or tended to get lost in other creative work. The Women's Movement from the 1960s to the present is significant because it has enough volume and depth to represent significant power, that is, it holds the possibility of exerting an influence on how Americans think about the relations between the sexes, about sexuality, and what a reconceptualized, degendered humanity might mean for the nature of society and its politics.

The explanation for the rise of the Women's Movement lies with the logic of American society and American-style liberalism. The stark atomism of American liberalism in which (male) individuals are the basic social reality eventually led to a demand for liberty and equality for women as individuals. The economic expansion of the United States produced an ever larger middle class (in terms of numbers and perhaps in relative size) and that meant that large numbers of women, like their fathers, brothers, and husbands, were spared the manual work of farm and factory. Indeed, middle- and upper-class American parents want the best for both sons and daughters and this led to a large number of educated women. Undisputable evidence that women were capable of both skilled mental and manual labor, along with the unmet labor needs of the economy, the special opportunities to display competence during wartime, and other causes, such as birth control, eventually led to a large reservoir of politically disaffected women.

Feminist theory blossomed from the 1970s on and has exerted considerable influence on social theory. In simple terms, feminist theory focuses on gender relations, which it regards as relations of power that are unnecessarily unequal and damage and shortchange women. For both liberal and radical feminists, gender relations are not natural, though they disagree on how to view gender inequality.

Miriam Johnson argues that liberal society is producing gender equality through its inherent processes of structural differentiation and value generalization. Building directly on Parsons and neofunctionalism, Johnson, like all feminists, focuses on marriage and the family as the institutional area in which men dominate women. She does not find much hope for women in sexual liberation or in equal parenting because both will still be conducted on male terms.

Johnson approves the trend toward maternal behavior outside the nuclear family, expressed in intergenerational links and in voluntary groups. The escape by women from the nuclear family has been aided by divorce and there are now many women free of marriage—single mothers, divorced women, never-married women, widows, lesbians, and abused women. She even cites with extra approval the matrilocality of African-American communities in which women exercise maternal influence in many contexts besides the nuclear family.

In all this, Johnson does not mention the need for political action; indeed, she notes that gender-neutral arguments and gender-blind laws are not necessarily good for women. The emancipation of women will come from the continued structural differentiation of capitalism (modern society), which runs counter to the nuclear family and will continue liberalism's historic forward thrust toward including all in its basic values: individualism, equality, and freedom. But the new version of liberal society will be focused more on feminine values.

Johnson's argument seems to be that a taken-for-granted capitalist political economy will pull women into the labor force and generate enough broken homes to free women from the confines of the nuclear family and deploy them into the public sphere. The coping strategies of African-American women struggling with crippled families may be the wave of the future. Liberal society (as in Saint-Simon and Comte) will be redeemed by feminine values somehow naturally embodied in women. Nowhere is there a reference to the power of the class system, in which it is clear that the men and women of the upper classes dominate the men and women of the lower-middle, the working, and the lower class. American society is not to be reformed or reconstructed by human agency. Somehow it is a natural force that must be allowed to follow its "evolutionary tractory" as posited by liberalism's premier spokesperson, Talcott Parsons.[7]

Janet Saltzman Chafetz also argues that the gender division of labor is feminism's central target, especially focused around a demand for greater access to elite positions by women.[8] Chafetz's indictment of gender inequality has a historical and economic focus. From agrarian society on, the gender division of labor has given men a highly disproportionate amount of economic resources. Men use these resources to dominate women in the home as well as outside. So strong is gender segregation that women and men each become different and women actually help to reproduce the society that affects them adversely by socializing children into distinct masculine and feminine personalities.

Chafetz argues that income equality as well as equality in holding elite positions must be achieved if women are to be genuinely equal. She says that the chief focus of attention must be on the causes that determine the economic division of labor. She concludes that the primary independent variable affecting the degree of gender inequality is technology and is certain that its future effects will continue to be positive for women. Technology will increase the demand for labor, drawing married women into the labor force. Technology will allow women to control their fertility, thus allowing them to forge careers outside of family life. Technology may reduce the time and energy spent on household duties. War and migration can cause a shortage of male labor. All in all, industrialized nations, including the United States, will tend toward an equal deployment of males and females in the occupational system, leading more to equal resources and a reduction of social definitions of masculinity. Past expansion of the economy, says Chafetz, has produced, not only women's labor force involvement, but women's movements of various kinds. Women have achieved a great deal over the past century, though their movements do not cause but rather reflect basic changes in the economy.

Chafetz's liberalism is apparent. The main engine of redemption is economic growth (by a taken-for-granted capitalist society). Modern society is differentiating itself by some inner dynamic logic to include everyone in its presumed meritocratic processes. There is no hint of economic concentration or of a class system in Chafetz's analysis in which those who own technology (the means of production) will continue the nonnatural inequalities generated by corporate capitalism. There is no mention of the additional increase in the already high inequality of household income that has resulted because those with similar incomes marry each other. There is no word on the stratification of societies in which economic growth and the well-being of both men and women in the middle class and above in the United States depends on the exploitation of Third World labor.

Chafetz's liberalism makes her see only the positive side of trends. But technology has not liberated women in the home, only made them more productive. Progress in the economy for women means progress in a male class system—to succeed women have to go through the same, overlong process of credential-getting that men go through. Not only is their behavior the same as men in their occupational roles, but white, female college graduates vote the same—a majority of them voted for Ronald Reagan, an avowed opponent of feminism and labor (whose most depressed reaches are disproportionately composed of women).

Johnson and Chafetz are both aware of the literature, both liberal and radical, that has indicted society's treatment of women. Both have chosen, however, to express their faith in the basic structure of power that characterizes liberal society. Both argue that women have not made progress by fighting for it. It is the overall economy that has generated progressive changes. Here they are voicing American liberalism's complacency about technology and the capitalist economy and its negative view of politics. But writing in the late eighties and early nineties, Johnson and Chafetz should have been aware that American society has contradicted their basic positions. That women are probably worse off today than they were fifty years ago is only one of the many facts that should have prompted serious reservations about liberal society and a reconsideration of their antipolitics stance.

Radical Feminism: Dorothy E. Smith

Radical feminists are varied, but they tend to reject (liberal) objective empirical science because it is impersonal and presupposes an outside observer studying a finished reality. Since that outside observer is male, the facts that are seen and the goals of knowledge tend to be those that are consistent with male values. To become radical, feminists have had to do what other radicals have done, namely, break with the positive or mainstream empirical tradition.

To achieve an epistemology of their own, radical feminists have drawn on Marx, on phenomenology (especially Foucault), and on Freud. At the same time, radical feminists, aware that both Marxism and phenomenology have neglected women and have gender biases, have tried to develop their own epistemology. Overwhelmingly, they have pointed to women's experiences as the source of that which can point them to a postmodern epistemology and eventually to a postliberal, postsexist society.

Relying on women's experiences means different things; for most, it means that women's experience has made them caring, nurturing, particularizing beings and from this must come a way of knowing that is infused with feeling and unashamedly evaluative. Most radical feminists agree that the abstractions of masculine rationality and impersonality cannot capture the distinctive world of women. Some feminists have changed the way in which we look on the history of natural science. Carolyn Merchant, for example, has argued that natural science, capitalism, and masculinity go together and represent a violation of the natural. The natural and the feminine are linked in Merchant's thought to give us a new perspective on society and environmentalism.[9] Some feminists add the experience of reproduction to their criticism of the impersonal masculine world, something considered more basic than (masculine) production.

Smith is a radical conflict feminist who began her career in the Marxist tradition. Her early radical feminism led her to a discussion of the relation between capitalism and the family, and of the relationship between the macro-order and everyday life.[10] The fundamental orientation of Smith's early work was derived from her concern about the direction taken by advanced corporate capitalism. Building on C. Wright Mills, she emphasizes that corporate capitalism has turned the middle class as well as workers into labor or employees. This means that managers and white-collar workers are now labor from whom surplus is extracted. The process whereby the concentrated bureaucratic capitalist economy spreads out to develop a supportive infrastructure is applied by Smith to the family with a particular focus on women.

For Smith (and others), the family under capitalism supplies the economy with marketable labor. Smith's special focus is on the middle-class family as a facility for and an image of the outer world of capitalism (she describes the working-class family as more obviously dependent on the income of the husband and thus more obviously a social structure dependent on the capitalist economy). The middle-class woman embodies the moral order enjoined by the capitalist economy. She loves her children and devotes herself to preparing her children for school, but hers, says Smith, is the unpaid work of an agent for the economy. She decorates her house and the members of her family via the latest information from the mass media. She uses products and services provided by capitalist industry and professionals. Her identity and her labor are not hers.

The foundations of Smith's thought have shifted and are now anchored in a combination of Marx and phenomenology.[11] Her main interest is to develop a sociology that will allow women to speak. Women are excluded from power (and thus have no voice), not only by the basic "relations of ruling" (politics, government, law, education, the economy), but by objective sociology. The latter tends to be the voice of the objective male ruling apparatus; this voice helps in the subjugation of women by insisting that knowledge consists of abstract statements devoid of subjectivity and particularity. Since the world to which women have been confined by capitalism is anchored in subjectivity and highly particular, their existence is denied by conventional (empirical, positive) sociology. The rational and impersonal is the way in which all sectors of capitalism, including sociology, function, and it also forms the basis of supersubordination by gender.

Smith acknowledges her debt to George Herbert Mead, Maurice Merleau-Ponty, Karl Marx, and Harold Garfinkel (there are also numerous references in her work to Alfred Schutz), but adds that she is not a symbolic interactionist, a phenomenologist, a Marxist, or an ethnomethodologist. She wants to develop a way that will allow women to express their experiences (raise their consciousness) in a problematic everyday world and has found ethnomethodology useful in homing in on the neglected world of the everyday life lived by women. But unlike ethnomethodologists, she insists on connecting that world to the oppressive outside world. To avoid the abstract, alienating concepts of sociology requires a language of escape from the seamless, pervasive world of male dominance through impersonality. Here Smith uses Foucault and the concept of *discourse* to build her new way of expressing immediate experience.

Smith's emphasis on the need to accept as knowledge only that which is a direct expression of personal experience is a welcome note, quite independently of her feminism. But while her overall work contains rich insights into a number of power relations affecting women negatively (case studies of suicide, mental illness, a murder inquiry, the relation of mother, child, and school), Smith's new feminist sociology remains unclear. Women, she argues, should not be studied from the outside by outsiders, even other women. This turns them into objects. They must become subjects and this requires a mode of inquiry that takes what they have to say about what they are doing and experiencing seriously. This Smith does in her enormously insightful collection of case studies. But it is clear that the everyday world is problematic, not to women, but to Smith. Thus, Smith consistently insinuates the knowledgeable outsider into her analysis, an outsider who must provide the linkage women need to connect their troubles to the oppressive power structure. Smith does this using a bland Marxism, that is, an analysis that is not anchored in class or class struggle, and which has no dynamic other than Smith's new perspective (which will presumably release women's unconscious anger).

Smith's depiction of traditional sociology as a complement to capitalist power relations is on target. But that same sociology also has the capacity (Vico-Weber-Cooley and the method of understanding, participant observation, case study, institutional analysis, micro-macro analysis) to uncover the world of women; what it lacks is the interest as long as men dominate research. Objective mainstream sociology also has a strong tradition that claims that subjectivity is knowable and a proper subject matter for empirical investigation. The above explains why Smith's valuable chapter outlining a feminist research strategy resembles (and all of it is easily assumable under) conventional sociology.[12]

Nonetheless, there is something unreal about a social theory based on women. The very power of society that Smith is so conscious of has made the category *women* unreal in a different and more conventional way than is found in feminist theory. The United States has six million women who earn more than their husbands. It has millions of women who own and run businesses. A majority of white women college graduates voted for Ronald Reagan, who was openly hostile to helping women. The United States has huge numbers of women who work in the pink ghetto, and even in sweatshops, to support their families with and without spouses. And millions of women lose self-esteem in their teens or are physically abused. Where in all this is the category *women*? If American women spoke, would they sound much different from American men? Probably, but only on a number of secondary issues. Would they say anything collectively that Smith would want to hear? Not likely. The same differentiation into classes and victims is true of men (and both sexes are further differentiated by race, ethnicity, and sexuality). The knowledgeable observer may have a bigger role to play in helping people speak than Smith acknowledges. Smith is aware of the power of social class and racism and has declared her intention to add them to her analysis of gender.

Racial Feminism: The Tension Between Socialist Feminism and Patriarchical Theory

The basic ideas of socialist feminism appear in the late eighteenth and early nineteenth centuries with the emergence of socialist theory as such. Socialists argue that the economy in historical context precedes all other relations and shapes the nature of the state, religion, and art, as well as the family and gender relations. Socialists, especially Marxists, also argue that democratic control over the economy will end exploitative relations in the economy, polity, and family. Making men free also means that women will be free, ending gender dualism. Under socialism, marriage will be based on love and full reciprocity, and work, including parenting and housework, will be shared. There will be no property to transmit and the rearing of children will be a public as well as a private responsibility.

The historical experience of women socialists with the overall socialist movement has not been positive. Actually, women socialists experienced the same kind of sexist treatment that socialism was allegedly against. Socialist women in nineteenth- and early twentieth-century Germany, France, and the United States were not only kept out of leadership positions, but were told that women's issues (the vote, equal pay, legal rights in the family, birth control, abortion) were secondary to the acquisition of power by socialism and the destruction of capitalism. Once socialism is established, they were told, women's problems will be solved.

Feminist socialists have criticized strict Marxian interpretations of domestic labor and of segregation by sex in the labor force. Women, they argue, may be exploited under the capitalist system as wives, mothers, paid workers, and as consumers, but the sex-based nature of that exploitation must be accounted for.[13]

The tension between feminism and socialism was heightened during the 1970s as women began to play a much larger role in theorizing. The climax was a full fledged theory of patriarchy, a theory that was attached to a wide variety of perspectives besides socialism. The essence of the partriarchal perspective is that sex-based inequality is universal, existing under capitalism and socialism (the USSR), is prior to other forms of inequality, and may even be the basis for other forms.

The basis of patriarchy is women's reproductive biology and it is the drastic definition of women as wives, mothers, and caretakers that turns them into inferiors. Today, socialist feminism still exists, but its most vital form is feminist socialism, a many-sided theory that argues that gender inequality is more important than class if judgments are to be made, though human liberation requires an escape from both.[14]

Theorists who combine feminism and socialism are aware that there are also other kinds of inequality. In a far-ranging critique of Marxism, Isaac Balbus argues that liberation from the Instrumental, Objectified world of capitalism can come about only through a combination of feminism, participatory democracy, and environmentalism. Employing Freudian ideas, Balbus argues that the starting point for liberation is to replace the mother-centered world of socialization that acts as an agent for Instrumentalism (capitalism).[15]

The feminist socialism of Ann Ferguson is also distinctive because while enunciating the need for socialism, she also asserts the failure of socialists to account for the unconscious, for gender oppression, for racial oppression (including the special condition of black women), and for gay-lesbian oppression. Ferguson tends to place gender and race before class, though she repeatedly cites the need to unite women and men across the boundaries of gender, race, style of life, and class to build coalitions that will work for a democratic socialism.[16]

Against this background, socialists have tried to square socialism, especially Marxism, with the feminist movement.[17] The key Marxian idea linking gender inequality to class inequality is to think of female household work (housework, giving birth, raising children) as unpaid labor on behalf of capitalism yielding extra surplus value.

When women participate in the labor force they are regarded in sexist terms as unworthy and thus get poorer jobs that pay much less. They are also paid less when they do comparable work. Because of their burden of housework and child care, women cannot commit themselves to paid work the way men can, and their outside careers and incomes suffer. Because they are not equal to their husbands economically, they continue to be inferior at home.

Shelton and Agger argue that Marxism can explain gender inequality fully, and that patriarchy (whether a left feminism appreciative of Marxism or a radical feminism that claims patriarchy as sovereign cause) is not a separate scheme of explanation. Actually, patriarchy ultimately shades off into liberal feminism or trendy postmodern relativism. Only Marxism is a comprehensive theoretical scheme organically connected to practice and, while historically remiss in regard to women's troubles, is capable of expanding to include gender issues and still be true to its central logic.

Readers can make up their own minds which of the above perspectives on gender relations makes the most sense as they follow the analysis of American gender inequality and its politics in the remainder of this chapter.

THE ECONOMIC PARTICIPATION OF AMERICAN WOMEN

Women have always performed economic tasks. Their economic participation in recent times (as measured by the percent of women in the labor force) is not so much an increase in the amount of economic work done by women but a change in type of work. In America's rural past, women made their primary economic contribution on the family farm and at home. Changes in how women participate in the economy correspond somewhat to that of men—from the nineteenth century on, more and more economic work by both men and women has been done off the farm and in factories, offices, and stores.

Three major patterns stand out in the economic participation of females since the nineteenth century: The number of working women has increased greatly (more than half of all women between the ages of eighteen and sixty-four are working, making up almost half of the work force), women are working before and *after* marriage and before and *after* having children, and large numbers of women have started their own businesses.

The major reason why women work is to support their families. Some work to find fulfillment in careers. Significantly, even working-class women find low-paying, unfulfilling jobs preferable to housework because they offer clear-cut responsibilities and escape from isolation.[18]

Gender and Occupations

The American occupational system is deeply segregated by sex. Though less true today than thirty years ago, almost all occupations are either female or male dominated. Income differences have also persisted with women earning about 65 to 75 percent of men's despite having the same education[19] and the same occupation.[20] In addition, many *comparable* occupations show large disparities in earnings (for a discussion see Box 19–1).

Some narrowing of the gender gap occurred from the 1970s to 1980s, but the reasons are no cause for optimism. A large part of the relative advance of women was due to setbacks suffered by males during the deindustrialization of the American economy. Another part was due to polarization among women as a small group advanced into the better paying occupations, while most women, especially black women, fell behind. The business world's accelerating thrust to lower labor costs by using temporary and part-time workers, or going abroad, will continue to hurt all workers, but lower-level women more than men and probably black women the most. In addition to a steepening hierarchy of income among all workers, including a cleavage between an upper level of well-protected knowledge workers, there appears to be a strong trend toward increased occupational segregation by gender and race.[21]

While much of the structure of sex segregation was publicized by feminist scholars during the 1970s, it is only in the past few years that research has isolated the relevant variables in this area and has been able to tackle concrete questions. In particular, recent research has been able to refute many of the erroneous reasons advanced as to why women fare less well than men in the workplace.[22] The major reasons alleged to explain gender inequality are: biology, lack of motivation, desire to have families, failure to invest in education, and lack of experience. All these assertions have been refuted. Women value success in business as much as men and they have actually invested more time in education than men. They are also discriminated against even when they are suitably experienced. By carefully controlling for factors that women share with men, recent studies have shown that disparities in income and authority are due to gender bias.

Women Managers and Professionals: Income and Authority Gaps Due to Gender Bias

In recent decades women have made considerable relative increases vis à vis men in college enrollment, graduate and professional education, and in entering management and professional occupations. Women's gains are impressive if one uses census categories—for example, they posted 30 percent and 40 percent increases in jobs classified as managerial, executive, and administrative in 1980 and 1990 respectively. But as Barbara Reskin and Catherine Ross show, women are concentrated near the bottom of organiza-

BOX 19–1 *Is It Possible to Determine the Comparable Worth of Occupations?*

The Equal Pay Act of 1963 and Title VII of the 1964 Civil Rights Act declared it illegal to pay women less than men when both do the same or similar work. Yet after more than thirty years, women as a whole still earn considerably less than men. Early on, efforts were made to expand on Title VII of the Civil Rights Act to include equal pay for *comparable* jobs. Why, say critics, should nurses be paid less than streetcleaners or parking meter repairmen? Why should librarians and teachers make less than janitors, truck drivers, or construction workers? There is no reason why clerks and secretaries should receive less than workers doing comparable work outdoors or in factories.

Comparable worth cannot be legislated or established by the courts, say opponents, because there is no scientific way to judge the worth of occupations. Occupations are based on value judgments found in our culture, and the best way to determine the hierarchy of job values is through the free labor market and the law of supply and demand. Only the market can determine who have the skills, the diligence, and the sense of responsibility that are the core attributes of occupations.

A more radical approach argues that comparable worth, even if successful, cannot do much to change the basic structure of labor in the United States. Far from having a free labor market, the United States' occupational system is a result of historical accidents and arbitrary power (slavery, immigration, and the general ebb and flow of cheap labor, the brain drain, excessive professional credentials, control of labor entry by trade unions, excessive qualifications for occupations established by licensing and certification boards, the flow of capital overseas, and so on). Women, no more than men, cannot get a fair shake in the employment market until the organized public structures the economy to prevent monopolies over good jobs (and thus excessive income and benefits) and outlaws exploitation and degradation in the lower reaches of the economy.*

*For a good review of the issues on comparable worth by the Committee on Occupational Classification and Analysis of the National Research Council, including a conservative disclaimer and a radical minority report, see Donald J. Treiman and Heidi I. Hartmann, eds., *Women, Work, and Wages: Equal Pay for Jobs of Equal Value* (Washington, DC: National Academy Press, 1981). For a report on reform efforts, comparable worth legislation at the state level, and court decisions, see *Pay Equity and Comparable Worth,* Bureau of National Affairs (Washington, DC, 1984).

tional hierarchies, supervise workers of their own sex, and have lower earnings and lower authority despite the fact that their education and experience is similar to that of men.[23]

Exact studies in the professions are still scarce. Earlier we reported John Hagen's study of the legal profession to illustrate the power that property has over income (see the section Power Over Income in Chapter 7). Hagen's study was actually focused on gender inequality and revealed a gender gap of 25 percent in income after controlling all other relevant variables.[24] And despite the fact that women have increased their numbers to half of law school enrollments and to 27 percent of all lawyers, they still lag badly in pay, promotions, partnerships, and professorships at law schools (according to a report of the American Bar Association[25]).

Research of this caliber in regard to other professions is still scarce. Women television writers earn considerably less than men controlling other factors.[26] Architecture is less than a fully established profession, but the unequal status of women architects is worth noting.[27]

In the case of sociology itself, women have made considerable progress in obtaining doctorates and now make up 25 percent of sociology faculty.[28] This increase was partly due to softness in the academic labor market in the 1970s and progress in sociology for women may have reached a plateau. And like in the rest of higher education, women sociologists have not obtained a proportionate share of upper rank and authority positions. In sociology, we also encounter another pattern in the professions—even when women make impressive entry gains, they tend to go (are shunted into?) less prestigious, less-rewarded specialties. In sociology women specialize in family, medical, population, aging, and gender studies. In medicine women doctors specialize in family and child medicine; in law, women lawyers are in family law. Even in the female-dominated fields of teaching, librarianship, nursing, and social work, women are subject to bureaucratic oversight by men in command positions.

The Feminization of Poverty

The capitalist economy of recent decades (along with other factors) has altered the American household and the composition of the poor. Today, women make up approximately two-thirds of poor people, and approximately half of all poor households are headed by women (a significant number of elderly widows are also poor). All this has occurred during and despite the women's movement.

The feminization of poverty appears to be a trend in other industrial societies although capitalist Sweden with its advanced welfare state, and socialist Poland and the former USSR appear to have offset the trend much better than the United States, France, or Canada.

Factors and policies relevant to female poverty and to poverty in general are:

1. Economic markets for labor
2. Government policies such as commitment to full employment, equal pay, and affirmative action
3. Government policies in regard to economic support for families such as money, housing, health care
4. Demographic factors such as teenage pregnancy, age of marriage, divorce, and life expectancy[29]

Minority Women and the Economy

Most minority women (African-American, Hispanic, Asian, Native American, Pacific Islander) face the triple burden of gender, class, and race and most have fared poorly in the labor market. The civil rights movement helped minority women, but their improved economic status in the postwar period was largely a result of America's economic expansion. Black women made gains in the 1960s and 1970s but these were stalled or reversed from the 1980s on (black women also suffered because black males experienced severe setbacks from the 1970s and 1980s on seriously disrupting black families).

The studies of gender inequality discussed earlier were focused on white women and were largely nonpolitical—while they went beyond the easy functionalism of an earlier period, they did not emphasize the need for women to use political power to erase gender inequities and they did not question whether the United States was capable of becoming gender-neutral. Studies of minority women cannot be as complacent. Two fine recent studies understand that the fate of minority women (in both cases, African-American women), as well as minority men and the majority of the labor, will be determined by better public policies, especially in regard to shaping the structure of the American economy.[30]

The Adverse Effects of the World Market

The economic status of women has been adversely affected by the growth of America's participation in the world market. The overall context for understanding this process is to recall that approximately 80 percent of the American labor force has had stagnant or declining real incomes for the past quarter of a century. Minority women have probably suffered the most, but white women have also been adversely affected by the ability of American capital to pit American labor against the labor of developing countries. All experts predict that the movement of American (and European) capital abroad will continue to grow since that represents the best opportunity for American capitalism to maintain and increase profit levels. Needless to say, feminists (and leaders in various other fields such as labor and environmental protection) must strive for humane labor standards, public services, and environmental protections in developing countries—this will make it less attractive for American (and European and Japanese) capital to move to such countries and help prevent the lowering of labor and environmental standards at home.

WOMEN AND EDUCATION

If education is seen as an important step toward climbing the class ladder, then women have made impressive gains all along the line. They now outnumber males in higher education and have made significant relative advances in medicine and law. Women are now prominent at military and maritime academies but still lag in the natural sciences and engineering.

Women have translated their educational gains into income gains when the same age groups are compared. But they still lag and they still face segregation and ceilings in various occupations and professions.

WOMEN AND SOCIAL MOBILITY

Mobility Through Achievement

American studies on female mobility patterns have appeared but it seems best to focus on Robert Erikson and John H. Goldthorpe's study of European patterns.[31] American studies still use variations on the U.S. Census classification of occupations; they still interpret education as evidence of universalism (or openness, equal opportunity), and they still confuse class processes with gender inequalities in the labor market.

Using class-based households rather than individuals as their unit of analysis, Erikson and Goldthorpe's study of nine European countries found no difference between the class (father) origins of males and their destinations and the class (father) origins of females and their destinations.

Mobility Through Marriage

Erikson and Goldthorpe also ask, do women experience more mobility through marriage than males experience through labor markets? Their conclusion is that both married and single women do not differ much from the mobility (up and down) of males in the labor market. In other words, they find no distinctive set of relations based on individual preferences based on personality, attractiveness, or romance; these may exist, but the authors conclude that occupational and marital mobility is structured by the same class resources and constraints.

What the above means is that individuals tend to marry within their class, a process that tends to widen income inequality when both spouses work.

American Mobility by Gender

Erikson and Goldthorpe do not analyze gender mobility in the United States but their analysis of the overall American mobility pattern shows that it does not differ from the European pattern (nor from those of Australia or Japan). With one exception, we can assume that overall gender mobility in the United States is largely the same as in Europe. The exception is that American women experience far more downward mobility to poverty (through marital breakdown) than in all other countries (which have better public programs mitigating poverty). It should be clear that gender inequities appear after women enter the labor force, that is, their upward mobility is curbed by gender discrimination.

CHANGING ATTITUDES BY AND TOWARD WOMEN

A revolution in attitudes about women (on the part of both men and women) has occurred in recent times. Both men and women have largely abandoned the idea that women are innately different and inferior to men. The long-held belief that women should confine themselves to being wives and mothers and develop passive, pious personalities has been abandoned by the majority of both male and female Americans.

Surveys over the last two decades have shown a large shift in attitudes among women at all age and educational levels toward a more liberal, equalitarian stance toward sex roles. In 1977, for example, only a third of women agreed that "most of the important decisions in the life of the family should be made by the man of the house," whereas in 1962 two-thirds agreed.[32] Surveys also show that most women now want to be wives, mothers, *and workers,* and most now expect to realize values in all three areas.

Though a clear majority of males and females now favors equality, changes in attitudes are not the same as changes in behavior. The same holds for new laws—a change in law does not automatically lead to a change of behavior. Remember, new attitudes and laws can be a burden to the extent that they shift responsibility from the power groups who control the distribution of opportunities and rewards to the individual (see the section "The Burden of Moral Equality," in Chapter 17). And despite the above convergence in attitudes, research reveals important gender differences in the value orientations of American adolescents that might have a bearing on who succeeds and who doesn't. From the mid-1970s to the early 1990s, females were "more likely than males to express concern and responsibility for the well-being of others, less likely than males to accept materialism and competition, and more likely than males to indicate that finding purpose and meaning in life is extremely important."[33]

Other forces also help explain why the relative position of women has not changed. In an interesting study of college women, Laurie Cummings found that feminist students projected a "Horatia Alger" image of success (the Protestant-bourgeois achiever plus luck). In addition, they resolved possible conflicts among marriage, motherhood, and career with the concept of *superwoman.* On the other hand, college women who were not feminists saw few difficulties in combining new work roles with old "female" roles. The study concludes that both types of women were conservative in that they saw progress for women within American society as presently constituted.[34]

THE POLITICS OF GENDER

Two distinct periods of struggle by women against sexual inequality stand out. In the nineteenth and early twentieth centuries, women fought to get the vote and succeeded with the nineteenth amendment to the U.S. Constitution (1919). Since the 1960s the women's movement has broadened its struggle to include equality in other areas, especially the economy, education, the law, and marriage.

Right Liberals and Women

Right liberals give women's equality low priority—indeed, they oppose it, though not always openly. The right liberal position is found in the Republican party, especially in its conservative wing. The main thrust of the Republican party is to protect and enhance the interests of propertied and professional groups. The Republican party is relatively indifferent to women's issues because resolving them threatens the interests of its main supporters. Republicans (and conservatives in general) argue that all will be well if the private economy is given first priority. Women and other minorities will benefit most, argue right liberals, if existing economic forces are left alone to produce wealth and opportunities for all (the trickle-down theory).[35]

Extreme right-wing liberals oppose many things that the majority of women want or that reform and radical groups want for them. They oppose the Equal Rights Amendment, abortion (whether paid for privately or with public funds), and nontraditional family practices or sexual preferences. In 1981, federal tax-supported abortions for women were eliminated (unless the mother's life was in danger, but not for rape[36] or incest), largely at the insistence of conservative forces. Conservatives were also influential in the defeat of the Equal Rights Amendment in 1982. The Reagan administration of 1980–1988 openly relaxed enforcement of all civil rights law. In 1983 it succeeded in getting the courts to agree that colleges receiving federal money could only be held accountable to civil rights laws for programs specifically funded. It also supported the state of Washington's appeal of a federal court decision upholding equal pay in a comparable worth case. The basic economic policy of the Reagan administration and its cuts in public programs for the poor, children, the elderly, and pregnant women all hit women, especially working, lower-class, and minority women very hard.

Conservative Republicans and conservative Democrats stress "family values," by which they mean the traditional nuclear family: male working, female as wife and mother. But their emphasis on family is hypocrisy since they do nothing about the absence of breadwinner jobs, have proposed cuts in the tax credit programs to help poverty families with full-time workers, and oppose family planning, especially sex education and access to contraceptives by teenagers.[37] In a broader context, right liberals oppose all government programs, which means they oppose publicly supported housing, child care, maternity leave, nutrition programs, and medical care. This despite the well-known fact that private enterprise cannot deliver on these services, especially for working women and women with modest to poverty income.

Left Liberals and Women

Female leaders, with help from men and other minority groups, have pushed for a full complement of rights for women and for an enhancement of their opportunities. Mainstream feminist groups such as the National Organization for Women (NOW) and the Women's Equity Action League (WEAL) engage in traditional political action and tend to be reformist in spirit. By and large, left liberals, including mainstream feminism, put their faith in new laws and in political reform to achieve their goals.

Right and left liberals do not question America's ability to absorb its minorities, including women. Given time and enough political and moral effort, the United States will realize all its ideals.

Radical Feminists

The radical position on women tends to be ambiguous, but by and large, women's issues are usually subordinated to economic questions. Radicals, including radical feminists, view the subjugation of women as merely part of the more general subjugation of working men and women to property groups. One difference among radical feminists is that some of them are opposed to masculine forms of domination, and they have taken a stance against what they feel is the uncritical acceptance by many liberals and radicals of competitive, achievement values. Feminine values of cooperation, sharing, and caring are seen as running counter to Protestant-bourgeois values and as the only basis for a nonsexist society.

Radical feminist groups are organized on a highly decentralized basis. Individuals are encouraged to exercise choice as to amount and type of participation and are given opportunities to change their life-styles in an atmosphere of mutual support. Though small in number, radical feminist groups have had considerable influence on mainstream feminism especially through their research and study reports.

Using These Perspectives to Understand the Abortion Battle

The fight over abortion represents a deep divide among Americans, much deeper than most are aware. The first level beneath the surface is the class nature of the opposing forces and the fact that pro and con forces represent, not merely the lower and upper classes, but forces that stand for a wide set of traditional values and forces that want a new set of values for women and society.[38]

The matter is complicated because the upper classes are not of one mind on abortion. Here, as in other gender issues, upper-class men want to look after the interests of their mothers, wives, and daughters. Thus moderate Republicans and liberal Democrats support the right to abortion. But conservative Republicans and Democrats, ever ready to use simplistic morality to support their worldview, vehemently oppose abortion. Their position also gains them support among some Christian groups and tradition-oriented sectors of the lower-middle and working classes. By and large, the opponents of abortion have managed to cut public funds for abortion, which in effect means that abortion is available differentially by social class.

The deepest meaning of the abortion issue is whether or not humans can bring collective life under control to serve stated human values. Women (and of course men too) are being held hostage to power groups who do not want to lose the meaning that tradition gives them or the power that obsolete beliefs support. More important than opposition to abortion is the opposition of a wide variety of traditionalists (secular conservatives, some Protestants, Orthodox Jews, and the Roman Catholic Church) to birth control and family planning.

Only a planned economy and society can curb the burden on women—as well as on men and society—of unwanted children. Citizens must not allow this issue to be discussed in conventional terms. They, especially educated white women, must realize that by supporting anti-abortion political parties, they are supporting the fantasy of laissez-faire, the power of paranoid Protestants, and a male Roman Catholic clerical hierarchy that practices celibacy to maintain its bureaucratic integrity.

Women, Voting, and Laws to Help Women

Women tend to vote a little differently from men but not as much as is supposed. They tend to favor government intervention to help working women and women with problems. By and large their voting, like men's, follows class lines. Their vote is important politically only in the sense that small amounts of votes can mean a lot in American elections.

Many laws were passed to help women from the 1960s on, especially civil rights laws supporting equality for women in being considered for jobs, equal facilities in schools, and affirmative action. Other programs sought to help with maternity leave, child care, abusive spouses, sexual harassment, rape reform, child support, and so on. Impressionistically (no exact studies exist), programs that help women in the upper classes have had some success, while most programs of most value to most women have been poorly funded and have been cut or underenforced even if they were succeeding.

Health Care and Research

Well-to-do women probably receive the best medical care possible. But the large majority of women are subject to the negative consequences of class and sexism. Working- and lower-class women, like their male counterparts, do not receive the same medical care received by the middle class and above. But in addition to deprivation by class, broad segments of the female population, including women above the working classes, are treated differently by the medical profession (see Box 19–2, "The Female Patient: The

BOX 19–2 *The Female Patient: The Double Jeopardy of Class and Gender*

Mary Healthy goes to the doctor (the chances are high that the doctor will be a male). Mary is getting a checkup—the doctor examines her heart, lungs, blood pressure, but not her breasts and does not give her a pelvic examination (general reproductive organs). Mary has had no problems with these overlooked regions of her body and is just as happy to leave them unexamined. What has happened? Why should a doctor overlook the obvious, distinguishing, and potentially troublesome parts of the female anatomy? The reason, however ludicrous it may seem, is that medical schools locate these parts of the body in a gynecology course—it follows, therefore, that if patients want those parts of the body checked they must go to a specialist. A few years later Mary enrolls in a prepaid group health plan. Her doctor sees her through some discomfort, advising against a hysterectomy. Mary is fortunate—if she had been in a program like Blue Cross, where doctors get paid only if they do something, her chances of having a hysterectomy (needed or not) would be 50 percent higher.

Mary's luck changes and her marriage sours. She begins to drink. Her self-esteem, not high to start with given the lower value accorded to women by American culture, suffers a double blow. Mary has internalized the double standard for alcoholics and thinks that women who drink are morally reprehensible (men who drink, on the other hand, are considered to be victims of the job, comic figures, and so on). And she believes herself a failure for not succeeding at marriage. Mary does not feel tip-top and begins to go to the doctor with vague symptoms (confirming his stereotype of women as complainers). Her doctor never spots her alcoholism (he was not trained in this area though he does tend to spot male alcoholics more often than women). Unsurprisingly, there are few treatment centers for women alcoholics.

Doctors tend to have different images of health for males and females. Healthy women are "more submissive, less independent, less adventurous, less competitive, more excitable in minor crises, more easily hurt, and more emotional than a mature healthy man." Their conception of a healthy adult closely parallels that of a healthy man (for sources, see Marian Sandmaier, "Alcoholics Invisible," p. 28). It is no accident, therefore, that her doctor uses drugs to cure (sedate) Mary since submissiveness is part of his definition of a healthy female. Women are not only far more likely to be given drugs than men but far more likely to become cross-addicted. It is not long before Mary becomes addicted to drink *and* pills.

Mary's luck changes for the better. A 1970 federal law requires provision for female alcoholics in centers receiving federal money. She is one of the few to get a place but the treatment doesn't work. The center has no program for job training, no provision to care for her children, no follow-up program once she is released, and the image used by the male staff to rehabilitate her is the same one that led her to drink in the first place. They want to give her a feminine personality, which she also wants deeply but which conflicts with a deep urge to be her own person (married women are much more likely than married men to become mentally ill—never-married women tend to have much lower rates).* Her troubles will appear all over again after leaving the treatment center since she will either be very poor, or, if she marries again, subject to unhealthy sex roles.

Both men and women in need of medical care benefit from the miracles of modern medicine but they are also mistreated. Mistreatment varies by age, class, and sex. The female as female is subject to all that befell Mary: excessive specialization in medical school by students, the profit motive, medical myths, popular myths in medicine, double standards, and poor public health-care policies. And by having her deviance (alcohol, mental illness, other behavior) "medicalized," she is being mistreated even when she receives the best of care since only her symptoms are being treated.

*Walter R. Gove, "Sex, Marital Status, and Psychiatric Treatment: A Research Note," *Social Forces* 58 (September 1979):89–93.

Double Jeopardy of Class and Gender."[39]) The different damaging treatment of female patients is no doubt a result of the pervasive sexism of American society. But it is also due to the fact that women are excluded from the upper reaches of the health-care professions.

THE MASS MEDIA AND GENDER: THE MORE THINGS CHANGE . . .

The backlash against attempts to promote equality for women that was reported earlier has also appeared in the mass media. The trends in the area of gender are similar to those in the area of race and ethnicity. From the 1960s on, the blatant sexism of the media diminished. Women were better represented in achievement roles—they appeared as doctors, lawyers, detectives, and so on. That movement in the depiction of women has continued. The fourth sequel (1995) to the television program *Star Trek* has a woman as its central character, the captain. A 1996 episode of *This Old House* featured female plumbers.

But the overwhelming bulk of media characters and stories still feature males in achievement roles. Women are still depicted—and it seems increasingly so since the backlash that began in the 1980s—as feminine, that is, as nurturing, engaged in household activity, by their appearance, including body shape, and by their relationships to others (mother, wife, daughter).

Underrepresentation on television is too abstract and, in any case, the idea of representing any aspect of American society accurately would not be entertaining and thus not profitable. The media not only reflect the American population's values and beliefs, but they sidestep problems and contradictions. For example, they may not be underrepresenting women in the medical or legal worlds, but they have little to say about the deep segregation of women in these professions into less-rewarded, less-prestigious specialties. When a woman does achieve standing in one of these specialties, she is apt to be referred to as a *female* surgeon.

The biased depiction of women, as well as class, race, ethnicity, and as we see, age, disability, and life-style, is difficult to see because it is communicated through images that reflect unconscious assumptions of what is real and legitimate. This feature of gender bias, its pervasiveness and therefore difficult-to-see nature, is featured in many critical analyses. But many (if not most or all) gender analyses, especially textbooks, have literally no reference to social class. In addition, most gender analyses are liberal, that is, they are critical of the media or society for not allowing women full participation in American society. Mainstream feminism assumes that the United States as presently structured can generate equality and full participation by all its members; that is, they do not ask whether the exploitation of women and other minorities is connected to the basic structure of power, or whether it is simply a question of not following through on the extension of legal and political rights to all. In the following sections, we will try to strike a balance between liberal and radical feminism.

Soap Operas

The soap opera (from the 1930s on)[40] stresses the importance of romantic interaction, the blossoming of true love, marriage, domesticity, and kinship values. The daytime soap opera presupposes and affirms an ideal family order: true love as the basis of marriage, having children as a woman's fulfillment, parent-child love and devotion, and generational continuity. All problems boil down to the need to maintain a happy, moral family life. Good people associate sex with love, marriage, and children. The world of everyday life is meaningful and small decisions have big implications. Life is filled with many different examples of human nature, all humans behave blindly, life is not always fair, but in the long run (which never comes) good triumphs and evil is punished.

Soaps have increased the number of women with careers, but these are token jobs, a ritual bow to the women's movement. (Actually, women on soap operas who devote too much time to their careers are punished.) Soaps are extremely popular and reflect deeply held values (at least among women who make up the main bulk of the audience). They no doubt help to maintain traditional family values, at least among women. In recent decades, the evening soap opera has developed the family theme (which dominates the daytime soaps) to include the world of big business, including the international economy. Here again, a variegated human nature reigns supreme, but unlike the daytime soaps the evening soaps have a greater tendency for individuals to do good and evil in personal relations as these bear on business relations and vice versa.[41] The (small) movement of women into the business world and the growing importance of the international economy are also reflected in the evening soaps.

The soaps do not have a straight narrative with a strong patriarchical climax and this has led some feminists to see the soap opera as a feminist text that can inspire resistance by viewers. But research has failed to produce such sophistication among soap audiences. As critics have pointed out, the soaps render the individual insignificant and its multiple characters and plots make it difficult for the viewer to identify with any of them. Soap operas have many limited egos in conflict and no one is really able to take charge because each is ignorant about what everyone else is going to do. Thus, far from inciting resistance to male power, the soap opera's format of narration without end; its themes of ideal love, marriage, and family constantly thwarted; its many-sided explanations for evil and failure; and its transgressions that offer vicarious enjoyment for hidebound housewives, reflects the unsatisfactory life of audiences and offers fake justifications and temporary solace for it. Unlike the masculine narrative, which has a strong character coping with his world, the feminine "story" is a never-ending mélange of episodic events in which self-oriented individuals struggle without avail in a world that is moral because people get what they deserve. Here one finds the social action tradition of sociology, the rational-choice tradition in economics, and the interest-group politics of political science—the capitalist world of eternal scarcity, except that in this case all instead of most fail.

Romance Novels

The romance novel has a predictable formula and is easy for busy women to read; it is also inexpensive. Aspiring authors are given a tip sheet spelling out the formula: a vulnerable woman meets a powerful man who excites her sexually. They spar, she makes clear that she wants love with sex, they separate. She fears that she has lost him, but in reality, he respects her. Some plot twist threatens their relationship, but they finally declare their love for each other, presumably a love that will last forever.[42]

Like much of the mass media, romance novel publishing is a lucrative monopoly using exploited female authors.[43] The readers are clear about why they read them—for escape. Janice Radway has studied a nonscientific sample of such readers and has offered contrasting interpretations of what the romance novel signifies. On the one hand, readers are escaping from patriarchical marriages into a world where love and commitment, not competitive pursuits for success, reign supreme. On the other, such reading and its content probably do very little to change the patriarchical marriage to which the women must return. Or rather, concludes Radway, we will not be sure until we trace what happens to readers and their spouses over time.[44]

Female Heroes

Popular culture has many females in heroic roles. A female in a heroic role was a heroine in the gothic novel because she triumphed over adversity pursuing a feminine goal, marriage to a man of substance. Today, females are heroic in male roles, for example, as detectives (Cagney and Lacy, *Murder She Wrote*), journalists (*Murphy Brown*), *Star Trek* captain, doctors (*E.R., Chicago Hope*), or predators (*Fatal Attraction, Disclosure, Thelma and Louise*). Some have even interpreted *Roseanne* as a feminine text because it features a housewife who openly ridicules feminine values.

The great romantic comedies of the 1930s and 1940s signaled the emergence of the capable, intelligent woman, largely among the upper classes.

The rise of the middle-class career women has been portrayed on *Mary Tyler Moore* and women can even be superheroes (Wonder Woman, Bionic Woman). The feminist movement, essentially a broadening of opportunities for middle- and upper-class women, is reflected in popular culture in many ways. Women have been given new motives, personalities, and statuses, often conforming to male values and usually according to their social class.[45] Significantly, the rise of the professional plot has included females among the professional group; this is necessary not only to satisfy liberal feminism, but because contemporary male elites are depicted as self-sufficient—no longer do male heroes return to the community when their work is done. Since elites are no longer organically connected to society, it would not do to have males appear to be homosexuals given America's prejudices. Actually, elites engage in sex and romance *during* their adventures, not after as in earlier heroic tales, thus creating the impression that the here and now is where everything worthwhile takes place (a reversal, obviously, of the Protestant-bourgeois, early capitalist theme stressing gratification postponement for the sake of a better future).

The Nancy Drew stories also suggest a new status for women, but have left an ambiguous legacy. Drawing on the Horatio Alger tradition but reflecting the new world of corporate America, the Nancy Drew stories (along with the Hardy Boys series by the same male author) stress success through intellectual-professional creativity rather than character. But Nancy remains feminine and attractive and is thus a superwoman.[46] Here again popular culture, increasingly working through professionalism, mediates a conflict rather than solving it.

Advertising and Gender

Women are still depicted in feminine roles in advertising. They are still used to sexualize commodities. They are still used to uphold unrealistic standards of beauty for women (and for men for that matter). In this regard, note should be taken that corporations do the advertising and they exert enormous influence over both advertising and content. A case study is Gloria Steinem's account of *Ms.* magazine's losing struggle with advertisers.[47]

Pornography and Slasher Films

Pornography is a $5 billion global business run by males for males. It depicts sex acts in which men initiate and control the interaction. It is obviously part of the generalized subordination of women and is rightly subject to attacks by feminist groups. Feminists object to pornography in general because of the explicit male power relation that it helps to sustain, and object to pornography with violence in particular because, they claim, it leads to sexual violence against women in real life.

The evidence for the causal impact of pornography with violence is highly suggestive, but far from conclusive[48] (the evidence is from experiments and registers attitudes, which of course are not the same as overt behavior). Beyond this, Gayle Rubin has argued that feminist antipornography campaigns are misguided. For one thing, pornography with violence is a very small part of the market and caters to a special clientele. The huge amount of violence in the media (films, music videos, television, books, and magazines), most of it directed at women, has nothing to do with sex. Antipornography feminists should pay more attention to slasher films and less to pornography. Rubin implies that clamping down on pornography and prostitution, however desirable from one point of view, may prevent a more open attitude by all toward sex—in short, the opposition to it by prolife, profamily conservative groups on moral grounds is not necessarily in the best interests of women.

In any case, Rubin argues that antiporn feminists cannot help women with the real problems they face "of unequal pay, job discrimination, sexual violence and harassment, the unequal burdens of child-care and housework, increasing right-wing infringements on hard-won feminist gains, and several millennia of unrelenting male privilege vis-à-vis the labor, love, personal service, and possession of women."[49]

SPORTS AND GENDER INEQUALITY

One can also note latent consequences to the positive gains made by women in the field of sport. Progress in giving girls and women equal opportunities in lower- and higher-education sports had been slow since Title IX of the Education Amendment Act of 1972 guaranteed gender equality for schools receiving federal aid. As late as the mid-1990s, women were still suing to get colleges and universities to provide them with equal treatment in sports. Given the economic constraints faced by schools, and resistance by male sports directors and organizations (resulting in slow motion enforcement by the Department of Education), schools dragged their feet in extending equality to women.[50]

In an important empirical study, Don Sabo explodes a number of myths about women's participation in sports. Contrary to myths, females are healthier both physically and psychologically if they participate in sports. And women do not become "macho" by playing sports; rather, they expand their feminine personality.[51]

Providing equality for women in sports has two latent consequences. Female athletes may not become "macho," but women athletes and programs have succeeded by imitating not merely masculine behavior, but class and class values as well. The second latent consequence of women's success, not only in school sports but also in the professional world, is to demonstrate in almost every sport their inferiority to men (one exception is horse racing, where female jockeys do as well as men).[52]

Despite golf tournaments for seniors and Special Olympics for the disabled, both male and female sports have the latent consequence of emphasizing youth and health as the basis of achievement, thus distracting attention from the fact that 15 to 20 percent of the population is handicapped, that we have an aging population with special needs, that large majorities of Americans get no exercise, and that America's governing class is made up of white males age fifty and older who do not operate in the world of clearcut rules and results characteristic of sports.

But perhaps the best way to see sports as a reflection and reinforcer of all forms of inequality is to read Douglas E. Foley's "The Great American Football Ritual: Reproducing Race [Ethnicity], Class, and Gender Inequality." [53] Foley's study of a small Texas town (80 percent Mexican American), based on participant observation and interviews, revealed a powerful, all-pervasive socialization process in which male athletes and their boosters promoted a way of life dominated by economically powerful white males. One need know little more than that coaches ranked higher than academic teachers in the high school, and provided the personnel for principals and superintendents, to understand sports as a legitimating practice and ideology for an illegitimate class system.

Perhaps the best way to deflate the use of sports to uphold the argument for widespread innate inequality is to note that experts have demonstrated that almost all of the ability that we observe in sports can be acquired by almost anybody through long years of systematic training and practice. It appears that the same holds true for fields as dissimilar as chess and violin playing.[54]

THE WOMEN'S MOVEMENT: ANY NET GAINS?

Since the 1960s, new laws have been passed to outlaw sex discrimination and guarantee equal pay; affirmative action programs have been mounted; social science research on women has grown dramatically; and women are now more visible in the world of business, the media, sports, the professions, government, and in elected offices. In 1981 President Ronald Reagan nominated and the Senate confirmed the first female United States Supreme Court Justice. In 1984 Geraldine Ferraro became the first woman to run for vice-president of the United States.

Appearance aside, a basic question remains: Has the overall women's movement resulted in any *net* gains? The same question can be asked differently: Is the latent function of the women's movement to strengthen the status quo by permitting handfuls of upper- and middle-class women to achieve some gains while dooming the vast majority of women to illegitimate inequalities? (See Box 19–3, "Is Women's Liberation a Movement Favoring Only the Upper Classes?") Most (including almost all introductory sociology textbooks and all books on sex roles) exaggerated the gains made by women, not least by overlooking negative evidence. What the facts show is that political and civil rights, favorable laws, and more education have not changed the relative position of women over the past thirty years (if anything, that position has deteriorated). Nor is the undoubted increase in participation by women in the general life of society an unmixed blessing. Women, for example, have rising rates of lung cancer. Women are also increasing their criminal behavior and becoming adept at more specialized types of crime as their opportunities become more varied.[55] And companies report that they are having problems with (and thus developing a negative attitude toward) over-thirty pregnancies by women executives and professionals, something that indicates that it is still difficult for women to combine career and motherhood.[56]

Assessing changes in the position of women is complicated. Women who work have more equality at home. Part of the low economic position of women stems from the breakup of marriages—here women may be losing economically but gaining in another sense because they are freed from unhappy marriages. No-fault divorce has not turned out to be the blessing that feminists once thought, because women are not getting a fair share of economic rewards from divorce settlements. On the positive side, some evidence indicates that the greater participation by women in formal work roles has reduced their incidence of mental illness, which up to now had appeared to be higher than the rates for men.

Nonetheless, progress in the crucial economic realm appears to be minimal. The main thrust of the women's movement has assumed that increased opportunity and favorable laws can bring about economic change. As such, women are still being subordinated by the basic norms that promote inequality in America. Achieving political and legal equality and formal equality of opportunity can only serve to legitimate sexual inequality in much the same way that formal equality legitimates the inequality of black and other minority Americans (the first to be victimized by this ideology were white Anglo-Saxon males). On balance, the evidence points to one conclusion—the basic outcome of the women's movement has been *to modernize the terms under which women will be dominated.* Until women's reform groups commit themselves to full employment and question the artificial scarcity of good jobs, the only result of their reforms will be to replace white and minority males with middle- and upper-class females. Once the upper classes have enough women in visible economic and professional positions, it will become harder for the vast bulk of women to argue that they are being victimized. Perhaps

BOX 19–3 *Is Women's Liberation a Movement Favoring Only the Upper Classes?*

The thrust of mainstream feminism has been to seek justice and progress for women through a redefinition of their political and legal rights. By and large, mainstream feminism has asked that women be accorded full and equal rights with men. The women's movement has also focused on issues that are of special importance to women: abortion, rape laws, maternity leaves with pay or coverage by insurance, tax subsidies for child-care centers, and enhanced educational opportunities.

These are certainly valuable reforms, but why not other reforms? Mainstream feminism has not focused on the problems of working women except to support the efforts of women to enter previously all-male occupations. It has not asked for a national system of child-care services. Little has been said of the exploitation of women by businesses that violate labor laws (there are now as many sweatshops in the United States as in the scandalous era of the early industrial period). Nothing has been said about the need for labor unions to protect workers, changes in the minimum wage, control of runaway plants, public housing, and comprehensive medical services for ordinary people. Mainstream feminism wants a fair share of the good jobs for women but has said nothing about the need to break down the artificial and wasteful barriers that keep such jobs scarce (and its occupants far less competent then they could be).

The single most important thing that would benefit women is a national commitment to full employment. But nothing is heard on this score.

As the wives and daughters of the middle and upper classes get an increasing share of good jobs, as their daughters marry men in the middle and upper classes, and as the structure of family income resembles a bell shape (a shrinkage of middle-level households has already begun—see Chapter 7), there will be less and less heard about the reforms women need most.

The Women's Movement has little to do with the interests of the majority of women. It is primarily a class phenomenon. The American upper classes treat their sons and daughters equally. From roughly 1875 to 1960, the American middle and upper classes built up a large backlog of educated daughters with no outlets for their abilities (aside from nursing, teaching, or library work). From the 1960s on, the upper classes (remember that educated men have given strong support to the women's movement) have worked hard to make it possible for the women of the upper classes to enter the world of business and the professions. By calling these actions a *women's* movement, the historic middle class (propertied and professional groups) continues (falsely) to associate its own interests with humanity at large.

better said, the women's movement will become more effective on behalf of women when upwardly mobile females realize that they will continue to be exploited even as members of the upper classes.

SUMMARY

The inequality of women can be analyzed along gender lines: all women regardless of class or race are considered and treated as inferiors.

The inequality of women can also be analyzed along racial lines: white women have a better social life than minority women.

The inequality of women by class means women in the upper classes are better off than women in the lower classes.

White women do not receive the same income and authority as men holding education and experience constant. Women have and are making relative gains in education but these are not being translated into income and occupational status.

Minority women (African-American, Hispanic, Asian, Native American, Pacific Islander women) are a depressed portion of the labor force facing the triple burden of gender, class, and race.

The bulk of women has faced the same negative economic consequences as men in recent decades, especially because of corporate downsizing and the world-market economy.

Women from the various classes fare the same in terms of class mobility when it comes to first job (or marriage) as men. Gender inequality occurs after they spend some time in the labor force.

Gender issues are prominent in American politics and women appear to be suffering setbacks as conservatives hammer away at affirmative action, abortion, and welfare for the poor.

The Women's Movement has largely benefited white women in the upper classes, though black women have done better than black males in recent years.

NOTES

1. Margaret Mead, *Sex and Temperament in Three Primitive Societies* (New York: Dell, 1935).
2. C. W. M. Hart and Arnold R. Pilling, *The Tiwi of North Australia* (New York: Holt, Rinehart & Winston, 1979).
3. Rae Lesser Blumberg, *Stratification: Socioeconomic and Sexual Inequality.* (Dubuque, IA: Wm. C. Brown, 1978).
4. Marvin Harris, *Cannibals and King: The Origins of Culture* (New York: Random House, 1977), ch. 6.
5. For a superb comparative-historical analysis of gender inequality in terms of specific types of society (forager, horticultural, pastoral, agrarian, and devel-

oped and developing capitalist and socialist), see Charlotte G. O'Kelly and Larry S. Carney, *Women and Men in Society: Cross-Cultural Perspectives on Gender Stratification,* 2nd ed. (Belmont, CA: Wadsworth, 1986).

6. For example, Plato and John Stuart Mill advocated the right and ability of women to participate in the male world. Saint-Simon and Comte focused, not on recruiting female talent for the male world, but on using female values as the moral cement to make that world work. Radical liberals and socialists included women in their demand for the liberation of males from oppressive conditions or from capitalism in general.
7. Miriam M. Johnson, "Liberalism and Gender Equality: Problems of Social Integration," in Paul Colomy, ed., *The Dynamics of Social Systems* (Newbury Park, CA: Sage, 1992), pp. 175–189.
8. Janet Saltzman Chafetz, "Gender Equality: Toward a Theory of Change," in Ruth A. Wallace, ed., *Feminism and Sociological Theory* (Newbury Park, CA: Sage, 1989), pp. 135–160.
9. Carolyn Merchant, *The Death of Nature: Women, Ecology, and the Scientific Revolution* (San Francisco: Harper & Row, 1980).
10. Dorothy E. Smith, "Corporate Capitalism," in M. L. Stephenson, ed., *Women In Canada* (Toronto: Newpress, 1973), pp. 5–35.
11. Smith's latest work and some of her earlier essays may be found in *The Everyday World As Problematic: A Feminist Sociology* (Toronto: University of Toronto Press, 1987); *The Conceptual Practices of Power: A Feminist Sociology of Knowledge* (Boston: Northeastern University Press, 1990), and *Texts, Facts, and Femininity: Exploring the Relations of Ruling* (New York: Routledge, 1990). The most accessible source to Smith's sociology of knowledge and indictment of male sociology is "Sociological Theory: Methods of Writing Patriarchy," in Ruth A. Wallace, ed., *Feminism and Sociological Theory* (Newbury Park, CA: Sage, 1989), ch. 2.
12. Dorothy E. Smith, *The Everyday World as Problematic: A Feminist Sociology* (Toronto: University of Toronto Press, 1987), ch. 5.
13. See the articles under Capitalist Patriarchy and Female Work in Zillah R. Eisenstein, ed., *Capitalist Patriarchy and the Case for Socialist Feminism* (New York: Monthly Review Press, 1979).
14. For an early and perhaps the best statement of this position, including a valuable critique of liberal feminism (John Locke, Jeane-Jacques Rousseau, Mary Wollstonecraft, John Stuart Mill and Harriet Taylor, and Betty Friedan), see Zillah R. Eisenstein, *The Radical Future of Liberal Feminism* (Boston: Northeastern University Press, 1981).
15. Isaac D. Balbus, *Marxism and Domination: A Neo-Hegelican, Feminist, Psychoanalytic Theory of Sexual, Political, and Technological Liberation* (Princeton, NJ: Princeton University Press, 1981).
16. Ann Ferguson, *Sexual Democracy: Women, Oppression, and Revolution* (Boulder, CO: Westview, 1991).
17. The following is based on Beth Anne Shelton and Ben Agger, "Shotgun Wedding, Unhappy Marriages, No Fault Divorce? Rethinking the Feminism-Marxism Relationship," in Paula England, ed., *Theory in Gender/Feminism on Theory* (New York: Aldine De Gruyter, 1993), pp. 25–41.
18. Myra M. Ferree, "The Confused American Housewife," *Psychology Today* 10 (September 1976):76–80.
19. U.S. Bureau of the Census, "Money Income of Households, Families, and Per-

sons in the United States: 1992," *Current Population Reports,* P60–184 (Washington, DC: U.S. Government Printing Office, 1993), Figure 2.

20. U.S. Bureau of the Census, *Statistical Abstract of the United States 1995* (Washington, DC: U.S. Government Printing Office, 1995), Table 677.
21. Annette Bernhardt, Martina Morris, and Mark S. Handcock, "Women's Gains or Men's Losses? A Closer Look at the Shrinking Gender Gap in Earnings," *American Journal of Sociology* 101, no. 2 (September 1995):302–328.
22. For two readers that reflect this new research, see Ann Helton Stromberg and Shirley Harkess, eds., 2nd ed., *Women Working* (Mountain View, CA: Mayfield, 1988) and Jerry A. Jacobs, ed., *Gender Inequality at Work* (Thousand Oaks, CA: Sage, 1995).
23. Barbara F. Reskin and Catherine E. Ross, "Jobs, Authority, and Earnings Among Managers: The Continuing Significance of Sex," in Jerry A. Jacobs, ed., *Gender Inequality at Work,* ch. 5.
24. John Hagen, "The Gender Stratification of Income Inequality Among Lawyers," *Social Forces* 68 (March 1990):835–855.
25. Nina Bernstein, *New York Times,* January 8, 1996, p. 9.
26. William T. Bielby and Denise D. Bielby, "Cumulative Versus Continuous Disadvantage in an Unstructured Labor Market: Gender Differences in the Careers of Television Writers," in Jerry A. Jacobs, ed., *Gender Inequality at Work,* ch. 8.
27. Gwendolyn Wright, "On the Fringe of the Profession: Women in Architecture," in Spiro Kostof, ed., *The Architect: Chapters in the History of the Profession* (New York: Oxford University Press, 1977), ch. 11.
28. Patricia A. Roos and Katherine W. Jones, "Shifting Gender Boundaries: Women's Inroads Into Academic Sociology," in Jerry A. Jacobs, ed., *Gender Inequality at Work,* ch. 11.
29. For a valuable analysis of female poverty in five capitalist and two socialist societies, see Gertrude S. Goldberg and Eleanor Kremen, "The Feminization of Poverty: Only in America," *Social Policy* 17 (Spring 1987):3–14.
30. Natalie J. Sokoloff, *Black Women and White Women in the Professions: Occupational Segregation by Race and Gender, 1960–1980* (New York: Routledge, 1992) and Bette Woody, *Black Women in the Workplace: Impacts of Structural Change in the Economy* (New York: Greenwood Press, 1992).
31. Robert Erikson and John H. Goldthorpe, *The Constant Flux: A Study of Class Mobility in Industrial Societies* (New York: Oxford University Press, 1992), ch. 7.
32. For a report of a study using data from 1962, 1963, 1966, and 1977 by Arland Thornton and Deborah Freedman, see *ISR Newsletter,* Institute for Social Research, University of Michigan (Winter 1980), 3. Similar shifts in attitudes have been found by the Roper Organization in its survey for the 1980 Virginia Slims American Women's Opinion Poll—see *New York Times* (March 13, 1980), C1.
33. Ann M. Beutel and Margaret Mooney Marini, "Gender and Values," *American Sociological Review* 60 (June 1995):446.
34. Laurie Davidson Cummings, "Values Stretch in Definitions of Career Among College Women: Horatia Alger as Feminist Model," *Social Problems* 25 (October 1977):65–74.
35. Readers are reminded that while right liberals continue to enunciate this view with knee-jerk conviction, it has been thoroughly discredited by history and social analysis.

36. Newspaper accounts of the abortion controversy cite estimates from an undisclosed source that place the number of pregnancies from rape at 15,000 per year. Neither side of the abortion controversy dispute this estimate, which may or may not be accurate.
37. In a study of thirty-seven developed countries, the Alan Guttmacher Institute found that the United States had by far the highest rate of teenage pregnancy. The reason seemed to be that the United States is alone in not publicly promoting sex education and birth control, *New York Times,* March 13, 1985, p. 1.
38. Kristen Luker, *Abortion and the Politics of Motherhood* (Berkeley: University of California Press, 1984).
39. Much of this discussion is based on Susan Schiefelbein, "The Female Patient: Heeded? Hustled? Healed?," *Saturday Review* 7 (March 29, 1980):12–16; and Marian Sandmaier, "Alcoholic Invisible: The Ordeal of the Female Alcoholic," *Social Policy* 10 (January–February, 1980):25–30.
40. The following is a composite interpretation of Deborah D. Rogers, "Daze of Our Lives: The Soap Opera as Feminist Text"; Karen Lindsey, "Reading Race, Sexuality, and Class in Soap Operas"; John Fiske, "Gendered Television: Femininity"; and Tania Modleski, "The Search for Tomorrow in Today's Soap Operas," all in Gail Dines and Jean M. Humez, eds., *Gender, Race, and Class: A Text-Reader* (Thousand Oaks, CA: Sage, 1995), pp. 325–354.
41. Mary S. Mander, "Dallas: The Mythology of Crime and the Moral Occult," *Journal of Popular Culture* 17 (Fall 1983):44–50.
42. Marilyn M. Lowery, "The Traditional Romance Formula," Gail Dines and Jean M. Humez, eds., *Gender, Race, and Class: A Text-Reader* (Thousand Oaks, CA: Sage, 1995), pp. 215–222.
43. Richard Pollack, "What's in a Pseudonym: Romance Slaves of *Harlequin,*" in ibid., pp. 223–227.
44. Janice A. Radway, *Reading the Romance* (Chapel Hill: University of North Carolina Press, 1984). The 1991 reprint has a new introduction.
45. By 1980, popular music had begun to drop the traditional sex role standards that had prevailed in the 1960s and 1970s; see Kathleen L. Endres, "Sex Role Standards in Popular Music," *Journal of Popular Culture* 18 (Summer 1984):9–18. In addition, women rock stars like Madonna have assumed the same aggressive, sexual, calculating, money-hungry swagger that has long been characteristic of male rock stars. For other changes in the depiction of women, see Cornelia Butler Flora, "Changes in Women's Status in Women's Magazine Fiction: Differences by Social Class," *Social Problems* 26 (June 1979):558–569, and Victor Gecas, "Motives and Aggressive Acts in Popular Fiction: Sex and Class Differences," *American Journal of Sociology* 77 (January 1972):680–696.
46. Susan P. Montague, "How Nancy Gets Her Man: An Investigation of Success Models in American Adolescent Pulp Literature," in W. Arens and S. P. Montague, eds., *The American Dimension: Culture Myths and Social Realities* (Port Washington, NY: Alfred, 1976), pp. 99–116.
47. Sut Jhally, "Image-Based Culture: Advertising and Popular Culture"; Robert Goldman, "Constructing and Addressing the Audience as Commodity"; Jean Kilbourne, "Beauty and the Beast of Advertising"; and Gloria Steinem, "Sex, Lies, and Advertising," all in Dines and Humez, *Gender, Race and Class in Media,* selections 10, 11, 16, 15.
48. For a summary of research, see Richard Jackson Harris, "The Impact of Sexually Explicit Media," in Jennings Bryant and Dolf Zillman, eds., *Media Effects: Ad-*

vances in Theory and Research (Hillsdale, NJ: Lawrence Erlbaum and Associates, 1994), pp. 247–272.

49. Gayle Rubin, "Misguided, Dangerous, and Wrong: An Analysis of Anti-Pornography Politics," in Dines and Humez, *Gender, Race and Class in Media,* ch. 28. For a counterargument by Andrea Dworkin, a leading antipornography feminist, see "Pornography and Male Supremacy," in ibid., selection 27.
50. For a history of how male athletic directors and organizations took over women's sports, including a marked reduction in women coaches and athletic directors even as the number of female athletes swelled, see Linda Jean Carpenter and R. Vivian Costa, "Back to the Future: Reform with a Woman's Voice," in D. Stanley Eitzen, ed., *Sport in Contemporary Society: An Anthology,* 4th ed. (New York: St. Martin's Press, 1993), pp. 388–395.
51. Don Sabo, "Psychosocial Impacts of Athletic Participation on American Women: Facts and Fables," in Eitzen, *Sport in Contemporary Society,* pp. 374–387.
52. Margaret A. Ray and Paul W. Grimes, "Jockeying for Position: Winnings and Gender Discrimination on the Thoroughbred Track," *Social Science Quarterly* 74, no. 1 (March 1993):46–61.
53. In Eitzen, *Sport in Contemporary Society,* pp. 326–354.
54. For a review of research in these areas, see Daniel Goleman, "Peak Performance: Why Records Fall," *New York Times,* October 11, 1994, p. C1.
55. *New York Times,* January 21, 1980, p. A18; for general background, see Freda Adler and Rita James Simon, eds., *The Criminology of Deviant Women* (Boston: Houghton Mifflin, 1979).
56. *Wall Street Journal,* July 20, 1981, p. 1.

20
The American Class System: A Summary and Interpretation

◆ ◆ ◆ ◆

◆ ◆ ◆ ◆

THE GENERAL STRUCTURE OF AMERICAN CLASSES

A social class is made up of families and unrelated individuals who share similar benefits across the three dimensions of class, prestige, and power. Our analysis of the three major dimensions and numerous subdimensions of stratification indicates that the distribution of American social and cultural values (material comfort and convenience, psychic development and satisfaction, political-legal power and every conceivable subcategory of behavior and benefit) can be subsumed by the concept of *social class,* now understood to mean the location of families and individuals across the three major dimensions of inequality. The essence of social stratification is the existence of a hierarchy of valued things, traits, and behaviors, which, lodged in households, are transmitted by means of social processes to children.

Looked at broadly, America's social stratification by social class is continuous with the past. It has legitimate elements (things work the way norms say they should) and illegitimate elements (behavioral phenomena that contradict basic norms and values: hereditary wealth, class advantages, oligarchic competition, racial-ethnic-sexual discrimination). Changes have taken place, of course, in the various elements that make up a social class. The occupational skill levels of the various classes have risen consistently, and the nature of the American household—the means by which the class system is transmitted from one generation to the next—has been modified by various factors. But contrary to both popular and elite belief, social mobility in the United States exhibits no movement toward meritocracy, or nonegalitarian classlessness. The upper classes tend to stay where they are or move up, the lower-working and lower classes tend merely to stay where they are, and the lower-middle and upper-working classes exhibit a trendless up-and-down movement depending on the state of the political economy.

Recent data suggest strongly that the first break in America's system of social stratification may have occurred: slow economic growth, a stagnant standard of living, and a shrinking middle class over the past three decades have resulted in a bipolar class structure, a decline in social mobility, and a loss of overall adaptive capacity. The general relation between legitimate and illegitimate elements has not changed much and there has been no significant increase in equality of opportunity, competition, or social justice (remembering, of course, that the civil rights and women's movements have simply moved blacks into the class system and given females in the upper classes a better chance to use their class advantages). Simply put, our social classes represent significant and enduring differences in the benefits Americans derive from society. By referring to these strata, therefore, one can predict outcomes in a wide range of areas, including family life; health; civic, political, and cultural participation; voting; type and amount of crime; justice; and so on. Obviously, some overlap between the various strata, some differences within them, and some regional and local variations exist. Despite these qualifications, however, America's social classes are real because each is a network of social groups sharing unequally and often illegitimately in the totality of social benefits.

Existing research points to five relatively distinct strata in the United States, and to a fairly pronounced integration of the three dimensions, whose center of gravity is the class dimension.

The Upper Class

The United States has a small collection of upper-class families (about 1 to 2 percent of all households) that enjoy a thoroughgoing consistency of class, prestige, and power statuses.[1] More specifically, this class of families has great economic power derived from its ownership and control of economic enterprises; its wealth is secure over generations; and it enjoys high and dependable income. Furthermore, it enjoys high family stability, life expectancy, and mental health; high-quality socialization and education; high occupational prestige and satisfaction; high levels of comfort and diversion; high psychic satisfaction from material and symbolic consumption; high psychic satisfaction and high prestige from primary and secondary associations; and great access to, influence over, and protection from political and legal processes.

The basic causal process that maintains such families at the top is readily explicable; each of the foregoing categories of benefits reinforces the others, producing a web of causation that enables upper-class families to weather and prevail over adversity, whether in the form of economic depression, or an occasional mental illness or retarded child. No understanding of this group of families is possible if one restricts oneself to individualistic explanations. On the contrary, their social position derives from the historical accumulation and consolidation of advantage, including careful attention to the socialization structures and processes that ensure continuity from one generation to the next.

It can be assumed that upper-class families are fairly self-conscious about their position in society, though they do not characteristically emphasize their superiority by demanding deference or recognition from society-at-large. The main evidence for imputing self-consciousness about social class to this group is the careful and comprehensive way in which they raise their children and manage their lives and the fact that membership in this stratum is restricted to those who qualify on both class and prestige criteria. This class also derives considerable unity and social power from common upbringing, education, intermarriage, socializing and associational membership, and overlapping economic statuses. Finally, surveys have shown that in general the upper classes are more conscious of social class than are the lower classes.

The upper class is very secretive and we must infer most of its characteristics. It is tradition-conscious without being backward or reactionary; it is civic minded without being much interested in politics or public service. It is a leisure class, though its males work at occupations. It supports charitable, educational, and cultural activities and organizations, though its role may be declining as hard-pressed colleges, museums, service agencies, and research institutes become increasingly dependent on tax funds and business contributions to support themselves.

The power of the upper class derives from its wealth, which gives it control over the fundamental process of capital investment. The wealth of the upper class is intertwined and there is extensive overlap and cooperation among its various members. The upper class is also intertwined with the upper classes of other capitalist societies. The power of the upper class also derives from its ability to set the terms of membership for new wealth—here its control of both elite private schools and elite prestige groups is important. Its control over corporations and secondary organizations as well as government gives it the power to determine how the upper middle class should behave. Its power is also secured by good works (especially through foundations), by reform (corporate liberalism or support of moderate Republicans and Democrats), and by the liberal ethos of individualism, competition, and progress.

The Upper Middle Class

Families whose breadwinners are proprietors of substantial businesses or farms or upper-level managers or professionals, in either "private" or "public" life, enjoy a high level of sociocultural-personality benefits and a high level of consistency in their various benefits and statuses (about 10 to 15 percent of all households). In recent years women have increased their share of this group either alone or as the working partner of their spouse.

This class of families lacks the wealth of the upper class; it also lacks certain prestige assets, but it appears not to suffer much on this account. As we have noted, one of the characteristics of a stable class system is the existence of many different ways by which individuals and families can obtain satisfaction. In any case, to join the ranks of the upper class, upper-middle-class families must learn to consume and to associate according to upper prestige standards and protocols. For real and lasting success in this regard, they must place their children in the socialization structures (especially private schools and prestige colleges) that old-rich families have established for their own offspring. In the meantime, upper-middle-class families participate in a full range of voluntary organizations, founding their own clubs and frequenting new resorts if need be. While they may occasionally experience discomfort when they consume or when they apply for membership in exclusive clubs, they tend to enjoy high consistency in all their statuses.

An upper-middle-class family is by definition characterized by high income, high education, high occupation (in terms of both prestige and other satisfactions), high participation in voluntary associations, and high awareness and participation in political life. Such families enjoy stable family life, privacy, pleasant surroundings, and stimulating associations. Their children of both sexes receive higher education as a matter of course, and their members enjoy the comfortable feeling that they are fully normal.[2]

Post-1945 America witnessed a significant growth in the absolute numbers of the upper middle class, though there appears to have been only slight growth in its relative size. Basically, the upper middle class is made up of individuals (and their families) who rode the wave of post–World

War II corporate and professional expansion. Subject to the long-range process of rationalization, there has been a steady bureaucratization of the economy (the growth of corporate concentration), the professions (hospitals, law firms, universities, and so on), voluntary organizations (professionally run charitable organizations, foundations, trade and professional organizations, labor unions, churches, and so on), and, of course, government.

Thought of in terms of class (and not of the ideology of "nonegalitarian classlessness"), much of what has occurred in post-1945 America makes sense as class modernization, not as the reduction of ascription and the realization of merit and equality. As the upper and upper middle classes have grown in absolute numbers (not in relative size), elite institutions of higher education have been enlarged and others have been upgraded. As maturing industrial society has experienced long-term and short-term pressures and crises (technological displacement of labor and large-scale migration, boom and bust, labor unrest, war, racial conflict, student unrest, pollution, and the like), it has increasingly turned to political solutions, which are defined by the upper middle class and its political allies—the rich, entrenched small-town business people and professionals, and small farmers. It is not surprising, therefore, that the upper middle class is a major beneficiary of most legislation, reform and otherwise. It goes without saying that this class is not a ruling class in any traditional sense. For one thing, it is too diverse in composition to have clear-cut common economic and political interests. Furthermore, it is too deeply committed to economic functions to be committedly political. On the whole, it is conservative on most domestic economic issues and liberal on foreign policy, civil rights, and personal behavior.

The Lower Middle Class

The lower middle class is a very diverse group, unified loosely by the fact that it is not a manual (factory) laboring class, and, more importantly, by an overall level of social existence that places it above the working class and gives its children a much greater probability of rising to the upper middle class (about 30 to 35 percent of all households). The lower middle class includes small-business people and small farmers; various self-employed or marginal professionals[3] and semiprofessionals (teachers, clergy, local elected officials, social workers, nurses, police officers, firefighters); and middle-management personnel, both private and public. On the whole, members of this class enjoy stable family lives and a certain measure of occupational prestige; they are civic minded; and while they participate in political life less than the upper classes, they are more political than the classes below (each of the segments of this class can exhibit different shades of political behavior depending on issue and context). The various segments of this class have diverse histories, and each is potentially subject to various forms of inconsistency.[4] Small-business people, small farmers, and independent professionals are still committed to the laissez-faire ethic of rugged individualism, even though each of these groups has suffered a decline in relative class, prestige, and power status over the past century. Quasi-professionals, as well as middle-management personnel, enjoy a measure of prestige because of their education, because they are associated with valued social functions, and because their work is clean and allegedly cerebral, but their class position is not always congruent with their prestige. One of the persistent trends in this area is the growing unionization of teachers, firefighters, police officers, and nurses on a "professional" basis—that is, without associating themselves with factory and other service workers with whom they share many basic economic problems. Among these groups, small-business people and small farmers experience peculiar inconsistencies in their economic (class) positions. Small-business people are subject to many economic markets (credit, labor, commodity) as both buyers and sellers, and thus are unlikely to develop a coherent class ideology. The inconsistency of their position probably goes a long way toward explaining the appeal of that magical mechanism, the free market, for small-business owners. Farmers also have an inconsistent market relation: They are often buyers of credit in a seller's market and sellers of commodities in a buyer's market.

Both small farmers and owners of small businesses have made a considerable effort to shore up their difficult economic positions by stressing prestige factors. Both stress the moral value of their respective ways of life (self-sufficiency, competition) and both link their activities to the health of society. Neither group, however, is above using government to lower its costs—such as of transportation and credit—to stabilize the price of what it sells ("fair trade" laws, farm price supports), or to prevent collective bargaining by labor unions. The basic defensive posture of the semiprofessions, on the other hand, is collective action (increasingly collective bargaining) and the upgrading of their professional images, especially through increased and unnecessary educational requirements promoted by professional associations.

The Working Class

When we turn our attention from the lower middle class to the working class (about 40 to 45 percent of all households), we cross a rather deep cleavage in the American class system. The evidence points overwhelmingly to a significant gap between the level of social and cultural benefits received by blue-collar and lower-level white collar workers and those received by the classes above them. (A gap of similar magnitude separates the working class and the lower class.) The term *working class* obviously refers to a broad, diverse group of families encompassing highly skilled as well as semiskilled and unskilled workers—a group, in other words, that subsumes quite varied levels of income, work satisfaction, and prestige. If by *working class* one means workers who are steadily employed in manual, clerical, and retail sales occupations, regardless of other attributes, then inconsistency of class, prestige, and power statuses seems to be the normal condition of the working class. There is, first of all, the confining routine of their work and its lack of prestige (see Table 14–1). Working-class marriages are significantly more unstable than are marriages in the classes above. At best, marriages at this level are deeply segregated into masculine and feminine roles; there is considerable isolation and even estrangement between working-class husbands and wives. In comparison with the classes above, working-class families manifest a significantly lower level of participation in community affairs and in the aesthetic and intellectual life of the nation. All in all, working-class life is seriously inconsistent with the American emphasis on freedom and individual choice; happiness; moral, political, and legal equality; and personal fulfillment and identity through work and success.

Some elite elements in the working class receive incomes in the middle-class range of income levels, and are thus somewhat difficult to classify. It is of great importance that this group accounts for the bulk of the working class with college-bound children. However, extreme caution must be exercised in interpreting high working-class incomes. The hourly wages of plumbers, steamfitters, bricklayers, and the like are quite misleading, since seasonal and other forms of underemployment make it difficult to translate hourly wages into true annual incomes. Secondly, a comparison of total work-related economic benefits (pensions, insurance, sick leave, material comforts and safety on the job, and paid holidays and vacations) and power-related economic benefits (taxation, housing policies, recreational facilities, public services in general) would undoubtedly differentiate many lower-middle-class and working-class individuals who earn similar incomes. And, of course, it is of the utmost importance not to confuse individuals with family income data: The bulk of high working-class incomes belong to families with two or more wage earners.

By and large, members of the working class earn incomes that permit only a modest level of comfort. Many working-class families live austere and even impoverished lives. Few can save—accumulation is very slow—and many live on credit. Economically, they are best characterized as living close to their incomes, which has obvious psychological implications. While members of the working class are less self-conscious about residential prestige differentials than the classes above, and do not worry much about being excluded from membership in middle-class clubs, they do face serious psychological insecurity and pain. Workers are typically not protected against serious medical illness, and historically their pensions were not vested—that is, workers lost all rights when they changed jobs or were laid off.[5] Many working-class males experience drudgery or heavy exertion (or both) in their work, compounded by the knowledge that they have little chance of improving their economic status. The working-class female typically faces a life of drudgery, revolving around too many children,[6] and isolation; she often remains closer to her relatives than to her husband.

Trade unions protect only 16 percent of the working class, and misconceptions about the power of unions to the contrary, many unskilled workers are not well paid—that is, they do not enjoy even a modest level of living—even when they are represented by unions. Trade unionism has not resulted in a monolithic struggle between labor and management, as the popular image has it. Employers still find it possible to appeal to workers against trade unions, and employers and trade union officials often reach agreements against the wishes of workers (sometimes legally and sometimes not). The Reagan administration of the 1980s openly undermined labor strength through its appointees to the National Labor Relations Board, by its open promotion of overseas investment, its curb on social services, and its lack of interest in full employment.

Politically, the working class tends to be more apathetic than the classes above it; when it votes or otherwise participates in politics, it tends to be liberal on economic-welfare issues and conservative on foreign policy and civil rights (with the obvious exception of African Americans and some other minorities). The working class gets into a great deal of trouble as a result either of criminal activities or of credit and marital-family problems, but its access to justice and public aid is deeply biased by class factors. Despite the pronounced particularities of the working-class life experience, however, it cannot be said that there exists anything resembling a working-class subculture. Nothing so poignantly expresses the plight of the American working class as the fact that it is subject to the full force of the middle-class ethos.

The Lower Class

The lower class in America is made up of a diverse collection of families and individuals: the permanently unemployed; the erratically employed; the underemployed; the badly underpaid; the old who are poor; abandoned mothers; and the physically, mentally, and psychologically sick, disabled, or different (about 20 to 25 percent of all households). This group is not united by any common consciousness, nor do its members have much to do with each other. What these individuals have in common, basically, is their worthlessness on the labor market, a class position that renders them fairly worthless in terms of prestige and power as well.

The lower class, therefore, is a composite of different types of individuals and families. Some are multigenerational members of the lower stratum who have inherited their class position as the children of migratory workers, seasonal laborers, hospital help, and the like. Others, unlucky enough to have physical characteristics that do not conform to the country's definition of normality, are destined from birth for the lower class. Still others gravitate downward as a result either of defeat in economic combat or of having or developing undesired or dysfunctional personalities. In the past two decades female-headed one-parent homes have burgeoned, many of which are poor (the feminization of poverty). Still another category of poor appeared in the 1980s, full-time workers below the poverty level. And there are now significant numbers of young white males, often with families, who are among the poor. From 1987 on the majority of the new homeless have been families with children.

THE CLASS SYSTEM AND RACIAL-ETHNIC MINORITIES

The norms and values governing majority-minority relations have been fully embodied historically only by a relatively small group of white, largely Protestant upper- and upper-middle-class families. At this level, remember, there is great consistency among the three hierarchies of social worth. The group that first achieved preeminence in America happened to be white, Anglo-Saxon, and Protestant, and its members simply assumed or asserted the superiority of all they did and believed in. Today, the upper class appears to contain significant numbers of Roman Catholics and Jews; however, because no exact studies exist, we cannot specify exact numbers or determine whether such newcomers are full or only partial members.

Families that do not exhibit unusually high or low achievement in the spheres of occupation, education, or income occupy the next rung of the class ladder. White Protestants—both Anglo-Saxons of long duration in the United States and immigrant groups from Germany and Scandinavia—exhibit normal class achievement; in other words, they are well represented above the manual labor rank. As white Protestants, they also have normal prestige despite the fact that the occupations white Protestants hold and the churches they attend vary widely in class composition and prestige worth.[7]

Roman Catholics of European origin (French, Irish, German, Polish, Italian) and European Roman Catholics who entered the United States via Canada (French Canadians) are now represented on all rungs of the class ladder. Thanks to their location in urban centers, Roman Catholics have been assimilated culturally, which is to say that socioeconomic status predicts more about a Roman Catholic than does religion. Even on basic issues such as birth control and parochial education, it cannot be said that there is a Roman Catholic position (among the laity) that varies much from the class views of non-Catholics. And in the field of politics it appears that the historic proclivity of (underdog, working class) Roman Catholics to support the Democratic party has come to an end. As they diversify by class, Roman Catholics vote along the same class lines that divide other Americans. While basic religious attitudes have no doubt changed, there is still a prestige ranking that affects European Roman Catholics adversely. Because of both national origin (long associated with working-class status) and religion, European Roman Catholics do not mingle easily with other Americans outside the dimensions of class. Associational life in the United States is pervasively segregated along religious-ethnic lines, though such segregation is not necessarily enforced or characterized by feelings of resentment. Indeed, a relatively full way of life is available to the Irish of Boston, the French Canadians of Burlington, Vermont, and their counterparts elsewhere. While complaints may be expressed about this or that grievance or injustice, resentment of the system of society is minimal. Indeed, as we saw earlier, prestige segregation plays an important role in making the American system of stratification work.

A number of minorities in the United States enjoy normal-to-high class achievement but suffer from subnormal prestige and power. This category of minorities includes Jewish, Japanese, and Chinese Americans, and Americans from India. By and large, these groups have matched or exceeded the class achievements of majority Americans, but they suffer from adverse prestige evaluations on religious, ethnic, and racial grounds. While these groups have taken on the American cultural identity, they live and associate separately from other Americans. The position of Japanese and Chinese Americans in Hawaii is somewhat different from that of their counterparts in the continental United States: the latter has a deeper racist tradition than Hawaii, though no exact comparative studies exist.

It is no exaggeration to say that the United States possesses a substantial group of families and unrelated individuals who exhibit all the earmarks of a "permanent" proletariat. This category of minorities includes significant numbers of African Americans, Native Americans, Eskimos, Mexican Americans, Puerto Ricans, and to some extent Filipinos. It also includes a diverse group of white Protestants who are not readily identifiable and thus not easily denied prestige.

Though each of these minorities is itself stratified, containing middle- and upper-class members, in the aggregate these minority groups have not made any significant relative gains vis-à-vis the class standing of mainstream white Protestants and white European Roman Catholics. They also suffer from a low prestige evaluation (largely associated with their historic economic subordination), which is largely expressed in racist terms. By force of class, prestige and power, these groups are barred from full or even adequate participation in American society. The vicious process in which low class (income, wealth, occupation, education) leads to low prestige (through racist values and beliefs, ethnic prejudice, residential segregation, interactional segregation), which in turn reinforces low class is an institutionalized pattern that will not be easy to break.

In addition, the power position of this group of minorities has been compromised throughout American history. Despite the rhetoric and the promises of American society, the most that can be claimed for the strenuous reform movements of recent decades is that they have lifted these groups out of "caste" subordination into class subordination. Though these minority groups achieved significant power mobility in the 1960s through the acquisition of a more effective franchise, they remain weak politically because they are weak economically; do not have access to politically relevant voluntary pressure groups; and are gerrymandered by the economics of transportation and housing, by discrimination, by various forms of public policy, and by explicitly drawn political boundaries.

THE CLASS SYSTEM AND GENDER

Measured in terms of movement out of their origins in the existing class hierarchy, women fare pretty much the same as men when they enter the labor market (either analyzed by mobility through marriage or through occupation.) Women have made gains in education, and young, better-educated women have made relative gains in comparison to men in income and occupation. The narrowing of the gender gap in the 1980s, however, occurred largely because males in middle-management and blue-collar positions suffered setbacks and because a small number of women did well. In recent decades, structural changes in domestic and international capitalism have adversely affected men and especially women in the bottom 80 percent of the labor force and revived occupational segregation by gender and race. Holding education, experience, and motivation constant, recent empirical research has clearly established a significant gender bias in the distribution of income and occupational authority.

THE STRUCTURE OF SOCIAL POWER

Expressed in the vocabulary of stratification analysis, *social power* refers to a social class or classes possessing class, prestige, and power assets of such an order, intensity, and magnitude that it controls the structure and direction of society. The more sophisticated formulations of this idea specify the type of social system that produces such (social) power.

Three different images of social power can be distinguished: the power elite, the pluralist, and the semi-pluralist.

Is There a Power Elite?

C. Wright Mills argued that the main trend in the development of American capitalism is economic and political concentration. He argued further that there was already in evidence a small power elite drawn from and coordinating the upper reaches of the corporate world, the federal executive branch of government, and the military, which had come into being because of processes inherent in advanced industrial society. Perched atop the stratification dimensions of class and power, this group possesses, according to Mills, significantly more power than Congress, trade unions, farmers, small business, or the general public.[8]

G. William Domhoff, who has set himself the task of trying to substantiate Mills' thesis more fully, has investigated the upper levels of the various hierarchies in American society and offers what he considers conclusive evidence that a small homogeneous, stable, and interchangeable collection of very rich individuals (and families) occupies the command positions of American society.[9]

Our study of social stratification found considerable concentration of power along the lines suggested by Mills, Domhoff, Dye, van der Pijl, and Useem. This should not be interpreted to mean that a tiny clique is running the country. The upper levels in the United States exercise hegemonic power, but there is quarreling among elites and conflicts between elites and the secondary levels of power. The tiny American upper class (and its immediate allies in the small business world and many of the professions) prevails in the sense that it has succeeded in committing America to abstract economic growth under private auspices—this is vital to its main interest, profit and power from property. Beyond this priority, there are quarrels about means and a lack of clear priorities and policies about a variety of sociopolitical issues. But these qualifications should not be interpreted to mean that the United States has approximated either a nonegalitarian classless society or a pluralistic self-equilibrating system of power, or that it is even making progress toward pluralism or a democratic meritocracy.

Pluralism: The Myth of an Adaptive Equilibrium of Power

Pluralist theorists believe that American society is adaptive because it is characterized by creative competition among relatively equal social actors. Pluralists argue that competition among individuals and groups (within the framework of free markets, law, toleration, and professionalism) transforms group diversity and conflict into social integration, stability, harmony, justice, and progressive adaptation. Pluralists argue that social differentiation has led to a society whose various parts check and balance each other. They argue that American society is open and fluid, allowing individuals and groups to rise and fall according to ability. Pluralists see society as a natural, objective system, and oppose views suggesting that society has to be explicitly managed. When "artificial" human actions are taken, argue pluralists, they should be directed toward helping the natural society struggling to emerge from history.

American pluralists allege that no single group or combination of groups can dominate the others. The plurality of groups makes for overlapping group membership, which in turn inhibits groups from acting unilaterally. Our pluralist group structure, they argue, avoids cleavage between large contending blocs—there is stability if religious disputes occur among 200 denominations as opposed to two. A pluralist society produces a "strange bedfellow" set of relations. Those who want to ban abortion do not agree on the need for nuclear energy. Those who want gun control do not necessarily agree that school prayer is a good thing. The insurance company that argues against government interference in its investment policies wants the government to control hospital costs or require safer automobiles. Segments of Protestantism and Roman Catholicism oppose gay rights but other segments join secular groups to support them.

This criss-crossing of interests and values makes it impossible, argue pluralists, for arbitrary and unilateral power to emerge. A pluralistic power structure forces groups to make alliances with one another and promotes the arts of negotiation and compromise. Given this pluralistic power structure the public is always provided with alternatives to choose from and is constantly supplied with a wide variety of information to help it make up its collective mind about public issues. Under pluralism the public interest is guaranteed, or is at least being pursued and approximated.

Pluralist theorists defend both elites and ordinary people. American pluralism, they argue, allows the talented to rise to the top. Each area of human endeavor gradually develops standards to ensure competence, and society is led by its true aristocracy—the achievers in science, business, medicine, law, art, and so on. Ordinary people have their rights, including the right to compete for high position, and an indirect right as consumers, voters, or volunteer workers to influence how society works.

Pluralists argue that the United States is ruled by a shifting coalition of elite groups that comprise a moving equilibrium, not a unified upper class. Elites can get their way only in certain areas and have to yield to other elites on other issues. Ordinary Americans have at least some power to influence events in their everyday lives. But their real power derives from elite competition to gain their support, especially in economic and political markets. American society, pluralists argue, is flexible enough to achieve reforms when needed and no group will remain powerless or be victimized over the long run.

The evidence against pluralism (and a power elite) is large. In every sector of American society, there is competition but also hierarchical power. Business firms compete, but the economy is also deeply concentrated and excludes many from effective power and renders many powerless. The professions are based on significant competition and have developed achievement standards, but they are also deeply marked by artificial scarcity and incompetence, and by significant amounts of unethical and criminal behavior. The American polity is a hurly-burly of competition, but the economically powerful prevail while many are powerless. Government officials and legislators are drawn from the upper classes. Legislation and the law in general favor the powerful. Three-quarters of the seats in the U.S. House of Representatives are noncompetitive. Almost half of the eligible voters stay away from elections, many undoubtedly because they believe that they are powerless to influence events. The free press is useful in clarifying issues and protecting the rights of some, but it is also a powerful force in favor of the upper classes and the status quo. Education is not a fair contest to determine the natural elite, but deeply biased in favor of the upper classes and the status quo. Voluntary groups perform many functions and help to disperse power, but their policy-making boards and committees are dominated by the upper classes. All these institutions and groups work to depoliticize social problems, thus leaving their solution in the hands of those who cause them, the upper classes.

No matter what process, issue, or outcome is analyzed, the pattern is clear. The benefits of American life (income, wealth, occupation, education) are distributed unequally and with no close, positive relation to merit or functional outcomes. The lower classes bear the brunt of unemployment, insecurity, and occupational disease and disability, and it is their sons that bear the burden of war. And the government supports this overall process through its tax, spending, and other policies.

No assessment of power in the United States, therefore, can ignore three basic aspects of American life:

1. The existence of significant amounts of powerlessness, exploitation, waste, and privilege
2. The fact that these phenomena are deeply institutionalized and thus not easily eradicated
3. That oligarchic relations are *systemic,* that is, they characterize all aspects and apexes of American society

Semi-Pluralism: The Reality of Oligarchy

Our study of the American class system does not substantiate the pluralist argument. Indeed, it is probably true to say (judging from introductory sociology textbooks) that this position is now on the wane in sociology—few sociologists would argue that the United States is characterized by a relative equality of power, by responsible (professionalized) elites, or by a relative equality of opportunity and competition.

If American society does not conform to the pluralist model, to what model does it correspond? The best answer is that we are probably governed by an upper-middle-class to upper-class power structure with strong overtones of oligarchy.[10] The model of a "middle-class" establishment resembles the pluralist model up to a point. There is some truth, for example, in the argument that the liberal democracies are unique because the people rule. Power *is* shared by more people than was the case in the past. But this is not the same thing as saying that the people-at-large participate actively in the business of running society, which they do not, or that they have equal shares of power, which they do not. It is also true that the many groups in contemporary society tend somewhat to check and balance each other as they jostle for advantage. But closer scrutiny reveals that the articulated groups in American society are overwhelmingly upper-middle and upper class in leadership, composition, and social philosophy. This fact is evidence of social power rather than of a natural distribution of ability, since the processes and agencies of achievement in the United States are heavily ascriptive and arbitrary. Far from being a society based on equality of opportunity, the United States has *no* equality of opportunity—except among members of the same class—and cannot as long as children are raised in families steeply differentiated by class, and thus by prestige and power.

Stated differently, it is social power that explains individualism rather than the reverse: A minority of white males and their families from middle-, upper-middle, and upper-class backgrounds (along with an increasing handful of their wives and daughters, the Women's Movement) has managed to monopolize important social positions in the name of nonegalitarian classlessness, or the philosophy of individualism. This has led to a hierarchy of ascriptive and arbitrary power in the United States because the dominant groups believe in achievement, excellence, and progress, and continously raise the norms required for admittance to upper-level occupations. Because these norms are largely unrelated to functional performance, their latent function is to maintain an artificial scarcity of qualified personnel. This practice is imitated at all levels as semiprofessionals and skilled workers use the state or their unions to establish unnecessary occupational qualifications. The net result is not pluralistic competition or power but a scramble for a socially created shortage of desirable positions in which the winners are largely preordained by the rules of the game.

The dominant power groups in American society have succeeded, by and large, in inculcating their explanation of how society works in the remainder of the population. Americans not only accept large concentrations of private power, especially corporations and the professions, but also regard this situation as normal and therefore legitimate. And the same thing is true of other basic features of American society: the primacy of economic status and occupation over other institutions; the stress on work and gain; the assumed validity of highly unequal rewards; faith in the automatic beneficence of science, technology, and education; the use of religion as a secular faith; reliance on an individualized and psychologized human nature as the ultimate explanation of behavior; and the assumed fiduciary benevolence of private power blocs.

Of course, there is evidence that Americans are highly critical of the specific ways in which their society works and, as public opinion polls have consistently revealed, have considerably less than full confidence in their leaders and institutions.[11] The important point, however, is that the lower classes find it difficult to articulate a philosophy that would challenge the existing system of power since their Americanism predisposes them away from the concept of power and the institutional explanation of behavior. And underlying the maintenance of the status quo is the fact the upper and lower classes are all implicated in the existing division of labor. Daily experience, interpreted in terms of the ideology of classless inequality and progress through reliance on existing processes (or variations on them), locates the various classes in orbits that seem normal and natural.

Within the upper and upper middle classes there is an intricate intermeshing of interests that the pluralist model invariably overlooks or slights. Interests are coordinated across competing groups in the same class by intermarriage; interlocking directorships; informal agreements; common experiences, such as schooling, socializing, religion, and business; and "fiduciary" organizations, such as law firms, banks, professional associations, voluntary organizations of various kinds, and governments. The intermeshing of interests can take the form of reciprocal backscratching and support, such as when the insurance industry supports the American Medical Association (AMA) in its fight against a public system of medical care and in turn receives support from the AMA in its own opposition to public insurance programs. Or it can take the form of reciprocal inaction, an important feature of our professional life. Indeed, the existence of noncompeting clusters of power within specific sectors of society, the economy, the professions, education, prestige groups, and politics is a salient feature of American society. These features, together with (1) economic insecurity and competition for scarce jobs and resources at lower levels, and (2) ethnic, religious, and racial hostilities, go a long way toward explaining the nature of social power in America.

THE PROBLEM-SOLVING RECORD

The American problem-solving system has had notable failures over the past few decades. Its inability to direct the economy into sustained productivity, full employment, use values, and price stability is far and away its biggest failure. Economic failure is also the cause of failure elsewhere. Declining investment in infrastructure and public services, including health and education, is part of the decline of cities and living standards, and these feed back, both directly and as social overhead, to retard and reduce productivity. Unemployment and job insecurity breed crime and waste and these too reflect back to burden the economy.

The problem-solving failure of the past few decades is well-nigh absolute in the area of blue- and white-collar crime. The United States has been unable to curb family dissolution or the serious problem of violence within the home. There appears to be no overall progress in protecting the environment. The Index of Social Health, compiled by Marc L. Miringoff and the Fordham Institute for Innovation in Social Policy, provides data about problems in sixteen areas: infant mortality, child abuse, children in poverty, teen suicide, drug abuse, high school dropouts, average weekly earnings, unemployment, health-insurance coverage, the elderly in poverty, health insurance for the elderly, highway deaths due to alcoholism, homicides, food-stamp coverage, housing, and the gap between rich and poor. The Institute reports that between 1970 and 1991 (the last year for full data on all indicators), there has been a consistent downward drift in the social health of the nation as measured by these indicators.[12]

There is other evidence that the United States is not making progress against its problems. For over a decade the United States has no longer enjoyed the world's highest standard of living and many countries now have better health care, far less crime, and much more livable cities. Under the joint pressures of economic and political rationalization and reform, the general nature of group life has become even more hierarchical as more of life is run by professions embedded in bureaucratic structures. Almost no sphere of life has remained immune from this process, though the results are not unilaterally bad or easy to evaluate. Workers and professionals alike find themselves earning their livelihoods in vast impersonal structures. Political parties find it hard to build political followings as government welfare agencies and direct-action groups steal their former supporters. Volunteers find themselves drawn into bureaucratic structures run by career professionals. Voluntary organizations find themselves drawn into orbits controlled by governments. A large network of interest groups, many of them single-issue groups that practice a paranoid style of politics, clog up public life. And everyone finds a bureaucratic rationality substituted for individual rationality.

With the rise of a complex and interdependent economy and social system ever on the threshold of stalemate and conflict, economic power groups have resorted to political means (especially central governments) to achieve economic and social objectives even as they continue to denounce politics and government, uphold the virtues of self-reliance, and affirm the vitality of grassroots politics. Faced with the need to plan, American society has undertaken a considerable amount of "public" planning, often using personnel whose experience and outlook have been derived from a lifetime of affirming antiplanning, entrepreneurial values and ideas. When policymakers attempt serious planning or reforms, they find themselves deadlocked by an interlocked structure of veto groups that makes it difficult to enunciate any policy unless it is so abstract or compromised as to be virtually meaningless. Given the experience of much of its personnel and given the "veto" power structure contained in a mature industrial economy, the remorseless trend of turning politics into administration grows apace.

The irrelevance of American political institutions to social problems is now widely acknowledged. The ideology of relying on private actions to solve public ills is so deeply planted that no effective urban, state, or national politics or planning appears possible. The United States has no coherent and effective economic, energy, transportation, health, educational, housing, urban, family, or youth policy. Its system of taxation is inequitable and badly related to public purposes. The problems of retirement and the elderly are far from met. It has no meaningful, reality-oriented foreign policy, relying largely on military force and the abstraction of a laissez-faire, world-market economy. From the late 1970s on, huge, chronic domestic and foreign trade deficits began to appear, indicating not only that the United States was living beyond its means but that it lacked the capacity to stop doing so.

Failure can be measured on many dimensions: the United States has been unable to provide full employment or equal competition and opportunity. There appear to be sizable amounts of poverty with significant increases since 1960. Minority groups have made no relative economic advances since they acquired their civil rights over two decades ago. The economy and the environment are still on a collision course, despite a quarter-century of warnings and efforts. The United States has a poor healthcare system, perhaps the worst in the capitalist world. Its private and public educational system is largely irrelevant to the needs of contemporary citizenship and fails to provide skilled workers or competent professionals.

Few can argue that the natural and social sciences have produced the knowledge needed to run an advanced industrial system. Certainly the news media have not provided the knowledge or awareness needed by modern publics.

The slowdown in the American economy and the relative stagnation in living standards from the 1970s on are unique occurrences in American history. Are they temporary or do they herald a more permanent condition? The easy optimism that has marked America's past, an optimism derived from unprecedented economic growth, may be a false guide. The United States may be facing a future that its past does not prepare it for. Not only are energy sources dwindling but all planetary resources are going to become increasingly scarce. America may no longer have the flexibility it once had as a white, Protestant, middle-class male monopoly. Today, a vast new array of groups are clamoring for their share of America's benefits and the American polity appears overloaded with demands. For the first time in its history, the United States cannot buoy its fortunes on a dependable supply of victims: the poor; women and children; racial and ethnic minorities; the elderly; the handicapped; and gays and lesbians.

Has the United States lost its enchanted world of Manifest Destiny and inevitable progress, its sense of being in tune with the cosmos? Fifty years of economic growth seem to have created rather than solved problems. Not only have the consequences of prosperity contradicted basic American beliefs, but little has been done to prepare Americans for coping with what may be a qualitatively different future. Instead of a creative set of elites able to deal with problems one by one, the United States has an interlocked set of power groups that seem unable to tackle the deep tangle of intertwined social problems.

The elaborate welfare state erected during the past century is no doubt a source of stability for American society and has helped to correct some injustices and prevent some hardship and suffering. But the welfare state has also locked all power levels of American society into a structure of dependency and immobilization. The attempt by the Reagan administration of 1980–1988 to unclog American society by reducing the role of government and returning it to its past condition (an alleged era of individualism and free market competition) failed largely because of resistance by the wealthy and well-to-do who are the main beneficiaries of the welfare state and the main supporters of the Reagan administration. The Republican Congress of 1994–1996 made a ferocious attempt to return to the nineteenth century (one that had never occurred) and to squeeze the weak, but it too failed because its proposals threatened established interests.

The basic group dynamic in American society is competition among the various levels and types of propertied groups to maintain or increase relative advantage. The higher morality guiding rivalry among the "haves" is economic growth, not as measured by meaningful work, healthy consumption, or husbandry of resources (use economy) but in the abstract (exchange economy). Ominously, economic growth is no longer easily equated with rising levels of social welfare. Ever-larger portions of our gross national product are going into unproductive, unsatisfying social overhead: military preparations, fighting crime, repairing the physical and human costs of pollution, unsafe workplaces, and unhealthy life-styles, welfare subsidies for unproductive people at all class levels, and debt service.

The 1960s may be a watershed by another criterion—it may mark new heights of formalism and reliance on myth. Our assorted indices and theories do not provide meaningful categories for judging economic and social outcomes. Earlier we reported on a valuable change in the poverty index to aid public policy (see Chapter 7). A far more important change has been proposed in the GDP, which currently records all economic transactions without discriminating among activities that promote human well-being; enhance productivity in socially useful areas; represent waste, pollution, and other harmful costs; or deplete natural resources. And it utterly ignores unpaid household work and community service. As such, the GDP is an irrational way to keep national accounts and it contaminates all areas of public policy.[13] In the meantime, expectations soar beyond what society can deliver, and widespread deviance is the order of the day. Absolutist, single-interest groups multiply as demands are unmet. Meanwhile, elites orient themselves to vague, often empty abstractions: freedom, excellence, research, economic growth, and so on. Far from being tied to social functions, elites have given themselves the right to look after their own interests and provide solutions to their own problems, under the master myth that both self- and public interest are the same. In the meantime, the public becomes alienated and the legitimacy of elites declines.

THE SEPARATION OF ELITES AND PROFESSIONS FROM SOCIAL FUNCTIONS

Americans are wrong to be puzzled about why their problems are not being solved. The answer is fairly simple. The United States has gone further than any other capitalist society in divorcing its productive property and its professions from performing social functions. Because of our broad and false consensus about the nature of property and professional practice, few can really see what has happened. The major reason for recessions, periods of inflation, family problems, crime, unemployment and underemployment, urban decay, productivity decline, and an ineffectual foreign policy is the highly concentrated and self-oriented economic-professional world.

The major power relation (institutional and group structure) that makes up American society is the autonomy of property (including human capital) from accountability. Americans have been led to believe that market forces and open competition determine the hierarchy of wealth and income. This is not true of wealth and not true of the incomes of professionals. The American upper class, by and large, have the power to determine their own incomes and to enhance and protect their wealth. In turn, the high incomes they give themselves (leading to the largest gap, by far, between their incomes and ordinary people in the capitalist world) allows them to live apart and keeps them ignorant of how ordinary people live. Perhaps more important is the fact that their separation from ordinary people means that they do not experience the full negative consequences of the decisions they make about the running of America, especially their decisions about the generation and uses of material and human capital.

We Americans are problem-oriented, but our approach to problems protects the status quo and creates as many problems as it solves. We tend to individualize the cause of problems; instead of evaluating the medical profession, for example, we initiate malpractice suits. The mythology of doctor-patient relation hides the service-for-fee profit system undergirding medicine. When the cost of American medicine outstripped the number of customers who could afford it, we never got a chance to discuss the best way to deliver health care. We foolishly allowed health care to be defined by collective bargaining, which means that the unemployed and many of the employed have to do without health-care insurance. We blundered through piecemeal reform into financing medicine indirectly through taxes, Medicare, Medicaid, and private insurance, including Blue Cross–Blue Shield, thus ensuring plenty of money for private-profit health care with few questions asked about it and even less evaluation and accountability. Incidentally, does our productivity index capture the fact that doctors (a minority of them) are performing over one million unnecessary operations every year, or the fact that doctors (again a minority) are stealing more from the public than all the muggers, burglars, and stickup-persons in the country put together?

In all areas of behavior we have an elaborate system that blames victims and individual evildoers, but rarely the real cause, the organized groups that dominate particular areas. When we focus on problem solvers, our characteristic focus is on heroes (profiles in courage, Nobel Laureates, whistleblowers) and empty abstractions (excellence, the gold standard, balance the budget, nonpartisanship, voluntarism). The closest we get to real causes is when we complain about unrepresentative and thus unresponsive policy-making bodies: Congress, labor unions, the Supreme Court, the United Way, colleges, professional boards, foundations, and of course, corporations. *But few see the absence of broad public participation in decision making as a system-wide pattern and few can relate apathy and alienation to the oligarchic nature of our economic, social, and political life.*

The failure of our various elites has led to a significant and steady decline of popular trust in political leaders and the professions, a decline that threatens the legitimacy of institutions. (For a discussion, see Chapter 14.) The failure is evident in the political stalemate that prevents the United States from generating majority coalitions with a mandate to govern. Failure shows up on many fronts. Our insecure, alienated, and depoliciticized citizenry is easy prey for demagogues, and with the help of lawyers vents its experience with professional failure in malpractice and liability lawsuits. Economists have failed to develop practical theories to help citizens and the government deal with the economy. Political scientists have yet to learn that political institutions do not have much independent impact on society (the same is true of education, public and private). Textbooks seem not to promote learning, while biased and incomplete high school history texts (which characterizes all of them) have probably done much harm. Government cannot generate useful data on crime, energy, unemployment, inflation, and productivity.[14] Economists and sociologists have done poorly in forecasting social and economic developments; the CIA misses revolutions right under its nose. It may be no exaggeration to say that because of our knowledge elites we don't know where we've been, where we are, or where we're going.

Failure is far more pervasive than we are aware because elites have ready excuses for their inadequacies—who can tell if they are really saving souls, removing a dangerous uterus, formulating a good system of taxes, developing a sound energy or foreign policy, and so on. When you think of it, we do not value our elites because of what they know or can do. People who know how to do something predictably, like making a shoe, cutting hair, teaching elementary school, or delivering a letter are looked down on. We value elites because they claim to know how to deal with our collective ignorance and fears. Elites have a great stake in keeping the world unpredictable and dangerous. They have a lot to lose if peace breaks out, if health care or education becomes routinely available, if personal identities are easily formed, if meaningful jobs are plentiful, and so on. Is this why research results are so little used? A leading sociologist estimates that no more than 5 percent of the data reported in sociology journals treats variables that policy makers would ever dream of changing. Seen from this perspective, scientific research is a way of indefinitely postponing the application of science to our problems.

Elite failure is also difficult to identify because elites define problems and give us what they claim is the only path to follow. In effect, the professionalization of problem solving closes the door on alternatives and leaves us with no outside standards to judge elites by. The crash program on cancer research, from the early 1970s on, for example, was a relative failure (large amounts of money were wasted and stolen, basic research was distorted) and yet the full magnitude of failure could not be assessed because as a people we did not decide between genuine alternatives and therefore could not imagine what would have happened had the unneeded cancer research money been put into known ways of *preventing* cancer. Incidentally, the crash program of cancer research is instructive on another account: it illustrates how elites cooperate to solve their own problems while failing to solve the public's. Rich people supported a tax-supported program because private wealth was not up to the job (and no amount of money could buy the rich a cancer cure). The American Cancer Society, Sloan-Kettering, and other medical centers, along with government agencies, had many motives for medicalizing cancer, not least because it diverted attention from the interests (their own included) threatened by cancer prevention: dairy farming, tobacco growers and manufacturers, food processors, polluting corporations, and nuclear arms plants. And the whole idea appealed strongly to then-president Richard Nixon—what better use of billions of tax dollars than to spend them on an apple-pie-and-mom program that would help his reelection.

Our magical market is our most conspicuously incompetent problem solver. Magic is extremely useful to elites because they get the credit if something goes right while evil spirits (communism, OPEC, terrorists, Cuba) get the blame if something goes wrong. Our economic and political elites—from corporation executives, MBAs, lawyers, accountants, foundation executives, reform groups, strategic planners, the Federal Reserve Board, the Congress, and the president—do not really do much to attack the economic problems of the country (which are also the main source of almost all other problems) because to do so puts them in conflict with their own interests. Again and again the American people respond to polls stating that they are in favor of government action, including wage and price controls, to cure economic ills. In contrast, the Republican party and large segments of the Democratic party call for voluntary efforts, the magical market, moral effort, or local government to solve our problems.

Problem solving in the United States is a vital and effective tradition among powerful groups as long as they are acting on their own problems. But in solving their problems they create problems for others. The movement of capital out of Cleveland or New York to cheap labor, low-cost areas such as Orlando or Seoul is an imaginative solution for those faced with rising labor costs and taxes, and a problem for stranded workers and cities. The movement of elites (and the broad middle class) into the suburbs solves their problems of getting decent housing and education, but erodes the tax base of cities, undermines communities, and reduces the forces of law and order. Computers are installed to make corporations more efficient, but do not. Instead, they enhance bureaucratic power, creating electronic sweatshops, economic concentration, and overseas investments not sanctioned by public discussion or legislation.

The upper classes solve their various health, education, travel, housing, and other problems under the general principle that if each is successful the whole will be too. This obsolete market mentality is alive and well in America and no doubt solves some problems, creates others, and aggravates still others, leaving the country dynamically the same at best. When the hustle and bustle is over, little will have been done to change the fundamental process by which one group's victory is another's loss. Economic growth and a well-managed system of victimization (liberalism, racism, sexism) had hidden this process for much of American history. The decline in real wages and stagnant living standards for two decades, plus the recession of 1989–1992, brought a little realism into the presidential campaign of 1992. The victory of the Democratic party in 1992 brought a more active, reform party into (plurality) power. But regardless of administration, the drag on creative problem solving of our unmanaged economy and professions will continue unseen and unattended. Far from noticing that the American economy (and polity) has been increasingly disconnected from the American people and that the American professions and disciplines are largely ways to hide economic and political failure, administrations consider it the height of adaptive creativity to intensify our reliance on that same economy and its auxiliary, the professions and disciplines.

THE IDEAL OF AN ADAPTIVE SOCIETY

An adaptive or functional society (not to be confused with functionalist social theory) is a problem-solving entity not a problem-free utopia. The members of a functional society can feed themselves, reproduce, settle disputes, and adjust to new conditions. Adaptive power groups are able to develop the motives, ideas, and skills needed for replenishing, sustaining, and adapting a given way of life to both old and new circumstances. A functional society has *legitimacy,* which means that people take it on faith that power groups deserve their power. Hierarchy, laws, taxes, unequal wealth and income, discipline, high standards, and competition are not suspect because ordinary citizens see direct and beneficial consequences flowing from them. Setbacks and failures are not resented because they appear to occur in a *just* society. A functional society has statuses and norms that, by and large, produce intended and desired results. The adaptive society is an ideal, but it is not beyond reach—to repeat, it is a problem-solving entity rather than a utopian one.

The Dream of Directed Change

Human beings have long dreamed of a society subject to human control and direction. Auguste Comte, a founder of sociology, thought of knowledge as a scientifically determined prediction about, and thus control over, collective existence. Despite disagreements on other matters, most sociologists agreed with Comte in this respect. Whether functional, conflict, or interactionist, whether pure or applied in orientation, most sociologists have always thought of sociology as a way to help individuals and groups take conscious charge of their collective affairs. In adapting this outlook, sociology has been at odds with the main current of American society. By and large, American elites have argued that society needs no explicit direction. Our knowledge, they argue, should help us understand and conform to society's basic principles.

Today we know that the alleged principles of society are merely misplaced analogies between nature and society. All groups have used government to overcome problems despite their theories. Nonetheless, government intervention and social planning remain dirty words in the United States. Today, the United States is the only developed country in the world that has no open, officially acknowledged planning process. But the United States has always been planned—by Congress, corporations, professional associations, local governments, commissions, and institutes. All policy-making is an attempt to predict the future. *The choice is not between planning or not planning but between good and bad planning.* Perhaps things are changing—certainly policy occupations, policy research, and policy programs are booming.

Social planning gained some respectability in American history thanks largely to wars and depressions. During the Great Depression of the 1930s the United States actually committed itself to a limited form of planning. Ever since the 1930s the federal government has openly tried to direct the economy by using its monetary, tax, and spending policies to balance supply and demand (Keynesianism). Democratic administrations have favored stimulating consumer demand while Republicans favor producers. But Keynesianism appears to have failed. The reason is not difficult to undercover. Like so much else in American society the Keynesian state is abstract to a fault. Its purpose is economic balance and growth in the abstract leaving all the major decisions about how and where to invest resources up to private, self-interested groups. Reliance on broad abstractions is formalism not policy.

Lifetime habits are not shed easily. Freedom from government interference (free enterprise economics) and survival of the fittest (social Darwinism) have been the dominant philosophy of American elites for almost a century and a half. But the relative economic decline of American society, its apparent inability to make headway against its problems, and its frustrations abroad may be leading to changes. In the late 1970s some American leaders called for the United States to give its economy some explicit direction. The term used was *industrial policy.* The United States has always had an industrial—that is, economic—policy, but it has always been secretive, implicit, and on a backdoor basis.

Reducing the Power of Wealth

So far, however, American leaders have shown little interest in social planning in the full meaning of the term. Meaningful social planning would require control over the basic investment process by the organized public. It requires fresh approaches to basic questions. Can we achieve full employment *and* price stability? Can public investment make the economy more efficient and equitable? How should human resources be developed? What proportion of the economy should go into health services, education, recreation, food, clothing, housing, the military, research?

The American public cannot expect to have a functional, adaptive society unless more public direction is given to capital investment. There are any number of ways to do this, from direct government investment in strategic industries and services to outright nationalization. There is also the option of socialism. Regardless of how policy in this area proceeds, the concentrated wealth of the upper class must be reduced through taxation.[15] And political reforms, especially eliminating the role of wealth in the financing of political campaigns and abolishing the gerrymander, must be made to reduce the political power of the upper (and upper middle) class.

Curbing the power of wealth means strict enforcement of scientifically sensible labor, consumer, and environmental laws, and a refusal to invest in countries that are remiss in these regards.

The value of small business to American society and to maintaining healthy local communities needs to be better understood. In addition, semi-professionals, such as teachers, police officers, and nurses, need better work environments.

America needs to follow practices developed in other capitalist societies and make it easier for workers to shift from one line of work to another. And there should be a greater stress on the value of manual work, something that will follow if the upper and upper middle classes are harnessed to social functions.

The lower class is the creation of an unsatisfactory society. The reforms outlined above, especially if better public services for all are developed, will help cut down on the size of the lower class.

Electoral Reform: Eliminating Plutocracy

The stalemate of the American political process is evident to most people. There has been an ominous drop in political participation. People may have lost their sense that they have power to influence government. Many are aware and often cynical about the way government works to help the strong, the wealthy, and the educated more than their opposites.

Proposals to revitalize the American polity include the following:

1. Abolishing the gerrymander to force candidates and parties to compete in mixed electoral districts
2. Financing all elections with tax money, thus curbing the special power that goes to those with money
3. Making it easier to register and vote

The overall thrust of electoral reform is to make politics more meaningful, and to make political actors accountable and their discourse clear and relevant.

Prospects for electoral reform do not look good. Those who benefit from existing arrangements are the same ones who must make the reforms, and that is asking a great deal. Existing arrangements fragment the electorate and allow entrenched power groups to veto electoral and other reforms. The gerrymander separates the population into relatively homogeneous enclaves that elect candidates tied to narrow interests. The financing and running of campaigns tends to emphasize candidates' personality, not issues or overall policy programs. Laws to control contributions to political parties and to limit campaign expenditures have not been effective—power groups ignore them for the most part or find it easy to go around them. In addition, the United States Supreme Court has declared that property interests (corporations) have the right to free speech (on ballot issues) thereby loosening the limits that reformers had hoped to place on the power of corporations to influence politics.[16]

The flow of money directly to candidates frees them from party discipline and makes them the agents of the suppliers of money. Public money to help finance presidential campaigns has been a step toward reforming elections, but Congress has refused to finance congressional elections with public money (for the obvious reason that incumbents have a huge advantage over challengers). The present arrangements benefit business and professional interests, and it is doubtful if their power over elections and candidates can be curtailed without strenuous effort. An aspect of this problem that is also detrimental to creative, pluralist politics is that over 90 percent of the money contributed to candidates goes to incumbents, and it is not uncommon for private power groups to contribute to *both* Republican and Democratic candidates. No wonder then that three-quarters of the seats for the U.S. House of Representatives are noncompetitive!

Reformers argue that curtailing the power of private money will force interest groups to argue their positions on their merits. Forcing power groups to explain why what they want is good for all is the meaning of a democratic polity. Reformers argue that Great Britain puts very strict limits on how much can be spent on elections and no harm has come to their democratic processes. Great Britain also allots free time on television for political parties (after all, the airwaves are public property). This reduces the party's need to solicit funds from private groups and it curtails the use of political commercials focused on irrelevant slogans and images.

Curbing Secrecy, Corruption, and Deception in Public Life

Secrecy, corruption, and deception sometime receive separate treatment. However, each makes the other possible and the three should be seen as a single problem.

Secrecy has been curtailed somewhat in recent years by the Freedom of Information Act and by the opening up of public hearings and legislatures. But, argue experts, there is still a large amount of unnecessary secrecy, especially among intelligence and law enforcement agencies.

Corruption in public life consists largely of private groups controlling public officials. This is a pervasive feature of the American polity especially at the local and state levels. Corruption at the federal level is not absent, but here it takes a different form. If one thinks of federal politics and government as primarily ways to prevent change and to protect the interests of established groups, then much of what appears strange and backward at the federal level makes good sense: Regulatory agencies regulate in favor of their respective interest groups and against the public; executive agencies are often administered by officials who have private interests in their areas of responsibility and administer the law accordingly; a gerrymandered Congress is filled with people who owe allegiance to special-interest groups and with people who often have direct interests in matters that they legislate on.

Deception in public life takes many forms starting with the selling of candidates all the way to committee, commission, and government reports. The United States Army Corps of Engineers has a long history of misleading the Congress and the American people about construction projects favored by itself and other special interests. Few people believe proposals from the Department of Defense because of a long history of misleading and undependable estimates of military costs. American foreign policy is conducted without benefit of openly debated and carefully researched policy studies.

Public and private groups consistently exaggerated Soviet military buildups and American vulnerability. Myths about government spending, debt, size, and taxes continue because power groups find them useful. The Nuclear Regulatory Commission has a long history of deceiving the American public about nuclear energy. Even government agencies that collect scientific data mislead—government data on population, crime, unemployment, and so on are misleading unless the assumptions under which facts are collected are kept clearly in mind.

Secrecy, corruption, and deception go together and feed on each other. This is nowhere more apparent than in the behavior of our many unelected, nonresponsible agencies, authorities, boards, and commissions that run so much of American public life. Secrecy, corruption, and deception emerge from even seemingly innocent and useful traditions. For example, a breeding ground of secrecy, corruption, and deception is our tradition of bipartisan foreign policy and nonpartisan politics and government. In effect, what these do is to let existing power groups remain in the saddle while public policies go unexamined and unevaluated.

The Reagan administration of the 1980s was the lowest point of federal politics since the Harding Administration of the 1920s. With its contempt for government and politics, the Reagan administration relaxed public supervision of federal programs and made no effort to improve the conduct of politics. No pay raises for Congress, federal judges, or federal civil servants, for example, resulted in a large loss of talent and violation of law—congressional members, caught in a financial squeeze and in the awkward, inconsistent position of having to deal with lobbyists who earned more than twice what they did, circumvented the law to increase their income. The result was the ethics scandal of 1989, which forced the Speaker of the House of Representatives to resign. The federal executive branch also oozed corruption as one political appointee after the other was forced to resign. The Reagan administration's contempt for public service and its open invitation to Americans to enrich themselves (under the false assumption that self-interest leads to the public good) resulted in a huge orgy of mismanagement at most federal departments, resulting in enormous costs to the taxpayer (or, rather, additions to public debt) and damage to the environment.

Corruption and incompetence are routine at the federal level and the Reagan administration's unusual record in these regards is not the issue. All federal administrations and all elected officials come from the American electorate, actually from the class system. The key thing to keep in mind, therefore, is the sociology of power. The defects of public life reflect the defects of private life. The key question to ask is: What illegitimate things are going on in private life that require the debasement of public ideals?

Economic and Social Planning

The question to ask here is: Must professionalism be wedded to a laissez-faire capitalist society, or can it serve a planned capitalist society or a socialist society? Certainly the crucial thing here is to stop the excessively abstract nature of professional education and focus it instead on policy. This requires a breakdown of artificial disciplines and an emphasis on relating professional problem solving to social causation, especially the economy.

One beneficial result of demanding performance from professional elites is that the excessive qualifications now required for elite occupations can be reduced and this can be followed by a reduction down the line. There is also a need to reduce the incomes of the presently overpaid members of the upper middle class: Executives in large corporations and elite doctors and lawyers come immediately to mind.

Planning requires knowledge about how society works. But knowledge is acquired and used by social groups. People must do the planning but people see the world from their location in groups. Above all, directed change and better policy-making means structuring groups so that they can function better.

The major change needed is to put less faith in nonexistent market solutions. Basic decisions about the economy must be made by a public organized for that purpose. The second major change is to improve our political institutions, especially by freeing them from the power of private money. The third is to transform education to emphasize applied knowledge from kindergarten on with a view toward generating competent, adaptive citizens and improving our professions and occupations. And all reform must be guided by the overriding principle that policy groups are effective if they have heterogeneous memberships and are operating in a genuinely pluralistic system of power. Only when all social groups are adapative will the Owl of Minerva fly by day instead of by night.

American power groups are sincerely striving to improve the performance of American society. Here it is important to distinguish between better policies with which to address problems, and policies designed to improve adaptive capabilities (our main focus should be on the latter). Societies do not unfold naturally nor do they improve (or decay) naturally. If we want a society to work, it must be designed to work. Ultimately, the sociologist must have an image of a workable society, one composed of groups and institutions that foster creative, competent, adaptive personalities.

The American polity, argue reformers, must play a bigger role in explicitly guiding American society. Our present policy of pretending that we do not have policies is not working. Calling all this free enterprise and democracy obscures the issue: The lack of policies to run the country is itself a policy and deserves to be evaluated as such. The American economy must be directed, if not actually planned, so that recessions, unemployment, and bankruptcy can be prevented. Explicit government direction can help modernize and adjust the economy to new conditions—at present threatened businesses dig in and use government to protect obsolete ways. Explicit government direction can help the professions evaluate their performance according to their own achievement criteria—at present threatened professionals dig in and use government to protect the incompetent and preserve obsolete practices. Once the planning process is started in regard to corporations and professionals, labor unions, farmers, and other groups will be obliged to follow suit. The main objective of planning is to make it possible for groups to adjust to new conditions. *An all-important condition for developing adaptive personalities and an adaptive society is to create a public in which all have faith that losses and gains will be shared equitably.*

Planning, it must be repeated, does not mean adhering to an alleged rational scheme concocted by those in power, by those with more education, or by those who claim to have a better science. Planning is a political process in which the many discuss and decide how to design groups and institutions, and allocate resources to achieve a given structure of values.

Strengthening Social-Policy Research

Social-policy research has emerged in recent years as an encouraging development both in education and American public life. Despite impressive beginnings much remains to be done. Relations between social researchers and government data-collection agencies must be improved. A wide range of data must be recast to make them relevant to policy formation. Relations between fact collectors and policy makers must be improved. And evaluation, already well underway, must be improved so that officials can see if public policies and programs are achieving their goals.

The use of advisory committees and consulting firms to formulate reports and make policy recommendations to our legislatures and political leaders must be reexamined. Critics charge that such bodies disguise the exercise of power and allow partisan power holders to appear disinterested and objective while blocking or mismanaging needed reforms. There is also a need to reexamine our policy of burying or postponing issues by asking for more research, as well as using Congressional commissions, independent regulatory agencies, and presidential panels and commissions to make believe that we are basing public policy on objective knowledge.

Public-policy educational programs must also come abreast of the new realism about the professions. At both the undergraduate and graduate levels, education for the professions must deal with the real world faced by problem solvers. They must recognize that running public affairs is not a matter solely for technical knowledge, not a matter to be approached only in a value-neutral way. Ultimately, problems make sense only if they are put in a sociopolitical context and solved through a mixture of cognitive and value judgments. So far the record is not encouraging. America's public-policy education lacks a historical-comparative dimension and a sense of the realities of power (groups pursuing contradictory, unreal, and antisocial goals). Both our public-policy education and research tend to stress narrow technical studies, for example, of housing, health care, land use, taxation, air and water pollution, transportation, education, and recreation. Such studies are based on the fallacy that science can provide answers and that subjective human decision can be transcended. The largely technocratic nature of our approach to social problems denies the reality of power and fails to promote the ideal of informed decision making by humans living in a moral universe.

The ultimate insight is that science and professionalism are political activities and that politics reflects social structure, especially the corporate economy. If we want better thinking, we must redesign the groups that our thinkers belong to: the federal executive, Congress, corporations, churches, schools, hospitals, academic departments, professional associations, and so on. If we want a better society we must not be content merely to study it or reform it—we must also be prepared to redesign it to yield the behavioral and symbolic results we want.

NOTES

1. Obviously, this definition excludes the new rich (instant business millionaires, entertainment celebrities) and the criminal rich.
2. Remember that we are speaking about relative modal tendencies. The upper middle class obviously experiences trouble of various sorts, notably as a result of the pressure on children at this level to match or exceed the attainments of their successful fathers (and increasingly, mothers). And new difficulties have appeared at this level—for example, among dual-career couples as indicated by the fact that women with graduate-professional degrees have experienced high divorce rates.
3. These same professionals could well be members of the upper middle class or even upper class in their local class hierarchies but become lower middle class when ranked nationally. The reader will recall that professionals are themselves stratified internally on various grounds; see "Stratification Within and Among Professions" in Chapter 6.

4. For a discussion of class inconsistency *within* class, see "America's Unique Class Politics" in Chapter 14.
5. Starting in 1974, Congress has strengthened pension rights for workers but much remains to be done. The 1994–1996 Republican Congress tried unsuccessfully to weaken pension protection.
6. Family planning and legalized abortion may have modified this aspect of working-class life for some.
7. There is also a depressed white Protestant Anglo-Saxon group, largely rural but also concentrated in urban "hillbilly" enclaves.
8. C. Wright Mills, *The Power Elite* (New York: Oxford University Press, 1956).
9. G. William Domhoff, *Who Rules America?* (Englewood Cliffs, NJ: Prentice-Hall, 1967), *The Higher Circles: The Governing Class in America* (New York: Random House, 1971), *Who Rules America Now? A View for the '80s* (Englewood Cliffs, NJ: Prentice-Hall, 1983), and *The Power Elite and the State: How Policy is Made in America* (New York: Aldine De Gruyter, 1990). Thomas R. Dye has also provided persuasive evidence of oligarchic power in America emphasizing institutional elites rather than property and social class—see his *Who's Running America? The Clinton Years,* 6th ed. (Upper Saddle River, NJ: Prentice Hall, 1995).

   Other theorists—for example, Kees van der Pijl and Michael Useem, have found evidence that the American upper class has succeeded in linking its interests with the upper class of Great Britain and Europe. The evidence suggesting the existence of an international capitalist class (now including Japan) deserves further research. For an earlier discussion of links among the upper classes of capitalist societies, see Chapter 15.
10. An *oligarchy* is a propertied or occupational power group, or collection of such groups, that consciously or unconsciously does not honor the ideals of its society.
11. See the section "Declining Legitimacy?" in Chapter 14.
12. Marc L. Miringoff, *The Index of Social Health, 1993* (Tarrytown, NY: Fordham Institute for Innovation in Social Policy, 1993). However valuable, the Index of Social Health is not a full coverage of social problems. For example, it does not focus on productivity, crime by the upper classes, or the spoilation of the environment.
13. Clifford Cobb, Ted Halstead, and Jonathan Rowe, "If the GDP Is Up, Why Is America Down?" *The Atlantic Monthly,* 276, no. 4 (October 1995):59–78.
14. There are important qualifications to this global indictment. The General Accounting Office (GAO), which is an assembly of a wide variety of professionals, has a reputation for scientific rigor, honesty, and a flair for knowing what kinds of questions to ask (though it works for Congress, both political parties and a wide variety of groups, while protesting its findings, concede that its standards are beyond reproach). The EPA is one of the many examples of federal agencies that do not supply useful data on which to base policy; essentially it does no basic research and its regulations lack credibility. The history of the EPA also provides insight into the dependence of professionals on the wider business elite—its budget was cut consistently by the Reagan administration and by the 1994–1996 Republican Congress and is significantly lower than it was in 1981.
15. For a carefully researched proposal, based on the way in which other capitalist countries tax wealth, see Edward N. Wolff, *Topheavy: A Study of the Increasing Inequality of Wealth in America* (New York: Twentieth Century Fund Press, 1995).
16. This continues the nineteenth-century legal fiction that corporations are persons entitled to constitutional rights.

Name Index

...ject Index